THE TORN VEIL

Daniel M. Gurtner examines the meaning of the rending of the veil at the death of Jesus in Matthew 27:51a by considering the functions of the veil in the Old Testament and its symbolism in Second Temple and Rabbinic Judaism. Gurtner incorporates these elements into a compositional exegesis of the rending text in Matthew. He concludes that the rending of the veil is an apocalyptic assertion like the opening of heaven, revealing, in part, end-time images drawn from Ezekiel 37. Moreover, when the veil is torn, Matthew depicts the cessation of its function, articulating the atoning role of Christ's death which gives access to God not simply in the sense of entering the Holy of Holies (as in Hebrews), but in trademark Matthean Emmanuel Christology: "God with us." This underscores the significance of Jesus' atoning death in the first gospel.

DANIEL M. GURTNER is Assistant Professor of New Testament at Bethel Seminary.

SOCIETY FOR NEW TESTAMENT STUDIES

*MONOGRAPH SERIES*

General Editor: John Court

**139**

THE TORN VEIL
MATTHEW'S EXPOSITION OF THE DEATH OF JESUS

SOCIETY FOR NEW TESTAMENT STUDIES

*MONOGRAPH SERIES*

*Titles in the series*

125. Jesus' Defeat of Death
PETER G. BOLT
0 521 83036 2

126. From Hope to Despair in Thessalonica
COLIN R. NICHOLL
0 521 83142 3

127. Matthew's Trilogy of Parables
WESLEY G. OLMSTEAD
0 521 83154 7

128. The People of God in the Apocalypse
STEPHEN PATTEMORE
0 521 83698 0

129. The Exorcism Stories in Luke–Acts
TODD KLUTZ
0521 83804 5

130. Jews, Gentiles and Ethnic Reconciliation
TET-LIM N. YEE
0 521 83831 2

131. Ancient Rhetoric and Paul's Apology
FREDRICK J. LONG
0 521 84233 6

132. Reconstructing Honor in Roman Philippi
JOSEPH H. HELLEMAN
0 521 84909 8

133. Theological Hermeaneutics and 1 Thessalonians
ANGUS PADDISON
0 521 84983 7

134. Greco-Roman Culture and the Galilee of Jesus
MARK A. CHANCEY
0 521 84647 1

135. Christology and Discipleship in the Gospel of Mark
SUZANNE WATTS HENDERSON
0 521 85906 9

136. The Judaean Poor and the Fourth Gospel
TIMOTHY J. M. LING
0 521 85722 8

137. Paul, the Stoics, and the Body of Christ
MICHELLE LEE
0 521 86454 2

138. The Bridegroom Messiah and the People of God
JOCELYN MCWHIRTER
0 521 68425 9

# The Torn Veil

## Matthew's Exposition of the Death of Jesus

DANIEL M. GURTNER

CAMBRIDGE UNIVERSITY PRESS
Cambridge, New York, Melbourne, Madrid, Cape Town, Singapore, São Paulo

Cambridge University Press
The Edinburgh Building, Cambridge CB2 2RU, UK

Published in the United States of America by Cambridge University Press, New York

www.cambridge.org
Information on this title: www.cambridge.org/9780521870641



First published 2007

Printed in the United Kingdom at the University Press, Cambridge

*A catalogue record for this publication is available from the British Library*

*Library of Congress Cataloguing in Publication Data*

Gurtner, Daniel M., 1973-
The torn veil: Matthew's exposition of the death of Jesus / Daniel M. Gurtner.
p. cm. – (Society for New Testament Studies monograph series; 139)
Includes bibliographical references and indexes.
ISBN-13: 978-0-521-87064-1 (hardback)
ISBN-10: 0-521-87064-X (hardback)
1. Bible. N. T. Matthew XXVII, 51 – Commentaries. 2. Veil of the Temple (Jerusalem)
I. Title.
BS2575.53.G87 2007
226.2′06 – dc22
2006029203

ISBN-13 978-0-521-87064-1 hardback
ISBN-10 0-521-87064-X hardback

*To Beth*
*With all my love*

# CONTENTS

# PREFACE

This volume is a minor revision of my Ph.D. thesis completed under the supervision of Prof. Richard J. Bauckham at the University of St Andrews, Scotland. I am grateful for Prof. Bauckham's very capable supervision, as he patiently corrected careless oversights and fallacious reasoning. Not only has his gracious supervision has informed my work in the Gospels and Second Temple Judaism, but his honest scholarship, done at the highest level, has been a formative example for me. I am likewise grateful to Prof. Ron Piper, who, though late in coming to my supervisory aid, was nonetheless decisively influential in crafting my argumentation with care and precision.

I am particularly grateful to Dr G. K. Beale for his enduring encouragement in my research, for his rigorous, thorough, and worshipful exegetical fervor, and for his love for Jesus Christ that is evident through it. I am grateful to my parents, Donald and Marilyn Gurtner and Wayne and Sharon Greenwood, for unwavering support of my calling and studies. I am grateful to Prof. John Court for accepting this piece for the SNTS Monograph Series, and to Dr Donald A. Hagner for recommending that he do so, along with offering some valuable suggestions for how to introduce the subject.

While the present work has been submitted to the scholarly community for scrutiny and critique, it is, more importantly, submitted to the glory of my Lord and Savior Jesus Christ as an act of obedient worship, of which he alone is worthy. It was in joyful obedience to his calling that this project was undertaken, and it is a testimony to his faithfulness that it is completed. Errors that remain throughout this study simply testify to the enduring frailty of its author.

Though many have contributed in numerous ways to this project, it is dedicated to Elizabeth Ann, my love for whom is surpassed only by my love for our Lord. She has heard all of my triumphs, struggles, and daily reports on my research, and she has listened patiently to the minutiae of lexicographic research and endured the profundity of my wrestling with theological hypotheses while she sacrificially worked to allow me the luxury of research. This book is for Beth,

*With all my love.*

Daniel M. Gurtner
Bethel Seminary
St Paul, Minnesota

# LIST OF ABBREVIATIONS

## Biblical

Old Testament

| | | | |
|---|---|---|---|
| Gen. | Genesis | Neh. | Nehemiah |
| Exod. | Exodus | Est. | Esther |
| Lev. | Leviticus | Ps(s) | Psalms |
| Num. | Numbers | Prov. | Proverbs |
| Deut. | Deuteronomy | Isa. | Isaiah |
| Josh. | Joshua | Jer. | Jeremiah |
| Jdg. | Judges | Lam. | Lamentations |
| 1 Sam. | 1 Samuel | Ezek. | Ezekiel |
| 2 Sam. | 2 Samuel | Dan. | Daniel |
| 1 Kgs | 1 Kings | Nah. | Nahum |
| 1 Chron. | 1 Chronicles | Hab. | Habakkuk |
| 2 Chron. | 2 Chronicles | Zech. | Zechariah |

New Testament

| | | | |
|---|---|---|---|
| Matt. | Matthew | Col. | Colossians |
| 1 Cor. | 1 Corinthians | Heb. | Hebrews |
| Gal. | Galatians | Jas. | James |
| Eph. | Ephesians | Rev. | Revelation |

## Philo

| | | | |
|---|---|---|---|
| *Abraham* | *on the life of Abraham* | *Moses* | on the life of Moses |
| *Contempl. Life* | *on the Contemplative life* | *Names* | *on the Changing of Names* |
| *Giants* | on Giants | *QE* | Questions on Exodus |
| | | *Spec. Laws* | *Special Laws* |

## Josephus

| | | | |
|---|---|---|---|
| *Ant.* | *Jewish Antiquities* | *Life* | *Life* |
| *J. W.* | *Jewish War* | *Ag. Ap.* | *Against Apion* |

## Apocrypha and Pseudepigrapha

| | |
|---|---|
| *Apoc. Ab.* | *Apocalypse of Abraham* |
| *Apoc. El. (H)* | *Apocalypse of Elijah* |
| *Apoc. Sedr.* | *Apocalypse of Sedrach* |
| *Ascen. Isa.* | *Ascension of Isaiah* |
| *2 Bar.* | *2 Baruch* |
| *4 Bar.* | *4 Baruch* |
| *1 En.* | *1 Enoch* |
| *3 En.* | *3 Enoch* |
| Ep. Jer. | Epistle of Jeremiah |
| *1 Esd.* | *1 Esdras* |
| *Jos. Asen.* | *Joseph and Aseneth* |
| *Jub.* | *Jubilees* |
| *Liv. Pro.* | *Lives of the Prophets* |
| 1 Macc. | 1 Maccabees |
| 2 Macc. | 2 Maccabees |
| 3 Macc. | 3 Maccabees |
| 4 Macc. | 4 Maccabees |
| *Pss. Sol.* | *Psalms of Solomon* |
| *Sib. Or.* | *Sibylline Oracles* |
| Sir. | Sirach |
| *T. Ash.* | *Testament of Asher* |
| *T. Benj.* | *Testament of Benjamin* |
| *T. Dan* | *Testament of Dan* |
| *T. Iss.* | *Testament Issachar* |
| *T. Jud.* | *Testament of Judah* |
| *T. Levi* | *Testament of Levi* |
| *T. Naph.* | *Testament of Naphtali* |
| *T. Sol.* | *Testament of Solomon* |
| *T. Zeb.* | *Testament of Zebulun* |
| Wis. | Wisdom of Solomon |

## Rabbinic

| | |
|---|---|
| *b. B. Bat.* | *Babylonian Talmud Baba Batra* |
| *b. B. Me'il.* | *Babylonian Talmud Baba Me'ilah* |

| | |
|---|---|
| *b. Giṭ.* | *Babylonian Talmud Giṭṭin* |
| *b. Ḥag.* | *Babylonian Talmud Ḥagigah* |
| *b. Sanh.* | *Babylonian Talmud Sanhedrin* |
| *b. Soṭah* | *Babylonian Talmud Soṭah* |
| *b. Yoma* | *Babylonian Talmud Yoma* |
| *Eccles. Rab.* | *Midrash Rabba Ecclesiastes* |
| *Exod. Rab.* | *Midrash Rabba Exodus* |
| *Gen. Rab* | *Midrash Rabba Genesis* |
| *Lam. Rab.* | *Midrash Rabba Lamentations* |
| *Lev. Rab.* | *Midrash Rabba Leviticus* |
| *m. Meg.* | *Mishnah Megillah* |
| *m. Ber.* | *Mishnah Berakhot* |
| *m. ʻErub.* | *Mishnah Erubin* |
| *m. Ned.* | *Mishnah Nedarim* |
| *m. Shek.* | *Mishnah Shekalim* |
| *Num. Rab.* | *Midrash Rabba Numbers* |
| *Pes. K.* | *Pesiqta of Rab. Kahana* |
| *Pesiq. Rab.* | *Pesiqta Rabbati* |
| *Pirqe R. El.* | *Pirqe Rabbi Eliezer* |
| *Ruth Rab.* | *Midrash Rabba Ruth* |
| *Song Rab.* | *Midrash Rabba Song of Solomon* |
| *t. Meʻil.* | *Tosefta Meʻilah* |
| *t. Sukkah* | *Tosefta Sukkah* |
| *Tg.* | *Targum* |
| *Tg. Neof.* | *Targum Neofiti* |
| *Tg. Ps.-J.* | *Targum Pseudo-Jonathan* |
| *y. Taʻan.* | *Jerusalem Talmud Taʻanit* |

## Secondary Sources

| | |
|---|---|
| ABC | Anchor Bible Commentary |
| ABD | Anchor Bible Dictionary |
| *ANF* | *Ante-Nicene Fathers* |
| *AS* | *Aramaic Studies* |
| *AUSS* | *Andrews University Seminary Studies* |
| *BAR* | *Biblical Archaeology Review* |
| *BASOR* | *Bulletin for the American Society of Oriental Research* |
| BDB | Brown, F., S. Driver, and C. Briggs. *The Brown-Driver-Briggs Hebrew and English Lexicon.* Peabody, Mass.: Hendrickson, 1996. Repr. Boston, Mass.: Haughton, Mifflin, 1906. |

| | |
|---|---|
| BDF | Blass, F., A. Debrunner, and Robert W. Funk. *A Greek Grammar of the New Testament and Other Early Christian Literature* Chicago, Ill.: University of Chicago Press, 1961 |
| BECNT | Baker Exegetical Commentaries on the New Testament |
| BHB | *Biblisch-historisches Handwörterbuch* |
| *Bib.* | *Biblica* |
| *BN* | *Biblica Notizen* |
| *BSW* | *Biblical Studies on the Web* |
| *BTB* | *Biblical Theology Bulletin* |
| BZAW | Beihefte zur Zeitschrift für die alttestamentliche Wissenschaft |
| CB | Cultura biblica |
| *CBQ* | *Catholic Biblical Quarterly* |
| CBQMS | *Catholic Biblical Quarterly Monograph Series* |
| CJ | Classical Journal |
| ConBNT | Coniectanea neotestamentica or Coniectane biblica: New Testament Series |
| ConNT | Coniectanea neotestamentica or Coniectane biblica: New Testament Series |
| *CR: BS* | *Currents in Research: Biblical Studies* |
| CSCO | Corpus scriptorium christianorum orientalium |
| *CurBS* | *Currents in Research: Biblical Studies* |
| *CurTM* | *Currents in Theology and Missions* |
| *DCG* | *Dictionary of Christ and the Gospels* |
| DDD | *Dictionary of Demons and Deities* |
| DJD | *Discoveries in the Judean Desert* |
| *DJG* | *Dictionary of Jesus and the Gospels* |
| *DNTB* | *Dictionary of New Testament Backgrounds* |
| *DOTP* | *Dictionary of Old Testament Pentateuch* |
| *DSD* | Dead Sea Discoveries |
| ECDSS | Eerdmans Commentaries on the Dead Sea Scrolls |
| ECSNU | Edenda curavit Seminarium Neotestamenticum Upsaliense |
| EDSS | Encyclopedia of the Dead Sea Scrolls |
| EJL | Early Judaism and Its Literature |
| EKK | Evangelisch-katholischer Kommentar |
| ETL | Ephemerides theologicae lovanienses |
| *EvQ* | *Evangelical Quarterly* |
| *Exp.* 5th Series | *Expository Times 5th Series* |

| | |
|---|---|
| *ExpTim* | *Expository Times* |
| GAP | Guides to Apocrypha and Pseudepigrapha |
| HAT | Handbuch zum Alten Testament |
| *HBT* | *Horizons in Biblical Theology* |
| HCOT | Historical Commentary on the Old Testament |
| *HeyJ* | *Heythrop Journal* |
| HNT | Handbuch zum Neuen Testament |
| HSS | Harvard Semitic Studies |
| *HTR* | *Harvard Theological Review* |
| *HUCA* | *Hebrew Union College Annual* |
| *HvTSt* | *Hervormde teologiese studies* |
| *IBS* | *Irish Biblical Studies* |
| ICC | *International Critical Commentary* |
| *IEJ* | *Israel Exploration Journal* |
| *Interp.* | *Interpretation* |
| ISBE | International Standard Bible Encyclopedia |
| *JAOS* | *Journal of the American oriental Society* |
| *JBL* | *Journal of Biblical Literature* |
| *JETS* | *Journal of the Evangelical Theological Society* |
| *JNES* | *Journal of Near Eastern Studies* |
| *JNSL* | *Journal of Northwest Semitic Languages* |
| *JQR* n.s. | *Jewish Quarterly Review*, New Series |
| JSJSupp | Journal for the Study of Judaism Supplement Series |
| *JSNT* | *Journal for the Study of the New Testament* |
| JSNTSup | *Journal for the Study of the New Testament, Supplement Series* |
| JSOT | *Journal for the Study of the Old Testament* |
| JSOTSup | *Journal for the Study of the Old Testament, Supplement Series* |
| JSP | *Journal for the Study of the Pseudepigrapha* |
| JSPSup | *Journal for the Study of the Pseudepigrapha, Supplement Series* |
| *JTS* | *Journal for Theological Studies* |
| LSJ | Liddell, H. G., and R. Scott. *A Greek-English Lexicon*. 9th ed. Oxford. Oxford University Press, 1996 |
| MSU | Mitteilungen des Septuaginta-Unternehmens |
| MTL | Marshalls Theological Library |
| MTS | Marburger Theologische Studien |
| NCB | New Century Bible |
| *Neot.* | *Neotestamentica* |
| NES | Near East Studies |

| | |
|---|---|
| NICNT | New International Commentary on the New Testament |
| NICOT | New International Commentary on the Old Testament |
| *NIDOTTE* | New International Dictionary of Old Testament Theology and Exegesis |
| NIGTC | New International Greek Testament Commentary |
| *NKZ* | *Neue kirchliche Zeitschrift* |
| *NovT* | *Novum Testamentum* |
| NovTS | *Novum Testamentum, Supplement Series* |
| NSBT | *New Studies in Biblical Theology* |
| *NSK* | *Neue sächliche Kirchenblatt* |
| PC | Proclamation Commentaries |
| NTG | New Testament Guides |
| NTM | New Testament Message |
| *NTS* | *New Testament Studies* |
| NTT | Norsk Teologisk Tidsskrift |
| OTP | Old Testament Pseudepigrapha |
| *OtSt* | *Oudtestamentische Studiën* |
| PH | The Pentateuch and Haftorahs |
| *RA* | *Revue d'assyriologie et d'archéologie orientale* |
| *RB* | *Review biblique* |
| *RBL* | *Review of Biblical Literature* |
| REG | Revue des etudes grecques |
| *RelSBul* | *Religious Studies Bulletin* |
| RevQ | *Revue de Qumran* |
| *RHR* | *Revue de l'histoire des religions* |
| SBLDS | Society of Biblical Literature Dissertation Series |
| SBLSCS | Society of Biblical Literature Septuagint and Cognate Studies |
| *SBLSP* | *Society of Biblical Literature Seminar Papers* |
| SCS | Septuagint and Cognate Studies |
| SDC | Scripture Discussion Commentaries |
| SFSHJ | South Florida Studies in the History of Judaism |
| SFSMD | Studia Francisci Scholten memoriae dicta |
| SJLA | Studies in Judaism in Late Antiquity |
| *SJT* | *Scottish Journal of Theology* |
| SNT | Studien zum Neuen Testament |
| SNTSMS | Society for New Testament Studies Monograph Series |
| SP | Sacra Pagina |
| Str-B | Strack-Billerbeck, *Kommentar zum Neuen Testament aus Talmud und Midrasch.* |
| *Syria* | *Syria* |

| | |
|---|---|
| *T&G* | *Theologie und Geschichte* |
| *TDNT* | Theological Dictionary of the New Testament |
| TDOT | Theological Dictionary of the Old Testament |
| *Them.* | *Themelios* |
| TSAJ | Texte und Studien zum antiken Judentum |
| *TWAT* | *Theologische Wortbuch zum Alten Testament* |
| *TynB* | *Tyndale Bulletin* |
| UUA | Uppsala Universitetsårskrift |
| *VE* | *Vox Evangelica* |
| *VT* | *Vetus Testamentum* |
| WBC | Word Biblical Commentary |
| WMANT | Wissenschaftliche Monographien zum Alten und Neuen Testament |
| WUNT | Wissenschaftliche Untersuchungen zum Neuen Testament |
| *ZAW* | *Zeitschrift für die Alttestamentlische Wissenschaft* |
| *ZNW* | *Zeitschrif für die Neuestestamentlische Wissenschaft* |
| *ZST* | *Zeitschrift für systematische Theologie* |

## Miscellaneous

| | |
|---|---|
| C.E. | common era |
| B.C.E. | before the common era |
| *Fr.* | *Fragments* |
| *Hom.* | *Homily* |
| LXX | Septuagint |
| LW | Luther's Works |
| LCL | Loeb Classical Library |
| MT | Masoretic Text |
| *Cr.* | *Crations* |
| *Pasch* | *Pascha* |
| *Aq* | Aquilla |
| *Sm* | Symmachus |
| *Th* | *Theodocian* |

## Select Ancient Works: Christian and Secular

| | |
|---|---|
| Apollinaris, *Fr. Jo.*, | *Fragments on John* |
| Apollonius, *Lex. Hom.* | *Homeric Lexicon* |

| | |
|---|---|
| Athanasius, *Ep. Cast.* | *Hom. Illud Homilia in illud: Ite in castellum* |
| Athanasius, *Hom. Pass.*, | *Homilia de passione et cruce domini* |
| Athanasius, *Sermo asceticus*, | |
| Augustine, *Civ. Dei* | *City of God* |
| Augustine, *Comm. Ps.* | *Commentary on Psalm* |
| Augustine, *Cons.* | *Harmony of the Gospels* |
| Augustine, *Pecc. orig.* | *Original Sin* |
| Augustine, *Serm. NT* | *Sermons on the New Testament* |
| Augustine, *Spir. Et litt.* | *The Spirit and the Letter* |
| Chrysostom, *Comm. Heb.* | *Commentary on Hebrews* |
| Chrysostom, *Cruc.* | *De cruce et latrine homiliae II* |
| Chrysostom, *Hom. 1 Cor.* | *Homily on 1 Corinthians* |
| Chrysostom, *Hom. Jo.* | *Homily on John* |
| Chrysostom, *Hom. Matt.* | *Homily on Matthew* |
| Chrysostom, *Orat. Hyp.* | *Oratio de hypapante* |
| Chrysostom, *Scand.* | *Ad eos qui scandalizati sunt* |
| Chrysostom, *Trid. Res.* | |
| *Clem. Recogn.* | *Clementine Recognitions* |
| Clement of Alexandria, *Exc.* | *Excerpts from Theodotus* |
| Clement of Alexandria, *Paed.* | *Christ the Educator* |
| Clement of Alexandria, *Strom.* | *Miscellanies* |
| Concilia Oecumenica, *Concil. Univ.* | |
| *Const. ap.* | *Apostolic Constitution* |
| Cyril of Alexandria, *Comm. Jo.* | *Commentary on John* |
| Cyril of Alexandria, *Comm. Matt. 27.51* | *Commentary on Matt 27.51* |
| Cyril of Alexandria, *Comm. Minor Proph.* Or *Commentarius in xii prophetas minores* | *Commentary on the Minor Prophets* |
| Cyril of Alexandria, *Fr.* | fragments |
| Cyril of Alexandria, *Fr. Acts et Ep. Cath.* | *Fragments on Acts and the Catholic Epistles* |
| Cyril of Jerusalem, *Catech. illum.* | *Catecheses ad illuminandos* |
| Euripides, *Phoenisae* | *Phoenician Maidens* |
| Eusebius, *Dem. ev.* | *Demonstration of the Gospel* |
| Eusebius, *Fr. Luc.* | *Fragments on Luke* |
| Eusebius, *Hist. ecc.* | *Ecclesiastical History* |

| | |
|---|---|
| Herodotus, *Hist.* | *Histories* |
| Hippocrates, *De morbis popularis* | *Diseases* |
| Jerome *Ep.* | *Epistle* |
| Origen, *Cels.* | *Contra Celsum* |
| Origen, *Comm. Jo.* | *Commentary on John* |
| Origen, *Ezech.* | *Fragmenta ex commentaries in Ezechielem* |
| Origen, *Fr. Cant.*, | *Libri x in Canticum canticorum* |
| Origen, *Fr. Luc.* | *fragments on Luke* |
| Origen, *Sch. Cant.* | *Scholia in Canticum canticorum* |
| *Prot. Jas.* | *Protevangelium of James* |
| Tertullian, *Adv. Jud* | *Against the Jews* |
| Tertullian, *Marc.* | *Against Marcion* |
| Theodoretus, *Interp. Daniel* | *Interpretation of Daniel* |
| Vettius Valens, *Anth.* | *Anthology* |
| Xenophon, *Apol.* | *Apologia Socratis* |
| Xenophon, *Mem.* | *Memorabilia* |

# 1

# INTRODUCTION

The narrative flow of Jesus' Passion account in Matthew 27 shifts abruptly when Jesus 'gave up his spirit' (27:50). Up to this point, the reader follows Jesus as he is interrogated by Pilate in Jerusalem (27:11–26), taken to the Praetorium to be beaten and mocked (27:27–31a) and led away to Golgotha for crucifixion (27:31b–44). The narrative continues by recounting the darkness (27:45), Jesus' recitation of a portion of Psalm 22 (27:46) and the responses of 'those standing there' (27:47–49). Then the narrative presents Jesus crying out in a loud voice and giving up his spirit (27:50). At this point in the account the reader is propelled from the narrative sequence and scene at Golgotha into a meta-narrative (vv 51–53) in which, among other events, the veil of the temple is torn in two. What is remarkable is that although each Synoptic Evangelist records this event, none of them stops to explain it.[1] The lack of explanation on the part of the Evangelists, it seems, has contributed to the great variety of interpretations of this event offered throughout the history of Christendom. Scholars both ancient and modern have addressed the enigmas raised by this text from a variety of methodological perspectives with discouragingly differing, often contradictory conclusions. Some scholars have lamented that the meaning of the rent veil in Matthew will probably never be discerned with any degree of certainty.[2] While the present volume is by no means the final word on this complicated text, I contend that the history of the interpretation of the rending of the veil (*velum scissum*) provides significant data from which we can glean sound methods towards modest progress in moving the discussion of the rent veil forward. Therefore each

[1] D. A. Hagner presumes that 'the evangelist can leave this unexplained because it was so familiar to the early church'. *Matthew* (2 vols.; WBC 33A–B; Dallas, Tex.: Word, 1995), II, p. 849. R. Brown, *The Death of the Messiah: A Commentary on the Passion Narratives in the Four Gospels* (New York, N.Y.: Doubleday, 1994), argues that neither the author nor his readers understood the symbolism.

[2] M. de Jonge, 'Matthew 27:51 in Early Christian Exegesis', *HTR* 79 (1986), 74; A. Barnes, *The Gospels* (2 vols.; Edinburgh: Blackie & Son, 1841) I, p. 320.

method will be categorised, documented and analysed for its effectiveness in bringing together relevant data for a coherent interpretation of the rending of the veil in Matthew 27:51a.

## 1 The State of the Discussion

Discussion of the rending of the temple veil begins with Ephraem the Syrian,[3] who represents an early trend in scholarship that endures to the present day. In his *Commentary on Tatian's Diatessaron* (written c. 363–373), he illustrates the ambiguity of this event by providing a variety of interpretations.[4] He begins by commenting that the rending shows 'that [the Lord] had taken the kingdom away [from the Jews?] and had given it to others who would bear fruit'.[5] He then provides a diverse and lengthy list of 'alternative' interpretations, including the destruction of the temple because God's Spirit had departed from it, the Spirit's rending the veil in mourning as the high priest tore his robe during the wrongful accusations against Jesus and God's throwing down the curtain of the temple as Judas threw down the gold he received for his betrayal, to mention only a few.[6] Indeed, throughout his commentary Ephraem moves 'freely from one interpretation to another . . . without really choosing one of them'.[7] As we shall see, prior to Ephraem and since, scholars have been occupied with interpreting the rending of the veil, regardless of its synoptic context, by a variety of means which often relate to which veil (inner, outer, both or neither) is in view and what the implications of its rending are for the then-present (Herodian) temple. This variety, surveyed below,[8] includes arguing for a particular view based on **lexical**

[3] For a survey of the earliest interpretations, cf. de Jonge, 'Matthew 27:51 in Early Christian Exegesis', 67–79. An earlier version of this chapter first appeared in D. M. Gurtner, 'The Tearing of the Temple Curtain: A Look Back and a Way Forward', *Them.* 29 (2004), 4–14. See also A. Pelletier, 'La tradition synoptique du "Voile déchiré" à la lumière des réalités archéologiques', *RSR* 46 (1958), 161–66; M. de Jonge, 'De berichten over het scheuren van het voorhangsel bij Jesus' dood in de Synoptische evangeliën', *NTT* 21 (1966), 90–114.

[4] While we appreciate pre-critical scholarship's desire to recognise a plurality of meanings to enrich interpretation, we will see below (pp. 124–8) that such plurality is not necessarily warranted by the compositional whole of Matthew's Gospel.

[5] *Commentary on Tatian's Diatessaron* 41.4–6 (*Mark* [ACCS: NT2; trans. and ed. T. C. Oden and C. A. Hall; London: Fitzroy Dearborn, 1998], *ad loc.*). See Matt. 21:43.

[6] See Oden and Hall, *Mark, ad loc.*; de Jonge, 'Matthew 27:51 in Early Christian Exegesis', 74.

[7] de Jonge, 'Matthew 27:51 in Early Christian Exegesis', 74. Elsewhere, however, Ephraem cites the rending of the veil as evidence for the divine nature of Christ (*Serm. on the trans.* 7.4).

[8] For a list of the thirty-five (undocumented) interpretations counted by one scholar, see T. J. Geddert, *Watchwords: Mark 13 in Markan Eschatology* (JSNTSup 26; Sheffield:

discussions of the use of καταπέτασμα, the necessity of the veil's being **visible** to the centurion who subsequently (especially in Mark) professes his faith or an **apologetic** interpretation. Other arguments are **Christological** in orientation and based largely on the relationship between Jesus' death and the three veil texts in Hebrews. A final group of **miscellaneous** interpretations are largely historical in nature and seem to fit into none of the other categories. A few scholars have proposed a single rationale for their interpretation but most prefer to employ a variety of overlapping bases for their conclusions. Therefore the survey provided below does not intend to account for the extremely complicated mixture of methods and resulting interpretations employed throughout Christendom, but rather serves to illustrate both the complexity of the issues involved and the lack of substantial agreement among scholars evaluating precisely the same evidence. We will see that use of familiar methods that are to date inadequately applied to this issue is in order.

## 1.1 The Lexical Argument

The most obvious, although least fruitful, argument on which an interpretation is based is lexical in orientation. The text of Matthew 27:51a reads, 'καὶ ἰδοὺ τὸ καταπέτασμα τοῦ ναοῦ ἐσχίσθη ἀπ' ἄνωθεν ἕως κάτω εἰς δύο'.[9] The question is, to which (if any) of the two (or more) 'veils' described first in Exod. 26:4–33 that Matthew presumably alludes to does his use of τὸ καταπέτασμα refer? Whereas most scholars draw attention to the ambiguity of the lexical evidence,[10] a handful of scholars have based a significant portion of their interpretation of the rending of the veil upon the lexical evidence of καταπέτασμα.

Some have speculated that the 'specification of "*the*" curtain (27:51) strongly favors the inner curtain'.[11] Others have argued that in the LXX, καταπέτασμα is the preferred term for the inner veil, whereas

Sheffield Academic Press, 1989), pp. 140–45. For a more comprehensive account of particularly ancient Christian interpretations, see Pelletier, 'La tradition synoptique', 161–66; Gurtner, 'The Tearing of the Temple Curtain', 4–14.

[9] Textual variations and the varying synoptic accounts will be considered in Chapter 6.

[10] Seemingly only Philo makes a distinction between καταπέτασμα and other terms for curtains in the temple, a point overlooked by T. Zahn, 'Der zerrissene Tempelvorhang', *NKZ* 13 (1902), 730. See C. Schneider, 'Καταπέτασμα', *TDNT* III, p. 629; D. Juel, *Messiah and Temple: The Trial of Jesus in the Gospel of Mark* (SBLDS 31; Missoula, Mont.: Scholars Press, 1977), p. 140.

[11] C. S. Keener, *A Commentary on the Gospel of Matthew* (Grand Rapids, Mich.: Eerdmans, 1999), p. 686, n. 243. Similarly Eta Linnemann, *Studien zur Passionsgeschichte* (FRLANT 102; Göttingen: Vandenhoeck & Ruprecht, 1970), p. 159.

ἐπίσπαστρον[12] or κάλυμμα[13] refers to the outer.[14] Similarly scholars have looked to extracanonical sources (esp. Philo, *Moses* 2.101,[15] and Josephus[16]) that allegedly make such a lexical distinction to insist that the inner veil in front of the holy of holies is in view for the Evangelists.[17] While those who argue from a lexical standpoint are unanimously in favour of the inner veil, their subsequent interpretations are less consistent. W. Grundmann interprets the rending of the veil as among other 'kosmisch-apokalyptisch' events at Jesus' death, which is a 'Hinweis auf die Heilsvollmacht Jesu: Er eröffnet den Zugang zu Gott'.[18] Similarly, C. F. Keil takes his lexical conclusions to the only other New Testament references to the καταπέτασμα (Heb. 6:19, 9:3, 10:20) and insists that 'Das Zerreißen des Vorhangs beim Tode des Herrn bezeichnet also diesen Tod als das Mittel der Versöhnung der Menschen mit Gott', thus allowing access to God himself. The temple and the temple-cult are therefore no longer necessary.[19] F. Bleek claims that by means of the rending of the καταπέτασμα, 'der Blick und Zutritt in das Allerheiligste eröffnet'.[20] He concludes that the Evangelists record a 'poëtische Darstellung' with 'symbolischer Bedeutung', namely that Jesus' death provides redemption, by means of which believers enter into the holy of holies.[21]

How scholars arrive at such interpretations solely on the basis of a dubious evaluation of lexical evidence is often not clarified and is typically devoid of any discussion of the Matthean context.[22] C. E. B. Cranfield, to name but one such scholar, is tentative in his identification of the veil because of the lexical inconclusiveness of καταπέτασμα in the LXX.[23] Even C. Schneider in his lexical work exclusively on καταπέτασμα

[12] E. Lohmeyer, *Das Evangelium des Matthäus* (4th edn; Göttingen: Vandenhoeck & Ruprecht, 1967), p. 395.

[13] F. Bleek, *Synoptische Erklärung der drei ersten Evangelien* (ed. H. Holtzmann; Leipzig: Engelmann, 1862), p. 475, adds κάλυμμα to the discussion of ἐπίσπαστρον, and also suggests καταπέτασμα is the preferred LXX rendering of פרכת.

[14] Lohmeyer (*Matthäus*, p. 395, n. 3) draws this distinction, erroneously insisting that 'diese Underscheidung wird fast durchweg festgehalten'. Similarly L. C. Fillion and M. A. Bayle, *Évangile selon S. Matthieu* (Paris: P. Lethielleux, 1878), p. 554, suggest καταπέτασμα is an ordinary name ('appellation ordinaire') for the inner veil, although their interpretation lies more in its relation to Heb. 9:8.

[15] Philo is the primary evidence for W. Grundmann, *Das Evangelium nach Matthäus* (Berlin: Evangelische Verlagsanstalt, 1968), p. 562.

[16] Josephus is the primary evidence employed by C. F. Keil, *Kommentar über das Evangelium des Matthäus* (Leipzig: Döfferling und Franke, 1877), p. 590.

[17] Grundmann, *Matthäus*, p. 562. See Str-B III, p. 733.

[18] *Ibid.*, p. 562. [19] Keil, *Matthäus*, p. 590.

[20] Bleek, *Erklärung*, p. 475. [21] *Ibid.*, p. 476.

[22] An exception being Fillion and Bayle, *Matthieu*, p. 554, who clearly use their lexical data as one among other arguments for their conclusion.

[23] C. E. B. Cranfield, *The Gospel according to Saint Mark* (Cambridge: Cambridge University Press, 1959), pp. 459–60. So also G. R. Driver, 'Two Problems in the New

favours the inner veil for its 'cultic significance' rather than lexical evidence.[24] It was 'the most important curtain of the temple'.[25] Although careful consideration of lexical issues pertaining to the veil will be thoroughly explored in Chapter 2 of this work, most scholars suggest that there is insufficient consistent use of the term καταπέτασμα in canonical texts to determine with certainty which veil is being referred to, let alone to base an interpretation solely upon this term, and it is therefore rightly given proportional weight in the overall arguments. The lexical identity of the καταπέτασμα must then be considered with other factors.

## 1.2 The Visibility Argument

Another way to interpret the rending of the veil is by the centurion's apparent response to it. All three synoptic references to the event (Matt. 27:51; Mark 15:38; Luke 23:45) place the centurion's confession 'ἀληθῶς θεοῦ υἱὸς ἦν οὗτος' (Matt. 27:54; Mark 15:39; Luke 23:47)[26] *after* the rending of the veil. Origen (c. 185–254; *Comm. Matt.* 140), although focusing on the response of fear, follows the text closely and literally to suggest 'the centurion and those with him *saw* how the veil of the Temple was rent from top to bottom'.[27] Scholars, then, see the centurion's remark as a response to the rending of the veil, which is among τὰ γενόμενα he beheld.[28] This view argues that the (Gentile) centurion would be permitted to see only the *outer* veil. Moreover, in order to be seen from Golgotha the veil must have been quite tall. Josephus describes the outer veil as being 55 cubits high (*J.W.* 5.5.4 §§211–12), which not only would allow the centurion to see the veil from that distance but also would conceal the inner veil from his view.

The strongest and most thorough modern proponent of this view, H. M. Jackson, argues that owing to its size[29] and its 'hanging where and how it

Testament', *JTS* 16 (1965), 336; J. E. Yates, *The Spirit and the Kingdom* (London: SPCK, 1963), p. 232; Str-B I, p. 1044.

[24] Schneider, *TDNT* III, p. 629. Similarly K. H. Maahs, 'Curtain', *ISBE* I, p. 838; Keener, *Matthew*, pp. 686–87; G. Lindeskog, 'Vorhang', *BHB* III, p. 2119; Linnemann, *Studien*, p. 159; Str-B can only decide 'nur theologische Gründe den Ausschlag geben' (Str-B I, p. 1045), and favours the inner because of 'der hohen kultischen Bedeutung des inneren Vorhangs'.

[25] F. Ó Fearghail, 'Sir 50, 5–21: Yom Kippur or the Daily Whole-Offering?' *Bib.* 59 (1978), 310.

[26] The accounts are slightly different, and will be considered in detail in Chapter 6.

[27] *Matthew* 140 (*ANF* VI, p. 90) (emphasis mine).

[28] What precisely is 'seen' will be discussed in Chapter 6.

[29] W. D. Davies and D. C. Allison, *The Gospel according to Saint Matthew* (3 vols.; ICC; Edinburgh: T. & T. Clark, 1988, 1991, 1997), III, p. 630, suggest the outer veil is in mind partially because 'the effect is less dramatic if the words concern the much smaller

did' (*J.W.* 5.5.4 §§207–9) the veil 'must have been capable of being seen from a great distance'.[30] In a detailed topographical discussion on the subject, he argues that Golgotha was on the Mount of Olives, 'for it is the only place of sufficient elevation outside the walls of the city from which the outer curtain of the Temple, facing east, could be clearly seen, away across the Wadi Kidron'.[31] Jesus' death being a very visual event,[32] the rending of the veil must also have been a visual phenomenon to which, it is argued, the profession of faith by the centurion bears witness. As were the other 'signs associated with Jesus' death', the rending of the veil is likely to have been 'public'.[33] Moreover, if the inner veil *were* in mind, only the Jewish priests would have witnessed the rending, and they certainly would not have publicised this event![34]

As with the lexical arguments, interpretations based on visibility are quite diverse. Origen proposes, among other things, 'a moral interpretation' which brings one to the 'fear of God' that will 'bear witness that He who has suffered these things is the Son of God'.[35] T. E. Schmidt suggests that the 'rending may foreshadow God's judgment on the Temple; but, at a deeper level, it signifies the departure of God's Spirit from the Jews'.[36] D. Bock concludes, however, that whichever veil is in mind, 'it suggests an opening up of access to God'.[37] Marshall sees the outer veil's being in view for Luke, while for Mark it may represent 'the new way into the presence of God opened up by Jesus'.[38] Seeming to merge two interpretations, McNeile uses the rending of the veil to somehow associate the

inner veil'. Surely, though, Matthew is not concerned so much with the physical difficulty (cf. 8:23–27; 19:26, etc.) as with the metaphorical significance and resulting theological implications, which are indeed miraculous. He need not say how large the rocks are that split, how deep the graves are that opened, nor how many saints were raised. The mere fact of the occurrence is of sufficient magnitude to inspire faith in the centurion (27:54)!

[30] Jackson, 'Death of Jesus in Mark', 24. Similarly Davies and Allison, *Matthew* III, p. 631.

[31] Jackson, 'Death of Jesus in Mark', 24. He concedes, however, that the location of Golgotha on the Mount of Olives is not necessary for his exegesis of Mark 15:37–39, although it seems essential in order for the veil to be seen.

[32] Jackson, 'Death of Jesus in Mark', 24; S. T. Lachs, *A Rabbinic Commentary on the New Testament: The Gospels of Matthew, Mark, and Luke* (Hoboken, N.J.: Ktav, 1987), p. 434; D. Ulansey, 'The Heavenly Veil Torn: Mark's Cosmic Inclusio', *JBL* 110 (1991), 124 and T. E. Schmidt, 'The Penetration of Barriers and the Revelation of Christ in the Gospels', *NovT* 34 (1992), 237–40. Cf. I. H. Marshall, *The Gospel of Luke* (NIGTC; Exeter: Paternoster, 1978), p. 875.

[33] D. L. Bock, *Luke* (BECNT; 2 vols.; Grand Rapids, Mich.: Baker, 1996) II, p. 1860. Bock's conclusion, however, is cautious, and he first highlights the lexical difficulties with any decision.

[34] See discussion below, p. 14.

[35] *Matthew* 140 (*ANF* VI, p. 90). A more thorough explanation of the evangelistic or 'vindication' interpretation is discussed below, pp. 7–8.

[36] Schmidt, 'Penetration of Barriers', 236–37.

[37] Bock, *Luke* II, p. 1860, n. 28.

[38] Marshall, *Luke*, p. 874.

'Lord's Death, the fall of Jerusalem,[39] and the End of the Age', concluding that 'the rending of the veil was a warning sign (cf. *Clem. Recogn.* 1.41, "lamentans excidium loco imminens")' in addition to being a sign of mourning.[40]

The fundamental difficulty with the visibility argument, as with many attempts to press the historical details, is that it does not seem to acknowledge the distinctly apocalyptic language in which the evangelist places this event. Surely Matthew, whose distinct voice is not acknowledged here, places the *velum scissum* between the death of Christ and the explicitly apocalyptic 'events' of the splitting of rocks, opening of tombs, and raising of the holy ones,[41] intending the rending of the veil in some way to relate to this motif. The visibility arguments place the event in a purely historical narrative context and make no provision for Matthew's apocalyptic milieu. Indeed, L. Sabourin rightly comments 'the *interpretation* of history lies in the center of apocalyptic thought'.[42]

## 1.3 The Apologetic Arguments

Scholars from the third century on have suggested a variety of what can be broadly called 'apologetic' interpretations of the *velum scissum*. They have often taken careful note of Jesus' prediction of the destruction of the temple (Matt. 23:38) and, seeing the rending of the veil as a symbol of temple destruction, have interpreted the event as a means of vindicating, or fulfilling, Jesus' prediction. Similarly, other scholars have suggested that the rending of the veil is simply an act of vengeance on the part of God for the unjust execution of his son. Still others have taken a slightly different approach to the 'apologetic' concept and suggested that the *velum scissum* is a sort of 'authentication', a divine 'sign' affirming that although Jesus was crucified as a felon, God is 'speaking' through the rending of the veil to affirm that Jesus is in fact who he claimed to be, God's (divine) Son. In addition to affirming the divinity of Christ, other

[39] Similarly, W. L. Lane, *The Gospel of Mark* (NICNT; Grand Rapids, Mich.: Eerdmans, 1974), p. 575, comments, 'The rending of the veil is a public sign that the rejection of the Messiah by the leaders of the people discloses a failure in sensitivity to the divine purpose so serious that it seals the disaster of A.D.70. Jesus' death and the destruction of the formal structures of Judaism are inseparably bound together'.

[40] A. H. McNeile, *The Gospel according to St Matthew* (London: Macmillan, 1915), p. 423. See discussion of 'Mourning' below, pp. 17–18.

[41] See Sabourin, 'Apocalyptic Traits', 19–36.

[42] *Ibid.*, 19 (emphasis mine). Stanton (*A Gospel for a New People*, p. 2) comments, 'The evangelist writes with several strategies in mind. He intends to set out the story *and significance* of Jesus as a 'foundation document' for his readers: his primary aims are Christological and catechetical' (emphasis mine). The apocalyptic imagery employed by the evangelist at the rending of the veil will be explored more fully in Chapter 6.

scholars use the *velum scissum* to argue for his humanity and for the historical reality of the sufferings he endured on the cross.

In Matthew 23:38, Jesus is recorded as saying 'ἰδοὺ ἀφίεται ὑμῖν ὁ οἶκος ὑμῶν ἔρημος',[43] a saying which many ancient and modern scholars intuitively associate with the *velum scissum*.[44] This interpretation comes in a variety of combinations normally associated with the destruction of the Jerusalem temple in 70 C.E., including pure vindication of prophecies whether they are Old Testament prophecies[45] or Jesus' prediction in 23:38 and elsewhere[46]; a combination of this vindication with judgment/ retaliation on the part of God[47];

[43] See Luke 13:35. The possible allusions to Isa. 5:9, 24:10; Jer. 26:9, 33:10–12; Ezek. 35:14–15 will be addressed in Chapter 5.

[44] *Const. ap.* (c. 350–400) 6.5.26; Eusebius, *Dem. ev.*, 8.2.116.4; *Catena in Marcum* 440.26, 441.8; John Chrysostom (c. 347–407). *Hom. Jo.* 59.361.41; *Cruc.* 10.15; *Trid. Res.* 50.824.19–20; Ps.-Macarius, *Hom. sp.*, 50.4.331; John Philoponus, *De opificio* 97.5, refers to the tearing of the veil as a τὰ εἰρημένα σημεῖα; Ps.-Macarius *Serm.* 64.49.5.3.3; see Catecheses ad illuminandos 13.32.19.

[45] Cyril of Alexandria, *Fr. Acta et Ep. Cath.* 74.760.27 (of Joel 2:31 in Acts 2:20); *Comm. Minor Proph.* 1.341.22 (of Joel 2:31); Eusebius, *Dem. ev.* 8.2.112.3 (Dan. 9:27); Tertullian (fl. c. 200), *Marc.* 4.42 (of Amos 8:9; Ezek. 11:22, 23; Isa. 1:8); C. G. Montefiore, *The Synoptic Gospels* (3 vols.; London: Macmillan, 1909) II, p. 744 (of Ezek. 37:12); Cf. also Eusebius, *Dem. ev.* 6.18.41.3; Cyril of Jerusalem, *Catech. illum.* 13.32.19–33.1; Cyril of Alexandria, *Fr.* 315, *On Matt.* 27:51.

[46] Eusebius, *Fr. Luc.*, 24.605.29; *Dem. ev.* 6.18.41.3; A. Schlatter, *Der Evangelist Matthäus: Seine Sprache, sein Ziel, seine Selbständigkeit* (Stuttgart: Calwer Verlag, 1957), pp. 783–84; J. P. Heil, *The Death and Resurrection of Jesus: A Narrative-Critical Reading of Matthew 26–28* (Minneapolis, Minn.: Fortress, 1991), p. 85. Curiously, few have looked to Jesus' prediction in 24:2.

[47] R. Hummel, *Die Auseinandersetzung zwischen Kirche und Judentum im Matthäusevangelium* (München: Kaiser, 1966), pp. 84–85; U. Luz, *The Theology of the Gospel of Matthew* (trans. J. B. Robinson; Cambridge: Cambridge University Press, 1995), p. 136; J. Lange, *Das Erscheinen des Auferstandenen im Evangelium nach Mattäus: Eine traditions- und redaktionsgeschichtliche Untersuchung zu Mt 28, 16–20* (Würzburg: Echter Verlag, 1973), pp. 337–38; D. Patte, *The Gospel according to Matthew: A Structural Commentary on Matthew's Faith* (Philadelphia, Pa.: Fortress, 1987), p. 390; J. D. Kingsbury, *Matthew* (PC; Philadelphia, Pa.: Fortress, 1986), p. 55. Cf. Dahl ('The Passion Narrative in Matthew', p. 63), who combines views saying, 'The rending of the temple veil signifies the end of the earthly temple service and judgment upon Judaism. (Also, the providing of access to God? Cf. Heb. 10:19f)'. M. Davies, *Matthew* (Sheffield: JSOT Press, 1993), pp. 198–99, suggests it refers to 'the human and theological significance of [Jesus'] death', a 'graphic intimation of the temple's profanation', which 'reminds the readers of Jesus' prophecy about the temple's destruction' (24:2). It also 'represents the endorsement of Jesus' fidelity and God's warning to his enemies'. For Luke, E. E. Ellis, ed., *The Gospel of Luke* (NCB; London: Nelson, 1966), p. 269, lists the prediction of the temple destruction (Luke 21:5–38), Christ opening the way to God for all people (Luke 23:43), and the cessation of 'temple rites' as the necessary means 'for the true worship of God' all as being in view. See K. Stendahl, 'Matthew', in *Peake's Commentary on the Bible* (ed. M. Black and H. H. Rowley; London: Nelson, 1962), p. 797. Perhaps also, E. Lohmeyer, *Das Evangelium des Markus* (12th edn; Göttingen: Vandenhoeck & Ruprecht, 1953), p. 347. See Origen, *Fr. Luc* 151.4; Jerome *Ep.* 46; J. T. Carroll and J. B. Green, *The Death of Jesus in Early Christianity* (Peabody, Mass.: Hendrickson, 1995), p. 47.

or simply pure judgment in response to the execution of God's Son.[48]

These often complicated and overlapping views have recently been summarised by Davies and Allison, who for a variety of such reasons prefer to relate the tearing of the veil to the destruction of the temple in 70 C.E.[49] In addition to Matt. 23:38, they look to Matt. 27:40, where passers-by speak of Jesus' alleged claim that he would destroy the temple and rebuild it in three days. They conclude that 'it is most appropriate that, immediately after people mock Jesus for his prophecy about the temple (v. 40), his words should be vindicated'.[50]

Although many in this category see the *velum scissum* as a sign of judgment in some sense, ancient scholars particularly specify the means by which the veil was rent. Some have apparently drawn from a tradition not unlike that of Tacitus (*Hist.* 5.13), who records reports that during the 70 C.E. siege of Jerusalem, 'the doors of the shrine (temple) opened and a superhuman voice cried: "The gods are departing": at the same moment a mighty stir of their going was heard'.[51] Some have understood the association of this tradition with the rending of the veil as depicting abandonment. It normally involves an angel abandoning its role of protecting Israel.[52] Others have stated that what has departed from the temple, again in judgment, is either the Holy Spirit or even God himself.[53]

In a classic 'apologetic' sense, some, especially ancient scholars, have proposed that the *velum scissum*, being a miraculous event of divine

[48] Georgius Cedrenus, *Comp. hist.* 1.482.19; R. T. France, *The Gospel of Mark* (NIGTC; Grand Rapids, Mich.: Eerdmans, 2002), pp. 656–57. Seemingly also, Sim, *Gospel of Matthew and Christian Judaism*, p. 226; R. Watts, *Isaiah's New Exodus in Mark* (Tübingen: Mohr Siebeck, 1997), p. 330; R. Brown, *The Death of the Messiah: A Commentary on the Passion Narratives in the Four Gospels* (2 vols.; New York, N.Y.: Doubleday, 1994) II, p. 1100; perhaps also A. Schlatter, *Das Evangelium nach Matthäus* (Stuttgart: Calwer Verlag, 1947), p. 415.

[49] Davies and Allison, *Matthew* III, p. 631.

[50] *Ibid.*, III, p. 630. The texts they cite for support, however (II, p. 630, n. 100; Tertullian, *Marc.* 4.42; Chrysostom, *Hom. Matt.* 88.2), say nothing about the identity of the veil but rather allude to the concept of judgment only.

[51] Tacitus, *Hist.* 5.13 (LCL).

[52] Tertullian, *Marc.* 4.42; Hilary, *Comm. Matt.* 33.7; *Hom. Ps.* 57.10; Melito of Sardis, *Pasch.* 98.

[53] Tertullian, *Adv. Jud.* 13.15; *Const. ap.* (c. 350–400), 6.5.26; Clement of Alexandria, *Paed.* 3.2; Isho'dad of Merv (c. 850 C.E.); Isho'dad of Merv, *The Commentaries of Isho'dad of Merv: Bishop of Hadatha (c. 850 A.D.) in Syriac and English*, vol. 2, *Matthew and Mark in Syriac* (trans. and ed. M. D. Gibson; Cambridge: Cambridge University Press, 1911), pp. 113–114, using ܬܪܥܐ, probably 'gate' or 'door', but is also the standard (Peshitta) term for the Hebrew פרכת 'inner veil' (cf. Appendix ), and is likewise used in the Syriac of Matt. 27:51a; Ps.-Macarius, *Sermones* 64.16.3.5.2; John Chrysostom, *Cruc.* 10.15; Ephraem the Syrian, *Serm. pass.*, 36.2 (presumably his reference to the departure of a dove is symbolic of the Holy Spirit).

origin, is therefore a witness or declaration of the divinity of Christ,[54] which is itself sufficient grounds for faith.[55] It is also cited as historical evidence for the reality of Christ's crucifixion.[56] Interpretations of these arguments are too diverse to discuss in full here, and some of them, as is often the case with discussions of the *velum scissum*, are mere interpretations, with less apparent methodological rationale than many modern scholars would find adequate. Moreover, they rarely give careful attention to each of the respective synoptic contexts, and none do so for Matthew. According to Ephraem the Syrian, the veil was among the innocent sufferers for the sins of humanity.[57] Cyril of Alexandria declares that the rending of the veil marks the advent of the 'great day of the Lord' from Joel 2:30–31.[58] Eusebius represents the rending of the veil as the stripping away of the old covenant (ἡ κατὰ Μωσέα παλαιὰ διαθήκη περιῃρητο).[59] Tertullian argues that the *velum scissum* demonstrates that it is Christ who is the 'true temple'.[60] Melito of Sardis sees the rending of the veil as a sign of mourning.[61] For R. Brown, the 'sanctuary as such went out of existence; the building that continued to stand there was not a holy place'.[62]

[54] Origen, *Cels.* 2.33; Concilia Oecumenica, *Concil. Univ.* 431, 1.1.5.89.37; Epiphanius *Hom. div.*, 43.445.27; Origen, *Comm. Jo.* 19, 16; §-103; Arnobius, *Against the Heathen* 53; John Chrysostom, *Oratio de hypapante* 66.1; *Scand.*, 20.9.1; *Exp. Ps.*, 55.210.44; *Precatio* 64.1065.26; Athanasius (c. 296–373), *Homilia de passione et cruce domini* (addi-tamenta), 28.249.18; *Homilia in illud: Ite in castellum* 7.4.1; Athanasius, *Quaest. Script.* 28.725.17; Ephraem the Syrian, *Serm. trans.*, 7.4; Stendahl, 'Matthew', p. 797; H. Wansbrough, 'Matthew', in *Matthew and Mark* (SDC 7; London: Sheed & Ward, 1971), p. 241; perhaps also Gregory Nazianzus, *Pasch.*, 36.661.45; M. Dibelius, *From Tradition to Gospel* (trans. B. L. Woolf; Philadelphia, Pa.: Westminster, 1971), p. 195; R. H. Gundry, *Matthew: A Commentary on His Handbook for a Mixed Church under Persecution* (Grand Rapids, Mich.: Eerdmans, 1994), p. 575.

[55] Jerome (from Aquinas, *Catena Aurea* 1.963); Leo, *Serm. de Pass.* (from Aquinas, *Catena Aurea* 1.963); Michael Psellus, *Orationes hagiographicae* 3b.60.

[56] Eusebius, *Ecl. Proph.* 164.1; *Comm. Ps.*, 23.729.46; *Hist. ecc.* 3.8.1–9; *Dem ev.* 19; *Ecl. Proph.* 3.48; Perhaps also Georgius Acropolites, *Carm. Sabb.*, 7; John Chrysostom, *Orat. Hyp.*, 74.7; G. Dalman, *Jesus-Jeshua: Studies in the Gospels* (trans. P. P. Levertoff; London: SPCK, 1928), p. 220; Athanasius, *Hom. pass.*, 28.249.18.

[57] *Sermo asceticus*, 125.8.

[58] *Comm. Minor Proph.*, 1.341.22. He also sees the rending as symbolic of the fate of those who incurred Christ's sufferings. Moreover, it is symbolic of the passing away of the old temple and the opening up of the holy of holies 'τοῖς διὰ πίστεως τῆς εἰς Χριστὸν δεδικαιωμένοις', who can then follow in Christ's footsteps. *Comm. Mat. 27.51, Fr.* 315; Cf. J. Reuss, *Matthäus-Kommentare aus der griechischen Kirche* (Berlin: Akademie-Verlag, 1957), pp. 266–67.

[59] *Dem. ev.*, 8.2.119.8. Similarly, H. N. Ridderbos, *Matthew's Witness to Jesus Christ: The King and the Kingdom* (New York, N.Y.: Association Press, 1958), p. 87, sees a new creation motif.

[60] Tertullian, *Adv. Jud.*, 13.15.

[61] *Pasch.* 98, cf. discussion of Daube below, pp. 17–18.

[62] Brown, *Death* II, p. 1102.

Others interpret the *velum scissum* as a sign that the temple was handed over to the Gentiles.[63]

To date, only one scholar has claimed that the rending of the veil does not in *any* way signify the destruction of the temple,[64] and few have articulated precisely *why* the *velum scissum* (whichever veil is intended) symbolises the destruction of the temple. While it seems that the rending of the veil was occasionally used in the earliest church as a 'proof-text' for God's rejection of the Jews and, by implication, acceptance of Christians, this was not clearly articulated until well into the second century. Instead, the New Testament describes the *resurrection of Jesus* as vindicating Jesus, not his *death*, although Matthew associates the *velum scissum* with the latter. More significantly, G. Lindeskog argues that in other references to the destruction of the temple there is no mention of a veil.[65] Although the word καταπέτασμα need not be present for the meaning to exist, the assumption that 'rent veil = temple destruction' is a speculation that to date has not been substantiated. There is, quite simply, no documented evidence that establishes the association between a rent veil and the destruction of the temple.

## 1.4 The Christological Arguments

By far the most common interpretation of the *velum scissum* associates this event with the veil tradition discussed at three locations in Hebrews. Here, the believer's hope lies 'behind the καταπέτασμα' (6:19) in the holy of holies, where Christ offered himself as a sacrifice (9:3) and has opened for believers a 'new and living' way to God through the καταπέτασμα, which, the author says, is Christ's body (10:20). The use of these references, which are the only New Testament uses of καταπέτασμα other than the three Synoptic rending texts, is thought by some to add unwarranted and foreign interpretations to the rending of the veil in the synoptic texts.[66] Nonetheless, this is the 'traditional' interpretation and by far the most common among modern and not a few ancient scholars.

J. Calvin is the most noteworthy and influential proponent of this view. When harmonising the synoptic accounts of the events, he noted that the

63 Ps-Macarius, *Hom. Spirit*, 50.4.331.

64 M. Hengel, *Studies in the Gospel of Mark* (Eugene, Ore.: Wipf and Stock, 1985), p. 14.

65 G. Lindeskog, 'The Veil of the Temple', in *In honorem A. Fridrichsen sexagenarii* (ECSNU; ConNT 11; Lund: Gleerup, 1947), pp. 132–37.

66 Brown, *Death* II, pp. 1098–99; so also Lane, *Mark*, p. 575, n. 79. Similarly S. G. F. Brandon, 'The Date of the Markan Gospel', *NTS* 7 (1961), 132; Zahn, 'Der zerrissene Tempelvorhang', 729–56; Schmidt, 'Penetration of Barriers', 229.

veil's being rent 'at the completion of the sacrifice of expiation' is important because it was then that Christ 'opened for us the way to the celestial Sanctuary, that we should no longer stand away in the courtyard, but freely advance into the sight of God'.[67] The destruction of the Jerusalem temple

[67] J. Calvin, *A Harmony of the Gospels, Matthew, Mark, and Luke* (ed. D. W. Torrance and T. F. Torrance; trans. A. W. Morrison and T. H. L. Parker; Grand Rapids, Mich.: Eerdmans, 1972), p. 211; trans. of *Harmonia ex tribus Euangelistis composita* (Geneva: Vignon, 1555). Similarly, C. S. Mann, *Mark* (ABC 27; New York, N.Y.: Doubleday, 1986), p. 653; P. Bonnard, *L'Évangile selon Saint Matthieu* (Neuchatel: Delachaux & Niestlé, 1963), p. 407; Schlatter, *Das Evangelium nach Matthäus*, p. 415; idem, *Der Evangelist Matthäus*, pp. 783–84; Cranfield, *Mark*, pp. 459–60; D. Hill, *The Gospel of Matthew* (NCB; London: Oliphants, 1972), p. 355; H. B. Swete, *The Gospel according to St Mark: The Greek Text with Introduction Notes and Indices* (London: Macmillan, 1909), pp. 365–66; L. Morris, *The Gospel according to Matthew* (Grand Rapids, Mich.: Eerdmans, 1992), p. 724; A. W. Argyle, *The Gospel according to Matthew* (Cambridge: Cambridge University Press, 1963), p. 216; H. Anderson, *The Gospel of Mark* (NCB; London: Oliphants, 1976), p. 347; F. V. Filson, *A Commentary on the Gospel according to St Matthew* (London: A. and B. Black, 1971), p. 297, although he has the outer veil in mind. So also, S. Freyne, 'Mark', in *Mark and Matthew* (SDC 7; London: Sheed & Ward, 1971), p. 133; D. Senior, *The Passion Narrative according to Matthew: A Redactional Study* (Leuven: Leuven University Press, 1975), p. 311; G. E. P. Cox, *The Gospel according to St Matthew: A Commentary* (London: SCM Press, 1952), p. 164; R. H. Lightfoot, *The Gospel Message of St Mark* (Oxford: Clarendon Press, 1950), pp. 55–56; J. P. Lange, *The Gospels of St Matthew and St Mark* (3 vols.; Edinburgh: T. & T. Clark, 1862) III, p. 75; H. Goodwin, *A Commentary on the Gospel of S. Matthew* (Cambridge: Deighton, Bell, & Co., 1857), p. 539; D. A. Hagner, *Matthew* (2 vols.; WBC 33A–B; Dallas, Tex.: Word, 1993, 1995) II, pp. 848–49; R. T. France, *The Gospel according to Matthew: An Introduction and Commentary* (Grand Rapids, Mich.: Eerdmans, 1985), p. 400; E. A. Abbott, *The Founding of the New Kingdom: Or Life Reached through Death* (Cambridge: Cambridge University Press, 1917), p. 623; W. Kelly, *Lectures on the Gospel of Matthew* (London: G. Morrisch, 1868), p. 398; F. W. Beare, *The Gospel according to Matthew: Translation, Introduction, and Commentary* (Peabody, Mass.: Hendrickson, 1987), p. 536; T. H. Weir, 'Veil', in *Dictionary of Christ and the Gospels* (2 vols.; ed. J. Hastings; Edinburgh: T. & T. Clark, 1917) II, pp. 790–91; J. C. Fenton, *The Gospel of St Matthew* (Harmondsworth: Penguin, 1963), p. 444; J. E. Powell, *The Evolution of the Gospel: A New Translation of the First Gospel with Commentary and Introductory Essay* (New Haven, Cann.: Yale University Press, 1994), p. 215; Barnes, *The Gospels* I, p. 20; M. W. Jacobus, *Notes on the Gospels, Critical and Explanatory: Matthew* (Edinburgh: Oliphant, 1862), p. 289; H. A. W. Meyer, *Critical and Exegetical Commentary on the New Testament: Matthew* (2 vols.; Edinburgh: T. & T. Clark, 1879) II, pp. 276–77; J. A. W. Neander, *The Life of Jesus Christ* (trans. J. M'Clintock and C. E. Blumentahl; London: H. G. Bohn, 1851), pp. 421–22; Pelletier, 'La tradition synoptique', 161–80; C. F. D. Moule, *The Gospel according to Mark* (Cambridge: Cambridge University Press, 1965), pp. 127–28; Photius Lex., *Comm. Matt.*, *Fr.* 94.2.1, Cf. also *Fr.* 94.1.1; *Epist. et Amphil.*, 125.2; A. Carr, *The Gospel according to St Matthew* (Cambridge: Cambridge University Press, 1887), p. 311; V. Taylor, *The Gospel according to St Mark* (London: Macmillan, 1952), p. 596; A. D. Plummer, *An Exegetical Commentary on the Gospel according to S. Matthew* (London: Paternoster Row, 1909), pp. 401–2; B. Weiss, *Das Matthäus-Evangelium* (Göttingen: Vandenhoeck & Ruprecht, 1890), p. 485; J. P. Lange and P. Schaff, *The Gospel according to Matthew* (New York, N.Y.: Charles Scribner's Sons, 1915), p. 527; Maahs, *ISBE* I, p. 838; Alford, *The Greek Testament* I, pp. 280–81; H. Lutteroth, *De L'Evangeline selon Saint Matthieu* (Paris: Librairie Sandoz et Fischbacher, 1876), pp. 495–97; Perhaps also, Cosmas Indicopleustes, *Top. Christ.*, 5.24.1; J. M. Gibson, *The Gospel of St Matthew* (2nd edn; London: Hodder and Stoughton, 1892), p. 427; F. W. Green, *The Gospel according*

was a product of its cultic ineffectiveness vis-à-vis Christ's sacrifice of himself:

> Christ, blotting out the handwriting that was against us (Col 2:14), tore away every obstacle, that we might be all one royal priesthood dependent on Him as sole Mediator. The rending of the veil not only abrogated the ceremonies that flourished under the law but also opened heaven, that God might now, intimately, welcome the members of His Son to Himself.[68]

Calvin's has become the traditional view and assumes that the inner veil of the epistle to the Hebrews is meant. The era of the old covenant is over, and that of the new has begun.[69] Kingsbury declares that 'Jesus himself supplants the temple as the "place" where God mediates salvation to people'.[70] For others, the *velum scissum* represents *both* vindication of

*to St Matthew* (Oxford: Clarendon Press, 1936), pp. 254–55; Keener, *Matthew*, pp. 686–87, who adopts at least three interpretations. Similarly, Lindeskog, 'The Veil of the Temple', 136–37, although he sees the account in Hebrews as a later allegorical interpretation of the reality of Christ's atonement as recorded, especially in Mark. H. Sahlin, 'Zum Verständnis der christologischen Anschauung des Markusevangeliums', *ST* 31 (1977), 7–8, argues that the veil in mind was Christ's body and makes no distinction between the inner and outer veils of the temple. F. J. Matera, *The Kingship of Jesus: Composition and Theology in Mark 15* (Chico, Calif.: Scholars Press, 1982), pp. 139–40.

68 Calvin, *A Harmony of the Gospels*, p. 211.

69 P. F. Ellis, *Matthew: His Mind and Message* (Collegeville, Minn.: Liturgical Press, 1974), p. 97, n. 193; W. F. Albright and C. S. Mann, *Matthew: A New Translation with Introduction and Commentary* (ABC 26; New York, N.Y.: Doubleday, 1971), p. 353; D. E. Garland, *Reading Matthew: A Literary and Theological Commentary on the First Gospel* (London: SPCK, 1993), p. 260; E. Lohse, *History of the Suffering and Death of Jesus Christ* (trans. M. O. Dietrich; Philadelphia, Pa.: Fortress, 1967), p. 99; A. Sand, *Das Evangelium nach Matthäus* (Regensburg: Friedrich Pustet, 1986), pp. 465–66; H. K. LaRondelle, *The Israel of God in Prophecy: Principles of Prophetic Interpretation* (Berrien Springs, Mich.: Andrews University Press, 1983), pp. 177–78, who argues for the end of the sacrificial system in fulfillment of Dan. 9:27. G. Künzel, *Studien zum Gemeindeverständnis des Matthäus-Evangeliums* (Stuttgart: Calwer Verlag, 1978), p. 102. Similarly, D. Hill, 'Matthew 27:51–53 in the Theology of the Evangelist', *IBS* 7 (1985), 85. See especially Theodoretus, *Interp. Dan.*, 81.1481.43. Probably also, J. Jeremias, *New Testament Theology* (trans. J. Bowden; London: SCM Press, 1974) I, pp. 308–10; F. Schleiermacher, *The Life of Jesus* (trans. S. M. Gilmour; Philadelphia, Pa.: Fortress, 1975), pp. 420–21; trans. of *Das Leben Jesu. Vorlesungen an der Universität zu Berline im Jahr 1832* (ed. K. A. Rütenik; Berlin: Georg Reimer, 1864), although he insists that the author of Hebrews knew nothing of the veil's rending.

70 Kingsbury, *Matthew as Story*, p. 30; D. A. Carson, 'Matthew', in vol. 8 of *The Expositors Bible Commentary* (ed. F. Gaebelein; Grand Rapids, Mich.: Zondervan, 1984), p. 580; R. Thysman, *Communauté et directives éthiques: La catéchèse de Matthieu* (Gemblous: Éditions J. Duculot, 1974), p. 43, n. 1; H. L. Chronis, 'The Torn Veil: Cultus and Christology in Mark 15:37–39', *JBL* 101 (1982), 111; W. Carter, *Matthew: Storyteller, Interpreter, Evangelist* (Peabody, Mass.: Hendrickson, 1996), p. 221. A 'temple Christology' is more properly found in John. See S. Um, 'The Theme of Temple Christology in the Fourth Chapter of John's Gospel in Light of the Early Jewish Understanding of Water and the Spirit'

Christ's death and access to God.[71] It reveals 'hidden things', normally meaning salvation for the Gentiles (the centurion), although more often than not scholars fail to specify precisely what is revealed and to whom.[72]

Some have argued that if the evangelists are thinking of the inner veil, then the priests (who would be present at that hour for the evening sacrifices)[73] would by no means disclose that information.[74] Others have objected that the priests who were later converted (Acts 6:7) could have made such information known.[75] God has accepted Christ's atoning self-sacrifice for the benefit of sinners,[76] and the priests' sacrifices for sins are no longer necessary.[77]

(Ph.D. diss., The University of St Andrews, 2001); M. Kinzer, 'Temple Christology in the Gospel of John', *SBLSP* 37 (1998), 447–64; A. R. Kerr, *The Temple of Jesus' Body: The Temple Theme in the Gospel of John* (JSNTSup 220; Sheffield: Academic Press, 2002).

[71] J. Gnilka, *Das Matthäusevangelium* (2 vols.; Freiburg: Herder, 1988) II, p. 476; W. Wiefel, *Das Evangelium nach Matthäus* (Leipzig: Evangelische Verlagsanstalt, 1998), p. 481; S. de Dietrich, *The Gospel according to Matthew* (Richmond, Va.: John Knox, 1961), p. 147.

[72] Origen, *Fr. Cant*., 2.8.25; *Comm. Matt. 27:50–54*; *Fr. Luc*.151, 251; Cyril of Alexandria, *Comm. Jo*. 1.558; 2.143; *Comm. Matt. 27.51*, *Fr*. 315.266–67; Augustine, *Spir. Et litt*. 27 [15]; *Pecc. orig*. 29 (relating to Rom 3.21); *Serm. NT* 87.6 (relating the temple veil to that of Moses); Gregory Nazianzus, *Or*. 29, 'On the Son', 20; Clement of Alexandria, *Strom*. 5.6; John Chrysostom, *Hom. 1 Cor*. 61.203.44; *Exp. Ps*. 55.272.52; *Comm. Heb*., 15.4 says veil is his body that hides the Godhead; Tertullian, *Adv. Jud*. 13 (applying Jer. 2:10f; Amos 8:9); Clement of Alexandria, *Exc*. 1.27.1.1; 1.27.2.2, 4; 2.38.2.1–3.5; Matera, *Kingship of Jesus*, p. 139. M. Luther, *Lectures on Titus, Philemon, and Hebrews* (LW 29; ed. J. Pelikan; St Louis, Mo.: Concordia, 1968), p. 203, sees the rending as a sign of the end of the 'synagogue' and the appearance or revelation of the Church. Cf. Pelletier, 'La tradition synoptique', 161, who rightly sees these interpretations being similar to the revelation described in 1 Cor. 13:10–12 and 2 Cor. 3:13–18. For a concise survey of the origins and development of this interpretation, see pp. 179–80 therein. Cf. A. Pelletier, 'Le "Voile" du Temple de Jérusalem est-il devenu la "Portière" du Temple d'Olympie', *Syria* 32 (1955), 302.

[73] Jacobus, *Matthew*, pp. 289–90.

[74] So D. Brown, 'The Veil of the Temple Rent in Twain from the Top to the Bottom', *Exp*. 5th Series 2 (1895), 158–60; Keener, *Matthew*, p. 687; P. Gaechter, *Das Matthäus Evangelium: Ein Kommentar* (Innsbruck: Tyrolia, 1963), pp. 931–32; McNeile, *St Matthew*, p. 423.

[75] Alford, *The Greek Testament* I, p. 281; Plummer, *S. Matthew*, pp. 401–2; Carr, *St Matthew*, p. 311; Lange and Schaff, *Matthew*, p. 527. Brown (*Death* II, p. 1112, n. 32) suggests such speculation belongs to 'those who push the historical issue to the extreme'. Scholars such as Kingsbury, however, likely would not think the event historical and so are not bothered by this issue.

[76] T. Hegg, 'Separating the Most Holy from the Holy: The "Veil" in the Tabernacle and First and Second Temples' (Paper presented at the Northwest Regional Conference meeting of the Evangelical Theological Society; Portland, Ore., March 4, 2000), 16; cf. Gregory of Nyssa, *Res*. 9.318.2; Cyril of Alexandria, *Thes. Trin*., 75.400.6; Athanasius, *Hom. Pass*., 28.229.9.

[77] J. P. Meier, *The Vision of Matthew: Christ, Church and Morality in the First Gospel* (New York, N.Y.: Paulist Press, 1979), p. 33.

Interpretations based on this method are quite complicated; because, since so many *assume* the inner veil is intended on the basis of the Hebrews texts, with no discussion, it is difficult to distinguish between the method and the interpretation. Admittedly, though, one need not consider the Hebrews accounts to hold to the view of the inner veil's being opened to God. Bonnard emphasises the access of Gentiles to God and the abolition of the priestly regulations, while adding the *velum scissum* as a figure for the destruction of the temple itself.[78] L. Morris says the curtain 'no longer functioned to keep what lay on the other side of it a secret from those outside'.[79] Riches insists that it 'strongly suggests that the presence of God which was previously associated with the Temple has now passed to Jesus himself'.[80] Others suggest the rending of the curtain refers to the work of Christ, particularly his atoning work. R. H. Lightfoot claims that 'a barrier so strongly emphasized in Jewish religion had been broken down' in an atoning sense.[81] For Hagner, 'The death of Jesus establishes the priesthood of all believers'.[82] Abbott says, 'In the moment when He died, the Lamb of the Passover was slain, and the old Temple was "loosed" or destroyed on earth in order to give place to a new Temple in heaven'.[83] W. Kelly sees the rending as a necessity because 'Unrent, it had been the symbol that man could not draw near to God'.[84] T. H. Weir relates his discussion of the temple veil to women's face veils and spiritual blindness.[85] For Neander, it is 'the wall of partition between the Divine and the Human broken down; and a spiritual worship substituted for an outward and sensible one'.[86] Finally, Origen himself offers a myriad of allegorical interpretations largely centred on removing the 'veil' of unbelief.[87]

Noteworthy of nearly all of these scholars is their lack of attention to the Matthean context, to the referentiality of the symbolism employed, or to the Old Testament cultic function of the veil– or, in most cases, to all of these. Certainly, with the word καταπέτασμα occurring only six times in the New Testament, one should[88] consider the occurrences in Hebrews, which account for half of them. However, giving full credence

[78] Bonnard, *Matthieu*, p. 407. Cf. also D. J. Harrington, *The Gospel according to Matthew* (SP 1; Collegeville, Minn.: Liturgical Press, 1983), p. 400, who favours the inner veil (although with no discussion) and offers the same two interpretations.

[79] Morris, *Matthew*, p. 724.

[80] Riches, *Matthew*, p. 98.

[81] Unfortunately for the present purposes, he does not document a single text.

[82] Hagner, *Matthew* II, p. 848–49.

[83] Abbott, *Founding*, p. 623.

[84] Kelly, *Lectures on the Gospel of Matthew*, p. 398.

[85] Weir, *DCG* II, pp. 790–91.

[86] Neander, *The Life of Jesus Christ*, pp. 421–22.

[87] *Comm. In Matt.* 27:50–54; *Fr. Luc.* 151, 251.

[88] Contra Brown *et al.*; cf. n. 66.

to *Hebrews* without consideration of the veil in its *original Old Testament* function would certainly distort its meaning in *Matthew*.

## 1.5 Miscellaneous Arguments

A lengthy list of various methods and still more various interpretations belongs to a final category. Foremost among the methods is the one that takes a historical approach and seeks to reconcile the event with the accounts of Josephus (*J.W.* 6.5.2–4 §§281–315) and the Talmud (*b. Yoma* 39b; *y. Yoma* 6:43c).

### *(a) Temple Lintel*

I begin, however, with Jerome,[89] who in his *Epistle* 120:8 refers to a gospel in *Hebraicis litteris*, from which he sees the *superliminare* (lintel) of the temple destroyed by an earthquake (see also *Comm. Matt.* 27:51; *Comm. Isa.* 3). The identity of this 'Hebrew Gospel' has been the subject of some discussion,[90] and Jerome's lack of clarity only serves to further confuse the issue. De Jonge points out that in his *Epistle* 18:9 Jerome seems to almost equate *superliminare* and *velum*.[91] Moreover, although he explicitly makes reference to Josephus (*J.W.* 6.5.3 §300), the points where he depends on Josephus and where he depends on his 'Hebrew Gospel' are unclear. Scholars have been perhaps most creative in their attempts to reconcile the destruction of the 'lintel' with the tearing of the veil.[92]

[89] For a more complete discussion of Jerome's evidence, cf. Brown, *Death* II, pp. 1116–17; de Jonge, 'Matthew 27:51 in Early Christian Exegesis', 72–73.

[90] Cf. M. J. Lagrange, 'L'Évangile selon les Hébreux', *RB* 31 (1922), 321–49; de Jonge, 'Matthew 27:51 in Early Christian Exegesis', 72; P. Vielhauer and G. Strecker, 'The Gospel of the Nazareans', in *New Testament Apocrypha* (2nd rev. edn; 2 vols.; ed. W. Schneemelcher; trans. edn R. M. Wilson; Louisville, Ky.: Westminster John Knox, 1991) II, pp. 154–65; A. F. J. Klijn, *Jewish-Christian Gospel Tradition* (Supplements to Vigiliae Christianae 17; Leiden: Brill, 1992), pp. 1–43, 93, 94. K. Aland *et al.*, eds., (*Synopsis Quattuour Evangeliorum* [9th edn; Stuttgart: Deutsche Bibelstiftung, 1976], p. 489, note a later tradition found in the later *Historia Passionis Domini* (fol. 65$^r$), though (probably rightly) sees influence of Jerome.

[91] 'Matthew 27:51 in Early Christian Exegesis', p. 72.

[92] W. Bauer, *Das Leben Jesu im Zeitalter der neutestamentlichen Apokryphen* (Tübingen: J.C.B. Mohr, 1909), pp. 230–33, argues that it is a textual variant in the gospel's text. E. Nestle, 'Matt. 27,51 und Parallelen', *ZNW* 3 (1902), 167–69), argues for a scribal error in transmitting כפתר rather than the original פרכת. Similarly G. Dalman, *The Words of Jesus: Considered in the Light of Post-Biblical Jewish Writings* (trans. D. M. Kay; Edinburgh: T. & T. Clark, 1902), p. 56; H. Laible, 'Der zerissene Tempelvorhang und die eingestürzte Oberschwelle des Tempeleingangs vom Talmud bezeugt', *NKZ* 35 (1924), 287. Abbott (*Founding*, pp. 622–23) places the blame with Tatian's *Diatessaron* and its transmission of

Although Jerome himself does not claim this, T. Zahn[93] nonetheless turns to him to insist that the rending of the veil was a natural result of the breaking of the lintels,[94] caused by an earthquake. He depends on the work of E. Nestle[95] to trace how the canonical texts (in particular, Hebrews) wrongly interpreted the event.[96] The importance of these discussions is obvious, as they raise the question of Matthew's account as it relates to those of Josephus, Jerome and the Talmud. That is, is Matthew intending to record a historical event with which the aforementioned records should be reconciled *historically*? Or, is there another option? The issue will be addressed to some extent in Chapter 6. Some scholars have taken the theological and historical together, noting the theological symbolism as a portent of the historical destruction of the temple. In another article, Zahn places the event in the Matthean context, citing Jesus' escalating hostility towards the temple.[97]

### (b) Mourning

Another interpretation depends on the Jewish tradition of tearing one's clothes as a sign of mourning. Although it is among the more common

'surface', ܐܦ *aph*, which means in Hebrew 'nose' or 'face', and the Diatessaron has '*the face of the door of the temple* (or, *the door of the* temple) was rent'. Possibly the writer of the Hebrew Gospel may have interpreted this 'front' or '*face*' as meaning the '*lintel*'. But, if he did this, he would not have had in mind the first biblical mention of 'lintel'– the only one in the Law–where the Israelite is instructed to 'strike the *lintel*', n. 1. (Exod. 12:22–23 'lintel'; משקוף). Such conjecture is rightly dismissed by Dalman, *Words of Jesus*, p. 56; Bauer, *Leben Jesu*, p. 233.

93 Zahn, 'Der zerrissene Tempelvorhang', 729–56; cf. also P. Fiebig, 'Der zerrissene Tempelvorhang', *NSK* 40 (1933), 227–36.

94 Zahn ('Der zerrissene Tempelvorhang', 730) dismisses the accounts in Hebrews as pure dogmatisation of the more likely historical accounts of Jerome, the Talmud, and Josephus, citing the closeness in dating between the gospel record and that of Josephus.

95 Nestle, 'Matt. 27,51 und Parallelen', 167–69.

96 Curiously, he gives no other consideration to the context in any of the evangelists' pericopae. Similarly W. C. Allen, *A Critical and Exegetical Commentary on the Gospel according to S. Matthew* (Edinburgh: T. & T. Clark, 1912), p. 296; P. A. Micklem, *St Matthew* (London: Methuen, 1917), pp. 274–75; cf. also R. Schnackenburg, *Matthäusevangelium* (2 vols.; Würzburg: Echter Verlag, 1987) II, p. 281. From a similar school, although arguing that the veil tradition (in Hebrews) is a product of Gnostic influence, cf. Käsemann (*The Wandering People of God*) and a response that argues contrarily for a strong Jewish tradition, Hofius, *Vorhang*.

97 T. Zahn, *Das Evangelium des Matthäus* (Leipzig: Deichert, 1922; repr., Wuppertal: R. Brockhaus, 1984), p. 716. Though perhaps the strongest argument for the outer veil, and the most evident from the Matthean corpus, it fails to deal with the immediate apocalyptic imagery surrounding the death of Christ, especially that particular to Matthew's account. Moreover, he sees the rending as also resulting in equality between priesthood and laity: 'durch den Tod Jesu dieser Unterschied zwischer Priester und Volk aufgehoben und eine neue Kultusgemeinde gestistet sei'. Zahn, 'Der zerrissene Tempelvorhang', 732.

interpretations of the early church,[98] this view has been most clearly developed by D. Daube.[99] For him, 'the action of Elisha on Elijah's ascension' (2 Kgs 2:12) is a 'prototype' for the veil event. In this view, Daube points to similarities between the Elisha and Elijah narrative, confusion over Elijah during the crucifixion (Matt. 27:47, 49), the high priest rending his garments (Matt. 26:65), and linguistic parallels with Targum texts, to conclude that the rending was a sign of lament for the death of Jesus.[100] McNeile poetically summarizes this view as follows: 'The very temple rent its veil in mourning, as the earth had clothed itself in darkness'.[101]

### *(c) Breath of Jesus*

Among the most creative (as well as most ancient) interpretations of the rending of the veil is one which highlights its close proximity to the statement of Mark 15:37: 'ὁ δὲ Ἰησοῦς ἀφεὶς φωνὴν μεγάλην ἐξέπνευσεν'.[102] Evans insists that 'the force' of Jesus' 'powerful shout' is what 'actually tears the temple veil'.[103] Moreover, drawing largely from *Liv. Pro.* 12:11–12 and *T. Levi* 10:3, he concludes that the symbolism is one primarily of vindication of Jesus' prediction for the destruction of the temple (Mark 13:2) and the judgment of Jesus' 'priestly judges' (Mark 14:62).[104]

[98] *Recog. Clem.* 1.41; Hippolytus, *Pasch.* 55.2; Ps.-Cyprian, *De laude martyrii* 29; Ps.-Cyprian, *De montibus Sina et Sion* 8; Origen, *Fr. Luc.* 250; *Frg. On Matt.* No. 560; Aphrahat, *Demon.*, 21.17; Nicephorus Basilaces, *Progymnasma* 4.143. 206; John Chrysostom, *Hom. Matt. 26:39* 51.32.40; Ps.-Macarius, *Sermones* 64.2.6.5.13; Eznik of Kolb (fl. c. 430–c. 450), *De Deo* 358.

[99] D. Daube, *The New Testament and Rabbinic Judaism* (London: Athlone Press, 1956), pp. 23–24.

[100] *Ibid.*, pp. 23–24. Cf. also *Recog. Clem.*, 1.41; R. A. Edwards, *Matthew's Story of Jesus* (Philadelphia, Pa.: Fortress, 1985), p. 92; McNeile, *St Matthew*, p. 423; and esp. R. D. Aus, *Samuel, Saul and Jesus: Three Early Palestinian Jewish Christian Gospel Haggadoth* (SFSHJ 105; Atlanta, Ga.: Scholars Press, 1994), pp. 147–58.

[101] McNeile, *St Matthew*, p. 423.

[102] Cf. Matt. 27:50: ὁ δὲ Ἰησοῦς πάλιν κράξας φωνῇ μεγάλῃ ἀφῆκεν τὸ πνεῦμα.

[103] C. A. Evans, *Mark 8:27–16:20* (WBC 34B; Nashville, Tenn.: Nelson, 2001), p. 509.

[104] Evans, *Mark 8:27–16:20*, pp. 509–10. So also *Catena in Matt.*, 237.30–31; *Catena in Marcum*, 440.26, 441.1; *Catena in Acta*, 36:4; Chrysostom, *Hom. Matt.*, 88.2. Others further associate this interpretation with Jesus' prediction of the desolation of the temple (Matt. 23:38), So also *Catena in Marcum*, 441.8, 12; Apollinaris, *Fr. Jo.*, 145.1. Still others suggest what was breathed out and subsequently rent the veil was the Holy Spirit. Cf. Jackson, 'Death of Jesus in Mark', 27. This 'punitive' use of his breath, France (*Mark*, 657) regards as 'bizarre'. Schmidt ('Penetration of Barriers', 229) sees it as both a prediction of temple destruction *and* the departure of God's Spirit from the Jews.

Rather than Christ's breath, G. R. Driver insists that violent winds, common in Palestine, tore the veil.[105]

### *(d) Structure of Mark*

Others have turned to the structure of Mark for their understanding of the rending of the veil. K. Bailey characteristically sees a chiastic structure to Mark's crucifixion narrative (borrowed from Old Testament prophets), which juxtaposes the rending of the veil and the death of Christ. While one need not see a chiastic structure in this account, Bailey's interpretation based upon it concludes that 'for Mark, Jesus and his cross were a *replacement* for both the city of Jerusalem and the temple'. Mark's 'messianic secret' is out, revealing a '*dying saviour* . . . unveiled on a hill before the *entire world*'.[106] S. Motyer, also looking at Mark's structure, sees an 'inclusio' with the *velum scissum* in 15:38 and the rending of the heavens in 1:9–11. Therefore, the veil is 'a Markan Pentecost, a proleptic bestowal of the Spirit analogous to the proleptic destruction of the temple'.[107]

### *(e) Prayer*

In an innovative interpretation of the rending of the veil, which only works in Luke, D. Sylva highlights the close proximity of Jesus' death to the *velum scissum*, using the rending of the veil to interpret Christ's death.[108] With Jesus' death at the ninth hour, the hour of prayer, and other less-convincing arguments, he concludes that 'Jesus' commitment of his

[105] Driver, 'Two Problems', 337. He asserts, 'No one, certainly no educated man, can have supposed such a portent possible'.

[106] K. Bailey, 'The Fall of Jerusalem and Mark's Account of the Cross', *ExpTim* 102 (1991), 102, 4.

[107] S. Motyer, 'The Rending of the Veil: A Markan Pentecost?' *NTS* 33 (1987), 155. Similarly Ulansey ('Mark's Cosmic Inclusio', 124) adds that Josephus' description of the *outer* veil in *J.W.* 5.5.4 §§212–14 with its heavenly decoration confirms Motyer's view. However, Ulansey overlooks the possibility that the inner veil may have been quite similar as Josephus' ὁμοίως καταπετάσματι πρός τὸ ἔξωθεν 'in like manner from the outer portion by a veil' (Josephus, *J.W.* 5.5.5 §219 [Thackeray, LCL]) is inconclusive.

[108] D. D. Sylva, 'The Temple Curtain and Jesus' Death in the Gospel of Luke', *JBL* 105 (1986), 241. While it is acknowledged that the rending of the veil *is* a commentary on Christ's death, Sylva seems to be basing his explanation of that commentary on very shaky ground. The present work will argue from precisely the opposite direction. That is, although the rending of the veil is unexplained by the evangelist, Matthew has much to say about the death of Christ. Therefore, this study will use Matthew's understanding of *Christ's death* to illuminate an interpretation of the *rending of the veil.*

spirit is an address to the God revealed to him by the tearing of the temple curtain, as Stephen's commitment of his spirit is an address to the Lord revealed by the opening of the heavens'.[109]

### (*f*) *Markan Context*

Although few have sought to explain the rending of the veil outside of its Jewish setting, S. G. F. Brandon has put forth an interesting proposal from a Gentile perspective in the Gospel of Mark. Uniquely, he highlights the inappropriateness of the (Jewish) veil event in its Markan (Gentile) context, presuming Mark had a purpose different from that of his (Semitic?) source. He turns to the historical record of the 'Flavian triumph', when, according to Josephus (*J.W.* 6.6.3 §§288–309; cf. Tacitus, *Hist.* 5.13), the ornate veil was part of the loot pillaged from Jerusalem and taken to the imperial palace in Rome.[110] Suggesting that the Romans would have flaunted their spoils, he concludes, 'If the Christians of Rome were thus made familiar with these furnishings of the Temple and their significance, it is probable also that they were acquainted with stories about the prodigies which heralded the destruction of the Jerusalem sanctuary such as Josephus has recorded' (*J.W.* 6.6.3 §§288–309; Tacitus, *Hist.* 5.13).[111] With the Romans' tearing down of the temple, Brandon conjectures, the tradition of the *velum scissum* was probably conflated and appropriated to Jesus' death to respond to the Jewish notion of its acceptance by God as symbolised by his presence in the temple. This, naturally, was associated with the death of Jesus.[112]

### (*g*) *Temple*

Among the most promising studies, at least from a methodological standpoint, was one recently put forth by J. B. Green, which deals with the *velum scissum* in relation to destruction of the temple as portrayed in Luke-Acts.[113] The differing order of the account by Luke, coupled with

[109] Sylva, 'The Temple Curtain', 245. For an excellent critique of this view, which had found no support prior to 1986 and very little since, see J. B. Green, 'The Death of Jesus and the Rending of the Temple Veil: A Window into Luke's Understanding of Jesus and the Temple', *SBLSP* 30 (1991), 550. For a sympathetic voice, see J. Nolland, *Luke* (3 vols.; WBC 35A–C; Dallas, Tex.: Word, 1989, 1993) III, p. 1157, although he argues more cautiously and more emphatically of the apocalyptic nature of the event.

[110] Brandon, 'Date of the Markan Gospel', 132. [111] *Ibid.*, 132.

[112] This view is not without its serious difficulties and assumptions. For a helpful, though brief, critique cf. Yates, *Spirit and the Kingdom*, pp. 232–37.

[113] Green, 'Death of Jesus', 543.

the largely positive view of the Temple itself in Luke-Acts, leads Green to 'a source-critical analysis of the death scene in Luke 23 and to a literary-theological and sociological reading of the temple material in Luke-Acts'. He argues that the rending of the veil symbolises 'the obliteration of the barriers between those peoples previously divided by status and ethnicity'.[114] The attractiveness of this view is that Green has very carefully drawn a distinctively Lukan picture of the temple as a key hermeneutical element, a method which will similarly be employed in the present work for Matthew.[115]

### *(h) Various*

Again the ambiguity of the synoptic accounts of the veil has left a wide-open door for interpretative creativity.[116] To borrow a phrase from Beaton's accounts of the diversity of scholarly opinion on Old Testament text-forms in Matthew, interpretations of the rending of the veil are 'as diverse as they are creative'.[117] Ephraem the Syrian (*Comm. on the Diatessaron* 21.4–6) speaks of 'using the rent veil to clothe honorably the naked body of Jesus on the cross'.[118] Symeon the New Theologian (*Hymn* 36.41) calls the *velum scissum* among οἱ παράνομοι (the unlawful things) that no one fully understood. Leontius of Constantinople (*In sanctam parasceven*, 39–40) describes the rending of the veil as analogous to the fate of ἐκείνων δὲ αἱ καρτίαι οὐ κατηνοίγοντο (the hearts of those not understanding). J. Lightfoot insists that 'both

[114] *Ibid.*, 543. Similar conclusions are reached by Jerome, *Commentary on Matthew* 27:51; M. H. Crosby, *House of Disciples: Church, Economics, and Justice in Matthew* (Maryknoll, N.Y.: Orbis Books, 1988), p. 89; C. L. Blomberg, *Matthew* (Nashville, Tenn.: Broadman Press, 1992), p. 421; Stendahl, 'Matthew', p. 797; P. Benoit, *The Passion and Resurrection of Jesus Christ* (trans. B. Weatherhead; New York, N.Y.: Herder & Herder, 1969), pp. 201–2; D. Marguerat, *Le Judgment das l'Evangile de Matthieu* (Genève: Labor et Fides, 1981), p. 376; H. Frankemölle, *Jahwe-Bund und Kirche Christi: Studien zur Form- und Traditionsgeschichte des, Evangeliums' nach Matthäus* (Münster: Aschendorff, 1974), p. 118; similarly p. 167; R. Walker, *Die Heilsgeschichte im ersten Evangelium* (Göttingen: Vandenhoeck & Ruprecht, 1967), p. 73.

[115] While this is critical, it fails to give credence to a number of vital factors, not least of which is Luke's view of Christ's *death*, for it is in the context of the death of Christ that Luke places this event. Surely the subject of the crucifixion narrative is the death of Christ rather than the temple. We will revisit Green's method in Chapter 5.

[116] Although more of a vivid description than an interpretation, Asterius Sophista (fourth century) uses nautical language to compare with the tearing of the veil, which is rent like a great sail in the sea (τὸ καταπέτασμα ὡς ἄρμενον περιεσχίζετο; *Comm. Ps.*, 20.17.4; cf. 31.7.7).

[117] R. Beaton, *Isaiah's Christ in Matthew's Gospel* (SNTSMS 123; Cambridge: Cambridge University Press, 2002), p. 25.

[118] Brown, *Death* II, p. 1108, n. 22.

(inner and outer veils) are rent in the very middle'.[119] Finally, there is a considerable group of notable scholars who either make theological conclusions about the *velum scissum* with no justification or discussion whatsoever[120] or simply gloss over it while commenting on other portions of the pericope.[121]

## 1.6 Modern Attempts

Here it is appropriate to examine two works published to date, apart from commentaries and monographs on other topics, that purport to speak solely of the rending of the veil *in Matthew*. First, M. de Jonge's article considers the verse 'against the background of the interpretations in early Christian literature'.[122] He suggests that up to now, many approaches

[119] J. Lightfoot, *A Commentary on the New Testament from the Talmud and Hebraica, Matthew — 1 Corinthians* (trans. unknown, Peabody, Mass.: Hendrickson, 1989) I, p. 371; trans. of *Horae Hebraicae et Talmudicae* (Oxford: Oxford University Press, 1859); repr. of *Horae Hebraicae et Talmudicae* (Cambridge: Johan, 1674).

[120] J. A. Fitzmyer, *The Gospel according to Luke* (2 vols.; AB 28–28A; New York, N.Y.: Doubleday, 1981–1985) II, pp. 1518–19; E. Klostermann, *Das Markusevangelium* (HNT; Tübingen: Mohr, 1926), pp. 186–87; J. A. Bengel, *Gnomon of the New Testament* (2 vols.; trans. A. R. Fausset; Edinburgh: T. & T. Clark, 1877) I, p. 480; Lachs, *Matthew, Mark, and Luke*, pp. 434–35; A. Edersheim, *The Temple: Its Ministry and Services* (London: Religious Tract Society, 1874; repr., Peabody, Mass.: Hendrickson, 1994), p. 34; J. Wellhausen, *Das Evangelium Matthaei* (Berlin: Georg Reimer, 1904), p. 148; A. B. Bruce, 'The Synoptic Gospels', in vol. 1 of *The Expositor's Greek Testament* (ed. W. Robertson Nicoll; London: Hodder & Stoughton, 1897), p. 332; D. F. Strauss, *The Life of Jesus Critically Examined* (trans. G. Eliot; London: SCM Press, 1973), p. 692; H. B. Green, *The Gospel according to Matthew in the Revised Standard Version: Introduction and Commentary* (Oxford: Oxford University Press, 1975), p. 224; H. Ridderbos, *The Coming of the Kingdom* (trans. H. de Jongste; Phillipsburg, N.J.: P&R, 1962), p. 467; E. W. B. Nicholson, *A New Commentary on the Gospel according to Matthew* (London: C. Kegan Paul, 1881), p. 234; T. H. Robinson, *The Gospel of Matthew* (London: Hodder & Stoughton, 1928), p. 231; J. Morison, *Commentary on the Gospel according to Matthew* (London: Hamilton & Adams, 1870), p. 601.

[121] Hippolytus, *Noet.* 18.8.3; *Catena in Joannem*, 343.17; Cyril of Jerusalem, *Catech.* 1–18, 13.39.7; Theodoretus, *Ps.*, 80.1645.39; Augustine, *Cons.* 17–19; Origen, *Comm. Jo.* 19.16.103.4; Romanus Melodus, *Cantica dubia*, 43.10.6; 80.6.3; Lactantius, *Institutions* 4.19; D. J. Weaver, *Matthew's Missionary Discourse* (Sheffield: JSOT Press, 1990), p. 219, n. 75; E. Schweizer, *The Good News according to Matthew* (trans. D. E. Green; London: SPCK, 1976), p. 515; R. Kratz, *Auferweckung als Befreiung: Eine Studie zur Passions- und Auferstehungstheologie des Matthäus (besonders Mt 27,62–28,15)* (Stuttgart: KBW, 1973), pp. 38, 50; D. C. Sim, *Apocalyptic Eschatology in the Gospel of Matthew* (SNTMS 88; Cambridge: Cambridge University Press, 1996), pp. 110–11; J. Schmid, *Das Evangelium nach Matthäus* (Regensburg: Friedrich Pustet, 1965), pp. 373–76; Sabourin, 'Apocalyptic Traits', 19; G. Strecker, *Der Weg der Gerechtigkeit: Untersuchung zur Theologie des Matthäus* (Göttingen: Vandenhoeck & Ruprecht, 1962), p. 182.

[122] De Jonge, 'Matthew 27:51 in Early Christian Exegesis', p. 67. Harrington's (*Matthew*, p. 400) suggestion that there was a 'debate' on the veil in the early church surpasses the

that are used to interpret the account are unsatisfactory for three reasons: (1) 'The Gospel accounts do not seem to be interested in the question as to which of the two curtains is meant.' He states that only Hebrews 9:3 raises the issue, which is not picked up again until Origen. (2) Citing the work of A. Pelletier, he criticizes the tendency of recent scholars to identify the 'names, functions, and outward appearance of the curtains' according to Philo and Josephus on the grounds that the Gospel writers show no familiarity with these details.[123] (3) He is critical of scholarly citation of the historical accounts of Josephus (*J.W.* 6.6.3 §§288–31), the Talmud (*y. Yoma* 6:43c; *b. Yoma* 39b), and Jerome (*Ep.* 120:8) referred to with respect to a sign of the impending destruction of the temple and drawn upon as 'historical parallels to the veil-event'.[124] Surveying other scholars, notably D. Senior, R. Kratz, and M. Riebl, de Jonge rightly complains that they (as do most scholars) 'unfortunately concentrate completely on Matt. 27:51b–54 and seem to regard vs 51a as an element taken over from Mark which is connected with, but need not necessarily fit into, the apocalypticizing description of events which is peculiar to Matthew'.[125] He then goes on to survey the rending of the veil in the works of Jerome, Ephraem The Syrian, Melito of Sardis, Tertullian, and Origen, and in other lesser works, only to conclude that

> it is very unlikely that 'the' meaning of Matt. 27:51a will ever be established beyond doubt. Perhaps, however, the scrutiny of the early Christian material will induce modern exegetes to review their own interpretations critically and to present them with utmost modesty. Many of them are not all that new, and all of them are tenuous.[126]

Curiously, however, de Jonge never develops his criticism of the modern scholar's tendency to interpret the veil solely in light of its following context (27:51b–54), and offers no alternative approach.

A second, more recent and promising attempt was undertaken by D. Andreoli.[127] He argues that the *velum scissum* should be read in light of the Matthean special material (27:51b–53) which, he contends, is an early Easter liturgical hymn advocating a 'new exodus' based on Ezekiel 37.

evidence. No author, to our knowledge, refutes another's interpretation of the event but simply develops his own.

123 Pelletier ('La tradition synoptique', pp. 179–80) argues for the outer veil from an 'archaeological' perspective, though based on the Josephus and Philo texts. His contribution will be discussed more fully in Chapters 4 and 6.

124 De Jonge, 'Matthew 27:51 in Early Christian Exegesis', pp. 67–69.

125 *Ibid.*, p. 71. 126 *Ibid.*, p. 79.

127 'Il velo squarciato nel Vangelo di Matteo', *BSW* 1 (1998), 20–42.

He further asserts that when one examines Matthew's view of the temple and the temple's role in Jewish apocalyptic eschatology, the evangelist is clearly anti-temple and is therefore alluding to its destruction in the *velum scissum* text. There is much in Andreoli's proposal which I will examine with more care in Chapter 6, for his location of the veil in an apocalyptic setting and his examination of Matthew's view of the temple are decisive elements in solving the puzzle of Matthew's *velum scissum*. However, as we will also see in Chapter 6, Andreoli's suggestion falls short of identifying the referent in Matthew's use of the apocalyptic image and overlooks several essential texts, with the result that he misinterprets Matthew's understanding of the temple and its cult.

## 2 A New Approach

The preceding summary illustrates the complexities and ambiguities that are involved in interpreting the *velum scissum* in general, let alone in a specifically Matthean context. The present work will employ several methods to take an approach to the *velum scissum* that is not yet fully considered, in order to see whether additional light may be shed on this problematic subject. These methods are outlined as follows:

The veil, a very Jewish symbol, is often interpreted from Mark's (Gentile?) Gospel rather than Matthew's, which R. T. France calls 'at the same time the most Jewish and the most anti-Jewish of the gospels'.[128] Consideration of the 'Jewish' origin of the veil is perhaps both the most essential and the most overlooked element for interpreting the veil, particularly in Matthew. H. Alford's statement, 'A right and deep view of the O. T. symbolism is required to furnish the key to it',[129] has been largely overlooked. In 1970, E. Linnemann articulated what is curiously perhaps the most *unusual* methodological statement on interpreting the rending of the veil when she simply said, 'Wir werden diese Deutungen an dem zu prüfen haben, was *wir über die Funktion des Vorhangs im Tempelkult in Erfahrung bringen und für das Verstehen der Perikope durch ihre ersten Leser oder Hörer voraussetzen können*'.[130] Although her work gives only brief attention to the function of the veil in the Old Testament and none to its role in the Matthean Passion Narrative, her comment is an important place to begin. The method employed here, then,

[128] R. T. France, *Matthew: Evangelist and Teacher* (Downers Grove, Ill.: InterVarsity Press, 1989), p. 19.

[129] Alford, *The Greek Testament* I, p. 281.

[130] Linnemann, *Studien*, p. 160 (emphasis mine).

will initially be historical–critical in orientation.[131] Why begin here? It is largely recognised that Matthew is highly dependent upon Old Testament motifs and texts in the formation of both his Passion Narrative in particular and his gospel text in general. Therefore it seems most sensible to begin the study proper with Old Testament references to the veil, particularly because these references inform one's understanding of the cultic function and identity of the veil in subsequent texts. Even after Linnemann's assertions in 1970, few have given serious attention to the Old Testament origin of the veil, except as the locus of lexical data in an attempt to distinguish which veil Matthew had in mind. Yet even those who look to the Old Testament for lexical data fail to afford these texts sufficient attention and quickly leave them behind to pursue other avenues. Furthermore, I am convinced that the relative importance of the Old Testament and its fulfillment reflects at least an assumption on the part of Matthew that his readers were familiar with – if not steeped in – the Old Testament. Kingsbury's comment regarding Matthew's 'gospel of the kingdom' saying (13:9) is no less relevant here: '[Matthew] simply assumes that the reader will know what it means'.[132] Such a readership, which is typically called

[131] The nature of this historical–critical study will be evident when texts are discussed. For the present, however, this approach should not be confused with that of R. Bultmann, who classifies the events surrounding Jesus' death as 'rein novellistische Motive' (*Die Geschichte der synoptischen Tradition* [Göttingen: Vandenhoeck & Ruprecht, 1921], p. 172), nor with that of E. Käsemann, who insists that the veil motif (in Hebrews) is a development of the 'Gnostic tradition of the heavenly *Urmensch*-high priest' (*The Wandering People of God: An Investigation of the Letter to the Hebrews* [trans. R. A. Harrisville; Minneapolis, Minn.: Augsburg, 1984], p. 230). Käsemann's work first appeared as *Das wandernde Gottesvolk: Eine Untersuchung zum Hebräerbrief* (Göttingen: Vandenhoeck & Ruprecht, 1957). See also E. Grässer, *Der Glaube im Hebräerbrief* (MTS 2; Marburgh: Elwert, 1965) and G. Theissen, *Untersuchungen zum Hebräerbrief* (SNT 2; Gütersloh: Mohn, 1969). For a rebuttal, see O. Hofius, *Der Vorhang vor dem Thron Gottes: Eine exegetisch-religionsgeschichtliche Untersuchung zu Hebräer 6,19f. und 10,19f.* (WUNT 14; Tübingen: Mohr Siebeck, 1972), who argues the veil motif is solely derived from Hellenistic Jewish tradition rather than that of Gnosticism. Hofius' contribution will be considered in detail in Chapter 4. Modern scholars have recognised Käsemann's attempt to propose Merkabah mysticism as the primary backdrop for Hebrews' thought has failed. See C. R. Koester, 'The Epistle to the Hebrews in Recent Study', *CurBS* 2 (1994), 123–45, esp. 132; G. H. Guthrie, 'Hebrews in Its First-Century Contexts: Recent Research', in *The Face of New Testament Studies: A Survey of Recent Research* (ed. S. McKnight and G. R. Osborne; Grand Rapids, Mich.: Baker Academic, 2004), pp. 425–27; H.-M. Schenke, 'Erwägung zum Rätsel der Hebräerbriefes', in *Neues Testament und christliche Existenz* (eds H. D. Betz and L. Schottroff; Tübingen: Mohr Siebeck, 1973), pp. 433–34; R. Williamson, 'The Background of the Epistle to the Hebrews', *ExpTim* 87 (1975), 232–37. Instead, significantly, it is recognized as having come from common traditions in early apocalyptic Judaism. See L. Hurst, *Epistle to the Hebrews: Its Background of Thought* (SNTSMS 65; Cambridge: Cambridge University Press, 1990), esp. pp. 82–85.

[132] J. D. Kingsbury, *Matthew: Structure, Christology, Kingdom* (Minneapolis, Minn.: Fortress, 1975), p. 130. W. R. Telford (*Mark* [Sheffield: Academic Press, 1997], p. 106)

the 'implied reader',[133] would have seemingly recognised allusions and images and made theological connections which Matthew felt no need to explain. The present work, then, will begin (Chapter 2) by exploring each Old Testament text where *any* curtain translated καταπέτασμα in the LXX in order to determine what light, if any, it may shed on the veil's rending in Matthew's Passion Narrative. From there I will examine the respective cultic functions of the curtains (Chapter 3) to help determine which, if any, Matthew had in mind in depicting its rending.

I will then proceed (Chapter 4) to examine the veil in Second Temple Jewish and rabbinic texts, giving particular attention to texts which are partially or wholly apocalyptic in orientation. As is the case with the Old Testament, it is further assumed that the Jewish–Christian people among Matthew's readership[134] were also familiar with some of the texts or concepts reflected in 'Second Temple' Jewish writings.[135] We will see that from an early date the veil of the temple began to represent something beyond itself, and that by the rabbinic period a firmly established tradition identified the veil of the temple with the firmament of heaven from Gen. 1:6 within what can broadly be called a Jewish 'temple' cosmology.

I will then address the Matthean text itself (Chapters 5 and 6), where the method employed will be primarily 'composition-critical',[136] both

makes a similar point for Mark: 'One of the competencies expected of the implied reader . . . is intertextual competence, the ability to recognize, interpret and respond to the rich tapestry of Old Testament quotations and allusions which embroiders the text.'

[133] Here the definition of Kingsbury (*Matthew as Story*, p. 38) is accepted: 'an imaginary person who is to be envisaged, in perusing Matthew's story, as responding to the text at every point with whatever emotion, understanding, or knowledge the text ideally calls for. Or, to put it differently, the implied reader is that imaginary person in whom the intention of the text is to be thought of as always reaching its fulfillment'.

[134] For some discussion of the identity of Matthew's readership as well as its relationship to Judaism see D. J. Harrington, 'Matthew's Gospel: Pastoral Problems and Possibilities' in *The Gospel of Matthew in Current Study: Studies in Memory of William G. Thompson, S. J.* (ed. D. Aune; Grand Rapids, Mich.: Eerdmans, 2001), pp. 62–73; Stanton, *A Gospel for a New People*, pp. 113–91. For a discussion of the Matthean Community, see esp. D. C. Sim, *The Gospel of Matthew and Christian Judaism: The History and Social Setting of the Matthean Community* (Edinbrugh: T.&T. Clark, 1998); A. J. Saldarini, *Matthew's Christian-Jewish Community* (Chicago, Ill.: University of Chicago Press, 1994); R. S. Ascough, 'Matthew and Community Formation', in *The Gospel of Matthew in Current Study: Studies in Memory of William G. Thompson, S.J.* (ed. D. Aune; Grand Rapids, Mich.: Eerdmans, 2001), pp. 96–126; P. Luomanen, *Entering the Kingdom of Heaven: A Study on the Structure of Matthew's View of Salvation* (WUNT II, 101; Tübingen: Mohr Siebeck, 1998), pp. 262–86.

[135] Helpful sources which summarise what Jewish texts were known by Matthew include D. C. Allison's *The New Moses: A Matthean Typology* (Edinburgh: T. & T. Clark, 1993) and, to a lesser degree, L. Sabourin's 'Apocalyptic Traits in Matthew's Gospel', *RelSBul* 3 (1983), 19–36. See also D. E. Orton, *The Understanding Scribe: Matthew and the Apocalyptic Ideal* (JSNTS 25; Sheffield: Academic Press, 1989), pp. 137–63.

[136] The term is borrowed from Riches, *Matthew*, and will be developed more fully in Chapter 5.

seeking to treat the text as a single literary whole (though clearly not without outside textual, historical and theological influences) and presuming that the author (or final redactor whom, for convenience, I call Matthew) was fully aware of the imagery he was employing.[137] It also recognises that Matthew was employing imagery from a broad pool of thought and literature in Second Temple Judaism and particularly the Old Testament.

Chapter 5 will cover broader Matthean topics to inform our reading of the *velum scissum*. Whether in Matthew or Mark, most scholars see the rending of the temple veil as some sort of comment on the death of Jesus.[138] With an argument based exclusively on the Markan context, J. E. Yates provides an innovative approach to the relationship of the death of Jesus and the rending of the veil: 'The central and undoubted historical fact is Jesus dead on the Cross. Surely, here is the true centre of attention: why, then, should not the comment at 15:38 be a direct reference to Jesus himself?'[139] He then traces Mark's portrayal of Jesus' death throughout the Gospel to highlight the 'positive significance of the death of Jesus'.[140] It is important to note that while Yates does suggest that both Matthew and Luke have the *outer* veil in mind (i.e., his approach does not hold for the first or third evangelists), each of his most convincing arguments for holding that Mark had the *inner* veil in mind hold equally as well, and in places better, in the Matthean context. Therefore, this chapter will likewise employ a sort of hermeneutical algebra to examine Matthew's portrayal of the death of Jesus *throughout* the gospel (for which we have a good deal of data) and use that information to interpret the *velum scissum* (for which we have so little data). That is, I will attempt to discern the meaning of the unknown element in the Matthean equation (the *velum scissum*) by means of the known element (Matthew's portrayal of Jesus' death). The method employed here will also be 'composition-critical'[141] in that precedence will be given to the final text of Matthew as a whole for a contextual interpretation of the event, with credence also being given to sources other than Matthew's Gospel. Indeed, we will see that attention to the role of the *velum scissum* in the particular Matthean context has been largely neglected even among commentators on the first gospel. We will see if and how Matthew's consistent portrayal of the death

[137] Contra Brown, *Death* II, p. 1113.

[138] Whereas most see it as a comment on the death of Jesus, the basis for that association (which may well be right) needs to be firmly established. In Chapter 6 we will demonstrate that the veil, as well as the other Matthean events, are 'commenting' on Jesus' death and explore what the evangelist is, and is not, saying about it.

[139] Yates, *Spirit and the Kingdom*, p. 234. [140] *Ibid*., p. 232.

[141] The term is borrowed from J. Riches, *Matthew* (NTG; Sheffield: Academic Press, 1997), p. 14, and will be defined more fully in Chapter 5.

of Jesus throughout his Gospel informs our understanding of the *velum scissum*, which occurs immediately after that death.

Chapter 5 also includes a similar analysis of Matthew's portrayal of the temple. In a method not unlike that of J. B. Green in Luke, I will explore Matthew's attitude toward the Jerusalem temple in general to try to define, as much as possible, the relationship between Jesus and the temple and to look at possible implications for the relationship between the death of Jesus and the *velum scissum*. A similar approach was employed in Matthew by D. Andreoli, with whom I will interact to some extent. As with Andreoli, we will see if and how Matthew's consistent portrayal of the temple throughout his gospel informs our understanding of the rending of its veil in Matt. 27:51a.

Chapter 6 mainly explores the implications of the data discussed in Chapters 2–5 in an exegesis of the Matthean pericope (27:45–54), naturally focusing on Matt. 27:51a and the so-called special material (27:51b–53). I will address the implications for the cessation of the functions articulated in Chapter 3 within the Matthean corpus. I will also address whether and how we may identify the *velum scissum* as 'apocalyptic', examine the referentiality for the symbolism employed, and relate the symbolism to that employed in the Matthean special material. This is followed by a Conclusion, in which I will summarise the work as a whole and provide some suggestions for where it can be taken from there.

The present study does not pretend to have the final word on a complicated text. Instead, I hope to provide an initial word towards a new direction in examining this issue, which will serve both to illuminate a contextual interpretation of the rending of the veil, particularly in Matthew, and to encourage scholars to regularly evaluate the validity of their methods in examining this particularly troublesome text.

# 2

## VEILS IN THE OLD TESTAMENT

### Introduction

While many scholars have rightly looked to the Old Testament to explain Matthew's resurrection narrative in 27:53,[1] few have granted the same favour to his veil account in 27:51a.[2] Lange and Schaff declare, 'There is neither a prophecy of the Old Testament, nor a Jewish popular belief, which could explain a myth in this case.'[3] Perhaps, then, it is this fact, coupled with lexical ambiguity regarding Matthew's καταπέτασμα τοῦ ναοῦ, that has caused synoptic scholars to look either to Mark or Second Temple Jewish texts (Philo and Josephus in particular, whom I will consider in Chapter 4) for explanations of the rending of Matthew's veil. We will see, though, that while lexical evidence shows us there are three curtains translated καταπέτασμα in the LXX, syntactical and functional evidence are decisive factors in determining which of those three is referred to by Matthew.

The key term for which we must account, καταπέτασμα, is found first and most abundantly in Greek Old Testament traditions of the tabernacle.[4] It is largely agreed that at least the general framework of both the first

[1] Notably D. Hill, 'Matthew 27:51–53 in the Theology of the Evangelist', *IBS* 7 (1985), 76–87.

[2] The notable exceptions being Alford, *The Greek Testament* (4 vols.; London: Rivingstons, 1871–74), I, p. 281 and E. Linnemann, *Studien zur Passionsgeschichte* (FRLANT 102; Göttingen: Vandenhoeck & Ruprecht, 1970), p. 160. Indeed, most scholars prior to Bornkamm have sought historical reconstruction from Philo and Josephus, and since Bornkamm scholars have seemingly looked to Matthew's Markan 'source' while neglecting the Old Testament. This is especially true of Brown, *The Death of the Messiah: A Commentary on the Passion Narratives in the Four Gospels* (2 vols.; New York: Doubleday, 1994).

[3] J. P. Lange and P. Schaff, *The Gospel according to Matthew* (New York, N.Y.: Charles Scribner's Sons, 1915), p. 527.

[4] An exception is the rather recent discovery of an inscription at Samos Island. See D. M. Gurtner, 'Καταπέτασμα: Lexicographical and Etymological Considerations to the Biblical "Veil"', *AUSS* 42 (2004), 105–11. A possible exception also occurs in *Joseph and Aseneth*. See Chapter 4.

and second temples was patterned after the layout of the tabernacle. Ideologically, Second Temple texts made very smooth and natural transitions from Old Testament tabernacle texts to their respective discussions of either the Second Temple itself or the idealised, heavenly counterpart of the first.[5] This transition itself seems to have Old Testament precedents. R. E. Friedman has suggested that in 2 Chron. 29:5–7, King Hezekiah 'speaks of the Tabernacle as present in the Temple'.[6]

> Then he said to them, 'Listen to me, O Levites. Consecrate yourselves now, and consecrate the house of the LORD (בית יהוה), the God of your fathers, and carry the uncleanness out from the holy place (קדש). For our fathers have been unfaithful and have done evil in the sight of the LORD our God, and have forsaken Him and turned their faces away from the dwelling place of the LORD (משכן יהוה), and have turned their backs. They have also shut the doors of the porch and put out the lamps, and have not burned incense or offered burnt offerings in the holy place (קדש) to the God of Israel.' (NAS)

Yet the historical fate of the tabernacle is quite unclear.[7] Though some see Ps. 74:7 and Lam. 2:6–7 as indicating that the tabernacle was destroyed along with Solomon's temple, this is by no means certain. Whether these statements are meant to indicate the historical fate of the Pentateuchal structure, the functional continuity between the tabernacle and temple, or both, is not entirely clear. It seems best, then, to let stand the tension between the end of the tabernacle and the beginning of the temple. However, the fact that accounts of the tabernacle seem to fade into the narrative background of the Old Testament as the temple glares on the narrative foreground, with seemingly no disruption in cultic

[5] This is particularly apparent in the Temple Scroll. See Chapter 4.

[6] R. E. Friedman, 'Tabernacle', *ABD* VI, p. 293.

[7] Friedman (*ABD* VI, p. 294) hypothesises, based on the aforementioned 2 Chron., Ps. and Lam. texts, that the Old Testament 'presents a picture of the Tabernacle's place in history from its construction in the wilderness to its erection at Shiloh and then Gibeon to its placement inside the First Temple until its destruction in the burning of the Temple ca. 587 B.C.'. S. Légasse, 'Les voiles du temple de Jérusalem: Essai de parcours historique', *RB* 87 (1980), 566, presumes that the tabernacle account is post-exilic. For a discussion of the structure of the Solomonic temple with respect to other, similar ancient Near Eastern structures, see J. Ouellette, 'The Basic Structure of the Solomonic Temple and Archaeological Research', in *The Temple of Solomon: Archaeological Fact and Medieval Tradition in Christian, Islamic and Jewish Art* (RA 3; Missoula, Mont.: Scholars Press, 1976), pp. 1–20.

worship, strongly suggests that the tabernacle, for all intents and purposes, has been replaced by the temple.[8]

With it being likely, then, that the tabernacle was the historical, structural, and ideological predecessor of the Old Testament temple and, presumably, Matthew's ναός,[9] and with its accounts holding the highest number of occurrences of καταπέτασμα and similar language, we naturally look first to these texts for discussion of the veil.[10] A problem arises, however, because Matthean scholarship has become increasingly aware that the question of what textual tradition the first evangelist follows in his extensive use of the Old Testament is a very complicated issue.[11] Though in Matt. 27:51a we do not have a quotation from the Old Testament, the question of whether the strong Old Testament allusions throughout the Gospel, as well as those found in the subsequent events in the Matthean Passion Narrative (splitting of rocks, raising of saints, etc.), suggest the possibility of an Old Testament allusion for the veil itself must be left open for consideration.[12] It seems, however, that with respect to Matthew's καταπέτασμα τοῦ ναοῦ we are left with at least five options regarding the source of the language he employed: (1) the LXX,[13] (2) a Greek version similar to the MT,[14] (3) his own translation of a Hebrew text,[15]

[8] See also 1 Chron. 6:31–32 (MT 6:16–17), which describes the singing of ministers before the tabernacle 'until' Solomon built the temple.

[9] Matthew's particular temple language will be examined in Chapter 5 and considered in the broad context of other literary references to the temple and its environs by texts roughly contemporaneous with Matthew.

[10] The occurrences of καταπέτασμα in Second Temple Jewish texts, likewise, are dependent upon its use in the LXX.

[11] For a helpful survey of the varying views, see Stanton, *A Gospel for a New People: Studies in Matthew* (Louisville, Ky.: Westminster John Knox, 1992), pp. 349–58. For a more recent discussion, see Beaton, *Isaiah's Christ in Matthew's Gospel* (SNTSMS 123; Cambridge: Cambridge University Press, 2002), pp. 17–34. This subject will be broached with more careful attention in Chapters 5 and 6, where we consider the Old Testament background imagery and narrative formation of the gospel in general and passion narrative.

[12] This issue will be explored more fully in Chapter 6.

[13] D. S. New, *Old Testament Quotations in the Synoptic Gospels and the Two-Document Hypothesis* (SBLSCS 37; Atlanta, Ga.: Scholars Press, 1993).

[14] Beaton, *Isaiah's Christ*, pp. 21, 112, 141. Beaton qualifies this conclusion by asserting that its validity largely depends on 'the question whether the modifications bear any relationship to the surrounding context or Matthew's general theological interests' (p. 141). Cf. Stanton, *A Gospel for a New People*, pp. 354–55.

[15] The suggestion that Matthew's Old Testament text forms are likely drawn from his own translation of the Hebrew is a recent proposal put forth by Davies and Allison, *A Critical and Exegetical Commentary on the Gospel according to Saint Matthew* (3 vols.; ICC; Edinburgh: T.&T. Clark, 1988, 1991, 1997), III, pp. 573–77, cf. I, pp. 32–58; II, p. 37; Schlatter, *Das Evangelium nach Matthäus* (Stuttgart: Calwer Verlag, 1947), pp. 282–83. Beaton (*Isaiah's Christ*, p. 27) argues that the most common view for Matthew's formula quotations involves presumably the evangelist's own translation with modification by 'drawing upon Hebrew, Aramaic and Greek sources'.

(4) his Markan 'source'[16] and (5) his simply drawing from common Jewish Greek usage. There can of course be significant overlap among these categories.[17] Historically speaking, however, I have shown elsewhere that that the term καταπέτασμα mostly developed from the Old Testament LXX tradition[18] as used by Mark and adopted by Matthew. In order to examine veil language of the Old Testament as it may have been understood by Matthew, in light of its abundance in the Old Testament, we must cast our net very broadly and begin by considering both Greek and Hebrew synonyms for Matthew's καταπέτασμα τοῦ ναοῦ. The issue is further complicated by the fact that the phrase rendered by the evangelist, τὸ καταπέτασμα τοῦ ναοῦ, occurs nowhere in the Greek Old Testament, or indeed anywhere in Greek literature, except in the synoptics and subsequent references to them.[19] The first of these, an LXX reading not found in the Masoretic tradition, is discussed below. The others will be considered in their proper Second Temple context (Chapter 4).[20]

Veil language in the Old Testament is rather diverse, and in the Greek tradition it is by no means limited to καταπέτασμα. While at times relatively consistent, the Greek rarely uses the same word all the time for any single 'curtain' in the tabernacle. This is clearly demonstrated in the diagram titled 'Veil Language in the Structure of the Tabernacle'. This diagram provides graphic illustration of the diversity of language employed to describe the various hangings in the tabernacle. Of particular interest

[16] This, of course, presumes that Mark is in fact a source for Matthew, is most forcefully supposed by Brown (*Death* II, pp. 1098–1102). It begs the question, though; from where does Mark draw his veil language? Moreover, it is largely agreed that at least at his Old Testament citations, Matthew is doing his own creative redaction, regardless of whether he used Mark, Q, and M or not. Of course, the fact that it appears in Mark puts on the agenda the question of how reflective Matthew was on the use of the terminology for his own part. This will be addressed in Chapter 6.

[17] These sources, particularly Josephus and Philo, will be explored in Chapter 4.

[18] Gurtner, 'Καταπέτασμα: Lexicographical and Etymological Considerations to the Biblical "Veil"', *AUSS* 42 (2004), 105–11.

[19] This is made apparent by an exhaustive TLG search of Matthew's word construction. Its closest parallels are found when καταπέτασμα is used in close proximity with ναός e.g, 1 Kgs 6:36; 1 Macc. 1:22, Josephus, *Ant.* 14.7.1 §107; *J.W.* 5.5.7 §232.

[20] The exceedingly complex issue of the fluid versus the static state of Old Testament text forms present during the time of Matthew's writing will not be discussed here. The fact that Matthew's τὸ καταπέτασμα τοῦ ναοῦ does not occur in any extant recension from the Greek tradition suggests, as with the other portents surrounding Jesus' death, that if Matthew is drawing on the Old Testament he is doing so by making allusion to it. See discussion in Chapter 6. For a survey of modern discussions on the Old Testament text forms present at Matthew's time, cf. Beaton, *Isaiah's Christ*, pp. 52–61. Though it may seem appropriate to some that we begin with the MT and explore the LXX deviation from it, we are here primarily concerned with the LXX use of καταπέτασμα and use that term as the point of entry into the discussion.

for our purposes is to note that Matthew's term καταπέτασμα is used for *three different* hangings. Καταπέτασμα is the translation for the 'inner veil' before the holy of holies (31 times), the 'screen' between the holy place and the courtyard (2 times), and the 'curtain' of the entrance to the courtyard (5 times). These apparent translational inconsistencies are further complicated by inconsistency in the Syriac and Latin versions.[21] Moreover, it is at times difficult to distinguish which veil is in view in any specific reference.[22] Therefore, consideration of the various veils, curtains, and coverings must be given comprehensive treatment to isolate the precise identity and function of each in its Old Testament context. Here our attention will be primarily on a survey of the hangings and a description of them, naturally focusing on the three hangings in the tabernacle which are called καταπέτασμα. Distinguishing them according to their respective functions is the subject of Chapter 3.

## 1 Curtains of the Tabernacle

Rather than a veil τοῦ ναοῦ, as Matthew mentions, the Old Testament begins its veil discussion with various veils, curtains, and coverings τῆς σκηνῆς or τοῦ σκηνωματος[23] 'of the tabernacle'.[24] Significantly, the Old Testament has little to say about the veil τοῦ ναοῦ, but has a great deal more to say about what is largely agreed to be its precedent, the veil τῆς σκηνῆς. Yet the differences between the MT and the LXX, particularly in the tabernacle accounts, have been troublesome since Origen[25] and

[21] Please see Appendix 1 for an exhaustive chart of word uses. F. Ó Fearghail, 'Sir 50,5–21: Yom Kippur or the Daily Whole-Offering?' *Bib.* 59 (1978), 309, shows that in the Syriac version, ܦܪܣܐ is used for inner and outer curtains as well as for those within the temple court (cf. Exod. 26:7, 14, 33, 36, 37; 27:16, 21; 30:6, etc.). While we recognise that the Peshitta is dependent on LXX (E. Würthwein, *Text of the Old Testament* [2nd edn; trans. E. F. Rhodes; Grand Rapids, Mich.: Eerdmans, 1979], pp. 93–94), it is included for the sake of completeness. The Vulgate is chosen rather than the Old Latin because the former at times reflects a different Hebrew *Vorlage* than the MT while the Old Latin is very closely related to the LXX tradition.

[22] S. Westerholm, 'Tabernacle', *ISBE* IV, p. 699, rightly notes that the repetition of the phrase 'according to all that I show you concerning the pattern of the tabernacle, and of all its furnishings, so you will make it' (Exod. 25:9; cf. 25:40; 26:30; 27:8), likely excludes the necessity for an exhaustive *written* account. Though this begs the question of what Exod. 25–40 is for, this discussion is beyond the scope of our present interests.

[23] These Greek terms seem to be used rather interchangeably for the Hebrew אהל and מִשְׁכָּן. Westerholm, *ISBE*, IV, p. 698.

[24] MT מִשְׁכָּן, Peshitta ܡܫܟܢܐ, Vulgate *tabernaculum*.

[25] On this issue Origen says, 'What needs there speak of Exodus, where there is such diversity in what is said about the tabernacle and its court, and the ark, and the garments of the high priest and the priests, that sometimes the meaning even does not seem to be

are today well documented.[26] I will not here deal with the question of Greek expansions to clarify what may have been an otherwise ambiguous Hebrew text.[27] That A. Aejmelaeus has cautioned that the translation of the Exodus tabernacle traditions is 'one of the greatest textual problems in the Greek Pentateuch'[28] requires us to approach these texts with a great deal of caution. M. L. Wade has recognised that while the Greek translation of the first tabernacle account (Exod. 25–31) is fairly accurate (despite its ambiguities), the second (Exod. 35–40) is marked by 'unique vocabulary, significant reordering of the material in the central portion of the account, the abbreviated nature of the text, and internal conflicts'.[29] Wade's observation is significant and easily observable with respect to veil language in these texts. In Appendix 1 ('Veil Language in the Old Testament'), one can quickly see that in Exod. 25–31 the Greek is admirably consistent in its rendering of פרכת, יריעה and מסך, respectively, even to the point of changing from αὐλαία to δέρρις where the Hebrew has only יריעה, though clearly two different sheets are in view. Significantly, in only one

akin?' *Epistula ad Africanum* 4. Translation from M. L. Wade, *Consistency of Translation Techniques in the Tabernacle Accounts of Exodus in the Old Greek* (SBLSCS 49; Leiden: Brill, 2003), p. 3.

[26] For a helpful overview of the problems, see D. W. Gooding, *The Account of the Tabernacle: Translation and Textual Problems of the Greek Exodus* (Cambridge: Cambridge University Press, 1959), pp. 3–7; though see also G. S. Glanzman, Review of D. W. Gooding, *The Account of the Tabernacle: Translation and Textual Problems of the Greek Exodus, Theological Studies* 23 (1962), 106–108. For a more detailed account, see A. H. Finn, 'The Tabernacle Chapters', *JTS* 16 (1915), 449–82, who was among the first to argue that the differences in the tabernacle accounts are the result of translation techniques employed by but one translator. For a discussion particular to cultic articles, see J. W. Wevers, *Notes on the Greek Text of Exodus* (SCS 30; Atlanta, Ga.: Scholars Press, 1990), pp. 577–78. See also J. W. Wevers, 'PreOrigen Recensional Activity in the Greek Exodus', in *Studien zur Septuaginta – Robert Hanhart zu Ehren: Aus Anlass seines 65. Geburtstages* (ed. D. Fraenkel, U. Quast and J. W. Wevers; MSU 20; Göttingen: Vandenhoeck & Ruprecht, 1990), pp. 121–39; D. Fraenkel, 'Die Quellen der asterisierten Zusätze im zweiten Tabernakelbericht Exod. 35–40', in *Studien zur Septuaginta* (ed. D. Fraenkel*et al.*; MSU 20; Göttingen: Vandenhoeck & Ruprecht, 1990), pp. 140–86. For a survey of the history of the major views of the LXX translation accounts of the tabernacle, see Wade, *Consistency*, pp. 4–9.

[27] See Finn, 'The Tabernacle Chapters', 458.

[28] A. Aejmelaeus, 'Septuagintal Translation Techniques – A Solution to the Problem of the Tabernacle Account', in *Septuagint, Scrolls and Cognate Writings* (ed. G. J. Brooke and B. Lindars; SCS 33; Atlanta, Ga.: Scholars Press, 1992), p. 382.

[29] Wade, *Consistency*, p. 3. For a discussion of the ordering of the construction account in Exod. 35–40, see R. W. Klein, 'Back to the Future: The Tabernacle in the Book of Exodus', *Interp.* 50 (1996), 264–76. V. A. Hurowitz, 'The Priestly Account of Building the Tabernacle', *JAOS* 105 (1985), 21–30, has shown that the general construction and erection patterns of Exod. 25–40 reflect a common pattern of such accounts in the ancient Near East. R. E. Averbeck ('Tabernacle', *DOTP*, p. 816) calls the second account (Exod. 35–40) the 'compliance section' because of the repetition of the phrase 'Moses did everything just as the Lord had commanded him'.

(Exod. 26:37)[30] of its nine occurrences in Exod. 25–31 is καταπέτασμα *not* a translation of פרכת. It seems to be one of only three inconsistencies in the Greek translation of veil language throughout Exod. 25–31 (the others being in 26:36 and 26:14a). The second section (Exod. 35–40) is, as again observable from Appendix 1 as well as Appendix 2 ('Veil Language in the Two Tabernacle Accounts'), less rigorous in its handling of technical terminology, variant readings and simply omissions on the part of the Greek translator(s).[31] The significance of this phenomenon will be considered below.

Tabernacle texts, the texts in which the veil is found most abundantly, are broadly located between Exod. 27:21 and Num. 31:54 in the Old Testament.[32] In his helpful analysis of the tabernacle in biblical tradition, Koester outlines its three primary functions as follows: (1) 'a place of divine revelation', (2) 'where sacrifices would be offered and atonement made', and (3) 'God's presence in the tent would be a sign of his covenant faithfulness, since it would fulfil his promise to dwell with Israel and to be their God'.[33] These functions in Israelite worship are perhaps best reflected in the primary terms used to describe it: מקדש ('sanctuary'), משכן ('tabernacle') and אהל מועד ('tent of meeting').[34] Naturally, then, I begin

[30] That reading is by no means certain and is replaced in some texts by κατακαλυμματι and other readings, though this is largely seen in seventh-century cursive corrections to Codex Ambrosianus. It may have been dependent on a different, errant *Vorlage*, as is apparently the case in Exod. 26:34. See D. M. Gurtner, '"Atonement Slate" or "Veil"? Notes on a Textual Variant in Exod. XXVI 34', *VT* 54 (2004), 396–98. See discussion of the Exod. 26:37 text later.

[31] This is especially apparent in Exod. 39–40, where the diversity in Greek terms multiplies. For a list of Hebrew texts absent from the Greek translation of the second account, see Wade, *Consistency*, p. 4, n. 10.

[32] R. E. Averbeck, 'מוֹעֵד', *NIDOTTE* II, p. 873.

[33] C. R. Koester, *The Dwelling of God: The Tabernacle in the Old Testament, Intertestamental Jewish Literature and the New Testament* (CBQMS 22; Washington, D. C.: Catholic Biblical Association of America, 1989), p. 7. Friedman (*ABD* VI, p. 293) calls the tabernacle 'the place of communication between the deity and Moses for the remainder of Moses' life'. For a discussion of similar tent shrines in the ancient Near East, see F. M. Cross, 'The Priestly Tabernacle', in *The Biblical Archaeologist Reader* (ed. G. E. Wright and D. N. Freedman; Garden City, N.Y.: Doubleday, 1961), I, pp. 201–28. Légasse ('Les voiles', 567) calls it, like Moses, a 'prophetic mediator of divine wills'. H. L. Kessler, 'Through the Veil: The Holy Image in Judaism and Christianity', *Kairós* 32 (1990), 67, summarises: 'For Jews, the tabernacle/temple embodied God's presence among his Chosen People. It was the locus of the ancient cult with its priests and blood sacrifices and the site where God's laws were promulgated. Destroyed, replaced, and destroyed again, it symbolized the promised restoration during a messianic age, especially after AD 70'. Westerholm (*ISBE* IV, p. 699) says that the 'tabernacle was designed . . . as a dwelling place for Yahweh Himself, a place where His cultic worship would be conducted'. Cf. also P. P. Jenson, *Graded Holiness: A Key to the Priestly Conception of the World* (JSOTSup 106; Sheffield: Academic Press, 1992), pp. 111–14.

[34] See Averbeck, *DOTP*, pp. 807–27.

with the first accounts of veil language in the Pentateuchal narratives,[35] which include a detailed list of materials that are needed (Exod. 25:1–8), beginning with the various metals (Exod. 25:3), fabrics (Exod. 25:4–5a), wood (Exod. 25:5b), oils (Exod. 25:6) and precious stones (Exod. 25:7). The importance of Aejmelaeus's warning is quickly seen, however, as the (often significant) differences between the Greek and Hebrew traditions in precisely these texts preserved in the LXX and MT, respectively, become more apparent.[36] Fortunately, and apparently due to its importance in Old Testament cultic life, the detailed record of the construction of the tabernacle is discussed in a first account (Exod. 26–31) and repeated in a second account (Exod. 35–41),[37] at times clarifying these issues.[38]

### 1.1 The Tabernacle Proper[39]

The materials for the tabernacle were collected from the offerings of 'each man whose heart prompts him to give' (Exod. 25:2). The materials listed (Exod. 25:2–7) are likely a combination of their own property (Exod. 12:32) and the goods plundered from the Egyptians (Exod.

[35] While it is recognised that modern Pentateuchal scholarship has attributed this material largely to its 'priestly' (P) source, the present work will not acknowledge this distinction because it probably had no bearing on the first evangelist's employment of these texts (so also Koester, *Dwelling of God*, p. 6). Nor will this work address the criticism of those who challenge Israel's ability to obtain the listed resources in the Sinai wilderness or even the existence of such a structure, proposed most notably by J. Wellhausen, *Prolegomena zur Geschichte Israels* (6th edn; Berlin: Gruyter, 1927), pp. 38–51; so also R. E. Clements, *Old Testament Theology: A Fresh Approach* (MTL; London: Marshall, Morgan & Scott, 1978), p. 68. Cf. Westerholm, *ISBE*, IV, p. 699; Averbeck, *NIDOTTE* II, p. 874. For a helpful overview, see Légasse, 'Les voiles', 568–71; Jenson, *Graded Holiness*, pp. 27–29.

[36] For a helpful overview of the problems involved, cf. Gooding, *Account of the Tabernacle*, pp. 1–7.

[37] Gooding, *Account of the Tabernacle*, p. 3. M. Haran, 'The Priestly Image of the Tabernacle', *HUCA* 36 (1965), 191, comments that P's 'tendency to indulge in technicalities and stereotyped repetitions has reached its furthest limits here. There is no doubt, however, that it was intensified in this case by the importance and appeal of the subject'.

[38] Wade (*Consistency*, pp. 1–2) recognises the translation of the second account (Exod. 35–40) as being the work of a second hand, 'using the translation of the first tabernacle account (25–31) as a point of reference'. Moreover, she argues, the first section of the Greek is ambiguous while the second is normally considered less accurate because of its 'abbreviated nature', though they both take a similar approach to the translation of grammatical structures (2). For a discussion of theories behind the repetition in the second account, cf. Jenson, *Graded Holiness*, pp. 99–100.

[39] For a detailed account of the entire tabernacle structure, see Friedman, *ABD* VI, pp. 292–300; Westerholm, *ISBE* IV, pp. 698–706; Haran, 'Priestly Images', 191–226; Averbeck, *DOTP*, pp. 807–27.

12:35–36) upon their hasty departure from Egypt (Exod. 12:31–42). The task of construction itself was accomplished by Bezalel and through the empowerment of the Spirit of God (Exod. 35:30, 36:1). Long after Bezalel began working on the project, however, gifts were brought to the project, forcing Moses to put an end to the collecting (Exod. 36:3–6).[40] The expression used for the tent of meeting (σκηνῇ τοῦ μαρτυρίου) occurs first in Exod. 27:21 and 34 times in Exod. thereafter, where the MT reads אהל מועד 'tent of meeting', or, a place 'where God and man meet'. The LXX of Exodus, however, understands מועד as though related to עדות 'testimony' and, as Wevers says, 'the tent is thus thought of as the place where העדות, the tablets of The Ten Words, here translated τῆς διαθήκης, were placed. As the tent of the divine "testimony", the tabernacle symbolised the centrality of the עדות/τὰ μαρτύρια, or διαθήκη, in the cultic life of Israel'.[41]

## 1.2 The First Layer of the Roof (Exod. 26:1–6)

The tabernacle (σκήνη, משכן Exod. 26:1),[42] also known as the 'tent of meeting' (ἡ σκήνη τοῦ μαρτύριου, אהל מועד),[43] was made of materials previously listed in Exod. 25:4. It comprised ten sheets (αὐλαίας, יריעת)[44] which were of 'fine twisted linen' and 'blue and purple and scarlet material' (Exod. 26:1; 37:1 [LXX; MT 36:8]), each 28 cubits by 4 cubits (Exod. 26:2). It was to have cherubim (χερουβιμ, כרבים) woven into it, the 'work of a skillful workman' (ἐργασίᾳ ὑφάντου, מעשה חשב Exod. 26:1). Two large tapestries were made by fastening two sets of five of these 'sheets' (αὐλαίας, יריעת), fitted with fifty violet loops (Exod. 26:4) set against each other at the ends of the sheet (Exod. 26:5), joined by fifty gold clasps (Exod. 26:6), thus making the two larger tapestries (αὐλαίας, יריעת) subsequently fastened together to form a single 'roof' 40 cubits by

40 Haran, 'Priestly Images', 191.

41 Wevers, *Notes on the Greek Text of Exodus*, p. 442.

42 In 1 Chron. 17:5 משכן is curiously translated as κάλυμμα.

43 For a more comprehensive treatment of the semantic overlaps of משכן and אהל, particularly with respect to Hebrew and Ugaritic poetry, see U. Cassuto, *Commentary on the Book of Exodus* (trans. I. Abrahams; Jerusalem: Magnes Press, 1967), pp. 347–48.

44 Peshitta: ܝܪ̈ܝܥܬܐ, '*a hanging, covering, curtain, a tent, the inhabitants of a tent, a family*' (J. Payne Smith, *A Compendious Syriac Dictionary* [Oxford: Clarendon Press, 1903], p. 197). Vulgate: *cortinas*. Sarna says the Hebrew 'invariably refers to the fabrics of which tents are made' (cf. 2 Sam. 7:2, 1 Chron. 17:1; cf. Isa. 54:2; Jer. 4:20; 49:29; Hab. 3:7; Song 1:5). N. M. Sarna, *The JPS Torah Commentary: Exodus* (New York, N.Y.: JPS, 1991), p. 167.

28 cubits (Exod. 26:3).[45] This larger tapestry (αὐλαίας, יריעת), a single unit (ἔσται ἡ σκηνὴ μία, והיה המשכן אחד Exod. 26:6), would extend over the entire length of the 30-cubit structure from front to back and extend on the back from the top 10 cubits down to the ground forming the western end of the structure.[46] The 28-cubit width of the large tapestry would cover the 10-cubit width of the tabernacle proper and extend down each side (north and south) 9 cubits of its 10-cubit height and 1 cubit from the ground.[47] Strictly speaking, these ten sheets (משכן) were 'the tabernacle' proper,[48] while the covering of the tabernacle was generally called מכסה and καλύμμα (Exod. 35:11; Num. 4:25).[49]

## 1.3 The Second Layer of the Roof (Exod. 26:7–13)

The next layer was called the 'tent curtains' (Exod. 26:13; יריעת האהל). While the Hebrew retains the same generic word יריעת, the Greek tradition has recognised a slight difference in material and function for the next hanging, changing from αὐλαίαις to δέρρις.[50] There was a second layer atop the 'roof' that comprised 11 sheets (δέρρεις, יריעת) of goats' hair (Exod. 26:7), which was placed over the tabernacle proper (על־המשכן, ἐπὶ τῆς σκηνῆς). Each sheet (δέρρεις, יריעת) was 30 cubits by 4 cubits (Exod. 26:8). These were fastened together into two larger sheets, one of five smaller sheets (δέρρεις, יריעת) and the other of six (δέρρεις, יריעת; Exod. 26:9). Again fifty loops were affixed to the sheets (δέρρεις, יריעת; Exod. 26:10) and again the sheets were fastened together with clasps, though these were made of bronze (Exod. 26:11) rather than the gold of the clasps for the first covering (Exod. 26:6). The entire unit, then, measured 44 cubits by 30 cubits.

Although the Exodus account does not clarify, it seems most natural to assume that the 30-cubit width stretched over the 10-cubit width of the structure proper, thus providing the 10-cubit walls for each side (north and south).[51] How this second layer (44 cubits long) was situated lengthwise over the 30-cubit long tabernacle proper is less clear.[52]

45 Westerholm, *ISBE* IV, p. 700.

46 *Ibid.* 47 *Ibid.*

48 Gooding, *Account of the Tabernacle*, p. 16. Cf. also Exod. 40:19a.

49 Syriac ܟܣܝܐ 'an outer covering, roof', etc. (Payne Smith, *Syriac Dictionary*, p. 221); Latin *tectum*.

50 δέρρις is, more specifically, a 'skin', 'leather covering' or 'curtain made of skins'. H. G. Liddell *et. al. A Greek-English Lexicon* (9th. edn; Oxford: Oxford University Press, 1996), *ad loc.*

51 Westerholm, *ISBE* IV, p. 700. 52 *Ibid.*

Westerholm suggests that the 44 cubits would cover the 30-cubit length of the tabernacle proper and 10 would cover the back (western) wall. The remaining 4 cubits, he argues, were divided: two for additional coverage of the back (western) wall, and two folded (Exod. 26:9) over at the front (east) entrance.[53]

### 1.4 The Third (rams' skin; Exod. 26:14a) and Fourth (leather; Exod. 26:14b) Layers of the Roof

There was an additional covering (κατακάλυμμα, מכסה) of 'rams' skins' dyed red (26:14a) and 'coverings' (ἐπικαλύμματα, מכסה) of 'fine leather' (תחשים; cf. Num. 4:6, 8, 10, 11, 12, 14)[54] spread over that (26:14b; Exod. 40:19b; Num. 3:25a). It has been argued (Cole)[55] that these layers were used only while the structure was in transport.[56] Durham notes, 'The sea-cow leather may have been cured only; in this case, there may be here a descending value in these materials'.[57] The entire structure was supported by an intricate framework (Exod. 26:15–30), patterned after the model shown to Moses on Mt Sinai (Exod. 27:30), and seemingly kept in place by ropes held to the ground by bronze tent pegs (Exod. 27:19).[58]

[53] *Ibid.*, pp. 700–1. It seems more natural, though, to presume that the entire extra 4 cubits was folded over in front (Exod. 26:9) allowing no extra material in the back (west) beyond that needed to cover its wall (10 cubits). 'Goats' hair' (עזים) referred to natural, undyed wool, the least expensive of the fabric material mentioned. The ram-skin leather was tanned, or dyed red (or both). See J. I. Durham, *Exodus* (WBC 3; Waco, Tex.: Word, 1987), p. 354.

[54] The identity of this animal is perplexing. M. Haran, *Temples and Temple-Service in Ancient Israel* (Oxford: Clarendon Press, 1978), p. 152, n. 6, notes the following translations: KJV: badgers; RV: seals; RSV: goats; AT: porpoises; NJPS: dolphins. Cf. Sarna, *Exodus*, pp. 157–58. Cf. P. J. Budd, *Numbers* (WBC 5; Waco, Tex.: Word, 1984), p. 48; B. A. Levine, *Numbers* (AB 4A–B; New York, N.Y.: Doubleday, 1993, 2000), I, pp. 166–67; F. M. Cross, 'The Priestly Tabernacle and the Temple of Solomon', in *From Epic to Canon: History and Literature in Ancient Israel* (Baltimore, Md.: Johns Hopkins University Press, 1998), pp. 88–89. For a discussion and references for diverging views, cf. Haran, 'Priestly Images', 204. Num. 4:14b contains an addition by the LXX and Samaritan Pentateuch. Milgrom comments, 'This addition is essential since the laver is elsewhere ranked among the most sacred objects, as in Exod. 30:28–29, hence requiring covering for transport'. J. Milgrom, *The JPS Torah Commentary: Numbers* (Philadelphia, Pa.: JPS, 1990), p. 28.

[55] R. A. Cole, *Exodus* (Downers Grove, Ill.: InterVarsity, 1973), p. 194.

[56] Westerholm, *ISBE* IV, p. 701.

[57] Durham, *Exodus*, p. 354. The concept of descending value, 'material gradation', was first developed by Haran and will be discussed more fully in Chapter 3. See Haran, *Temples and Temple-Service*, pp. 162–63.

[58] Westerholm, *ISBE* IV, p. 701.

## 1.5 Curtains of the Courtyard

There were also curtains (קלעים, ἱστία)[59] of the courtyard which were likewise of finely twisted linen on the south (Exod. 27:9), north,[60] and west (Exod. 27:12; 38:12) sides of the courtyard. Similar curtains (קלעים, ἱστία) 15 cubits long were at one side of the entrance (Exod. 27:14; 38:14) and another set was opposite it (Exod. 27:15; 38:15[61]). A similar curtain[62] was hung at the entrance of the courtyard.[63]

## 1.6 Other Screens, Veils, and Curtains

Exodus refers to another 'curtain'[64] for the entrance to the tent.[65] There was also a cover of skin (מכסה, κάλυμμα) over the table of the Presence in transport (Num. 4:8) and coverings (מכסה, κάλυμμα) for accessories to the tabernacle while in transport.[66] Another veil (מסוה, κάλυμμα),[67] which is peripheral to our discussion, is the veil on Moses' face.[68]

59 Syriac ܣܕܪܐ '*a hanging, curtain*' (Payne Smith, *Syriac Dictionary*, p. 362); Latin *tentorium*.

60 Exod. 27:11; 37:16b (LXX; MT 38:18b); 38:16; 39:19a (LXX; MT 39:40a); 39:20a (LXX; MT 39:34a); Num. 3:26a; 4:26a. Syriac ܐܠܠܐ 'something which is drawn back' (Payne Smith, *Syriac Dictionary*, p. 70).

61 LXX 37:13, αὐλαία.

62 מסך, κάλυμμα/ καταπέτασμα. Syriac ܦܪܣܐ '*a hanging, curtain*' (Payne Smith, *Syriac Dictionary*, pp. 462–63); Latin *tentorium*. Wevers (*Notes on the Greek Text of Exodus*, p. 439, n. 16) notes that Aquila and Symmachus translated מסך by παρατάνυσμα 'something that is stretched out from' παρατείνω (cf. Exod. 37:5, 40:5).

63 Exod. 27:16; 37:16a (LXX; MT 38:18a); 39:19b (LXX; MT 39:40b); 39:20b (LXX; MT 39:34b); 40:5; Num. 3:26b; 4:26b; cf. also Exod. 27:18; Num. 4:32.

64 מסך, ἐπίσπαστρον/ καταπέτασμα. Syriac ܦܪܣܐ, Latin *tentorium*; cf. Légasse, 'Les voiles', 581, 83.

65 Exod. 26:36, 37; 35:15; 37:5 (LXX; MT 36:37); 40:28; Num. 3:25b; 4:25c. At Exod. 37:5 (LXX; MT 36:37) the curtain in the Greek tradition is called καταπέτασμα. See discussion that follows. For a more detailed discussion of this hanging, cf. Levine, *Numbers*, I, pp. 159–60.

66 Num. 4:10, 11, 12, 14a, b. Haran ('Priestly Images', 204) argues their weave is according to the *roqem* workmanship with no figures of cherubim.

67 Syriac ܬܟܣܝܬܐ 'a veil, covering; chalice veil . . . napkin, towel, handkerchief', etc. (Payne Smith, *Syriac Dictionary*, p. 569); Latin *velamen*.

68 Exod. 34:33, 34, 35. Translated by Symmachus as κάλυμμα (MT צמה). For a discussion of the radiance of Moses' face and his veil, see J. Morgenstern, 'Moses with the Shining Face', *HUCA* 2 (1925), 1–27; M. Haran, 'The Shining of Moses' Face: A Case Study in Biblical and Ancient Near Eastern Iconography', in *In the Shelter of Elyon: Essays on Ancient Palestinian Life and Literature in Honor of G. W. Ahlstrom* (ed. W. B. Barrick and J. R. Spencer; Sheffield: JSOT Press, 1984), pp. 159–73; Sarna, *Exodus*, pp. 220–21; Wevers, *Notes on the Greek Text of Exodus*, p. 573. Also peripheral is a woman's face veil (Song 4:3; 6:6[7]). Cf. D. J. Lane, '"The Curtains of Solomon": Some Notes on the "Syriacizing" of *ŠÎR-HAŠŠÎRÎM*', in *The Peshitta as a Translation: Papers Read at the II Peshitta Symposium Held at Leiden 19–21 August 1993* (MPIL; ed. P. B. Dirksen and A. Van der Kooij; Leiden: Brill, 1995), pp. 73–84. Once κάλυμμα is used by Aquila and an unknown source as a 'city wall' (Song 5:7; MT רדיד). Κάλυμμα is also used by Aquila and Symmachus in Gen. 8:13 to represent the 'surface of the ground' (MT מכסה).

## 2 The Inner Veil

### 2.1 The Veil of the Tabernacle

The next covering discussed in some detail (Exod. 26:31–37) is the inner veil, rendered mostly by καταπέτασμα[69] and פרכת[70] respectively.[71] The Hebrew term occurs in tabernacle contexts in several syntactical forms and descriptive contexts. This veil (פרכת, καταπέτασμα) was to be made of blue, purple, and scarlet yarn and finely twisted linen, with cherubim worked into it by a skilled craftsman (Exod. 26:31; 36:35). It was to be hung probably 20 cubits from the eastern end of the tabernacle, [72] forming a holy of holies that was a perfect cube of 10 cubits per side.[73] There were gold hooks on four posts of acacia wood overlaid with gold and standing on four silver bases (Exod. 26:32). The veil (פרכת, καταπέτασμα) was hung on its acacia wood frame, which itself was overlaid with gold by gold hooks, represented by the Hebrew letter *waw* (ו), which in its Paleo-Hebrew script resembled a two-pronged fork.[74] It was also hung by silver sockets (Exod. 26:32) or 'sockets of the sanctuary' (Exod. 38:27).[75] The veil (καταπέτασμα, פרכת) was hung under the clasps (Exod. 26:33a), and the ark of the testimony (ἡ κιβωτὸν τοῦ μαρτυρίου, ארון העדות) was

[69] The exceptions are that most critical texts preserve ἐπισπάστρον at 26:36, whereas Origen's Aquila renders it καταπέτασμα. Also, in 26:37 Origen's Theodotion preserves ἐπισπάστρον, though all other witnesses retain καταπέτασμα. For a discussion of the use of ἐπίσπαστρον, cf. A. Pelletier, 'Le 'Voile du Temple' de Jérusalem en termes de métier', *REG* 77 (1964), 70–75. Pelletier ('Le 'Voile' du Temple de Jérusalem est-il devenu la 'Portière' du Temple d'Olympie', 297) shows that the term in the LXX is related to the entrance to the tent. He says, 'In Exodus 26:36, ἐπίσπαστρον would be the technical term that would specify the system of the καταπέτασμα, a curtain activated by a circulation cord' (p. 298, my translation).

[70] The exception is that the MT curiously has כפרת at 26:34, though correctly preserved by Origen's Hebrew as פרכת. Also 26:36, 37 preserve מסך, and the confusion with respect to the Greek rendering of this word may reflect its unexpectedness. Wevers (*Notes on the Greek Text of Exodus*, p. 427) suggests that καταπέτασμα is the only word which translates פרכת throughout the LXX, with the possible exception of 39:20b (MT 34b). Moreover, he insists, 'פרכת is specifically the inner curtain whereas מסך is the outer curtain in front of the tabernacle'. The LXX of Exodus, however, 'does not make this sharp distinction since מסך is also sometimes translated by καταπέτασμα (cf. v. 37). The word basically means 'something that is stretched over' (cf. καταπετάννυμι), hence, a 'curtain'. Wevers, *Notes on the Greek Text of Exodus*, p. 427. Averbeck's suggestion (*NIDOTTE* III, p. 688) that the meaning of the term has been 'much debated' seems unfounded. Its meaning is clear; its function is not.

[71] Syriac ܦܪܣܐ, 'a cover, curtain, veil, screen; rit. The veil placed over the consecrated bread; a mat, rug, carpet; a measured allowance, portion, rations; a cedar-cone' (Payne Smith, *Syriac Dictionary*, pp. 462–63); Latin *velum*.

[72] Hegg, 'Separating the Most Holy from the Holy', 4–5.

[73] Westerholm, *ISBE* IV, pp. 700–1. [74] Sarna, *Exodus*, pp. 170–71.

[75] *Ibid.*; see Wevers, *Notes on the Greek Text of Exodus*, pp. 427–28; Durham, *Exodus*, p. 372.

brought in *behind*[76] the veil (καταπέτασμα, פרכת; Exod. 26:33b). The word פרכת is translated in twenty-five of its twenty-six occurrences in Greek by καταπέτασμα.[77] While this means that *most* of the time (96%) that פרכת occurs it is translated καταπέτασμα, καταπέτασμα has also been used for two other curtains of the tabernacle, namely the 'screen' and the 'curtain' of the entrance to the courtyard (see diagram 'Veil Language in the Structure of the Tabernacle'). Mere statistics, then, *favour* the inner veil, as most New Testament scholars have recognised, but they fall short of providing sufficient evidence to *affirm* that the 'inner veil' was in the mind of the evangelist when he wrote καταπέτασμα. Thus a great deal more evidence must be considered from the Old Testament, including such factors as the physical descriptions and materials for the curtains, their specified function in the cultic worship of Israel, and syntactical features that may help distinguish one καταπέτασμα from another. All of these factors I will revisit in due course.

For the present, however, it is sufficient to survey broadly the function of the פרכת veil. Generally, it served to separate the holy place from the holy of holies (Exod. 26:33a, b, c). According to most Greek traditions, it was shielding the atonement cover of the ark (Exod. 26:34).[78] The table was to be placed outside of it (*extra velum*; Exod. 26:35), and it was here (*extra velum*) that Aaron and his sons were to keep lamps burning from evening until morning as 'a lasting ordinance among the Israelites for the generations to come' (Exod. 27:21; Lev. 24:3). The altar of incense was placed in front of this veil (פרכת, καταπέτασμα; Exod. 30:6). The relation between the veil (פרכת המסך, καταπέτασμα) and the atonement cover will be explored later.[79]

The cost of the bases for the sanctuary and its (unspecified) curtain was 100 talents of silver.[80] Against the פרכת (*contra velum*) sin offerings were made (Lev. 4:6, 17), and it is here that Aaron would enter behind the curtain (*intra velum*) on the Day of Atonement (Lev. 16:2, 12, 15). An impure priest was not to approach the veil or the sanctuary behind it (Lev. 21:23; Num. 3:10 [a unique LXX reading]) or risk defiling the sanctuary. Access to the holy of holies through it was restricted to Aaron and his sons (Num. 18:7). The veil (פרכת, καταπέτασμα) was also used to cover the ark of the testimony while in transport (Num. 4:5).

[76] MT has והבאת שמה מבית לפרכת את ארון העדות here taking the hiphil perfect הבאת in an imperatival sense and the ל of לפרכת in a locative sense; so LXX εἰσοίσεις ἐκεῖ *ἐσώτερον* τοῦ καταπετάσματος.

[77] The lone exception being Exod. 39:20a (34a). See comments that follow.

[78] See detailed discussion later.

[79] Latin *velum quod ante illud oppanditur*.

[80] Exod. 39:4 (LXX; MT 38:27); cf. also Exod. 39:34; 40:21, 22, 26.

## 2.2 The Veil of the Temple

In Solomon's temple hung a פרכת veil corresponding to its tabernacle prototype.[81] As can be seen in Appendix 1, the term καταπέτασμα is present in 1 Kgs 6:36[82] (a reading unique to the LXX) and 2 Chron. 3:14.[83] Though not explicitly mentioned, it is presumably among the furnishings listed in 2 Chron. 5:5a, though Averbeck suggests that its close association with Moses and the scarcity of reference to it after his death (Deut. 34) indicates that it was not brought into the promised land.[84] Myers has noted its absence in both 1 Kings, except for the LXX insertion, and the portrayal of Ezekiel's temple,[85] and suggests, along with Curtis, that its description in Chronicles is derived from that of the tabernacle.[86] Rudolf, however, argues that פרכת was originally present in 1 Kgs 7:21b but was lost (haplography) due to the similarity of the Hebrew consonants in 'curtain' (פרכת) and 'capital of a pillar' (כתרת; 1 Kgs 7:17).[87] Hegg points out that though 2 Chron. 3:14 (the only such text with a corresponding

[81] Légasse ('Les voiles', 562) claims that the absence of curtains on the east side of Solomon's temple is contradicted by certain exegetes and archaeologists (noting W. Rudolph, *Chronikbücher* [HAT; Tübingen: Mohr, 1955], pp. 204–5 and T. A. Busink, *Der Tempel von Jerusalem von Salomo bis Herodes* [SFSMD 3; Leiden: Brill, 1970], pp. 206–7). These, Légasse contends, suppose that the word פרכת, designating the curtain of the דביר, disappeared from 1 Kgs 6:21 by haplography.

[82] Cf. Légasse, 'Les voiles', 568, 571.

[83] The absence of mention of the veil from Ezekiel's temple does not necessarily mean it was not present. For a description of the many articles left out of the description, see W. Eichrodt, *Ezekiel: A Commentary* (OTL; trans. C. Quin; London: SCM Press, 1970), p. 549. Koester (*Dwelling of God*, p. 21) says, 'Solomon's temple was the legitimate successor to the tent sanctuaries'. H. E. Faber van der Meulen, 'One or Two Veils in front of the Holy of Holies', *TE* 18 (1985), 23, takes this verse to mean that there are 'two doors which form the entrance to the holy place and the holy of holies', whereas 'Previous to this (2 Chron. 3:14), a veil (parokhet) in front of the holy of holies (LXX: *katapetasma*) is mentioned'. He also says, 'We may thus judge that the Chronicler has combined both descriptions concerning the partitioning of the holy of holies – that of the Deuteronomist and that concerning the tabernacle and he has done this in such a manner that it appears he is speaking of doors with one veil'. 'One or Two Veils', 24.

[84] Averbeck, *NIDOTTE* II, p. 873. For a survey of the various disappearances and reappearances of the tabernacle from Old Testament literature, see Koester, *Dwelling of God*, pp. 11–17.

[85] J. M. Myers, *II Chronicles* (AB 13; Garden City, M.J.: Doubleday, 1965), p. 18.

[86] E. L. Curtis, *The Books of Chronicles* (ICC; Edinburgh: T. & T. Clark, 1910), p. 327. C. Meyers ('Screen', *ABD* V, p. 1011) suggests that its presence in the temple (2 Chron. 3:4) 'may be the result of the influence of P material'.

[87] Rudolph, *Chronikbücher*, p. 204; cf. Légasse, 'Les voiles', 562, n. 8, who thinks haplography is unlikely. Cf. Busink, *Tempel*, pp. 206–7. A. Pelletier, 'Le "Voile" du Temple de Jérusalem est-il devenu la "Portière" du Temple d'Olympie', 299. For a detailed discussion of the 1 Kgs 6 text vis-à-vis the Ezekiel temple, cf. Légasse ('Les voiles', 562–63), who argues that in the Solomonic temple, as in Ezekiel's, there were no curtains but doors to the sanctuary.

Hebrew referent) mentions a פרכת veil constructed by Solomon, the summary verse at 2 Chron. 4:22 describes only doors for the holy of holies, leading some scholars to question whether the veil was actually present in this temple.[88] Moreover, though the Greek tradition adds a phrase in 1 Kgs 6:36 containing καταπέτασμα, its context reads καὶ ᾠκοδόμησε καταπέτασμα τῆς αὐλῆς τοῦ αἴλαμ[89] τοῦ οἴκου τοῦ κατὰ πρόσωπον τοῦ ναοῦ ('and he made a curtain of the gate of the porch of the house at the front of the temple'). It has been argued that this reading is perhaps a corruption of the Hebrew of 1 Kgs 7:12b,[90] though such observations remain speculative. The text in 2 Chron. 4:22 should not be taken as evidence for the exclusion of the veil, but merely as an indication that the veil itself was not included among the articles made of gold.[91] In 2 Chron. 3:14 we read that Solomon 'made the curtain (פרכת, καταπέτασμα)[92] of blue, purple, and crimson yarn and fine linen, with cherubim worked into it'. Other curtain language is found in 1 Chron. 17:5, where the Lord complains that to date he had only dwelt in a tabernacle or a 'tent' (κάλυμμα, אהל).[93]

## 2.3 Lexical Distinction: καταπέτασμα and פרכת

The Hebrew tradition unanimously describes this 'inner veil' as פרכת.[94] While every time[95] the word פרכת occurs in the Hebrew text the Greek uses καταπέτασμα, the opposite does not always hold true. There are occasions where καταπέτασμα is used without, apparently, the translator

[88] Hegg, 'Separating the Most Holy from the Holy', 7; so also S. Japhet, *I & II Chronicles* (OTL; London: SCM Press, 1993), pp. 557–58.

[89] Seemingly, this word is a transliteration of the Hebrew אולם 'porch'.

[90] S. J. DeVries, *1 Kings* (WBC 12; Waco, Tex.: Word Books, 1985), p. 88. For a discussion and proposed reconstruction of the complicated corruption of 1 Kgs 6:36b with 1 Kgs 7:12b, cf. especially C. F. Burney, *Notes on the Hebrew Text of the Books of Kings* (Oxford: Clarendon Press, 1903), p. 78; cf. also A. Šanda, *Die Bücher der Könige: Übersetzt und Erklärt* (2 vols.; Münster: Aschendorffsche Verlagsbuchhandlung, 1911) I, p. 150.

[91] In the Qumran texts, as we shall see, the veil itself is said to be made of gold (see Chapter 4).

[92] Perhaps in recognition of the lack of Syriac vocabulary thus far employed in translating the Hebrew, the Syriac translator transliterates פרכת into Syriac as ܦܪܘܟܬܐ.

[93] Cf. discussion in Japhet, *I & II Chronicles*, p. 330; Curtis, *Chronicles*, p. 227.

[94] Budd (*Numbers*, p. 35) argues that the מסך in Num. 3:31 'must be the curtain which separates the Holy of Holies from the Holy Place,' because 'most of the door hangings are the responsibility of the Gershonites (v. 25)'. So also Levine, *Numbers* I, p. 160. However, the curtain to which he refers in Num. 3:25b, מסך and κατακάλυμμα respectively, is surely the curtain at the entrance to the tent of meeting (τὸ κατακάλυμμα τῆς θύρας τῆς σκηνῆς τοῦ μαρτυρίου). The same Greek and Hebrew terms, κατακάλυμμα and מסך, are used in Num. 3:31. Thus this curtain is clearly *not* the inner veil.

[95] Except for the curious reading in Exod. 39:20b (34b), where מסך הפרכת is translated ἐπικαλύμμα.

seeing פרכת in his *Vorlage*. The point is that there is not quite a simple, one-to-one relationship between these terms. This has understandably caused New Testament scholars, particularly those considering the rending of the veil in Matt. 27:51, to look elsewhere for a more decisive indication of which, if any, particular veil is in the mind of the evangelist(s).

The complicated overlap of these terms is the subject of the present section. If it were fair to presume that the LXX translator had something nearly identical to the present MT before him as his *Vorlage*, then it would seem that he has been relatively consistent in his rendering of the minutiae with respect to tabernacle terms in Exod. 25:30.[96] Nearly all veil language, particularly the use of καταπέτασμα and פרכת respectively, occurs in the Pentateuch. Fortunately, it is recognised that where the LXX and MT agree most strongly is in the Pentateuch in general, which is likewise thought to be the earliest Greek translation of any part of the Hebrew Bible, depicted in the *Letter of Aristeas*, originating as early as the third century B.C.E.[97] Unfortunately, Aejmelaeus notes, 'Exodus has proved to be one of the most freely translated books in the LXX and one of those in which the requirements of Greek idiom have been best taken into account'.[98]

Within these texts it is necessary to evaluate the identity of the καταπέτασμα in relation to the פרכת veil. As I said earlier, most scholars have suggested lexical ambiguity between καταπέτασμα and other curtain language, such as κάλυμμα, in the LXX and Second Temple texts, especially Josephus, as the basis for looking elsewhere to identify which (if either) veil is meant by the evangelist, and thus his hermeneutical use of it in the passion narratives. While lexical identity alone is insufficient grounds for a contextual interpretation of the rending of the veil in Matthew, an exhaustive *syntactical* analysis of the use of καταπέτασμα in the Old Testament, an often overlooked Matthean 'source' in this discussion, is a necessary endeavour which, when coupled with further analysis (Chapter 3), proves more decisive than is usually thought.

## 2.4 Καταπέτασμα and the פָּרֹכֶת: Translational Considerations

Elsewhere I have argued that the LXX offers syntactical keys for identifying which of the three curtains designated καταπέτασμα is in view in a

96 This is certainly not an undisputed assumption. See discussion that follows.

97 Cf. Würthwein, *Text of the Old Testament*, pp. 50–52, 63.

98 Aejmelaeus, 'Septuagintal Translation Techniques', 388. For a discussion of particular translational techniques, see A. Aejmelaeus, 'What Can We Know about the Hebrew *Vorlage* of the Septuagint', *ZAW* 99 (1987), 58–89, esp. the discussion of Exodus on pp. 71–77. See also J. E. Sanderson, *An Exodus Scroll from Qumran* (HSS 30; Atlanta, Ga.: Scholars Press, 1986), pp. 247–55.

given context. In that article, I argued that for the LXX καταπέτασμα is the 'default' term for the inner veil (פרכת), and that where καταπέτασμα is used for any other curtain, the LXX translator employed syntactical qualification, in particular a locative genitive, to clarify which of the three curtains designated καταπέτασμα is in view.[99] Καταπέτασμα is the primary term for the inner veil, and each time it occurs alone, without a locative genitive, it refers to the inner veil (פרכת). This is apparent in Appendix 3. When the LXX translator wanted to make clear that a particular use of καταπέτασμα was *not* a reference to that veil, he did so by the use of a locative genitive clarifying to which part of the tabernacle the curtain belonged, as a means of distinguishing it from the primary καταπέτασμα. Since the synoptic locative genitive of καταπέτασμα (τοῦ ναοῦ) clearly does *not* make such distinction, we are left to suppose that the evangelists, like their LXX 'source', are referring to the inner veil by their use of καταπέτασμα τοῦ ναοῦ.[100]

As clear as this distinction seems to be, it must be considered as only one of many factors to be weighed in determining Matthew's meaning of the *velum scissum*. Linnemann, who is perhaps the most vocal proponent of viewing the veil in its Old Testament context, bypasses the lexicographical issue for a theological and functional one. She argues,

> Nur die symbolische Bedeutung des inneren Vorhangs konnte das Zeichen eindeutig machen; *deshalb kann mit dem καταπέτασμα nicht der äußere, sondern nur der innere Vorhang gemeint sein*.[101]

In order to extract a 'symbolische Bedeutung des inneren Vorhangs', however, we must carefully distinguish the stated functions of each of the three hangings translated καταπέτασμα in their respective Old Testament contexts. This is the subject of Chapter 3. We must also consider a broad understanding of the ideology of the veil within the thought world of Second Temple and Rabbinic Judaism to inform our understanding of the symbolism. This is the subject of Chapter 4.

[99] Wade, *Consistency*, p. 171, n. 39.

[100] For a fuller discussion, cf. D. M. Gurtner, 'LXX Syntax and the Identity of the NT Veil', *NovT* 47 (2005), 344–53. Cf. also my 'Καταπέτασμα: Lexicographical and Etymological Considerations to the Biblical "Veil"', *AUSS* 42 (2004), 105–11, where I argue that the term designates that the veil hung downward in a covering manner and that it is used exclusively in cultic contexts.

[101] Linnemann, *Studien*, p. 159. My emphasis.

# 3

## FUNCTIONALITY AND IDENTITY OF THE 'VEIL OF THE TEMPLE'[1]

### Introduction

S. Jellicoe insisted that it is 'primarily to the Greek Old Testament that we should look . . . for the theological significance of the terminology of the New (Testament)'.[2] As we have seen, however, lexical evidence for which veil Matthew had in mind in his *velum scissum*, let alone what is meant by it, in itself is inconclusive since the LXX knows three curtains it translates καταπέτασμα. While syntactical evidence (the locative genitive) is much more helpful in identifying which of these curtains the evangelist had in mind, it is neither the only nor the most decisive means by which such a verdict regarding the identity of Matthew's veil and the significance of its rending can or should be made. As we have seen in the introduction, one of the few points of agreement among scholars who address the rending of the veil is that whatever else it means, it surely refers to the cessation of the veil's function.[3] How did it function? If Matthew's term refers to the inner veil before the holy of holies, D. Senior claims it 'signified the locus of God's presence at the heart of Israel's cultic life' and 'served as a wall of separation between the people and Yahweh, the "wholly other"'.[4] C. Meyers says 'it guarded the . . . Ark, from the profanity of contact with humans'.[5] S. Motyer says it 'is taken to embody the whole religious system of the Temple'.[6] L. Morris says the curtain kept 'what lay on the

[1] For a more concise discussion of this subject, as well as some explorations into its implications for Matthew, see D. M. Gurtner, 'Functionality, Identity, and Interpretation: The Tearing of the Temple Curtain (Matt. 27:51a) in Light of Pentateuchal Tabernacle Texts', Paper Presented at the International Meeting of the Society of Biblical Literature (Groningen, 2004).

[2] S. Jellicoe, *The Septuagint and Modern Study* (Oxford: Clarendon Press, 1968), p. 332.

[3] I will demonstrate the validity of this assumption in Chapter 6.

[4] 'The Death of God's Son and the Beginning of the New Age', in *The Language of the Cross* (ed. A. Lacomara; Chicago, Ill.: Franciscan Herald Press, 1977), p. 41.

[5] 'Veil of the Temple', *ABD* VI, p. 685.

[6] 'The Rending of the Veil: Markan Pentecost?' *NTS* 33 (1987), 155.

other side of it a secret from those outside'.[7] D. Madvig claims it simply 'was symbolic of the separation between God and man'.[8] A. Pelletier says the curtains in general had the 'rôle de tenir caché le lieu de la Demeure de Yahvé: ils étaient le *signe* du mystère de sa présence'.[9] R. Brown asserts it served 'to shut the Holy Place off from the profane'.[10] Others have presumed that it refers to the outer veil, and its rending suggests the breaking of the barrier between Jew and Gentile.[11]

These are important comments, because they reflect various assumptions on the part of scholars with respect to the function of Matthew's veil. For many, particularly those who assume it is the inner veil and who look to Hebrews, it is a wall, of sorts, a divine 'keep out' sign that keeps the high priest out of the most holy place on all occasions save the Day of Atonement. Yet while most presume that the inner veil served to keep people out of the holy of holies, and the outer curtain kept Gentiles from worship, no one has given careful consideration to *precisely how the veils functioned in the Old Testament*, a corpus of texts upon which the first evangelist draws so heavily throughout, and particularly in his 'special material' (27:51b–53). Only Linnemann has insisted that we carefully consider its function in the temple cult (in the Old Testament) as a preface to the understanding of this pericope for its first readers or hearers.[12] Therefore, in the present chapter I will exhaustively explore the functions, implicit and explicit, of each of the three curtains designated καταπέτασμα, to determine as far as possible which, if any, of the three curtains Matthew may have had in mind.[13] I will do so by surveying each of the three curtains called καταπέτασμα, focusing on the functions of each, and then summarising the *potential* significance of the cessation of those functions.[14] We will see not only that the inner veil (פרכת) is the only καταπέτασμα for which a particular cultic function is designated, but also that this cultic function is important and necessary data

[7] *The Gospel according to Matthew* (Grand Rapids, Mich.: Eerdmans, 1992), p. 724.

[8] 'τὸ καταπέτασμα', *NIDNTT* III, p. 794.

[9] 'La tradition synoptique du 'Voile déchiré' à la lumière des réalités archéologiques', *Recherches de science religieuse* 46 (1958), 167.

[10] *The Death of the Messiah: A Commentary on the Passion Narratives in the Four Gospels* (2 vols.; New York, N.Y.: Doubleday, 1994), II, p. 1101.

[11] Cf. especially M. Barth, *Ephesians 1–3* (ABC 34; Garden City, N.Y.: Doubleday, 1974), p. 284.

[12] *Studien zur Passionsgeschichte* (FRLANT 102; Göttingen: Vandenhoeck & Ruprecht, 1970), p. 160.

[13] I will demonstrate the importance of underscoring Matthew's eye to the Old Testament in his account of the *velum scissum*, which he took from Mark, in Chapter 6.

[14] Here we emphasise potential significance because, naturally, the Matthean context will direct any conclusions we may draw here.

for determining the contextual meaning of the cessation of its function in the Matthean *velum scissum* account.

## 1 Καταπέτασμα #1: Curtain of the Entrance of the Courtyard

The first curtain called καταπέτασμα is the one at the entrance of the courtyard (see diagram).[15] This courtyard could be entered by the entrance of the tent of meeting[16] by any Israelite, provided he or she brought the appropriate sacrifices and offerings and were in a state of ritual purity (Lev. 12:4). The Israelite community gathered at the entrance to this courtyard for Moses to communicate a message from God to them (Lev. 8:3f; Num. 10:3, 27:2; etc.). Here also is where 'holy things' were to be eaten (Lev. 6:16, 26).[17] This curtain is explicitly mentioned six times in the Old Testament (Exod. 27:16, 37:16a [MT 38:18a], 39:19b [MT 40b], 40:5; Num. 3:26b, 4:32), once (Exod. 27:16) as κάλυμμα, once (Exod. 40:5) as κάλυμμα καταπετάσματος and in the rest as simply καταπέτασμα with its appropriate locative genitive.[18] Each of these Greek expressions translates the Hebrew מסך.

This curtain (called κάλυμμα in its first appearance in the LXX, Exod. 27:16) is translated 'hanging' (KJV), 'screen' (NAS, NRS) and 'curtain' (NIV). It is mentioned only here in the first account of the tabernacle (Exod. 25–30), where it is described as a curtain of the entrance of the courtyard (τῇ πύλῃ τῆς αὐλῆς κάλυμμα) made 'of blue and purple and scarlet material and fine twisted linen, the work of a weaver' (Exod. 27:16 NAS). The remaining three references to this curtain in the LXX of Exodus are by the translator of the second account (Exod. 35–41), with the two in Numbers seemingly following the latter Exodus translator. In the second Exodus account (Exod. 35–41) this same curtain is called τὸ καταπέτασμα τῆς πύλης τῆς αὐλῆς (Exod. 37:16a [38:18a]) or τὸ καταπέτασμα τῆς θύρας τῆς σκηνῆς (Exod. 39:19b [40b]).[19]

[15] In Exod. 27 it is called κάλυμμα. Aquila and Symmachus call it a παρατάνυσμα 'something that is stretched out'. Wevers, *Notes on the Greek Text of Exodus* (Septuagint and Cognate Studies 30; Atlanta, Ga.: Scholars Press, 1990), p. 439, n. 16.

[16] τὴν θύραν τῆς σκηνῆς τοῦ μαρτυρίου; Lev. 1:3; 12:6; 14:23; 15:14, etc. Westerholm, 'Tabernacle', *ISBE* IV, p. 702.

[17] Westerholm, p. 702.

[18] τῆς πύλης τῆς αὐλῆς at Exod. 37:16a (38:18a); Num. 3:26b 4:32 and τῆς θύρας τῆς σκηνῆς at Exod. 39:19b (40b). Exod. 37:16a (38:18a), 39:19b (40b); Num. 3:26b. Wade, *Consistency of Translation Techniques in the Tabernacle Accounts of Exodus in the Old Greek* (SBLSCS 49; Leiden: Brill, 2003), p. 171, n. 39.

[19] Num. 4:32 contains an alternative reading in the LXX not found in the MT, listing this curtain (καταπετάσματος τῆς πύλης τῆς αὐλῆς) among the things the Merarites

While surely this curtain had a structural function within the tabernacle, this function is nowhere made explicit, and allusions to a cultic function are conspicuously absent. Its function may be indicated by what occurs within its precincts. For here was located the altar of burnt offering (Exod. 27:1–8) to which the Israelites brought burnt offerings and sacrifices (Lev. 17:8). Its fire was never to go out (Lev. 6:8–13) as a 'symbol of God's character and constant presence among His people'.[20] To this altar were brought the morning and evening burnt offerings (Exod. 29:38–42; Num. 28:3–8).[21] Here atonement was made for the offerer (Lev. 1:4),[22] whose complete consecration is symbolised by his laying his hands on the head of the victim and blood's being thrown (זרק) against the altar (על־המזבח) at the door of the tent of meeting.[23] Carpenter notes that it 'will be a pleasant odor before Yahweh when carried out correctly' and that 'the entire ritual is a process that makes the offerer and his sacrifice acceptable . . . before God and pleasing to him'.[24]

While these texts make no explicit comment regarding the function of this curtain, it seems reasonable to assume that its locus in Israelite worship and the requirement of ritual purity for those who enter through it suggests the exclusion of Gentiles and, presumably, ritually impure Jews. The presence of the altar of burnt offering may suggest that this curtain separates the sanctified from the unsanctified; however, this is not stated, and it seems to refer more to the altar than to the curtain. While one could see the validity of Carter's contention that the curtain was the *locus* of communal activity between God and Israel,[25] this is not the same as its *function*. Instead it is the location of an event in which the veil itself is entirely passive. Moreover, should we consider the cessation of this function in Matthew, then it would depict a severing of a communal relationship, clearly contrary to Matthew's Emmanuel

were to carry. The unique LXX reading includes, among other things, the carrying of this curtain by the Merarites, who were descendents of Levi (Gen. 46:11; Exod. 6:16; Num. 3:17; 1 Chron 6:1, 16 [MT 48, 62]), which may speak of its sanctity (Cf. M. J. Horsnell, 'Merari, Merarites', *ISBE* III, p. 321; S. A. Reed, 'Merarites', *ABD* IV, pp. 698–99), along with the other articles they carried. Yet all of the sanctuary was carried by one of three clans, of which the Merarites were the least holy. Cf. P. P. Jenson, *Graded Holiness: A Key to the Priestly Conception of the World* (JSOTSup 106; Sheffield: Academic Press, 1992), p. 90. For potential influence from Canaanite enthronement practices, cf. K. Koch, *Spuren des hebräischen Denkens: Beiträge zur alttestamentlichen Theologie* (ed. B. Janowski and M. Krause; Neukirchen-Vluyn: Neukirchener Verlag, 1991), pp. 37–43.

20 E. E. Carpenter, 'Sacrifices and Offerings in the OT', *ISBE* IV, p. 268.

21 Westerholm, p. 701. 22 Carpenter, p. 268. 23 *Ibid.* 24 *Ibid.*

25 Carter, *Matthew: Storyteller, Interpreter, Evangelist* (Peabody, Mass.: Hendrickson, 1996), p. 221.

Christology. Therefore it seems unlikely that this καταπέτασμα is the one in view in the Matthean *velum scissum* text.

## 2 Καταπέτασμα #2: The Screen of the Door of the Tent of Meeting

The next curtain that is called καταπέτασμα is the 'screen' hung between the holy place and the courtyard, called καταπέτασμα in two of the four texts in which it is mentioned (Exod. 26:37, 37:5 [MT 36:37]), though elsewhere it is ἐπισπάστρον (once, Exod. 26:36) and κάλυμμα (once, Num. 4:25c). Beginning in Exod. 26:36, the MT knows this 'screen' only as מסך, in place for the doorway of the tent and made 'of blue and purple and scarlet material and fine twisted linen, the work of a weaver' (ποικιλοῦ; רֹקֵם).[26]

As was the case with the 'curtain of the entrance of the courtyard', the screen does not have a particular designated function in the cultic worship of Israel. Its presence between the courtyard and the holy place presumably suggests that it served as a structural and cultic separation between the two, expressing the barrier between a higher and lesser degree of holiness[27] – that is, between Levite and lay Israelite. The altar of incense (Exod. 30:1–10) was the locus of morning and evening incense offerings. Atonement was made for this altar annually by smearing blood on its horns (Exod. 30:10).[28] There was also the lampstand (Exod. 25:31–40; cf. Lev. 24:1–4; Num. 8:1–4), which was made of gold and which was situated in the holy place and kept burning continually (Exod. 27:20; Lev. 24:2) and served to illuminate the sanctuary.[29] Finally, within the holy place stood the table for the bread of presence (Exod. 25:23–30), located on the north side, depicting the sustaining power and presence of God.[30]

The rending of such a curtain could suggest cessation of the function of the lampstand – that is, darkness within the tabernacle similar to the darkness in the Matthean passion narrative. Yet the relative obscurity of this curtain (mentioned only four times, and only twice called καταπέτασμα) would make it difficult to presume that Matthew's readers would have thought of this curtain (as opposed to others) in the *velum scissum* text. Moreover, as we will see in Chapter 6, it is difficult to associate the cessation of any of these functions with the death of Jesus, the focal

[26] It was also called κάλυμμα καταπετάσματος ἐπὶ τὴν θύραν τῆς σκηνῆς τοῦ μαρτυρίου ('veil for the doorway to the tent of meeting', Exod. 40:5; so also Num. 3:26b).

[27] Cf. Jenson, pp. 102, 108. [28] Westerholm, p. 702.

[29] R. H. Smith, 'Lampstand', *ISBE* III, p. 70.

[30] G. L. Carr and N. J. Opperwall, 'Presence, Bread of the', *ISBE* III, pp. 955–56.

point of the Matthean passion narrative with which the evangelist links the *velum scissum*.

## 3 Καταπέτασμα #3: The Veil between the Holy Place and the Holy of Holies

Where the importance of the functionality of what the LXX translates καταπέτασμα becomes most apparent is in reference to the inner פרכת veil. The term represents the only καταπέτασμα found in what R. E. Hendrix has shown to be the literary core of the *function* of the tabernacle within Israelite cultic worship.[31] Though פרכת appears only twice in this section (Exod. 27:21, 30:6, both translated καταπέτασμα), its exclusive presence in tabernacle cultic function texts merits careful examination of both its implicit and explicit functions within the tabernacle.

### 3.1 Implicit Functions of the Veil

Implicit functions of the veil are best considered in six (overlapping) categories. These include *lexicographical and etymological* features of the term פרכת, the veil's *location* in the tabernacle, the *materials* from which it is made, the *colours* of those materials, the *workmanship* with which it is made and the presence of *cherubim* on it. Although other curtains in the tabernacle/temple possess features *similar* to these, the פרכת is the only curtain, and thus the only καταπέτασμα, to possess *all* of these distinctive features.[32] It has been rightly recognised as the most important curtain in the Old Testament.

With respect to *lexicographical and etymological* characteristics, the 'inner veil' appears as פרכת 26 times in the MT,[33] and פרכת never refers to anything but the 'inner veil'.[34] Of its 26 occurrences in the MT, 25

[31] Exod. 27:20–33:7. See R. E. Hendrix, 'A Literary Structural Overview of Exod. 25–40', *AUSS* 30 (1992), 123–38; S. Bar-Efrat, 'Some Observations on the Analysis of Structure in Biblical Narrative', *VT* 130 (1980), 170.

[32] The פרכת veil was identical to both other curtains called καταπέτασμα with respect to materials and colours. It greatly differed, however, with respect to the workmanship involved in its creation, the presence of cherubim on it, and thus similarly and most significantly, its function in the cultic worship of Israel.

[33] R. E. Gane, 'Re-opening Katapetasma ("Veil") in Hebrews 6:19', *AUSS* 38 (2000), 7, n. 7, suggests that the מסך at Num. 3:31 'must be the inner veil here because it was assigned to the care of the Kohathites, following assignment of the other two screens to the Gershonites (vv. 25–26)'. He also notes that the term פרכת falls within the category of the more general term מסך.

[34] So also J. Milgrom and R. Gane, 'פרכת', *TWAT* VI, p. 755; N. M. Sarna, *The JPS Torah Commentary: Exodus* (New York, N.Y.: Jewish Publication Society, 1991), pp. 170–71; U. Cassuto, *Commentary on the Book of Exodus* (trans. I. Abrahams; Jerusalem: Magnes Press, 1967), p. 361.

refer to the inner veil of the tabernacle and 1 (2 Chron. 3:14) to the inner veil of Solomon's temple.[35] It is also called the פרכת העדת 'veil of the covenant' (Lev. 24:3) for its role in concealing the ark of the covenant, and פרכת הקדש, 'the veil of the holy [place]' (Lev. 4:6); the latter can also mean 'holy veil'.[36] Milgrom and Gane look to the Akkadian origin for their understanding of its function.[37] They argue, 'Der Vorhang diente als Schranke, um Eingang una Sicht zu verhindern, und markierte zugleich den Ort, in/auf dem Gott thronte'.[38] פרכת may derive from the Sumerian *bára* or the Akkadian *parakku* or the verb *parāku*,[39] which can mean simply 'to spread open' but most commonly means to 'lay something across' something else, perhaps in a prohibitive manner.[40] Abbott argues that the Hebrew term denotes something that 'separates the king from people'; its radical meaning is 'breaking', and it may indicate an abrupt 'breaking off' or even 'crush'.[41] As limited as etymological analyses are, here they seem to be congruent with explicit functions of the veil and thus will be revisited later in this chapter.

M. Haran argues that its *location* within the tabernacle suggests the superiority of the veil 'both in quality and in rank of holiness'.[42] Haran further argues that in the tabernacle accounts, the hangings and curtains are listed from the least valuable and cultically significant to the most. The

[35] Milgrom and Gane, p. 755. B. A. Levine, *The JPS Torah Commentary: Leviticus* (Philadelphia, Pa.: JPS, 1989), p. 21, n. 11, notes the lack of a curtain mentioned in 1 Kgs 6:31 (where doors are mentioned), whereas in 2 Chron. 3:14 there are both a curtain and a door.

[36] Sarna (pp. 170–71) acknowledges this but says that it refers to the holy place in front of the veil. He further comments, 'In later Hebrew the term *parokhet* was transferred to the ornamented curtain covering the Ark that contains the Torah scrolls in the synagogue'. Cf. Jenson, p. 92. Jenson says that the distinction between holy objects and holy persons is that 'the holiness of objects is permanent, and they can never again enter the profane sphere' (p. 49).

[37] Milgrom and Gane, p. 756. Légasse, 'Les voiles du temple de Jérusalem: Essai de parcours historique', *RevB* 87 (1980), 582, says that the curtain at the entrance of the holy of holies always is designated feminine substantive *paroket*, suggesting a kinship with the Phoenician with the word *prkm*.

[38] Milgrom and Gane, p. 756; so also A. H. McNeile, *Exodus* (3rd edn; London: Methuen & Co., 1931), p. 172; cf. J. Milgrom, *Leviticus 1–16* (ABC 3; New York, N.Y.: Doubleday, 1991), p. 234.

[39] *TWAT* VI, p. 755. For a summary of the debate regarding the etymology of this word, cf. R. E. Averbeck, 'פרכת', *NIDOTTE* III, p. 688. Milgrom (*Leviticus 1–16*, p. 234) notes its relation to the Akkadian verb *parāku*, which means 'go across, block, bar', and which can describe a curtain. Cf. also Cassuto, *Exodus*, p. 359.

[40] Cf. W. von Soden, ed., *Akkadisches Handwörterbuch* (3 vols.; Wiesbaden: Harrasowitz, 1972), II, pp. 828–29. See the use of פרס in *Tg. Neof.* on Gen. 1:2; 9:14; 13:3, 10; 31:25; 33:19; Exod. 12:42; 25:20; 37:9; Lev. 11:26; 26:20; Deut. 32:11.

[41] Abbott, *The Fourfold Gospel*, sect. 5, *The Founding of the New Kingdom; or, Life Reached through Death* (Cambridge: Cambridge University Press, 1917), p. 617. Cf. also n. 3. *b. Sota* 11b.

[42] M. Haran, 'The Priestly Image of the Tabernacle', *HUCA* 36 (1965), 206–7.

mention of the inner veil at the end of the veil lists and in the innermost parts of the tabernacle in the Exodus texts, then, suggests both its value and its cultic significance vis-à-vis the other hangings of the tabernacle.[43] This notion of 'material gradation' has been strongly advanced by an important work by P. P. Jenson, who argues that the entire priestly code is based on varying degrees of sacredness of an object, person, space, time and so forth, on a 'holiness spectrum'.[44] This spectrum, Jenson contends, is 'most clearly represented by the spatial dimension' in which the centre of the tabernacle is the locus of the most holy and sacred space in the community, with lessening degrees as one proceeds farther away from its centre.[45] Thus the פרכת, being the innermost curtain, was the most holy.[46] Haran and Jenson both apply this idea of gradation also to materials, to the weaving of materials and to colours; these issues will be further discussed.

All the curtains that are translated καταπέτασμα were made of the same *materials*.[47] At times scholars have exaggerated the differences between these curtains on the basis of their materials.[48] Each curtain was made of 'finely twisted linen'.[49] It was made of 'a fine grade of linen',[50] which was probably Egyptian in origin.[51] 'Blue' (probably purple-blue) and 'purple' (probably purple-red) represent wool materials dyed to these colours with dyes extracted from different species of shellfish. The term for 'scarlet stuff' (שני) is derived from the kermes worm (*coccus ilicis*)

[43] Haran, *Temples and Temple-Service in Ancient Israel* (Oxford: Clarendon Press), p. 160. Milgrom, *The JPS Torah Commentary: Numbers* (Philadelphia, Pa.: JPS, 1990), pp. 25–26; J. I. Durham, *Exodus* (WBC 3; Waco, Tex.: Word), p. 354.

[44] Jenson, p. 37. Jenson has several charts illustrating this important observation. Two concern graded holiness in general (p. 102), one (accompanied by a diagram) illustrating the 'zones of holiness' and showing the holy of holies to be in the most sacred zone (p. 90). A table of spatially graded holiness is also displayed (p. 64), and his 'gradation' is defined this way: 'When an object (or person) is classified according to a particular trait, it is assigned to one of several classes or levels, and these are often ordered in a certain hierarchy or priority' (p. 62). 'For example, the extreme holiness which the high priest embodies (the personal dimension) is matched by the extreme holiness of the innermost sanctum (the spatial dimension)' (p. 64).

[45] Jenson, p. 37. [46] *Ibid.*, p. 92.

[47] Pelletier ('La tradition synoptique', p. 167) says, 'The decoration of the exterior curtain remains, otherwise indifferent, in any case indeterminate' (my translation).

[48] Cf. Durham, p. 354. For a discussion of the suggested material and cultic differences between the פרכת and מסך veils, see M. Haran, 'Priestly Image', 203–4.

[49] For a more comprehensive treatment of tabernacle material, cf. Sarna, p. 157. Κεκλωσμένου καὶ βύσσου νενησμένης, שש משזר; Exod. 26:31. Sarna (p. 167) argues that משזר is a technical term found exclusively in tabernacle contexts.

[50] Sarna, p. 167; cf. Wevers, p. 393.

[51] Durham, p. 354. The account of 2 Chron. 3:14 says that it was made of בוץ, which A. Hurvitz, 'The Usage of שש and בוץ in the Bible and Its Implication for the Date of P', *HTR* 60 (1967), 118, 120, suggests is a later synonym that is the result of post-exilic association with northeastern peoples.

from which this dye was produced. 'Fine twisted linen' (שׁשׁ), a superior Egyptian variety, would also be needed.[52] Other materials were 'goats' hair', coming from the Israelite flocks, and 'tanned rams' skins', though the precise meaning of תחשׁ is uncertain.[53]

As is the case with the materials, each of the three καταπέτασμα curtains was made of the same variety of *colours* (Exod. 26:31) that also point to their value. Again M. Haran strongly argues that although both colours and materials for the inner veil are similar to those of the other veils of the tabernacle, the order in which they are listed for the פרכת veil, as in other aspects of the tabernacle account, is one of 'material gradation'. That is, the order of these lists highlights the elevated sanctity of the פרכת veil above all other hangings in the tabernacle.[54] The curtains were violet (ὑακίνθος, תכלת), or some suggest 'blue-purple' or perhaps a darker purple compared with the lighter (ארגמן) purple.[55] This colour was occasionally thought to be the colour of the sky (cf. *b. Soṭah* 17a), which may help account for its association with the heavenly firmament (Gen. 1:6) in later Judaism.[56] Durham notes that 12,000 murex snails were needed to yield only 1.4 grams of pure dye![57] This colour, normally associated with the Phoenicians, was known for its association with both divinity and royalty in the ANE,[58] which lends itself to the notion that Yahweh was both the sacred deity and the king enthroned in the midst of Israel within the tabernacle.

The curtains were also (light) purple (πορφόρα, ארגמן), perhaps better 'red-purple'.[59] This comes from a rich, expensive dye, often used in royal contexts.[60] Scarlet (κόκκινος, תולעת שׁני), perhaps 'crimson thread',[61] refers properly to a material produced by the kermes worm (*coccus ilicis*) but is often[62] extended to refer to material dyed the same colour.[63] In addition to its use in tabernacle furnishings, this colour is associated with

52 Westerholm, p. 698. 53 *Ibid.*

54 Haran, 'Priestly Image', 203–4. So also Durham, p. 373; similarly C. Houtman, *Exodus* (3 vols.; HCOT; Leuven: Peeters, 2000), III, pp. 417–18; Jenson, pp. 104, 106.

55 A. Brenner, *Colour Terms in the Old Testament* (JSOTSup 21; Sheffield: JSOT Press, 1982), p. 146.

56 *Ibid.*, p. 146. We will revisit this association in Chapter 4.

57 Durham, p. 354; cf. R. Gradwohl, *Die Farben im Alten Testament* (BZAW 83; Berlin: Töpelmann, 1963), pp. 66–78; L. B. Jensen, 'Royal Purple of Tyre', *JNES* 22 (1963), 104–18.

58 For a complete survey, especially the history, origin, and chemical composition of this purple, cf. Jensen, pp. 104–18.

59 Cf. Jdg. 8:26; Est. 1:6; 8:15; esp. Dan. 5:7, 16, 29. Brenner, p. 147.

60 Cf. Brenner, p. 147. 61 *Ibid.*, p. 143.

62 All of its 26 uses in the Old Testament occur in the tabernacle accounts.

63 Wevers, p. 392. Wevers also notes that the LXX interprets its *Vorlage* with κόκκινον διπλοῦν, meaning 'doubly scarlet', 'taking the free noun as related to שׁני "second", though at the same time aware that it also means "scarlet"'.

the cleansing of lepers (Lev. 14), ceremonies of purification (Num. 19:6) and royal apparel (2 Sam. 1:24; Jer. 4:30; Nah. 2:3).[64] Brenner suggests that uses of both ארגמן and תכלת in the same context serve as 'signifiers for royal attire, that is, as a symbol of power and government'.[65] The use of 'royal' colours and materials should come as no surprise, as the tabernacle in general and the angelic wings over the כפרת in particular are often thought to represent the kingly presence of Yahweh among his people. This is confirmed by the description of Yahweh's presence with Israel as being 'enthroned between the cherubim' (1 Sam. 4:4; 2 Sam. 6:2; 2 Kgs 19:15; 1 Chron. 13:6; Pss 80:1, 99:1; Isa. 37:16), which when coupled with a reference to God's enthronement 'in heaven' (Ps. 2:4) may support the notion that the holy of holies was thought to be a replica of heaven.[66]

Jenson indicates that the costliness of a curtain in the tabernacle is 'proportional to its closeness to God'.[67] This becomes most apparent in the distinction between the inner (פרכת) veil and the other (מסך) curtains with respect to the *workmanship* with which they are crafted. Westerholm argues that the screen 'required the same materials as the veil, but less elaborate workmanship; because the screen involved no cherubim figures, the work could be assigned to an embroiderer rather than a more skilled pattern weaver'.[68] The more skilled weaving is designated by two of the three terms for such workmanship (חשׁב and רקם)[69] that, Haran argues, 'are always mentioned only in connection with a mixture of all kinds of dyed wool with the linen . . . [and] taken as a hallmark of holiness'.[70] According to Jenson, such mixtures, particularly with respect to colours, 'are associated with holiness'.[71] Thus, for Haran, the order in which the materials are listed and the quality of workmanship employed on the 'veil' and its close proximity to the ark of the covenant, properly designate it as the pre-eminent of all 'veils' and hangings of the tabernacle, with the royalty of its colours suggesting that simply from appearance alone the פרכת may function as a visible indicator that what lies behind is a divine king. It was an appropriate article to hang in front of the enthroned Yahweh. Milgrom goes so far as to suggest that it 'had the same sacred status as the sancta (Exod. 30:29)'.[72]

[64] E. J. Banks, 'Color', *ISBE* I, p. 743. [65] Brenner, p. 146.

[66] God is said to be 'enthroned': 'in Zion' (Pss 9:11; 132:13–14; Isa. 14:13); 'as the Holy One' (Ps. 22:3); 'over the flood' (Ps. 29:10a); 'as king forever' (Ps. 29:10b); 'forever' (Pss 55:19; 102:12); 'on high' (Ps. 113:5) and 'above the circles of the earth' (Isa. 40:22).

[67] Jenson, p. 101. [68] Westerholm, p. 701.

[69] The three techniques for weaving in the tabernacle texts are: חשׁב workmanship (Exod. 26:1, etc.), רקם workmanship (Exod. 26:36) and ארג workmanship (Exod. 39:22).

[70] Haran, 'Priestly Image', p. 202. [71] Jenson, p. 86. [72] Milgrom, *Numbers*, p. 20.

As we have seen, the unique workmanship required for the veil is directly related to the presence of *cherubim* on the veil (Exod. 26:31), which itself may point to its function in the tabernacle cult.[73] These figures, DeVries suggests, 'symbolized the presence of Yahweh'[74] and were woven of elite quality, 'the work of a skillful workman'.[75] Borowski suggests that cherubim are among the earliest expressions of divine characteristics in the ancient Near East.[76] Drawing largely from an Assyrian figure of ivory thought to date from the ninth or eighth century B.C.E. and from another artefact from Arslan Tash (near the Syria–Turkish border, though of Egyptian influence) that dates from the ninth century B.C.E., Borowski argues that 'in addition to being guardians, cherubim served as a throne or resting place for God's invisible presence'.[77] Interestingly, Jenson shows that, like the cherubim, the priests who served to 'guard at the entrance would prevent unauthorized entrance',[78] especially against 'the approach of any impurity which could threaten its holiness'.[79] Priests served a similar role in the tabernacle. That is, they were charged with 'guarding' the

[73] *Pace* Pelletier ('La tradition synoptique', 166), who claims there were simply decorative.

[74] S. J. DeVries, *1 Kings* (WBC 12; Waco, Tex.: Word, 1985), p. 94.

[75] Ἔργον ὑφαντὸν, מעשב יעשה; Exod. 26:3. Cf. R. J. Forbes, *Studies in Ancient Technology* (4 vols.; Leiden: Brill, 1964) IV, p. 211–17. For various readings, see Wevers, p. 427. Haran ('Priestly Image', p. 203 n. 26) notes that 'the Talmudic sages depicted *ḥoshev* workmanship as a combination of threads interwoven in such a way that different figures emerge on the two sides of the fabric', citing *Yoma* 72b, Rashi on Exod. 26:1, 36. He further asserts that *ḥoshev* workmanship is normally used with respect to cherubim work. 'It seems likely, therefore, that this workmanship is mainly distinguished for containing figures, whereas *roqem* workmanship, though it also involves a mixture of colors and varieties, contains no figures.'

[76] E. Borowski, 'Cherubim: God's Throne?' *BAR* 21 (1995), 36. For a more complete description of tabernacles in general in the ancient Near East, see R. E. Averbeck, 'The Cylinders of Gudea', in *The Context of Scripture*, vol. 2, *Monumental Inscriptions from the Biblical World* (ed. W. W. Hallo and K. L. Younger; Leiden: Brill, 2000), pp. 417–33.

[77] Borowski, p. 37. Although many agree with Borowski that the cherubim represent a throne for God, Clements argues that the כפרת is not at all analogous to the cherubim throne. Instead, he insists, the association of cherubim with God's throne was a later development borrowed from the Canaanites, from whom they would adopt a number of 'mythological' features to their cultic worship practices. R. E. Clements, *God and Temple* (Philadelphia, Pa.: Fortress Press, 1965), pp. 34–35, following M. Dibelius, *Die Lade Jahves: Eine religionsgeschichtliche Untersuchung* (Göttingen: Vandenhoeck & Ruprecht, 1906), p. 95. So also T. N. D. Mettinger, 'Yhwh Sabaoth: The Heavenly King on the Cherubim Throne', in *Studies in the Period of David and Solomon and other Essays International Symposium for Biblical Studies, Tokyo, 1979* (ed. T. Ishida; Winona Lake, Ind.: Eisenbrauns, 1982), p. 116. Haran argues that Dibelius draws too sharp a distinction between the role of the cherubim on the ark and the ark itself. Clements, he argues, relies solely on his assumption of the historical origin of the cherubim coming from Shiloh (2 Sam. 6:2), which dates from 1050 B.C.E., and dates his 'P' source after that. Haran, 'The Ark and the Cherubim: Their Symbolic Significance in Biblical Ritual', *IEJ* 9 (1959), 36.

[78] Jenson, p. 92. [79] *Ibid.*, p. 93.

tabernacle,[80] though its integrity 'is maintained by God himself in cases where the human guard fails (e.g. Lev. 10:1–3)'.[81] Milgrom has shown that this point is underscored in P texts by distinct mention of the presence of God in these texts, '"guarding" against violation'.[82]

In biblical tradition, the cherubim likewise served a guardian role from their first appearance in canonical texts (Gen. 3:24), where they guarded 'the way to the tree of life'.[83] This seems to set a precedent for how they are to be understood in the tabernacle and in subsequent temple depictions on the veil and carved on walls around Solomon's[84] and Ezekiel's visionary temples.[85] That is, as the priests served to guard the tabernacle against intruders, so the cherubim, the only beings continuously allowed in the presence of God, depict a guarding of the way into the holy of holies by similar intruders. Elsewhere the cherubim are present at man's meeting with God (e.g., Moses; see Exod. 25:22; Num. 7:89) or the winged throne upon which God sits[86] or mounts to fly (2 Sam. 22:11; Ps. 18:10).[87] Yahweh instructs Moses to make 'two cherubim out of hammered gold at the ends of the cover' (Exod. 25:18) 'of one piece with the cover' (Exod. 25:19).[88] With wings spread upward and overshadowing the atonement

[80] Milgrom, *Studies in Levitical Terminology, 1: The Encroacher and the Levite; The Term 'Aboda* (NES 14; London: University of California Press, 1970), p. 9, says that their 'guard duty is a lifelong responsibility'. For a more detailed discussion of the guardianship role of the priests (משמרת), see Milgrom, *Levitical Terminology*, pp. 8–16.

[81] Jenson, p. 107. [82] Milgrom, *Levitical Terminology*, p. 10.

[83] Cf. M. Alexandre, 'L'épée de flamme (Gen. 3, 24): textes chrétiens et traditions juives', in *Hellenica et Judaica: Hommage à Valentin Nikipronetzky* (ed. A. Caquot, M. Hadas-Lebel and J. Riand; Leuven: Peeters, 1986), pp. 403–41; R. S. Hendel, '"The Flame and the Whirling Sword": A Note on Genesis 3:24', *JBL* 104 (1985), 671–74.

[84] Inner and outer rooms; 1 Kgs 6:29, 32, 35; 7:29, 36; 2 Chron. 3:7. Though also woven into curtains (αὐλαία, יריעה) of the tabernacle (Exod. 26:1, 31), of the three curtains translated καταπέτασμα are only found on that which translates פרכת (Exod. 26:31; 36:35; 2 Chron. 3:14).

[85] Cherubim were prominent figures in the holy of holies of Ezekiel's vision. They are found beneath God (presumably in temple; Ezek. 9:3) and as a throne (Ezek. 10:1). They are found in his vision of the temple (Ezek. 10:2 [2x], 3, 4, 5, 6, 7, 8, 11 [3x], 14 [2x], 15, 16 [2x], 17, 18, 19, 20; 11:22) and on carvings on doors of Ezekiel's vision of the outer sanctuary (Ezek. 41:18 [3x], 20, 25). For a discussion of the complicated differences between the Greek and MT texts of Ezekiel's temple vision and their cherubim, see G. A. Cooke, *The Book of Ezekiel* (ICC; Edinburgh: T. & T. Clark, 1936), pp. 317–18. For an interesting overview of the function of Ezekiel's cherubim, particularly in their ancient Near Eastern context, see W. B. Barrick, 'The Straight-Legged Cherubim of Ezekiel's Inaugural Vision (Ezekiel 1:7a)', *CBQ* 44 (1982), 546–50.

[86] 1 Sam. 4:4; 2 Sam. 6:2; 2 Kgs 19:15; 1 Chron. 13:6; Pss 80:1; 99:1; Isa. 37:16.

[87] Barrick, p. 547.

[88] Jenson (p. 103) indicates that the costliness of gold 'fittingly represents the dignity and power of those who are able to possess it, to a pre-eminent degree, God'. Moreover,

slate, they were to be arranged in such a manner as to face each other[89] where (Exod. 25:1–22) they were 'guardians of the mercy seat from which the . . . divine Glory . . . speaks to Israel'.[90] Their figures are present as olivewood statues overlaid with gold in the holy of holies of Solomon's temple.[91] That the cherubim figure so prominently in the tabernacle outer hangings is then a sign of the divine presence within, resonating with their original appearance in biblical tradition at Gen. 3:24, which is repeated for the פרכת. Scholars have come to recognise that the Garden of Eden is a temple-like sanctuary with cherubim set to guard the way to it (Gen. 3:24).[92] Perhaps the cherubim on the veil, then, similarly serve to guard the way to the sanctuary of God within the holy of holies. Their depiction in these cultic texts is significant, as their presence on the פרכת veil is thought particularly to reflect their function within the most holy place. It seems that they are representative not only of the presence of the enthroned Yahweh among his people, but more specifically of the presence of Yahweh *enthroned among his people*. Moreover, they served, like the priests, as guardians of the sanctity of the tabernacle but were uniquely the guardians of the holy of holies. I will revisit this notion in our discussion of explicit functions of the veil.

We see then that features of the veil lead nicely to its implicit functions. These, we will see, are congruent with *explicit* functions of the veil and include *etymological and lexicographical* features of the term פרכת that suggest a prohibitive barrier, spread out before the throne room of a king. Its *location* in the tabernacle suggests the utmost degree of sanctity, consistent with the sacred *materials* from which it is made and the *colours*

he shows that it is commonly associated with divinity and holiness throughout the ancient Near East (see Jenson, p. 103 n. 3, for references).

[89] Exod. 25:20; cf. Heb. 9:5. For a brief overview of the use of similar postures by angelic figures and their depiction of a deity, cf. T. Ornan, 'Symbols of Royalty and Divinity', *BAR* 21 (1995), 38–39. Cf. also Houtman, *Exodus* III, pp. 382–85.

[90] Mettinger, 'Cherubim', *DDD*, p. 365. Following M. Görg, 'Keruben in Jerusalem', *BN* 4 (1977), 13–24, Mettinger (*DDD*, p. 365) argues that the cherubim 'iconography of P must thus have a different, Egyptian background' than that found in prophetic texts and those of the Solomonic temple. Cf. esp. R. DeVaux, 'Les chérubins et l'achre d'alliance, les sphinx gardiens et les trônes divins dans l'ancien orient', in *Bible et Orient* (ed. R. DeVaux; Paris: Cerf, 1967), esp. pp. 235–54. For a survey of other opinions regarding the origin of cherubim, see Haran, 'Ark and the Cherubim', pp. 92–94.

[91] 1 Kgs 6:23, 24, 25 [2x], 26, 27 [2x], 28; 8:6, 7; 2 Chron. 3:10, 11 [3x], 12 [2x], 13; 5:7, 8.

[92] G. Wenham, 'Sanctuary Symbolism in the Garden of Eden Story', in *Proceedings of the Ninth World Congress of Jewish Studies*, division A, *The Period of the Bible* (Jerusalem: World Union of Jewish Studies, 1986), pp. 19–24.

of those materials. The *workmanship* with which the veil was crafted also suggests a higher degree of sanctity, as does the presence of *cherubim* on it, a unique feature among the καταπέτασμα curtains, suggesting the unapproachable divine presence within, resonating with the image of the cherubim first placed at the Garden of Eden in Gen. 3:24.

## 3.2 Explicit Functions of the Veil

In addition to *implicit* functions of the veil, the καταπέτασμα that is translated פרכת and thus refers to the inner veil before the holy of holies is the only καταπέτασμα designated with *explicit* functions both structurally and cultically. We will see, however, that the implicit functions of the veil coalesce with and richly inform its explicit functions. We have seen that the veil serves as a 'keep out' sign before the holy of holies, but the Old Testament is much more specific than that. In particular, Pentateuchal tabernacle texts indicate that the veil provided (בדל) *general cultic separation between the holy and the less holy*. Von Rad indicates that the tension created between clean and unclean, holy and secular, blessing and curse, 'was a basic datum of all life – it was so universally valid that it has to be assumed as present and taken for granted even where it is not mentioned *expressis verbis*, as for instance in the prophets'.[93] Of the various sheets, hangings and veils, only this *inner* veil (καταπέτασμα, פרכת) is accompanied by any clear explanation of its function with respect to this tension.[94] In Exod. 26:33c we read לכם בין הקדש ובין קדש הקדשים והבדילה הפדכת. This can be translated literally as 'the veil separates for you the holy place and the most holy place'. The verb הבדילה, a hiphil perfect from בדל, means generally 'to separate'. Occurring 44 times in the MT, בדל can most simply convey a sense of separation,[95] though a separation of divine origin or purpose.

Normally בדל separation is carried out by priests or even the Lord himself; thus I have called this the 'priestly' function of the veil. In the Pentateuch, however, where half the occurrences of בדל in the MT occur, such separation begins with God, who is said to have separated (בדל)

[93] G. Von Rad, *Old Testament Theology* (2 vols.; trans. D. M. G. Stalker; Edinburgh: Oliver & Boyd, 1962) I, p. 272, quoted in Jenson, p. 61.

[94] Within the tabernacle itself, this occurs after a manner not unlike other cultic vessels, such as the lampstand (Exod. 25:31–40), laver (Exod. 30:17–21), etc. Linnemann (p. 159) argues that the inner veil is the 'allein kultisch bedeutsamen Vorhang'. So also C. Schneider, *TDNT* III, p. 629.

[95] L. Kohler and W. Baumgartner, *Lexicon in Veteris Testamenti Libros* (2 vols.; Leiden: Brill, 1958) I, p. 106, say 'trennen unterscheiden an' 'Unterschied machen' 'abtrennen' 'aussondern'. See also BDB, p. 95.

light from darkness (Gen. 1:4). God also sets a 'firmament' (Gen. 1:6; רקיע, στερέωμα) which separated (בדל) 'water from water' (בין מים למים, διαξωρίζον ἀνὰ μέσον ὕδατος καὶ ὕδατος; Gen. 1:6). He also creates 'lights' (Gen. 1:14; מארת, φωστήρ), which serve to separate (בדל) והיו בין היום ובין הלילה 'between the day and the night' (LXX: ἀνὰ μέσον τῆς ἡμέρας καὶ ἀνὰ μέσον τῆς νυκτὸς). Similarly in Gen. 1:16, 18, God creates 'two great lights' (שני המארת הגדלים, τοὺς δύο φωστῆρας τοὺς μεγάλους) which separated (בדל) 'light' from 'darkness' (האור ובין החשך בין, διαχωρίζει ἀνὰ μέσον τοῦ φωτὸς καὶ ἀνὰ μέσον τοῦ σκότους; Gen. 1:18). In a general sense the creation narrative of Gen. 1 depicts separation (בדל) 'in terms of separating what does not belong together and separating for a specific task'.[96] We will see that later Jewish authors recognised the correlation between the separating function of the heavenly firmament (Gen. 1:6) and of the veil to depict its role in Second Temple and rabbinic cosmology (Chapter 4).

In the so-called Priestly material ('P', and cultic texts elsewhere) בדל seems to be a technical term used to articulate what must take place between the holy and the less holy: 'distinction'. For example, the priest was not to sever (בדל) the body of a dove or young pigeon (Lev. 1:14) that is offered for burnt offering (Lev. 1:17), or the neck of the doves or pigeons (Lev. 5:7) offered for sin offering (Lev. 5:8). In a curious command to abstain from 'wine or strong drink' (Lev. 10:9), Aaron and his sons are threatened with death as an aspect of their distinction (בדל) of 'the sacred' (הקדש) and 'the profane' (החל), 'the unclean' (הטמא) and 'the clean' (הטהור; Lev. 10:10). Similarly, the entire priestly code of clean and unclean animals (Lev. 11:1–45) is summarised by its purpose: to separate (בדל) between 'the unclean' (הטמא) and 'the clean' (הטהר), the animals that may be eaten and those that may not (Lev. 11:47; similarly Lev. 10:10, 20:25).[97] In a similar cultic context (Ezek. 42:20), the prophet Ezekiel is

[96] C. Van Dam, 'בדל', *NIDOTTE* I, p. 604.

[97] The LXX rendering of בדל as used here at Exod. 26:33 is seemingly more sporadic. In Exod. 26:33, LXX has διορίζω ('draw a boundary through, delimit, separate' [LSJ]; 'to draw a boundary through, to separate' [J. Lust, E. Eynikel and K. Hauspie, *A Greek–English Lexicon of the Septuagint* {2 vols.; Stuttgart: Deutsche Bibelgesellschaft, 1996} I, p. 117]). As is the case in Exod. 26:33, בדל is rendered διορίζω in other key verses (Lev. 20:24; Ezek. 42:20). For the other references, it seems as though the translators saw a Hebrew word other than בדל, since the idea of 'separation' is nowhere present. Cf. Josh. 5:6; 15:47; 2 Chron. 32:4; Job 35:11; Isa. 45:18, 24–25; Ezek. 41:12–14; 42:1, 10. For a possible exception, see Ezek. 47:18. For a complete list of possible Hebrew words present in the LXX *Vorlagen*, see E. Hatch and H. A. Redpath, eds., *A Concordance to the Septuagint: And the Other Greek Versions of the Old Testament (Including the Apocryphal Books)* (2d edn; Grand Rapids, Mich.: Baker, 1998), p. 336. See also Jenson, p. 43.

given a vision of the temple (Ezek. 40:1–42:20)[98] and describes the 'protection wall' (חומה, προτείχισμα) that serves to separate (בדל) 'the holy from the profane' (בין הקדש לחל).[99] This type of בדל separation is not new to Ezekiel and is a function previously given to priests (Ezek. 22:26). This function and the task of instructing (הורה) Israel to observe בדל separation (Ezek. 22:26) are the primary tasks of the priests as depicted in Ezekiel[100] and in the Old Testament in general.[101] Their failure to uphold their duties of בדל separation (Ezek. 22:26) is among the other grounds (enumerated in Ezek. 26:25–30) for Yahweh's impending judgement (Ezek. 26:31). The only feature of Ezekiel's temple said to carry out בדל separation is this wall (Ezek. 42:20). It 'has the task of marking the division between the sacred and the profane'.[102] This is necessary because it is assumed throughout each theophany in Ezekiel's prophecy: 'The holy cannot be thought of or understood in the biblical sphere apart from the holy one. . . . The holy is found where God himself is present'.[103] It is perhaps not unfair to say, then, that the Lord established the wall of the temple to do in part what the priests could not (cf. esp. Ezek. 34): distinguish (בדל) between the holy and profane.[104]

Even the law itself engages in בדל separation (Lev. 11:47). As stated earlier, the entire priestly code regarding clean and unclean animals (Lev. 11:1–45) is summarised by its purpose: to separate (בדל) between 'the unclean' (הטמא) and 'the clean' (הטהר).[105] This description 'guides the priests in carrying out their responsibility of distinguishing between the clean and the unclean for the people (10:10)'.[106] The final use of 'separation' (בדל) in this sense is in Exod. 26:33, which, as noted earlier, refers to the פרכת veil. Here the veil makes distinction between the holy place

[98] For a helpful reconstruction of the plan of that temple, cf. W. Eichrodt, *Ezekiel: A Commentary* (Old Testament Library; trans. C. Quin; London: SCM Press, 1970), p. 537, or D. I. Block, *Ezekiel* (NICOT; Grand Rapids, Mich.: Eerdmans, 1998), pp. 572–73.

[99] LXX has the curious ἀνὰ μέσον τῶν ἁγίων καὶ ἀνὰ μέσον τοῦ προτειχίσματος τοῦ ἐν διατάξει τοῦ οἴκου.

[100] W. Zimmerli, *A Commentary on the Book of the Prophet Ezekiel, Chapters 1–24* (trans. R. E. Clements; Philadelphia, Pa.: Fortress Press, 1979), p. 336.

[101] Cf. Van Dam, *NIDOTTE* I, p. 604.

[102] Zimmerli, *A Commentary on the Book of the Prophet Ezekiel, Chapters 25–48* (trans. J. D. Martin; Philadelphia, Pa.: Fortress Press, 1983), p. 404.

[103] Zimmerli, *Ezekiel 25–48*, pp. 404–5; cf. L. C. Allen, *Ezekiel* (2 vols.; WBC 29; Dallas, Tex.: Word, 1990) II, p. 235.

[104] See 11Q20 xii 21–22.

[105] For a detailed study of dietary laws in Lev. 11, see Milgrom, 'Ethics and Ritual: The Foundations of the Biblical Dietary Laws', in *Religion and Law: Biblical–Judaic and Islamic Perspectives* (ed. E. Firmage, B. Weiss and J. Welch; Winona Lake, Ind.: Eisenbrauns, 1990), pp. 159–91; G. Wenham, 'The Theology of Unclean Foods', *EvQ* 53 (1981), 6–15; R. K. Yerkes, 'The Unclean Animals of Leviticus 11 and Deuteronomy', *JQR* n.s. 14 (1923), 1–29.

[106] J. E. Hartley, *Leviticus* (WBC 4; Dallas, Tex.: Word, 1992), p. 163.

(הקדש) and the most holy place (קדש הקדשים). Or, if we accept Haran's thesis, the function of the veil here may be more significantly to separate the most holy from, perhaps, the less holy, which, as seen in the Ezekiel vision, may have evolved into a distinction between the holy and the profane (Ezek. 42:20). That is, the veil made בדל distinction not just between two chambers of the tabernacle as an ordinary wall, but rather between two spaces of differing degrees of sanctity.

The inner chamber is 'most holy', while the outer is merely 'less holy'. To phrase this differently, the veil served to make distinction between what is of the utmost sanctity, by virtue of its association with the presence of Yahweh himself in the most holy place, and *anything that is of a lesser degree of holiness*. Indeed, the idea of the tabernacle/temple structure in general concerns degrees of holiness in concentric circles, with the utmost degree of holiness in the centre and its agent of separation the veil. This is, in a sense, the priestly function of the veil, for as the veil was to make a 'distinction' (בדל) from the most holy place, so the Lord commanded Aaron to make 'distinction' (בדל) between the sacred and the impure under penalty of death (Lev. 10:10) and pass that teaching on to all Israel (cf. Lev. 11:47).[107] Moreover, the ritual purity of the entrant was also bound up in his high priestly status. For only the high priest, the most sacred priest in Jenson's scheme, was able to enter the holy of holies. Precisely how this distinction is carried out is likewise specified in the Old Testament. For in the Old Testament we see that the distinction it provides is executed by means of prohibition of physical and visual accessibility to the holy of holies (and thus to the presence of God within).

Before we look at the accessibility issue, however, we must first consider whether the veil also has a role in the 'sin offering' (חטאת; Lev. 4:6, 17),[108] where the priest is to take the blood of the bull into the tent of meeting and 'dip his finger into the blood and sprinkle (הזה) some of it seven times before the Lord, in front of the curtain of the sanctuary' (Lev. 4:6). Precisely what it means to 'sprinkle' (הזה) and where it is done ('toward the veil of the sanctuary' or 'on the veil of the sanctuary'; את פני פרכת הקדש) has been the subject of some discussion.[109] J. Hartley

[107] Moreover, the call to make 'distinction' (בדל) between sacred and impure is inextricably linked to Yahweh's setting apart (בדל) Israel as his chosen people (Lev. 20:25–26).

[108] For a detailed analysis of the etymology, meaning, and implications of חטאת, see B. A. Levine, *In the Presence of the Lord* (SJLA 5; Leiden: Brill, 1974), pp. 101–14. Averbeck shows that the term can either refer to 'sin offering' or 'purification offering'. Cf. his discussion of the two in 'Sacrifices and Offerings', *DOTP*, pp. 717–18.

[109] For a more concise overview, see Hartley, *Leviticus*, p. 60. Cf. T. C. Vriezen, 'The Term *HIZZA*: Lustration and Consecration', *OtSt* (1950), 202; B. Janowski, *Sühne als Heilsgeschehen: Studien zur Sühnetheologie der Priesterschaft und zur Wurzel KPR im Alten Orient und im Alten Testament* (WMANT 55; Neukirchen-Vluyn: Neukirchener, 1982).

seems to indicate, with respect to the Day of Atonement ritual, that the sprinkling of blood *in the direction* of the mercy seat, or atonement slate, with some of it probably falling on it, is sufficient for the efficacy of the sacrifice.[110] Whether the blood actually reached the veil or not is unclear and has been the subject of some discussion.[111] Yet, as with other blood sprinklings in Leviticus, the *direction in which the blood is sprinkled* is indicative of the purpose of the sprinkling. This leads Kurtz to suggest that this sprinkling was a 'substitute for the sprinkling of the Capporeth',[112] which, he argues, 'was what was really necessary'.[113] Similarly, M. Haran suggests that in 'cultic ceremonies this veil sometimes serves as a kind of projection and 'shadow' of the *kapporeth* behind it (Lev. 4:6, 17)'.[114] Milgrom and Gane are surely correct when they suggest that the term פרכת העדת ('veil of the testimony'; Lev. 24:3) requires that one not make a significant distinction between the veil and the ark 'of the testimony'.[115] While the correlation between the veil and the atonement slate should be noted, the similarities are not expressed in terms of function. That is, the similarities with respect to the cherubim, for example, could simply serve to provide continuity for depicting the presence of God within. Though the veil as a projection of the atonement slate is particularly attractive when we examine the rending of the veil in the Matthean context, this function is less than clear in the Old Testament alone and therefore would be difficult to recognise in the Matthean *velum scissum* text.

While cultic separation is the primary function of the veil, how exactly was this separation executed? Again we find quite specific information on this matter in the Old Testament, where we see that the veil *executed*

110 Hartley, 'Atonement, Day of', *DOTP*, p. 57.

111 At issue is one's interpretation of את פני פרכת הקדש: '*against* the veil of the Holy Place' or '*toward*' it. For a concise overview of the varying opinions, see Hartley, *Leviticus*, p. 60. Cf. also Vriezen, pp. 201–35. G. Lindeskog suggests that 'on the great day of atonement sprinkled the blood onto the veil instead of, as in the First Temple, onto the mercy-seat'. See his 'The Veil of the Temple', in *In honorem A. Fridrichsen sexagenarii* (Edenda curavit Seminarium Neotestamenticum Upsaliense; Coniectanea neotestamentica; New Testament Series 11; Lund: Gleerup, 1947), pp. 134–35; see Str-B III, pp. 182, 184.

112 Kurtz, in our view, pushes beyond the evidence. With question as to whether the blood actually reaches the veil and with an air of incompleteness of the ritual apparent, its function to 'effect' atonement is speculative. Instead, it seems to represent quite the opposite. That is, rather than accomplishing proper expiation, the veil seems here either (1) to function effectively and *prevent*, block or 'shield' proper expiation from taking place or perhaps (2) to serve as a physical symbol that the proper expiation has not taken place.

113 J. H. Kurtz, *Sacrificial Worship in the Old Testament* (Edinburgh: T. & T. Clark, 1863), p. 217.

114 Haran, 'Priestly Image', p. 203. So also N. Kiuchi, *The Purification Offering in the Priestly Literature: Its Meaning and Function* (JSOTSup 56; Sheffield: Academic Press, 1987), p. 125.

115 Milgrom and Gane, p. 756.

*its cultic-separation role by prohibiting physical and visual accessibility to the holy of holies* (and thus to God's presence within). It seems that separation is the theological basis for the prohibition of access, its role as a 'keep out' sign. As I noted earlier, Milgrom and Gane suggest that the primary function of the veil (פרכת) was to articulate, or even enforce, a restriction of physical access to the throne of God and thus his very presence.[116] The Lord tells Aaron that he and his sons are the only ones permitted to serve as priests in relation to the articles behind the veil (ולמבית לפרכת),[117] and all others who come near the sanctuary are to be 'put to death' (Num. 18:7; cf. Lev. 16:2).[118] Exception for entering the most holy place is made only in the context of the Day of Atonement (Lev. 16:11–28), when the high priest takes the offering behind the veil (פרכת) as a 'sin' or 'purification' offering (חטאת, Lev. 16:11). Here the blood is taken into the holy of holies and sprinkled (הזה) on the atonement slate of the ark (Lev. 16:14; ולפני הכפרת יזה).[119] On the Day of Atonement, Aaron 'was to use the blood of the sin offering to purify and consecrate' the altar (Lev. 16:19).[120] Hartley observes that this sacrifice 'laid the foundation for God to forgive the people all sins committed since the previous Day of Atonement'. Moreover, he concludes that by this sacrifice 'God could continue to be present, blessing the covenant community'.[121] The veil marked a physical barrier which could only be penetrated in one particular sacrifice and when offering a sacrifice by blood, the means by

[116] *TWAT* VI, p. 756; so also McNeile, p. 172.

[117] For a discussion of the doubling of prepositions in early Phoenician and Ugaritic, cf. Levine, *Numbers* (2 vols.; ABC 4A–B; New York, N.Y.: Doubleday, 1993, 2000), I, pp. 442–43.

[118] Cf. Milgrom, *Levitical Terminology*, pp. 21–22.

[119] Note the similar expression used here, ולפני, as in Lev. 4. Whether one holds that the blood is actually sprinkled *on* the veil in Lev. 4 (seemingly more likely in light of the Lev. 16:14 parallel) or at least in the direction of it, the common expression of sprinkling (הזה) and the term for 'toward' or 'upon' (לפני) strongly suggest a parallel with the Lev. 4 rite. Lev. 16:14 ולפני הכפרת יזה; Lev. 4:6a והזה . . . לפני יהוה; Lev. 4:6b והזה . . . את־פני פרכת הקדש. Cf. Hartley, *DOTP*, p. 57. *Tg. Neof.* Lev. 16:2 (reading פרכתה) says nothing new about the veil, but in 16:3 adds to the prohibition of entry into God's presence 'before the mercy seat which is upon the ark *of the testimony* lest he die, because in *my* cloud, *the glory of my Shekinah, my Memra, is revealed* upon the mercy seat'.

[120] Averbeck, *DOTP*, p. 727. Whereas previously (Lev. 4:3–12) the blood was sprinkled outside the veil, here it is taken into the holy of holies and again sprinkled (הזה), but this time on the atonement slate of the ark (Lev. 16:14; ולפני הכפרת יזה). Whether one holds that the blood is actually sprinkled *on* the veil in Lev. 4 (seemingly more likely in light of the Lev. 16:14 parallel) or at least in the direction of it, the common expression of sprinkling (הזה) and the term for 'toward' or 'upon' (לפני) strongly suggest a parallel with the Lev. 4 rite.

[121] Hartley, *DOTP*, p. 55. Averbeck (*DOTP*, p. 710) shows that the basic meaning of כפר, as seen by its Akkadian cognate *kuppuru* ('to wipe clean') is 'to purge', particularly with reference to the tabernacle and altar.

which the presence of Yahweh with his people is enabled. This is the traditional understanding of the veil's function particularly informed by the Hebrew texts and Calvin's influence, mentioned in the introduction. Yet the intruder must be the high priest and may not enter 'whenever he chooses', says the Lord, 'because I appear in the cloud over the atonement cover' (Lev. 16:2; Num. 7:89).[122] Even on the Day of Atonement, when the high priest is permitted physical accessibility to God within the holy of holies,[123] the 'atonement slate' is 'hidden' from sight by the cloud, 'in this way saving him (the high priest) from death (Lev. 16:12–13)'. According to Lev. 10:3, the death of Aaron's sons was caused by the revelation of God's glory.[124] Being above the atonement slate, Jenson contends, 'is the

[122] כי בענן אראה על־הכפרת; ἐν γὰρ νεφέλῃ ὀφθήσομαι ἐπὶ τοῦ ἱλαστηρίου. The 'atonement slate' is often rendered ἱλαστήριον and כפרת, respectively. Haran claims that the veil 'conceals' the atonement slate from view and 'makes around it, as well as around the ark, a mysterious hiding place'('Priestly Image', p. 219).

[123] While a worshipper may 'come' to the temple and worship God, especially through sacrifice but also through prayer (H. D. Preuss, 'בוא', *TDOT* II, p. 22.), one may not do so at any time. Prior to entering God's presence, 'righteousness' (צדקה; Preuss, *TDOT* II, p. 23) must be present as well as purification and status as high priest. בוא is here used as a 'technical term of cultic language' for approaching Yahweh (Preuss, *TDOT* II, p. 23), and especially (for קרב) Milgrom, *Levitical Terminology*, pp. 16–22. From Lev. 21:23 no descendent of Aaron who has a defect may 'go near the curtain' (אל־הפרכת לא יבא) for fear of desecrating the sanctuary (*autem* is added by Sahidic Coptic MSS 566 [J. P. Morgan Library, New York] and the Louvain edition L. T. Lefort, *Les Manuscrits Coptes de l'Université de Louvain* [Louvain: Bibliothèque de l'Université, 1940]). That Yahweh was concerned with the sanctity of his sacred 'area' is perhaps seen in the plural מקדשי (cf. Jer. 51:51; Ps. 68:36; Levine, *Leviticus*, p. 146). Thus, prior to entering into the holy of holies, צדקה righteousness must be accomplished. While it could be argued that such an analysis obscures the distinction between the priestly and the lay worshipper, the notion of concentric circles of sanctity radiating from the centre of the tabernacle structure seems to lend itself to the conclusion that regulations for 'coming' were similar for these two groups, though clearly at a lesser degree for the laity.

[124] The precise nature of their violation in Lev. 10, to which Lev. 16 alludes, is disputed. For a survey of the various opinions regarding their possible offences, see Hartley, *Leviticus*, pp. 132–33; R. Gradwohl, 'Das "fremde Feuer" von Nadab und Abihu', *ZAW* 75 (1963), 288–96; J. Laughlin, '"The Strange Fire" of Nadab and Abihu', *JBL* 95 (1976), 559–65; P. Segal, 'The Divine Verdict of Leviticus X 3', *VT* 39 (1989), 91–95; R. Zuurmond, 'Der Tod von Nadab und Abihu', *T&K* 24 (1984), 23–27. Hartley (*Leviticus*, p. 131) argues that they were introducing some sort of (Egyptian?) pagan rite into the tabernacle worship. Wevers (p. 241) comments that such cloud theophanies were normally not lethal, though the account of the death of Aaron's sons (Nadab and Abihu; Lev. 10) placed at the beginning of this chapter serves 'to sternly warn the high priest to conduct himself properly when he enters the Holy of Holies on the Day of Atonement so that he does not lose his life as they did (cf. 22:2)' (Hartley, *Leviticus*, p. 234). A similar instance is found in 2 Sam. 6:6–7, where Uzzah was struck dead by God for his 'irreverence' in touching the ark when it nearly fell. For a brief survey, see A. A. Anderson, *2 Samuel* (WBC 11; Dallas, Tex.: Word, 1989), pp. 103–4. Anderson holds that Uzzah's sin was not allowing YHWH to determine his own resting place and that the man's actions frustrated the plans of God. Cf. 1 Chron. 15:13. The punishment of death seems harsh in light of the apparently valiant

most appropriate place for God to reveal himself, since it is at the heart of the tabernacle'.[125] Thus, it seems, restriction of physical accessibility to God was based on a restriction of visual accessibility to his glory.

This visual restriction is further depicted in the veil's description as the 'shielding veil' (פרכת המסך),[126] which is clearly indicative of the 'shielding' function it serves.[127] We see it 'shielding' the ark and the atonement slate (Exod. 35:12a; cf. 39:20b [MT 34b]), and Israel was instructed to use the 'shielding veil' (פרכת המסך) 'and shield upon the ark of the testimony' (ויסך על ארון העדות; Exod. 40:21).[128] In Exod. 40:3, we read that Moses was to 'shield the ark with the curtain' (וסכת על־הארן את־הפרכת; cf. Exod. 35:12).[129] Similarly, in Num. 4:5, we find that Aaron and his

deed on the part of Uzzah, and scholars have offered various explanations. Yet it seems that at least one factor for his death must involve his status as a non-priest touching the sacred ark, the interpretation offered by Josephus (*Ant.* 7.4.2 §81). The act of Uzzah is called 'irreverence' (שלה), a rare word in Hebrew, the Aramaic (שלי) sense of which is to 'act in error' or 'neglect'. S. R. Driver, *Notes on the Hebrew Text and the Topography of the Books of Samuel: With an Introduction on Hebrew Palaeography and the Ancient Versions* (2d edn; Oxford: Clarendon Press, 1913), p. 267. Some scholars have associated the term with the Babylonian *šullū* 'treat disdainfully' (Anderson, *2 Samuel*, p. 103).

125 Jenson, p. 114.

126 Exod. 35:12a; 39:20b [MT 34b]; 40:21 (τὸ κατακάλυμμα τοῦ καταπετάσματος); Num. 4:5.

127 So also B. Jacob, *The Second Book of the Bible: Exodus* (trans. W. Jacob; Hoboken, N. J.: Ktab, 1992), p. 798.

128 The 'protecting' or 'concealing' function of the פרכת veil is first seen in the Greek of Exod. 26:34, a reading not present in the Masoretic Hebrew tradition. Here the Greek translator apparently saw פרכת ('veil') rather than the correct reading, כפרת ('mercy seat') and, looking to Num. 4:5, noted one properly uses a veil to 'cover' (κατακαλύπτομαι) the ark of the covenant. Cf. Gurtner, '"Atonement Slate" or the "Veil"?' Notes on a Textual Variant in Exodus XXVI 34', *VT* 54 (2004), 396–98.

129 For a discussion of the textual discrepancies involved with this text, cf. Friedman, *ABD* VI, p. 295; V. A. Hurowitz, 'The Form and Fate of the Tabernacle: Reflections on a Recent Proposal', *JQR* 86 (1995), 127–51; Hurowitz, 'The Priestly Account of Building the Tabernacle', *JAOS* 105 (1985), 21–30. The 'protecting' or 'concealing' function of the פרכת veil is first seen in the Greek of Exod. 26:34, a reading not present in the Masoretic Hebrew tradition. Here the Greek translator apparently had a *Vorlage* פרכת ('veil') rather than the correct reading, כפרת ('mercy seat'), and, looking to Num. 4:5, noted that one properly uses a veil to 'cover' (κατακαλύπτομαι) the ark of the covenant (see Gurtner, '"Atonement Slate" or "Veil"?' pp. 396–98). Though again seen in Exod. 35:12, the concept of the veil's protection or concealment is more explicitly articulated in Exod. 40:3, where we read that Moses was to 'shield the Ark with the curtain' (וסכת על־הארן את־הפרכת). Here, however, the Samaritan Pentateuch has a strong tradition of reading הכפרת for the MT's הפרכת (cf. Jenson, p. 95 and n. 2; Cassuto, p. 479). The Peshitta reads ܦܪܣܐ, the Vulage *Velum*. The Samaritan Pentateuch reading הכפרת is witnessed in A (c. 1345); C (c. 1480/1); D (c. 1181); E (c. 1484); F (c. 7th century); H (c. 1452); I (c. 1476/7); P (c. 1441/2); Q (c. 1394/5); Y3 (c. 1340) 𝔄 (c. early/mid 1500s); 𝔅 (c. 1321/22); 𝔇 (c. 1532); ℭ (1413); 𝔊 (1431/32); 𝔍. (1867). For Samaritan Pentateuch texts, these are considered quite old. Cf. E. Würthwein, *The Text of the Old Testament* (2d edn; trans. E. F. Rhodes; Grand Rapids, Mich.: Eerdmans, 1994), p. 47. Dates are from A. F. von Gall, ed., *Der Hebräische Pentateuch der Samaritaner*

sons were to take down the 'shielding veil' (פרכת המסך) and cover (כסה, κατακαλύπτομαι) the ark with it when in transport.[130] Here the ark is concealed from sight, as it is the most sacred object of the tabernacle (Exod. 25:10–22), where the Lord (יהוה) spoke to Moses.[131]

Milgrom notes that the priests, like all others, were forbidden to view the ark. In his view, 'the curtain would function like the cloud of incense that Aaron raised in the shrine on the Day of Atonement (Lev. 16:2, 13); even for the High Priest, the sight of the exposed ark was considered to be fatal'.[132] We find a similar injunction in Num. 4:20, where the Lord commands the Kohathites not to look at the 'holy things', including those in the holy place, or they will die (cf. 1 Sam. 6:19–20). The severity of the violation is perhaps illustrated by the punishment's being enforced against even the briefest offence, commonly translated 'for a moment'.[133] Linnemann suggests that the concern seems to be what she calls 'der Anblick der unverhüllten Majestät Gottes'. Lev. 16:13 warns that the smoke was present in the holy of holies 'lest he [the high priest] die' (ולא ימות).

As we have seen before, the concept of death in the presence of Yahweh is not new here. Elsewhere we come upon the 'hidden face of God',

(Gießen: Töpelmann, 1914), I, pp. I–LXX. Likewise the Old Latin tradition preserves *super eam propitiatorium*, though no trace of that reading is found in extant Greek manuscripts upon which the Old Latin was dependent. The discrepancy seems to be in transmission of the Exodus text rather than a characteristic modification for theological purposes by the Samaritan scribe, for the parallel text in Num. 4:5 reads פרכת with no sign of a כפרת reading. Friedman (*ABD* VI, p. 295) argues that the פרכת must be a 'pavilion' because it is used to cover the ark and *not* a veil. This seems to confuse the evidence that the hanging veil in a portable structure could not be taken down and used to cover the ark while in transport. For a strong rebuttal of Friedman, see Hurowitz, 'Form and Fate', pp. 127–51. Cf. also Hurowitz, 'Priestly Account', pp. 21–30. Similarly in Num. 4:5 we find that Aaron and his sons are to 'take down' the פרכת המסך and cover the ark with it (כסה, κατακαλύπτομαι) when in transport (cf. Levine, *Numbers* I, p. 166). Although the Kohathites were responsible for carrying it along with other cultic articles, their lack of sacred status (Num. 3:9) would cause their viewing of the sacred articles to bring death (Num. 4:15–20; Milgrom, *Numbers*, p. 25).

[130] Cf. Levine, *Numbers*, p. 166.

[131] Westerholm, pp. 699–700; cf. W. Lotz, M. G. Kyle and C. E. Armerding, 'Ark of the Covenant', *ISBE* I, pp. 291–94. Concealment of the ark is made more explicit in rabbinic texts, which say that the ark was to 'lay hidden' (*m. Shek.* 6:1, 2), a requirement for which the veil was essential (*Num. Rab.* 4:13 [on Num. 4:5]).

[132] Milgrom, *Numbers*, pp. 25–26. Levine, *Leviticus*, pp. 100–101. Hartley (*Leviticus*, p. 239) comments that Keil and Delitzch (p. 339) see the smoke as representing the continuous prayers of the people, though he rightly concludes that the phrase 'lest he die' requires a reading that prefers the protection of the high priest. So also Jenson, pp. 107–8.

[133] Levine (*Numbers* I, p. 170) comments that the duration of looking on the atonement slate 'for a split second' 'literally connotes the time it takes to swallow one's spittle (Job 7:19)'.

particularly in Exod. 33:19–23 (also פני יהוה 'face of the Lord').[134] In Exod. 33:20, the Lord passes by Abraham, but declares that he may not see his face כי לא־יראני האדם וחי ('because man may not see my face and [yet] live'). They met 'face to face', but Moses was not to see God's face properly; it was covered with smoke. Linnemann argues that here the smoke functions just as the veil, preventing the priest from viewing the lethal glory of the Lord.[135] This is an essential observation, for according to Jenson, the physical restrictions within his scheme of graded holiness point to the reality that 'the primary emphasis is on the visible and realized holiness of the sanctuary, mediating his nearness and accessibility ("before Yahweh")'.[136] Thus it seems that the veil served as a physical and visual barrier, ostensibly protecting the priest from the lethal presence of the enthroned Lord and reinforcing the distinction (בדל) between God and humankind. The veil served to provide cultic separation, which it executed by restricting physical and visual accessibility to God. The execution of this function is graphically depicted by the cherubim woven into the veil, which depict *angelic guardianship of the presence of God.*

As we have seen, the veil is also called פרכת המסך ('shielding veil', Exod. 35:12a; 39:20b [MT 34b]; 40:21 [τὸ κατακάλυμμα τοῦ καταπετάσματος]; Num. 4:5), which is probably indicative of the 'shielding' function of the veil.[137] The significance of this function may be indicated by the unique presence of cherubim on it. Interestingly, the description of the veil 'shielding' (סכך) the ark is a function shared only by the wings of the cherubim, which are placed above the atonement slate (כפרת, ἱλαστήριον) in the tabernacle (Exod. 37:9), as well as in the temple (1 Kgs 8:7; 1 Chron. 28:18).[138]

M. Haran argues that the cherubim 'cover' (סככים) something 'with their wings' in a variety of places, notably the 'atonement slate' (in the

[134] Cf. H. Simian-Yofre, 'פָּנִים', *TWOT* XI, pp. 595–96; S. E. Balentine, *The Hidden God: The Hiding of the Face of God in the Old Testament* (Oxford: Oxford University Press, 1983), pp. 164–76.

[135] Linnemann, p. 161. Similarly J. H. Hertz, *Leviticus* (PH; London: Oxford University, 1932), p. 156; Hartley, *DOTP*, p. 57; so also G. J. Wenham, *The Book of Leviticus* (NICOT; Grand Rapids, Mich.: Eerdmans, 1979) p. 231, who adds that Keil argues that the incense was to prevent *God* from seeing the *priest*. Milgrom (*Leviticus 1–16*, pp. 1024–31) suggests that since this smoke was insufficient to obscure completely the priest's view of YHWH, rabbinic tradition indicates that the priest added a smoke-producing agent to the incense to enhance the cloud.

[136] Jenson, p. 43. This is because 'the priestly perception of holiness is that it may be transmitted by sight as well as touch' (p. 107).

[137] So also Jacob, p. 798.

[138] For other uses of סכך, cf. Job 1:10; 40:22; Pss 139:13; 140:7–8; Lam. 3:44; Ezek. 28:14, 16 (in reference to 'guardian cherubim').

tabernacle), the ark and its poles (in the temple; 1 Kgs 8:7), and the Garden of Eden (Ezek. 27:13–16).[139] The presence of these cherubim on the veil, it seems, is no small matter. Steinmann suggests that the cherubim were woven into the curtains of the outer walls of the tabernacle, 'making cherubim visible to the priests no matter where in the tabernacle they would be'.[140] It points to the divine presence enthroned within the most holy place. It is while enthroned above the cherubim here that God meets with the high priest. This meeting, occurring in the divine presence, is accomplished by means of atonement. Previously, I said that where there are cherubim there is God. Furthermore, where there is God among people, there must also have been atonement. For without atonement, there is a barrier, or veil, between God and his chosen people. Cassuto argues that the cherubim 'recall the garden of Eden, the place where Man dwelt when he was free from sin, and they link thereby the *kappōreth* to the idea of the atonement of sin, the main intent of the priest's service before the *kappōreth* on the Day of Atonement'.[141] Thus it seems possible that the *velum scissum* in Matthew's gospel could depict the removal of the angelic guardianship against entering into the (edenic) presence of God.

## Function of the Veil: Conclusion

We have seen that with respect to functionality, all καταπέτασμα curtains, except those that translate פרכת, can be largely removed from the discussion as none of them is afforded particular cultic functions in the Old Testament. With respect to this veil, its implicit function as seen by particular features converges with the explicit function articulated in the text of the Old Testament itself. The function of the veil was to effect *separation (בדל) between the most holy and the less holy*. This is a structural feature based on a theological necessity. Moreover, this separation was executed by means of the veil's *prohibiting physical and visual accessibility to the God* enthroned in the holy of holies. Finally, this prohibition

139 Haran, 'Ark and the Cherubim', p. 36. He insists, however, that the סכך in P and Kings denotes only physical posture and not 'covering' in a more symbolic sense. He argues this, though, because seemingly, in his opinion, the role of the veil's 'screening' (Exod. 40:3, 21) forbids understanding 'screening' in a symbolic or theological sense and must merely refer to a literal, physical posture of both the veil and the cherubim wings (Haran, 'Ark and the Cherubim', p. 36). However, this argument seems less convincing in light of the largely theological *and* symbolic function of בדל attributed to the veil discussed earlier. That is, there seems no reason to assert the סכך posture of the veil serves as both a description of its physical position and a statement of its theological function, as it seems to have in Gen. 3:24.

140 Steinmann, *DOTP*, p. 113.

141 Cassuto, p. 335.

is *depicted graphically by the presence of cherubim* woven into the veil, which resonates with the guardian function they serve in Gen. 3:24, where inaccessibility to the presence of God is first seen in biblical tradition. While I will consider the implications of the cessation of this function within the particular Matthean context (Chapter 6), I can note here that the cessation of functions depicted by the *velum scissum* indicates, in some way, the cessation of the cultic necessity of distinction between most holy and less holy, which therefore removes the need for such distinction to be executed by a prohibition of physical and visual accessibility to God, and removes the cherubim that graphically depict this distinction.

# 4

## THE VEIL IN SECOND TEMPLE AND RABBINIC JUDAISM

### Introduction

Traditions in Second Temple and rabbinic literature pertaining to either of the temple curtains are not as prevalent as one might expect, given the centrality of the temple to Jewish identity.[1] Yet this has not hindered New Testament scholars from looking largely to these sources for their understanding of the rending of the veil in the synoptic passion accounts.[2] To complicate matters, the few relatively early sources that are available and that contain data pertaining to the veil provide confusing and, at times, contradictory historical accounts of the curtains in the Herodian temple.[3] Because many New Testament scholars see the *velum scissum* as in some sense symbolic, it is important to see whether the veil developed any symbolic qualities during this time. It is also important to attempt to discern what it symbolised and whether those symbols were fixed to any degree by the time of the writing of Matthew's veil account in the latter half of the first century, particularly in sources that may have been accessible to Matthew. To address these, and questions of identity and function, I will here provide a comprehensive treatment of Second Temple and Rabbinic Jewish texts as they pertain to the veils and curtains of the 'heavenly sanctuary' and each of Jerusalem's temples. I will approach

[1] Perhaps the Qumran sectarians' view that the present temple in Jerusalem was defiled may account for both their scant attention to the temple and their replacement of it with an idealised, 'heavenly' sanctuary. See C. A. Newsom, *EDSS* II, p. 889. J. D. G. Dunn, *Jews and Christians: The Partings of the Ways AD 70 to 135* (Tübingen: J. C. B. Mohr, 1992), recognises the temple as one of the 'four pillars of Second Temple Judaism', while E. P. Sanders, *Judaism: Practice and Belief 63 BCE – 66 CE* (London: SCM Press, 1992), p. 10, sees it as an essential element of 'common Judaism'. R. J. Bauckham, 'The Parting of the Ways', *ST* 47 (1993), 141, claims that the temple was 'central' to 'Jewish self-identity'.

[2] See D. M. Gurtner, 'The Veil of the Temple in History and Legend', *JETS* 49 (2006), 97–114.

[3] Although not referring to the Herodian temple, 1 Kgs 6:31–34 speaks of doors, while 2 Chron. 3:14 speaks of a veil leading into the holy of holies. R. E. Brown, *The Death of the Messiah: A Commentary on the Passion Narratives in the Four Gospels* (2 vols.; New York, N.Y.: Doubleday, 1994), II, p. 1110.

these issues by considering the veil in both the physical structure of the historical (Herodian) temple in Jerusalem and any ideological, theological or symbolic developments in these various Jewish traditions.

## 1 History and Structure of the Jerusalem Temple

The Jerusalem temple had a long and tumultuous history. Though it was the product of David's desire to house the Ark of the Covenant, the temple was built by Solomon.[4] When Jerusalem fell to the Babylonians in 587 B.C.E., the temple was destroyed but soon rebuilt by those returning from exile beginning in 538 B.C.E. Named after the governor of the period, this structure is known as the temple of Zerubbabel and was completed in 515 B.C.E. Lacking the Solomonic temple's rich adornment (cf. Hag. 2:1–9), Zerubbabel's temple was apparently damaged several times over the years and was ultimately rebuilt by Herod the Great.[5] It is this phase of the temple's structural and ideological history that provides the backdrop for the temple portrayed in Matthew's gospel.

Herod's work on the temple began in either the eighteenth (19/20 B.C.E.; Josephus, *Ant.* 15.11.1 §380) or the fifteenth (23/22 B.C.E.; *J. W.* 1.22.1 §401)[6] year of his reign and was completed, with the exception of detailed additions and adornments, within 10 years.[7] Yet such additions, it seems, were continually added to the structure right up to the outbreak of the Jewish revolt in 66 C.E. As particularly the interior structure of Herod's temple was largely patterned after Solomon's, Herod's temple also had curtains. Yet, as in the LXX, Second Temple texts referring to the Herodian temple are by no means uniform in identifying either how many curtains there were, or which ones were designated καταπέτασμα. Therefore I will examine mostly the inner curtain(s) (these sources provide relatively little information on any other curtain in the temple) from all non-canonical texts up through the first century C.E. and beyond, where these texts are helpful.[8]

[4] 1 Kgs 5:17–19; 8:15–21; 1 Chron. 22:8–10; see the description of Solomon's temple in 1 Kgs 6:1–7:51; 2 Chron. 3:1–4:22.

[5] For a concise survey, see C. Meyers, 'Temple, Jerusalem', *ABD* VI, pp. 362–64.

[6] Sanders, p. 57.

[7] M. O. Wise, 'Temple', *DJG*, p. 812. The entire project took much longer, 46 years so far, according to John 2:20, which well surpassed the lifetime of Herod. For a helpful overview of the layout of the temple, see M. Hengel, 'The Geography of Palestine in Acts', in *The Book of Acts in Its First Century Setting*, vol. 4, *Palestinian Setting* (ed. R. Bauckham; Grand Rapids, Mich.: Eerdmans, 1995), pp. 35–45.

[8] Although we will focus on Matthew's term, καταπέτασμα, we will also draw attention to the fact that the structure typically associated in ancient sources with the exclusion of

The inner temple (ναός) was surrounded by a massive court of the Gentiles; together these comprise the entire complex (ἱερόν) of nearly 40 acres.[9] Within the temple (ναός), or 'sanctuary', hung a series of curtains, though scholars have debated how many there were and what their configuration was vis-à-vis a set of doors.[10] Elsewhere I indicate why I favour Josephus' account in *J.W.* 5, which concludes that both the holy place and the holy of holies were screened by a single veil each (καταπέτασμα; *J.W.* 5.5.4 §212; 5.5.5 §219).[11] While it is difficult to be fully confident about this conclusion, it seems to make the most sense of the evidence.

## 2 Καταπέτασμα within the Non-canonical LXX

In addition to LXX references to the veil in canonical texts discussed in Chapter 3, there are three other uses of καταπέτασμα in other LXX documents: one in Sirach and two in 1 Maccabees. The **Sirach** text (50:5) refers to the priest Simeon's coming out of the temple after offering a sacrifice. The Hebrew reads that he came out מבית הפרכה, which could be understood as 'from behind the veil' or, as the Greek takes it, 'from the house of the veil' (ἐν ἐξόδῳ οἴκου καταπετάσματος). The Syriac seems to affirm the former understanding of the Hebrew when it has ܡܢ ܬܚܝܬ ܦܪܣܐ ('from underneath the veil'). Scholars have debated which sacrifice Simeon had offered in this text, based on the ambiguity of this phrase.[12]

Gentiles, which many New Testament scholars presume to be the *outer* veil (called the κάλυμμα by Philo), is in fact the dividing wall (τὸ μεσότοιχον), which in Pauline tradition is a barrier between Jews and Gentiles broken down by Christ's death (Eph. 2:14) and which is nowhere called καταπέτασμα. Moreover, it cannot be the outer veil (in front of the holy place). It enclosed the court of the Israelites and the court of the priests. Gentiles could not enter these.

[9] Such a strict distinction between ναός and ἱερόν cannot always be maintained. See O. Michel, 'Ναός', *TDNT* IV, pp. 884–85, n. 19. Particular temple language will be explored in Chapter 5.

[10] For a description of how the veils were hung, cf. *b. Sukkah* 7b.

[11] Gurtner, 'The Veil of the Temple in History and Legend', *JETS* 49 (2006), 97–114.

[12] See P. W. Skehan and A. A. Di Lella, *The Wisdom of Ben Sira* (ABC 39; New York, N.Y.: Doubleday, 1987), p. 550; S. Légasse, 'Les voiles du temple de Jérusalem: Essai de parcours historique', *RevB* 87 (1980), 560–89; Ó Fearghail, 'Sir 50,5–21: Yom Kippur or the Daily Whole-Offering', *Bib.* 59 (1978), 301–13; B. G. Wright, *No Small Difference: Sirach's Relationship to its Parent Text* (SCS 26; Atlanta, Ga.: Scholars Press, 1989), p. 177; O. F. Fritzsche, *Die Weisheit Jesus-Sirach's* (Wäysenhauses: Leipzig, 1859), p. 297; V. Ryssel, 'Die Sprüche Jesus' des Sohnes Sirachs', in *Apokryphen, Die Apokryphen und Pseudepigraphen des Alten Testaments* (ed. E. Kautzsch; Tübingen: Mohr Siebeck, 1900) I, p. 468; R. Smend, *Die Weisheit des Jesus Sirach: Erklärt* (Berlin: Reimer, 1906), p. 477; W. O. E. Oesterley, *The Wisdom of Jesus the Son of Sirach or Ecclesiasticus* (London: SPCK, 1916), p. 338; B. G. H. Box and W. O. E. Oesterley, 'Sirach', in *Apocrypha, The Apocrypha and Pseudepigrapha of the Old Testament in English* (2 vols.; ed. R. H. Charles; Oxford: Clarendon Press, 1913), I, p. 293.

Yet I have argued elsewhere that the reference is almost certainly to his emergence from within the inner veil, the holy of holies, and thus it was the Day of Atonement Sacrifice, with the Greek translator simply misunderstanding the sense of his Semitic *Vorlage*.[13] The Greek text, however, is not without its significance for our purposes, for it seems that the Greek translator understood οἴκου καταπετάσματος as a circumlocution for the temple building (ναός). This is a unique understanding, for it may suggest that the temple is to be identified with respect to its veil, providing early (and apparently the first) explicit indication that the veil stood for something beyond itself, in this case the temple.[14]

1 Maccabees contains two mentions to the curtains of the temple. The first (1:22) figures in the list of the objects of worship that Antiochus Epiphanes plundered from the Jerusalem shrine upon his return from Egypt in his attempt at 'erasing the telltale signs of their Jewish heritage'.[15] Here a single veil is mentioned (καταπέτασμα), which Légasse, because of its presence again among cultic objects mentioned in the temple re-dedicated under Judas Maccabeus (4:49–51), identifies with the curtain of the holy of holies,[16] though Faber van der Meulen may be right in being less certain.[17] The second use of καταπέτασμα is found in this restoration context (1 Macc. 4:51), though it speaks of the rehanging of the veil*s* (τὰ καταπετάσματα). That this reference is to more than one veil, and that the context refers to numerous cultic objects with this being the only instance of hanging something, suggests that this use of καταπέτασμα is intended to refer collectively to all the curtains in that temple.[18]

[13] See Gurtner, 'The "House of the Veil" in Sirach 50', *JSP* (2005), 187–200.

[14] If this were the case, it would support the notion that the rending of the veil in Matthew refers to the destruction of the temple, for if by saying 'veil' (καταπέτασμα) one could be expected to have the entire temple in mind, its rending would more strongly suggest temple destruction.

[15] D. A. deSilva, *Introducing the Apocrypha: Message, Context, and Significance* (Grand Rapids, Mich.: Baker, 2002), p. 244.

[16] Légasse, p. 566. On this point he is critical of F.-M. Abel, *Les Livres des Maccabées* (Paris: Librairie Lecoffre, 1949), p. 12, who identifies the 1 Macc. 1:22 veil 'without hesitation' as the exterior curtain (n. 28). See also H. Vincent, 'Jérusalem d'après la letter d'aristée', *RB* 6 (1909), 558.

[17] H. E. Faber van der Meulen, 'One or Two Veils in front of the Holy of Holies', *Theologia Evangelica* 18 (1985), 23. So also J. Goldstein, *I Maccabees* (ABC 41; New York, N.Y.: Doubleday, 1976), pp. 209–10.

[18] Looking to 1 Macc. 1:22 as well as the *Letter of Aristeas* text, C. Clermont-Ganneau, *Le dieu satrape et les Phéniciens dans le Péloponèse* (Paris: Imprimiere nationale, 1878), pp. 56–60, has proposed an interesting thesis. He suggests that the curtain (παραπέτασμα) in the Olympian temple to Zeus (Pausanias, *Descr*. 6.12.4), built in part by Antiochus Epiphanes, was the same as that taken from Jerusalem by Antiochus Epiphanes (c. 215–164 B.C.E.; *J.W.* 6.6.1 §317; *Ant*. 12.5.2 §245; 2 Macc. 6:2). Many have followed this conjecture (see Pelletier, 'Le "Voile" du Temple de Jérusalem est-il devenu la "Portière" du Temple d'Olympie', *Syria* 32 [1955], 291–92). Yet Légasse (pp. 586–87) says that Josephus

The Sirach and 1 Maccabees sources provide no decisive data on the use of καταπέτασμα. Yet they do provide some information on the value of the veil to the reestablishment of the Jerusalem temple and on a potential use of it as a circumlocution for the temple itself.

## 3 Καταπέτασμα outside the LXX

Apart from the LXX and prior to the end of the first century C.E., καταπέτασμα occurs only twenty-nine times.[19] Six are found in the New Testament (Heb. 6:19, 9:3, 10:20; Luke 23:45; Mark 15:38; Matt. 27:51), one in *Letter of Aristeas* (86), and one in *Joseph and Aseneth* (10:2). The remaining twenty-one occurrences are found in Josephus (10 times) and Philo (11 times) respectively. Veil traditions, without the use of καταπέτασμα, are also found in the *Lives of the Prophets* and rabbinic literature, and will be discussed in another section. The use of καταπέτασμα is not only inconsistent but frequently vague. In Josephus's ten uses, three could refer to either the outer or the inner veil,[20] perhaps four refer to the inner,[21] and one clearly refers to the outer.[22] While again we find the use of a locative genitive, suggesting Matthew may have the inner veil in view, two references are insufficient to determine this with any degree of certainty.[23]

*J.W.* 6.6.1 §317 and 5.5.5 §219 are unreliable in recording the veil's fate. Such would refer to the curtain in Zerubbabel's, rather than Herod's, temple. Clermont-Ganneau (pp. 56–60) argues that Pausanias could have shortened his description of the curtain (παραπέτασμα) and its function had he simply called it a καταπέτασμα. Yet Pelletier (pp. 292–94) has shown that the identity of Antiochus, III (the Great, d. 187 B.C.E.) or IV (Epiphanes), is by no means certain among scholars of Pausanias, Pelletier himself arguing for the former, though the latter had a reputation for pillaging temples (Polybius, *Fr.* 31.4.10). See M. Hadas, *Aristeas to Philorates (Letter of Aristeas)* (DCHCL; New York, N.Y.: Harper & Brothers, 1951), p. 133; Pelletier, pp. 289–91; B. Celada, 'El velo del Templo', *CB* 15 (1958), 109–12; J. C. Dancy, *A Commentary on I Maccabees* (Oxford: Basil Blackwell, 1954), p. 68; Vincent, pp. 556–57; Abel, p. 12; J. C. VanderKam, *An Introduction to Early Judaism* (Grand Rapids, Mich.: Eerdmans, 2001), p. 200; R. Tramontano, *La Lettera di Aristea a Filocrate* (Naples: Uniffico Succursale della civiltà cattolica in Napoli, 1931), chap. 3.2.

19 It seems that for many centuries after the New Testament, the term is used exclusively in reference to the synoptic and Hebrews traditions of the veil.

20 *Ant.* 8.3.3 §75; *J.W.* 6.8.3 §389; 6.8.3 §390.

21 *J.W.* 7.5.7 §162; see 5.5.5 §219; 5.5.7 §232 (τὰ τοῦ ναοῦ καταπετάσματα; perhaps referring to two inner veils or inner *and* outer); *Ant.* 8.3.7 §90 (καταπέτασμα τοῦ ἀδύτου).

22 *J.W.* 5.5.4 §212.

23 M. Barker, 'Beyond the Veil of the Temple: The High Priestly Origins of the Apocalypse', *SJT* 51 (1998), 1, insists that 'Josephus, who was himself a priest (*Life* 1), says that the tabernacle was a microcosm of the creation (*Ant.* 3.7.7 §181). Thus the veil which screened the holy of holies was also the boundary between earth and heaven'. Though this observation may be quite valid, it is difficult to substantiate on the evidence of her single reference.

In Philo we find eleven uses of καταπέτασμα. Scholars have frequently noted that Philo explicitly says that there were two curtains in the temple (ὑφάσμασι), with the inner one called 'the veil' (καταπέτασμα) and the outer one called 'the covering' (κάλυμμα; *Moses* 2.87, 101).[24] While he does use the term for the inner veil (*Names* 192; *Spec. Laws* 1.231a; *Moses* 2.81), Philo uses it elsewhere for what can only be the *outer* veil (*Spec. Laws* 1.171, 1.231b, 1.274, 1.296) and is therefore inconsistent in his own use and contrary to his own assertion in *Moses*.[25] Though he uses καταπέτασμα metaphorically as a 'veil' of unbelief (*Giants* 53), it would be difficult to prove that Philo's Alexandrian tradition was also held by a Palestinian, or perhaps Antiochan, Greek writer such as Matthew. I will revisit another reference in Philo in what follows.

Several references to καταπέτασμα are also found in Josephus. Though he uses καλύμμα only once (*J.W.* 5.12.3 §516, a cover over a dead body), he uses καταπέτασμα 10 times. Naturally, these references are found most abundantly in texts describing the Roman assault on Jerusalem and its temple. He provides a lavish and helpful description of the inner veil as καταπέτασμα (*J.W.* 5.5.4 §212), explicitly describing its presence before the holy of holies (*J.W.* 5.5.5 §219). Elsewhere, however, in language similar to that of Matthew, he refers to veil*s* of the temple (τὰ τοῦ ναοῦ καταπετάσματα; *J.W.* 5.5.7 §232) which, later, he says were delivered into Roman hands (cf. *J.W.* 6.8.3 §389) and taken to Rome as plunder (*J.W.* 7.5.7 §162). Not only were the veil*s* taken as plunder, but Josephus records that the sacred material used to repair the 'veil' was also taken (*J.W.* 6.8.3 §390). Elsewhere he refers to veils over the doors in Solomon's temple (*Ant.* 8.3.3 §75), yet presumes that there is a single veil is before the Ark of the Covenant (*Ant.* 8.3.7 §90; though he uses another word in §91, διπλασίονας). Returning again to the plural, he records how Antiochus plundered the veils (*Ant.* 12.5.4 §250), but they were recovered by the righteous Crassus (*Ant.* 14.7.1 §107). Although it is difficult to say with certainty, and his apparent contradictions are addressed elsewhere,[26] it seems that when he refers to curtains of the temple, he uses the plural of

[24] M. Dods, 'The Epistle to the Hebrews', in *The Expositor's Greek Testament* (ed. W. R. Nicoll; Grand Rapids, Mich.: Eerdmans, 1970), p. 305, argues that this distinction is to be carried over into the New Testament, though B. F. Westcott, *The Epistle to the Hebrews* (London: Macmillan, 1903), p. 163, discounts this argument on the grounds that Philo's is a 'spiritual interpretation'. Indeed Rice is correct in noting that in Heb. 9:3, the presence of the numerical adjective *δευτερον* καταπετασμα (second veil) suggests that the word καταπέτασμα 'was *not* reserved for the inner veil as Philo and Dods suggest'. G. Rice, 'Heb 6:19: An Analysis of Some Assumptions Concerning Katapetasma', *AUSS* 25 (1987), 66. His emphasis.

[25] Cf. Pelletier, p. 300; Légasse, p. 584, n. 133; Faber van der Muelen, p. 23.

[26] Gurtner, 'History and Legend'.

καταπέτασμα, yet when referring to the inner veil, he uses the singular. The fact that he does not clearly speak of the *outer* curtain makes this difficult. Another important reference to the veil in Josephus will be addressed later.

Brief mention of a καταπέτασμα is found in *Joseph and Aseneth* 10:2.[27] The theme of chapters 1–21 largely deals with the need to convert to Judaism,[28] which has been argued to be the theme of the whole work.[29] The book in general is an expansion of the account in Gen. 41:45, where Pharaoh gave Joseph Aseneth, the daughter of Potiphera, priest of On, as his wife. G. Bohak sees its symbolism as depicting Onias' understanding of Isa. 19:18 as a divine directive to establish the temple cult in Heliopolis, Egypt. That is, the work is largely an allegory 'relating to the Jewish military colony and temple founded by the exiled high priest Onias IV in the Heliopolitan nome of Egypt'.[30] Specifically, Bohak suggests that the details in the description of Philometor's house are comparable to those of the temple in Ezek. 37. Its tower was like a temple and is depicted with '"graded holiness" whereby the inner sanctuary of Aseneth's room is depicted as a holy of holies'.[31] The significant text for our purposes relates to Aseneth's conversion to Judaism. Leaving the companionship of the seven virgins (10:1), she stole away in secret 'and hurried and took down from the window the skin (which hung there for a) curtain (τῆν δέρριν τοῦ καταπετάσματος), and filled it with ashes from the fireplace, and carried it up into the upper floor, and put it on the floor' (10:2).[32] The first section here (10–13) seems to be a place of inner reflection, repentance and preparation, while the following section (14–17) takes a more symbolic tone in announcing her conversion.[33] What is meant by this is seemingly made clear in the following context (10:7–17), where Aseneth removes all her Egyptian attire, puts on black cloths in

27 The discussion of whether a shorter or longer version of the text is preferred has no bearing on this text, as it largely focuses on chapters 14–17. See E. M. Humphrey, *Joseph and Aseneth* (GAP; Sheffield: Academic Press, 2000), pp. 18–28. The earliest extant text of this work, however, is preserved in Syriac. Found in a manuscript dating from the first half of the sixth century, the expression is there rendered ܦܪܣܐ. E. W. Brooks, ed., *Historia Ecclesiastica Zachariae Rhetori Vulgo Adscripta* (CSCO 83; Louvain: Imprimerie Orientaliste L. Durbecq, 1953), p. 30.

28 C. Burchard, 'Joseph and Aseneth', *OTP* II, p. 189.

29 See K. Kohler, 'Asenath, Life and Confession or Prayer of', *The Jewish Encyclopedia* (12 vols.; ed. I. Singer *et al.*; New York, N.Y.: Funk & Wagnalls, 1901–6), II, pp. 172–76.

30 H. W. Attridge, Review of G. Bohak, *'Joseph and Aseneth' and the Temple at Heliopolis*, *CBQ* 60 (1998), 556.

31 Humphrey, pp. 34, 101.

32 Translation throughout is that of Burchard, pp. 202–47.

33 Humphrey, p. 105. So also R. S. Kraemer, *When Aseneth Met Joseph: A Late Antique Tale of the Biblical Patriarch and His Egyptian Wife, Reconstructed* (Oxford: Oxford University Press, 1998), p. 33.

mourning and grinds her Egyptian idols. The process of her conversion has clearly begun.

Although Bohak's suggestion for an Egyptian provenance is debatable, it has no bearing on our understanding of καταπέτασμα here, for the position that *Joseph and Aseneth* depicts temple symbolism and conversion to Judaism is doubtless true. Regardless of which 'veil' of the temple may be alluded to here, Bohak's further recognition of temple imagery finds particular support from the presence of the word καταπέτασμα. He comments,

> The Greek word used here for 'curtain', καταπέτασμα, is such a rare word that we could base our entire argument on it alone. It is a word that appears almost exclusively in Jewish and Christian texts, and refers to the curtains which hung first in the Tabernacle, and then in the Jerusalem temple. To a Jewish author, and to a Jewish audience, this word would have had an immediate cultic connotation. If Aseneth's tower is described as having a καταπέτασμα, it must have been thought of, in some ways at least, as a temple.[34]

Translation of this text is debatable. While it is possible to translate the τοῦ καταπετάσματος epexegetically, as earlier, it can also be translated 'skin of the curtain'.[35] The former would seem to make more sense of her subsequent conversion. For if we are to accept Bohak's allegorical interpretation, it seems that the pulling down (καθεῖλεν) of the veil (which served as a curtain) is closely related to her conversion to Judaism, a concept seemingly related to the concept of 'unveiling' the previously hidden God articulated more carefully in rabbinic texts.[36] But it is less

[34] G. Bohak, *'Joseph and Aseneth' and the Jewish Temple in Heliopolis* (EJL 10; Atlanta, Ga.: Scholars Press, 1996), pp. 70–71. This point is missed by Humphrey. Asking why the term καταπέτασμα occurs here, rather than *outside* Aseneth's chambers, Humphrey may be overlooking an important LXX allusion – that is, that καταπέτασμα is the preferred term for the inner, פרכת, veil of the tabernacle/temple. Humphrey, p. 93; cf. Kraemer, p. 119. Bohak also notes, 'As far as I know, the tearing down of Aseneth's καταπέτασμα has not been noted by New Testament scholars, in spite of its possible significance for the study of Mark 15:38 par' (p. 70, n. 18).

[35] Although the subject is the 'skin' (δέρριν) 'of the veil' (του καταπετάσματος) and not the 'veil' itself, Bohak may have underestimated his own case by not recognising that the term καταπέτασμα, as noted earlier, occurs *exclusively* in cultic contexts. See Gurtner, 'Καταπέτασμα: Lexicographical and Etymological Considerations to the Biblical "Veil"', *AUSS* 42 (2004), 105–11.

[36] Yet this interpretation could be highly significant, because it shows evidence of the rabbinic interpretation prior to the first century C.E. Kraemer (pp. 225–44) argues for a date perhaps as late as the early third century C.E. The potential contribution of these interpretations will be more fully considered later.

than clear that this is the intent of the text, for what is revealed is not indicated. Perhaps it is likely that the 'skin of the curtain' reading is rather in view, for it would associate her conversion with a stated sacred object, the veil. It could be derived from a text such as Num. 4:5, which calls the inner veil a פרכת המסך (cf. LXX Exod. 40:5 κάλυμμα καταπετάσματος) or 'screened *paroket*'.[37] If we are to see the 'skin' perhaps as a covering for the veil, then perhaps the allegorical meaning is that previously there was a visual obstacle, obscuring view of the veil itself, perhaps as a means of revelation leading to conversion, as with the Gentile centurion (Matt. 27:54). This concept of an obscured view is a common biblical metaphor for unbelief in the Old Testament (i.e., spiritual 'blindness'; cf. Deut. 28:29; Isa. 42:19, 43:8, 44:9, 56:10, 59:10; Lam. 4:14; Zeph. 1:17) and borrowed in the New Testament (Matt. 15:14; 23:16–17, 19, 24, 26; John 9:39, 41; Rom. 2:19; 2 Pet. 1:9). Yet with the veil itself having a veil, the καταπέτασμα seems to be taking on a rather different function. That is, rather than the veil concealing what is then revealed, the veil itself is the object that is revealed, having previously been shielded and protected. Perhaps it should not come as a surprise that something that initially had a function of protecting something else begins to be revered in its own right. That is, it is not here properly a masking of God, but is a symbol in its own right apparently beyond its immediate function in the temple, and may serve as a step for the veil's standing for something else. Despite this symbolic value, it is important to note that the reference to the veil here does not seem to be the focus of attention for her conversion but rather a step towards it. The author seems more concerned that the skin of the veil was removed and used to collect hot ashes to symbolise her repentance. While this can be held only tentatively in the present text, we will see that the symbolic value of the veil seems to evolve into a symbol not so much for faith *per se*, but for the heavenly firmament (Gen. 1:6). There is, then, a precedent for a development of an ideology of the veil beyond and, perhaps independently of, its original intent.

A less helpful occurrence of καταπέτασμα is found in the *Letter of Aristeas*.[38] In his alleged account of being sent to Jerusalem by the Egyptian king Ptolemy II (285–47 B.C.E.), Aristeas recounts his being chosen as an ambassador in his letter to Philocrates. Upon arriving in Jerusalem, Aristeas reports a description of the topography of the environs of the city

[37] B. A. Levine, *Numbers* (2 vols.; ABC 4A–B; New York, N.Y.: Doubleday, 1993, 2000), I, p. 443.

[38] For a history of the text and critical editions, see H. St J. Thackeray, 'The Letter of Aristeas', in *An Introduction to the Old Testament in Greek* (ed. H. B. Swete; Cambridge: Cambridge University Press, 1900), pp. 501–18.

and especially the temple and its precincts. While this letter is notoriously difficult,[39] and its date and historicity are considered highly suspect,[40] the author records his experience of the temple's curtains:

> (*86) The configuration of the veil (καταπέτασμα) was in respects very similar to the door furnishing, and most of all in view of the continuous movement caused to the material by the undercurrent of the air.[41] It was continuous because the undercurrent started from the bottom and the billowing extended to the rippling at the top – the phenomenon making a pleasant and unforgettable spectacle.[42]

Vincent has conjectured that the details of the veil may be provided to give the *impression* of eyewitness accounts to further validate the overall purpose of the letter.[43] But which curtain is in view is not clear.[44] If the alleged Aristeas (the letter, of course, is pseudonymous) were a priest, he could be providing eyewitness accounts[45] of either the inner or outer veil, as both would be accessible to him. If he were not a priest, however, only the outer veil would be visible to him and we are left to presume that the use of καταπέτασμα in this text refers to the outer curtain. Since it seems that Aristeas was not a priest, the reader is left to presume that the use of καταπέτασμα in this letter refers to the outer veil.[46]

[39] See R. J. H. Shutt, 'Letter of Aristeas: A New Translation and Introduction', *OTP* II, p. 8; A. Pelletier, *Letter d'Aristée à Philocrate* (SC 89; Paris: Les Éditions du Cerf, 1962), p. 8; K. Jobes and M. Silva, *Invitation to the Septuagint* (Grand Rapids, Mich.: Baker, 2000), pp. 33–35.

[40] See Shutt, p. 9; VanderKam, *Introduction to Early Judaism*, pp. 81–84; Pelletier, *Lettre d'Aristée*, pp. 57–58. VanderKam (p. 81) contends that there are 'really no firm grounds for assigning it to a particular period', though he notes the first clear reference to it, in Josephus's *Antiquities* (written in the 90s C.E.).

[41] Cf. Pelletier, 'Le "Voile"', p. 300. [42] Shutt, p. 2:18.

[43] Vincent, pp. 555–75; Cf. also Vincent, pp. 520–32; Hadas, p. 47; S. Jellicoe, *The Septuagint and Modern Study* (Oxford: Clarendon Press), p. 38–41. Vincent builds on the work of Clermont-Ganneau, p. 58; Cf. also R. Tramontano, *La Lettera di Aristea*. The presence of the καταπέτασμα may suggest a date prior to 170 B.C.E. either for the alleged journey or the writing of the letter, as the καταπέτασμα is said to have been taken by Antiochus Epiphanes c. 170 B.C.E. Cf. 1 Macc. 1:21 later. Clermont-Ganneau (p. 58) has argued that the veil described by Pausanias (c. 115–180) in his *Description of Greece* (LCL; 5.12.4) as being presented by Ephipanes to the temple of Zeus at Olympia is the same curtain described by Aristeas.

[44] Faber van der Muelen (p. 22) suggests that the reference here is to the 'curtain in front of the entrance to the temple'. So also C. T. R. Hayward, *The Jewish Temple: A Non-Biblical Sourcebook* (London: Routledge, 1996), p. 31.

[45] This issue will be addressed in our discussion of rabbinic texts later.

[46] See Hayward, *Jewish Temple*, p. 31. E. R. Goodenough, *Jewish Symbols of the Greco-Roman Period* (12 vols.; New York, N.Y.: Pantheon, 1953), II, p. 174, suggests that a late inscription reading καταπέτασμα refers to a curtain before the Torah shrine in a synagogue.

While lexicographically inconclusive, the cited sources serve as a caution as to how we analyse Second Temple and rabbinic texts. That is, I shall henceforth in this chapter broaden our discussion beyond the particular language of καταπέτασμα and פרכת, for to do so in these texts, where lexical distinctiveness fades in comparison with the MT and LXX, may impose artificial lexical restraints on the varied language used to describe these cultic articles.[47] Instead, we must cast our nets more broadly while recognising that these texts are extremely valuable for a physical description of the curtains and veils in the Herodian temple and perhaps the significance of its rending.

## 4 The Veil outside Καταπέτασμα Language[48]

Though the subject is commonly debated,[49] it seems most fitting to respect the individuality of the texts and conclude with an analysis of the divergent portraits these sources paint of the temple veil. I will generally try to observe both the unique elements and commonalities of various Jewish texts as well as consider the broader issue of how various texts of Second Temple and Rabbinic Judaism employed the sacred texts pertaining to the veil for their own ideological usage.[50] Yet favour will be afforded to the individuality of each text, and an analysis will be provided at the end. Maier suggests that in contrast with the Dead Sea Scrolls, Second Temple texts such as the *Letter of Aristeas*, *3 Esdras*, and *Judith* 'contain positive evaluations of the Second Temple' and bear characteristics of 'of pro-Maccabean literature'.[51] Yet the temple in Qumran texts is not as easily pinpointed in the Dead Sea Scrolls ideology as it is in other Second Temple texts.

[47] For a succinct account of the diversity of veil language, see Fearghail, p. 309. Barker's (p. 1, n. 1) contention that there is a strict lexical distinction between inner and outer veils in the LXX and Philo, which presumably carry over to other Second Temple and New Testament texts, simply overlooks significant evidence as outlined earlier.

[48] I consider references to the *velum scissum* found in the Testaments of the Twelve Patriarchs (discussed later) to post-date the synoptic account, and therefore offer no background information pertinent to our discussion here.

[49] See Bauckham, 'Parting of the Ways', pp. 135–51; Sanders, pp. 45–314.

[50] R. Beaton, *Isaiah's Christ in Matthew's Gospel* (SNTSMS 123; Cambridge: Cambridge University Press, 2002), p. 50, rightly observes that 'the value of these texts for NT studies depends . . . upon their dating, geographical distribution and the degree to which they represent the ideological framework of the general populace'. See E. Slomovic, 'Toward an Understanding of the Exegesis in the Dead Sea Scrolls', *RevQ* 7 (1969), 3; also, D. Patte, *Early Jewish Hermeneutics* (Missoula: SBL, 1975), L. V. Rutgers *et al.*, eds., *The Use of Sacred Books in the Ancient World* (Louvain: Peeters, 1998) and J. H. Charlesworth, 'The Pseudepigrapha as Biblical Exegesis', in *Early Jewish and Christian Exegesis* (ed. C. A. Evans and W. F. Stinespring; Atlanta, Ga.: Scholars Press, 1987), pp. 139–52.

[51] J. Maier, 'Temple', *EDSS* II, p. 924. See discussion of 1 Maccabees below.

Elsewhere I have shown where several references to the veil of the temple occur in documents found at Qumran,[52] and will summarise that material here. For the 'Temple Scroll', we look primarily to 11QTemple[a] (11Q19),[53] where there are only two fragmentary references to the פרכת veil in the heavenly sanctuary.[54] In line 13 it seems to refer to Exod. 26:31[55] and speaks of making a 'gold veil' (פרוכת זהב).[56] It may be that the significance of a *gold* veil may be found in similar descriptions of gold cultic vessels (11Q19 iii 8, 9, 12; xxxi 8–9; xxxii 10; xxxvii 11; xxxix 3; xli 17; xli 16). These seem to be an attempt by the author to represent a temple to be built in Jerusalem in the future. The text also contains a badly damaged fragment at line 14, which reads היה הפרוכ]ת and seems to simply recount the 'skilled workmanship' mentioned in the Exodus text.[57] As was the case in the MT, Qumran documents seem to unanimously know the פרכת as the single 'inner' veil.[58]

In the *Songs of the Sabbath Sacrifice*, a document Newsom summarises as 'largely concerned with invoking and describing the praise of angelic priests in the heavenly temple',[59] we find brief mention of the veil (פרוכת) in the tenth song. Here the reader is led through the heavenly sanctuary where the curtain of the inner chamber of the King is visible and

[52] Gurtner, 'The Biblical Veil in the Dead Sea Scrolls' Qumran Chronicle 14 (2006), 57–79.

[53] For a survey of the potential relationship of other manuscripts (11Q20, 4Q524, 4Q365a, 11Q21) to 11Q19, see F. García Martínez, 'Temple Scroll', *EDSS* II, pp. 927–29.

[54] García Martínez, 'Temple Scroll', *EDSS* II, p. 930, notes that its literary genre, relationship to biblical texts, origins and date have been 'hotly disputed during the last twenty years with no consensus reached to date'. However, no one has proposed a date later than the first century C.E. Most are comfortable with a date of 150 to 60 B.C.E., though various layers of redaction are apparent. M. O. Wise, 'Temple Scroll (11QTemple)', *DNTB*, p. 1185.

[55] D. D. Swanson, *The Temple Scroll and the Bible: The Methodology of 11QT* (Leiden: Brill, 1995), p. 223, notes that its order is that of 2 Chron. 3:14, but J. Maier, *The Temple Scroll: An Introduction, Translation & Commentary* (trans. R. T. White; JSOTSup 34; Sheffield: JSOT Press, 1985), p. 68, suggests that the adjustments are in conformity to 1 Kgs 6:15.

[56] While 'gold' (זהב) is present in the Exodus 26 account, from which this text is drawn, the mention of a gold curtain (פרוכת זהב) is not found elsewhere, except the account of the *Prot. Jas.* 10:2. Golden objects and the veil in 1 Macc. 1:22 may have led to the golden veil tradition of the DSS.

[57] Cf. E. Qimron, 'New Readings in the Temple Scroll', *IEJ* 28 (1978), 162.

[58] The Temple Scroll presumably speaks of a 'screen of the vestibule entrance' in Column 10, though it is so poorly preserved that only portions of its description are extant, and not the term itself. Yadin suggests that the biblical sources for this column are Exod. 26:36; 36:38; 27:16–17 and 38:18–19, which, as is apparent in Appendix 1, use the term מסך for this curtain exclusively. Though, as we will see, others have argued that there were actually two veils in front of the holy of holies. See Faber van der Meulen, p. 22–27. Though, see 4Q365[a] 2 ii, 6–10, which seems to speak of the holy of holies with *doors* made of gold.

[59] Newsom, *EDSS* II, p. 887.

where animated cherubim, embroidered in the curtain, sing praises to God.[60] The veil (again, פרוכת) appears twice in this context (4Q405 f15ii–16:3 and 4Q405 f15ii–16:5). First, we read of 'the appearance of flames of fire [b]eauty upon the veil of the shrine of the King' (line 3).[61] It is unclear whether this description is of the veil itself or of its inscriptions, which have 'a luminous and fiery appearance'.[62] Second, line 5 reads, 'glorious from their two sides . . . curtains of the wondrous *inner chambers*[63] and they bless [the *God of all*]'.[64] Davila suggests that the reference in line 5 reflects the notion of a second side to the veil.[65] It is the product of 'wondrous embroidery work'[66] and is probably 'the heavenly counterpart of the curtain concealing the holy of holies' in the tabernacle and Solomon's temple.[67] More significantly, the 'heavenly beings' on the veil (פרוכת) are even more pronounced in the Songs of the Sabbath Sacrifice than their mere mention in the Pentateuchal accounts and are depicted as animated participants in heavenly worship. The praise is further elaborated in the same text when 11Q17 v 2–10 is combined with 4Q405 15.ii–16. In a partially restored text (of the former), it reads as follows:

> *5* they [will] cause [wonderful] . . . to be heard [inside the precious place, the inner shrine at the ex]it of the vesti[bules] . . . won[derful] figures . . . [give thanks to the king of] *6* [glor]y [with joyful voice] . . . gods . . . their . . . and effigies . . . *7* . . . the ap]pea[rance of] . . . they will hear (?) . . . god of divinitie[s] . . . *8* . . . eternal thrones . . . *9* . . . their [f]orms are cherubs of . . . *10* . . . foundations . . .[68]

The presence of angels in heavenly worship is well attested in Qumran texts, where their primary function is to praise God, while knowledge, particularly of God, is their primary quality.[69] Thus they are said to be revealers of divine mysteries to the faithful community (4Q402 14 ii 7).[70] As both priests and revealers, Newsom argues, the primary focus of the

[60] J. R. Davila, *Liturgical Works* (ECDSS 6; Grand Rapids, Mich.: Eerdmans, 2000), p. 139.

[61] DJD 11:335. [62] DJD 11:336.

[63] Underlines represent Davila's reconstruction based on 11Q17 v.

[64] כבוד משני עבריהם [. . .] פרכות דבירי הפלא וברכו ל[אלוהי כול . . .]. [65] Davila, p. 140.

[66] J. M. Baumgarten, 'The Qumran Sabbath Shirot and Rabbinic Merkabah Traditions', *RevQ* 13 (1988), 202.

[67] Davila, p. 140.

[68] F. García Martínez and E. J. C. Tigchelaar, *The Dead Sea Scrolls: Study Edition* (Grand Rapids, Mich.: Eerdmans, 1997), II, p. 1215.

[69] C. Newsom, *Song of the Sabbath Sacrifice: A Critical Edition* (HSS 27; Atlanta, Ga.: Scholars Press, 1985), pp. 29–30.

[70] *Ibid.*, p. 30.

Songs of the Sabbath sacrifice is ‘on the role of the angels as priests in the heavenly temple’.[71] In these texts the barrier between heaven and the temple is blurred, and heaven itself is depicted as the temple in which the angels minister.[72]

Within the *Damascus Document*, largely a legal text concerned with the purity of the priesthood and the community,[73] we find a fragmentary reference to the veil. In the midst of injunctions for priestly purity, ‘[Anyone] of the sons of Aaron’ (4Q266 5 ii 4–5; cf. lines 8, 10, 12), so as to avoid contamination, impure priests are commanded not to ‘approach the service of . . . מבית לפרוכת’ (4Q266 5 ii 6–7; אל יגש לעבודת [. . .] מבית לפרוכת). However, there is some question as to what מבית לפרוכת is referring, a problem recognised by the Greek translator of Sir. 50:5. The translation of this text is complicated greatly by the lack of a preceding context. The phrase itself (מבית לפרכת) occurs several times in the MT (cf. Exod. 26:33; Lev. 16:2, 12, 16), each with reference to the inner veil, and may be a technical term referring to the location of the priest ‘within the veil’ to perform his cultic duties.[74] If this is what 4Q266 intends, then it may simply mean no more than the physical location of the priest with respect to the inner veil and discusses regulations appropriate for it.[75]

The final reference to the veil found at Qumran, apart from biblical texts identical to those discussed in Chapters 2 and 3, is in the so-called Apocryphon of Moses. The language of 4Q375 1 ii 7 (Apocryphon of Moses B[a]) is nearly identical to that of Lev. 16:2, and the blood of the offering is likewise sprinkled לפני פרוכת: ‘And Aa[ron shall sprinkle with some of the blood] 7 before the veil of [the sanctuary and shall approach] the ark of the testimony’.[76] Again we encounter the same problem of whether the blood was sprinkled ‘against’ or ‘before’ the veil,[77] and the role of the veil in this rite is unclear.

[71] *Ibid*. Newsom further notes that these functions are not unique to Qumran, but are likewise found in *Jubilees*, *1 Enoch*, and *Testament of Levi*.

[72] Newsom, *Song of the Sabbath Sacrifice*, p. 48.

[73] J. C. VanderKam, *Dead Sea Scrolls Today* (Grand Rapids, Mich.: Eerdmans, 1994), p. 56.

[74] So goes the translation of J. M. Baumgarten in DJD 18:50. See R. E. Gane, ‘Re-Opening Katapetasma (“Veil”) in Hebrews 6:19’, *AUSS* 38 (2000), 7–8.

[75] Another option, though quite tenuous, suggests that the phrase means ‘house of the veil’. See Gurtner, ‘“House of the Veil” in Sirach 50’.

[76] García Martínez and Tigchelaar, II, p. 743. See J. Strugnell, ‘Moses-Pseudepigrapha at Qumran: 4Q375, 4Q376, and Similar Works’, in *Archaeology and History in the Dead Sea Scrolls: The New York University Conference in Memory of Yigael Yadin* (JSOTSup 8; Sheffield: JSOT Press, 1990), p. 232. See also G. Brin, ‘Issues Concerning Prophets (Studies in 4Q375)’, in *Studies in Biblical Law: From the Hebrew Bible to the Dead Sea Scrolls* (JSOTSup 176; Sheffield: JSOT Press, 1994), pp. 128–63.

[77] See discussion in Chapter 3.

C. A. Evans notes that a prediction found in the *Lives of the Prophets* offers a strong parallel to the rending of the veil in the synoptics (in this case, Mark). *Lives of the Prophets* is a Jewish composition from perhaps prior to 70 C.E., but preserved, like all Second Temple Jewish literature apart from the Dead Sea Scrolls, only in Christian contexts. Hare indicates that it is therefore 'not surprising that many contain Christian interpolations'.[78] Satran goes so far as to insist that it is a Christian document.[79] Indeed, 12:10–13 says of Habbakuk:

> He gave a portent to those in Judea, that they would see a light in the Temple and so perceive the glory of the Temple. And concerning the end of the Temple he predicted, 'By a western nation it will happen'. 'At that time', he said, 'the curtain of the *Dabeir* will be torn into small pieces (τότε τὸ ἅπλωμα, φησί, τοῦ δαβεὶρ εἰς μικρὰ ῥαγήσεται), and the capitals of the two pillars will be taken away, and no one will know where they are; and they will be carried away by angels into the wilderness, where the tent of witness was set up in the beginning'.[80]

Satran is forced 'to admit bewilderment regarding [this text's] original context or significance'.[81] Yet he has clearly identified it with *Liv. Pro.* 5:1–2 (Hosea), which is surely Christian and therefore suggests dependence upon the synoptic rending texts or at least dependence upon a common tradition.[82] *Lives of the Prophets* 5:1–2 speaks of Hosea's giving a 'portent (τέρας), that the Lord would arrive upon the earth if ever the oak which is in Shiloh were divided from itself and the twelve oaks came to be'.[83] Yet D. R. A. Hare 'believes this is a genuine pre-70 prediction that reflects growing unease over the increasing presence of Gentiles in and around Jerusalem'.[84] The context is Habbakuk before the Babylonian

78 D. R. A. Hare, 'Lives of the Prophets', *DNTB*, p. 653.

79 D. Satran, *Biblical Prophets in Byzantine Palestine: Reassessing the "Lives of the Prophets"* (Leiden: Brill, 1995), p. 118. See also A. M. Schwemer, *Studien zu den frühjüdischen Prophetenlegenden* Vitae Prophetarum (TSAJ 49; Tübingen: Mohr Siebeck, 1995), pp. 66–69.

80 *OTP* II, pp. 393–94. Hare notes that ἅπλωμα is an unusual term for a curtain, but is found in *T. Benj.* 9:4. *OTP* II, p. 393 n. f. 'Curtain' here (ἅπλωμα) is recognised as something which is unfolded, or an expanse (LSJ).

81 Satran, p. 67.

82 *Ibid.*, pp. 2–8. See M. de Jonge, 'Christelijke elementen in de Vitae Prophetarum', *NTT* 16 (1962), 170–74, 176–77, who argues that the Christian elements are far more pervasive than many have believed, and that this collection of Jewish traditions first attained literary form in a Christian context. See *OTP* II, p. 384.

83 *OTP* II, p. 391. See Schwemer, *Vitae Prophetarum* I, p. 123.

84 Evans, *Mark 8:27 – 16:20* (WBC 34B; Nashville, Tenn.: Nelson, 2001), p. 509.

captivity and clearly relates the rending of this curtain to the destruction of the temple, yet in *Liv. Pro.* 12:11 Habbakuk is speaking with respect to the second temple.[85] It seems that, following Hare, this tradition is genuinely free from Christian interference, for the dissimilar contexts and language employed in *Liv. Pro.* 12:10 would make it difficult to make a case for a Christian revision. That this account of a torn veil directly relates to the destruction of the temple[86] leads Schwemer to claim that the veil before the holy of holies is used 'pro toto für die σκηνή'.[87]

Yet there are three distinct features which preclude its influence upon the Matthean 'rending' texts. First, the dating of this document is quite problematic, and Hare's early date is not widely accepted. Satran demonstrates that it is surely Christian and after 70 C.E.[88] Second, even if it could be established to have a date prior to that of the synoptic accounts, the contexts and language are so decidedly different that it would be difficult to associate the clear temple destruction context of *Lives of the Prophets* with the death of Jesus context of the synoptics. Third, the tearing of the curtain in *Lives of the Prophets* is described with such striking similarity to the rabbinic tradition of Titus cutting it to shreds upon his assault on the Jerusalem shrine in 70 C.E. that it not only affirms a later date but places it more firmly in that tradition, which we will examine more fully later.[89]

In a similar post–70 C.E. text, *2 Baruch*, a decidedly apocalyptic document, the veil (ܐܦ̈ܝ ܬܪܥܐ, lit. 'face of the door' 6:7) was said to be one of the cultic items of the tabernacle taken by an angel from the holy of holies (ܒܝܬ ܩܘܕܫ ܩܘܕ̈ܫܐ) to be 'swallowed . . . up' by the earth, in an account of the 587 destruction of Jerusalem (*2 Bar.* 6:7–10)[90] and the

[85] Schwemer, *Vitae Prophetarum* II, p. 120.

[86] Cf. A. G. Van Aarde, 'Matthew 27:45–53 and the Turning of the Tide in Israel's History', *BTB* 28 (1998), 16–26; W. Trilling, *Das Wahre Israel: Studien zur Theologie des Matthäus-Evangeliums* (Müngen: Kösen, 1964), p. 221; D. C. Allison, *The End of the Ages Has Come* (Philadelphia, Pa.: Fortress, 1985), pp. 80–103.

[87] Schwemer, *Vitae Prophetarum* I, pp. 123–24. Although she suggests this is like the veil in the *Life of Jeremiah*, she cites no text in that document for such a claim. Moreover, she insists that the veil symbolises not the heavenly firmament, but the earth. See B. Ego, *Im Himmel Wie Auf Erden: Studien Zum Verhältnis Von Himmlischer Und Irdischer Welt in Rabbinischen Judentum* (WUNT II, 34; Tübingen: Mohr-Siebeck, 1989), pp. 15, 21f, 40, 111f, 123, 189. Contra O. Hofius, *Vorhang vor dem Thron Gottes: Eine exegetisch- religionsgeschichteeliche Untersuchung zu Hebräer 6,19f. und 10,19f* (WUNT 14; Tübingen: Mohr Siebeck, 1972), pp. 24f, who says the inner veil is the firmament, though Schwemer seems to contradict herself later (II, p. 127).

[88] See Satran, pp. 118–19. See also Schwemer, *Vitae Prophetarum*, pp. 66–69.

[89] See Gurtner, 'The 'Cut-Up' Veil and the Dating of *Lives of the Prophets* 12' (in production).

[90] *OTP* I, p. 623.

guardian of the 'house' has abandoned it (*2 Bar.* 8:2; cf. *4 Bar.* 4:1; *J.W.* 6.5.3 §300; Tacitus, *Hist.* 5.13). *2 Baruch* narrates the 587 destruction as a type of the 70 C.E. destruction, though in the latter no cultic objects were present as in the former. Thus the sacred articles were removed prior to the invitation to enter was extended to the Babylonians (8:2).[91] As with the Aristeas text, this provides little additional information regarding the veil, save its importance. Yet that it occurs within an apocalyptic context, which I will define carefully in Chapter 6, is an observation we will see again in what follows.

Rabbinic sources are among the most frequently cited texts for New Testament scholars' discussion of the veil in the synoptic accounts for their historical configuration and various legends related to it. I discuss these issues in some detail elsewhere.[92] Though rabbinic writings are largely much too late to have influenced an ideology of the veil(s) upon Matthew, they do represent some valuable developments which at times can be traced to much earlier traditions and are thus worthy of consideration here, especially as they reflect an apocalyptic worldview (which I will define carefully in Chapter 6).[93] In particular, they depict the veil as symbolic of the heavenly firmament from Gen. 1:6. From the rabbinic corpus, McKelvey argues that the temple was considered a gateway from earth to heaven,[94] where heavenly beings lived and worshipped in a distinctly apocalyptic literary context.[95] Within this scheme, some have understood the veil to be the barrier between heaven and earth, behind which divine secrets are kept.

The veil of the temple, called פרגוד in many traditions and וילון in others (*b. Ḥag.* 15a), derives its name from the Latin *paragganda*, which is a garment ornamented with a border, so called because of its Phrygian origin.[96] P. Alexander notes that this curtain (פרגוד) corresponds to the veil before the holy of holies in the tabernacle and temple (Exod. 26:31; 2 Chron. 3:14). He suggests that פרגוד is the preferred term, even over פרכת, and that it indicates a curtain in heaven that 'separates the immediate

[91] Brown, *Death* II, p. 1110. [92] Gurtner, 'History and Legend'.

[93] For a very helpful discussion of apocalypticism in early rabbinic traditions, see M. Bockmuehl, *Revelation and Mystery in Ancient Judaism and Pauline Christianity* (Grand Rapids, Mich.: Eerdmans, 1990), pp. 104–26.

[94] *b. Yoma* 54b; *Gen. Rab.* 4:2 (on Gen. 1:6); *Gen. Rab.* 68:12 (on Gen. 28:12); *Pirqe R. El.* §32.35; *Num. Rab.* 12:4 (on Num. 7:1).

[95] See Ps. 11:4; *T. Levi* 5:1f; *1 En.* 14:16–18, 20; *2 Bar.* 4:6–8. R. J. McKelvey, *The New Temple* (London: Oxford University Press, 1969), pp. 25–41. From E. Best, *A Commentary on the First and Second Epistles to the Thessalonians* (London: Black, 1972), p. 287.

[96] M. Jastrow, *A Dictionary of the Targumim, the Talmud Babli and Yerushalmi, and the Midrashic Literature* (2 vols.; London: Shapiro, Vallentine & Co., 1926), II, p. 1214.

presence of God from the rest of heaven'.[97] *3 Enoch* 45:1–2a speaks of 'the curtain of the Omnipresent One (פרגוד של מקום), which is spread before the Holy One (*Pirqe R. El.* §4; *Gen. Rab.* 4:1 [on Gen. 1:6]), blessed be he, and on which are printed all the generations of the world and all their deeds, whether done or to be done, till the last generation'[98] (cf. *m. Mid.* 1:1). A tradition found in an extended comparison between the tabernacle instructions of Exod. 26–36 and God's creation in Gen. 1 in *Num. Rab.* 12:13 (on Num. 7:1) is telling of the relationship between this veil and heaven. Here the author compares the tabernacle with the created order:

> The Tabernacle denotes that its importance was equal to that of the world, which is called 'tent', even as the Tabernacle is called 'tent'. How can this statement be supported? It is written, *In the beginning God created the heaven*, etc. (Gen. 1:1), and it is written, *Who stretched out the heaven like a* curtain (Ps. 104:2), while of the Tabernacle it is written, *And thou shalt make curtains of goat's hair for a* tent *over the Tabernacle*, etc. (Exod. 26:7). It is written in connection with the second day (of creation), *Let there be a firmament . . . and let it divide*, etc. (Gen. 1:6), and of the Tabernacle it is written. *The veil shall* divide *unto you* (Exod. 26:33).[99]

This text clearly identifies the inner veil of the temple with the heavenly firmament from Gen. 1:6 within a wider tabernacle/temple cosmology. Similarly, where Job 26:9 mentions no veil,[100] its Targum (*Tg.* Job 26:9) describes God's spreading clouds over his glory like a curtain:[101] 'He

[97] '3 Enoch', *OTP* I, p. 296, n. 45a. These important observations fit nicely with the functions we outlined in Chapter 3. Hofius (p. 16, n. 82, 83, 84) says that the veil 'markiert den tiefen Abstand, der zwischen Gott und seinem himmlischen welt besteht. Er ist damit Austruck für die überweltliche Hoheit, Reinheit und Heiligkeit (*Sipre* Lev. 11:44; 11:45; 20:26; *Lev. Rab.* 24:4 [on Lev. 19:2]) dessen, der in einem unzugänglichen Lichte wohnt (1 Tim. 6:16) und so von allen seinem Geschöpfen qualitative geschieden ist'.

[98] Alexander, *OTP* I, p. 296, cf. *3 En.* 10:1. The veil was also thought to hide human failings from God's sight (*b. B. Meṣi'a* 59a; *b. Yoma* 77a; cf. also *Pirqe R. El.* §4.7). See O. Mulder, *Simon the High Priest in Sirach 50: An Exegetical Study of the Significance of Simon the High Priest as Climax to the Praise of the Fathers in Ben Sira's Concept of the History of Israel* (JSJSup 78; Leiden: Brill, 2003), pp. 123–124, n. 150.

[99] *Midrash Rabbah: Numbers* (2 vols.; trans. J. J. Slokti; London: Soncino Press, 1939), I, p. 483.

[100] 'He obscures the face of the full moon, And spreads His cloud over it'.

[101] 'He holds tightly *the thick darkness* about his *throne so that the angel(s) will not see him*; he spreads the clouds *of his glory* over it *like a curtain*'. The term פרגוד was originally of Persian origin (cf. *Tg. Ps.-J.* Gen. 37:17; Lev. 16:15). 'In the Pseudepigrapha and later Rabbinic literature it was used to designate the separation of the immediate presence of God from the heavenly court' (C. Mangan, 'The Targum of Job', in *The Aramaic Bible* 15

holds tightly *the thick darkness* about his *throne so that the angel(s) will not see him*; he spreads the clouds *of his glory* over it *like a curtain*'.[102] Though often thought too late to be of value for New Testament exegesis,[103] the correlation between the veil and the heavens for concealing purposes is already established. Behind the veil (מאחורי הפרגוד) is a place of secrecy where things that could be known only to God are present in profoundly apocalyptic texts (*Tg. Ps.-J.* Gen. 37:17; *Pirqe R. El.* §7; cf. *b. Ḥag.* 15a).[104]

Those who either hear or see what occurs behind it are thought to be let in on a heavenly secret or revelation.[105] The veil is thought to conceal things, with its removal depicting the revelation of biblical truths: 'R. Aḥa b. Ḥanina said: Neither is the veil drawn before him, as it is said, "*Thy teacher shall no more be hidden*"' (*b. Soṭah* 49a). Secret things such as knowledge of tribulations in store for the world are contained within (*b. Ber.* 18b).[106] The heavenly secret of the location of Joseph's brothers was overheard 'from behind the veil' (*Tg. Ps.-J.* Gen. 37:17). From behind the curtain Moses' prayer to extend his life was received,[107] and from behind the veil answers to prayers are announced (*Mek.* Exod. 19:9). Sometimes angels and even demons can, from the outside, hear the secrets contained within (*b. Ḥag.* 16a; cf. *b. Sanh.* 89b; *b. Ḥag.* 15a; 2 Sam. 14:20). Alexander notes that 'only the Prince of the Divine Presence

[Edinburgh: T. & T. Clark, 1991], p. 63, n. 5; cf. *3 En.* 45:1; *b. Yoma* 77a). Cf. L. Ginzberg, *The Legends of the Jews* (7 vols.; trans. H. Szold and P. Radin; Philadelphia, Pa.: Jewish Publication Society, 1936–47), V, p. 250.

102 C. Mangan, *The Targum of Job* (AB 15; Edinburgh: T. & T. Clark, 1991), p. 63.

103 Alhough Qumran contains a copy of a Job Targum (11QtgJob = 11Q10 = Job 17:14–42:11), and *b. Šabb.* 115a refers to a Job Targum from 50 C.E., the Qumran version is probably dissimilar from the later version. The 11Q10 text leaves off at Job 26:2 and continues at 26:10! The Qumran reading in vv 10ff varies from that of *Tg.* Job 26, and it is recognised that the 'Qumran Job Targum is totally different from the Targum of Job transmitted by rabbinic Judaism' (M. McNamara, *Targum Neofiti 1: Genesis* [AB 1A; Edinburgh: T. & T. Clark, 1992], p. 43). Cf. M. Sokoloff, *The Targum of Job from Qumran Cave XI* (Ramat-Gan: Bar-Ilan University, 1974); J. A. Fitzmyer, 'Some Observations on the Targum of Job from Qumran Cave 11', *CBQ* 36 (1974), 503–24; C. Mangan, 'Some Observations on the Dating of Targum Job', in *Back to the Sources: Biblical and Near Eastern Studies in Honour of Dermot Ryan* (ed. K. J. Cathcart and J. F. Healey; Dublin: Glendale, 1980), pp. 67–78; C. A. Evans, *Non-Canonical Writings and New Testament Interpretation* (Peabody, Mass.: Hendrickson, 1992), p. 106. Cf. Légasse, p. 583.

104 See Ginzberg, *Legends* II, pp. 10–11; *b. Ta'an* 10a; *b. Pesaḥ* 94a.

105 We note here the strong correlation between this view and the rending of the heavens/veil in the Markan account described in the introduction.

106 H. Odeberg, *3 Enoch* or *The Hebrew Book of Enoch* (Cambridge: Cambridge University Press, 1928), p. 141. Cf. M. Barker, *The Gate of Heaven: The History and Symbolism of the Temple in Jerusalem* (London: SPCK, 1991), pp. 104–32.

107 Hofius, p. 11.

is allowed to go within the curtain' (see *b. Yoma* 77a; *3 En.* 48D:7; *Pirqe R. El.* §4).[108] For the others, the veil them from the 'destructive glare of the divine glory' (*Tg.* Job 26:9; cf. *3 En.* 22B:6; *b. B. Meṣi'a* 59a).[109] For them the veil served to prohibit access not just to God himself but more explicitly the Ark of the Covenant, which is repeatedly said to have lain 'hidden',[110] a requirement for which the veil was essential (*Num. Rab.* 4:13 [on Num. 4:5]). Within the curtain was the locus of the most holy sacrifices (*b. Meg.* 9b–10a; cf. *m. 'Ed* 8.7; *b. Zebaḥ.* 107b), a locus which, as in Lev. 16:2, was forbidden to be entered (*b. Menaḥ.* 27b; *Tg. Onq.* Lev. 16:2). The concealing role of the veil in such contexts may have originated in a tradition like that of *b. Ḥag.* 12b, which develops God's stretching out heavens like a curtain in Isa. 40:22: God 'stretches out the heavens like a curtain, And spreads them out like a tent to dwell in' (כדק שמים וימתחם כאהל לשבת), or the comparison of creation with the temple in *Num. Rab.* 12:13 (on Num. 7:1). Regardless, for Hofius the veil before the most holy place corresponds to the רקיע ('firmament'). He also finds in Isa. 40:22 that God stretches 'the sky (שמים) out like a veil (דק)'.[111] He dates the tradition to the time of Philo and Hebrews, with rabbinic traditions probably in place by the second century, and concludes 'both

[108] *OTP* I, p. 296, n. 45a. Cf. Hofius, p. 11. A Hekhalot text comprising §1–80 of *SH-L* and translated by P. Alexander, *OTP* I, pp. 223–315. Passages not included in *SH-L* are cited according to the edition of Odeberg, *3 Enoch*. Cf. Davila, pp. 140–41. P. Schäfer *et al.*, *Synopse zur Hekhalot-Literatur* (TSAJ 2; Tübingen: Mohr Siebeck, 1981). Hekhalot texts published in the *Synopse* are cited by the traditional names of the given 'macroform' (*Hekhalot Rabbati*, *Hekhalot Zutarti*, etc.) followed by the relevant paragraph number(s) in *SH-L*. Passages not found within the boundaries of the traditional named texts are cited as '*SH-L*' followed by the relevant paragraph number(s). G. Friedlander, *Pirḳê de Rabbi Eliezer* (trans. G. Friedlander; New York: Sepher-Hermon Press, 1916), p. 23, n. 5; cf. *b. Ber.* 18b; *b. Ḥag.* 15a. It is 'the veil which separates the Shekhinah from the angels' (*b. Yebam.* 63b). He notes, 'The B. M MS. Reads here: "The seven angels which were created at the beginning, minister before the veil which is spread before Him".' Cf. *1 En.* 90:21; Rev. 4:5; and *b. B. Meṣi'a* 59a.

[109] Alexander, *OTP* I, p. 296, n. 45a.

[110] *m. Sheq.* 6:1, 2. When the Israelites went into battle with the ark, their camp was that 'of the ark' (*m. Soṭah* 8:1). Yet one could go before it with prayers (*m. Ber.* 5:3; *cf. m. 'Erub.* 3:9), and 'before the Ark' was where prayers were received (*m. Ta'an* 1:2; 2:2; *cf.* 2:5; *m. Meg.* 4:3, 5, 8). And it belongs to the people (*m. Ned.* 5:5). This seems to support the shielding function of the veil, explored in Chapter 3.

[111] Hofius, p. 25. דק is a hapax in the MT. Cf. S. M. Olyan, *A Thousand Thousands Served Him: Exegesis and the Naming of Angels in Ancient Judaism* (Tübingen: Mohr Siebeck, 1993), p. 116; D. L. Penney, 'Finding the Devil in the Details: Onomastic Exegesis and the Naming of Evil in the World of the New Testament', in *New Testament Greek and Exegesis: Essays in Honor of Gerald F. Hawthorne* (ed. A. M. Donaldson and T. B. Sailors; Grand Rapids, Mich.: Eerdmans, 2003), pp. 37–52, esp. p. 43.

in the rabbinic and in the Hellenistic-Jewish texts, the curtain delimits the heavenly world as the area of highest holiness of the earthly world'.[112]

An objection to the identification of the veil with the heavens may be put forth on the grounds that many rabbinic texts spoke not of a single layer of heaven but of seven distinct tiers. If this is the case, which one is associated with the veil? It is the case that perhaps from the time of *2 Enoch* (late first century C.E.?) and *3 Baruch* (first to third century C.E.?), Jewish texts richly develop the notion of the layering of heaven. The layering of heaven is most explicitly found in *b. Ḥag.*, which is classical rabbinic tradition and may well reflect relatively early material. *b. Ḥag.* 12b depicts a dispute among rabbis: 'R. Judah said: There are two firmaments, for it is said: *Behold, unto the Lord thy God belongeth heaven, and the heaven of heavens* (Deut. 10:14). Resh Laḳish said: [There are] seven'.[113] The text then goes on to name those seven (*b. Ḥag.* 12b–c). It is important to note that in rabbinic texts where the layers of heaven are depicted, there is no association, which I have found, between any of these layers and any of the curtains of the tabernacle/temple.

Although one would expect that the different curtains – at least the outer and inner veils – represent different layers of the heavens, this is decidedly not the case. First, while there are frequently several layers to heaven in rabbinic texts, there is only mention of a single veil, the פרכת. Indeed, there is no discussion of the outer curtain (מסך) in the Mishnah.[114] Moreover, the veil is associated with the heavens only in texts where no layering is clearly in view.[115] Finally, and most importantly, J. E. Wright has shown that 'there never was only one dominating view of the structure, contents, and population of the heavenly realm in early Judaism and Christianity but several'.[116] He has also shown that the notion of a layered heaven, which ranges from a single layer, to as many as 955, and further to an unlimited number, was a later development under Greco-Roman influence.[117] Thus, though there were many traditions that held to a multi-layered scheme of

[112] Hofius, p. 27.

[113] *Hebrew–English Edition of the Babylonian Talmud: Ta'annith* (trans. J. Rabbinwitz; ed. I. Epstein; London: Soncino Press, 1984).

[114] Légasse, 'Les voiles', 579–80. And only three in Qumran (4Q167 3 iii; 4Q375 1 ii 7; 4Q525 35 ii).

[115] An exception may be found in *Hekhalot Zutarti* §346//§673, in which R. Akiva reached 'the curtain' (פרגוד) after passing the 'entrances of the firmament'. Davila, pp. 140–41.

[116] J. E. Wright, *The Early History of Heaven* (Oxford: Oxford University Press, 2000), p. 118.

[117] The earliest texts 'seem to presuppose a single heaven cosmography' (Wright, *Early History*, p. 137), including *Gk. Apoc. Ezra*, most of New Testament, *4 Ezra*, *Jos. Asen.*, DSS and most of *1 En*.

heaven, most of the earliest texts did not. This indicates that subsequent authors who employ a symbolic view of the veil corresponding to the heavenly firmament from Gen. 1:6 at the very least need not, perhaps even could not, have identified that heavenly firmament with one within a multi-layered scheme.

## 5 Philo and Josephus (Revisited)

While I have noted that these fully developed notions of the symbolic quality of the veil of the temple are articulated quite late, it seems quite probable that widespread and firm association points to a notion quite early in the tradition. Indeed, the association between tabernacle/temple curtains and the heavenly firmament is at least as early as Josephus, and fits within a wider temple cosmology that dates two centuries before him.[118] The physical descriptions of the veil provided by Josephus and Philo are insightful. Pelletier suggests that for both Philo and Josephus the veil served to obscure from the 'views of the public the mystery of the abode of God to reserve it to the privileged priesthood'.[119] Philo describes the veil (τό καταπέτασμα) as being made of the same colours as the other curtains: 'dark red and purple and scarlet and bright white' (*Moses* 2.87 LCL). Pelletier argues that this reflects Philo's view of the four elements, which originated from Stoic philosophy. For him the veil symbolises the separation between κόσμος αἰσθητός (sensual world) and κόσμος νοητός (intellectual world). This, Hofius argues, is a 'philosophical modification' of the older Hellenistic-Jewish interpretation of the curtain before the holy of holies.[120] For Philo the number of materials is significant in that 4 was the number of cosmological elements. Pelletier sees Philo's portrayal of the more important, inner veil as an allegorical projection from the Pentateuch. He argues that Hellenism had deeply penetrated into the Jewish environment and attributed to this curtain a 'symbolisme cosmique dans le goût de l'époque'.[121]

[118] See Wright, *Early History*, pp. 117–83. See further discussion in Chapter 6.

[119] Pelletier, 'La tradition synoptique du 'Voile déchiré' à la lumière des réalités archéologiques', *Recherches de science religieuse* 46 (1958), 172.

[120] Hofius, p. 24. *QE* 2.91 [to Exod. 26:31]; 2.94 [to Exod. 26:33b]; *Moses* 2.74ff; see G. W. Macrae, 'Some Elements of Jewish Apocalyptic and Mystical Tradition and their Relation to Gnostic Literature' (2 vols.; Ph.D. diss.; Cambridge University, 1966) II, pp. 43ff.

[121] 'Cosmic symbolism in the taste of Enoch'. Pelletier, 'La tradition synoptique', pp. 167, 169. D. Rudman uses this symbolism of the elements of the universe to argue the rending of the veil depicted the destruction of the cosmos in line with his contention for a *Chaoskampf* in the synoptic Passion Narratives ('The Crucifixion as *Chaoskampf*: A New Reading of the Passion Narrative in the Synoptic Gospels', *Bib.* 84 [2003], 107).

Yet Josephus, perhaps because of his priestly heritage, is more descriptively specific. The outer curtain as well as the veil (both καταπέτασμα) was

> of Babylonian tapestry (Βαβυλώνιος ποικιλτὸς), with embroidery of blue and fine linen, of scarlet also and purple, wrought with marvelous skill. Nor was this mixture of materials without its mystic meaning: it typified the universe. For the scarlet seemed emblematic of fire, the fine linen of the earth, the blue of the air, and the purple of the sea; the comparison in two cases being suggested by their colour, and in that of the fine linen and purple by their origin, as the one is produced by the earth and the other by the sea. On this tapestry was portrayed a panorama of the heavens, the signs of the Zodiac excepted.
>
> (*J.W.* 5.5.4 §§212–214 LCL)

The Babylonian tapestry and the scarlet purple and skill clearly depict royalty. Such Babylonian tapestry likewise served as the coverlet for Cyrus's golden sarcophagus when it was visited by Alexander the Great (Arrian, *Anabasis of Alexander* 6.29.5) who 'founded the Persian Empire, and was King of Asia' (6.29.8; cf. 3.21.1; 4.18.3). Yet Josephus's elaboration for us shows the rich symbolism of its 'mystic meaning'. Pelletier claims that for Josephus 'the embroidery of the curtain represented the stars of the firmament'[122] (presumably the רקיע of Gen. 1:6). Hofius says that for Josephus the veil symbolises the separation between heaven and earth.[123]

[122] Pelletier, 'La tradition synoptique', p. 171.

[123] Hofius, p. 23. While from a rabbinic standpoint one could sympathise with Barker's insistence that 'those who entered the holy of holies were entering heaven' (though surely not from the texts she cites ['Beyond the Veil of the Temple', p. 3]), her insistence that 'those who entered heaven became divine' is without evidence. There are several other reasons why we find Barker's work to be of limited use for our purposes. First, she conflates Old Testament, rabbinic and Second Temple texts to draw a single, coherent picture of the historical veil with no acknowledgement of the contradictions among them (p. 1). Second, she presumes that because Josephus claims the tabernacle was a 'microcosm of creation', he implies that 'the veil which screened the holy of holies was also the boundary between earth and heaven' (p. 1). While this conclusion may be true, there is nothing in Josephus's statement, to which she alludes, that suggests it. Third, she cites rabbinic references (*b. Hor.* 12a; *b. Ker.* 5b) as being 'second temple' rather than properly rabbinic (p. 2), and otherwise displays no discretion regarding the dating and chronology of the documents she cites. Fourth, although she rightly enumerates the different elements which the colours of the veil depicted, it does not necessarily follow that 'the veil represented matter', as she asserts (p. 4). Fifth, although she rightly places the veil in an apocalyptic milieu, she fails to define the term and seems to use its connotations idiosyncratically (8). I will define the term in detail in Chapter 6. Sixth, she indirectly compares the holy of holies to the Garden of Eden without paying attention to Wenham's seminal work on the subject (p. 9). Seventh, she claims that calling figures 'sons of God' 'implies that they were begotten not created'

The colours depicted the elements of the universe, and describing it as portraying the 'panorama of the heavens' (τὴν οὐράνιον θεωρίαν) suggests the firmament imagery associated with the veil summarised from rabbinic texts discussed earlier. Precisely what does he mean by 'panorama' and how does it relate to 'the heavens'? Θεωρίαν generally refers to a sight or spectacle.[124] In Josephus the term refers to a design, plan, or something visually depicting something else (Josephus, *Ant.* 2.9.5 §226, 8.5.2 §138, 12.2.9 §66, 12.2.12 §99, 16.5.1 §140, 19.1.12 §81, 19.1.13 §89; *J.W.* 5.5.2 §191). Moreover, Josephus tells his readers what that 'something else' is, ἅπασαν τὴν οὐράνιον. Οὐράνιος is a relatively rare adjectival form of οὔρανος and can, itself, mean a 'panorama of the heavens' (Xenophon, *Mem.* 1.1.11) but mostly means 'heavenly' or 'dwelling in heaven' as a place for the gods, and so on (Euripides, *Ion* 715; *Phoenisae* 1729; Plato, *Phaedr.* 247a; *Inscriptiones Graecae* 12(2).58b4; Aeschylus, *Prometheus vinctus* 165; *Agamemnon* 90).[125] What Josephus tells us, then, is that on the veil was portrayed, presumably woven ('tapestry'), something that looked like heaven. That is, whatever else Josephus is saying, he asserts that the veil itself, in some sense, looked like heaven. This need not say that the veil is in some sense *equated* with the heavens, as we have seen in rabbinic literature, but it does draw our attention to an association being made between heaven and the veil which is within the first-century period. Moreover, as I will demonstrate in Chapter 6, the identification of the veil as the heavenly firmament is found in an important document widely agreed to be the primary source for the writing of the gospel of Matthew, the gospel of Mark.[126]

## The Veil in Second Temple and Rabbinic Judaism: Conclusion

We have seen that in at least one Qumran text the veil had a place in the heavenly sanctuary, was revered as golden, and was interwoven with animated cherubim praising God as one entered the heavenly *debir*. Yet

(p. 12), when that does not necessarily follow, and certainly not for Second Temple and rabbinic literature other than Philo, and it may be a misreading even of Philo.

[124] LSJ, *Lexicon*, p. 797.

[125] *Ibid.*, p. 1272. It is quite rare in the LXX and New Testament: 1 Esd. 6:14; 2 Macc. 7:34; 9:10; 3 Macc. 6:18; 4 Macc. 4:11; 9:15; 11:3; Dan. (Th) 4:26; Matt. 5:48; 6:14, 26, 32; 15:13; 18:35; 23:9; Luke 2:13; Acts 26:19. I owe credit to J. T. Pennington for help on these observations.

[126] Although this is not an apocalyptic context, as in other Jewish writings similarly depicting the veil, it is no longer valid to discredit Josephus's connection with Jewish apocalypticism. See P. Bilde, 'Josephus and Jewish Apocalypticism', in *Understanding Josephus: Seven Perspectives* (ed. S. Mason; JSPSup 32; Sheffield: Academic Press, 1998), pp. 35–61.

there is also evidence in this corpus of material that the veil of the temple began to evolve an ideology of its own. For example, it began to be a symbol of something beyond itself (the temple) as early as the Greek translation of Ben Sira (Sir. 50:5). In another instance the veil itself, rather than concealing what is sacred, is itself concealed as sacred and given its own covering, the removal of which is perhaps a symbol for the conversion of Aseneth (*Jos. Asen* 10:2). As early as Josephus the veil was associated with 'heaven' (in some sense). The identity of the veil with the heavenly firmament seems to be most readily developed in texts of an apocalyptic, though is also found in narratives such as that of Josephus. Rabbinic tradition shows that the veil, by that time, was quite firmly associated with the heavenly firmament, particularly from Gen. 1:6 and particularly in texts where no discussion of the layers of heaven is apparent. Indeed, there is little evidence that the veil was symbolic of anything else. The veil is thought to conceal heavenly secrets, with its removal depicting the revelation of biblical truths. Yet that such an association was so widespread and present in such a variety of texts strongly suggests it was developed from a much earlier tradition. Thus, if it is not yet firmly in place by Matthew's time, it was surely in the beginning stages of a fixed ideology that associated the veil that is torn in Matthew, with the heavenly firmament. Before I can explore how this functions in Matthew, however, two contextual elements are necessary for understanding the meaning of Matthew's rending of the veil: Matthew's portrayal of the temple (for it is the veil *of the temple* which was torn), and Matthew's portrayal of the death of Christ (for it is subsequent to the death of Jesus that this portent occurs). These will serve as the subjects of our next chapter.

# 5

# MATTHEW'S TEMPLE AND JESUS' DEATH: HERMENEUTICAL KEYS TO THE RENDING OF THE VEIL

## Introduction

As I have argued throughout, all of the analyses of Old Testament, Second Temple and rabbinic portrayals of the veil must be subjected to the Matthean text to evaluate adequately their role in a contextual interpretation of the rending of Matthew's temple veil. This, in part, is the subject of the present chapter, where I will undertake a composition-critical approach to what I have identified as two hermeneutical keys to interpreting Matthew's rending of the veil: Matthew's portrayal of the temple and his portrayal of the death of Jesus. Here I will employ a sort of hermeneutical algebra. There are three elements to this equation carefully linked by the evangelist: the tearing of the veil, the temple and the death of Jesus. I will examine Matthew's portrayal of the temple and the death of Jesus *throughout* the gospel (for which we have some evidence) and use these items to interpret the rending of the veil (for which we have but a single piece of evidence).[1]

'Composition criticism' can be variously understood.[2] Stanton says that it 'considers the overall structure of each gospel, the structure of individual sections and subsections and the order in which the evangelists have placed the traditions at their disposal'. It has a 'strong insistence that the gospels must be viewed as whole units whose various parts are interrelated'.[3] However, this has very strong affinities with redaction criticism

[1] We will not concern ourselves here with the issues of the historical Jesus, or even necessarily how Jesus understood his own death (surveyed admirably by S. McKnight, 'Jesus and His Death: Some Recent Scholarship', *CR*: *BS* 9 [2001], 185–228).

[2] W. G. Olmstead, *Matthew's Trilogy of Parables: The Nation, the Nations and the Reader in Matthew 21.28–22.14* (SNTSMS 127; Cambridge: Cambridge University Press, 2003), has provided a helpful starting point by showing the weaknesses of both redaction (tradition-historical) and narrative criticisms and by illustrating how they can be mutually corrective.

[3] *The Gospels and Jesus* (Oxford: Oxford University Press, 1989), pp. 24, 26, 27, 41. Cf. O. L. Cope, *Matthew: A Scribe Trained for the Kingdom of Heaven* (CBQMS 5; Washington, D.C.: Catholic Biblical Association of America), pp. 6–10.

as it is traditionally employed. Essentially, our definition of composition criticism is identical to redaction criticism except for two important factors. First, I will try to carefully relate Matthean redaction to the overall corpus of his entire gospel (a feature lacking in some modern uses of the method). Second, I will not try to probe a tradition history prior to Matthew, but will try to see how Matthew's modifications of his sources contribute to the wider articulation of Matthean themes.[4] These departures from some modern applications of redaction critical work feed into a more holistic approach of composition criticism.

## 1 The Temple in Matthew's Gospel

The first half of this analysis, which concerns the temple, is modelled by J. B. Green, whose methodological approach to the tearing of the veil in Luke I mentioned in the introduction. He approaches the problem by examining the event in relation to destruction of the temple as portrayed in Luke-Acts.[5] The order of the account by Luke, coupled with the largely positive view of the temple itself in Luke-Acts, leads Green to conclude that the rending of the veil (in Luke) symbolises 'the obliteration of the barriers between those peoples previously divided by status and ethnicity'.[6] The attractiveness of this view is that in it Green has carefully drawn a distinctively Lukan picture of the temple, within the entire composition of the gospel itself, as a determinative hermeneutical element.[7] I will undertake a similar approach to the temple in Matthew. Yet, as is the case with Matthew's Christology, it is difficult to reconstruct a clear portrait of the temple,[8] for though statements *about* the temple are present and important, they are scant. They must, then, be pieced together with the evangelist's compositional portrayal of the temple to arrive at a coherent picture. We will see that the temple seems to be both a 'character' in

[4] For a further summary of the method, see Telford, *Mark* (T. & T. Clark Study Guides; Sheffield: Academic Press, 1997), pp. 88–89.

[5] J. B. Green, 'The Death of Jesus and the Rending of the Temple Veil: A Window into Luke's Understanding of Jesus and the Temple', *SBLSP* 30 (1991), 543. The destruction of the temple is another element in our equation of Matthew's interest in the temple, one that we will discuss later.

[6] Green, p. 543.

[7] While this is critical, it alone fails to give credence to a number of vital factors, not least of which is Luke's view of Jesus' *death*, for it is in the context of the death of Jesus that Luke places this event. Surely the subject of the crucifixion narrative is the death of Jesus rather than the temple.

[8] R. T. France, *Matthew: Evangelist and Teacher* (Downers Grove, Ill.: InterVarsity, 1989), p. 279. See F. W. Barnett, 'Characterization and Christology in Matthew: Jesus in the Gospel of Matthew', *SBLSP* 28 (1989), 588–603.

the Matthean narrative and a (deliberate) 'setting' for pivotal scenes in Matthew's depiction of the primary subject of his gospel, naturally, Jesus. When the composite elements of this portrait are brought together, we recognise that Matthew is positive towards the temple in general, affirming the validity of its sacrifices and the presence of God within it. Yet the temple's destruction is imminent not because Matthew sees intrinsic problems with it, but because it is mismanaged by a corrupt Jewish leadership.

At a surface level, however, Matthew could be seen to present somewhat contradictory views of the temple. Is it a place to be 'cleansed' and preserved for prayer (21:13)? Or is it a place to be left desolate (23:38) and ultimately destroyed (24:2)? Matthew presumes the presence of God in the temple, thereby making it sacred (23:21), while the temple itself makes sacred its gold (23:17). Some contend that Matthew's Jesus seems to replace the function of the Jerusalem temple[9] as he immediately provides healing for the lame and blind within its courts (21:14), for which praise was offered for the 'son of David' (21:15).[10] Others have claimed that this 'cleansing' text illustrates that the Herodian temple was 'judged inadequate as the place of God's presence and authentic worship'.[11] But it was also an appropriate place for Jesus to teach (21:23; 26:55) as well as *still* a place to offer sacrifices (5:23–24; 8:4). One wonders why Matthew

[9] J. D. Kingsbury, *Matthew as Story* (2d edn; Philadelphia, Pa.: Fortress, 1988), p. 30, declares 'Jesus himself supplants the temple as the "place" where God mediates salvation to people'. See D. A. Carson, 'Matthew', in *The Expositors Bible Commentary* (ed. Frank Gaebelein; Grand Rapids, Mich.: Zondervan, 1984), p. 580; R. Thysman, *Communauté et directives éthiques: La catéchèse de Matthieu* (Gemblous: J. Duculot, 1974), p. 43, n. 1; H. L. Chronis, 'The Torn Veil: Cultus and Christology in Mark 15:37–39', *JBL* 101 (1982), 111; W. Carter, *Matthew: Storyteller, Interpreter, Evangelist* (Peabody, Mass.: Hendrickson, 1996), p. 221. Kessler, 'Through the Veil: The Holy Image in Judaism and Christianity', *Kairós* 32 (1990), 67, has argued that although Jews looked for a restoration of the temple, Christians held that the temple would be replaced by the Messiah as the old covenant was replaced by the new. Philo predicted that the 'temple and the offerings that supported it would endure for ever' (*Spec. Laws* 1.76; quoted from E. P. Sanders, *Judaism: Practice and Belief, 63 BCE – 66 CE* [London: SCM, Press, 1992], p. 52). M. Knowles, *Jeremiah in Matthew's Gospel: The Rejected-Prophet Motif in Matthean Redaction* (JSNTSup 68; Sheffield: JSOT Press, 1993), p. 175, contends that Jesus' 'ultimate intention in Matthew's Gospel was not simply to "cleanse" or restore the Temple to its proper use, but to replace it with something "greater than the temple"' (12:6; cf. 26:61; citing L. Goppelt, *Typos: Die typologische Deutung des Alten Testaments im Neuen: Anhang Apoklyptik und Typologie bei Paulus* [Darmstadt: Wissenschaftliche Buchgesellschaft, 1969], p. 76); Carter, pp. 220–22; P. Luomanen, *Entering the Kingdom of Heaven* (WUNT II, 101; Tübingen: Mohr Siebeck, 1998), p. 228.

[10] Alternatively, the healings enable those people to worship in the temple, from which the lame and blind were barred.

[11] J. P. Heil, *The Death and Resurrection: A Narrative-Critical Reading of Matthew 26–28* (Minneapolis, Minn.: Fortress, 1991), p. 85. So Josephus, *Ant.* 20.8.5 §166; cf. *J.W.* 5.1.3 §19.

later indicates Jesus' superiority to the temple (12:6) and declares that the 'house' will be left desolate (23:38). Does the parable of the wedding banquet (22:7) presume the temple's destruction? Answering these questions may lead us to a more comprehensive picture of Matthew's understanding of the temple. In light of Matthew's infamous 'anti-Jewish polemic', scholars frequently conjecture that he is likewise anti-temple. We will see, however, that the first evangelist has a remarkably consistent and positive portrayal of the temple. No negative word is uttered by either the evangelist or his Jesus about the temple *itself*. Indeed, Matthean redaction seems to stifle texts where Mark's Jesus could be understood as anti-temple, and Matthean negative statements about it, such as its impending (or past?) destruction, are centred on confrontations with the religious leaders who mismanage it. Destruction allusions and statements about the temple also resonate with language and theodicy found in Jeremiah, where God's displeasure with those managing the Solomonic temple finds expression in judgement executed against the temple itself.[12] Fault lies with *them* and, as in Jeremiah's time, the temple, so to speak, took the fall.

What is the compositional function of the temple? Does Matthew portray a reasonably consistent view of it? And, if so, what attitudes does he intend to evoke in his readers particularly regarding the temple's relationship to Jesus? Matthew's temple language is a helpful but limited place to begin an analysis of his view of the temple. It is, after all, his qualification of the καταπέτασμα with *τοῦ ναοῦ* that primarily calls for a study of his view of the temple. This evangelist, as is common in the New Testament, can use any of four terms for the temple: οἶκος, οἰκία, ἵερον or ναός. His use of οἶκος is rather straightforward (9 times). Naturally, it refers to a private home (9:6, 7), the 'house' of Israel (10:6; 15:24) and a king's 'palace' (11:8). In a parable it refers to a 'house' vacated by an evil spirit (12:44). In reference to the temple, οἶκος is used only in allusions to or citations from the Old Testament without necessarily any further intention than to connote the Semitic circumlocution of God from his Old Testament source.[13] Matthew uses οἰκία similarly (25 times). It is likewise used of a private home (2:11; 8:6, 14; 9:10, 23, 28; 10:12–14;

[12] B. W. Longenecker, 'Rome's Victory and God's Honour: The Jerusalem Temple and the Spirit of God in Lukan Theodicy', in *The Holy Spirit And Christian Origins: Essays In Honor of James D. G. Dunn* (ed. G. N. Stanton, B. W. Longenecker and S. C. Barton; Grand Rapids, Mich.: Eerdmans, 2004), p. 93, defines this as 'theodicy', in which 'God is said to have permitted disasters to fall on [his] people as a means of disciplining them, since [he] had grown dissatisfied with their infidelity as a covenant people'.

[13] 12:4 (1 Sam. 21:7). No temple term is used here in the LXX, only references to ἐκ προσώπου κυρίου (21:7) and ἐνώπιον κυρίου (21:8); 21:13 (Isa. 56:7; 60:7, using οἶκος); 23:38 for 'house' of Jerusalem' (Ps. 118:26, using οἶκος).

13:1, 36; 17:25; 19:29; 26:6) or a hometown (13:57). Οἰκία is also used in parables or illustrations, such as reference to a light shining to everyone in a house (5:15) or to a man building his house upon the stability of a rock (7:24–27), or to a 'household' divided among itself (12:25). Matthew also uses it in a similar context with reference to robbing a man's house (12:29) or not going onto the roof of one's house or taking things out of the house while awaiting the parousia (24:17; cf. 24:43). The possibility of οἰκία referring to the temple is only remotely present in the 'house upon a rock' analogy (7:24–27).

Τὸ ἱερόν typically refers to the general structure of a temple and its courts in extra-canonical texts.[14] Yet in the LXX it is almost exclusively reserved for pagan shrines (Ezek. 45:9; 1 Chron. 29:4; 2 Chron. 6:13), perhaps emphasising the particularity of Israel's sanctuary.[15] It is the extra-canonical use that seems to be more prevalent in the New Testament, where τὸ ἱερόν most frequently refers to the temple, generally (cf. Matt. 12:6; Acts 24:6; 1 Cor. 9:13), and Matthew seems to favour using the term for the general temple complex, including its courts and sanctuary (ναός). Jesus is placed upon the highest point of the temple (ἱερόν) when tempted by Satan (4:1–11), and its courts are the location of his confrontation with the priests on a Sabbath controversy (12:5). Jesus is said to be greater than the ἱερόν (12:6), and from there he drove out 'all who were buying and selling' (21:12). Here he also heals the blind and lame (12:14), and here he evokes the acclamation of the children who shouted, 'Hosanna to the Son of David' (21:15), an act about which the chief priests and teachers were indignant. He was teaching in the temple (ἱερόν) when the chief priests and elders challenged the origin of his 'authority' (τὴν ἐξουσίαν; 21:23). And only after leaving the temple (ἱερόν) and having his attention called to its buildings (24:1) does Jesus predict that every one of its stones will be thrown down (24:2). Finally, Jesus is arrested in Gethsemane even though he sat teaching in the temple (ἱερόν) daily (26:55). Within the temple (ἱερόν), Jesus was not to be touched, a point raised by Jesus himself at his arrest (26:55), which may indicate the generally positive relationship Matthew's Jesus has with the temple, as we will see.

Ναός in classical Greek was long known to refer to an 'abode of the gods' with respect to a temple[16] or the innermost shrine in which the deity dwells.[17] Though the LXX can use the term to translate אולם (also אילם;

[14] Herodotus, *Hist.* 1.183; 2.63; Polybius, *Fr.* 16.39.4; Josephus, *Ant.* 6.14.8 §374; *J.W.* 7.5.4 §123; 1 Macc. 10:84; 11:4.

[15] G. Schenk, 'τὸ ἱερόν', *TDNT* III, p. 235.

[16] See Michel, *TDNT* IV, p. 880.

[17] Herodotus, *Hist.* 1.183; 6.19; Xenophon, *Apol.* 15; *UPZ* 1.c; *PGnom.* 79; LSJ, *Lexicon*, p. 1160. See J. H. Moulton and G. Milligan, *Vocabulary of the Greek Testament* (Peabody,

'vestibule' or 'porch'),[18] it overwhelmingly translates היכל ('temple' or 'main room of a temple').[19] This refers to the temple, holy place and the holy of holies, within the precincts of the ἵερον. Dalman's claim that this distinction holds firm in the gospels seems likely.[20] The term ναός does not occur in Matthew's gospel until the 'woes' chapter (23), where Jesus rebukes 'blind guides' for their oaths 'by the temple' or 'the gold of the temple' (23:16). Yet Jesus affirms that it is the temple (ναός) that makes the gold 'sacred' (ὁ ἁγιάσας; 23:17). He further affirms that the importance of swearing by the temple is compounded by the presence of 'one who dwells in it' (ἐν τῷ κατοικοῦνι αὐτόν; 23:21). The curious event of the murder of Zechariah, son of Berekiah, occurred just outside the ναός: 'between the temple (ναός) and the altar' (23:35).[21] Testimonies, clearly said to be false, accuse Jesus of claiming he will destroy the temple (ναός; 26:61; 27:40), and Judas throws his money into the ναός prior to going away and hanging himself (27:5). Indeed, Matthew's temple language is helpful in discerning how he uses terms, but does not provide apparent indications of his view of the temple and its cult in general. For that we must cast our nets more broadly to examine how the evangelist portrays the temple generally both in his redactional use of temple language and pericopae and in his depiction of it and its cult in the narrative as a whole.

At the beginning of his gospel, Matthew shows no knowledge of Luke's introduction of the 'temple of the Lord' (1:9; τὸν ναὸν τοῦ κυρίου) in the extended scene of Zechariah's vision, through the infant Jesus' circumcision and presentation at the temple (Luke 2:21–38) and the scene

Mass.: Hendrickson, 1997), p. 422; repr. of *Vocabulary of the Greek Testament* (London: Hodder & Stoughton, 1930).

[18] 1 Chron. 28:11; 2 Chron. 8:12; 15:8; 29: 7, 17.

[19] W. L. Holladay, *A Concise Hebrew and Aramaic Lexicon of the Old Testament: Based upon the Lexical Work of Ludwig Koehler and Walter Baumgartner* (Leiden: Brill, 1988), p. 79. Cf. Lust, *Lexicon* II, p. 313. LXX 1 Sam. 1:9; 3:3 (A = οἴκῳ κυρίοὺ; 2 Sam. 22:7; 1 Kgs 6:3, 5, 17 (בית and A adds οἶκος), 33, 36; 7:21, 50 (A adds τοῦ οἴκου, בית); 2 Kgs 18:16; 23:4; 24:13; 2 Chron. 3:17; 4:7, 8, 22; 26:16; 27:2; 36:7; Ezra 5:14; 6:5; Pss 5:7; 10:5; 17:6; 26:4; 27:2; 28:9; 44:15; 64:4; 67:29; 78:1; 137:2; 143:12; Amos 8:3; Joel 3:5; Jonah 2:5, 8; Hab. 2:20; Hag. 2:16, 19; Zech. 8:9; Mal. 3:1; Isa. 66:6; Jer. 7:4; 24:1; Ezek. 8:16; 41:1, 4, 15, 21, 23, 25; Dan. 4:26; 5:2, 3. See Michel, *TDNT*, IV, p. 882, n. 6, 7.

[20] G. Dalman, *Orte und Wege Jesu* (3d edn; Gütersloh: C. Bertelsmann, 1924), p. 301. See Michel, *TDNT* IV, p. 882, n. 8.

[21] C. Deutsch, 'Wisdom in Matthew: Transformation of a Symbol', *NovT* 32 (1990), 43–44, contends that this pericope (23:35f) has Matthew's Jesus place himself among the tradition of rejected prophets, wise men and scribes from Israel's past, which was later transferred to Wisdom's history (see Wis. 7:27; 10:1–11:14; 1 Kgs 18:1–16; 2 Chron. 24:17–23; *Mart. Isa.* 5:1–16; *Liv. Pro.* 2:1; 3:18; 6:2; 7:1–3; D. E. Aune, *Prophecy in Early Christianity and the Ancient Mediterranean World* (Grand Rapids, Mich.: Eerdmans, 1983), pp. 158f.

there in Jesus' youth (Luke 2:41–52). Instead, Matthew's introduction to the temple itself (ἱερὸν) appears neither with a Zechariah episode nor with reference to a sacrifice (as in Mark), but in his 'temptation' narrative (4:1–11), where the devil (ὁ διάβολος) takes Jesus into the 'holy city' and places Jesus 'on the highest point of the temple' (ἐπὶ τὸ πτερύγιον τοῦ ἱεροῦ; 4:5), a feature absent from Mark and appearing a bit later in Luke (4:9). Matthew perhaps preserves the 'Q' reading: Jesus is 'taken' (παραλαμβάνει 4:5; 'Q' 4:9), whereas in Luke he is 'led' (4:9; ἤγαγεν) to the Holy City.[22] Also, in Matthew the devil 'stood him' (ἔστησεν αὐτὸν; so 'Q' 4:9) on the pinnacle of the temple; in Luke, Jesus stands himself (ἔστησεν) there. Since Matthew seems to be preserving his source, it is difficult to tell whether he is making a point. It may be that his preservation of the devil's standing Jesus begins to indicate Matthew's developing notion of authority confrontations that occur in the ἵερον.

Readers are given their first glimpse of the evangelist's view of the temple cult in 5:23–24, a text perhaps loosely related to Mark 11:25. Here the worshipper who brings his gift (προσφέρω + δῶρα 8:4; 2:11)[23] upon the altar (τὸ θυσιαστήριον, probably the altar of burnt offering in Jerusalem[24]) and is to be reconciled with his brother prior to offering it. That the gift is given[25] at all seems to presume the validity of this sacrifice. Yet Matthew's favour towards the cult is subservient to reconciliation, which must occur first (πρῶτον; 5:24) and then the gift is given (5:24). Though elsewhere no such injunction is proposed, it is apparent that here at least 'participation in the sacrificial system', far from being replaced or mooted, is 'presupposed'.[26]

Further indirect reference to the temple by virtue of its cult is found in Matt. 8:1–4 (Mark 1:40–45; Luke 5:12–16), which Matthew has removed from the Markan introductory material to place the reference immediately after the Sermon on the Mount and at the head of his section concerning miraculous healings and so forth (Matt. 8:1–9:34). In this scene Matthew takes Mark's account of the healing of a leper, which reads 'the leprosy

[22] Matthew seems to change his source ('Q' 4:9, Ἰερουσαλήμ to τὴν ἁγίαν πόλιν) for the name of the city, the significance of which we will re-visit later. Cf. J. M. Robinson, P. Hoffmann and J. S. Kloppenborg, *The Critical Edition of Q* (Hermeneia; Minneapolis, Minn.: Fortress, 2000), pp. 28–29.

[23] This is a favourite Matthean combination. See W. D. Davies and D. C. Allison, *A Critical and Exegetical Commentary on the Gospel according to Saint Matthew* (3 vols.; ICC; Edinburgh: T. & T. Clark, 1988, 1991, 1997), I, pp. 248, 517.

[24] Davies and Allison, *Matthew* I, p. 517.

[25] Davies and Allison (*Matthew* I, p. 517) suggest that it is understood to be given to the priest.

[26] *Ibid.*, p. 518.

left him and he was cleansed' (Mark 1:42; ἀπῆλθεν ἀπ' αὐτοῦ ἡ λέπρα, καὶ ἐκαθαρίσθη), and simply asserts that the man was 'cleansed of his leprosy' (ἐκαθαρίσθη αὐτοῦ ἡ λέπρα). Immediately (καὶ εὐθέως)[27] Jesus tells the man to tell no one of his healing but to go to the high priest (omitting Mark's 'concerning your cleansing', Mark 1:44, also Luke 5:14). As in 5:24, Matthew alone records that the man is to offer a 'gift' (8:4; τὸ δῶρον) *after* the cleansing, again presuming the legitimacy of offering the appropriate sacrifice. Although Mark (1:44–45) and Luke (5:15–16) know more to the story, Matthew ends it rather abruptly here, perhaps content to finish his narrative with Jesus insisting on the man's offering the gift that Moses commanded,[28] as a testimony to 'them'. The 'testimony to them' (εἰς μαρτύριον αὐτοῖς) is difficult, though it was a 'fixed expression' in the LXX[29] for covenant faithfulness. While some take it to function negatively *against* the priesthood,[30] Luz's insistence that it be taken positively, to affirm that 'As Israel's Messiah Jesus keeps the Torah', seems to be most cogent to Matthew's concern for legal matters (cf. 5:17–19).[31] Yet this is not just any legal matter, but a *cultic* legal matter, which the evangelist seems to indicate Jesus is concerned to observe. Luz's observation is still quite important, for it suggests that the legal matters that Matthew's Jesus is uniquely concerned not to abolish but fulfil extends to those that pertain to the temple.[32] This point will be important when we bring together our reading of Matthew's temple and his portrayal of the death of Jesus.

Another problem with this text is that although the antecedent of αὐτοῖς is not specified, the person in the immediate context and most naturally understood to be in view is the *singular* priest (τῷ ἱερεῖ; cf. Jer. 13:2–3), presumably the priest on duty at the time. Perhaps, though, Matthew is using the singular term for a priest to represent the collective body of priests. If this is so, why does Matthew, of all the evangelists, concern himself with Jesus' displaying his obedience to the Torah *to the priests*? Similarly, some have understood there to be an implicit need

[27] Here Matthew is uncharacteristically preserving this from Mark. U. Luz, *Matthew 8–20* (Hermeneia: Minneapolis, Minn.: Fortress, 2001), p. 6.

[28] Luz, p. 6.

[29] Gen. 31:44; Deut. 31:26; Josh. 24:27; Job 29:14; Hos. 2:12; Amos 1:11; Micah 1:2; 7:18; Zeph. 3:8; cf. Jas. 5:3; Ignatius, *Trall.* 12.3; *Barn.* 9:3; Davies and Allison, *Matthew* II, p. 16 n. 23. For a discussion of the different ways to understand this statement, cf. Davies and Allison, *Matthew* II, p. 16.

[30] Cf. Davies and Allison, *Matthew* II, p. 16; Luz, p. 6, n. 17.

[31] Luz, p. 6.

[32] R. Bauckham, 'Jesus' Demonstration in the Temple', in *Law and Religion: Essays on the Place of the Law in Israel and Early Christianity* (ed. B. Lindars; Cambridge: James Clarke, 1988), p. 73.

to be pronounced clean by the priest, to fulfil a cultic requirement and provide a 'witness' or 'testimony'.[33] Elsewhere Matthew's Jesus is concerned to pay the temple tax so as to not *cause offence* to the priests (17:27). Later he will even affirm that people are to 'do and obey' (ὅσα ἐὰν εἴπωσιν ὑμῖν ποιήσατε καὶ τηρεῖτε) what the scribes and Pharisees say because they sit on 'Moses' seat' (whatever that refers to), but they are *not* to do what the scribes and Pharisees do (κατὰ δὲ τὰ ἔργα αὐτῶν μὴ ποιεῖτε; 23:3). The concern seems to be that, although Jesus explicitly chastises the teachings of those in this office (cf. 9:10–11, 14; 12:1–2, 10–14; 15:1–20; 19:3–9), Matthew's concern is to affirm Jesus' 'loyalty to the righteousness of Torah'.[34] Although it seems out of character for *Matthew* to be concerned about 'testimony', 'offense' or 'obedience' to the Jewish religious leaders, it is essential to recognise that Matthew may condemn their *hypocrisy*, but he affirms the *teaching of Torah*, executed by those sitting on Moses' seat. While surely this is indicative of Matthew's concern that Jesus 'fulfils' the law (5:17), the cultic implications are important. For as Matthew has previously assumed the legitimacy of sacrifices offered (5:23–24; 8:4), he also seems to affirm the validity Torah. Indeed it is only because of their position on 'Moses' seat' that Matthew's Jesus is so deeply scornful of the behaviour of those who presently occupy them.[35] If their posts were not legitimate, Jesus could presumably simply say so and resolve the matter there. Instead, he *affirms their offices* with respect to the Law, but condemns their execution of their roles.

It seems curious that although Matthew affirms the validity of the priesthood and sacrifices, he elsewhere asserts that God desires 'mercy and not sacrifice' (ἔλεος θέλω καὶ οὐ θυσίαν; 9:13; also 12:7; cf. Hos. 6:6). The first citation is a direct response by Jesus to criticisms by the Pharisees that Jesus is eating with 'tax collectors and sinners' (τῶν τελωνῶν καὶ ἁμαρτωλῶν; 9:11). This citation is unique to Matthew among the synoptics (Mark 2:17 reads οὐκ ἦλθον καλέσαι δικαίους ἀλλὰ ἁμαρτωλούς) and matches precisely with Aquila's version of the LXX of Hos. 6:6.[36] It is largely accepted that Matthew's καὶ οὐ is not a starkly contrastive assertion but a Hebraic idiom of 'dialectical negation' meaning 'I desire mercy

[33] Davies and Allison, *Matthew* II, p. 15. [34] Hagner, *Matthew* II, p. 659.

[35] These affirmations of priestly offices are overlooked by Olmstead (*Trilogy*) in his narrative characterisation of the Jewish leaders. Moreover, he overlooks statements affirming temple sacrifices (5:23–24; 8:4) and positive statements about the temple itself. Cf. D. M. Gurtner, Review of W. G. Olmstead, *Matthew's Trilogy of Parables: The Nation, the Nations and the Reader in Matthew 21.28–22.14*, *Them.* 30 (2004), 63–64.

[36] Davies and Allison, *Matthew* II, p. 104.

*more* than sacrifice'.[37] Luz further asserts that this understanding 'was clearly the understanding of Hosea himself, the Targum, and contemporary Jewish exegesis. It also best fits the thought of Matthew himself, who did not abolish the cultic law but made it inferior to the love command (5:18–19; 5:23–24; 23:23–28)'.[38] The affirmation of this reading of the Hosea citation is seen in 12:7 in a Sabbath controversy. Here Matthew, again in a text unique to his gospel, quotes the Hosea text immediately following his declaration that Jesus was greater than the temple (12:6).[39] In this reference Matthew provides the same meaning in a differing context. Indeed, that Matthew's Jesus did not intend to abolish the sacrificial laws is affirmed by his argument based upon them in the immediate context (12:5–6).[40] He thus makes the same point that 'unless informed by a spirit of mercy, observance of the Torah can become uninformed slavery to the traditions of men'.[41]

These are the only explicit references to sacrifices in Matthew (though perhaps implicit in Matt. 8). However, in Mark (1:44; Luke 5:14; cf. Luke 2:24), the healed leper is commanded to offer sacrifices for his cleansing, and loving God and one's neighbour is 'more important than all burnt offerings and sacrifices' (12:33). That this is omitted by Matthew may indicate that he viewed the statement as potentially nullifying the sacrifices that he has elsewhere affirmed. Though, for Matthew, God desires mercy *more than* sacrifices (just as Jesus is *more than* [greater than] the temple), he nonetheless affirms the validity of the sacrifice being offered.

The temple and its cult are discussed in several key texts in Matthew 12. In 12:4 Matthew recounts a Sabbath controversy, asserting that the disciples are innocent of any wrongdoing for picking grain on the Sabbath just as David was innocent when he 'entered the house of God and ate the consecrated bread' (εἰσῆλθεν εἰς τὸν οἶκον τοῦ θεοῦ; 1 Sam. 21:1).[42] How could David, who was not a priest, enter the 'house of God' to get the bread from the holy place?[43] The full story reveals that David was

[37] Luz, p. 34. G. Strecker, *Der Weg der Gerechtigkeit: Untersuchung zur Theologie des Matthäus* (Göttingen: Vandenhoeck & Ruprecht, 1962), p. 32; J. P. Meier, *Matthew* (NTM 3; Wilmington, Del.: Michael Glazier, 1981), p. 94.

[38] Luz, p. 34; Davies and Allison, *Matthew* II, pp. 104–105.

[39] Presumably in both cases, 'sacrifice' stands for mere obedience to Torah requirements of outward action.

[40] Luz, p. 182.

[41] Davies and Allison, *Matthew* II, p. 105; cf. D. J. Moo, 'Jesus and the Mosaic Law', *JSNT* 20 (1984), 10.

[42] Matthew omits, as does Luke, Mark's 'in the days of Abiathar the priest' (Mark 2:26).

[43] There is general agreement that David ate of the 'bread of the Presence', which consisted of twelve loaves arranged in two rows upon the table in the holy place. Exod. 25:23–30; 40:22–3; Lev. 24:5–9; Num. 4:1–8; 1 Sam. 21:4–6; 1 Chron. 9:42; Davies and Allison, *Matthew* II, p. 309, n. 25.

not violating the sacred space, in that he himself did not enter the holy place to get the bread, but the bread was brought to him by the priest (1 Sam. 21:6). Moreover, David is explicitly said to have met the cultic cleanliness requirements to eat of the bread (1 Sam. 21:5).[44] Although the disciples faced no such dire situation, Jesus nonetheless absolves them from guilt apparently by concerning himself with 'the weightiest matters of the Law'.[45] The subject is not the temple, but the Sabbath.

More explicit discussion of the temple is found in 12:5–6, unique to Matthew, where Jesus demonstrates his lordship over the Sabbath (12:1–14). This text is an insertion into the Markan pericope (Mark 2:23–28) concerning the action of David in the temple and asserting that 'the priests in the temple desecrate the day [Sabbath] and yet are innocent' (12:5). Jesus then asserts that 'one greater than the temple is here' (τοῦ ἱεροῦ μεῖζόν ἐστιν ὧδε; 12:6). While the identity of the 'one greater' than the temple (ἱερόν; 12:6) has been disputed, surely the saying is associated with Jesus himself, and what is greater (μεῖζόν) than the temple is likely Jesus.[46] Mark's 'greater than' statements have nothing to do with the temple.[47] Yet though Matthew adopts Mark's use of the 'greater than' formula elsewhere,[48] he uses it with respect to the temple three times: here Jesus is greater than the temple, later the temple is greater than its gold (23:17) and finally the altar is greater than the gift given on it (23:19). With respect to Jesus, Matthew affirms that he is greater than the temple (12:6), than Jonah (πλεῖον, 12:41) and than Solomon (πλεῖον, 12:42).[49] Matthew seems to have perhaps adapted Mark's and 'Q's' (or perhaps extending a 'Q' pattern) 'greater than' statements to elevate first Jesus (12:6, 41, 42 ['Q' 11:31, 32])[50] and then the temple (23:17, 19).

[44] Luz (p. 181) indicates that rabbis likewise were quick to absolve David from guilt by citing that hunger has precedence over Sabbath observance. Cf. *b. Menaḥ*. 95b/96a; Str-B I, pp. 618–19; Davies and Allison, *Matthew* II, p. 308.

[45] B. Gerhardsson, *The Gospel Tradition* (ConBNT 15; Lund: Gleerup, 1986), p. 26; Davies and Allison, *Matthew* II, p. 308.

[46] R. H. Gundry, *Matthew: A Commentary on His Handbook for a Mixed Church under Persecution* (Grand Rapids, Mich.: Eerdmans, 1994), p. 223; so also Davies and Allison, *Matthew* II, p. 314. France (p. 215) claims that this text is a means by which 'Matthew has prepared the way for this focus even before Jesus' actual arrival in Jerusalem in chapter 21'. Cf. D. C. Kupp, *Matthew's Emmanuel: Divine Presence and God's People in the First Gospel* (SNTSMS 90; Cambridge: Cambridge University Press, 1996), pp. 75–76.

[47] They are simply made with respect to the mustard plant (4:32), the priority of the disciples (9:34), the greatest commandment (12:31) and the significance of a poor widow's offering (12:43).

[48] He uses it with respect to the mustard seed (Matt. 13:32) and the disciples (18:1, 4; 23:11; see 11:1). See Cope, *Scribe*, p. 35.

[49] Matthew also uses 'greater' expressions in the escalated shouts of Hosanna (Matt. 20:31), the greater righteousness Jesus demanded (πλεῖον, 5:20) and to underscore the importance of non-material things (6:25; cf. 20:10). Cf. Cope, *Scribe*, p. 43.

[50] Cf. Robinson *et al.*, pp. 252–55.

Yet the first of these uses (12:6) puts things in perspective: the former (Jesus) is greater than the latter (the temple).[51] It seems that Matthew, in his affirmation of the temple and its cult elsewhere, is careful in these statements to put it in its place with respect to Jesus. It is a valid place to offer sacrifices and (later) to pray, but ultimately it is secondary (as a means of a relationship with God) to Jesus.

Mark's Sabbath healings (2:23–3:6), other than mentioning priests in the house of God, have nothing to do with the temple. Yet for Matthew, immediately after Jesus' teaching on his superiority to the temple and thus his innocence of Sabbath violation, Jesus goes out to a synagogue and heals a man with a shrivelled hand (12:9–14). Whether by retaining Mark's juxtaposition of these two accounts, as he did, Matthew intended to provide the unfortunate man with the means by which he may then go and participate in temple worship (Gerhardsson) is a complicated question, for Matthew presumably preserves Mark's setting of the event in the Capernaum synagogue (Mark 2:1; 3:1; Matt. 12:9). How the man then gets to temple worship is curious, unless Mark extends his view of the temple to the synagogue. Later we will see that Jesus actually performs a similar healing within the temple precincts, which may further connect Jesus' healing ministry with that of the temple.[52] In light of Jesus' directives to offer sacrifices in 5:23–24 and 8:4, it is possible that Matthew is presuming that his readers will recognise that what Jesus is doing in the temple is cleansing these people so that they are then free and able to participate in sacrificial worship right there at the temple. Notice that neither the temple nor its services are portrayed in a negative light.[53] Instead, as Gerhardsson contends and we have already seen, Matthew has simply looked to put the temple in its proper perspective with respect to Jesus.[54]

Some have suggested a temple allusion in 16:18, where Peter is called the 'rock'. This argument reads Matthew's 'my church' statement in light

[51] See R. Beaton, *Isaiah's Christ in Matthew's Gospel* (SNTSMS 123; Cambridge: Cambridge University Press, 2002), p. 184.

[52] A 'temple Christology' is more properly found in John. Cf. note.

[53] One would question whether indeed God's presence was to have left the temple at the death of Jesus. Surely the apostles in Acts recognise the legitimacy of temple worship even *after* this event, presumably affirming that God's presence is still there. See A. Pelletier, 'La tradition synoptique du "Voile déchiré" à la lumière des réalités archéologiques', *Recherches de science religieuse*', 46 (1958), 173; Cf. D. C. Sim, 'Matthew's Anti-Paulism: A Neglected Feature of Matthean Studies', *HvTSt* 58 (2002), 767–83; J. Becker, 'Die Zerstörung Jerusalems bei Matthäus und den Rabbinen', *NTS* 44 (1998), 59–73, 71.

[54] B. Gerhardsson, 'Sacrificial Service and Atonement in the Gospel of Matthew', in *Reconciliation and Hope: New Testament Essays on Atonement and Eschatology Presented to L. L. Morris on His 60th Birthday* (ed. R. Banks; Exeter: Paternoster Press, 1974), p. 31.

of 2 Sam. 7 and presumes the church to constitute a new temple, noting that 'in Jewish tradition the rock at the base of the temple on Zion, the so-called *'eben šĕtîyyâ*, is at the centre of the world'.[55] While this is congruent with other groups in Judaism and early Christianity conceiving of people as a temple,[56] Matthew does not here make a clear transition from identifying the temple as a legitimate cultic enterprise in itself to identifying it as a group of people.[57] A stronger argument could be in the evangelist's use of οἰκοδομέω with respect to the church, a term that is used elsewhere with respect to accusations against Jesus in both 26:61 (from Mark 14:58) and 27:40 (from Mark 15:29), regarding his apparent threat to tear down the temple (ναός) and raise it up (οἰκοδομέω).[58] From Mark 14:58, Davies and Allison contend that the reference here to a ναός 'not made with hands' is to the church.[59] Yet the Markan account bears no more evidence of an ecclesiastical reading than does Matthew's. Moreover, they argue that the Davidic motifs in Matt. 16:13–20 suggest that 2 Sam. 7 and 1 Chron. 17 are in view, which evokes a temple imagery.[60] Yet even if such contexts were in view, it does not necessarily follow that the temple images present in the Old Testament texts are brought to the Matthean pericope, let alone that they apply to the newly formed church. We cannot say for certain that Matthew identified his church with the temple.[61]

Matthew again alludes to the temple in the account of the temple tax (17:24–29), which is entirely unique to his gospel. In this scene, Jesus declares his exemption from the temple tax but nonetheless pays his and Peter's taxes by invoking a miraculous provision of the funds from the mouth of a fish (17:27). He pays it not out of obligation, but 'so that we may not offend them' (17:27). Davies and Allison, following

[55] Davies and Allison, *Matthew* III, pp. 627–28.

[56] See *ibid.*, III, p. 627, n. 86; B. Gärtner, *The Temple and the Community in Qumran and the New Testament: A Comparative Study in the Temple Symbolism of Qumran Texts and the New Testament* (Cambridge: Cambridge University Press, 1965).

[57] Davies and Allison, *Matthew* III, p. 627, claim that an allusion to 2 Sam. 7 'evokes the idea of a temple', which seems a rather weak basis to claim that the people *are* the temple. They also say that the notion of the church being the temple is here 'implicit'.

[58] Davies and Allison, *Matthew* III, p. 627.

[59] *Ibid.* III, p. 627; cf. n. 89; III, p. 335, n. 54; D. Juel, *Messiah and Temple: The Trial of Jesus in the Gospel of Mark* (SBLDS 31; Missoula, Mont.: Scholars Press, 1977), pp. 144–57.

[60] Davies and Allison, *Matthew* II, p. 603.

[61] J. P. Heil, 'The Narrative Strategy and Pragmatics of the Temple Theme in Mark', *CBQ* 59 (1997), 76–100, furnishes a promising, but ultimately disappointing, narrative pragmatic analysis of the 'Temple Theme in Mark'. In it, he presumes that the church replaces the temple and examines how the church is to function in light of the ways the temple failed. Ultimately, however, his presumption that the church supplants the temple cannot be substantiated, at least with much clarity, in Matthew as it is in Mark.

Bauckham,[62] comment that here Matthew affirms the temple cult but questions 'the idea that taxation is the appropriate means of maintaining that divine institution'.[63] This verdict is underscored by the conclusion that Jesus gives Peter instructions to pay the tax (17:27). Yet why is Matthew here concerned that his Jesus not offend people, when only a few chapters later such concerns are by no means obvious? Luz suggests the concern is to 'compromise for the sake of peace and love' on matters that are not fundamental to faithfulness to the Torah.[64] Davies and Allison, however, capture more of Matthew's view of the temple when they assert that 'voluntary payment should be made in order to prevent others from inferring that Peter or Jesus has rejected the temple cult'.[65]

The temple itself (τὸ ἱερὸν)[66] first appears in Mark's gospel in 11:11, a pivotal point in this gospel to introduce the second evangelist's Passion Narrative.[67] In this climactic scene in Matthew's gospel (21:1–27), Jesus enters Jerusalem (21:1–11) and the temple (ἱερόν; 21:12), where he performs his notorious 'cleansing'. Carter, to name but one scholar, insists that Jesus' actions here demonstrate the completion of the necessity of the temple's sacrificial system, and that Jesus now replaces the temple and is the location where 'God's presence and atonement were experienced'.[68] Yet this contention seems to violate the plain sense of the pericope. For, as Bauckham contends, by his insistence on the temple's being a house of prayer, accompanied by his actions, Jesus is not rejecting or downplaying the sacrificial cult.[69] Instead he looks for it to be 'the expression of the prayer of those who came to the temple to worship'. That Matthew's Jesus asserts that the temple 'will be called' (κληθήσεται) a house of prayer (a reading found in neither the Isa. 56:7 nor Isa. 60:7 texts, to which he alludes) seems to affirm the legitimacy of its function and a desire on the part of Matthew to see that function restored: that is, it has a future.[70] Although κληθήσεται may be simply a 'prophetic' future and

[62] R. Bauckham, 'The Coin in the Fish's Mouth', in *Gospel Perspectives 6: The Miracles of Jesus* (ed. D. Wenham and C. Blomberg; Sheffield: JSOT Press, 1986), pp. 219–52.

[63] Davies and Allison, *Matthew* II, p. 745. [64] Luz, p. 418.

[65] Davies and Allison, *Matthew* II, p. 746.

[66] Cf. Longenecker, 'Rome's Victory and God's Honour', p. 95.

[67] M. Kähler, *The So-Called Historical Jesus and the Historic Biblical Christ* (Philadelphia, Pa.: Fortress Press, 1964), p. 80 n. 11, has suggested that the gospels could be called 'passion narratives with extended introductions'.

[68] Carter, p. 221.

[69] While Bauckham's analysis seems to attend more to issues relating to the historical Jesus, his conclusions are congruent with the theological interests of the First Evangelist.

[70] Although it is possible to see this reference as being to the future of the church (see Gundry, p. 413), again we find no clear evidence that the church is equated with, let alone supplanting, the temple in Matthew's gospel.

may not indicate a future in this sense in the Matthean context, surely the contrastive element (21:13; ὑμεῖς δὲ αὐτὸν ποιεῖτε σπήλαιον λῃστῶν) serves to underscore the culpability of the temple management. That is, the intended function of the temple was being frustrated by corruption and exploitation within the temple precincts,[71] and Jesus, as messianic king, comes to the temple 'to purge it of practices that mocked its divinely intended purpose'.[72]

Immediately upon entering Jerusalem (21:12–13), Matthew has Jesus entering the temple (ἱερόν; 21:12), whereas Mark claims that Jesus entered the next day (11:12). Although such urgency is typically associated with Mark (his καὶ εὐθύς statements), Matthew is particularly concerned with Jesus' location in the temple.[73] After he entered the temple, the 'blind and lame' (τυφλοὶ καὶ χωλοὶ) came to Jesus and he healed them *there* (ἱερόν; 21:14),[74] presumably in the outer courts, where they were permitted, and where Jesus also found the merchants and tax collectors (21:12). However, each of Mark's healings of the blind occurs not only outside the temple, but outside the city.[75] Matthew knows that the 'blind and lame' (τυφλοὶ καὶ χωλοὶ) were to keep their distance from the house of the Lord.[76] Why does Matthew seem to clearly diverge, partly by means of relocation, from Mark's account? Moreover, why does he bring the unfortunate people within the temple's outer courts? The reader may be intended to recall Jesus' claim to superiority over the temple, but Gerhardsson has offered a more tenable solution.[77] He proposes that Matthew's Jesus is not violating the Law by acknowledging these outcasts in the temple but by upholding it. Jesus does this by removing the quality that forbade them entrance in the first place: he heals their disabilities 'so that they may then

[71] Bauckham, 'Jesus' Demonstration in the Temple', p. 84.

[72] Hagner, *Matthew* II, p. 598. Moreover, as Hagner argues, 'Matthew's juxtaposition of this pericope with the triumphal entry of Jesus into the city has the effect of emphasizing the identity of the one who now enters the temple: it is the messianic king, the Son of David' (*Matthew* II, p. 600). See Beaton, p. 183.

[73] See R. T. France, 'Chronological Aspects of "Gospel Harmony"', *VE* 16 (1986), 38.

[74] He has seen them before in Matthew and healed them (15:30), apparently in ironic contrast to the 'blind' Pharisees who refuse to be healed and whom Jesus commands his disciples to leave (15:14). See Knowles, pp. 234–35, who associates this text with the Davidic Messiahship of Jesus.

[75] Mark 8:22–23; 10:46, 49, 51.

[76] And so Matthew presumably means that they were in the court around the temple (the 'court of gentiles'). According to 2 Sam. 5:8, the blind and lame are forbidden to enter εἰς οἶκον κυρίου. Cf. Lev. 21:18–19; 1Q28[a] ii 5–22; CD xv 15–17; *m. Ḥag.* 1:1; 1QM vii 4–6; xii 7–9. See Strecker, p. 19, n. 1.

[77] Hagner (*Matthew* II, p. 601) seems to suggest that this is an ironic narrative device intended to show the kingdom blessings which transformed the temple precincts 'from a commercial center to a place of healing'.

enter'.[78] So it seems possible that Matthew is presuming that the healed person is then permitted to go offer the sacrifice after he is healed, as Jesus encourages the leper to do. Sacrifices, on at least one occasion in Matthew, followed healings (cf. 8:4). Surely Matthew in this pericope is concerned that Jesus restore the temple to its intended function by making it a 'house of prayer',[79] and this pericope seems best understood in that light, to prepare the unfortunate man to participate in its worship by healing him.[80]

The temple setting is important, for though Matthew (21:9), Mark (11:9–10) and John (12:13) all record Jesus' 'triumphal entry', only the First Evangelist explicitly states that the children's praises of 'Hosanna', apparently in response to Jesus' healing, likewise occurred *in the temple* (ἱερόν, 21:15).[81] Davies and Allison suggest the locus is a portent, and that a temple, as the locus of special revelations, joined with a (frequently oracular) acclaim of children, forcefully confirms 'God's approval of Jesus'.[82] From here, Jesus departs from the temple to spend the night in Bethany (21:17; Mark 11:11), only to return 'early in the morning' (πρωΐ), whereas Mark has 'on the next day' (τῇ ἐπαύριον; 11:12).[83] The Markan Jesus' departure from the temple (cf. 11:28–30)[84] has been seen as contributing to his Wisdom Christology, whereby Jesus is depicted as the personification of Wisdom, who departs in judgement because one is unwilling to heed the wisdom conveyed.[85] Apparently Matthew's adjustment intends to lend narrative continuity with the previous pericope,

[78] See B. Gerhardsson, *The Mighty Acts of Jesus according to Matthew* (Lund: Gleerup, 1979), p. 30, cf. n. 16; see especially Gerhardsson's contribution in C. H. Martling and S. E. Staxäng, eds., *Kommentar till evangelieboken, Högmässotexterna* (Part 3; Stockholm: Uppsala, 1964), pp. 484–486.

[79] See Davies and Allison, *Matthew* III, p. 132.

[80] Beaton (pp. 183–85) asserts that particularly during Hezekiah's restoration of the temple (2 Chron. 29:3–7) the 'cleansing of temple and healings therein point to motifs of purification and wholeness'. See 'Son of David' in *Pss. Sol.* 17:30; Davies and Allison, *Matthew* III, p. 139.

[81] D. Daube, *The New Testament and Rabbinic Judaism* (London: Athlone Press, 1956), pp. 20–21, notes that traditionally rabbis thought this Psalm (118) would be recited upon the appearance of the Messiah. See Knowles, pp. 234–5, n. 4. Here we also see a polemic against the Jewish leaders: *they* were indignant, while the *children* shouted praise.

[82] Davies and Allison, *Matthew* III, p. 141.

[83] It is possible here to recognise Matthew's identity of Jesus with Wisdom, as he does more explicitly in 11:19, 25–30. See Deutsch, 'Wisdom in Matthew', pp. 33–39.

[84] See M. J. Suggs, *Wisdom, Christology, and Law in Matthew's Gospel* (Cambridge, Mass.: Harvard University Press, 1970), pp. 77–98.

[85] For a discussion of Wisdom in Matt. 11:25–30, see C. Deutsch, *Hidden Wisdom and the Easy Yoke; Wisdom, Torah and Discipleship in Mt11, 25–30* (JSNTSup 18; Sheffield: Academic Press, 1987); T. Arvedson, *Das Mysterium Christi: eine Studie zu Mt. 11.25–30* (Leipzig: Alfred Lorentz, 1937); H. D. Betz, 'The Logion of the Easy Yoke and of Rest (Mt. 11:28–30)', *JBL* 86 (1967), 10–24. For Wisdom in Matt. 23:34–36, 37–39, see F. Burnett,

though typically such urgency depicted by action is expected in Mark. Along the way Jesus causes the fig tree to wither explicitly to demonstrate the power of faith (21:21–22).[86] This subject has been discussed in some detail by W. R. Telford, whose *Redaction-Critical Analysis of the Cursing of the Fig-Tree Pericope in Mark's Gospel and Its Relation to the Cleansing of the Temple Tradition* has much to say about Matthean redaction of the account.[87] Telford's work, though somewhat dated, is an excellent starting point of decisive importance for the present discussion. For he demonstrates that Matthean redaction of the Markan pericope lays emphasis on the power of Jesus and resulting faith,[88] as is common in Matthean redaction of Markan miracles,[89] rather than associating the miracle of the cursed fig tree with the temple. France asserts that in his pericope Matthew has 'subordinated strict chronology to a more dramatic presentation of the incident in order to draw out more powerfully what he understands to be its theological implication'.[90] Matthew has removed 'practically all' elements from Mark that suggest the account was primarily symbolic.[91] Moreover, with 'Jesus' miracles of healing in the Temple (21.4), the cursing of the fig-tree no longer stands out as it does in Mark as the *only* miracle performed by Jesus in Jerusalem . . . The story has been removed from the sphere of judgment and eschatology, and is treated as if it were a normal miracle story'.[92] Thus the saying regarding the throwing of the mountain into the sea (Mark 11:23; Matt. 21:21) is no longer suggestive of the Temple Mount, as it is in Mark.[93] We find, then,

*The Testament of Jesus-Sophia; a Redaction Critical Study of the Eschatological Discourse in Matthew* (Washington, D.C.: University Press of America, 1979).

[86] In Mark's account (11:20–26) it was a statement against faithless Israel. Gerhardsson (*Mighty Acts*, p. 59) sees the withering in such a way, emphasising here an 'ecclesiastical interpretation' applicable to Jesus' *followers* over against a *Christological* reading that moves Jesus himself to the fore. Cf. D. Duling, 'The Therapeutic Son of David: An Element of Matthew's Christological Apologetic', *NTS* 24 (1978), 393.

[87] This is the lengthy subtitle of the work, the full title of which is *The Barren Temple and the Withered Tree: A Redaction-Critical Analysis of the Cursing of the Fig-Tree Pericope in Mark's Gospel and Its Relation to the Cleansing of the Temple Tradition* (JSNTSup 1; Sheffield: JSOT, 1980).

[88] See Telford, *Barren Temple*, p. 81. [89] *Ibid.*

[90] France, 'Chronological Aspects', p. 38.

[91] Telford (*Barren Temple*, p. 81) notes that Matthew has removed or altered Mark's account with respect to 'Jesus' survey of the Temple (11:1), his disappointed search for fruit, the show of leaves, the curious "for it was not the season for figs", the delay in the effect of the curse . . . The strange position of the story before and after the cleansing episode has been altered . . . The position of the story in Mt. 21, while derivative of Mark, appears logically unrelated to the surrounding material, despite Matthew's attempt to provide closer contextual links'.

[92] Telford, *Barren Temple*, p. 80.

[93] *Ibid.*, p. 79. Cf. Davies and Allison, *Matthew* III, pp. 152–53. Many have seen mountain references in Matthew's gospel as alluding to Sinai rather than the 'Temple Mount'. Yet

that Matthew, while clearly escalating Mark's polemic against the Jewish leaders, softens his polemic against the temple.

Immediately after this event Jesus once again enters the temple courts (ἱερόν; 21:23), an account found likewise in Mark (11:27) and Luke (20:1). Yet whereas Mark says that again Jesus went into Jerusalem and entered the temple, and Luke casually mentions Jesus' being in the temple teaching the people, Matthew's account may emphasise the temple (ἱερόν) by placing it earlier in the sentence than it appears in the other Synoptic accounts and making it the first noun in that sentence. A conflict arises *here*, of all places, with the chief priests and elders of the people regarding Jesus' 'authority' (ἐξουσίᾳ) to do 'these things' (ταῦτα)[94] – both by what authority he does these things and who gave him such authority.[95] Thus Matthew seems to provide a wording that emphasises that the conflict here concerns authority, with the context of Jesus' priestly critics, a theme we have found consistently throughout.

Another possible allusion to the temple is found in 21:33–46.[96] This, the 'parable of the Wicked Tenants', seems to be a thinly veiled illustration of the Jews' rejection of Jesus. Scholars have recognised that v. 33b is clearly dependent upon the LXX of Isa. 5:2, and that in the *Targum* of that text (*Tg.* Isa 5:1b–2, 5) the tower becomes the temple, and the wine vat the altar (cf. *t. Suk.* 3:15; *t. Me'il.* 1:16), and 'the song as a whole has become a prediction of the temple's destruction'.[97] Here Jesus responds to the self-condemning words of his listeners (21:41) by citing Ps. 118:22.

some would see Sinai itself as a temple. See G. K. Beale, *The Bible and the Church's Mission: A Biblical Theology of the Temple* (NSBT; Downers Grove, Ill.: InterVarsity, 2004), pp. 105–7.

[94] Hagner (*Matthew* II, p. 609) says it refers to the events of the preceding day, while Davies and Allison (*Matthew* III, p. 159) presume it to include everything in chapter 21 (save the withering of the fig tree). Cf. J. T. Carroll and J. B. Green, *The Death of Jesus in Early Christianity* (Peabody, Mass.: Hendrickson, 1995), p. 54.

[95] See Beaton (p. 185), who contends that the 'healings in Matthew appear to be linked to a broader concern for justice and the renewal/reconstitution of the people of God. Central to this theme is Jesus' role as ideal Davidic King/leader/messianic ruler, which Matthew articulates throughout the narrative'.

[96] Other than 21:33b, Matthew's set of three parables featuring a departure and return (21:28–22:14) provide no indication that the temple is involved. Instead, it is traditionally understood as a polemic against the Jewish leaders or, recently, all of Israel. Cf. Olmstead, *Trilogy*; R. J. Bauckham, 'Synoptic Parousia Parables Again', *NTS* 29 (1983), 129–134.

[97] Olmstead, *Trilogy*, p. 110; cf. pp. 113–16; 116 n. 95. Although there is some discussion about the dating of the Isaiah Targum, C. Evans and G. Brooke have found similar tower/temple allusions in *1 En.* 89 (cf. *1 En.* 89:3, 56, 66b–67; *Barn.* 16.1–2, 4, 5) and 4Q500 respectively, both of which predate the New Testament (cf. Olmstead, *Trilogy*, pp. 110–11 and nn. 67–69, citing C. A. Evans, 'God's Vineyard Parables of Isaiah 5 and Mark 12', *BZ* 28 [1984], 82–85; B. Chilton, *A Galilean Rabbi and His Bible: Jesus' Own Interpretation of Isaiah* [London: SPCK, 1984], pp. 111–14; *idem*, 'God's Vineyard and Its Caretakers', in *Jesus and His Contemporaries* [Leiden: Brill, 1995], 401; G. J. Brooke, '4Q500 1 and the

This indicates that they have, in fact, rejected the 'cap stone' (κεφαλὴν γωνίας; cf. Isa. 28:16). Though this stone likely refers to the 'keystone' or 'capstone' at the top of a doorway,[98] *T. Sol.* 22–23 suggests that this refers to the stone that completed Solomon's temple.[99] It is possible that, as Jesus 'fulfils' the law (5:17), he is here depicted as 'completing' the temple – that is, providing what is presently lacking: a communion with God embodied in Matthew's 'God with us' Christology. This is difficult to substantiate, however, because it is not clear that Jesus is here associating himself with the stone that completes the temple, which would indicate that they have rejected what makes the temple complete.

A potential allusion to the temple is found in the parable of the Wedding Banquet (22:1–14). Here is a description of the 'kingdom of heaven' (22:2), in which a king was enraged by the mistreatment of his servants and rejection of his invitation (22:3–7a). As a result, 'he sent his army and destroyed those murderers and burned their city' (22:7). McNeile, to name but one scholar, insists this text refers to the fall of Jerusalem and thus uses it as a basis for dating the first gospel after the tragedy of 70 C.E.[100] Yet scholars such as Gundry contend that the allusion is rather to Isa. 5:24–25, a context behind Matt. 21:33 (cf. Isa. 5:1–7), suggesting that Matthew edited his parable, borrowed from a previous tradition, to conform to the Isaiah text. Thus he insists that the reference is not to the fall of Jerusalem in 70 C.E.[101] Davies and Allison see that *both* the Isa.

Use of Scripture in the Parable of the Vineyard', *DSD* 2 [1995], 279–85, 87–89; 293; W. J. C. Weren, 'The Use of Isaiah 5, 1–7 in the Parable of the Tenants [Mark 12, 1–12; Matt. 21, 33–46]', *Bib.* 79 [1998], 15–17; E. Lohmeyer, 'Das Gleichnis von de bösen Weingärtnern', *ZST* 18 [1941], 242–59; M. Black, 'The Christological use of the Old Testament in the New Testament', *NTS* 18 [1971], 12–14; and K. Snodgrass, *The Parable of the Wicked Tenants: An Inquiry into Parable Interpretation* [Tübingen: Mohr Siebeck, 1983], pp. 63–4; 113–18).

[98] Hagner, *Matthew* II, p. 622.

[99] Davies and Allison, *Matthew* III, pp. 185–86.

[100] McNeile, *St Matthew*, p. xxvii. Hagner (*Matthew* II, p. 630) is less certain of its original intent, but does insist that 'it is virtually impossible for post-70 readers of the Gospel not to see the destruction of Jerusalem alluded to in these words'. Cf. also Longenecker, 'Rome's Victory and God's Honour', pp. 98–99. For a survey of the arguments and representative scholars holding to an *ex eventu* prophecy, see Olmstead, *Trilogy*, p. 119, n. 115. For a survey of those who argue against an *ex eventu* reading, see Olmstead, *Trilogy*, p. 119 n. 116. See also his n. 117 for some analysis.

[101] Gundry (pp. 436–37) further argues that Matthew's τότε (22:7, 8) would push the Gentile mission past that date, which is clearly not in the scope of Matthew (28:19–20). C. H. Dodd, *The Parables of the Kingdom* (London: Nisbet, 1935), pp. 61–65, sees it as a prediction of coming eschatological/historical events. Such predictions were by no means rare among Jewish prophets of antiquity. See C. A. Evans, 'Predictions of the Destruction of the Herodian Temple in the Pseudepigrapha, Qumran Scrolls, and Related Texts', *JSP* 10 (1992), 89–147; S. J. D. Cohen, 'The Destruction: From Scripture to Midrash', *Prooftexts* 2 (1982), 18–39; R. Goldenberg, 'Early Rabbinic Explanations to the Destruction of Jerusalem', *SBLSP* 21

5 text *and* the events of 70 C.E. are in view.[102] Regardless of whether before or after, conspicuously absent in this statement about the temple is any statement which could be read negatively against the temple itself. Instead we find that the siege upon the city (22:7) was because the invited guests abused the king's servants. The city (and its temple?) had done nothing wrong though it was destroyed as an act of judgement against those who refused the king's invitation to the banquet.[103]

The temple is a prominent feature in Matthew's 'seven woes' section (chapter 23). In this unique Matthean material, Jesus chastises the 'blind guides' for thinking that swearing by the temple (ναός) means nothing, but swearing by the gold of the temple (ναός) is binding (23:16). They are criticised for making distinctions between oaths taken 'by the temple' (ἐν τῷ ναῷ) and 'by the gold of the temple' (ἐν τῷ χρυσῷ τοῦ ναοῦ) on the one hand, and 'by the altar' (ἐν τῷ θυσιαστηρίῳ) and 'by the gift upon it' (ἐν τῷ δώρῳ τῷ ἐπάνω αὐτοῦ, cf. 5:23) on the other.[104] Both the gold and the gift, he states, have significance because of the altar with which they are associated.[105] Furthermore, Jesus insists that the value of such gold is found in the *temple* (ναός; 23:17), and swearing by this temple (ναός) is the same as swearing by the one who dwells in it (23:21, 22). Although the subject here is surely the use of oaths, Matthew explicitly cites the Pharisees' misappropriation of their oaths *with respect to the temple and its sacrifices*. This observation, as we have seen throughout, underscores Matthew's concern to portray the temple as being misused by those in charge of it.[106] Moreover, Matthew brings this woe to a climax by first *presuming* God to still be present within the temple (23:21; ἐν τῷ κατοικοῦντι αὐτὸν)[107] and adding to it a new charge of swearing by heaven and acknowledging God's presence there (23:22).

(1982), 517–25; and A. J. Saldarini, 'Varieties of Rabbinic Response to the Destruction of the Temple', *SBLSP* 2 (1982), 437–58. For the view that there may be no reference to the 70 C.E. events, see R. J. Bauckham, 'The Parable of the Royal Wedding Feast (Matthew 22:1–14) and the Parable of the Lame Man and the Blind Man (*Apocryphon of Ezekiel*)', *JBL* 115 (1996), 447–64.

[102] Davies and Allison, *Matthew* I, p. 132. Though they fail, in our view, to account for the issue of the Gentile mission.

[103] Gundry (p. 436) provides a helpful summary of how this language should be taken as judgment language against the Jewish leaders.

[104] Hagner, *Matthew* II, p. 669.

[105] Davies and Allison, *Matthew* III, p. 292. See U. Luz, *Das Evangelium nach Matthäus* (EKK; 4 vols.; Zürich: Benziger Verlag, 1985–2002) III, pp. 326–28.

[106] Davies and Allison (*Matthew* III, pp. 292–93) rightly observe that they are chastised precisely for disobeying the *cultic* law.

[107] On potential implications for the dating of the gospel in light of this observation, see Davies and Allison, *Matthew* III, p. 293; France, *Matthew: Evangelist and Teacher*, p. 88.

Moreover, 'between the temple (ναός) and the altar' is the location of Matthew's curious account of the murder of Zechariah, son of Berekiah (23:35), apparently a 'Q' text ('Q' 11:50),[108] providing details absent from the Lukan version (11:50).[109] Moreover, Matthew has changed the reading, as found in Luke 11:49, from 'wisdom of God sends you prophets' to 'I send you prophets' (cf. 'Q' 11:50), clearly ascribing a Wisdom identity to his Jesus.[110] Although which Zechariah is in view has been disputed, it seems probable that the one in 2 Chron. 24:20–22, who was stoned to death in the courtyard of the temple, is the best choice. If this is so, then Matthew changed his source.[111] The LXX of this account (24:21) reads that the murder occurred ἐν αὐλῇ οἴκου κυρίου (so also Luke 11:51; MT בחצר בית יהוה), yet Matthew changes it to ναός. Why Matthew changes οἴκου κυρίου to ναός here, as he does in 27:5, is not immediately apparent. It may be, as we will see below, that Matthew's aversion to speaking negatively against the temple is heightened even further when it is associated with God (κύριος). That is, when Matthew speaks negatively of the temple, he avoids associating it with God.[112] His point of contention, as we have seen before and will revisit, in typical prophetic (Jeremiah) fashion, is misuse of the temple.[113]

[108] Robinson *et al.*, pp. 286–88.

[109] For a helpful survey of the issue, see Hagner, *Matthew* II, pp. 676–78, where he takes the position that the Zechariah referred to here is that of 2 Chron. 24:20–22, who was stoned to death in the courtyard of the temple (ἐν αὐλῃ οἴκου κυρίου; 24:21), interpreting 'from the blood of Abel to the blood of Zechariah' to mean from the beginning to the end of the Hebrew Bible. Cf. R. Beckwith, *The Old Testament Canon of the New Testament and Its Background in Early Judaism* (Grand Rapids, Mich.: Eerdmans, 1985), pp. 211–22; Str-B I, pp. 422–23; see Becker, 'Die Zerstörung Jerusalems', 59–73.

[110] Deutsch, 'Wisdom in Matthew', p. 41. See Aune, *Prophecy*, p. 237; E. Schweizer, *Matthäus und seine Gemeinde* (Stuttgart: K. B. W. Verlag, 1974), p. 283; Suggs, *Wisdom*, pp. 59f; U. Wilckens, *Weisheit und Torheit: eine exegetisch-religions-geschichtliche Untersuchung zu 1. Kor. 1 und 2* (Tübingen: Mohr Siebeck, 1959), p. 197.

[111] Robinson *et al.*, pp. 286–88. Knowles (p. 107) notes that the slaying of this Zechariah is often associated with the fall of Jerusalem. 2 Chron. 24:21–22; *Tg.* Lam 1:19; 2:20; 5:11, 13; *y. Ta'an.* 4:9; *b. Giṭ.* 57b; *b. Sanh.* 96a; *Pes. K.* 15.7; *Lam. Rab.* 1:16 §51; 2:20 §23; *Eccles. Rab.* 3:16 §1; cf. *b. Yoma* 38b; S. H. Blank, 'Death of Zechariah in Rabbinic Literature', *HUCA* 13 (1938), 327–46; Becker, 'Die Zerstörung Jerusalems', 59–73. The destruction of Jerusalem is also associated with Israel's rejection of Jesus, the Jeremiah-like prophet (*2 Bar.* 2:1; *Par. Jer.* 1.1–3; Knowles, p. 142).

[112] We find that the Old Syriac ($Sy^s$) goes even further to dissociate God with the temple when discussion is polemical. This is the case, for example, at 26:61 where the Greek reads ὁ ναὸς τοῦ θεοῦ ('the temple of God') while $Sy^s$ reads ܗܢܐ ܗܝܟܠܐ ('this temple'). See also Mark 11:15a; A. G. Lewis, *Old Syriac Gospels* (London: Williams & Norgate, 1910), p. 75; T. Nicklas, 'Die altsyrische Sinaiticus-Handschrift (Sys) als Zeuge antijüdischer Tendenzen', *AS* 1 (2003), 29–54, esp. 36–37.

[113] This point is most explicitly seen in Matthew's allusion to Jer. 7:11 (Matt. 21:13; cf. Isa. 56:7; Knowles, p. 188). It may be possible that Matthew chooses ναός, the holiest

The pericope culminates in two further 'judgement' texts. The first (23:38) recounts Jesus' declaration: 'Look, your house is left to you desolate (ἔρημος)'. Although Matthew may allude to Jer. 12:7,[114] he does not seem to have a particular Old Testament prophecy in view. Deutsch sees this as a clear consequence of Jerusalem's refusal to accept Jesus, the personification of Wisdom.[115] This is underscored by the depiction (in Second Temple Jewish texts) of Wisdom looking for a place to dwell in the temple, but finding none, withdrawing again, in judgement (Sir. 24:8–12). Traditionally, scholars have seen this as a reference to God's abandonment of his own temple, resonating with the language of his abandonment of the first temple just prior to its destruction (Ezek. 8:6, 12; 9:3, 9; 11:23; cf. *Barn.* 4:12).[116] Davies and Allison contend that the reference was originally to the departure of the Shekinah from the temple (cf. 1 Kgs 9:6–9; Isa. 64:10–11),[117] though scholars have argued that the referent is Jerusalem, or even 'the house of Israel'.[118] Knowles is correct that these texts describe God's *departure* from the temple, not its destruction, but the departure of God's presence from the temple was a prelude to the city's destruction (Josephus, *J.W.* 5.9.3 §§412–13; 6.5.3 §§295–300; Tacitus, *Hist.* 5.13; *2 Bar.* 8:2; 64:6–7; *Par. Jer.* [*4 Bar.*] 4:1). However, one should not move too quickly from abandonment to destruction[119] so as to simply conflate the temple with its inept leaders.[120]

The destruction of the temple was seen as subsequent to God's departure, both of which were inescapably the result of the sins of God's people. This is apparent in a similar use of Matthew's 'desolation' (ἔρημος) saying, which occurs in *T. Levi* 15:1, announcing that 'the sanctuary

portion of the temple complex, to heighten the sense of sacrilege produced by the deeds. That is, the offence is done not just against the temple, but against the holiest part of the temple. Yet this option seems less likely because it fails to account for Matthew's dissociation of the temple from God. If the evangelist were simply heightening the degree of sacrilege involved, would he not *preserve* the name of God, the presence of whom is what makes the temple holy (Matt. 23:21)?

[114] Cf. Knowles, pp. 185–8. [115] 'Wisdom in Matthew', p. 45.

[116] Hagner, *Matthew* II, p. 681. France (*Matthew: Evangelist and Teacher*, pp. 215–16) sees this text as the 'first explicit prediction of the future desolation of the temple', which is strategically located at 'the climax of the extended denunciation of the scribes and Pharisees in chapter 23'. It is particularly related, he contends, to 'the statement that the sins of the fathers have culminated in 'this generation', upon whom punishment is now at last to fall. Jesus' last, earnest appeal to Jerusalem has met with no response (23:37)'. As we have shown in the introduction, many ancient scholars associated this verse, along with the rending of the veil, with the destruction of Jerusalem.

[117] Davies and Allison, *Matthew* III, p. 321.

[118] For a brief survey, cf. Davies and Allison, *Matthew* III, p. 322.

[119] Knowles, *Jeremiah in Matthew's Gospel*, p. 143. See Longenecker, 'Rome's Victory and God's Honour', pp. 90–96.

[120] Carter, *Matthew*, pp. 170, 221.

which the Lord chose shall become desolate through your uncleanness, and you shall be captives in all the nations'.[121] Similarly, Josephus says 'God himself . . . turned away from our city . . . because he deemed the temple to be no longer a clean dwelling place for Him' (*Ant.* 20.8.5 §166; cf. *J.W.* 5.1.3 §19).[122] This view is underscored by the departure of Jesus' presence, which he has already identified with the Shekinah (Matt. 18:20; cf. *m. 'Abot.* 3:2),[123] from the temple (ἱερόν), in prophetic fashion going towards the Mount of Olives (24:1; cf. Zech. 14:4).[124] This is significant, Knowles contends, because God's presence in that shrine was an affirmation of Israel's election, sanctification and protection. Yet the realities of 586 B.C.E. indicate 'that the covenantal sanction afforded by God's "presence" was not inviolable'.[125] It would seem natural, then, for a first-century Jewish reader to see Jesus' departure as a similar act of abandonment[126] and, perhaps, the removal of the mark of Israel's identity as the people of God.

The second judgement text in this pericope is related to the first. Immediately, his disciples marvel at the structure, yet Jesus emphatically

[121] *OTP I*, p. 793. Knowles (p. 101) indicates that, in true Jeremiah fashion, rejection of the words of God's prophets and of the just are among the other sins leading to the temple's destruction (cf. *T. Jud.* 23:1–5; *T. Iss.* 6:1–4; *T. Zeb.* 9:5–8; *T. Dan* 5:7–9; *T. Naph.* 4:1–5; *T. Ash.* 7:2–7; *Pesiq. Rab.* 29 (138a); 31 (146a); *Exod. Rab.* 31:16 (on Exod. 22:27); O. H. Steck, *Israel und das gewaltsame Geschick der Propheten: Untersuchungen zur Überlieferung des deuteronomistischen Geschichtsbildes im Alten Testament, Spätjudentum, und Urchristentum* (WMANT 23; Neukirchen-Vluyn: Neukirchener Verlag, 1967), pp. 147–62; M. A. Knibb, 'The Exile in the Literature of the Intertestamental Period', *HeyJ* 17 (1976), 264–66. Knowles also is careful to note that the destruction of the temple in 70 C.E. is the product of a Deuteronomistic cycle of people's rejection of God (pp. 115–16; cf. Ezra 3:30; 5:28; *b. Yoma* 9b: 'Why was the first Sanctuary destroyed? Because of three things which prevailed there: idolatry, immorality, and bloodshed').

[122] Longenecker, 'Rome's Victory and God's Honour', p. 94.

[123] Knowles, *Jeremiah in Matthew's Gospel*, p. 144. For more discussion of Matthew's identification of Jesus with the Shekinah, cf. Davies and Allison, *Matthew* II, pp. 789–90.

[124] Cf. France, *Matthew: Evangelist and Teacher*, p. 215; Luomanen, *Entering the Kingdom of Heaven*, pp. 227–28.

[125] Knowles, *Jeremiah in Matthew's Gospel*, p. 267. Yet in the Herodian temple, Knowles shows, some rabbis held the Shekinah was never present there (*b. Yoma* 21b; *Num. Rab.* 15:10 [on Num. 8:2]), or at least 'not as helpful' as before (cf. *2 Bar.* 68:5–6). God was thought to dwell with Israel in Zion, his holy mountain (Joel 2:27; 4[3]:16–17). Knowles notes that 'the security of both the city and the Temple constituted a sign of divine favor and covenant faithfulness'. With the destruction of the temple, acts of piety (prayer and obedience to the Torah) replaced temple sacrifices (1QS ix 3–6; cf. Gärtner, *Temple and the Community*, pp. 15, 20–21; 44–46; J. Neusner, 'Judaism in a Time of Crisis: Four Responses to the Destruction of the Second Temple', *Judaism* 21 (1972), 318; Saldarini, 'Varieties of Rabbinic Responses to the Destruction of the Temple', 437–58; Knowles, p. 270. Cf. G. I. Davies, 'The Presence of God in the Second Temple and Rabbinic Doctrine', in *Templum Amicitiae. Essays on the Second Temple Presented to Ernst Bammel* (ed. W. Horbury; JSNTSup 48; Sheffield: JSOT Press, 1991), pp. 32–36.

[126] Kupp, pp. 93–94; Davies and Allison, *Matthew* III, p. 333.

predicts, in a tradition found in each Synoptic account, that 'not one stone here will be left on another; every one will be thrown down' (24:2; cf. Mark 13:1; Luke 21:5).[127] Although the evangelist provides no immediate explanation of this saying, the fact that it is placed right after Jesus' statement about his return (23:39, citing Ps. 118:26) and before his extended monologue regarding signs of the end of the age (24:3–25:46) strongly suggests that his prediction of the temple's destruction is an integral factor in Matthew's eschatology[128] and bears defining characteristics of divine judgement.[129] Yet Jesus' implicit and explicit statements regarding the destruction of the temple do not themselves 'question the legitimacy of the cult'.[130] Instead, 'what we have here is not a repudiation of a divinely founded institution but a tragic forecast by Jerusalem's king of a disaster fostered by human sin. The destruction of the temple is God's verdict upon the capital'.[131] Davies and Allison have shown that Jesus is not alone in this prophetic tradition of foretelling the destruction of Jerusalem and its temple[132] for identical reasons: the sins of Israel's leadership in mismanaging the temple. This is culminated when Jesus goes to the Mount of Olives (24:3), where he sees the temple which will be destroyed and indicates a return to the Mount of Olives (cf. 27:53; Acts 1:9, 12).[133] This resonates with Zech. 14:4, which asserts that the Lord will stand on the Mount of Olives at the great day of judgement upon Jerusalem (14:1–21). The prophetic judgement is announced.

Among the signs of the end of the age (Matt. 24), the evangelist includes mention of 'the abomination that causes desolation' (τὸ βδέλυγμα τῆς ἐρημώσεως) standing in the holy place (24:15). The citation is taken from Daniel (9:27; 11:31; 12:11; and partially via Mark 13:14), where it refers to a pagan altar or image of Zeus set up in the Jerusalem temple by Antiochus IV Epiphanes (167 B.C.E.; cf. *T. Levi* 15:1; *Apoc. El. (H)* 2:41; 4:21).[134] The referent in the Matthean context is uncertain, though it may allude to the attempted desecration by Caligula (40 C.E.), to the destruction of the temple itself (as in Luke 21:20) or to a future 'eschatological defilement' associated with the anti-Christ.[135] Regardless of the precise referent, Matthew seems to identify the defilement of the temple with

[127] Olmstead (*Trilogy*), arguing for the collective guilt of all Israel for the sins against Jesus rather than just her leaders, asserts that this is how one should read Matt. 27:25 that Jesus' blood should 'be on us and on our children'.

[128] See Knowles, pp. 188–89. [129] France, *Matthew: Evangelist and Teacher*, p. 216.

[130] Davies and Allison, *Matthew* III, p. 334. [131] *Ibid.* III, p. 335.

[132] *Ibid.* III, p. 335, citing Micah (Mic. 3:12), Jeremiah (Jer. 7:8–15; 9:10–11; 26:6, 18), and Jesus bar Ananias (Josephus, *J.W.* 6.5.3 §300ff.).

[133] *Ibid.* III, p. 347. [134] *Ibid.* III, p. 345. [135] *Ibid.* III, pp. 345–46.

some eschatological 'sign'. Olmstead contends this 'signals God's judgment on rebellious Israel for the rejection of his servants which spans her history' for which the 70 C.E. tragedy is a 'precursor'.[136] We see, then, that this abandonment and impending destruction are the *consequences* of Israel's failed leadership.

A further allusion to the temple with respect to the leaders' (mismanaged) stewardship of it is found in 24:45, where Jesus refers to a servant 'whom the master has put in charge of the servants in his household' and who is expected to be found faithful upon the master's return (24:46–51). This is part of a parable given privately to the disciples regarding the end of the age (24:3). The symbolism again refers to the leaders of Israel, though the 'household' may simply refer to their leadership in general over the 'house' of Israel, including their management of the temple.

Chapter 26 begins Matthew's Passion Narrative, in which Jesus is arrested, protesting that 'every day I sat in the temple courts (ἱερόν) teaching, and you did not arrest me' (26:55). Although this complaint is mentioned in each of the canonical gospels (Mark 14:49; Luke 22:53; John 18:20), in Matthew's narrative it seems to point back to the events in 21:1–27. Matthew takes this pericope from Mark, and though he condenses it to a degree, he edits points where the temple (ναός) is soon to become a central issue of controversy. First, Mark's 'this man-made temple' (τὸν ναὸν τοῦτον τὸν χειροποίητον; Mark 14:58) becomes 'God's temple' (τὸν ναὸν τοῦ θεοῦ; Matt. 26:61). This is a strange redaction, since as we have seen previously Matthew seems careful to avoid identifying the temple with God where it is spoken against. Yet since these charges are explicitly said to be false (26:59–60), perhaps Matthew was emphasising the illegitimacy of accusations that Jesus betrayed animosity towards the divinely instituted temple. Next Jesus is accused of saying 'I am able to destroy the temple (ναός) of God and rebuild it in three days' (26:61), whereas Mark's accuser says that Jesus claimed that he *will* destroy the temple (καταλύσω; 14:58). Explanations for Matthean redaction have been various, with some suggesting that it is inappropriate for Matthew to preserve Mark's 'will destroy' after 70 C.E. But it would seem just as inappropriate for Matthew's Jesus to tell people to offer sacrifices (5:23–24; 8:4) and presume that God was still in the temple (23:21) when it was already destroyed. It seems more plausible that Matthew is trying to mute Mark's polemic against the temple with respect to Jesus. That is, perhaps Matthew is concerned that, though his Jesus speaks against the mismanagement of the temple and of its

[136] Olmstead, *Trilogy*, p. 116.

imminent destruction, he is cautious that Jesus not speak directly against it.[137] Although both accusations are clearly said to be 'false witnesses' (ψευδομαρτύρων; Matt. 26:60; cf. Mark 14:56, 57), Matthew seems to emphasise Jesus' ability, while identifying the temple as God's (τοῦ θεοῦ; cf. 26:61). Matthew stresses the *power* of Jesus, but not his instrumentality in the destruction of the temple. Moreover, Matthew's Jesus speaks of the destruction of the ἱερον (cf. 24:1–2), while the false accusations suggest that he spoke against the ναὸς. Some scholars suggest the temple 'not made with hands' refers to the church, suggesting that Matthew was concerned that his Jesus founded the church after his resurrection.[138] This cannot be the case, for Matthew clearly depicts the founding of the church during Jesus' ministry.[139] Davies and Allison suggest the temple reference is to Jesus himself, so 'I am able to destroy the temple of God' means 'I am able to lay down my life'.[140] Yet this is not entirely satisfactory, since Matthew's Jesus emphasises not his *ability* to lay down his life but the fact that, in each of his passion predictions, he *will*. Instead, perhaps Matthew is concerned to emphasise the power of Jesus over the temple to affirm his superiority to it (12:6), yet still recognises it as belonging to God. Moreover, Luz suggests Jesus' ability to destroy the temple underscores his power as the son of God (4:3, 6; 26:53; 27:40–42) to do so, but his obedience as son of God not to (cf. 27:43).[141] The importance of this observation will be addressed in Chapter 6.

We next come across the temple in 27:5, where Judas throws his ill-gained money into the temple (ναός) and leaves to hang himself. The early Christians understood Judas' suicide, found only in Matthew among the gospels, as an act of judgement (Acts 1:18). Scholars are widely agreed that the gesture is symbolic of the priests' guilt accompanying that of Judas.[142] This pericope (Matt. 27:3–10) is a redactional addition between Mark 15:1 and 15:2 (cf. Acts 1:15–20; Jerome, *Com. Matt.* 27:9). Here the temporal sequence of his narrative is clearly broken, as 27:2 leaves the priests and elders leading Jesus to Pilate, while 27:3–10 places them in the temple sanctuary.[143] The account itself is apparently a Matthean redaction of the Old Testament, for his source (LXX Zech. 11:13) says

[137] Telford, *Barren Temple*, p. 83.

[138] See Davies and Allison, *Matthew* III, p. 526; Lohmeyer, *Matthäus*, pp. 367–68; Luz, *Matthäus* IV, p. 176.

[139] See Davies and Allison, *Matthew* II, p. 628.

[140] *Ibid.* III, p. 526, n. 38, citing Gundry (p. 543), who observes that Matthew's 'I am able' statement harmonises with the voluntary nature of Jesus' death in that gospel. Cf. Luz, *Matthäus* IV, p. 176, n. 20.

[141] Luz, *Matthäus* IV, p. 176.

[142] Davies and Allison, *Matthew* III, pp. 564–65.

[143] Brown, *Death* I, p. 637.

the money will be 'thrown' (ἐμβάλλω)[144] 'into the house of the Lord' (εἰς τὸν οἶκον κυρίου).[145] Yet Matthew says it was 'cast' (ῥιπτειν) 'into the temple' (εἰς τὸν ναόν).

The ναός is almost surely referring to the inner sanctuary of the temple complex,[146] accessible only to the priests, and quite a long distance to throw a handful of coins from the outer court into which Judas would be permitted.[147] Judas could enter the court of the Israelites, which was adjacent to the court of priests. If the latter is loosely designated ναός (properly the sanctuary building), then he does not have to throw far. Apparently, though, Matthew does presume a long distance because he intensifies Zechariah's term 'throw' (ἐμβάλλω) to 'cast' (ῥίπτειν) perhaps to compensate for a longer distance. That is, he seems to have first changed the destination of the throwing (into the sanctuary), and then modified the verb accordingly. Why, however, is he so concerned to read ναὸς for τὸν οἶκον κυρίου? Brown suggests the emphasis upon the ναὸς here is to 'communicate the horror of profanation'.[148] That is, to emphasise the degree of sacrilege involved. But why could Matthew not do that by retaining τὸν οἶκον κυρίου, particularly given his tendency to retain οἶκος from an Old Testament source when alluding to it, as he is doing here?[149] The uniqueness of this pericope may supply the answer, for in two of the other texts where Matthew retains the LXX οἶκος reading (Matt. 12:4 [1 Sam. 21:7]; 21:13 [Isa. 56:7; 60:7]) there is nothing negative said about the temple. And, it is only *after* Jesus' lament over Jerusalem's lack of repentance that he will speak a negative word towards the οἶκος when alluding to Old Testament texts (Matt. 23:38 [Ps. 118:26]). Then, perhaps, there is nothing negative to say about the temple, a divinely instituted enterprise established in the Old Testament (cf. 5:17), until after Jesus has lamented the lack of repentance of its leaders. *Then* its destruction, despite its legitimacy, is depicted using Old Testament οἶκος language.

144 Although Aquila and Symmachus use ῥιπτειν. For a discussion of the textual variations in the Zechariah text, see C. C. Torrey, 'The Foundry of the Second Temple at Jerusalem', *JBL* 55 (1936), 247–60.

145 See Knowles, *Jeremiah in Matthew's Gospel*, pp. 56–57. Josephus refers to the allusion to Zechariah as τὸν ἱερὸν θησαυρόν, καλεῖται δὲ κορβωνᾶς (*J.W.* 2.9.4 §175). See also R. Gundry, *The Use of the Old Testament in St Matthew's Gospel: With Special Reference to the Messianic Hope* (NovTS 18; Leiden: E. J. Brill, 1967), p. 124; J. A. Upton, 'The Potter's Field and the Death of Judas', *CJ* 8 (1982), 214–16; P. Benoit, 'La mort de Judas', in *Exégèse et théologie* (Paris: Cerf, 1961), I, pp. 341–59.

146 This is usually the case in Matthew. Davies and Allison, *Matthew*III, p. 564.

147 Scholars conjecture, then, that the money was thrown over a wall or through a gate. Cf. Hagner, *Matthew* I, p. 812.

148 Brown, *Death*, I, p. 642.

149 Matt. 12:4 (1 Sam. 21:7); 21:13 (Isa. 56:7; 60:7); 23:38 (Ps. 118:26).

Perhaps more plausibly, if, as is sometimes recognised, this gesture is in part a demonstration that the priests bear some of the blame in Judas' betrayal,[150] Matthew may have been concerned to remove κυρίος from association with it.[151]

Perhaps that it was cast into the ναός depicts that the guilt incurred by Judas is to be shared with those who conduct services therein, for which οἶκος κύριου would be too general. That the guilt is some way intended to be shared with the priests is supported by the fact that immediately the priests are on the scene. They take the money away from the temple treasury and purchase a field (27:7), literally 'the field of the potter' (τὸν ἀγρὸν τοῦ κεραμέως). It was used to buy a field called 'Field of Blood', and Matthew justifies it in characteristic fashion by citing the Old Testament,[152] likely a combination of texts from Zechariah and Jeremiah, indicating that even this was within God's sovereign control.[153] The ναός continues to be a point of contention even on the cross, where passers-by, apparently hearing and believing the (false) accusations against Jesus, mock him by saying, 'You who are going to destroy the temple (ναός) and build it in three days, save yourself! Come down from the cross, if you are the Son of God!' (27:40; cf. Mark 15:29–30). Again, it is important to recognise that accusations of Jesus' polemic against the temple itself are said to be false. For the present, I will suspend judgement on the temple (ναός) reference in 27:51 until I can profile a more decisive view of Jesus' death in Matthew's gospel in general.

## 2 Matthew's Temple: Conclusion

We have seen that frequently Matthew is deliberate about his choice of location and issues surrounding the temple and its cult. Telford has also made this observation in his analysis of Matthew's redaction of the Markan fig-tree pericope examined earlier. Yet he adds that such a

[150] Davies and Allison, *Matthew* III, pp. 564–65.

[151] Yet another reading is worthy of consideration. It could be that, as Judas is first said to recognise his error (27:4–5; ἥμαρτον is a standard term for 'confession', Davies and Allison, *Matthew* III, p. 263 and n. 22), throwing his money into the inner sanctum could be understood as an attempt to make a sin offering. Previously we have seen that Matthew is concerned that one first make reconciliation, then offer his gift on the altar (5:23–24), and, though it is difficult to be certain, it would not be surprising if he were indicating a similar scenario with Judas.

[152] Although Matthew says his citation comes from Jeremiah (19:1–13; 32:6–9), it more closely fits with the LXX of Zech. 11:12, 13. See Brown, *Death*, I, pp. 648–51.

[153] Brown, *Death* I, p. 652.

conclusion is supported by what Matthew *omitted* from Mark, including Mark 11:16, which seems to allude to Jesus' obstruction of sacrificial worship, and Mark 12:32–35, which could be taken to disparage the temple cult. Matthew retains but modifies Mark's account of Jesus' prediction of the destruction of the temple, as I showed earlier. Yet where he retains Mark's prophecy concerning the destruction of the temple (Matt. 27:1–2; Mark 13:1–2), 'he does precede it by the Lament over Jerusalem (23.37–39), which shows Jesus' attitude to be one of regret over the imminent demise of the city and its Temple . . . For Matthew (5.17), Jesus is one who has come to fulfill (πληρῶσαι) rather than to destroy (καταλῦσαι)'.[154] Davies and Allison concur:

> Matthew, writing after A.D. 70, had no need to attack the Jerusalem temple, nor did he. Rather did he assume its propriety, that is, its foundation in the Torah, and its one-time sanctity: God intended the temple to be a house of prayer (21.13), a place for offering of sacrifices (5.23–4), and a holy site sanctifying the objects within it (23.16–22). If the temple had ceased to be these things, and then ceased to be altogether, the explanation was simply that God's judgment had come upon Jerusalem: the corruption of the priests and others (21.13; 23.35) and the rejection of Jesus (21.42–43; 22.7) brought divinely ordained destruction.[155]

The assertions by Lohmeyer that Matthew is anti-temple fail to distinguish between the temple and the leaders responsible for it.[156] Andreoli's argument that Matthew is against the temple because it represents the 'old order' fails to account for Matthean redaction of Markan texts or for positive statements about the temple's cult.[157] Instead, Matthew is

[154] Telford, *Barren Temple*, p. 83.

[155] Davies and Allison, *Matthew* III, p. 143, cf. n. 64; 2 Kgs 21:10–15. In all this, Davies and Allison (*Matthew* III, p. 143, cf. n. 65–67), Matthew falls in line with late first-century Jewish thought. *4 Ezra*, *2 Bar.* and *Apoc. Ab.*, for instance, likewise attribute Jerusalem's tragic demise and the leveling of its sanctuary to Jewish failing. Cf. G. W. E. Nickelsburg, *Jewish Literature between the Bible and the Mishnah: A Historical and Literary Introduction* (London: SCM, 1981), pp. 294–99; J. Z. Smith, 'The Temple and the Magician', in *God's Christ and His People: Studies in Honour of Nils Alstrup Dahl* (ed. J. Jervell and W. A. Meeks; Oslo: Universitetsforleget, 1977), pp. 233–47.

[156] Telford, *Barren Temple*, p. 83, n. 106; Lohmeyer, *Matthäus*, p. 184.

[157] Andreoli, 'Il velo squarciato nel Vangelo di Matteo', 35–40. He only discusses: 12:1–8, suggesting that one is permitted to break the law because Jesus is greater than the temple; 21:13–16, suggesting that Jesus obliterates the commands of 2 Sam. 5:8; 21:14–15, suggesting the confrontation with leaders in the temple foreshadows the creation of a new

an author 'emphasizing the sovereignty of Jesus over the Temple rather than one reflecting an antagonism towards it'.[158] Matthew's references to its destruction are made only following a lament over the unwillingness of its leaders to repent. The lament, found only in Matt. 23:37–39 and Luke 13:34–35 (cf. 'Q' 13:34–35), is nearly identical in each text, with Matthew apparently preserving the original.[159] A similar lament was pronounced by Jeremiah (Jer. 2:30; cf. Neh. 9:26), and that the destruction of Jerusalem is depicted on the heels of this account has led scholars to conclude that the destruction is necessitated not because of fault with the temple but because of the unrepentance of the Jewish leaders.[160]

## 3 The Death of Jesus in Matthew's Gospel

As we saw in the introduction, Yates provides an innovative approach to the rending of the veil in Mark by tracing Mark's portrayal of Jesus' death throughout the gospel to highlight the 'positive significance of the death of Jesus'.[161] This fact is then used to interpret the rending of the veil, which Mark so closely associates with the death of Jesus. His method applies just as well, and in places better, in the Matthean context.[162] Thus as Yates has done in Mark, so I will examine Matthew's portrayal of

people; 26:60–61, arguing that Matthew sees no role for the temple in his eschatological program; 23:37–39, suggesting Jesus is abandoning the temple as God did (Jer. 22:5). We cannot interact with all Andreoli has done here, except to say that his selection of texts and his discussion of them are quite idiosyncratic, and he favours interpretations that support his thesis without discussion of alternative views of respective pericopae. Not the least of what Andreoli overlooks is cultic references in 5:23–24; 8:1–4 and the temple tax in 17:24–29.

[158] R. A. McConnell, 'Law and Prophecy in Matthew's Gospel' (Ph.D. diss.; University of Basel, 1964), pp. 72–75, esp. 75. Telford, *Barren Temple*, pp. 83–84.

[159] Cf. Robinson *et al.*, *The Critical Edition of Q*, p. 420.

[160] Cf. Davies and Allison, *Matthew* III, p. 324; cf. Olmstead, *Trilogy*, p. 83; D. C. Allison, 'Matt. 23.39 = Lk 13.35b as a Conditional Prophecy', *JSNT* 18 (1983), 75–84; Deutsch, 'Wisdom in Matthew', pp. 13–47. Such a reading would depict the incarnate wisdom departing as a pronouncement of judgement on those who reject wisdom (cf. Prov. 1:20–33; Matt. 11:16–19, 20–24); R. J. Miller, 'The Rejection of the Prophets in Q', *JBL* 107 (1988), 225–40; Steck, *Israel und das gewaltsame Geschict der Propheten*, pp. 280–97. For further support of the notion that the lament is from a Jeremiah-like tradition (and represents an *intra muros* discussion), see David M. Moffitt, 'Righteous Bloodshed, Matthew's Passion Narrative and the Temple's Destruction: Lamentations as a Matthean Intertext', *JBL* 125 (2006): 299–320.

[161] J. E. Yates, *The Spirit and the Kingdom* (London: SPCK, 1963), p. 232.

[162] Careful attention to detail will illustrate that *each verse* cited by Yates as support for his view of the veil in Mark is also present in Matthew (though *not* Luke): Yates (p. 235) points out the positive nature of Jesus' death as portrayed in Mark (Mark 10:45 = Matt. 20:28; Mark 14:22ff = Matt. 26:26ff) which 'point to a positive significance and not merely to judgment' (p. 234). He also argues that 'public signs' were 'contrary to the prejudice of Jesus himself', citing Mark 8:12 (= Matt. 12:39; 16:4).

the death of Jesus throughout his gospel as a means of informing our interpretation of the *velum scissum*, with which he associates it.[163]

D. Senior's *Passion of Jesus in the Gospel of Matthew*[164] has provided a compositionally sensitive examination of the topic in the first gospel. In this work he unfolds a 'survey of the first twenty-five chapters of the gospel in order to show how the death of Jesus has been looming before the reader almost from the very beginning of Matthew's narrative' and an examination of the Passion Narrative itself with a synthesis of 'Matthew's passion theology'.[165] This book provides the compositional results, in a more concise and readable form, of his Ph.D. dissertation, which examines the same topic from a strongly redaction-critical perspective,[166] and is a helpful starting point for our discussion. In it, Senior shows that the whole of Matthew's gospel portrays the death of Jesus in a consistent manner, cogently summarised in 26:28: that his death saves people from their sins.[167] 'No other Gospel presents the salvific impact of Jesus' passion in such explicit terms. Through his obedient death Jesus triumphs over death and that breakthrough is extended to all of God's people'.[168] While Senior's suggestion is certainly valid as a summative conclusion, we will see that Matthew's portrayal of the significance of Jesus' death is not so much a consistent theme as it is an unfolding disclosure of the fact that the Jesus who will save people from their sins (1:21) will do so by his sacrificial, atoning death (26:28).[169] Moreover, this unfolding portrait is bracketed by 1:21 and 26:28, which serve as a framing, or inclusio, for his entire discussion of the relationship between Jesus' death and the forgiveness of sins. The effect of Jesus' death, in some way, counters the

[163] In Chapter 6, I will discuss the nature of the relationship between the death of Jesus (Matt. 27:50) and the *velum scissum* (27:51a).

[164] (Wilmington, Del.: Glazier, 1985).

[165] Carroll and Green, *Death of Jesus*, p. 9. See A. R. Warner, 'Fulfilling All Righteousness: The Death of Jesus in Matthew', *CurTM* 29 (2002), 12–19. For a very helpful narrative summary, cf. M. A. Powell, *What Is Narrative Criticism?* (Minneapolis, Minn.: Fortress, 1990), pp. 45–46: 'Jesus has not come to give speeches but to give his life'. Unfortunately, Brown's magisterial *Death of the Messiah* provides no comprehensive summary of the significance of Jesus' death in the respective gospel accounts.

[166] D. P. Senior, *The Passion Narrative according to Matthew: A Redactional Study* (Leuven: Leuven University Press, 1975).

[167] Senior, *The Passion of Jesus in the Gospel of Matthew* (Wilmington, Del.: Glazier, 1985), p. 166.

[168] *Ibid.*, pp. 167–68.

[169] The subject of the death of Jesus, however, is entirely ignored in Luz's *The Theology of the Gospel of Matthew*. This omission is, as Carter puts it, 'puzzling'. For Matthew Jesus is a purpose-driven saviour, recognising clearly the necessity (δεῖ; 16:21; 26:54) of his coming in fulfilment (πληρόω) of God's plan (see Beaton, *Isaiah's Christ*, 18; W. Carter, Review of U. Luz, *The Theology of the Gospel of Matthew*, *RBL* [June 26, 2000], 2).

effects of people's sins. R. Troxel indicates that Jesus' death carries a 'positive value for Matthew, especially insofar as it confirms Jesus' obedience'.[170] That is, Jesus' death is particularly portrayed by Matthew as an act of willing obedience to his father (26:42). In Chapter 6, I will revisit the importance of Troxel's observation when discussing the centurion's profession of Jesus as 'son of God'.

Typically, scholars have begun their analyses of the significance of Jesus' death, ironically, at his birth, where Joseph is instructed by an angel of the Lord (1:20) to name the child Mary will bear 'Jesus' 'because he will save his people from their sins'.[171] What is not explicit in 1:21 is that it is achieved in any way through death, martyrdom, obedience and so on. Matthew leaves it open deliberately. That σώζω in Matthew's gospel can refer to a deliverance from physical danger (8:25), disease (9:21–22), or death (24:22)[172] suggests that Jesus offers forms of 'salvation' through various aspects of his ministry as well as through his death; otherwise Jesus' ministry itself would be reduced to a means of arriving at his death. Matthew's use of σώζω does, however, give us a glimpse of the unfolding progression of the significance of Jesus' death, which is made explicit in 26:28. That the evangelist regards deliverance as being *from sins* (ἀπὸ τῶν ἁμαρτιῶν) and directly associates Jesus' identity with the deliverance term ישע clearly indicates a soteriological function of Jesus.[173] For in

[170] R. L. Troxel, 'Matt. 27.51–54 Reconsidered: Its Role in the Passion Narrative, Meaning and Origin', *NTS* 48 (2002), 39; so also Carroll and Green, *Death of Jesus*, p. 47.

[171] καὶ καλέσεις τὸ ὄνομα αὐτοῦ Ἰησοῦν αὐτὸς γὰρ σώσει τὸν λαὸν αὐτοῦ ἀπὸ τῶν ἁμαρτιῶν αὐτῶν; 1:21 (cf. Luke 2:17). Cf. R. Gnuse, 'Dream Genre in the Matthean Infancy Narratives', *NovT* 32 (1990), 97–120. Hagner (*Matthew*, I, p. 19) suggests the evangelist here looks forward to 26:28, where Jesus speaks of pouring out blood, while cognizant of Ps. 130:8: 'And He will redeem (λυτρώσεται; יפדה) Israel from all his iniquities'. Gerhardsson ('Sacrificial Service', p. 26) contends that the 'interpretation of Jesus' name says nothing about the way in which Jesus saves his people from their sins. There is no suggestion that this is to happen exclusively through his sacrificial death'. Indeed, Gerhardsson further contends, 'The saying about the service and sacrifice of the Son of man does not appear in the context of a discussion on atonement'. He claims these are largely exemplary statements for those who want to be greatest in the Kingdom of Heaven. Moreover, he claims that the sacrificial language in Matthew is related more to the typical, rather than exclusive, human interests of Jesus and they are better understood in rabbinic terms of a 'spiritual sacrifice'. Yet there is no indication from the language and text of Matthew that the sacrifice of Jesus, ultimately seen at the crucifixion, is anything other than atoning. Acknowledged by Davies and Allison (*Matthew* I, p. 210), though, the association of Jesus' 'saving' (9:2) with healing does not preclude its soteriological function here. Cf. Harrington, *Matthew*, p. 35; Carson, 'Matthew', p. 76; Morris, *Matthew*, p. 30; Kingsbury, *Matthew*, p. 42; Gundry, *Matthew*, pp. 23–24; Carroll and Green, *Death of Jesus*, p. 50.

[172] Carson, 'Matthew', p. 76; Luomanen, *Entering the Kingdom of Heaven*, pp. 37–40, 225.

[173] Luomanen, *Entering the Kingdom of Heaven*, pp. 224–27. Moreover, it is precisely sinners that he has 'called' (Matt. 9:13; cf. Mark 2:17).

contexts where σώζω is used in reference to narrative times beyond those of the gospel itself (the eschaton), it is used explicitly with soteriological implications for the one who is associated with Jesus (10:22; 24:13, 22), the particulars of which unfold as the narrative develops.

The first reference to Jesus' death is found implicitly in Matt. 12:40, where Matthew, building upon Mark (8:12) regarding the request for a sign, adds a reading from 'Q' (11:30) indicating that the sign he will give is that of Jonah.[174] Yet Matthew adds a distinctively Matthean saying[175] to both traditions, that the sign he will give (that of Jonah, cf. Jonah 2:1) pertains to the Son of Man's being three days and nights in the heart of the earth (ἐν τῇ καρδίᾳ τῆς γῆς).[176] This is clearly an allusion to Jesus' death (and resurrection).[177] This reference is given in response to a request for a sign (σημεῖον; 12:38), presumably authenticating Jesus' identity.[178] What this pericope tells us of Jesus' death, then, is that it is an integral aspect of Jesus' identity. Perhaps the evangelist expects his readers to piece together this statement of Jesus' identity, tied to his death, with his earlier statement regarding Jesus' identity, tied to his saving people from their sins (1:21), but the correlation is not immediately apparent.

More explicit references to the nature of Jesus' death are found in his passion predictions, where the necessity (δεῖ)[179] of his death becomes more apparent.[180] The 'sign of Jonah', which Matthew explicitly associates with Jesus' death (12:40), is again alluded to (16:1–2) prior to the first passion prediction (16:21–23), though without explicit reference to his death (perhaps the reader is to recall that notion from before). On the heels of Peter's confession (Matt. 16:13–20), Matthew's Jesus begins what will remain the subject for the rest of his gospel (ἀπὸ τότε; 16:21): his suffering, death and resurrection.[181] That Matthew, following Mark, has preserved this account so close to Peter's confession should perhaps lead readers to understand Jesus' identity as 'the Christ, the son of the living God' (16:17), as (at least partially) defined by his passion. The text predicting his death (16:21) is almost identical to that of Matthew's Markan source (Mark 8:31).[182] Here Matthew's Jesus makes

[174] Robinson *et al.*, p. 250; Davies and Allison, *Matthew* II, p. 355.

[175] Luz, *Matthew 8–20*, p. 217.

[176] The sign is again mentioned in Matt. 16:1–2, though only the sign of Jonah without the statement about being in the belly of the earth.

[177] Luz, *Matthew 8–20*, p. 217; Gundry, p. 245. Whether Jesus' descent here is simply to the grave or to hell has been the subject of some discussion. Cf. Davies and Allison, *Matthew* II, p. 356.

[178] Luz, *Matthew 8–20*, p. 216.

[179] Carter, *Matthew*, p. 212.

[180] Hagner, *Matthew* II, p. 479.

[181] Luz, *Matthew 8–20*, p. 381.

[182] See Luz, *Matthew 8–20*, p. 380, n. 4.

explicit what is implicit in 12:40, though only to his disciples,[183] and the 'divinely decreed necessity that Jesus must suffer and die' (δεῖ) becomes apparent.[184] Yet *why* it is a necessity and *what is accomplished* by it is, again, not made clear. We may be able to associate Matthew's correlation between the necessity of Jesus' death (16:21) and his identity as 'the Christ' (16:17) with his identity as the one who will save people from their sins (1:21), but, again, the association is not explicit. What is explicit, however, is that Jesus' death in Matthew's gospel is *expected* and *necessary*. Other pieces regarding Jesus' death in Matthew's gospel will have to be pieced together with these as the narrative unfolds.[185]

Another implicit passion prediction is found in Matt. 17:9, where Jesus speaks of being 'raised from the dead'. When the disciples ask about the priority of Elijah's arrival (Matt. 17:10), Jesus asserts that Elijah has come (in John the Baptist, 17:13) and that Jesus will 'suffer' in the same way as he has.[186] Matthean redaction of Mark (Mark 9:12b) heightens the parallelism 'between the fate of John and the fate of Jesus'.[187] Readers of Matthew's gospel already know of the death of John (Matt. 14:2–10; cf. 16:14), and that Matthew's Jesus anticipates the same treatment (οὕτος καὶ . . ., 17:12) likewise suggests his death. Here several elements of Jesus' death are revealed. First, not only is it expected, but Jesus will be raised from it (17:9; i.e., it is only a *temporary* condition). Second, what the disciples saw at the transfiguration was not to be disclosed to others until after that resurrection (17:9). Third, Jesus' death is like John's, which is apparently depicted as the death of an innocent prophet inaugurating the restoration of 'all things' (17:11–12; cf. 3:1–15).

The second explicit passion prediction in Matthew is found in 17:22–23. Verse 23 of this text, where explicit mention of Jesus' death is made, is very similar to its Markan source (Mark 9:31).[188] The Matthean context seems to be an isolated account of a saying given by Jesus after a healing, when he and the disciples came together in Galilee (17:22). All we are told is that Jesus knows that it will happen, but that he will rise from the dead on the third day. The disciples, in response, are filled with grief. As

[183] Note Matthew's omission of Mark 8:32a. Luz, *Matthew 8–20*, p. 381, n. 8.

[184] Pace Luz, *Matthew 8–20*, p. 381. Cf. Davies and Allison, *Matthew* II, pp. 656–57. Note in 16:21 only the leaders, and not the Jews in general, are mentioned (Olmstead, *Trilogy*).

[185] Matthew's statement 'What can a man give in exchange for his soul?' (16:26) connotes a type of death and some sort of exchange, though it is not apparent that Jesus' death is in view.

[186] See D. C. Allison, 'Elijah must come first', *JBL* 103 (1984), 256–68.

[187] Davies and Allison, *Matthew* II, p. 716, cf. 475–76. Moreover, the passive Son of Man in Mark 9:12b becomes the subject in Matt. 17:12.

[188] Except that Matthew omits the redundant Markan variant ἀποκτανθεὶς (Mark 9:31) reading after 'and they will kill him' omitted in Markan mss B 2427 k sa$^{mss}$.

opposed to the necessity (δεῖ, 16:21), Luz asserts this account speaks of 'the imminence of Jesus' dying and rising'.[189] Perhaps also, by his choice of ἀποκτανθῆναι, Matthew associates the death of Jesus with the deaths of the prophets (cf. Matt. 23:34, 37) and of Christian disciples (10:28; 24:9), where the same term is used. 'Thus Jesus stands at the end of one line of martyrs and at the beginning of another.'[190] However, the explicit purpose and implications of Jesus' death are not made clear, though the readers are perhaps left to presume that they are related to his identity.

The next passion prediction is in two parts. The first simply predicts Jesus' being condemned to death and is taken verbatim from Mark (10:33) in Matt. 20:18. Additions to the following verse (Mark 10:34) are purely Matthean and indicate that Jesus' death will be by crucifixion (καὶ σταυρῶσαι, 20:19), unfolding some of the details of his death rather than, as done previously, describing it in 'summary form' (16:21; 17:22).[191] This form of death is first introduced here, but will again be disclosed as the means of the Jewish leaders' execution of Jesus later in the gospel (26:2; 27:26, 31). Polemic against the Jewish leaders is also made explicit as the role of the high priests and scribes is heightened.[192]

In an illustration to his disciples about humble leadership, Jesus indicates that his leadership is characterised by service in which he gives his life as a ransom for many (Matt. 20:28).[193] This is, in part, a purpose statement, that he came (ἦλθεν) to serve (διακονῆσαι). Moreover, he asserts that he will give up his life as a 'ransom' for many (λύτρον). The entire pericope (Matt. 20:20–28) is taken from Mark (10:35–45), and Matthean redaction is slight. Whereas Mark's Jesus says that a disciple is to be a slave of all (πάντων, 10:44), Matthew reserves the servant role to being among the disciples (ὑμῶν, 20:27). The next verse (Matt. 20:28) begins with ὥσπερ, whereas Mark has καὶ γὰρ (10:45). The difference is slight but important: for the latter suggests that Jesus' service and sacrifice are the bases for the humble nature of leadership among the disciples. In this way, the leadership among the disciples remains the main subject of the pericope, with Jesus' own service serving as an example and a ground or basis for their own humble leadership. Matthew's transitional term (ὥσπερ) is quite different. Matthew uses the term only ten times, each purported to have come from Jesus.[194] When Jesus uses the term

[189] Luz, *Matthew 8–20*, p. 411. [190] Davies and Allison, *Matthew* II, p. 734.

[191] Luz, *Matthew 8–20*, p. 539. [192] *Ibid.*

[193] καὶ δοῦναι τὴν ψυχὴν αὐτοῦ λύτρον ἀντὶ πολλῶν.

[194] It is used as a negative illustration for disciples not to imitate (6:2, 7), or to illustrate how an unrepentant congregant should be treated *as you would* treat a pagan or tax collector (18:17). Matthew's Jesus mostly uses the term in parables or illustrations of how things will be at the end (13:40; 24:27, 37; 25:14, 32).

in reference to himself (12:40), as here, it indicates 'something in like manner' to himself. Thus here (26:28), Jesus could be telling the disciples to serve *in like manner* (though not necessarily the same) to his service. Moreover, the general description of service is made specific in that we read that he will give his life as a ransom for many. This is important because it could be understood that, rather than Jesus' ransom logion being the basis for servant leadership among the disciples (as in Mark), servant leadership among the disciples is illustrated by Jesus' example, which is to the highest degree, Jesus giving up his life not simply in an exemplary self-sacrifice (as in John 15:13), but as 'ransom' (λύτρον).

Jesus interprets his death as 'ransom' (λύτρον),[195] which is a term meaning 'deliverance by payment' and which is used in extra-canonical Greek 'of the manumission of slaves and release of prisoners of war'.[196] Here the 'payment' is made not with money but with Jesus' life (τὴν ψυξὴν αὐτοῦ, 20:28). It is used in the LXX of people as 'ransom-price' for payment to save one's life after one person has killed another (Exod. 21:28–32), buying back an enslaved relation (Lev. 25:51–52) and redemption of a first-born child (Num. 18:15).[197] Davies and Allison have recognised that the 'principle of "life for life" is operative here'.[198] Luz asserts that 'from the many New Testament concepts of atonement and redemption the idea that the believers are redeemed by Christ (1 Cor. 6:20; 7:23 [τιμή instead of λύτρον]) comes the nearest to what might be meant here'.[199] Scholars have traditionally recognised Isaiah 53 behind this logion.[200] Yet it is important to note the reservation of Davies and Allison:

> As it stands in Matthew, 20.28 states that Jesus was – note the one-time aorist – an atonement offering, a substitution, a ransom for sins. But almost every question we might ask remains unanswered. What is the condition of 'the many'? Why do they need to be ransomed? To whom is the ransom paid . . .? Is forgiveness effected now or at the last judgment or both? How is it appropriated? Even when 1.21 and 26.26–9 are taken into account it is impossible to construct a Matthean theology

[195] Luz, *Matthew 8–20*, p. 546.
[196] Davies and Allison, *Matthew* III, p. 95. Cf. Carter, *Matthew*, pp. 217–20.
[197] Davies and Allison, *Matthew* III, p. 95. [198] *Ibid.*
[199] Luz, *Matthew 8–20*, p. 546.
[200] Cf. Davies and Allison, *Matthew* III, pp. 95–96 for a full summary. Others have seen Isa. 43:3–4 (see Davies and Allison, *Matthew* III, pp. 96–97). *Pace* Luz, *Matthew 8–20*, p. 546.

> of atonement. We have in the Gospel only an unexplained affirmation.[201]

This is an important concession, though as we have seen earlier and will further piece together later, there is a great deal more material pertaining to Jesus' death to draw from than the three texts they cite. Indeed, Luz indicates that the saying in Matt. 20:28 'is not a foreign element that is incidental to the text; it is the high point of an organic train of thought that begins (v. 18) and ends (v. 28) with the suffering of the Son of Man'.[202] Yet he, like Davies and Allison, suggests that 'there is little in Matthew that provides an answer for the question [about the nature and meaning of Jesus' atoning death]'.[203] And 'for Matthew the idea of a ransom or "substitute" is probably less important here than the radical nature of Jesus' service'.[204] But to what effect? This reading stifles the very significance of this unique logion, which I will develop more later.

The next mention of Jesus' death is made in Matt. 26:2, a Matthean insertion into the briefer Markan text recounting the plot against Jesus (Mark 14:1–2). It seems to indicate that the First Evangelist wanted to make readers aware that Jesus knew that the plot was under way (26:2), whereas Mark and Luke provide no such insight. Matthew 26:2 uniquely asserts that 'the Son of Man will be handed over and crucified'. Readers already know that he will be crucified (20:19), though we learn that he will be 'handed over' (betrayed, παραδέδοται)[205] in the process. Carroll and Green point out that whereas Mark's Passion Narrative begins with the plot to kill Jesus, Matthew has Jesus himself predict his death at the Passover, and only then (τότε) 'do the religious leaders proceed to hatch the plot to kill him (26:3–5).[206]

The most important statement about Jesus' death in Matthew is found in 26:28, where Jesus refers to the wine as 'my blood of the covenant, which is poured out for many for the forgiveness of sins'. This verse contains some significant redactions from its Markan source, for where Mark reads 'This is my blood of the covenant which is poured out for many' (14:24b),[207] Matthew's account reads 'For this is my blood of the covenant which concerning many has been poured out for the remission of

[201] Davies and Allison, *Matthew* III, p. 100.

[202] Luz, *Matthew 8–20*, p. 546.

[203] *Ibid.* [204] *Ibid.* [205] Cf. Luz, *Matthäus* IV, p. 52.

[206] Carroll and Green, *Death of Jesus*, p. 43. For a discussion of τοτε as a Matthean redaction, see S. L. Black, *Sentence Conjunctions in the Gospel of Matthew: καί, δέ, τότε, γάρ, οὖν and Aysndeton in Narrative Discourse* (JSNTSup 216; SNTG 9; Sheffield: Academic Press, 2002), pp. 218–53.

[207] Τοῦτό ἐστιν τὸ αἷμά μου τῆς διαθήκης τὸ ἐκχυννόμενον ὑπὲρ πολλῶν.

sins' (26:28).[208] First, whereas both Mark's and Matthew's accounts have Jesus giving the disciples the cup, Matthew replaces Mark's 'and they all drank from it' (Mark 14:23; καὶ ἔπιον ἐξ αὐτοῦ πάντες) with a command from Jesus to 'drink from it, all of you' (Matt. 26:27; πίετε ἐξ αὐτοῦ πάντες). Because Matthew already has Jesus speaking, he omits Mark's 'and he said to them' (καὶ εἶπεν αὐτοῖς Mark 14:24a). He retains verbatim Mark's 'this is my blood of the covenant' (Mark 14:24; Matt. 26:28), but inserts an important γάρ (26:28), indicating that the command to drink (26:28) is based on a truth claim, made in the following verse (26:28), that the drink is Jesus' blood of the covenant. The crucial insertion Matthew makes to the Markan statement is that the blood of the covenant was poured out 'for the remission of sins' (εἰς ἄφεσιν ἁμαρτιῶν, 26:28). Mark (14:24) says that his blood is simply for the many (πολλῶν),[209] while Luke says that it was 'poured out for you' (τὸ ὑπὲρ ὑμῶν ἐκχυννόμενον; 22:20). Matthew seems to take the phrase from Mark's account of Jesus' baptism (1:4; cf. Luke 3:3), the only other location of εἰς ἄφεσιν ἁμαρτιῶν in the Synoptics, and redacts it into the supper narrative:[210] It is not John's baptism of repentance that is for the forgiveness of sins (Mark), but Jesus' blood (Matthew; αἷμα), a clear metaphor for his death (27:4, 24, 25; cf. 27:6, 8).

What occurs at Matthew's account of John's baptisms is not the forgiveness of sins (Mark 1:4), but merely the confessing of sins (Matt. 3:6). 'Sin' and 'sins' occur only eight times in Matthew (1:21; 3:6; 9:2, 5, 6; 12:31; 26:28). We have already seen that Jesus will in some sense 'save his people from their sins' (1:21). Forgiveness of sins is in some way related to Jesus' healing of a paralytic (9:2, 5), and Jesus is said to have the authority for such forgiveness (9:6). Forgiveness of 'every sin' was expected to be available at the eschaton (12:31), and now Jesus' death occurs for the purpose of forgiveness of sins (26:28).

The atoning significance of Jesus' death has been variously understood. Some insist that the 'offering of blood sacrifices on the Day of Atonement, for instance, was understood as a way of removing the barrier of sin

[208] τοῦτο γάρ ἐστιν τὸ αἷμά μου τῆς διαθήκης τὸ περὶ πολλῶν ἐκξυννόμενον εἰς ἄφεσιν ἁμαρτιῶν. Some MSS read 'new covenant' (καινης διαθηκης), A C D W $f^{1.13}$ 892. 1006. 1342. 1506 𝔐 latt sys a bo; Ir$^{lat}$. Though the text reading is preferred by $\mathfrak{P}^{37}$ ℵ B L Z Θ 0298$^{vid}$ 33 *pc* mae bo$^{ms}$. It is also possible that Matthew follows the form of Jesus' work that he knew in the practice of the Lord's Supper.

[209] Though some manuscripts (W $f^{13}$ *pc* a vg$^{ms}$ [sa$^{mss}$ bo] bo$^{mss}$) take the Matthean addition for Mark's account.

[210] J. D. G. Dunn (personal conversation). So also A. Schweitzer, *The Mysticism of Paul the Apostle* (trans. W. Montgomery; London: A. & C. Black, 1931), p. 60.

(Lev. 16)',[211] similar to the sin offering (חטאת).[212] The atoning nature of the death is underscored by Matthew's abundance of blood language vis-à-vis Mark and Luke,[213] where αἷμα occurs only six times in both together. Mark's sole reference is found in the 'my blood of the covenant' statement (Mark 14:24). Of Matthew's eight uses of the αἷμα, only that of 26:28 is from Mark (14:24) and only one is from 'Q' ('Q' 11:51; Matt. 23:35).[214] Blood seems to be used in the Old Testament sense of containing life in 23:30, where the word is used for the murder of prophets,[215] as it is similarly used for the 'blood' of Abel and Zechariah, who were 'murdered' (Matt. 23:35).[216] Blood is also used in Matthew in connection with Judas, for the murder of Jesus ('blood money', 27:6; 'Field of Blood', 27:8). In addition to the reference in 26:28, Jesus' blood is said to be 'innocent' by Judas after his betrayal (27:4). Yet this is not an 'innocent blood' that cries out for vengeance (Gen. 4:11), but one which makes atonement (26:28).[217]

The next discussions of Jesus' blood are found in Matt. 27:24–25, an entirely unique Matthean text. First, Pilate washes his hands before a mob and declares that he is innocent of Jesus' blood (ἀθῷός εἰμι ἀπὸ τοῦ αἵματος τοῦ δικαίου τούτου),[218] to which the crowd responds, 'Let his blood be on us and on our children' (τὸ αἷμα αὐτοῦ ἐφ' ἡμᾶς καὶ ἐπὶ τὰ τέκνα ἡμῶν). This text seems to be an acknowledgement of responsibility for Jesus' death on the part of the speakers,[219] particularly in light of the fact that Pilate does not acknowledge responsibility. (There is considerable discussion of the extent of 'all the people' who share in this guilt and the implications of it.[220]) Perhaps it is an allusion to the disaster of the fall of

[211] Carter, *Matthew*, pp. 218–19. Cf. Gen. 2:15–17; 3:1–4; Deut. 29:1–30:20, esp. 29:20–29; 30:15–20; Jer. 25:1–38; Amos 1:3–4:13. Hagner, *Matthew* II, p. 773.

[212] McNeile, *St Matthew*, pp. 382–83. See Gerhardsson, 'Sacrificial Service', p. 25. Davies and Allison (*Matthew*III, p. 475) claim that the allusion to Exod. 24:8 is 'much firmer' than that to the Jeremiah tradition. Moreover, they add, in 'Jewish tradition the Sinai offering becomes explicitly expiatory', citing the Targumim Onkelos and Pseudo-Jonathan. Furthermore, they insist on a 'striking parallel' with Heb. 9:15–22. The importance of the congruity between Matthew and the Hebrews accounts is beyond the scope of this project. Cf. Schweitzer, *Mysticism*, p. 217.

[213] Knowles (p. 207, cf. pp. 74, 219) pays a great deal of attention to Matthew's blood language, comparing Jesus' death with those of prophets by the 'innocent blood' references. Yet only Jesus' blood in the first gospel is depicted as having atoning significance (26:28).

[214] Cf. Robinson *et al.*, p. 288. Luke's are in Luke 11:50, 51; 13:1; 22:20; 22:44.

[215] The term αἷμα is not found in the corresponding 'Q' text. Robinson *et al.*, p. 282.

[216] 'Q' 11:51; cf. Robinson *et al.*, p. 288. [217] Davies and Allison, *Matthew* III, p. 563.

[218] For a discussion of the Old Testament background, cf. Brown, *Death* I, pp. 834–36.

[219] See Lev. 20:9; Deut. 19:10; Josh. 2:19; 2 Sam. 1:16; Jer. 26:15; Ezek. 18:13; 33:4; Acts 5:28; 18:6; *T. Levi* 16:3–4; Davies and Allison, *Matthew* III, p. 591; cf. Luz, *Matthäus* IV, p. 279.

[220] For a discussion, see Brown, *Death* I, pp. 836–39.

Jerusalem in 70 C.E.[221] Some discount the potential to see in 26:28 that the crowd is unwittingly calling for the blood of Jesus to cover its sins (cf. 23:35).[222] Yet Brown is correct not to dismiss this notion so quickly, as the most significant statement pertaining to Jesus' blood in Matthew's gospel asserts that its shedding is for the purpose of forgiveness.[223]

A final allusion to Jesus' death, before that death actually occurs, is in Matt. 27:1. This text is redacted from Mark 15:1, where readers are told that the leaders reach a decision about Jesus, whereas Matthew adds that the decision is to put him to death (κατὰ τοῦ Ιησοῦ ὥστε θανατῶσαι αὐτόν, 27:1). Matthew's addition may be made to align with 26:59,[224] where the decision is made to put Jesus to death, further incriminating the Jewish leaders responsible for it.[225]

## 4 Jesus' Death in Matthew: Conclusion

We have seen that Matthew's portrayal of Jesus' death provides pieces of a developing portrait. Matthew intends his readers, presumably, to assimilate these unfolding pieces to arrive at a coherent picture of the significance of Jesus' death. To Matthew, Jesus' identity is related to his role of saving 'his people from their sins' (1:21). Yet we also know (12:40) that Jesus' death is an integral aspect of his identity. We learn that Jesus' death is necessary (δεῖ; 16:21), expected, and related to his identity as 'the Christ, the son of the living God' (16:17). Later we see that Jesus will be raised from the dead (17:9) and that his death, like John's, is depicted as the death of an innocent prophet inaugurating the restoration of 'all things' (17:11–12; cf. 3:1–15). Moreover, Jesus' death is imminent (17:22–23). We also see that his death will be by crucifixion (20:19) and brought about by the Jewish leaders. Significantly, Jesus' death is 'ransom' (λύτρον) for many (20:28). It is, in some sense, a payment offered to rescue another, perhaps borrowed from cultic texts of the Old Testament. We also see that Jesus' death will result from a betrayal (26:2; cf. 27:1). Although Pilate refuses to accept responsibility for Jesus' death (27:24), others do accept it (27:25). The most important statement about Jesus' death (26:28) asserts that Jesus' death is for the purpose of the forgiveness of

[221] Eusebius, *Dem. ev.* 8.3; *T. Levi* 16:3–4; Davies and Allison, *Matthew* III, pp. 591–92.

[222] Davies and Allison, *Matthew* III, p. 592.

[223] Brown, *Death* I, p. 839; see H. G. Reventlow, 'Sein Blut komme über sein Haupt', *VT* 10 (1960), 327; T. B. Cargal, '"His Blood Be upon Us and upon Our Children": A Matthean Double Entendre?' *NTS* 37 (1991), 109–10.

[224] Davies and Allison, *Matthew* III, p. 553.

[225] See Gundry, p. 552; Hagner, *Matthew* II, p. 809.

sins. The most natural way to understand the evidence seems to be that one cannot divorce Jesus' identity from the nature and purpose of his death and its significance. So, Jesus, as the Christ (16:17–21) came to save people from their sins (1:21). His death was the 'ransom' that paid for their release from captivity to death (20:28), and serves to take away sins (26:28). The 'saving' nature of Jesus' death is underscored even on the cross (27:42), where he is mocked for being unable to 'save' himself by coming down off the cross. The irony is that in remaining on the cross and dying, he is fulfilling his 'saving' role, which was depicted at the very outset of the first gospel. Senior asserts that 'for Matthew the death of Jesus is not only the final revelation of his identity but the most powerful expression of his redemptive mission'.[226] It would be difficult in 27:42 to fail to observe an atoning significance of Jesus' death, perhaps even as explicit as indicating a degree of penal substitution. Kupp suggests that the phrase 'which is poured out for many for the forgiveness of sins' (26:28) is an 'elaboration of the angel's first explanation of "Jesus" in 1.21'. He concludes, 'Here the implied reader sees in part the material shape to one of the fundamental questions of the opening narrative frame: *how* will Jesus bring salvation to his people?'[227]

### Matthew's temple and Jesus' death: Conclusion

Matthew's understanding of the temple and his portrayal of Jesus' death are important factors to be weighed in our interpretation of Matthew's account of the *velum scissum*. The former, we have seen, is strongly affirmed with respect to the validity of the temple's existence, the presence of God in it, its sacrifices, its being a legitimate place for prayer, those on 'Moses' Seat' associated with it. Yet its destruction is imminent, lamentably because of the mismanagement of it by the Jewish leaders. Matthew's portrayal of Jesus' death is explicit as a wilful, atoning act by which people are rescued from their sins. How these two factors contribute to a contextual reading of the *velum scissum* will be discussed in the next chapter.

[226] *The Passion of Jesus in the Gospel of Matthew*, p. 166. Senior (*Passion of Jesus*, pp. 166–67) further asserts that 'the thunderous events that follow upon the death of Jesus belie that mockery. The cosmic signs demonstrate that indeed Jesus in death saved others: the earth is split and the tombs broken open and those asleep in death rise to new life (27:51–53)'.

[227] *Matthew's Emmanuel*, pp. 96–97.

# 6

# ANALYSIS OF THE MATTHEAN *VELUM SCISSUM* PERICOPE

## Introduction

The objective of this chapter is to assimilate data from previous chapters to arrive at a conclusion about the significance of the rending of the veil in Matthew's gospel. I will argue that the Matthean *velum scissum* depicts two striking 'comments' on the significance of Jesus' death. First is that it occasions an apocalyptic opening of heaven whereby the following material is conveyed as a heavenly vision depicting the sovereignty of God despite the tragic event of Jesus' death. The second is that the rending of the veil depicts the cessation of its function, which I have argued is generally to separate God from people. Its rending then permits accessibility to God in a manner not seen since Genesis 3. These readings of the Matthean *velum scissum* text uniquely applied to the Matthean pericope. As I showed in the introduction, the most common views associate the *velum scissum* with the destruction of the Jerusalem temple in 70 C.E. and with statements about accessibility to God found in Hebrews. The former is not without its problems and warrants careful scrutiny and discussion, which I will attempt to undertake below. The latter, accessibility to God, is quite valid but in itself is incomplete and likewise warrants further review. An important starting place, however, is to define the Matthean pericope in question and examine Matthean redaction of his Markan source.

## 1 Text and Redaction

### 1.1 Text

The primary text under consideration is Matt. 27:51a, the *velum scissum* account taken from Mark (15:38). Yet I will also discuss Matthean expansion and redaction of the Markan text within the larger pericope, focusing on the prior material (Jesus' death, Matt. 27:50) and subsequent material (Matthew's 'special material' [27:51b-53] and the 'centurion's profession' [27:54; Mark 15:39]). The textual problem in 27:53b will be addressed with the text itself. The most satisfactory explanation of the Matthean *velum scissum* will, in part, account for all redactional elements in the pericope in question. Here, then, I will examine Matthean redaction in the larger pericope of 27:50–54 and offer some comments on the contribution that his redaction brings to the pericope. This will serve as an initial indication of the significance afforded to the *velum scissum* by the First Evangelist.

### 1.2 Redaction at 27:50: Jesus' Death

Readers of the Matthean pericope (27:50–54) note some striking redactions of the Markan source, which provide some, but not all, of our understanding of how Matthew understands the *velum scissum* account, which he adopts almost *verbatim* from Mark. Matthean redaction to the Markan death scene is significant (Matt. 27:50 = Mark 15:37), for Mark's Jesus yields a loud shout (ἀφεὶς φωνὴν μεγάλην, 15:37) and then simply 'breathed out' or 'expired', using a simple verbal form of ἐκπνέω and offering scant evidence 'for reading into the scene any reference to the Holy Spirit'.[1] Matthew's Jesus, however, cries out (again) in a great voice (πάλιν κράξας).[2] Although Matthew knows the term πνέω (7:25) from which Mark's 'breathed out' (ἐκπνέω)[3] is derived, his Jesus 'yields' not a shout but 'the spirit' (ἀφῆκεν τὸ πνεῦμα, 27:50), which *may* be the Holy Spirit. For Mark the shout and death are a single event[4] though they seem to be distinct in Matthew, whose redaction 'emphasizes the voluntary nature of Jesus' death'.[5] Although yielding of one's spirit is a familiar expression for death,[6] why would Matthew make Mark's single cry/death event into two and change his simple ἐξέπνευσεν to ἀφῆκεν τὸ πνεῦμα and have his Jesus yield his spirit, rather than a cry? Matthew uses ἀφίημι forty-six times with a variety of meanings,[7] though the use in 27:50 is unique in that what is 'released' by Jesus was given to him

[1] R. T. France, *Mark: Evangelist and Teacher* (Downers Grove, Ill.: InterVarsity, 1989), p. 655.

[2] For references to a scream in response to unjust affliction, see W. D. Davies and D. C. Allison, *A Critical and Exegetical Commentary on the Gospel according to Saint Matthew* (3 vols.; ICC; Edinburgh: T.&T. Clark, 1988, 1991, 1997), III, p. 627.

[3] Mark uses ἐκπνέω at 15:37, 39; cf. Luke 23:45.

[4] C. A. Evans, *Mark 8:27–16:20* (WBC 34B; Nashville, Tenn.: Nelson, 2001), p. 508.

[5] Cf. *Apoc. Sedr.* 10:3. Davies and Allison, *Matthew* III, pp. 627–28.

[6] Gen. 35:18 (death of Rachel); *1 Esd.* 4:21 (a man); cf. Josephus, *Ant.* 1.12.3 §218; 5.2.8 §147; 12.11.2 §430; 14.13.10 §369; *2 En.* 70:16.

[7] It is used for consenting to something (3:15) or permitting (7:4; 13:30; 19:14; 23:13; 24:2) something to happen. It is also used for leaving Jesus unmolested (4:11; 22:22; 27:49).

earlier: 'the Spirit' (τὸ πνεῦμα). Reception of the Spirit occurs at Jesus' baptism (3:16), where 'heaven was opened and [Jesus] saw the Spirit of God descending like a dove and lighting on him', where Matthean redaction may have been influenced by Isaiah 42:1.[8] This is one of only two occurrences of πνεῦμα in Matthew where Jesus is said to have received the Spirit. The second (12:18) quotes directly from Isaiah 42:1–4, depicting a commissioning of Jesus for his messianic mission.[9] The arrival of the Spirit upon Jesus refers not to an adoptionist Christology (Jesus was already of the Holy Spirit from his birth; 1:18–25), but to the inauguration of his messianic mission.[10] Perhaps Jesus' 'yielding of the Spirit' is a result of the fulfilment of his role. That is, the initiation of his messianic role is indicated by his reception of the Spirit at his baptism, and its completion is indicated by his yielding of the same Spirit at his death. It is, in effect, an indication that his messianic role is accomplished in his death.[11] This reading is congruent with our analysis (in Chapter 5) of the purposeful death of Jesus in relation to his mission and will again become important for structural purposes below.

### 1.3 Redaction at 27:51a: the *velum scissum* Proper

The *velum scissum* proper (Matt. 27:51a = Mark 15:38) is taken almost *verbatim* from Mark, with two slight but significant differences. First,

It is used for leaving behind something important for a greater purpose (4:20, 22; 5:24, 40; 8:22; 18:12; 19:27, 29). It is used for forgiving debts (6:12) or sins (6:14, 15; 12:31, 32; 12:32; 18:21), sins and illnesses (9:2, 5, 6) or even the cancelling of a debt (18:27, 32, 35) seemingly as a metaphor for forgiveness of sins. It can also be used for abandonment (apparently in judgement, 15:14; 23:28; 24:40, 41), the departure of an illness (8:15), forsaking of the law (23:23), giving a wife to someone else (22:25), simple physical departure (13:36; 26:44) or deserting Jesus and leaving him for his arrest (26:56).

[8] Davies and Allison, *Matthew* I, p. 334.

[9] Cf. R. Beaton, *Isaiah's Christ in Matthew's Gospel* (SNTSMS 123; Cambridge: Cambridge University Press, 2002), pp. 190–95. Elsewhere in Matthew (in which 19 occurrences of πνεῦμα are found), it is used of the Holy Spirit, which was the means by which Jesus was conceived (1:18, 20) and the instrument of the baptism with which he will baptise (3:11). The Holy Spirit led Jesus into the desert to be tempted (4:1), and the 'spirit of God' was the means by which Jesus drove out demons, as evidence that 'the kingdom of God has come upon you' (12:28). Πνεῦμα is used of evil spirits associated with demons that cause illness and that Jesus and his disciples drove out of people (8:16; 10:1; 12:43, 45). It is also used of the will of a person (26:41; cf. 5:3). The spirit of God gives people speech (10:20; 22:43), and blasphemy against it will not be forgiven (12:31, 32). Finally, the name of the Holy Spirit is, in part, what disciples are to be baptized into (28:20).

[10] Davies and Allison, *Matthew* I, p. 335.

[11] Cf. *Apoc. Sedr.* 10:3; Davies and Allison, *Matthew* III, pp. 627–28; M. Eloff, 'Restoration from Exile as a Hermeneutical Prism for a Theological Interpretation of Matthew's Gospel' (Th.D. diss.; Stellenbosch University, 2002), pp. 4–20 and n. 49.

Mark's καὶ becomes καὶ ἰδοὺ in Matthew, an expression carefully examined by A. Vargas-Machuca in the 'Narrative Style of Matthew'.[12] Vargas-Machuca shows that καὶ ἰδοὺ occurs as a demonstrative particle in Matthean redaction[13] and demonstrates that in the first gospel, 'the basic meaning of the particle *idou* in narrative context is to introduce something relatively new and of certain importance for the story'.[14] Indeed, Matthew's 24 uses of καὶ ἰδου[15] always introduce something unexpected in a narrative,[16] often theophanic in nature, such as the angelic appearance to Joseph (2:13) or to Jesus (4:11), the opening of heaven (3:16) and the voice from heaven declaring Jesus as God's Son (3:17; 17:5), or

[12] '(Καὶ) ἰδού en el estilo narrative de Mateo', *Bib.* 50 (1969), 233–44.

[13] His diagram illustrates the distribution of the expression:

| Frequencies | Mt | Mk | Lk | Jn |
|---|---|---|---|---|
| Of the particle ἰδού | 62 | 7 | 57 | 4 |
| Of the expression: καὶ ἰδού | 28 | 0 | 24 | 0 |
| In the narration: καὶ ἰδού | 23 | 0 | 15 | 0 |
| In the narration: ἰδού | 10 | 0 | 1 | 0 |

A. Vargas-Machuca, '(Καὶ) ἰδού en el estilo narrative de Mateo', *Bib.* 50 (1969), 233. Cf. M. Johannessohn, 'Die Wahrnehmungssatz bei den Verben des Sehens in der hebräischen und griechischen Bibel', *ZVS* 64 (1937), 141–260; *idem*, 'Das biblische καὶ ἰδού in der Erzahlung samt seiner hebräischen Vorlage', *ZVS* 66 (1939), 145–95 and 67 (1940), 30–84.

[14] Vargas-Machuca, p. 234; cf. W. Bauer, *Griechisch-deutsches Wörterbuch zu den Schriften des Neuen Testaments und der frühchristlichen Literatur* (5th edn; Berlin: De Gruyter, 1963), col. 733; D. A. Hagner, *Matthew* (2 vols.; WBC 33A–B; Dallas, Tex.: Word, 1993, 1995), I, p. 18.

[15] Matt. 2:13; 3:16, 17; 4:11; 7:4; 8:2, 24, 29, 32, 34; 9:2, 3, 10, 20; 12:10, 41, 42; 15:22; 17:3, 5; 19:16; 20:30; 26:51; 27:51; 28:2, 7, 9, 20. D. Andreoli, 'Il velo sqaurciato nel Vangelo di Matteo', *BSW* 1 (1998), 22, categorises them as follows: ten times it introduces a miracle (8:1–2, 23–24, 28–29; 9:1–2, 19–20; 12:9–10; 15:21–22; 20:29–30; 28:8–9), four times it introduces an extraordinary fact (2:9; 3:16; 19:16; 27:51) and four times it introduces a new episode (8:32, 34; 9:3; 26:50b–51). It serves to unite what follows with what precedes tightly, which is mostly Jesus (3:16; 8:1–2, 23–24, 28–29; 9:1–2, 10, 19–20; 12:9–10; 15:21–22; 19:15; 20:29–30; 27:50–51). In a narrative context it frequently begins a new pericope, but never an absolute beginning because it binds with the preceding sentence.

[16] These are: the presence of a plank in one's eye (7:4); a leper's coming to Jesus to be healed (8:2); the sudden appearance of a furious storm (8:24); the speaking of demons (8:29); the rush of a herd of pigs down a bank (8:32); the appearance of an entire town to drive away Jesus (8:34); the presence of unexpected faith (9:2); the shock of Jesus' forgiving sins (9:3); the shock of Jesus eating with tax collectors and sinners (9:10); a bleeding woman coming to Jesus to be healed (9:20); a man with a shriveled hand coming to Jesus to be healed (12:10); Jesus being greater than Jonah (12:41) and Solomon (12:42); the sudden appearance of Moses and Elijah (17:3); a man's asking Jesus about inheriting eternal life (19:16); two blind men by a roadside seeking healing from Jesus (20:30); Jesus' companion reaches for his sword (26:51); the resurrected Jesus' going into Galilee (28:7); the resurrected Jesus' suddenly appearing (28:9); despite his ascension into heaven, Jesus' proclaiming that he will be with his disciples (28:20).

the earthquake and appearance of an angel at the empty tomb (28:2).[17] Matthew's καὶ ἰδοὺ in 27:51a is likewise used to indicate something unexpected and theophanic in nature, for a theophanic understanding seems most congruent with the divine origin of the *velum scissum* and the subsequent 'special material' (27:51b-53), an origin which is depicted by employing the 'divine passives' (*passivum divinum*), as we will see below. Also, a theophanic understanding of καὶ ἰδοὺ appreciates the correlation between the *velum scissum* and two other places where the expression occurs: the opening of heaven (3:16) and the transfiguration (17:3),[18] which I will also examine with some care below.

Yet the unexpected theophanic nature of the expression is not the only way καὶ ἰδοὺ is used. The expression has also been shown to lend to the narrative coherence of the pericope (27:51a–52) *and* to serve as a 'commentary pragmatic marker'. S. Black, independently of Vargas-Machuca, notes that in Matthew's gospel καί lends narrative cohesion to our pericope, outlining it as follows:

> 27:51a καὶ ἰδοὺ τὸ καταπέτασμα τοῦ ναοῦ ἐσχίσθη ἀπ' ἄνωθεν ἕως κάτω εἰς δυό
> 27:51b καὶ ἡ γῆ ἐσείσθη
> 27.51c καὶ αἱ πέτραι ἐσχίσθησαν,
> 27:52a καὶ τὰ μνημεῖα ἀνεῴχθησαν
> 27:52b καὶ πολλὰ σώματα τῶν κεκοιμημένων ἁγίων ἠγέρθησαν . . .[19]

Black comments that 'by using this marked syntactical structure Matthew highlights each incident that takes place. At the same time, portraying the continuity of the clauses with καί signals the audience that the separate incidents form one significant event, an event of some prominence in Matthew's account of Jesus' death'.[20] Yet Black adds that καὶ with ἰδοὺ

[17] Vargas-Machuca (p. 240) argues that it resumes a narration after a quotation, or continues the narration with extraordinary facts. E.g. 2:19 (angel appears to Joseph); 3:16 (opening of heaven); 19:16 (the appearance of the rich young man); and 27:51 (*sic*) the rending of the veil. Although Vargas-Machuca entertains the possibility various sources for Matthew's use of ἰδού vis-à-vis Mark's use of the term, he concludes that Matthew's is a redactional use of Mark's. Cf. M. Johannessohn, 'Das biblische καὶ ἰδού', p. 61.

[18] See A. D. A. Moses, *Matthew's Transfiguration Story and Jewish-Christian Controversy* (JSNTSup 122; Sheffield: Academic Press, 1996), pp. 127–28.

[19] S. L. Black, *Sentence Conjunctions in the Gospel of Matthew: καί, δέ, τότε, γάρ, οὖν and Aysndeton in Narrative Discourse* (JSNTSup 216; SNTG 9; Sheffield: Academic Press, 2002), pp. 128. So also D. P. Senior, *The Passion Narrative according to Matthew: A Redactional Study* (Leuven: Leuven University Press, 1975), p. 307, who notes this is a 'rigid series of co-ordinate καί[s]', which is an unusual construction for Matthew (cf. p. 307, n. 4)

[20] *Ibid.*, p. 129.

in Matthew serves as a 'commentary pragmatic marker'[21] on the prior event to which it is related.[22] This leaves Jesus' death (which I identified as atoning) as the main subject upon which the subsequent material (the *velum scissum*, 'special material', and the 'centurion's profession') functions as commentary, explaining important facts concerning the death of Jesus.[23] Senior agrees, asserting that Matthew's addition of ἰδού to Mark's 'threadbare' καί 'serves as a connection between Jesus' death in 27:50 and the signs that follow'.[24]

Narrative analyses underscore the 'commentary' role of καὶ ἰδοὺ and following material by recognising that after Jesus' baptism, 'the narrator shifts to an internal viewpoint aligned spatially with Jesus, which is maintained until his death, whereupon the narrator's viewpoint again becomes external (27:51). Matthew 1–2 and 27:51–28:20 thus form the Gospel's narrative frame, on the basis of the narrator's external-internal shift viewpoint'.[25] A shift in the narrative frame supports the notion that the author is, by changing perspectives, commenting in some respect upon the last element in the narrative whole (3:1–27:50), which is the death of Jesus (27:50).[26] Thus Matthean use of καὶ ἰδοὺ in 27:51a seems to assert the unexpected, theophanic nature of the events following Jesus' death, upon

21 *Ibid*., p. 134, citing the phraseology of J. Fraser, 'An Approach to Discourse Markers', *JP* 14 (1990), 385–86. Black (p. 135) adds, 'καί generally contributes little to discourse processing when καὶ ἰδού appears'.

22 Examples include 1:20, 2:1, 9, 13, etc. See Black, pp. 134–36.

23 Similarly, J. E. Yates, *The Spirit and the Kingdom* (London: SPCK, 1963), p. 234, insists that in Mark (and surely Matthew as well), 'the central and undoubted historical fact is Jesus dead upon the Cross. Surely, here is the true centre of attention: why, then, should not the comment at 15.38 be a direct reference to Jesus himself?' From Lightfoot, Yates further says, 'The primary reference, accordingly, is to the *work* of Jesus, consummated in the Passion'. Senior, 'Death of God's Son and the Beginning of the New Age', in *The Language of the Cross* (ed. A. Lacomara; Chicago, Ill.: Franciscan Herald Press, 1977), p. 40; J. R. Donahue, *Are You the Christ? The Trial Narrative in the Gospel of Mark* (SBLDS 10; Missoula, Mont.: University of Montana Press, 1973), pp. 201–6; J. B. Green, 'The Death of Jesus and the Reding of the Temple Veil: A Window into Luke's Understanding of Jesus and the Temple', *SBLSP* 30 (1991), 551, n. 30.

24 Senior, *Redactional Study*, p. 307. So also M. de Jonge, 'Matthew 27:51 in Early Christian Exegesis', *HTR* 79 (1986), 69–70.

25 D. D. Kupp, *Matthew's Emmanuel: Divine Presence and God's People in the First Gospel* (SNTSMS 90; Cambridge: Cambridge University Press, 1996), p. 52. Kupp also puts forth several arguments 'for seeing 27.51–28.20 as the closing narrative frame of the story. The death of a protagonist forms a natural termination in itself. At the same point in our story the narrator's spatial alignment makes a significant shift away from Jesus, to an external point of view. The narrator's concern becomes the impact of Jesus' death on the cosmic level through various signs and miraculous events (27.51–4), which on the human level effect the soldiers' confession' (p. 100; cf. his chart on p. 101).

26 J. Knowles, *Jeremiah in Matthew's Gospel: The Rejected-Prophet Motif in Matthean Redaction* (JSNTSup 68; Sheffield: JSOT Press, 1993), pp. 78, 238–39, n. 4; M. A. Powell, *What is Narrative Criticism?* (Minneapolis, Minn.: Fortress, 1990), p. 42. R. D. Witherup,

which the following material serves as 'commentary'. The fact that ἰδοὺ is a visual term will be examined below.

The second Matthean redaction of the *velum scissum* text proper (Matt. 27:51a = Mark 15:38) is the order of events immediately subsequent to it. Matthew follows Mark in saying τὸ καταπέτασμα τοῦ ναοῦ ἐσχίσθη, but Mark says that it was rent εἰς δύο ἀπ' ἄνωθεν ἕως κάτω, whereas Matthew reads it was rent ἀπ' ἄνωθεν ἕως κάτω εἰς δύο.[27] Matthew's recording of the event – that it was split first, then into two – is recognised as providing a more natural reading of the sequence of the events than Mark's, which puts the results first.[28]

### 1.4 Redaction at 27:51b–53: The 'Special Material'

The third Matthean redaction to the Markan *velum scissum* is the most significant, because his account of the splitting of the stones, raising of the holy onesand so forth, is found nowhere else in extant Jewish or Christian literature prior to the Matthean text (27:51b–53). This begs the question of why Matthew elaborates on Mark at this point. Mark shows the centurion's confession seemingly in direct response to the rending of the veil at Jesus' death. Presumably Matthew considers this an inadequate cause for the centurion's confession, or at the very least an incomplete one. Why is this so? Moreover, why is there additional Matthean redaction to the centurion's confession itself? For not only has Matthew inserted the 'special material', but he has created a fourth redactional element to his Markan source by changing the singular centurion (Mark 15:39) to a centurion *and others* (Matt. 27:54) who did not simply hear Jesus' cry and see how he died (Mark 15:39) but also saw 'the earthquake and all that had happened' (Matt. 27:54). Finally, the single centurion's profession of Jesus as 'son of God' (Mark 15:39) is changed in Matthew to his first being 'terrified' and then stating that Jesus is 'son of God' (Matt. 27:54). So, Matthew is concerned not only with the addition of his 'special material'

'The Cross of Jesus: A Literary-Critical Study of Matthew 27' (Ph.D. diss; Union Theological Seminary in Virginia, 1985), p. 277 claims that vv 51–54 are 'the climax of the entire chapter'. Moreover, 'This passage (vv. 51–54) is inextricably bound to the prior section of material and is to be seen as portraying the consequences of Jesus' death'. D. Hill, 'Matthew 27:51–53 in the Theology of the Evangelist', *IBS* 7 (1985), 76, contends that 'the brief apocalypse is the vehicle of a theological (and eschatological) interpretation of Jesus' death'.

[27] Though mss A C[3] W $f^{1.13}$ 892 1006 1342 1506 ***M*** Sy[p.h] and mae conform the Matthean reading to Mark's.

[28] Andreoli, 'Il velo squarciato nel Vangelo di Matteo', 21; Senior, *Redactional Study*, p. 308.

but also that at least one element of it (the earthquake) is 'seen' and contributes to the spectators' 'fear'. Is all of this redactional activity simply for narrative purposes – making a more plausible basis for the centurion's confession by making more dramatic events that would create a sense of awe? While the Matthean special material does heighten the sense of awe, why would Matthew change the singular observer to plural, and indicate that 'they' responded in fear? The most satisfactory solution accounts for all the Matthean redaction and illustrates the significance of additional material in light of other Matthean texts and recognisable images from other influential texts in the first-century Jewish/Christian literary milieu. Adding these images surely contributes to the profundity that elicits the subsequent response, but why *these* images? That is, what was lacking in Mark's material subsequent to the *velum scissum* that Matthew felt it needed such profound elaboration using *these extraordinary depictions*?

To answer this question we must enter the complicated discussion of the nature and significance of the special material itself. I cannot discuss this material comprehensively, but I will examine each phrase to try to identify the contribution it lends to the Matthean insertion of his special material. The first item that he reports is an earthquake (27:51b; καὶ ἡ γῆ ἐσείσθη). Earthquakes were frequently present in theophanic scenes[29] and are expected to occur at the end of time,[30] particularly in apocalyptic literature (which I will define below).[31] Although such earthquakes can frequently accompany judgement themes,[32] for Matthew this does not seem to be the case. It seems that in light of the other positive portents surrounding Jesus' death and the use of an earthquake in 28:2, at a resurrection, the theophanic reading (without judgement) is preferable.[33]

[29] R. Bauckham, 'The Eschatological Earthquake in the Apocalypse of John', *NovT* 19 (1977), 224.

[30] Joel 2:10; 4:16; Isa. 24:18–23; 29:6; Mic. 1:4; Nah. 1:5. Cf. J. Lange, *Das Erscheinen des Auferstandenen im Evangelium nach Mattäus: Eine traditions- und redaktionsgeschichtliche Unterzuchung zu Mt 28, 16–20* (Würzburg: Echter Verlag, 1973), p. 366; P. Hinnebusch, *St Matthew's Earthquake: Judgment and Discipleship in the Gospel of Matthew* (Ann Arbor, Mich.: Servant, 1980), pp. 143–50.

[31] Bauckham, 'Eschatological Earthquake', pp. 226–27. In Rev. 11:19 such an earthquake takes place where 'the temple is opened so that the power and glory of God might be manifested on earth in the final judgment of the nations'.

[32] Davies and Allison (*Matthew* III, p. 632, cf. n. 113) note that Zech. 14:5 particularly serves as background to this earthquake, which ancients typically viewed as 'responses to human wickedness', though this is by no means the only occasion. They note that in *As. Mos.* 10:4–5 and *T. Levi* 4:1 eschatological earthquakes and darkness occur together, whereas in Rev. 11 resurrection and earthquakes are joined.

[33] See Davies and Allison, *Matthew* III, pp. 632, 664–65. Hagner, *Matthew* II, p. 849, citing Matt. 24:7; 28:2, with Old Testament background in Isa. 24:19; 29:6; Jer. 10:10; Amos 8:8, etc. So also P. Luomanen, *Entering the Kingdom of Heaven* (WUNT II, 101;

Matera concludes that Matthew's use of σείσμος indicates 'a manifestation of God's power in Jesus', which reaches a climax at the resurrection of the dead.[34] Further, in Matthew's gospel an earthquake has been understood to raise issues tied to Jesus' identity (as Son of God, v. 54).[35] It has also been widely recognised that Matthew draws, at least in part,[36] from Ezek. 37, where an earthquake (σεισμός; Ezek. 37:7 LXX) precedes the opening of graves and the resurrection of people who return to the land of Israel (Ezek. 37:12–13). McDonald asserts that the earthquake is 'Matthew's code for an apocalyptic act of God'.[37] For the present, it is important to recognise the theophanic nature of the event in light of Ezek. 37.

In 27:51c, again a *passivum divinum* of σχίζω is used. This time, rather than the veil's being rent (51a), the rocks are split (καὶ αἱ πέτραι ἐσχίσθησαν). Pelletier claims that whatever split the rocks split the veil,[38] and surely God is intended to be seen as the agent of both.[39] The splitting

Tübingen: Mohr Siebeck, 1998), p. 108. Cf. Allison, *New Moses: A Matthean Typology* (Edinburgh: T. & T. Clark, 1993); I. Maisch, 'Die Österliche Dimension des Todes Jesu: Zur Osterverkündigung in Mt 27,51–54', in *Auferstehung Jesus – Auferstehung der Christen: Deutungen des Österglaubes* (ed. A. Vögtle and I. Broer; Freiburg: Herder, 1986 ), p. 109.

[34] F. J. Matera, *Passion Narratives and Gospel Theologies: Interpreting the Synoptics through Their Passion Stories* (New York, N.Y.: Paulist Press, 1986), p. 116; cf. Hill, 'Matthew 27:51–53', 76; Witherup, 'The Death of Jesus and the Raising of the Saints: Matthew 27:51–54 in Context', *SBLSP* 26 (1987), 580; U. Luz, *Das Evangelium nach Matthäus* (EKKNT; 4 vols.; Zürich: Benziger Verlag, 1985–2002), IV, p. 364. For Carson ('Matthew', p. 581) an earthquake is *both* a 'symbol of judgment and theophanic glory', citing 1 Kgs 19:11; Isa. 29:6; Jer. 10:10; Ezek. 26:18, and Bauckham, 'Eschatological Earthquake', pp. 224–33. Cf. also M. Riebl, *Auferstehung Jesu in der Stunde seines Todes? Zur Botschaft von Mt 27, 51b–53* (Stuttgart: Katholisches Bibelwerk, 1978), pp. 75–77; de Jonge, 'Matthew 27:51 in Early Christian Exegesis', pp. 70–71; R. Kratz, *Auferweckung als Befreiung: Eine Studie zur Passions- und Auferstehungstheologie des Matthäus (besonders Mt 27,62–28,15)* (Stuttgart: Katholisches Bibelwerk, 1973), pp. 38–47. Harrington, *The Gospel according to Matthew* (SP 1; Collegeville, Minn.: Liturgical Press, 1983), p. 400, claims that 'the earthquake serves as the prelude to the resurrection of the dead'.

[35] Witherup, 'The Cross of Jesus', p. 283. A σείσμος, in Matthew, occurs where the Sea of Galilee is 'shaken' (8:24; cf. Luomanen, p. 106) and in the city of Jerusalem upon Jesus' entry (21:10). While Matthew's trial scene does raise the issue of 'judgement' in a nearby context, there is no apparent indication that the recipient of any type of judgement is anyone other than Jesus.

[36] Also earthquakes were expected to accompany God's filling of Zerubbabel's temple with his glory (Hag. 2:6–7). J. T. Carroll and J. B. Green, *The Death of Jesus in Early Christianity* (Peabody, Mass.: Hendrickson, 1995), p. 49; cf. Carter, pp. 223–25.

[37] J. I. H. McDonald, *The Resurrection: Narrative and Belief* (London: SPCK, 1989), p. 91, cited in N. T. Wright, *The Resurrection of the Son of God* (Minneapolis, Minn.: Fortress, 2003), p. 634 n. 5.

[38] A. Pelletier, 'La tradition synoptique "Voile déchiré" à la lumière des réalités archéologiques', *Recherches de science religieuse* 46 (1958), 174.

[39] It could be argued that this is simply a way of expressing past tense in a narrative. However, that notion would hold well for an aorist verb, while the use of aorist passives in

of the stones is also the result of a manifestation of God's power (Nah. 1:5–6; 1 Kgs 19:11; Ps. 114:7f; Isa. 48:21) and is used in some Second Temple texts to indicate God's victory over death in the final age.[40] Although scholars recognise allusions to a number of (Jewish) texts,[41] Allison has persuasively argued that Zech. 14:4–5 stands out as most appropriate.[42] In that text the Mount of Olives is 'split' and the Lord comes together with 'all the holy ones'.[43] In addition to Ezek. 37, Allison finds Zech. 14 in the Dura-Europa synagogue's north panel as important background for this Matthean text, for in that panel the resurrected dead come forth from a split Mount of Olives.[44] The significance of this background, for Allison, is that in Zech. 14 the allusions drawn by Matthew, where the rocks are the Mount of Olives, depict the turning of a new eschatological age.[45]

In v. 52a Matthew recounts the opening of tombs (καὶ τὰ μνημεῖα ἀνεῴχθησαν). Scholars have frequently noted the allusion to LXX Ezek. 37:12–13 (ἀνοίγω ὑμῶν τὰ μνήματα).[46] Here, again, we find a parallel in the opening of tombs after the splitting of the stones in the Dura Europa synagogue wall-painting, which portrays the resurrection of the dead as a vivid depiction of the 'enlivening of the dry bones in Ezek. 37'.[47] A figure,

this sequence has been recognised by most commentators on this pericope as designating divine origin, i.e., the so-called divine passive.

40 Senior, 'Death of God's Son', pp. 42–43.

41 Rocks are similarly split in 1 Kgs 19:11–12; Isa. 2:19; 48:21; Nah. 1:5–6; Zech. 14:4; *T. Levi* 4:1.

42 Allison, *The End of the Ages Has Come: An Early Interpretation of the Passion and Resurrection of Jesus* (Philadelphia, Pa.: Fortress, 1985), pp. 40–46. So also R. D. Aus, *Samuel, Saul and Jesus: Three Early Palestinian Jewish Christian Gospel Haggadoth* (South Florida Studies in the History of Judaism 105; Atlanta, Ga.: Scholars Press, 1994), pp. 117–19.

43 Carroll and Green, p. 49.

44 Allison, *End of the Ages*, p. 43. He finds support in *Tg.* Zech. 14:3–5; *Tg.* Song 8:5; *Song Rab.* 4:11 §1; *Ruth Rab.* 2; *Eccles. Rab.* 1:11 §1; cf. R. E. Goodenough, ed., *Jewish Symbols in the Greco-Roman Period* (12 vols.; New York, N.Y.: Pantheon, 1953–65), X, pp. 179–96; see XI, plate 21, for a good reproduction of this plate. Cf. H. Riesenfeld, *The Resurrection in Ezekiel XXXVII and in the Dura-Europas Paintings* (UUA 11; Stockholm: Amqvist & Wiksells, 1948), pp. 27–38; J. B. Curtis, 'An Investigation of the Mount of Olives in the Judaeo-Christian Tradition', *HUCA* 28 (1957), 170–72.

45 Allison, *End of the Ages*, p. 46.

46 Davies and Allison, *Matthew* III, p. 633; Cf. Luz, *Matthäus* IV, pp. 364–65. Senior, *Redactional Study*, p. 320; E. Schweizer, *The Good News according to Matthew* (trans. D. E. Green; London: SPCK, 1976), p. 515, and D. A. Hagner, 'Apocalyptic Motifs in the Gospel of Matthew: Continuity and Discontinuity', *HBT* 7 (1985), 62.

47 R. E. Brown, *The Death of the Messiah: A Commentary on the Passion Narratives in the Four Gospels* (2 vols.; New York, N.Y.: Doubleday, 1994), II, p. 1123. Riesenfeld, *Resurrection in Ezekiel*; R. Wischnitzel-Bernstein, 'The Conception of the Resurrection in the Ezekiel Panel of the Dura Synagogue', *JBL* 60 (1941), 43–55; A. Brabar, 'Le theme

perhaps the Davidic Messiah (Ezek. 37:24–25), is then depicted raising the dead. Significantly, Ezek. 37:12–13 'offers the only *opening* of tombs (as distinct from the simple raising of the dead) described in the OT'.[48] Furthermore, in the Ezekiel text the opening of the tombs is associated with knowing the Lord and his leadership of them into restoration from exile, which *may be* similar to the assertion that Matthew's holy ones come out of their tombs after Jesus' resurrection (v. 53b).

Many have recognised that Matt. 27:52b (καὶ πολλὰ σώματα τῶν κεκοιμημένων ἁγίων ἠγέρθησαν) is the thematic climax of this mini-narrative.[49] Alhough this text raises questions too numerous to be discussed here,[50] most see here a reference to Old Testament saints from Ezekiel 37,[51] surely with influence from such texts as Zech. 14:4–5[52] and

religieux des fresques de la synagogue de Doura (245–56 après J. C.)', *RHR* 123 (1941), 143–92. R. Aguirre Monasterio, *Exégesis de Mateo, 27, 51b–53: para una teologia de la muerte de Jesus en el Evangelio de Mateo* (Vitoria: Editorial Eset, 1980), pp. 84–97, relates various targumic and Jewish liturgical reflections to the Dura frescoes. Brown (*Death* II, p. 1123, n. 62) says, 'None of this material is a totally reliable guide to 1st cent AD folkloric understanding of the raising of the dead, but it may well be closer to that understanding than is modern exegesis of OT texts pertaining to the subject'.

[48] Brown, *Death* II, p. 1123. Following Brown, we doubt the conjecture connecting the giving of the Spirit (Ezek. 37:6) and Jesus' yielding his spirit (Matt. 27:50). For a full discussion, see Brown, *Death* II, p. 1123, n. 64.

[49] Senior, *Redactional Study*, pp. 314–15. Andreoli ('Il velo squarciato nel Vangelo di Matteo', pp. 25–26; cf. 29 n. 34) asserts that the raising of the holy ones is, for him, a 'literary summit' which requires the coherence of the special material (27:51b–53) as a whole and was written very early, prior to its incorporation into Matthew, though he agrees with Aguirre Monasterio (*Exégesis de Mateo, 27, 51b–53*) that Matthew was himself the final editor. D. Senior, 'Revisiting Matthew's Special Material in the Passion Narrative: A Dialogue with Raymond Brown (The Death of the Messiah, 1994)', *ETL* 70 (1994), 418.

[50] The identity of these 'fallen asleep holy ones' has been the subject of some discussion. Luz (*Matthäus* IV, p. 365) insists that since Matthew refers to πολλὰ ('many') rather than 'all' of the holy ones, he cannot refer to the general resurrection. Others ask whether this is a general or some other resurrection. D. Witherup ('The Death of Jesus', p. 574) looks solely to how the event 'functions within the context of Matthew 27 and the Gospel of Matthew as a whole'. R. H. Gundry, *Matthew: A Commentary on His Handbook for a Mixed Church under Persecution* (Grand Rapids, Mich.: Eerdmans, 1994), p. 576, suggests that τῶν ἁγίων is used to produce a parallel between 'the holy people' and 'the holy city' into which they enter, and this, if true, may underscore the visionary nature of the pericope, as it would then connect the raised people *and* Jerusalem with the visionary 'holy city' in Matt. 4:1–11.

[51] Senior, 'Death of God's Son', p. 45, referring to the general resurrection. Brown (*Death* II, p. 1125) suggests that τῶν κεκοιμημένων ἁγίων is an epexegetical expression to πολλὰ σώματα, denoting that the 'many bodies' *are* 'the fallen-asleep holy ones'. Thus it does not refer to every holy one of all time.

[52] LXX Davies and Allison, *Matthew* III, p. 633: 'saints in an eschatological context', citing LXX Isa. 4:3; Dan. 7:18, 22; Did. 16:7; *T. Levi* 18:11; *Liv. Pro.* (Jer.) 15. They note also that 'although the "many" came to be commonly equated with all the redeemed of pre-Christian times . . ., the text does not support this notion' (cf. Ignatius, *Magn.* 9.2 Contrast Isho 'dad, *Comm.* 22: only 500 saints were raised (an allusion to

Dan. 12:2,[53] who were simply 'the pious Israelites whose resurrection

1 Cor. 15:6; contra Gundry, p. 576, who claims that 'in Semitic speech, "many" often meant "all"'.). Allison, *End of the Ages*, p. 43–44, and J. Gnilka, *Das Matthäusevangelium* (2 vols.; Freiburg: Herder, 1986, 1988), II, p. 477. Zech. 14:4–5 is interpreted in the Dura Europa north panel, where the Mount of Olives split, 'the revived dead are emerging from the crack. The fallen building on the slopes of the mountain probably symbolizes an earthquake (Zech. 14:4), and those resurrected are in all likelihood here identified with the "holy ones" of Zech. 14:5'. Allison, *End of the Ages*, p. 43. *Tg.* Zech. 14:3–5; *Tg.* Song 8:3; and other rabbinics which see 'holy ones' of Zech. 14:5 as the ancient saints. For patristic material see the section on Christ's descent into Hades in R. J. Bauckham, 'Descent to the Underworld', *ABD* II, pp. 145–59. On identifications of 'the holy ones' of Zech. 14:5 in New Testament texts (usually dead Christians, sometimes angels), see R. J. Bauckham, 'A Note on a Problem in the Greek Version of I Enoch i.9', *JTS* 32 (1981), 136–38.

[53] Gundry, pp. 576–77. Perhaps it is difficult to divorce Dan. 12 from any discussion of resurrection in the New Testament. Scholars have argued for other sources of influence for Matthew's 'special material'. Very recently, R. L. Troxel, 'Matt. 27.51–54 Reconsidered: Its Role in the Passion Narrative, Meaning and Origin', *NTS* 48 (2002), 30–47, suggested that the evangelist drew from a tradition in *1 Enoch* for his depiction of the raising of the saints. While Matthew is, indeed, drawing upon apocalyptic imagery similar to that employed in *1 Enoch* (earthquakes, open heaven, resurrection, etc.), this does not mean that he employs them in the same way *1 Enoch* (93:6) does. Moreover, Troxel's proposal is not without its serious problems. Although he acknowledges broad scholarly consensus that the text is dependent on Ezek. 37:1–14 and Zech. 14:4–5, where raising and saints are present, Troxel curiously insists that 'aside from "the saints" there is no element in Matt. 27.51–3 that is distinctly related to Zech 14.4–5' (p. 42). Apparently he does not recognise the association of the splitting of the Mount of Olives in two with the splitting of the veil and says that the rending of the rocks in Matthew 'shows no necessary reliance on Zechariah's split mountain' (p. 43) (27:51/Zech. 14:4). He also overlooks the earthquake in Zech. 14:5 (referring to the earthquake in Uzziah's time; cf. Matt. 27:52), and discounts appeals to *Tg.* Zech. 14:4–5 and *Tg.* Song 8:5 and rabbinic traditions that 'Elijah will blow the trumpet summoning the dead to resurrection on the Mount of Olives' (Davies and Allison, *Matthew* III, p. 629, n. 89), because it does not identify them as 'holy ones' (p. 43, n. 75). How he then bypasses the Ezek. 37 background is not explained, yet he uses his (mis)understanding of the Zechariah and Ezekiel backgrounds to this pericope to look elsewhere, particularly the 'Apocalypse of Weeks' in *1 En.* 93:6. But this seems to entirely depend on the reference to *hagioi*, and he has not demonstrated any more parallels between Matthew and 1 *Enoch* at this juncture than he *supposes* (erroneously) to be present between Matthew and Zech. 14:4–5! Others have suggested a dependence on the Gospel of Peter (such as a 'cross gospel' behind Matthew and *The Gospel of Peter* by J. D. Crossan, *The Birth of Christianity: Discovering What Happened in the Years Immediately after the Execution of Jesus* (Edinburgh: T. & T. Clark, 1999), pp. 103–20; *idem*, *The Cross that Spoke* (San Francisco, Calif.: Harper & Row, 1988). Cf. esp. D. Hutton, 'The Resurrection of the Holy Ones (Mt. 27:51b–53): A Study of the Theology of the Matthean Passion Narrative', (Th.D. diss., Harvard University, 1970); Senior, *Redactional Study*, p. 277, n. 18. While still others look to 2 Samuel for influence upon the entire Matthean crucifixion scene. M. Gourgues stresses the influence of 2 Sam. 22:1–51 on the entire span of Matthew's crucifixion scene; cf. 'Il entendit de son temple ma voix': Échos du "Cantique de David" (Ps 18 = 2 S 22) en Mt 27,50–51 et dans le Nouveau Testament', in *Où demeures-tu? La maison depuis le monde Biblique* (ed. J.-C. Petit; FS G. Couturier; Montréal: Fides, 1994), pp. 323–41, cf. Senior, 'Revisiting', p. 419. Yet it is extremely difficult to disregard the prominence of Zechariah 14 and Ezekiel 37 for this unique material. Moreover, the contention that it came from a pre-Matthean tradition rather

had for some time formed part of the popular eschatology'[54] or 'righteous Jews (the δίκαιοι, 'righteous') of the time before Jesus, perhaps the patriarchs, prophets, or martyrs'.[55] Although Brown is perhaps right that Matthew's concern does not seem to be with the precise identity of the raised, his assertion that Matthew *is* concerned with 'the awesome power of God's action' and that 'an inbreaking of God's power signifying that the last times have begun' is true but incomplete.[56] For surely the raising of the saints in reference to the death of Jesus is not generally about God's power but is specifically related to God's activity displayed in Jesus' death. Hill is right in stating that it declares that 'the death of Jesus is life-giving'.[57] The causal relationship, then, relates back to Jesus' death. This is important for Matthew, for it underscores the life-giving, atoning nature of Jesus' death portrayed in the first gospel, as we have seen in Chapter 5.

That these holy ones are 'fallen asleep' (τῶν κεκοιμημένων) is clearly a metaphor for death[58] and perhaps the temporality of it, while their raising

than being a unique contribution of the evangelist simply lacks evidence. W. Schenk, *Der Passionsbericht nach Markus* (Gütersloh: Mohn, 1974), *ad loc*., tries to prove that Matthew took over a Jewish apocalyptic hymn dealing with the resurrection, inspired by Ezekiel 37. Senior has rightly criticised him on this point, but follows Schenk in assuming apocalyptic elements derived from Ezekiel 37 *and* perhaps from Psalm 22. Senior, *Redactional Study*, p. 324, n. 16.

[54] A. H. McNeile, *The Gospel according to St Matthew* (London: Macmillan, 1915), p. 424; J. P. Heil, *The Death and Resurrection of Jesus: A Narrative-Critical Reading of Matthew 26–28* (Minneapolis, Minn.: Fortress, 1991), p. 85; Hill, 'Matthew 27:51–53', p. 76.

[55] Davies and Allison (*Matthew* III, p. 633) assert that they are the 'pious Jews from ancient times'. Hagner (*Matthew* II, pp. 849–52) says that 'Matthew's readers will be thinking of the eventual resurrection of Christians'. That Brown (*Death* II, p. 1126) insists that 'relatively few of them were supposed to be buried in the Jerusalem area' is curious, since he does not consider this to be a historical account.

[56] Brown (*Death* II, p. 1126) insists 'all such speculation is unnecessary, for this popular, poetic description is deliberately vague – its forte is atmosphere, not details'. He notes that the factors in Matthew 28 with reference to Jesus' *real* resurrection (fear, lack of recognition, doubt, and demanded proof) 'are *not* found in Matt. 27:52–53'. Cf. Hill, 'Matthew 27:51–53', pp. 80–82. The notion of the dawn of a new eschatological age from this pericope, one related to Jesus' death, is almost universally accepted. Cf. Hill, 'Matthew 27:51–53', pp. 78–79; Powell, *What is Narrative Criticisim?* p. 79; D. Via, *Ethics of Mark's Gospel in the Middle of Time* (Philadelphia, Pa.: Fortress, 1985); Hagner, *Matthew* II, p. 852. Brown, *Death* II, p. 1126; Maisch, pp. 96–123; Senior, 'The Death of Jesus and the Birth of the New World: Matthew's Theology of History in the Passion Narrative', *CurTM* 19 (1992), 312–29. *Pace* Luz, *Matthäus*, IV, p. 365; R. L. Troxel, pp. 30–47. Witherup ('The Death of Jesus', pp. 584–85) argues that there are no 'new age' indications and that these events simply serve to vindicate Jesus in the narrative context. Cf. Senior, 'Death of God's Son', pp. 34–37; L. Sabourin, 'Apocalyptic Traits in Matthew's Gospel', *Religious Studies Bulletin* 3 (1983), 20; C. Rowland, *The Open Heaven: A Study of Apocalyptic in Judaism and Early Christianity* (Eugene, Ore.: Wipf & Stock, 1982), p. 353.

[57] Hill, 'Matthew 27:51–53', p. 79. Cf. Maisch, p. 122; Riebl, pp. 75f.

[58] Cf. *1 En*. 91:10; John 11:11; 1 Cor. 15:20; 1 Thess. 4:13; 2 Pet. 3:4; *4 Ezra* 7:32; *2 Bar*. 21:24; Davies and Allison, *Matthew* III, p. 634; Brown, *Death* II, p. 1124. Senior

(ἠγέρθησαν) connotes a traditional expression to describe the resurrection of the saints. Resurrection terminology (especially ἐγείρω) appears more than twice as many times in Matthew as in Mark (33 Matt.; 15 Mark), with fourteen instances referring to resurrection from the dead.[59] That Matthew is noted to have elsewhere used the term (11:5) to designate a sign of the authenticity of Jesus and his healing/proclaiming activity[60] will become important when we examine the centurion's profession. Furthermore, the saints' coming out of their tombs (27:53a, καὶ ἐξελθόντες ἐκ τῶν μνημείων)[61] is 'connected directly with the power of Jesus' death',[62] and again draws from Ezek. 37:12: 'and I will bring you forth out of your tombs' (μνημάτων).[63] Yet the timing is curious (27:53b, μετὰ τὴν ἔγερσιν αὐτοῦ)[64] and, of course, has been the subject of much discussion. Some have argued that this phrase was added at a later stage to be sensitive to the (later) belief that Jesus was the first to be raised from the dead,[65]

(*Redactional Study*, p. 315) suggests that the term 'is consistently used where the dead are spoken of in a context of resurrection expectations'.

59 Senior, *Redactional Study*, p. 315, n. 9; Brown, *Death* II, p. 1124, n. 65: see Matt. 10:8 [M] description of the disciples' activity, νεκροὺς ἐγειρετε: 11:5 [Lk]; 14:2 [Mk]; 16:21 [Mk 8:31 ἀναστῆναι]; 17:9 [Mk 9:10 ἀναστῆναι], 23 [Mk 9:31 ἀναστήσεται]; 20:19 [Mk 10:34 ἀναστήσεται ]; 26:32 [Mk]; 27:52 [M], 63 [M], 28:6 [M], 7 [+Mk]. All of these texts except 10:8; 11:5; 14:2; 27:52 refer to the resurrection of Jesus. For more on the language of resurrection in Matthew, see C. F. Evans, *Resurrection and the New Testament* (SBT 2d series 12; London: SCM Press, 1970), pp. 81–91.

60 Senior, *Redactional Study*, p. 316. Davies and Allison (*Matthew* III, p. 633, n. 123) note that though the favoured reading here is ἠγέρθησαν, some manuscripts read ηγερθη: A C W 090 Maj. Text: ℵ B D L Θ $f^{1.13}$ 33, while Tatian's *Diatessaron* simply reads the 'dead' were raised. For Witherup ('The Cross of Jesus', 284), raising of holy ones/entering 'are signs that God has vindicated his Son as he will vindicate all of the righteous whom he will make his sons and daughters in the eternal kingdom'. He adds, 'These holy ones are to be seen in conjunction with the Roman soldiers in v. 54. Both faithful Jew and faithful Gentile will be incorporated into the new kingdom'. 'The death of Jesus thus signals an end to the exclusivity of sacrificial worship and opens the way for faith on the part of the Gentiles. This first dramatic sign prepares the way for the climax of the passage, the exclamation of the Gentile soldiers' (281). Cf. M. H. Crosby, *House of Disciples: Church, Economics, and Justice in Matthew* (Maryknoll, N.Y.: Orbis Books, 1988), p. 89; W. F. Albright and C. S. Mann, *Matthew: A New Translation with Introduction and Commentary* (ABC 26; New York, N.Y.: Doubleday, 1971), pp. 350–51.

61 The phrasing ἐξελθόντες . . . εἰσῆλθον εἰς clearly depicts their departure and entrance to Jerusalem. Senior *Redactional Study*, p. 316; Gundry, p. 576.

62 Senior, *Redactional Study*, p. 322.

63 Davies and Allison, *Matthew* III, pp. 634–35

64 Davies and Allison, *Matthew* III, p. 634, n. 130, rightly indicate the reading 'after *their*' resurrection (αυτων instead of αυτου; so 30 220 Eth$^{mss}$), is weakly attested and is probably a secondary modification intended to avoid the difficulties of the text as it stands. Although Hagner (*Matthew* II, p. 850) adopts the plural reading as original, McNeile (p. 424, citing Ps. 138 [139]:2) tries to sidestep the issue by claiming that ἔγερσις is not used elsewhere of resurrection.

65 See 1 Cor. 15:20–23; Col. 1:18; Rev. 1:5. Davies and Allison, *Matthew* III, p. 634, cf. n. 135; Carroll and Green, *Death of Jesus*, p. 49; Gundry, p. 576. Brown (*Death* II, p. 1129, n. 78) rightly rejects such attempts to neutralise the phrase. Cf. Harrington, p. 400; Luz,

or it was a misplaced account of Jesus' resurrection (cf. Matt. 28:2),[66] or they offer a variety of other understandings of where the raised holy ones were and what they were doing in the interim time.[67] Historicising conjectures, however, seem to create more problems than they solve and, in particular, do not satisfactorily account for the apocalyptic nature of the events of the raising of the holy ones, the term 'holy city' and other apocalyptic images employed by the evangelist in this pericope. For it is important to realise that, as scholars have (rightly) described these images as 'apocalyptic', such 'apocalyptic writings are frequently far more tolerant of inconsistency and repetition'[68] than when read literally.

## 2 Apocalypticism and the *velum scissum*

### 2.1 Defining Terms

The Matthean *velum scissum* text and subsequent material draw upon apocalyptic images from the Old Testament. But what do we mean by 'apocalyptic' and what does it contribute to Matthew's insertion? These are important questions, for when they use the term 'apocalyptic' with

*Matthäus* IV, p. 365. While not necessarily seeing it as a later addition, Senior (*Redactional Study*, p. 317) says that 'the appearance of the ἅγιοι are not only later but *depend* on the resurrection of Jesus'. W. L. Petersen, in *Ancient Christian Gospels: Their History and Development* (ed. H. Koester; London: SCM Press, 1990), notes that several versions of the *Diatessaron* simply read 'dead' (27:52–53), which he takes to be more primitive because it is both simpler than Matthew's elaboration and less 'theologically loaded' (p. 425). This, however, is unlikely not only because there are no other manuscript traditions with this reading (particularly the Papyri), but also the *Diatessaron* is a source of dubious value for Matthean textual criticism. Cf. B. M. Metzger, *The Text of the New Testament: Its Transmission, Corruption, and Restoration* (3d edn; Oxford: Oxford University Press, 1992), pp. 89, 209. Moreover, there remain questions about the Syriac origin of the *Diatessaron* and the nature of Greek translations of it. Cf. K. Aland and B. Aland, *The Text of the New Testament: An Introduction to the Critical Editions and to the Theory and Practice of Modern Textual Criticism* (2d edn; trans. E. F. Rhodes; Grand Rapids, Mich.: Eerdmans, 1989), pp. 192–94, 215. Cf. Davies and Allison, *Matthew* II, pp. 634–35 and nn. 136 and 137; Schweizer, p. 516. The most satisfactory solution accounts for each element in the text as it stands.

[66] Hagner, *Matthew* II, p. 850. He, with McNeile (p. 423), suggests the earthquake material was placed there 'to relate the destruction (of Jerusalem and the temple) directly to the death of Jesus. Matthew seems clearly, however, to have two separate earthquakes in mind'.

[67] Some presume they simply stayed in their tombs. Gundry, p. 576. Others suggest the saints came out of their tombs on Friday, but did not enter into the holy city until after Jesus' resurrection (Sunday), giving priority to Jesus' resurrection. Brown, *Death* II, p. 1131.

[68] J. J. Collins, *The Apocalyptic Imagination: An Introduction to Jewish Apocalyptic Literature* (2d edn; Grand Rapids, Mich.: Eerdmans, 1998), p. 15. Cf. also M. Barker, 'Beyond the Veil of the Temple: The High Priestly Origins of the Apocalypse', *SJT* 51 (1998), 6–8. Cf. Philo, *QE* 2:91; *Apoc. Ab.* 20:3, 21:1; *3 En.* 45; *1 En.* 87:3; *Jub.* 1:26; *2 Bar.* 59:4–10.

respect to the veil and its context, scholars routinely fall short of defining what they mean by that term and how the veil of the temple fits into that category. Even K. L. Waters, in a recent article titled 'Matthew 27:52–53 as Apocalyptic Apostrophe', never defines what he means by 'apocalyptic'.[69] Matthew's 'special material' (27:51b–53) is sometimes called 'apocalyptic material' taken from an 'apocalyptic tradition',[70] while the resurrection of holy ones is an 'apocalyptic sign'.[71] By 'apocalyptic' many authors seem to mean either eschatological or symbolic (non-literal),[72] or both. While I am not questioning the legitimacy of locating these elements within an 'apocalyptic' milieu, it is my purpose here to try to define more carefully what I mean by the term 'apocalyptic'. Having identified Matthew's special material as 'apocalyptic' and having then defined what we mean by the term, we must then examine if and how an apocalyptic approach applies to Matthew's *velum scissum* (27:51a).

Although many scholars have recognised terminology regarding 'apocalyptic' as a slippery issue,[73] Aune has cleared the air a bit by deriving four categories in which to study this topic. Of these four, I can address only two: (1) 'apocalyptic eschatology' is defined as a system of religious beliefs, or worldview;[74] and (2) 'apocalyptic imagery' is defined as the

[69] K. L. Waters, 'Matthew 27:52–53 as Apocalyptic Apostrophe: Temporal-Spatial Collapse in the Gospel of Matthew', *JBL* 122 (2003), 489–515. His 'temporal-spatial collapse' is 'characteristic of most apocalyptic' (489).

[70] Senior, 'Death of Jesus', pp. 323, 328. Hagner (*Matthew* II, p. 851): 'symbolic-apocalyptic character of the language'. De Jonge ('Matthew 27:51 in Early Christian Exegesis', 71): 'apocalypticizing description of events'. Brown (*Death* II, p. 1126): 'apocalyptic trappings' and 'symbolic, poetic, and popular apocalyptic character'. Luz (*Matthäus* IV, p. 370): 'traditioneller apokalyptischer Hoffnungen' . . . 'apokalyptische Weltendwende' . . . 'apokalyptisch'. Geddert ('Apocalyptic Teaching', *DJG*, p. 25): 'apocalyptic motif'. See R. Brown, 'Eschatological Events Accompanying the Death of Jesus, Especially the Raising of the Holy Ones from their Tombs', in *Faith and the Future* (ed. J. P. Galvin; New York: Paulist Press, 1994), p. 43. Brown (*Death* II, p. 1145) calls all the events in the Matthean pericope, *except the veil*, 'apocalyptic signs wrought by God to interpret Jesus' death'.

[71] Senior, 'Death of Jesus', p. 323.

[72] Albright and Mann, p. 351; Brown, *Death* II, p. 1144. Cf. Bilde, 'Josephus and Jewish Apocalypticism', p. 39. D. Wenham, 'The Resurrection Narratives in Matthew's Gospel', *TynB* 24 (1973), 43–44, seems to draw an unnecessarily sharp distinction between 'apocalyptic' and literal.

[73] I am grateful to G. MacAskill for his valuable input into my research on apocalypticism and Matthew's gospel.

[74] D. E. Aune, *The New Testament in Its Literary Environment* (Philadelphia, Pa.: Westminster Press, 1987), p. 227. D. A. Hagner, 'Apocalyptic Motifs in the Gospel of Matthew: Continuity and Discontinuity', *HBT* 7 (1985), 56, says, 'Mt's eschatology has an apocalyptic orientation; it contains not simply an expectation of "end things", but also of a radical transformation of the present order by supernatural agency in the near future. It is furthermore deeply rooted in OT prophecy . . . By apocalyptic in this paper I mean perspectives in the Gospel that generally reflect this kind of an orientation'.

language and conceptions of apocalyptic eschatology found in bits and pieces in a variety of ancient literary settings.[75] While apocalyptic eschatology is a system of religious beliefs,[76] apocalyptic imagery is the means by which that worldview is conveyed. That is, when apocalyptic eschatology is conveyed in literary form it characteristically employs images and symbols, often expressed in specific, non-literal language[77] typically found in literature categorised within the 'apocalyptic' genre proper. A defining characteristic that such a worldview employs is the 'revelation of a supernatural world and the activity of supernatural beings'.[78] This is necessary because those who employ apocalyptic imagery frequently seek

[75] Aune, *Literary Environment*, p. 227. The others include 'apocalypticism' and 'millennialism', which are defined as forms of collective behavior based on these beliefs; and 'apocalypse', which is a particular type of literature giving written expression to those beliefs. For our purposes surely the first gospel is not an 'apocalypse' in the sense of a literary genre. Collins (p. 258) asserts, 'While apocalyptic writings can certainly include hortatory sayings (cf. the *1 En.* 91–107; *2 En.*), the overall form and style of the Gospels are very different from those of the apocalypses. The Gospels lack many of the typical apocalyptic forms and motifs, such as visions, heavenly ascents, or extended prophecies of the periods of history'. There is also no intermediary figure (Rowland, cf. p. 53), unless we consider the centurion to be so. For a further definition of the genre of 'apocalypse', cf. Collins, p. 5. Though, cf. Wright, p. 620, who argues that Mark is an 'apocalypse . . . designed to unveil the truth about who Jesus is through a series of revelatory moments'. See his *New Testament and the People of God* (London: SPCK, 1992), pp. 390–96; cf. Mark 1:10f; 8:29; 9:7; 14:61; 15:39. Hagner ('Apocalyptic Motifs', p. 60) says of Matthew that 'from beginning to end, and throughout, the Gospel makes such frequent use of apocalyptic motifs and the apocalyptic viewpoint that it deserves to be called *the apocalyptic Gospel*. Nearly every major section of the Gospel bears the stamp of apocalyptic in one way or another. This is true particularly of the beginning and the end of the Gospel, and also of the distinctively Matthean discourses'. D. C. Sim, *Apocalyptic Eschatology in the Gospel of Matthew* (SNTSMS 88; Cambridge: Cambridge University Press, 1996), p. 3, following Streeter (*Four Gospels*, p. 523) asserts that Matthew was written 'during a period of intense Apocalyptic expectation'. Moreover, he draws from P. D. Hanson's *The Dawn of Apocalyptic* (Philadelphia, Pa.: Fortress, 1975) to profile the social situation of the 'Matthean community' (esp. p. 63). However, I am not concerned with the sociological phenomena occurring in a political or religious movement. Thus we can restrict our discussion to 'apocalyptic imagery' and 'apocalyptic eschatology'. Cf. J. Nolland, Review of David C. Sim, *Apocalyptic Eschatology in the Gospel of Matthew*, *JTS* 49 (1998), 225–29; M. A. Powell, Review of David C. Sim, *Apocalyptic Eschatology in the Gospel of Matthew*, *RBL* (Jan. 15, 1998). With apocalyptic imagery we can only highlight a few key characteristic and isolate other more specific features as we find them in our discussion of the veil in its apocalyptic milieu.

[76] Aune, p. 107.

[77] Collins (p. 282) insists, 'The language of the apocalypses is not descriptive, referential, newspaper language, but the *expressive* language of poetry, which uses symbols and imagery to articulate a sense or feeling about the world. Their abiding value does not lie in the pseudoinformation they provide about cosmology or future history, but in their affirmation of a transcendent world'.

[78] Collins, p. 6. Sacchi's approach starts with the book of Watchers and the problem of evil, yet Collins doubts it can be traced to a single motif or theme (Collins, p. 11). Cf. Hagner, 'Apocalyptic Motifs', p. 57.

to address a crisis situation by showing that there is a transcendent reality beyond the immediate crisis in which that reality, located in heaven, is revealed often to distraught observers.[79] They provide a 'cosmic perspective' on the situation[80] in which God is sovereignly in control[81] despite the tragedy of the historical situation in which the revelation is conveyed.[82] In the midst of historical tragedy there are secrets[83] kept in heaven,[84] which are integral to God's 'salvific design'.[85] This transcendent reality is indiscernible by human reason alone[86] and can only be known by one of two means: 'Either the apocalyptic seer is told directly by God or an angel . . . or he is *shown* heavenly mysteries'.[87] This is a basic profile of *apocalyptic* that is *eschatological*,[88] which, again, is frequently conveyed by *apocalyptic imagery*: that is, images taken, at least in part, from sets of recognisable symbols. These symbols were understood to represent things beyond themselves, and identifying the referentiality of those symbols is crucial to understanding the meaning of a text that employs them.

These observations are fundamental to apocalyptic eschatology and, when taken into account here, pose no problem of chronology of the Matthean 'special material'. Although debatable, chronology likely has little role in apocalypses proper. The 'temporal and spatial collapse' employed by the evangelist[89] indicates that he seems to have no problem with jumping from Golgotha to the temple, to Jerusalem, perhaps to

[79] See Collins, p. 280. In addition to consolation, D. Hellholm, 'The Problem of Apocalyptic Genre and the Apocalypse of John', *Semeia* 36 (1986), 13–64, suggested that it might contain an element of exhortation as well. Collins, p. 41. Sim's 'dualism' (*Apocalyptic Eschatology*, pp. 35–41). See O. L. Cope, *Matthew: A Scribe Trained for the Kingdom of Heaven* (CBQMS 5; Washington, D.C.: Catholic Biblical Association of America, 1976), pp. 16–18; Bauckham, *Theology of the Book of Revelation* (Cambridge: Cambridge University Press, 1993), p. 7.

[80] Collins, pp. 261, 282–83.

[81] M. Bockmuehl, *Revelation and Mystery in Ancient Judaism and Pauline Christianity* (Grand Rapids, Mich.: Eerdmans, 1997, p. 27. Rowland (p. 144) says, 'There is no suggestion that the present age is in any sense abandoned by God'. Sim's 'determinism' (*Apocalyptic Eschatology*, pp. 41–42).

[82] Bockmuehl, p. 27; Rowland, p. 37 [83] Bockmuehl, p. 26.

[84] *Ibid.*, p. 31; Rowland, p. 3. G. Bornkamm says that 'the disclosure of divine secrets is the true theme of later Jewish apocalyptic' ('Μυστήριον', *TDNT* IV, p. 815; cf. Rowland, p. 9). 'Heaven is a kind of repository of the whole spectrum of human history which can be glimpsed by the elect' (Rowland, p. 56).

[85] Bockmuehl, p. 36. [86] Rowland, p. 75. [87] *Open Heaven*, p. 56.

[88] I am deliberately avoiding the term 'apocalyptic eschatology' because scholars frequently us it to refer to a sort of eschatology, that is, imminent transcendent intervention by God to bring this age to an end. I am using the term to describe something that is 'apocalyptic' while being 'eschatological'.

[89] See Waters, pp. 489–515.

the Mount of Olives, and back to Golgotha. He also seems to have no problem with the fact that at least part of what the centurion saw from Golgotha on a Friday occurred in Jerusalem after Sunday![90] The issue of where the raised ones were and what they were doing between Friday (when they were raised) and Sunday (when they appeared) likewise is not a concern. Therefore it seems best, in light of the apocalyptic nature of the material, to allow the apparent tension to stand while recognising the author's sensitivity to the tradition that Jesus must himself be raised first.

The identity of the 'holy city' is also disputed (27:53c, εἰσῆλθον εἰς τὴν ἁγίαν πόλιν). Although it clearly refers to Jerusalem, scholars have debated whether it refers to the literal or the 'heavenly' Jerusalem. Davies and Allison contend the literal Jerusalem is in view, insisting that suggestions for the others[91] are 'without foundation'.[92] Indeed, an apocalyptic reading of the rending of the veil would permit as plausible that Matthew is referring to the literal Jerusalem but in a visionary context. So the centurion and others are not witnessing what is happening in the literal Jerusalem at that moment from their location atop Golgotha. Instead, they are having a vision in which the raised saints of old enter into Jerusalem. The timing is likely immaterial in a visionary setting. A visionary reading of 27:53c is supported by recognising Matthew's general interest in Jerusalem[93] and looking to his use of the expression 'holy city' earlier in his gospel (4:5–6). The reference to τὴν ἁγίαν πόλιν in 4:5–6 has been understood by some as Jesus' having a 'trance-like vision'.[94] Davies and Allison point out the uncertainty whether the reader is to think of 'a visionary experience' or 'of a miraculous teleportation'. Yet that Jesus is shown 'all the kingdoms of the world' (4:8) leads them to favour the former.[95] By his use of 'holy city', a term that occurs only in Matt. 27:53c and in Matt. 4:5 in the first gospel, Matthew also seems to be making an inter-textual allusion. For in Matt. 4:5 the devil tests Jesus precisely on the issue that the centurion subsequently professes: Jesus' being the 'Son of God' (Matt. 4:5–6; 27:54). Although his sonship was challenged in the holy city previously (4:5), it is professed by the soldiers and affirmed by

[90] Collins, p. 15

[91] See Rev. 21:2, 10; Clement of Alexandria, *Strom.* 6.6; Origen, *Rom.* 5:1; Eusebius, *Dem. ev.* 4.12; 10.8.

[92] Davies and Allison, *Matthew* III, p. 635. So also Hagner, *Matthew* II, p. 850; Luz, *Matthäus* IV, p. 365. Cf. Acts 10:40–41. For more discussion of the 'holy city' as Jerusalem, see Davies and Allison, *Matthew* I, p. 365, n. 138. Brown (*Death* II, p. 1131) insists that their appearance to many' (27:53c) precludes a heavenly Jerusalem.

[93] Senior, *Redactional Study*, p. 317.

[94] Hagner, *Matthew* I, p. 66.

[95] *Matthew* I, p. 364.

the witnesses of raised holy ones in that very city later (27:53c–54).[96] Within a pericope that employs apocalyptic imagery, there is a disclosure of *heavenly* secrets and the 'events' viewed need not occur anywhere in a visionary experience. Instead, the importance of such a vision lies in the fact that it is revealed from heaven and seen in an apocalyptic vision.[97] I will discuss the significance of the 'Son of God' title for Jesus below. For the present, however, it is helpful to note that the 'holy city', rather than commenting on the precise location of the city – earthly or heavenly – informs a visionary reading of 27:53, provides an intertextual connection between the temptation narrative in Matt. 4 and the 'special material' in 27:53, and may serve a structural role in its location in Matt. 4 and 27.

After being raised, the holy ones 'appeared to many' (27:53d, καὶ ἐνεφανίσθησαν πολλοῖς). Matthew's ἐμφαινίζω is a hapax in the synoptics[98] and may be analogous to and symbolic of the actual resurrection

[96] However we are to understand the 'Jerusalem' in view, it is surely, as with that in 4:5, a city seen in a visionary context. This is affirmed by the transcendent nature of the pericope in which it occurs previously (4:5) and underscored by the revelatory context in which it appears subsequently (27:51a–53). Moreover, Waters traces the 'holy city' back to the earliest streams of apocalyptic thought in Christianity, draws upon the same tradition as the new Jerusalem in Revelation (p. 501), and sees it referring to the heavenly city in the 'apocalyptic future' (pp. 500, 503). Yet because he sees a 'spatial' and 'temporal' collapse, Waters jettisons 'after his resurrection'. Petersen (*Ancient Christian Gospels*, p. 425) indicates that some manuscript traditions of the *Diatessaron* record the resurrection and appearance of the risen dead simultaneously with Jesus' death on the cross. Thus 'the 'dead' were raised *and revealed there and then* as one more sign of the gravity of Jesus' death' (p. 425, his emphasis). Yet he asserts that 'in the canonical account, the delay of the appearance of those resurrected for three days defeats the whole purpose of having them raised when Jesus dies on the cross; but the delay *does* bring the canonical account into line with the Pauline theology' and 'it would appear that the *Diatessaron* preserves a more primitive version of the text at this point than does the canonical text, which has been revised to bring it into conformity with Pauline theology' (p. 426). In addition to the problems with using the *Diatessaron* as a text-critical source for Matthew, Petersen makes no room for a scribal omission, though he argues for it strongly elsewhere (cf. his Review of Robert F. Shedinger, *Tatian and the Jewish Scriptures: A Textual and Philological Analysis of the Old Testament Citations in Tatian's Diatessaron*, *JBL* 122 [2003], 394). More problematic is that Petersen fails to acknowledge that there are many scholars who argue that this text is part of an pre-Matthean tradition, perhaps allowing Matthew to add it to his tradition, though, as he recognises, sensitive to Pauline theology. The strongest rebuttal of Petersen's claim is that it finds no manuscript support outside of the *Diatessaron*. It may be that Tatian knew of the source from which Matthew drew, and preserved it without Matthew's addition of 'after his resurrection'. There is no manuscript support, outside of the *Diatessaron*, that the Gospel of Matthew ever existed without that phrase.

[97] Brown (*Death* II, p. 1131) urges that such a view would agree with other Christian portrayals of Jesus leading a host into heaven (e.g., Eph. 4:8; *Ascen. Isa.* 9:7–18). *T. Dan* 5:12 refers to the holy ones filing into the New (heavenly) Jerusalem after refreshing themselves in Eden. We will revisit Edenic allusions below, pp. 192–4.

[98] Senior, *Redactional Study*, p. 317. Matthew uses φαίνω to describe the appearances of the angel in the infancy narrative (1:20; 2:7, 13, 19).

appearance of Jesus himself.[99] Senior contends for a '*juridic* quality' to the verb, as it is used in the New Testament 'to indicate witness to an event'.[100] Surely Senior is correct that the thrust of the testimonial nature of the resurrected holy ones is 'a symbolic expression of the implication of Jesus' life-giving death'[101] that serves as a 'testimony to Jesus' victory over death',[102] a fitting understanding of the event in an apocalyptic context. Moreover, scholars who press this pericope into a temporal/spatial grid, rather than its occurring in a visionary context, have characteristically had trouble dealing with the problem that despite its enormous apologetic value, we have no reports of any raised holy ones being seen outside of Matthew's account of this startling event. Solutions proposed are admittedly 'completely in the realm of speculation'.[103]

With respect to the literary origins of 27:51b–53, most insist it is a purely Matthean redaction based on Old Testament and 'apocalyptic-eschatological themes',[104] and its origin has been the subject of some discussion.[105] Regardless of any pre-Matthean origin, Matthean redaction

[99] *Ibid.*, pp. 317–18, n. 1, citing D. Zeller, *Die weisheitlichen Mahnsprüche bei den Synoptikern* (Würzburg: Echter, 1977), p. 412.

[100] *Redactional Study*, p. 318, n. 2, citing Acts 2:13–15, 22; 24:1; 25:2, 15; and Heb. 9:24, where the word is used of Christ's role as 'advocate' before the Father . . . νῦν ἐμφανισθῆναι τῷ προσώπῳ τοῦ θεοῦ ὑπὲρ ἡμῶν.

[101] *Redactional Study*, p. 318. Cf. Zeller, *Die weisheitlichen Mahnsprüche*, p. 413, Zahn, *Matthäus*, p. 705. Witherup (cited in Hagner, *Matthew* II, p. 850) claims they testify *against Israel*. Others see it as an allusion to Christ's descent into Hades (McNeile, p. 424). Others a means of encouraging the persecuted (Gundry, p. 577). Some contend that the resurrection was to eternal life, others that it was only a temporary resurrection, still others that there only appeared to be a resurrection! see Brown, *Death* II, pp. 1131–33, cf. also his n. 87.

[102] Brown, *Death* II, p. 1131. Cf. Bauckham, *Theology of the Book of Revelation*, p. 73; F. Lapham, *An Introduction to the New Testament Apocrypha* (London: T. & T. Clark International, 2003), p. 99.

[103] Wenham, 'Resurrection Narratives, p. 44. It is also possible that the account could be legendary – purporting to be historical, but in fact not.

[104] Sim, *Apocalyptic Eschatology*, p. 111, n. 1. Although Allison (*End of the Ages*, pp. 41–46) argues that the evangelist has used a source that he redacted in only a minor way. Senior, *Redactional Study*, pp. 418–24; Hill, 'Matthew 27:51–53', p. 76.

[105] Waters says it is a 'Matthean addition to a pre-Matthean fragment' (p. 503); so also Allison, *End of the Ages*, p. 45, cf. p. 42, though cf. Davies and Allison, *Matthew* III, pp. 634–35. Andreoli agrees that it is a pre-Matthean fragment, but argues, based on syllable counts, that it was a hymn from Easter liturgy in early Jewish-Christian commuity, a song of victory like that of Exod. 15 (cf. *Jub.* 46:9). Andreoli, 'Il velo squarciato nel Vangelo di Matteo', p. 29. Cf. Maisch, p. 106. Andreoli's further argument, that the special material is connected to the two following scenes in Matthew (30) is less convincing. Andreoli's study would have been greatly enhanced by some analysis of early Christian hymnody and by placing his contention for a liturgical hymn within that arena. Cf. Maisch, pp. 112–21; J. Blinzler, 'Zur Erklärung von Mt 27, 51b–53. Totenauferstehung am Karfrietag?' *T&G* 35 (1943), 91–93. Wenham ('Resurrection Narratives', p. 46) rightly notes that, regardless of its origin, the Matthean special material (especially the resurrection) need not be 'considered

has been recognised throughout[106] and use of apocalyptic images is recognised as being more informed by the Old Testament texts from which it drew, and the immediate author's combination of them, than as a (hypothetical) pre-Matthean source.[107] As noted above, scholars have widely recognised the striking literary and thematic parallels between Matt. 27:51b–53 and Ezek. 37:1–14, which may assert an exodus-like deliverance from the Babylonian exile. Although it is unclear whether or not Matthew understood this pericope to indicate a restoration motif similar to that of Ezekiel 37, it is important to note that the Ezek. 37:1–14 pericope constitutes a vision,[108] which the prophet sees in a visionary context that is to be taken not for its literal but for its metaphorical importance.[109] Moreover, the metaphorical images employed in the heavenly vision symbolise something that will occur on earth in the future. In this famous vision the prophet sees bones coming together and being imbued with the breath of life as a metaphor for the restoration of Israel and Judah.[110] Although the desolate setting in which the vision occurs is frequently the site of judgement,[111] Ezekiel uses it, perhaps ironically, as a setting to proclaim salvation.[112] He uses the opening of the graves to depict the breaking of the 'prison door of Babylon'[113] and the image of resurrection as a counter-metaphor for death of the exile.[114] As we have

a sign of lateness'. For a discussion of the possible relationship between this resurrection account and the logion in John 5:25–26, see W. G. Essame, 'Matthew xxvii.51–54 and John v.25–29', *ExpTim* 76 (1964), 103.

[106] Andreoli, 'Il velo squarciato nel Vangelo di Matteo', pp. 22, 23, 25, and esp. 26, following Aguirre Monasterio (*Exégesis de Mateo, 27, 51b–53*) asserts that Matthew was himself the final editor. Senior ('Revisiting', p. 418) agrees that it was thoroughly rewritten with recognisable Matthean elements of style. In fact, Senior argues that it is a free editorial composition by Matthew (*Redactional Study*, pp. 207–23; 'Death of Jesus', 312–29; 'Death of God's Son', 31–59). Allison (*End of the Ages*, pp. 41–42) is less certain.

[107] See Collins, p. 20; Hill, 'Matthew 27:51–53', p. 77; Andreoli, 'Il velo squarciato nel Vangelo di Matteo', p. 29.

[108] Ezekiel's 'and the hand of the Lord came upon me' statements depict a visionary experience. Cf. M. Greenberg, *Ezekiel 21–37* (ABC 22A; New York, N.Y.: Doubleday, 1997), p. 742; M. V. Fox, 'The Rhetoric of Ezekiel's Vision of the Valley of the Bones', *HUCA* 51 (1980), 1–15. Moreover, this pericope (Ezek. 37:1–14) is recognised as being parallel with Ezekiel's inaugural vision (1:1–3:15), which provides precedent for the opening of heaven in later Judaism and Christianity and resonates with new-creation language. Cf. Zimmerli, *Ezekiel 25–48*, p. 266, citing 2 Cor. 5:17.

[109] Wright (p. 120) says, 'Ezekiel is no more envisaging actual bodily resurrection than he envisaged, when writing chapter 34, that Israel consisted of sheep rather than people'.

[110] Eichrodt, *Ezekiel: A Commentary* (Old Testament Library; trans. C. Quin; London: SCM Press, 1970), p. 506.

[111] *Ibid.*, p. 507; Greenberg, p. 748; F. C. Fensham, 'The Curse of the Dry Bones in Ezekiel 37:1–14 Changed to a Blessing of Resurrection', *JNSL* 13 (1987), 59–60.

[112] Eichrodt, p. 506. [113] *Ibid.*, p. 510.

[114] Greenberg, p. 747. The desolation left in Israel during the Babylonian captivity is known as the 'Babylonian gap' during which archaeological evidence affirms almost total

seen, Matthew likewise depicts the purpose of Jesus (especially his death) to be a means of deliverance (especially from sin),[115] and drawing a sharp distinction between the exile and the sin that caused it in Old Testament prophetic traditions would be a mistake. Although later Judaism seemed to understand this text to depict a literal, physical resurrection,[116] the text retained the metaphorical significance from the Ezekiel context.[117] This was understood in Christian writings to depict the dawning of 'the long-awaited messianic era',[118] here not so much associated with Jesus' resurrection (Grassi) as with his death.

## 2.2 The Significance of the Matthean 'Special Material' in Context

It may be possible that with Matthew's allusion to Ezekiel 37 he intended to draw from the broad context of that chapter in order to depict an eschatological restoration from exile. This theme in Matthew has been raised by M. Eloff[119] and P. Yokota[120] but has yet to be addressed fully in Matthean scholarship. That Matthew had Ezek. 37 in mind is not insignificant, for in that context we find recognisable Matthean themes, which we have seen before. Yokota indicates that Matthew appropriates the Ezekiel 37 pericope for his own eschatological purposes:

abandonment of Israelites cities during the time. See E. Stern, 'The Babylonian Gap', *BAR* 26.6 (2000), 45–51; *idem*, *Archaeology of the Land of the Bible* (4 vols.; New York, N.Y.: Doubleday, 2001) II, pp. 304–31, though cf. J. Blenkensopp, 'The Bible, Archaeology and Politics; or The Empty Land Revisited', *JSOT* 27 (2002), 169–71.

115 Andreoli, 'Il velo squarciato nel Vangelo di Matteo', p. 28.

116 4Q385 2 i 2–9; cf. 4Q386 1 i 1–10; 4Q388 8 i 4–7; Wright, *Resurrection*, p. 188 and n. 250; W. Neuss, *Das Buch Ezechiel in Theologie und Kunst bis zum Ende des XII. Jahrhunderts* (Münster: Aschendorff, 1912); Greenberg, pp. 749–50; *b. Sanh.* 92b. C. H. Kraeling, *The Synagogue, The Excavations at Dura-Europas: Final Report*, VIII/1 (New Haven, Conn.: Yale University Press, 1956), pp. 185–94; *idem*, 'The Meaning of the Ezekiel Panel in the Synagogue at Dura', *BASOR* 78 (1940), 12–18; R. Wischnitzer-Bernstein, 'The Conception of the Resurrection in the Ezekiel Panel of the Dura Synagogue', *JBL* 60 (1941), 43–55; *Gen. Rab.* 13:6 (on Gen. 2:5); 14:5 (on Gen. 2:7); *Deut. Rab.* 7:7 (on Deut. 28:12); *Lev. Rab.* 14:9 (on Lev 12:2). This is most starkly seen in the Dura Europas synagogue panel on the northern wall. Here there is a graphic depiction of the Ezekiel 37 text (and, perhaps, Zech. 14 and Dan. 12; also Allison, *End of the Ages*, pp. 40–46), though it is difficult to tell whether the rabbinic texts, as well as those of Matthew and rabbinic interpretations of Ezekiel 37, understood the resurrection here as a literal resurrection or as a metaphorical depiction of a return-from-exile motif, as does the Ezekiel 37 context.

117 J. Grassi, 'Ezekiel XXXVII.1–14 and the New Testament', *NTS* 11 (1965), 164.

118 *Ibid.*, p. 164.

119 M. Eloff, 'Restoration from Exile as a Hermeneutical Prism for a Theological Interpretation of Matthew's Gospel' (Th.D. diss. Stellenbosch University, 2002).

120 'Jesus the Messiah of Israel: A Study of Matthew's Messianic Interpretation of Scripture as a Contribution to Narrative Study of His Christology' (Ph.D. diss., University of St Andrews, 2004), pp. 304–5.

> Although the metaphor was understood by the first century as a literal prediction of the resurrection of the dead, given that the restoration of Israel is a permeating theme throughout the Gospel (that it seems likely) that the reader connects the resurrection of the dead in Matthew with the theme of Israel's restoration. If this is the case, the allusion to Ezek. 37 *assures* the reader that, as Jesus predicted beforehand (20:28; 26:28), his death put into effect the restoration of Israel.[121]

For example, the deliverance from political captivity is framed in a larger matrix of sin (v. 23): 'I will deliver them from all their dwelling places in which they have sinned'.[122] This, I have argued, is the purpose of Jesus' death as depicted in Matthew's gospel and may provide a point of contact: God's deliverance from the captivity of sin is achieved in the death of Jesus. That he was to deliver 'his people' from their sins suggests a collective deliverance, though we will need to see how Matthew defines Jesus' 'people' before we can identify the recipients of this deliverance. Finally, the temple imagery employed in the Ezekiel 37 pericope seems to cohere with Matthew's Emmanuel Christology. For upon the establishment of the new nation under an eternal Davidic kingship (Ezek. 37:24),[123] Ezekiel 'spiritualizes'[124] the assertion from Lev. 26:11 that God 'will set [his] tabernacle in their midst' (cf. Exod. 25:8; 29:44f) to promise an *eternal* (v. 26) dwelling place among them (v. 27),[125] seeming to make the temple superfluous. Greenberg suggests that this relates to Old Testament cloud theophanies (Isa. 4:5) as a means by which YHWH dwells among his people.[126] This coheres nicely with Matthew's Emmanuel Christology and provides some glimpse into the rationale behind his addition to

[121] 'Jesus the Messiah of Israel', pp. 304–5. Yokota further shows that though Wright (*Resurrection*, p. 634) doubts that Matthew associates the resurrection in Matthew's special material with the restoration of Israel because the final national restoration had not yet occurred, since Matthew 'redefines Israel in the course of his narrative, it is not unlikely that Matthew alludes to Ezek. 37 in such a way as to evoke the fulfillment of the restoration of Israel through the redemptive death of the Messiah' (p. 305, n. 994).

[122] Ezekiel makes no distinction between the physical captivity in which Israel finds herself and the sin that caused it. Greenberg, p. 756. Cf. Deut. 28:36, 64; Ezek. 14:3f; 20:39; 36:29.

[123] Greenberg, pp. 759–60. [124] *Ibid.*, p. 757.

[125] Eichrodt (pp. 514–15) comments, 'Just as, in the great temple vision of ch. 8–11, the temple was robbed of its status as the place of meeting between God and people by the general alienation of princes and people from God, and made into an assertion of the dominion of other gods, so in the time of salvation it is to fulfill its supreme purpose and mediate the realization of communion with God, the communion of God himself in abundant fullness.'

[126] *Ezekiel 21–37*, p. 757.

his Markan source. Andreoli contends that it was done because it deepens the eschatological hopes found in Jesus' death[127] which, he asserts, were already recognised in the appropriation of Ezek. 37 in Jewish apocalyptic literature of the Second Temple period.[128] As helpful as underscoring the restorative nature of this pericope is, it finds its climax in Ezek. 37:28, where God dwells among his people and affirms their covenant relationship (v. 27). Matthew has enhanced his Markan source to assert that the life-giving death of Jesus[129] inaugurates a new age[130] in which the final, eschatological deliverance from bondage to sin is achieved and God's presence now dwells among his people and permits a fellowship between man and God not seen since the Garden of Eden, a fellowship in which God dwells among his people.[131] Rather than God dwelling among his people in the tabernacle in the wilderness, God now dwells among his people in the person of Jesus. In his discussion of Jesus' resurrection with respect to the centurion's confession, Wright asserts that the coming of the new age reverses the effects 'of the present evil age', and that the resurrection of Jesus is the first of many resurrections that indicates the dawn of the new age and the renewing of the original relation.[132]

We have seen that Matthew's use of images from Ezekiel 37, which are frequently described as 'apocalyptic images' conveying theological

[127] Andreoli, 'Il velo squarciato nel Vangelo di Matteo', p. 29.

[128] *Ibid.*, 28. The notion of a sin-exile-return motif is precisely how *T. Benj.* 10:3 understands the *velum scissum*. See M. de Jonge, 'Two Interesting Interpretations of the Rending of the Temple-Veil in the Testaments of the Twelve Patriarchs', *Bij.* 46 (1985), 353.

[129] Hill, 'Matthew 27:51–53', p. 79.

[130] Harrington, p. 400. And, some insist, a raising *after* judgement. Luz (*Matthäus* IV, pp. 364–65) looks to *b. Sanh.* 92b, *Tg.* Ezek. 37:12, *Sib. Or.* 2:224, and 4Q385 2 i 1–10, which seems, in context, to connote raising after judgement. The dawning of a new era, presuming a dichotomy exists, is a defining characteristic of apocalyptic. Cf. G. E. Ladd, 'Apocalyptic and New Testament Theology', in *Reconciliation and Hope: New Testament Essays on Atonement and Eschatology Presented to L. L. Morris on His 60th Birthday* (ed. R. Banks; Exeter: Paternoster Press, 1974), pp. 286–87; W. A. VanGemeren, *Interpreting the Prophetic Word: An Introduction to the Prophetic Literature of the Old Testament* (Grand Rapids, Mich.: Zondervan, 1990), pp. 332–33; Troxel, pp. 41–42. Hagner ('Apocalyptic Motifs', p. 58, cf. pp. 62–66) says, 'If God had acted in a definitive way in Christ, then the long-awaited metamorphosis of the present age could not be far behind'. P. J. Achtemeier, 'An Apocalyptic Shift in Early Christian Tradition: Reflections on Some Canonical Evidence', *CBQ* 45 (1983), 241ff.; D. A. Hagner, 'Matthew's Eschatology', *SBLSP* 35 (1996), 170; W. Trilling, *Das Wahre Israel: Studien zur Theologie des Matthäus–Evangeliums* (Müngen: Kösen, 1964), p. 221; *idem*, *Christusverkündigung in den synoptischen Evangelien* (BH 4; München: Kösel, 1969), pp. 191–243; Maisch, p. 121.

[131] Moreover, the breathing of life into the dry bones has been widely recognised as recalling the creation context of Gen 2:7 and depicting a new-creation motif. Eichrodt, pp. 508. Senior (*Passion Narrative according to Matthew*, pp. 292ff; *Redactional Study*, pp. 307–12) asserts that 'Matthew's contribution is a dramatic embellishment of this Markan presentation by means of apocalyptic imagery' (p. 310). Schenk, p. 80; Maisch, p. 107.

[132] *Resurrection*, pp. 322, 337.

content,[133] expresses the theological value and eschatological meaning of the event upon which the *velum scissum* and subsequent material 'comment': the death of Jesus.[134] Both Ezek. 37 and Matt. 27:51b–53 employ apocalyptic imagery, each describing a scene in metaphorical terms, a scene set in a hopeless historical situation (exile and Jesus' death, respectively) in which a vision depicts a transcendent reality of God's ability miraculously to overcome the situation.[135] Moreover, Wright asserts that resurrection is always a description of the defeat of death.[136] Matthew's text, then, is best read with respect to the apocalyptic eschatology it asserts. So then, Matthew, in his use of this 'special material', has drawn strongly on recognisable images from the Old Testament and Jewish apocalyptic eschatology to assert that Jesus' death was the decisive factor in turning the page of salvation history to the new, messianic age.[137] Hagner asserts that 'the apocalyptic viewpoint permeates the Gospel of Matthew',[138] and this viewpoint must be taken seriously with respect to his *velum scissum* pericope.

If, then, these are apocalyptic images, they occur in a visionary context and their precise location is likely immaterial. This raises several issues that now must be addressed: (1) What did the soldiers 'see' (v. 54)? (2) Can Gentiles be said to be recipients of a heavenly (Jewish) vision? (3) What is the nature of the 'events' seen in a visionary context? Are they comments simply on the present situation at Golgotha, or are they predictions of some future reality on earth? Answers to these questions begin with an analysis of Matthew's addition to Mark, the comment about what the soldiers saw.

Mark's less common ὁ κεντυρίων, a *hapax* in the New Testament, is replaced by Matthew with the more usual biblical form ὁ ἑκατόνταρχος.[139] Yet Matthew's soldier is not alone; he is accompanied by others (καὶ οἱ μετ αὐτοῦ). While many arguments explaining Matthew's change

[133] Andreoli, 'Il velo squarciato nel Vangelo di Matteo', p. 30. Senior, *Redactional Study*, pp. 321–23.

[134] Andreoli, 'Il velo squarciato nel Vangelo di Matteo', p. 30; also Senior, *Redactional Study*, p. 321; Aguirre Monasterio, *Exégesis de Mateo, 27, 51b–53*, pp. 100, 102–6.

[135] Cf. Eichrodt, pp. 510–11. [136] *Resurrection*, p. 727 and esp. p. 728.

[137] Cf. Maisch, p. 101. [138] Hagner, 'Apocalyptic Motifs', p. 68.

[139] Senior (*Redactional Study*, p. 323, n. 3) shows that Mark's ὁ κεντυρίων occurs three times in Mark (15:39, 44, 45), whereas ὁ ἑκατόνταρχος (and alternate spelling –χης) does not occur in Mark at all but occurs 4 times in Matthew, 22 times in LXX and 17 times in Luke-Acts. Cf. C. Schneider, 'Der Hauptmann am Kreuz. Zur Nationalisierung neutestamentlicher Nebenfiguren', *ZNW* 33 (1934), 1–17; W. C. Allen, *A Critical and Exegetical Commentary on the Gospel according to S. Matthew* (ICC; Edinburgh: T. & T. Clark, 1912), p. 297; McNeile, p. 424; Senior, *Redactional Study*, pp. 323–28.

hold equally as well for just a single person, [140] Brown's theory that the appeal is to the requirement of Jewish law for two or more witnesses seems plausible[141] but speculative. Senior's contention that the plurality served to 'heighten the effect of the action' [142] is likely true but incomplete. For the escalation of the action is made apparent by the more plausible suggestion by Davies and Allison that the plurality of witnesses is necessitated to correlate his ἐφοβήθησαν σφόδρα (27:54) with the same phrase used at the transfiguration (17:6).[143] We will explore this intertextual allusion more fully below (pp. 166–8), but for the present it is worth recognising that many scholars take Matthew's καὶ οἱ μετ' αὐτοῦ with his τηροῦντες as indicating a prior relationship (vv. 27–36) and presume those 'keeping watch' to similarly be identified as Gentile soldiers.[144] Since those previously said to 'keep watch' over Jesus (ἐτήρουν, 27:36) are explicitly said to be 'the governor's soldiers' (οἱ στρατιῶται τοῦ ἡγεμόνος, 27:27), and no one else is said to 'keep watch' over Jesus in the entire Matthean Passion Narrative, the most natural reading of 27:54 is that the plurality of observers are likewise Gentile Roman soldiers.[145] Previously these soldiers were depicted as mocking Jesus in the Praetorium, leading him to Golgotha, giving him wine, crucifying him and dividing

[140] Harrington (p. 401) suggests the plurality of witnesses alludes to Ps. 22:27–28 and suggests the inclusion of Gentiles. So also N. Dahl, 'The Passion Narrative in Matthew', in *The Interpretation of Matthew* (ed. G. N. Stanton; Edinburgh: T. & T. Clark, 1995), p. 49. Cf. Gundry, pp. 577–78; Davies and Allison, *Matthew* III, pp. 635–37; Senior, *Redactional Study*, p. 324.

[141] Brown, *Death* II, p. 1143; D. J. Verseput, 'The 'Son of God' Title in Matthew's Gospel', *NTS* 33 (1987), 548.

[142] Senior, *Redactional Study*, pp. 323–28, citing precedent by Matthew in Matt. 8:29 (cf Mark 5:2) two demoniacs instead of Mark's one; 9:27 (cf Mark 10:46) two blind men instead of one (cf. also the doublet 20:30); 27:49 (cf. Mark 15:36) crowd instead of one speaker for the taunt. 'The taunts of 27:40–43 and especially 27:49 highlight Matthew's choral confession of Jesus in 27:54. Just as he was mocked by a group, he is proclaimed Son of God by a group.'

[143] Davies and Allison, *Matthew* III, p. 635. They also argue that Mark is sufficiently vague to allow for the possibility of more than one being present, and that 'Matthew's expansion "provides a confessing group to balance the mocking group of vv. 39–43, 49"' (*Matthew* III, p. 636 and n. 145, citing France, *Matthew*, 401. Cf. Brown, *Death* II, p. 1146; Hagner, *Matthew* II, p. 852). Although this is possible, it would be difficult to substantiate. Cf. also Pelletier, p. 175; C. F. D. Moule, *The Phenomenon of the New Testament: An Inquiry into the Implications of Certain Features of the New Testament* (London: SCM Press, 1967), p. 144.

[144] Davies and Allison, *Matthew* III, pp. 635–37; Andreoli, 'Il velo sqaurciato nel Vangelo di Matteo', 31. Matthew's use of τηρέω has two primary meanings: observing commandments (19:17; 23:3; 28:20) to the role of a soldier to keep watch (27:36; 28:4).

[145] Others present, such as Jewish bystanders at the cross, are said to 'pass by' (27:39), simply 'mock' (27:41), 'stand there' (27:47), run and get a sponge (27:48), and look for Elijah (27:49), and women 'watch from a distance' (27:55). Only Roman soldiers are said to 'keep watch'.

up his clothes (Matt. 27:36 added that they then sat and kept guard over him).[146] Yet their response, that Jesus was θεοῦ υἱὸς, in some way depicts a change of attitude. This is a striking change, particularly when placed alongside the 'Jewish' unbelief in the scene. We will see that this serves to underscore Matthew's elevated Christological interest[147] depicted in the 'centurion's profession'.[148]

What these soldiers saw (ἰδόντες) was the earthquake (τὸν σεισμόν) of 27:51b,[149] and (καὶ) τὰ γενόμενα.[150] The latter clearly refers to the incidents recorded subsequent to the earthquake.[151] Hill refers to them as 'apocalyptic events' (τὰ γενόμενα, 27:54) rather than signs.[152] 'Events' are particularly important to Matthew, for whom events surrounding the life of Jesus are said to occur to fulfil Scripture (Matt. 1:22) and inspire repentance (Matt. 11:21, 23). The same participial form found in 27:54 is

[146] Brown (*Death* II, pp. 1143–52, n. 1) notes that only Mark in the New Testament, 'with his penchant for Latinisms, uses [3 times] the loan word *kentyrion* from the Latin *centurio*, related to *centrum* ("a hundred"), a word found also in Greek literature [e.g. Polybius, *History* 6.24.5]'.

[147] So Senior, *Redactional Study*, p. 328, n. 3; A. B. Plummer, *An Exegetical Commentary on the Gospel according to S. Matthew* (London: Paternoster Row, 1909), p. 404; M. Lagrange, *Évangile selon saint Matthieu* (Paris: J. Gabalda, 1948), p. 533; Dahl, p. 28; W. Grundmann, *Das Evangelium nach Matthäus* (Berlin: Evangelische Verlagsanstalt, 1968), p. 563; G. Strecker, *Der Weg der Gerechtigkeit: Untersuchung zur Theologie des Matthäus* (Göttingen: Vandenhoeck & Ruprecht, 1962), p. 182; B. Gerhardsson, *The Mighty Acts of Jesus according to Matthew* (Lund: Gleerup, 1979), p. 225.

[148] Perhaps also Matthew's more immediate context is in view. That is, as there was a plurality of witnesses to the resurrected holy ones in the holy city, so there is a plurality of witnesses to the significance of that account, declaring Jesus to be the Son of God. See discussion below, pp. 173–4, 179–83.

[149] Gundry, p. 577.

[150] Senior (*Redactional Study*, p. 325, n. 4) notes the three occurrences of the term in Matthew. 'In 28:11 [M] it refers to the guards' report of the events at the tomb,' referring back to the appearance of the angel, which terrifies the soldiers (28:2; cf. 18:31), suggesting (p. 326) that 'hence the choral proclamation of faith that climaxes this scene should be read in the same theological light as the symbolic events of 27:51–53 . . . Matthew's statement is that the life-giving power of Jesus' death upon which God has set his seal of acceptance provokes faith in the gentiles', which fits the conclusion of Psalm 22, underscoring God's power among the people. Senior (*Redactional Study*, p. 325) insists that 'Matthew's phrase τὸν σεισμὸν καὶ τὰ γενόμενα is actually a definition of Mark's οὕτως', which is surely a reference to Jesus' death. Indeed, whatever he saw, Matthew clearly intends the reader to take the full list of 'events' together as a single unit, events which are, as we have seen, a result of Jesus' death (καὶ ἰδού, 27:51a) and which serve in the 'text as a symbolic description of God's legitimation of the life-giving death of his Son'.

[151] Brown, *Death* II, p. 1145, n. 6. Waters (p. 504) removes the statement regarding the other events as a later redaction and concludes that the centurion responds only to the earthquake.

[152] Hill, 'Matthew 27:51–53', p. 76. Indeed, 'signs' in Matthew are associated with unbelief (12:38; 16:1, 3–4; 24:2, 3), a request to which Jesus would not submit and would offer only the 'sign of the prophet Jonah' (12:39) with reference to his three days of death and to the coming of the 'Son of Man' (24:30).

found three other times in his gospel (18:31 [2x]; 28:11), each uniquely Matthean. Such events could happen temporally (28:11) or within a fictitious story (18:31), so there does not seem to be any reason to preclude Matthew's use of γίνομαι here in 27:54 as referring to 'occurrences', regardless of location, as it does in apocalyptic visionary texts.[153] The point seems to be, at least in Matthew's four occurrences of this form, that the 'events' elicit a response, which then becomes the focal point.

That the soldiers are seeing a heavenly vision is underscored by the nature of their first immediate response: fear. Davies and Allison suggest that the response of fear (ἐφοβήθησαν σφόδρα) is intended to connect this pericope to the disciples' fear in the account of transfiguration (17:6).[154] Some see it as indicative of an eschatological conversion[155] of Gentiles expected at the end of the age,[156] or of an 'attitude of worship'.[157] Yet 'fear' itself has been recognised in Matthean redaction as designating the manifestation of divine power,[158] in which there is likewise 'an attitude of explicit faith and proclamation'.[159] The proclamation aspect strongly underscores the importance of the testimony both of the centurion/group and of those in the 'holy city' – that is, testimony of the significance of Jesus' death, particularly indicating that he is the 'son of God' (ἀληθῶς θεοῦ υἱὸς ἦν οὗτος).[160] If Matthew is indeed glancing back to 17:6 in his ἐφοβήθησαν σφόδρα statement (the only other place in the New Testament where this phrase occurs),[161] this can inform our understanding of the 'profession' that follows and the nature of the soldiers' fear. For in 17:6 fear was the response of the three disciples on the Mount of Transfiguration to the voice from the cloud that declares: οὗτος ἐστιν ὁ υἱός

[153] Indeed, the entire book of Revelation concerns things that must 'take place' (γενέσθαι, Rev. 1:1; cf. Rev. 1:18, 19; 2:8, 10; 3:2; 4:1, 2; 6:12; 8:1, 5, 7, 8, 11; 11:13, 15, 19; 12:7, 10; 16:2, 3, 4, 10, 17, 18, 19; 18:2; 21:6; 22:6). Cf. 1 Kgs 22:54; 1 Esd. 1:10; Ezra 10:3; Dan. (Th) 9:12.

[154] This is supported by the affirmation of divine sonship of Jesus in both texts. Sim (*Apoclyptic Eschatology*, p. 144) asserts that Jesus' transfigured state 'prefigures the eschatological (resurrected) state of all the righteous'. See also Senior, *Redactional Study*, pp. 327–28.

[155] Gundry, p. 578.

[156] Allison, *End of the Ages*, p. 47, citing Matt. 12:41–42; Isa. 2:2–3; 11:9–10; 25:6–7; 45:20–25; Zech. 8; Tob. 13:11; *Pss. Sol.* 17:32–35 (30–31). Hagner, 'Apocalyptic Motifs', p. 59.

[157] Senior, *Redactional Study*, p. 326.

[158] *Ibid.*, p. 326, n. 3, 4, 5, 6; Lohmeyer, *Das Evangelium des Matthäus* (4th edn; Göttingen: Vandenhoeck & Ruprecht, 1967), p. 397; Strecker, p. 234.

[159] Senior, *Redactional Study*, p. 326.

[160] Their importance is underscored as witnesses, perhaps in anticipation of 28:10. Davies and Allison, *Matthew* III, pp. 635–37.

[161] W. G. Olmstead, *Matthew's Trilogy of Parables: The Nation, the Nations and the Reader in Matthew 21.28–22.14* (SNTSMS 127; Cambridge: Cambridge University Press, 2003), p. 87, n. 82.

μου ὁ ἀγαπητός, ἐν ᾧ εὐδόκησα ἀκούετε αὐτοῦ. Olmstead asserts that 'in both instances, then, ἐφοβήθησαν σφόδρα describes the fear that follows supernatural displays and in both instances the significance of the event revolves around Jesus' divine sonship'.[162] But is a 'supernatural display' an adequate description of the transfiguration text? A. D. A. Moses has shown that the pericope draws quite heavily from the Sinai theophany, blending Old Testament and Jewish apocalyptic images, where the response of fear was not to the biblical Moses but to the voice of God, which has close ties with Matthew's baptismal account and points heavily to the eschatological 'coming of God'.[163] This, then, could easily be understood as a recognition of Jesus' divinity, though that issue will need to be addressed in our discussion of θεοῦ υἱὸς below. For the present, the response in fear to a divine appearance subsequent to the *velum scissum* may underscore the cessation of the veil's function as a visual barrier. This is further seen in the presence of a cloud (νεφέλη) in the transfiguration text, a cloud which, like the veil, serves as a revelatory function[164] to conceal visual accessibility to God.[165] Although Senior doubts whether one should ask what the centurion 'saw' in history, this is an essential element of the apocalyptic eschatology of the pericope, in which 'seeing' is a defining characteristic.[166] What they saw in this heavenly vision included all the 'events' from the earthquake onwards (excluding the veil).[167] They are, then, having an apocalyptic vision, without necessarily having any

[162] *Ibid.* He adds, 'For Gundry, *Matthew*, 578, this connection between the disciples at the Transfiguration and the soldiers at the cross implies the conversion of the latter.' See Hagner, *Matthew* II, pp. 494–95.

[163] Moses, *Transfiguration*, pp. 27, 103, 157–58. It is also understood as an announcement of imminent resurrection (see 1 Cor. 15:51–52; *2 Bar.* 49:2–3; 51:3, 5, 9–12); Luz, *Matthew* II, p. 397; Moses, *Transfiguration*, p. 125. Cf. D. C. Sim, 'The "Confession" of the Soldiers in Matthew 27:54', *HeyJ* 34 (1993), 408–9.

[164] Moses, *Transfiguration*, p. 21, citing Exod. 13:21–22; 14:19–20; Num. 9:15–23; Deut. 5:22; Ezek. 10:3–4.

[165] For such vision language in Daniel and its use in Matt. 17, see Moses, *Transfiguration*, pp. 90–103; C. H. T. Fletcher-Louis, 'Narrative Christologies: The Transfiguration and Post-Resurrection Stories' (Third Oxford Lecture on the Development of Christology, undated, unpublished paper). See also D. Ulansey ('The Transfiguration, Cosmic Symbolism, and the Transformation of Consciousness in the Gospel of Mark' [paper presented at the annual meeting of the Society of Biblical Literature, New Orleans, La., November, 1996]), who compares the Markan transfiguration, in light of the *velum scissum* and the Markan baptismal account, to initiatory rites of the cults of Isis and Mithras.

[166] See R. J. Korner, '"And I Saw . . .": An Apocalyptic Literary Convention for Structural Identification in the Apocalypse', *NovT* 42 (2000), 160–83.

[167] So also E. Fascher, *Das Weib des Pilatus (Matthäus 27, 19). Die Auferweckung der Heiligen (Matthäus 27, 51–53): Zwei Studien zur Geschichte der Schriftauslegung* (Halle: M. Niemeyer, 1951), p. 33; Hagner, *Matthew* II, p. 852, *pace* Davies and Allison, *Matthew* III, p. 636, n. 146. Although Matthew does not say the centurion saw the veil, Beare (*Matthew*, p. 536) insists that since 'the curtain was not visible from outside the temple', 'its rending is not to be taken as a factual report'. Instead, it is to be taken 'as a symbol of

reality outside the vision itself.[168] The question of whether a Gentile can have a 'Jewish' vision and whether such a vision depicts something other than judgement is easily resolved elsewhere in the New Testament. Acts 10 relates the story of Cornelius, ironically a Gentile soldier, who is said to have a 'vision' in which he 'distinctly saw an angel of God' who gives him instructions about sending for Peter (10:4–7). Although Cornelius is a 'god-fearer' and likely knows about angels, he still provides an example of a Gentile given a 'Jewish' vision, with no sense of judgement whatsoever.

The final issue with the visionary nature of the Matthean special material pertains to the nature of the events seen in heaven. That is, are they comments simply on the present situation at Golgotha, or are they predictions of some future reality on earth? For this we must look both to the Ezek. 37 source from which Matthew drew and to other elements of Matthean eschatology. We have already said that Ezekiel's prophecy addressed the tragedy of the then current crisis of earthly exile by using heavenly images to depict a future reality, an earthly return from exile and all the eschatological blessings that this would include. Similarly, Matthew's use of this special material addresses the tragedy of the then current crisis of Jesus' death. As I indicated above, apocalyptic images are frequently employed to depict the transcendent reality that is going on 'behind the scenes' of a tragic event. They provide a 'cosmic perspective' of the situation in which God is sovereignly in control despite the tragedy of the historical situation in which the revelation is conveyed. In the midst of historical tragedy there are secrets kept in heaven that are integral to God's 'salvific design'. This transcendent reality is indiscernible by human reason alone and is known by the seer's being shown the heavenly mystery. Yet is Matthew, like Ezekiel, looking to a future reality? This

the thought that is made explicit in the Epistle to the Hebrews, that through the death of Jesus, the Holy of Holies is opened for all time'. See also Grundmann, p. 562.

[168] Although an apocalyptic seer typically sees heaven open (Ezek. 1:1), Matthew does not indicate that this is seen by the centurion. In the baptismal passages we find clues: at Mark 1:10 Jesus sees heaven open and the dove descend, yet in Matt. 3:16 heaven opens and then Jesus sees the dove descend. That is, Matthew has made a precedent for the visionary experience only said to be seeing what occurs after the indicator of the opening of heaven/veil. Thus in Matthew's (apocalyptic) opening of heaven the seer sees not the origin of the revelation but truly sees the content that is revealed. *Pace* Waters (pp. 489–515), who concludes the opening of the tombs, raising of the saints, and entering of the holy ones could not have been among those things seen, because the saints did not come out of the tombs until 'after his resurrection' (μετὰ τὴν ἔγερσιν αὐτοῦ). While logically consistent, this proposal fails to recognize that such temporal difficulties are not in the least troublesome to apocalyptic eschatology. He himself says a 'temporal-spatial collapse' is 'characteristic of most apocalyptic' (p. 489).

seems unlikely. Matthew seems to be appropriating the Ezekiel material to his own situation – applying it to Jesus' death. It seems more plausible that, as is typical for Matthew, he sees the events *foretold* in Ezekiel as being, in some sense 'fulfilled' in Jesus' death. This is particularly the case since, as I said above, the special material indicates the turning of the eschatological ages which is occasioned by the death of Jesus. Matthew is then proclaiming that the reality that Ezekiel intended to convey by using the images he employed in Ezek. 37 is occurring in heaven at the time of the death of Jesus. Moreover, Jesus' death has *occasioned* the eschatological turning of the ages depicted by the special material as revealed by the *velum scissum*. This underscores the 'commentary' nature of the events following Jesus' death.

## 2.3 Apocalyptic Imagery and Referentiality of the Veil

I have already said that Matthean redaction employs apocalyptic imagery, which suggests that an apocalyptic imagery approach to the *velum scissum* is therefore necessary. Indeed, many scholars have noted that the *velum scissum* is, in some sense, apocalyptic. In particular, it is best to categorise Matthew's *velum scissum* as 'apocalyptic imagery', imagery which in Judaeo-Christian traditions largely developed from Israelite prophetic traditions, and therefore frequently resonates with biblical images and phrases,[169] particularly in Matthew.[170] We have also seen that referentiality is an essential element in interpreting the use of apocalyptic imagery. With respect to the torn veil, however, scholars have rightly recognised there *is* no precedent in Judaism;[171] the referent is unclear, and conjecture has been dominant. Yet what about the veil itself? What does it symbolise?[172]

Scholars, to my knowledge, have not addressed this question. Instead, they tend to follow an interpretative tradition like that summarised by Davies and Allison, who for a variety of such reasons prefer to relate

[169] Collins, p. 17; Rowland, pp. 14, 60, 71; Bockmuehl, p. 31.

[170] Hagner, 'Apocalyptic Motifs', p. 56.

[171] Except, perhaps, in *Liv. Pro.* 12.

[172] S. Motyer, 'The Rending of the Veil: A Markan Pentecost?' *NTS* 33 (1987), 155, insists, 'The veil which stood before the Holy Place is taken to embody the whole religious system of the Temple.' Senior ('Death of God's Son', pp. 34–37) says that the veil before the holy of holies not only 'signified the locus of God's presence at the heart of Israel's cultic life' but also 'served as a wall of separation between the people and Yahweh'. J. D. G. Dunn insists that 'with apocalyptic language, the question of referentiality cannot be ignored' ('The Significance of Matthew's Eschatology for Biblical Theology', *SBLSP* 35 [1996], 161). He also asserts, 'It is in the nature of apocalyptic vision that what is seen and described is more symbolic than anything else' (p. 159) and that 'scenes drawn on the template of human history can function only metaphorically or allusively' (p. 160).

the tearing of the veil to the destruction of the temple in 70 C.E.[173] In addition to Matt. 23:38, they look to Matt. 27:40, where passers-by speak of Jesus' alleged claim that he would destroy the temple and rebuild it in three days. In their opinion, 'it is most appropriate that, immediately after people mock Jesus for his prophecy about the temple (v. 40), his words should be vindicated'.[174] They conclude that 'the context refers to Jesus' prophecy of destruction (v. 40)' to support their interpretation 'which relates the rending of the (outer) veil to the destruction of A.D. 70'.[175] Although they do not articulate the nature of that relationship, their observation of 27:40 is common and insightful. For there Matthew asserts (following Mark 15:29 closely, though not exactly) that Jesus is the 'one who is going to destroy the temple and in three days build it' (27:40). But this is apparently on the basis of the testimony in 26:61, which is explicitly said to be 'false' (26:59).[176] Previously, we saw, Matthew is explicitly and strongly affirming the temple with respect to the validity of its existence, the presence of God in it, its sacrifices, its being a legitimate place for prayer, and even the offices of administrators of the Law associated with it. Yet he also explicitly announces the imminence of its destruction, lamentably because of its mismanagement by the Jewish leaders. If it is so blatantly announced before, why, if the *velum scissum* does allude to the destruction of the temple, is it so terribly vague and indirect?

Lack of specific explanation means that I can only speculate on the hermeneutical rationale for equating the *velum scissum* with the destruction of the temple. Presumably one is to adopt Motyer's conjecture that the veil 'is taken to embody the whole religious system of the Temple'[177] and its rending depicts the destruction of both system and temple. Matthew's term for rending, σχίζω, does not mean destruction, but may suggest it as an effect of the rending.[178] But even given the importance of the veil within the temple, the destruction of the veil does not necessarily imply the destruction of the temple. Perhaps this view understands the veil as representative of the entire temple (veil = temple; therefore rending of veil = destruction of the temple). For this to be the case, however, one

[173] Davies and Allison, *Matthew* III, p. 631.

[174] *Ibid.*, p. 630. However, the texts they cite for support (II, p. 630, n. 100; Tertulliam, *Marc.* 4.42; Chrysostom, *Hom. Matt.* 88.2) say nothing about the identity of the veil but rather allude to the concept of judgement only.

[175] Davies and Allison, *Matthew* III, p. 631.

[176] *Pace* P. W. L. Walker, *Jesus and the Holy City: New Testament Perspectives on Jerusalem* (Grand Rapids, Mich.: Eerdmans, 1996), p. 29.

[177] Motyer, p. 155.

[178] This seems to be the case with his use of the cognate σχισμα in Matt. 9:16. Though LSJ (*Lexicon*, p. 1746) offer no such qualification.

would need to find a development of this imagery in other texts like, for example, that of the lamp-stand imagery in Rev. 1:12. Beale has shown that 'in Zech. 4:2–6 the lampstand with its seven lamps is a figurative synecdoche: part of the temple furniture stands for the whole temple, which by extension also represents faithful Israel (cf. Zech. 4:6–9)'.[179] The reader of Revelation, Beale contends, would have recognised the allusion to Zech. 4 and thus the part-for-the-whole imagery. Yet, as we have seen in Chapter 4, evidence for the veil as representative of the temple itself is scant. Only in the LXX of Sir. 50:5 (no later than the second century B.C.E.) and *Liv. Pro.* 12:10[180] (c. 70 C.E.?) is the veil symbolically associated with the temple. The same veil was understood by Philo, metaphorically of course, as a 'veil' of unbelief (*Giants* 53). In *Joseph and Aseneth* (10:2; c. 1c C.E.) the veil itself was covered by a skin (τῆν δέρριν) and its disclosure marked a decisive moment in the conversion of Aseneth to Judaism.[181] This, however, is where the variety of associations ends. For, as I have shown in Chapter 4, the symbolic referent for the veil was only one thing, the heavenly firmament of Gen. 1:6.

As we have seen in Chapter 4, identifying the symbolic referent of the veil with the heavenly firmament may have originated in a tradition like that of the Targum of Job 26:9, which describes God spreading clouds over his glory like a curtain. We have also seen that rabbis looked to Gen. 1:6ff (cf. *Num. Rab.* 12:16 [on Num. 7:1]) to say that the veil before the most holy place corresponds to the רקיע ('firmament').[182] We saw that Hofius shows that this veil served, in part, to conceal divine secret plans (common, as we have seen, in apocalyptic eschatology). Behind the veil (מאחור הפרגוד) is a place of secrecy where things that could only be known to God are present in profoundly apocalyptic texts.[183] Secret things such as knowledge of tribulations in store for the world are contained within (*b. Ber.* 18b).[184] God's heavenly secrets, kept behind the veil, are disclosed only when the barrier is breached either by one's hearing what is said behind it or, in rare occasion, when a heavenly being is permitted to penetrate it. Herein lies an apocalyptic element to the function of the veil within these texts, only some of which are formally 'apocalypses' in

179 G. K. Beale, *The Book of Revelation* (NIGTC; Grand Rapids, Mich.: Eerdmans, 1998), pp. 206–7.

180 See D. M. Gurtner, 'The "House of the Veil" in Sirach 50', *JSP* 14.3 (2005), 187–200.

181 Cf. e.g., *2 En.* 25 and Dan. 10:20ff.

182 Cf. Ego, *Im Himmel wie auf Erden*, pp. 112, 116, 119; Hofius, *Vorhang*, pp. 24–25. Cf. *Gen. Rab.* 4:1 (on Gen. 1:6); *y. Ber.* 1:2; *Gen. Rab.* 4:1 (on Gen. 1:6).

183 *Tg. Ps.–J.* Gen. 37:17; *Pirqe R. El.* §7. Cf. Ginzberg, *Legends* II, pp. 10–11. Cf. *b. Ta'an* 10a; *b. Pesaḥ.* 94a.

184 Odeberg, *3 Enoch*, p. 141. Cf. Barker, *Gate of Heaven*, pp. 104–32.

genre. And, as we have seen, this association of the veil with the heavenly firmament is found in Josephus (*J. W.* 5.5.4 §§214).

These texts, however, are notably late (except for Josephus) and, though the Jewish temple cosmology of which the veil as the heavenly firmament is a part can be dated as early as Ezekiel, the clear association between the veil and the heavenly firmament from these texts is too late to be of much value for Matthew's understanding of the symbolic value of the veil that is torn. Instead, a much firmer source for Matthew's view of the symbolism of the veil is found in the gospel of Mark. For Mark also makes a recognised association between the heavenly firmament torn at Jesus' baptism (σχίζω, Mark 1:10) and the splitting of the veil at the 'baptism' of Jesus' death (σχίζω, 15:38).[185] If these are both legitimate recognitions of the veil as the heavenly firmament, it not only establishes a very *early* recognition of the connection between the heavenly firmament and the veil of the temple, but locates that association within Mark's gospel, which scholars widely agree was a primary source for the composition of Matthew.[186]

## 2.4 Matthew's Adaptation of Mark's *Velum Scissum* Account

Mark's understanding of the function of the veil seems to be of lesser interest than that of Matthew when he considers its rending. For Mark makes no mention of an Emmanuel Christology, shows relatively little concern for seeing or being in the presence of God or the atoning nature of Jesus' death. Nor is he as concerned for separation in a cultically legal sense as is Matthew. Instead, Mark uses the *velum scissum* for two purposes: first, as a literary device connecting with his tearing of the heavens at the beginning of his gospel (1:10), and second, as an apocalyptic element indicating the disclosure of Jesus' identity as the Son of God (15:39).

Many scholars agree that readers of Mark's *velum scissum* should look to its theological importance rather than presume a literal history.[187] Yet theology is not the only concern of the second evangelist. Scholars have recognised a cogently structured literary style employed by the evangelist with respect to the veil. Motyer argues that 'incident picks up and forms an

[185] For a brief discussion of the *chiasmus* and *inclusio* in Mark's structure and the relation of these texts to it, cf. W. R. Telford, *Mark* (Sheffield: Academic Press, 1997), pp. 102–3.

[186] Although this is not an apocalyptic context, as in other Jewish writings similarly depicting the veil, it is no longer valid to discredit Josephus' connection with Jewish apocalypticism. Cf. P. Bilde, 'Josephus and Jewish Apocalypticism', pp. 35–61.

[187] Anderson, *Mark*, p. 347; France, *Mark*, p. 658; Taylor, *St Mark*, p. 596.

*inclusio* with the account of Jesus' baptism in 1.9–11'.[188] Drawing from the Markan use of the confessions of Jesus as υἱὸς θεοῦ, he draws attention to the close relationship between the opening narrative in chapter 1 of that gospel and the events surrounding the crucifixion. Ulansey builds upon Motyer's argument to suggest that he intended to bracket his entire gospel with a tearing of the veil/splitting of the heavens inclusio.[189] Yet there are more structural elements to Mark's gospel than previously recognised. It is true, as Motyer and Ulansey have recognised, Mark associates the splitting (σχίζω) of the heavens (1:10) with the splitting (σχίζω) of the veil (15:38), but Mark seems to bring his gospel to a degree of closure by asserting that God's declaration of Jesus as his son (ὁ υἱός μου, 1:11) is finally recognised by someone other than the 'evil spirits' (3:11) as the son of God (the centurion, υἱὸς θεοῦ, 15:39). Perhaps this can help alleviate the debate over the anarthrous υἱὸς θεοῦ by recognising that the God who identified Jesus at his son at the baptism (1:10) is the same God of whom Jesus is his son (15:39) at the 'baptism' of his death (Mark 10:38–39). Though Luke also refers to Jesus' suffering as a 'baptism' (Luke 12:50), he does not record a baptism of Jesus at all, and Matthew does not refer to Jesus' suffering as a 'baptism'. Thus Mark alone seems to describe the splitting of heaven and the announcement of Jesus' divine sonship at the baptism, describing Jesus' sufferings as a 'baptism', and round off the association by announcing Jesus' divine sonship again at the 'baptism' of his death and the splitting of the (heavenly) veil.

While Mark's literary device is intriguing, his *velum scissum* also serves a revelatory function, as it does in Matthew. Yet Matthew has taken the simple Markan account, which moves from the death of Jesus, to the torn veil, to the centurion's 'profession', and inserted his 'special material'. This seems to enhance the content of what is revealed, though Markan scholars, as with Matthean, have offered different explanations due to confusion about the referent of the symbolism employed. Of course, scholars have proposed the familiar discussion that the *velum scissum* is a Markan

[188] Motyer, p. 155. His further assertion that 'that it therefore represents a Markan Pentecost, a proleptic bestowal of the Spirit analogous to the proleptic destruction of the temple' has gained almost no support. He concludes this from C. K. Barrett's the suggestion that 'the lost ending of Mark actually contained an account of Pentecost' and because the promise of Spirit baptism in Mark is not fulfilled in the extant text. C. K. Barrett, *The Holy Spirit and the Gospel Tradition* (London: SPCK, 1947), p. 125; Pelletier, p. 179–80. Yet his insistence that the tearing of the veil 'reveals' desecration and judgement obscures his treatment of the 'special material' (in Matthew) and the centurion's profession (Matthew and Mark).

[189] Ulansey, 'The Heavenly Veil Torn: Mark's Cosmic Inclusio', *JBL* 110 (1991), 124. Is dependence on Josephus (*J. W.* 5.5.4 §§212–14) to argue the outer veil is in view has been discounted in the introduction and Chapter 4.

metaphor for the 'disenfranchisement of the temple and the displacement of the Jewish cultus that commence with Jesus' advent and are permanently sealed in his death'.[190] Yet this fails to acknowledge what the veil itself symbolised. Some contend that the veil simply represents itself, and the *velum scissum* was a revelatory device that simply revealed what was within the temple. This means that the inside of the holy of holies is opened up,[191] thus exposing the very face of God,[192] either depicting God's abandonment of it[193] or simply exposing its sanctity resulting in desecration that ends its sacrificial function.[194] Others mix the metaphor with that of Hebrews, asserting that the 'Temple on the cross was his body'.[195] Yet Lamarch, cognizant of the association of the veil with the heavenly firmaments (1:10) sees the veil as symbolic of the sky which is opened at 1:10, and the rending of the veil reveals God to all.[196] He also says that the opening of heaven is a new creation motif whereby a passage way is opened (cf. Heb. 9:11) by which Christ ascended to heaven to the right hand of God.[197] But 'God' is not what is revealed subsequent to the rending. Instead it is that Jesus is υἱὸς θεοῦ. As Chronis says, Mark's infamous 'Messianic secret' is out.[198] Matthew seems to have adopted the Markan revelatory function of the *velum scissum* while developing the content of what it reveals by inserting his special material and changing Mark's single centurion to a plurality of soldiers. Mark's lack of attention to themes which coalesce with the cessation of the veil's function seem to indicate he is less concerned with that aspect. Matthew, however, betrays important elements which dovetail very closely with the cessation of the veil's function by means of his portrayal of Jesus' death and the

[190] H. L. Chronis, 'The Torn Veil: Cultus and Christology in Mark 15:37–39', *JBL* 101 (1982), 111. The greatest weakness of this interpretation is that it fails to show the significance of the veil itself in any, let alone Mark's, context. He speculates on its meaning, what is understood to be behind the veil, and the implications of it. Stanton, *Gospels and Jesus*, p. 250; Brown, *Death* II, p. 1102; Evans, *Mark 8:27–16:20*, pp. 509–10; France, *Mark*, pp. 656–57. There are also those who would identify the veil with a garment, which is torn in lament as the high priest tore his robes (Mark 14:62; Brown, *Death* II, pp. 1100–1101).

[191] K. E. Bailey, 'The Fall of Jerusalem and Mark's Account of the Cross', *Expository Times* 102 (1991), 102. He further asserts (pp. 102–4) that Mark then equates Jesus with the holy of holies as that which is exposed. Therefore, 'Jesus and his cross were a *replacement* for both the city of Jerusalem and the temple'.

[192] Chronis, pp. 110–11; cf. Taylor, *St Mark*, p. 596

[193] H. M. Jackson, 'The Death of Jesus in Mark and the Miracle from the Cross', *NTS* 33 (1987), 27.

[194] Pelletier, p. 173; cf. Senior, 'Death of God's Son', 41

[195] Yates, *Spirit and the Kingdom*, p. 235; Lightfoot, *Gospel Message of St Mark*, p. 56.

[196] Lamarche, 'La mort du Christ et le voile du temple selon Marc', p. 588.

[197] Ibid., 589–90. [198] Chronis, pp. 110–11.

accessibility of God depicted in his Emmanuel Christology, as I will discuss below.

While this is recognised by some in Mark as a literary device,[199] does Matthew adopt Mark's association between the tearing of the veil and the opening of heaven? The Matthean baptismal text (3:13–15) has been recognised as employing eschatological imagery,[200] yet his account is slightly different from that of Mark. With Mark, the heavens were 'split' (σχιζομένους; 1:10[201]); in Matthew (3:16; and Luke 3:21) the heavens were 'opened' (ἠνεῴχθησαν [Matt. 3:16]; ἀνεῳξθῆναι [Luke 3:21]). Matthew's baptismal text, then, clearly adopts the apocalyptic opening-of-heaven scheme. Schneider suggests that Matthew likewise associated heaven with the firmaments of Gen. 1:6,[202] which serves to underscore the association I developed above. Moreover, J. T. Pennington suggests that there are no clearly considered levels of heaven in Matthew.[203] Any notion of levels of heaven in Matthew is the same vague sense that one finds in most of the apocalyptic and pseudepigraphical literature as well as in the Old Testament itself; i.e., there is a sense that God is *above* and beyond the visible heavens, but the specific levels of heaven that we find in Rabbinic and later apocalyptic literature are not found in Matthew.[204] Luz suggests the opening of heaven at Matt. 3:16 may allude to the similar event in Ezek. 1:1–4. [205] France notes that the typical word for the opening of the heavens in such visionary texts is ἀνοίγω, with Mark's σχίζω being 'vivid and unexpected'.[206] In Mark, though, the heavens are split

[199] Ulansey, 'Mark's Cosmic Inclusio', pp. 123–25. Cf. P. Lamarche, 'La mort du Christ et le voile du temple selon Marc', *NRth* 106 (1974), 585; Evans, *Mark*, p. 509.

[200] Rowland, pp. 362–63, 69. Cf. W. Bousset, *Die Religion des Judentums im späthellenistischen Zeitalter* (Tübingen: Mohr Siebeck, 1966), pp. 283ff; P. Volz, *Jüdische Eschatologie von Daniel bis Akiba* (Tübingen: Mohr Siebeck, 1903), p. 417; Jeremias, *New Testament Theology* I, pp. 69f.; Rowland, p. 367; F. Lentzen-Deis, *Die Taufe Jesu nach den Synoptikern: Literarkritische und gattungsgeschichtliche Untersuchungen* (Frankfurt: Josef Knecht, 1970), pp. 99f; G. Schneider, '"Im Himmel – auf Erden", Eine Perspektive Matthäischer Theologie', in *Studien zum Matthäusevangelium: Festschrift Für Wilhelm Pesch* (ed. L. Schenke; Stuttgart: Verlag Katholisches Bibelwerk, 1988), p. 290.

[201] Although D latt and geo read ηνοιγμενους, this is probably a secondary reading, perhaps looking to reconcile with that of Matthew and Luke, and cognizant of the fact that ἀνοίγω is the expected term for the opening of heaven.

[202] Schneider, p. 292.

[203] 'Heaven and Earth in the Gospel of Matthew' (Ph.D. diss., University of St Andrews, 2005), even in light of Matthew's frequent plural usage of οὖρανος, which Pennington argues serves a rhetorical rather than cosmological purpose.

[204] Pennington, 'Heaven and Earth'. See also J. J. Collins, 'A Throne in the Heavens: Apotheosis in Pre-Christian Judaism', in *Death, Ecstasy, and Other Worldly Journeys* (ed. J. J. Collins and M. Fishbane; New York, N.Y.: State University of New York Press, 1995), pp. 43–57.

[205] U. Luz, *Matthew 1–7: A Commentary* (Minneapolis, Minn.: Augsburg, 1989), p. 179.

[206] France, *Mark*, p. 77.

(σχίζω; 1:10) at Jesus' baptism, with a voice declaring his divine sonship, while at the 'baptism' of Jesus' death (Mark 10:38–39)[207] the veil (of the heavenly firmament) was split (σχίζω; 15:38), with another voice declaring his divine sonship (see below, and Conclusion). France notes that this literary cohesion in Mark resonates with Old Testament open-heaven language and indicates God's 'supernatural intervention to restore his people's fortunes'.[208] However, if Matthew is preserving Mark's association between the *velum scissum* and the opening of the heavens at Jesus' baptism, why has he apparently damaged Mark's inclusio structure by changing Mark's σχίζω to ἀνοίγω?

The answer to this question seems to lie in the fact that Matthew does not want to preserve an inclusio structure by associating the veil and the heavens but by connecting the descent of the Spirit at Jesus' baptism and the departure of the Spirit at Jesus' death. Thus the inauguration and completion of Jesus' messianic role, rather than a literary inclusio, are underscored by Matthean redaction. He also preserves a form of the Markan inclusio by conjoining his baptismal account (Matt. 3) and the temptation account (Matt. 4) – supporting the inclusio idea with the rending of the veil and the Jerusalem vision in his special material (27:51b-53). The correlation is further sealed by the 'son of God' statements linking the baptism and temptation accounts with each other and the centurion's profession (27:54). Thus Matthew does seem to preserve, to a degree, the Markan inclusio. By his adjustments, however, he changes the focus: whereas Mark attends to the splitting of the heavens at Jesus' baptism and the splitting of the veil at the 'baptism' of Jesus' death, Matthew adjusts the Markan narrative framework to enclose the core of his gospel with the reception of the Spirit for Jesus' messianic role at the baptism (3:16) and the yielding of the Spirit upon the completion of that role at his death (27:50). Matthew's association of the splitting of the heavens and the veil from Mark is preserved but weakened, not because he sought to dissociate the two but because his adjustments to the Markan structure sought to underscore Jesus' messianic mission more than Mark does.

[207] Yet the 'baptism' of Christ's death is a feature of Mark (10:38–39) and Luke (12:50) but absent from Matthew (cf. Matt. 20:22–23) – though added by C W 33 (892) 1006 1342 (1506) *M* f h q sy$^{p, h}$ bo$^{pt}$.

[208] France, *Mark*, p. 77, n. 65. Others who see such a background are Watts, *New Exodus*, pp. 102–8; C. Perrot, *Jésus et l'histoire* (Paris: Desclée, 1979), pp. 184, 198 n. 17, and J. Marcus, *The Way of the Lord: Christological Exegesis of the Old Testament in the Gospel of Mark* (Louisville, Ky.: Westminster/John Knox, 1992), pp. 49–50, 56–58, with Marcus contending for an 'apocalyptic theophany' seen only by Jesus. See also Davies and Allison, *Matthew* I, p. 329.

Thus there is no strong basis to suggest that Matthew has abandoned the association between the veil and the heavens portrayed by Mark.

If Matthew, then, identifies the veil with the heavenly firmament, his depiction of what happens to it and why it happens is significant. Immediately after Jesus' death, Matthew's τὸ καταπέτασμα τοῦ ναοῦ[209] 'was torn' (ἐσχίσθη).[210] This verb begins what Witherup (to name but one scholar) has identified as a series of divine passives, a frequent feature in apocalyptic writings as a 'circumlocution for divine activity'[211] which is understood to 'clearly show that Matthew is asserting the eschatological significance of Jesus' death'.[212] This suggests that, at least in part, the relationship between Jesus' death and the *velum scissum* is one of cause/effect. Jesus' death *caused* the veil to be torn (σχίζω).

Several LXX uses of σχίζω seem to be informative for Matthew's use of the term here.[213] It may reflect the action on the Red Sea at the exodus,[214]

[209] Only ms 1346 is at variant, where there is a *lacunae* reading κατ . . . ναου. Syr., interestingly, is quite specific and reads ܐܦ̈ܝ ܬܪܥܐ ܕܒܝܬ ܩܘܕܫܐ (lit. 'face of the door of the house of the sanctuary'), Shem-Tob's Hebrew: פרכת המקדש.

[210] Shem-Tob: נקרע.

[211] D. E. Aune, *Revelation* (3 vols.; WBC 52A–C. Dallas, Tex.: Word, 1997, 1998) I, p. 280. The curtain *was torn* (ἐσχίσθη, 27:51a), the earth *was shaken* (ἐσείσθη, 27:51b), the rocks *were split* (ἐσχίσθησαν, 27:51c), tombs *were opened* (ἀνεῴχθησαν, 27:52a) and bodies *were raised* (ἠγέρθησαν, 27:52b). Witherup, 'The Cross of Jesus', p. 280. Cf. Davies and Allison, *Matthew* III, p. 632; Senior, 'Death of God's Son', 42; Heil, *Death and Resurrection*, p. 85.

[212] Senior, 'Revisiting', p. 420.

[213] In this aorist passive form, σχίζω occurs 14 times prior to the second century C.E. (Anacreon, *Fragmenta* 96b.1; Thales, *Testimonia* 6.10; Herodotus, *Histories* 1.75.21; 4.119.3; Hippocrates, *De ossium natura* 7.1; Xenophon, *Symposium* 4.59.4; Antisthenes, *Fragmenta varia* 107.20; Matt. 27:51; Mark 15:38; Luke 23:45; John 21:11 Acts 14:4; 23:7; Plutarch, *Socrates* 594E.1). Yet other forms of the verb are more common in that era (Philolaus, *Frag.* 11.18; Herodotus, *Histories* 2.17.12, 18; 2.33.11; 4.49.6; Xenophon, *Anabasis* 1.5.12.6; *Cyropaedia* 8.2.5; Aeneas, *Poliorcetica* 15.6.4; Theophrastus, *Frag.* 6.11.9; 6.26.7; Apollonius Rhodius, *Argonautica* 4.325; Philoxenus, *Frag.* 146.4; Strabo, *Geographica* 17.2.2.23; Josephus, *Ant.* 3.9.1 §227).

[214] Exod. 14:21; Isa. (Aq) 63:12; also an unknown source of Exod. 14:16. We explore the correlation between the splitting of the 'heavenly waters' with respect to the baptismal texts above (pp. 172–77), particularly with respect to the 'baptism' of Jesus' death. If an exodus motif can be suggested in the Matthean Passion Narrative, one could suggest that the rending of the veil is providing deliverance similar to that of the splitting of the Red Sea. This could support Rudman's ('Crucifixion as *Chaoskampf*', pp. 102–107) notion that particularly the darkness and the *velum sicssum* in the Matthean Passion Narrative drawing on an Old Testament *Chaoskampf* typology in which 'Jesus is presented as a creator figure who confronts the powers of chaos. In this instance however, the powers of chaos emerge temporarily triumphant. The old creation is destroyed, paving the way for a renewal of creation with Jesus's resurrection' (p. 107). We will revisit the significance of a renewed creation depicted at the *velum scissum*. Other splitting (σχίζω) uses in the LXX occur for splitting wood for sacrifices (Gen. 22:3; 1 Sam. 6:14; cf. Eccles. 10:9), a violent wind (Aq and Sm Ezek. 13:13) or the wings of a bird (Wis. 5:11) splitting the air, and the heroics

which may be congruent with the 'new exodus' motif raised by Matthew's use of Ezek. 37 in his 'special material' (27:51b-53). Another prominent 'splitting' text which is probably in the background of the Matthean special material is the splitting (σχισθήσεται) of the Mount of Olives at the Day of the Lord (Zech. 14:4).[215] Yet the most important use of σχίζω for our consideration is probably that in Mark 1:10,[216] where heaven is split (σχιζ ομένους) and the Spirit descends as a dove. The use of σχίζω in Matt. 27:51a is generally recognised as a *passivum divinum* that clearly identifies God as the agent.[217] This is an important observation because it recognises that Matthew's Jesus had *not* been forsaken,[218] a defining quality in apocalyptic eschatology. Thus, for Matthew, the rending of the veil is an apocalyptic image depicting the opening of heaven, an apocalyptic assertion, and follows is the content of what it reveals.

## 2.5 What is Revealed

If the *velum scissum* is associated with the opening of heaven, as I have argued, then what follows serves as the content of the revelation – what is revealed. The first piece of the content that is revealed is Matthew's so-called 'special material'. That is, Jesus' death has itself occasioned a

of Eleazar killing men as they split before him left and right (1 Macc. 6:45). It is used for the tearing of garments in mourning (Isa. 36:22; 37:1) and for God's splitting the rock to provide Israel with water (Isa. 48:21; Aq Ps. 77 [78]:15). Cf. also Dan. LXX Su 55; Dan. Th Su 55; Aq Isa. 59:5; Th. Isa. 19:3.

[215] LSJ note two primary meanings for the σχίζω. The first is simply to 'split, cleave', (בקע) used of wood or of the tearing of a garment (*BGU* 928.20, 22); the other is to 'part, separate, divide' (קרע). LSJ, *Lexicon*, p. 1746. קרע is used here in Shem-Tob's Hebrew text of Matthew.

[216] The term occurs seven times in the New Testament, three times at the respective *velum scissum* texts (Matt. 27:51a; Mark 15:38; Luke 23:45) and once at Mark 1:10 (opening of heaven). Others include John 21:11 (tearing of Simon Peter's net at a miraculous catch of fish), Acts 14:4 (Jews and Gentiles were divided) and Acts 23:7 (Sanhedrin divided among itself).

[217] Hagner, *Matthew* II, p. 849; cf. Luz, *Matthäus* IV, p. 363. McNeile, p. 423; Brown, *Death* II, p. 1100. In note 7 on that page Brown comments, 'Later traditions will attribute the rending to the Temple itself or to the angels, but in either case the ultimate agency is God's'. R. Young, *Intermediate New Testament Greek* (Nashville, Tenn.: Broadman and Holman, 1994), p. 135. D. B. Wallace, *Greek Grammar Beyond the Basics: An Exegetical Syntax of the New Testament* (Grand Rapids, Mich.: Zondervan, 1996), pp. 437–38; cf. F. Blass, A. Debrunner, and Robert W. Funk, *A Greek Grammar of the New Testament and Other Early Christian Literature* (Chicago, Ill.: University of Chicago Press, 1961), p. 72 (§130.1); M. Zerwick, *Biblical Greek, Illustrated by Examples* (Rome: Scripta Pontificii Instituti Biblici, 1963), p. 76 (§236); Jeremias, *New Testament Theology* I, pp. 9–14; H. W. Smyth, *Greek Grammar* (Cambridge, Mass: Harvard University Press, 1956) §§590–96; 672–78. Kupp, *Matthew's Emmanuel*, p. 3. Linnemann, *Studien*, pp. 159–61.

[218] Brown, *Death* II, p. 1100.

revelatory assertion indicating its own significance. Upon the opening of heaven it is revealed, through the use of apocalyptic images, that Jesus' death has brought about the onset of the turning of an eschatological age from Ezekiel 37, in which exiles will return and God will dwell among his people. But this is not all that is revealed, for another item follows the *velum scissum* in both Matthew and Mark: that Jesus is 'son of God' (v. 54).

Ironically, those who (falsely) accuse Jesus of claiming to be able to destroy the temple, as son of God, now profess that very thing at the rending of its veil.[219] Davies and Allison comment,

> This is the third occasion on which the themes of Jesus as Son of God and the destruction of the temple have appeared in close connection: 26:61–4; 27:40, 51–4 . . . The sequence reflects Jesus' status as the messianic Son of David according to 2 Samuel 7, where it is promised that David's son will be God's son and that he will build a house (temple) in God's name.[220] The profession serves to contradict the bystanders' misunderstanding[221]

and to transform their mockery 'into a profession of faith in the crucified Jesus' profound identity', while ultimately vindicating Jesus.[222] It conforms to other professions by God, by Peter, by the disciples and by Jesus himself (3:17; 14:33; 16:16; 17:5; 26:63).[223] Senior has dubbed the 'profession' the 'keynote statement in the entire Passion story', providing stark contrast to the mockery scene, as 'belief in Jesus as the Son of God is the capital concern of Matthew in the Passion narrative'.[224] Hagner shows that Matthean redaction of the Markan text at this point shifts attention not to the manner of Jesus' death (ὅτι οὕτως ἐξέπνευσεν, 'that thus he died' [Mark 15:39]) but to the 'spectacular events referred to in vv. 51b-52'.[225] Thus the action of the soldiers is specifically the result of something that was revealed to them, culminating in the ἀληθῶς θεοῦ υἱὸς ἦν οὗτος statement.

[219] Sim ('Confession', p. 405) insists they are the same. Olmstead points out the stark contrast between the Jewish leaders who mock Jesus for claiming to be the son of God, and the soldiers who use it as a profession of faith (*Trilogy*, p. 87, cf. n. 85).

[220] Davies and Allison, *Matthew* III, p. 636.

[221] This suggests a 'royal messianic' category of Christology. Cf. Yokota, 'Jesus the Messiah of Israel', pp. 8–11, 154–270, 271–308.

[222] Matera, *Passion Narratives*, p. 87.

[223] *Ibid.*, pp. 87–88. Cf. Olmstead, *Trilogy*, p. 152, and nn. 85, 86; for Mark, Fascher, *Die Auferweckung der Heiligen (Matthäus 27, 51–53)*, p. 32.

[224] *Redactional Study*, p. 327. [225] Hagner, *Matthew* II, p. 848.

Much discussion has been made of Matthew's use of Christological titles and the anarthrous θεοῦ υἱὸς statement, and I cannot address all pertinent issues here.[226] France indicates the importance of the expression to connote the fatherhood of God,[227] though it echoes the servant motif of Isa. 42:1[228] and has been demonstrated by D. Verseput to serve 'to redefine the nature of Messiahship by emphasizing Jesus' filial obedience'.[229] In light of this, I must briefly comment on it in light of the revelatory function of the *velum scissum* that immediately precedes it in Mark, and that follows a series of apocalyptic eschatological images here in Matthew. Though not all will agree, most New Testament scholars concur: The reference is to 'the' son of God and subsequently, in part, a conversion by the (Gentile) centurion and company.[230] The title is recognised as a distinctive term of Jesus' obedience in Matthew. Jesus

[226] For a helpful overview, see France (*Matthew: Evangelist and Teacher*, pp. 292–93), who asserts 'Son of God' is the most important Matthean Christological title, and which depicts Jesus as obedient to the will of God and thus saves people from their sins. Kingsbury, *Matthew: Structure, Christology, Kingdom*, pp. 40–127, with criticism by D. Hill, 'Son and Servant: An Essay on Matthean Christology', *JSNT* 6 (1980), 2–26, response by Kingsbury, 'The Figure of Jesus in Matthew's Story: A Literary-Critical Probe', *JSNT* 21 (1984), 3–36, the criticism of D. Hill, 'The Figure of Jesus in Matthew's Story: A Response to Professor Kingsbury's Literary-Critical Probe', *JSNT* 21 (1984), 37–52, and response by Kingsbury, 'The Figure of Jesus in Matthew's Story: A Rejoinder to David Hill', *JSNT* 25 (1985), 61–81. Allison ('Son of God as Israel', 74–81; also Hill cited above) is critical of this approach for failing to account for the Isaianic servanthood of Jesus in this title, or anywhere in Judaism, early Christianity, Mark or Hellenistic world. Allison is particularly correct to dismiss the use of Christological titles as an adequate means in itself to arriving at a Matthean Christology. Cf. also France, *Matthew: Evangelist and Teacher*, pp. 298–311.

[227] *Matthew: Evangelist and Teacher*, pp. 292–98; see M. Hengel, *The Son of God: The Origin of Christology and the History of Jewish–Hellenistic Religion* (trans. J. Bowden; Philadelphia, Pa.: Fortress, 1976), pp. 21–56; J. D. G. Dunn, *Christology in the Making* (London: SCM, 1980), pp. 13–22.

[228] See France, *Matthew: Evangelist and Teacher*, p. 293; Beaton, *Isaiah's Christ*, pp. 64–83, 189–91.

[229] Verseput, 'Son of God', pp. 532–58, 296. France (*Matthew: Evangelist and Teacher*, p. 297) suggests Verseput may not go far enough, and hints that the title points to the divinity of Jesus.

[230] Cf. E. C. Colwell, 'A Definite Rule for the Use of the Article in the Greek New Testament', *JBL* 52 (1933), 12–21. So Davies and Allison, *Matthew* III, p. 636; Brown, *Death* II, p. 1146; Hagner, *Matthew* II, p. 852; Luz, *Matthäus* IV, p. 368. *Pace* Gundry, p. 577. Sim ('Confession', 401, cf. his n. 1) acknowledges that most Matthean scholars accept this reading, but he himself differs. He recognises that the soldiers present at 27:54 were the same as those present not just at 27:36 (recognised by Senior and others) but from 27:27–37. In these texts, he recognises, the soldiers are depicted as brutally torturing, degrading, and finally executing Jesus. Sim concludes that 'we may reasonably infer' (406) that because of their brutality '27:54 is motivated by [Matthew's] desire to incriminate the speakers'. This inference, however, is without textual evidence and though his indication of 'Matthew's full characterization of these soldiers' is helpful, it seems more likely that it provides an even starker contrast to the conversion exhibited in their 'profession' of faith in the Jesus whom they abuse and kill in 27:54 than Sim's contention (pp. 418–22) that their

'is the obedient Son of God who fulfils the Scriptures and is faithful to God's will unto death'.[231] Moreover, Jesus' 'obedience as the Son of God was tested (4:1–11; 26:18), and he summarises his entire mission in the upper room discourse (26:26–29), and remains committed to the will of his father (26:36–46) as revealed in the scriptures (26:47–56)'.[232] The same expression appears in 14:33, where after Jesus' calming of a storm, observers worshipped him and proclaimed 'ἀληθῶς θεοῦ υἱὸς εἶ'. This profession is understood as a revelation of the Father, which has developed from similar recognitions earlier in the gospel.[233] Matthew's portrayal of Jesus is 'not intended simply to give a compelling example of faithfulness' but is part of 'a larger canvas which conveys the unique identity of Jesus' as '*the* Israel' and '*the* Son of God'.[234] Obedience was often seen as the condition for God's presence to remain within the temple.[235] It seems, then, that Jesus' obedience is the means by which God can be 'with us' in Jesus. As we have seen in Chapter 5, 'No other Gospel presents the salvific impact of Jesus' passion in such explicit terms. Through his obedient death Jesus triumphs over death and that breakthrough is extended

statement 'bespeaks their sense of guilt and concession of defeat in the face of the divine, and foreshadows the attitude of the wicked on the day of judgment' (p. 422). For a discussion of this issue in Mark, cf. France, *Mark*, 660; and works cited in nn. 74–76. Evans, *Mark*, p. 510; M. Faessler, 'Marc 15,21–39: La Mort de Jésus', *BulCPE* 28 (1976), 28–30. R. Feldmeier, 'Der Gekreuzigte im "Gnadenstuhl": Exegetische Überlegungen zu Mk 15,37–39 und deren Bedeutung für die Vorstellung der göttlichen Gegenwart und Herrschaft', in *Trône de Dieu* (ed. M. Philonenko; Tübingen: Mohr Siebeck, 1993), pp. 213–32; E. S. Johnson, 'Mark 15,39 and the So-Called Confession of the Roman Centurion', *Bib.* 81 (2000), 406–13; Maisch, p. 98. R. L. Mowery, 'Son of God in Roman Imperial Titles and Matthew', *Bib.* 83 (2002), 100–110, asserts that Gentile readers of Matthew's gospel would identify Jesus with figures in the Roman imperial cult, though fails to acknowledge Peter's confession (Matt. 16) or any Old Testament or Jewish influences on the expression. Wright (*Resurrection*, p. 728) argues this was not part of the original Christian usage of the title.

231 Senior, *The Passion of Jesus in the Gospel of Matthew*, p. 164. So also Luz, *Matthew* II, p. 400. Olmstead, *Trilogy*, p. 102; G. Bornkamm, 'End Expectation and Church in Matthew', in *Tradition and Interpretation in Matthew* (ed. G. Borkamm, G. Barth and H. J. Held; Philadelphia, Pa.: Westminster Press, 1963), pp. 36–37.

232 Senior, *The Passion of Jesus in the Gospel of Matthew*, p. 164.

233 Davies and Allison, *Matthew* II, p. 510. Cf. Luz, *Matthew* II, p. 322.

234 Jesus 'is' Israel in that he obeys where Israel failed. Senior, *The Passion of Jesus in the Gospel of Matthew*, p. 164. Emphasis Senior's. Similarly Stanton, *Gospel for a New People*, pp. 378–79. Wright (*Resurrection*, pp. 727–28; cf. *New Testament and the People of God*, pp. 259–79) asserts that Matthew's use of 'son of God' indicates that he believed 'that Israel's god had acted in him to fulfil the covenant promises by dealing at last with the problem of evil'. And 'in [Jesus], the creator's covenant plan, to deal with the sin and death that has so radically infected his world, has reached its long-awaited and decisive fulfilment'.

235 Kupp, *Matthew's Emmanuel*, p. 131, citing J. Levenson, *Sinai and Zion: An Entry into the Jewish Bible* (Minneapolis, Minn.: Winston Press, 1985); 1 Kgs 6:1–13; 2 Sam. 7:14–16; Ps. 89:20–38. Clearly *disobedience* was behind God's departure from the temple in Ezekiel 10.

to all of God's people'.[236] Thus the profession is an acknowledgement of 'the final revelation of [Jesus'] identity'[237] introduced by the revelatory indicator of the *velum scissum.*

In Matthew's account of Peter's confession, the disciple acknowledges Jesus as 'the Christ, the son of the living God' (16:16), whereas Mark only has 'you are the Christ' (8:29; Luke 'the Christ of God' [9:2], and John 'you are the holy one of God' [6:69]).[238] That Matthew has added 'the son of God' to his source may help us with the centurion's profession. For Matthew further adds to Mark's account by saying μακάριος εἶ, Σίμων Βαριωνᾶ, ὅτι σὰρξ καὶ αἷμα οὐκ *ἀπεκάλυψέν* σοι ἀλλ' ὁ πατήρ μου ὁ ἐν τοῖς οὐρανοῖς (16:17). Whatever other intertextual allusions may be occurring here, it seems apparent that for Matthew the confession of Jesus as the Christ, the 'son of God', is a direct product of divine revelation (cf. also Matt. 14:33).[239] Such revelation also occurs in 27:51a, where the veil of the heavenly firmament is opened and the true identity of Jesus as the 'son of God' and the life-giving, new-age-inaugurating death of Jesus is revealed. And that his identity as Son of God is seen most vividly in his death[240] suggests that his role in bearing that title is most explicitly articulated in the atoning significance that his death is understood to carry in Matthew's gospel (26:28).

It seems likely that the soldiers may have actually spoken beyond what they knew, and Matthew expects his readers to accept his own notion of 'Son of God' placed on the lips of the soldiers. This understanding has led many to see in 27:54 a foreshadowing of the inclusion of Gentiles and the Gentile mission (28:18–20).[241] Regardless, it is recognised that Jesus' identity as Son of God is seen most vividly in his death[242] perhaps in that his role in bearing that title is most explicitly articulated in the atoning significance that his death is understood to carry. Our apocalyptic reading

[236] Senior, *The Passion of Jesus in the Gospel of Matthew*, p. 167. Senior then reviews all key texts (1:22; 4:16; 9:1–2; 11:3 [11:2–6]; 12:18–21; 20:28; 26:62–63, 67–68; 27:12–14, 27–31) (pp. 167–68).

[237] Senior, *The Passion of Jesus in the Gospel of Matthew*, p. 166.

[238] Wright, *Resurrection*, p. 621.

[239] For a helpful discussion of the intertextual relation between the identity of Jesus as son of God at Matt. 27:54 and Matt. 14:33, cf. Senior, *Redactional Study*, pp. 327–28. Cf. France, *Matthew: Evangelist and Teacher*, p. 294. Deutsch ('Wisdom in Matthew', p. 33) claims that themes of concealment and revelation in Matthew are very similar to wisdom themes in that gospel, and are both eschatological and apocalyptic, connoting 'the disclosure of the new order, the Reign of Heaven'. See also Matt. 10:26; G. MacAskill, 'Restored-Creation Eschatology in Matthew's Gospel and Early Judaism', Paper presented at the Annual Postgraduate Research Conference, University of Glasgow, June 2, 2004.

[240] Carson, 'Matthew', VIII, pp. 582–83. [241] See Olmstead, p. 87.

[242] Carson, 'Matthew', VIII, pp. 582–83. Cf. Andreoli, 'Il velo sqaurciato nel Vangelo di Matteo', p. 31, see his n. 69 for numerous others.

of the *velum scissum* affirms that, as is explicit with Peter's recognition of Jesus as the 'son of God', the soldiers' recognition of the same is the product of a divine revelation. It is the death of God's son that begins 'der eschatologischen Heilszeit'.[243] An apocalyptic reading of Matthew's *velum scissum* underscores that though his Jesus is beaten, bruised, and killed, God's power, which looms in the background by virtue of the *passivum divinum*, comes to the forefront in the material that follow Jesus' death, material that explicates precisely the transcendent significance of Jesus' death (while cognizant of his and others' resurrection).[244] The revelatory function of the torn veil in this pericope is congruent with Matthew's use of Mark's profession of faith by the centurion. That is, what is 'revealed' to him is that Jesus was the 'Son of God'. This may not be far from the Patristic readings I mentioned in the Introduction, which suggest that the rending of the veil reveals 'hidden things', normally meaning salvation to the Gentiles (the centurion), though more often than not failing to specify precisely what is revealed and to whom it was revealed.

## 3 Functionality and the *Velum Scissum*

The *velum scissum* reveals, in part, the eschatological nature of Jesus' death. It serves to reveal (in the special material) that Jesus' death inaugurates a turning of the ages depicted graphically in Ezekiel 37. Invoking these apocalyptic images may draw in a theme of restoration of the people of God from exile – a time which is also characterised by the unique presence of God among his people. But are there any further depictions in the *velum scissum* that support this notion? For the veil was not simply torn, but torn 'from the top to the bottom into two'. As I have shown in Chapter 3, scholars largely take this to indicate the cessation of the veil's function. But does Matthew's *velum scissum* support such a presumption, and if so, how does the cessation of the veil's function contribute to an interpretation of Matthew's *velum scissum* pericope? To answer these questions, we can again allow Matthean redaction of the Markan text to be our guide through this passage.[245] For his recording of the event – that it was split first, then into two – is recognised as providing a more natural

243 Maisch, p. 121–22.

244 Maisch (p. 123) asserts, 'Es kann also keine Rede davon sein, daß Tod, Auferstehung und endzeitliche Vollendung für Matthäus in einem einzigen Akt zusammenfallen'. Apocalyptic speech for the power of God is displayed most fully in Matt. 28:18–20.

245 I borrow this expression from Beaton, *Isaiah's Christ*, p. 170.

reading of the sequence of the events than Mark, who puts the results first.[246]

### 3.1 Matthean Redaction and Cessation of Function

Matthew's veil was torn ἀπ' ἄνωθεν ἕως κάτω εἰς δύο. The phrase is found nowhere else in Greek literature save in subsequent references to the Matthean *velum scissum*. Its individual components, however, are well attested and help us to understand the meaning of the phrase as a whole. Ἀπ' ἄνωθεν[247] is best indicative of a locular origin of the action and the motion of the action itself. LSJ note the use of ἄνωθεν as an adverb of place, meaning 'from above, from on high', though in narrative it can mean 'from the beginning, from farther back'.[248] Ἄνωθεν is an abundantly common word, occurring hundreds of times up to the second century C.E.[249] Ἀπ' ἄνωθεν is found only in the post-second century C.E. medical work of Pseudo-Galenus *De remediis parabilibus* (3.14.469.2). References using ἀπ' ἄνωθεν are only later, primarily in patristic works referring to the synoptic rending texts.[250] Yet it is the New Testament[251] and LXX[252] occurrences that are most informative for understanding the use of ἄνωθεν. In the New Testament it can refer to a beginning or place of origin in time (Luke 1:3; Acts 26:5; Gal. 4:9), or a special locale, such as the place from which Jesus' garments were torn (John 19:23), perhaps accounting for Daube's association of the rending of the veil with the tearing of a garment in mourning, cited in the Introduction. The most common use of ἄνωθεν, however, is to designate divine origin (John

246 Andreoli, 'Il velo squarciato nel Vangelo di Matteo', p. 21; Senior, *Redactional Study*, p. 308.

247 While B C* 33 u [w] read ἀπ' ἄνωθεν, several others, presumably following Mark's order, read εἰς δύο first (א Θ C$^c$ M 69 124 788 D 1346 A 𝔐 K U W Δ Π f$^1$ 2 28 157 565 579 700 1071 τ). D, however, inserts Luke's μέρη after εἰς δύο , while L [w] omits the preposition before ἄνωθεν altogether. 1424 retains the ἀπ' preposition but reads ἄνω for ἄνωθεν. Mss 69 and 543 read επ for απ, and A D Γ Δ Π Σ Φ ל do not employ elision and read απο ανωθεν.

248 LSJ, *Lexicon*, p. 169. 249 882 times, according to an exhaustive TLG search.

250 Cf. Origen, *Celsum* 2.33.7; Athanasius, *Homilia in illud: Ite in castellum* 7.4.1; Cyril of Jerusalem, *Catecheses ad illuminandos 1–18* 13.32.21; Eusebius, *Dem. ev.* 6.18.41.3; 8.2.112.4; *Generalis elementaria introductio (= Eclogae propheticae)* 164.1; Theodoretus, *Interp. Daniel* 81.1481.84; Cyril of Alexandria, *Commentarius in xii prophetas minores* 1.341.22; 1.521.8; 2.516.14; 3.97.9; *Comm. in Joannem* 3.99.5, etc. Cf. also Pseudo-Galenus, *De remediis parabilibus* 3.14.387.2.

251 Luke 1:3; John 3:3, 7, 31; 19:11, 23; Acts 26:5; Gal. 4:9; Jas. 1:17; 3:15, 17.

252 In LXX 23x: Gen. 6:16; 27:39; 49:25; Exod. 25:21, 22; 36:27, 38; 38:16, 19; 40:19; Num. 4:6, 25; 7:89; Josh. 3:16; Wis. 19:6; Isa. 45:8; Jer. 4:28; Ep. Jer. 1:61; Ezek. 1:11, 26; 4:17.

3:3, 7, 31; 19:11; Jas. 1:17; 3:15, 17). While the motion alluded to in John 19:23 may also be in view (by virtue of both the garment's and the veil's being of cloth material), that the divine origin is most prominent is apparent by both the dominant use of ἄνωθεν and the *passivum divinum* of ἐσχίσθη. The event of the *velum scissum*, like the death of Jesus, is an action 'purposed by God'.[253]

Further illumination of the term is found in LXX texts, where ἄνωθεν can refer to doing something afresh (Wis. 19:6; like the head of a river, Josh. 3:16) or the location of the atonement slate atop the ark (Exod. 25:21; cf. Gen. 6:16; Exod. 36:27, 38; 38:16, 19; 40:19; Num. 4:6). But in the LXX it commonly (10 out of 23 occurrences) refers to a heavenly locale as God's abode and source of his blessings (Gen. 27:39; 49:25; Isa. 45:8; Jer. 4:28; cf. Ezek. 1:11, 26; 4:17; Ep. Jer. 1:61) and, in a cultic sense, refers to the position of the glory of God *above* the ark and the atonement slate (Exod. 25:22, where God gives commands to Israel; Num. 7:89). As Matthew's use of καταπέτασμα has clearly drawn the reader into a cultic setting,[254] the cultic use seems the most likely, since Jesus' death is depicted as an atoning sacrifice (Chapter 5). This, Wevers has shown, reflects the importance of the Lord's speaking to Moses ἄνωθεν τοῦ ἱλαστηρίου (Exod. 25:21).[255] The cultic context, the death of Jesus, and the use of ἄνωθεν seem to fit nicely together to affirm an atoning function of Jesus' death as related to the veil. Again we see that the action of the *velum scissum* is wrought by God and may resonate with language of his presence above the atonement slate, which Hartley contends was 'the place where Israel could find full expiation for her sins in order to keep in force her covenant relationship with the holy God'.[256] Could this be an allusion to God's provision of atonement accomplished in the death of Jesus (26:28)?

The completion of the action is depicted in the veil's being torn not only 'from top' but also ἕως κάτω.[257] Ἕως is typically used temporally, but it also has a locative sense.[258] Κάτω here is an adverb of place,

[253] Carroll and Green, *Death of Jesus*, p. 43. So also Hagner, *Matthew* II, p. 848.

[254] See Gurtner, 'Καταπέτασμα: Lexicographical and Etymological Considerations to the Biblical "Veil"', *AUSS* 42 (2004), 5–11.

[255] J. W. Wevers, *Notes on the Greek Text of Leviticus* (SCS 44; Atlanta, Ga.: Scholars Press, 1997), p. 241.

[256] Hartley, *DOTP*, p. 57. For a discussion of the כפרת, its function, and diverse views of it, see Milgrom, *Leviticus 1–16*, p. 1014; Hartley, *Leviticus*, p. 235.

[257] MSS following Mark typically leave the ἕως κάτω until after ἄνωθεν and at the end of the clause: εἰς δύο . . . ἄνωθεν ἕως κάτω (א Θ C[c] M 69 124 788 D A M K U W Δ Π f[1] 2 28 157 565 579 700 1071 τ), cf. L [w].

[258] Cf. *BDF* §§ 403, 406.

designating the location or destination of the verb: *to the bottom*.[259] And ἕως + κάτω as we have here is a combination that is rare prior to the synoptic references.[260] There are subsequent references in secular literature,[261] but most occur in Christian traditions, in reference to the synoptic 'rending' texts.[262] This combination designates the locular sense of the opposite end from which the tearing began and the completion of the action at that end.

While the veil's being torn 'from the top' and 'to the bottom' depicts the origin and destination of the action of tearing, Matthew completes the phrase with the effect upon the curtain: It is rent into two (separate parts εἰς δύο).[263] While these two terms together occur scores of times through the first century C.E.,[264] they occur only in Matt. 27:51a and Mark 15:38 in all the New Testament, and only once in the LXX. The LXX reference (2 Kgs 2:12) says that, upon the slaying of an anointed person, Elisha tore his garments into two (εἰς δύο ῥήγματα). R. Aus conjectures that because εἰς δύο language is used both in 2 Kgs 2:12 and the *velum scissum* text, the synoptic rending refers to the rending of garments. Moreover, Aus insists that because God is said to rend his garments (Lam. 2:17), and that his garments and the veil were both purple, 'It was natural for the rabbis to think that God in mourning rent His royal purple garment in heaven when His dwelling on earth, the Temple, was destroyed by the Babylonians'.[265] Yet his conjecture that the veil is seen as the garment of God simply because, allegedly, both are said to be purple is highly speculative and fails to recognise the significance of that colour as a depiction of royalty found on other cultic curtains as well, as I have shown in Chapter 3. The expression εἰς δύο clearly means making something into two that was once one single unit.[266] It is used of a shield that is rendered irreparably useless for its task (*T. Jud.* 3:4), which seems to be its function here. Though it surely depicts a destruction of the shield and the veil, the object is destroyed precisely because it is unable to perform its function.

[259] *BDF* §103.

[260] Cf. Hippocrates, *De morbis popularis* 7.1.2.19; Heron, *De automatis* 30.2.3; Apollonius, *Lex. Hom.* 85.27; Cyranides 1.24.40.

[261] Julius Pollux, *Onomastricon* 1.143.6; Vettius Valens, *Anth.* 361.29; 9.19.8.

[262] Cf. *Acts of Andrew* 52.6; *Prot. Jas.* 47.15; Origen, *Contr. Cels.* 2.33.7; *Lib. X Cant.* 162.24; *Ezech.* 13.772.1; *Sch. Cant.* 17.257.51; *Comm. John* 19.16.103.5; Athanasius, *Hom. Illud* 7.4.2; *Ep. Cast.* 29.857.48, etc. Gundry (p. 575) suggests that Matthew put 'from top to bottom' first to 'stress that the event is a miraculous vindication of Jesus'.

[263] Εἰς takes the sense of 'becoming', which leads to δύο meaning two.

[264] 882 times, according to a search of the TLG.

[265] Aus, *Samuel, Saul and Jesus*, p. 151.

[266] *T. Jud.* 3:4; Philo, *Moses*, 1.205; 2.257; *Decal.* 50; *Creation* 56; *Heir* 219; Josephus, *Ant.* 3.7.6 §175; 8.3.3 §71; 11.8.4 §323; 14.4.4 §72; *J. W.* 2.4.3 §94, 2.18.2 §462; 5.3.1 §105; cf. *T. Zeb.* 9:4.

The veil that was once one piece of fabric (purportedly one handbreadth thick [*Exod. Rab.* 50:4 {on Exod. 36:35}; *m. Šeqal.*8:4–5; *Num. Rab.* 4:13 {on Num. 4:5}]) is now two pieces and is unable to perform its intended function.[267]

We have seen that Matthew's phraseology in 27:51a introduces something that is of particular importance and that is related to a revelatory statement (καὶ ἰδού). That the phrase correlates the subject of the preceding sentence (the death of Jesus) and the event that follows (the rending of the veil) is obvious. The καταπέτασμα is the inner veil before the holy of holies and is torn as an act of God (ἐσχίσθη). A directional statement, alluding to God in the heavenlies and perhaps to his location above the atonement slate, provides the locular origin of the rending—at its top (ἀπ' ἄνωθεν). Further providing directional indications, the evangelist records that the rending, begun at the heavenlies and atop the veil, proceeds to the bottom (ἕως κάτω); lest there be any doubt as to the extent of the damage, the singular veil before the holy of holies is now made into two (εἰς δύο), likewise indicating the cessation of its function.

## 3.2 Implications for the Cessation of Function

As we have seen in Chapter 3, there is general agreement that, whatever else the *velum scissum* indicates, that it is torn ἀπ' ἄνωθεν ἕως κάτω εἰς δύο refers to the cessation of its function. I will here explore the potential implications for the cessation of these functions as they are represented in the Old Testament corpus that was so formative at least for Matthew's Passion Narrative.[268] That is, it is important to look to the Old Testament functions of the veil because subsequent descriptions of its function depend on the Old Testament, and Matthew was cognizant of the Old Testament while redacting his Markan source.

Not all agree. Most notably, R. Brown presumes that Matthew took the tradition from Mark, yet questions whether any of the synoptic authors 'knew about the number of veils, or details about them and their symbolism'.[269] Brown suggests that the evangelist blindly followed Mark with little reflection. Yet Matthew has taken only the phrase

[267] This is an important observation, which we will revisit when considering the cessation of functions, examined in Chapter 3.

[268] We look to the Old Testament because Josephus and Philo do not speak of the cultic meaning of the inner veil. Schwemer, *Vitae Prophetarum* I, p. 125. Moreover, references to the καταπέτασμα subsequent to the LXX are greatly dependent upon the Pentateuchal tabernacle uses of the term and understanding of its role and identity. See Gurtner, 'Καταπέτασμα', pp. 5–11.

[269] Brown, *Death* II, p. 1113. One would think, though, that a learned Jewish Christian like Matthew would know the Torah inside out. So Allison, *New Moses*, p. 95.

καταπέτασμα τοῦ ναοῦ verbatim from Mark, while altering Mark's order of ἕως κάτω and εἰς δύο and contributing his own 'special material'. This makes it difficult to substantiate the view that Matthew gave less than careful reflection to his use of the Markan text. Moreover, the abundant influence of the Old Testament on the Matthean Passion Narrative in general has been widely recognised. Though there has been some discussion of from which Old Testament texts Matthew drew his 'special material' (27:51b–53), we have seen that there is widespread agreement that the material resonates with Old Testament eschatological images from Ezek. 37 and, surely, Zech. 14. Indeed, it would be difficult to assert that Matthew was cognizant of the Old Testament in 26:1–27:50 and 27:51b–54 but *not* at 27:51a. Instead, it seems much more plausible that while Matthew has indeed depended upon Mark's gospel for so much of his material, he has done so with a careful eye to the Old Testament. It is hardly credible to think that the First Evangelist did not reflect upon his Markan source, in view of the place he has given it in the drama he has created in 51b–53. Moreover, that Matthew has taken his veil text from Mark does not preclude his doing so with careful thought to the Old Testament, upon which he carefully reflected through the rest of the pericope. As Sim has argued in his discussion of Jewish-Gentile relations in the first gospel, Matthew was perfectly free to choose how he would employ his sources, and when he chose to 'reproduce intact a certain tradition, then we must conclude that his own view coincided with that of his source. If there were no such convergence of opinion, then we would expect the Evangelist to exercise his editorial right, as he does elsewhere, and alter the offending material'.[270] Thus we look for the Old Testament to inform our understanding of the veil's function which is ceased upon its rending.

The veil generally functioned to provide general *cultic 'separation' (בדל)*. If this separation ceased at the *velum scissum* (and, as a result of Jesus' death), the evangelist may indicate that there is no longer a distinction to be made between holy and less holy, in a cultic sense.[271] This supports the traditional view that there is a new accessibility to God created through the removal of the separating function of the inner veil, which I will develop more below, and is congruent with the eschatological hopes of Ezekiel 37. Yet it is important to note that it almost certainly does *not* (from a pure functionality standpoint) allude to the inclusion of Gentiles into Matthew's 'community' despite the (Gentile) centurion's profession of faith after it (27:54; cf. Mark 15:39). Instead, the inclusion

[270] D. C. Sim, 'The Gospel of Matthew and Gentiles', *JSNT* 57 (1995), 29–30.

[271] VanderKam (*Introduction to Early Judaism*, p. 200) argues that Alcimus's orders 'to tear down the wall of the inner court of the sanctuary' (1 Macc. 9:54, c. 159 B.C.E.), was an 'attempt to obliterate the distinction between the inner and outer courts'.

of Gentiles is better seen in the apocalyptic nature of the *velum scissum* and the Ezek. 37 (esp. v. 28) background to the special material. Suggesting that the cessation of separation refers to the inclusion of Gentiles confuses the function of the veil (which never separated Jew from Gentile) with the 'dividing wall' in the Herodian temple (which did separate Jew from Gentile and is recognised in Christian tradition in Eph. 2:14). Instead, as we have seen, the veil in Second Temple and Rabbinic Judaism is explicitly associated with the heavenly firmament from Gen. 1:6, and its rending then symbolises (in part) the tearing open of the heavens so readily recognisable in Jewish-Christian apocalyptic thought. This fits well with the apparently eschatological and 'apocalyptic imagery' of Matthew's special material and lends itself nicely to the revelatory nature of the identity of Jesus as the Son of God as recognised by the centurion who, presumably, mocked Jesus for that very charge beforehand.

The veil's separation function was executed by its prohibition of *physical and visual accessibility* to God. If this function ceases at the *velum scissum*, then the barrier that prohibits one from physically entering the presence of God, as well as from seeing his face, is effectively removed (again, as a result of the death of Jesus). Yet, as we have seen, *physical accessibility* could only be accomplished when the entrant bore gifts of atonement on the Day of Atonement, and only if the intruder had a high priestly status, lest those present die. Surely for Matthew, though, the raising of the saints (27:52–53) and the profession of the soldiers (27:54) connote *life* in various senses, rather than death.[272] He must then presume that the atonement necessary for physical accessibility to God and for the maintenance of his communal presence among his people[273] has been accomplished (Matt. 28:20), which Matthew *inextricably links with the death of Jesus*.[274] The accomplishment of atonement by the death of Jesus necessarily leads to the accessibility of humanity to God, depicted in Matthew not *just* as a person entering God's presence (as in Hebrews, and below), but also as God's being 'with us' (Emmanuel, 1:23).[275] This Emmanuel motif is cited as a lens through which the entire first

[272] Maisch, p. 122; Schenk, *Passionsbericht*, p. 90; Senior, *Redactional Study*, pp. 326–29.

[273] This is an essential element of the Day of Atonement sacrifice, as we have seen in Chapter 3.

[274] Even though Luke is often thought to have an 'undeveloped' atonement theology.

[275] Perhaps there is an allusion to Ezekiel 10, where the 'glory of the Lord' departed from the temple. Although judgement against the temple may be present in Matthew's assertion of the veil of the ναός being rent, this is only half of the story. In Ezekiel the Lord simply departs and nothing is said of where he goes. In Matthew nothing is *explicitly* said of his departure but much is said of where he goes: 'with us'.

gospel is to be read[276] and underscores Olmstead's assertion that the first gospel is to be read from the beginning 'but from the vantage point of the end'.[277]

The approachability of God in Jesus is a 'distinctive Matthean feature'.[278] This is seen in his abundant use of προσέρχομαι ('approaching Jesus'[279]), often used in association with προσκυνέω ('worship'; 8:2; 9:18; 20:20; 28:9), and recognised as a reverential[280] term borrowed from cultic, royal and worship settings in Judaism.[281] Yet for Matthew, Kupp contends, 'No longer was divine presence mediated through the cult and Temple of Jerusalem, but through the person and community of the Messiah',[282] which was accomplished 'by virtue of the atonement'.[283] This, however, is not a *rejection* of the temple, toward which Matthew has been so positive. Instead, it is an indication that the temple is superfluous: What it was intended to accomplish is surpassed by Jesus. This, then, is clearly associated in the first gospel with the death of Jesus, particularly as the evangelist has linked the rending of the veil to Jesus' death, as a consequence of that death.[284] Even more astounding is the agency of the veil's rending: It was not a by-product of the desecration of the Jerusalem shrine, as seen in rabbinic texts which record that Titus, upon his assault of the holy city, 'took a sword and slashed the curtain' (*b. Giṭ.* 56b). Instead Matthew, perhaps more than the other evangelists, recognises the

276 Kupp, *Matthew's Emmanuel.* 277 Olmstead, *Trilogy*, p. 73.

278 Black, *Sentence Conjunctions*, p. 221.

279 Which he uses 'far more frequently than do the other Evangelists' (51x; Mark 5x; Luke 10x; Black, *Sentence Conjunctions*, p. 239). See Olmstead, *Trilogy*, p. 134.

280 Black, *Sentence Conjunctions*, p. 240; Davies and Allison, *Matthew* I, p. 360; cf. J. R. Edwards, 'The Use of ΠΡΟΣΕΡΧΕΣΘΑΙ in the Gospel of Matthew', *JBL* 106 (1987), 65–74); Gundry, pp. 27, 55, 148. See the cultic use of בוא for 'approaching' God in the Old Testament. K. van der Toorn, *Sin and Sanction in Israel and Mesopotamia: A Comparative Study* (Assen: Van Gorcum, 1985), p. 37; Milgrom, *Numbers*, p. 29; *ANET* 649, lines 128–29; *ANET* 618, lines 449–50; D. R. Schwartz, 'Viewing the Holy Utensils (P Ox V,840)', *NTS* 32 (1986), 153–59; Wenham, *Leviticus*, p. 229; Segal, 'Divine Verdict', p. 93; Hartley, *DOTP*, p. 55.

281 E.g. Lev. 9:5; Num. 18:4; Deut. 25:1; Jer. 7:16; Heb. 10:1; 1 Pet. 2:4; Josephus, *Ant.* 12.2.2 §19.

282 Kupp, *Matthew's Emmanuel*, p. 2. Longenecker ('Rome's Victory and God's Honour', p. 95) contends that Matthew's Emmanuel Christology 'counters a theology of divine presence associated with the now destroyed Jerusalem temple'.

283 Kingsbury, *Matthew: Structure, Christology, Kingdom*, pp. 76, 82.

284 This point is more clearly seen by Kupp's designation of 27:51–28:20 as broken away from the narrative of Matthew's gospel proper and thus, perhaps, functioning as some sort of commentary on it (Kupp, *Matthew's Emmanuel*, p. 100). Matthew's Emmanuel Christology finds precedent in the Old Testament (cf. Exod. 24:16; Ezek. 37:27; Joel 2:27; 4[3]:16–17) as well as Second Temple and Rabbinic Judaism. Cf. *2 Bar.* 68:5–6; *b. Yoma* 21b; *Num. Rab.* 15:10 (on Num. 8:2); Aune, *Revelation* II, p. 476; Knowles, *Jeremiah in Matthew's Gospel*, pp. 240–41, 270), where like statements are said of God.

divine agency of its rending (as seen by the *passivum divinum* ἐσχίσθη and the use of ἀπ' ἄνωθεν). Moreover, the deed is irreparable (the veil was split εἰς δύο).

The permission for *visual accessibility* accomplished by the rending of the veil, however, is more difficult. For even the high priest was prevented from visual accessibility to God by the presence of a cloud. In the temporal world – both in Jewish and Christian traditions – it was impossible to see God and live (cf. Jdg. 13:22).[285] Yet Matthew has provided us with some help. Earlier in his gospel he affirmed that it is the 'pure in heart' (οἱ καθαροὶ τῇ καρδίᾳ) who will 'see God' (αὐτοὶ τὸν θεόν ὄψονται, 5:8; cf. Ps. 24:4).[286] Indeed, seeing God seems to be an eschatological blessing in Judaism[287] occasionally associated with eschatological events.[288] Seeing God's face is, among other things, a 'metaphor for a full awareness of the presence and power of God'.[289] Both the presence *and* the power of God are clearly demonstrated in the Matthean pericope by the widely recognised use of *passivum divinum*[290] and the dramatic account of the resurrection of the 'holy ones' (27:52). But what about God's 'lethal presence'? Moreover, if Matthew's rending text does allude to the visual accessibility to God, are we to presume that those who are now able to 'see God' are in fact 'pure in heart'? If *this* is so, Matthew clearly associates this apparent change, not in status but in essence, with the death of Jesus, providing *unprecedented* accessibility (both physical *and* visual) to God.[291]

[285] Gen. 33:10; Exod. 3:6; 19:21; 33:20, 23; Jdg. 13:22; *L. A. B.* 42:10; *Sib. Or.* 3:17; John 1:18; 1 Tim. 6:15–16; *Sipre* Num. 12:8.

[286] Cf. Sim, *Apocalyptic Eschatology*, p. 141. Sim further argues that since this is a privilege shared only with the 'holy angels' (cf. 18:10), it 'suggests the angelic status of the righteous in the new age' (p. 142).

[287] Job 19:26; Ps. 63:2; Isa. 52:6; 60:16; Jer. 24:7; 31:31–4; cf. 1 Cor. 13:12; Heb. 12:14; 1 John 3:2; Rev. 22:4; *4 Ezra* 7:98; *b. B. Bat.* 10a; Str-B I, pp. 212–14. Pss 11:7; 17:15; Job 19:26; Philo, *Contempl. Life* 11–12; *Abraham* 57–59; *Names* 81–82; Rev. 22:4; *Jub.* 1:28; *4 Ezra* 7:91, 98; *1 En.* 102:8. Vision is an important theme in biblical eschatology, as well as Matthew (Dunn, 'Significance', p. 159).

[288] Mark 14:62; *b. Sanh.* 98b. Davies and Allison, *Matthew* I, pp. 456–57. Cf. Origen, *Celsum* 7:33–34 and Augustine, *Civ. Dei* 22:29.

[289] '(Job 33.26; Pss 10.11; 17.15; 3 Jn 11), for worshipping God in the temple (Ps 42.2), or for seeing God in the context of a prophetic vision (Isa. 6.1)'. Aune, *Revelation* III, p. 1179; cf. W. Michaelis, 'ὁράω', *TDNT* V, pp. 329–30.

[290] The curtain *was torn* (ἐσχίσθη, 27:51a), the earth *was shaken* (ἐσείσθη, 27:51b), the rocks *were split* (ἐσχίσθησαν, 27:51c), tombs *were opened* (ἀνεῴχθησαν, 27:52a) and bodies *were raised* (ἠγέρθησαν, 27:52b). Witherup, 'The Cross of Jesus', p. 280. Cf. Davies and Allison, *Matthew* III, p. 632; Senior, 'Death of God's Son', 42; Heil, *Death and Resurrection*, p. 85; Aus, *Samuel, Saul and Jesus*, p. 117.

[291] Hagner ('Matthew's Eschatology', p. 168) asserts, 'Only in the future will the rewards of the righteous be fully experienced'.

Finally, the veil's separating function, which was executed by the prohibition of physical and visual accessibility to God, was depicted graphically by the presence of angelic guardians woven into it. Thus the rending of the veil could suggest that the *angelic protection of the presence of God* or divine 'keep out' sign was removed (again, as a result of Jesus' death).[292] As I have shown in Chapter 3, cherubim in the tabernacle and temple were understood to be guardians of its sanctity, resonating with themes from their initial role as guardians of the Garden of Eden, charged with keeping the expelled Adam and Eve from re-entering. G. Wenham has persuasively argued that the Garden of Eden was viewed 'as an archetypal sanctuary . . . a place where God dwells and where man should worship him'.[293] Moreover, the cherubim were stationed at its entrance,[294] the same location where they were woven into the inner veil of the tabernacle/temple.[295] Also, the angelic figure was girded with 'the flame of a revolving sword', which, though obscure, surely is understood by Old Testament scholars to reflect the presence of God in judgement (cf. Exod. 19:18; Ps. 104:4)[296] initiated in their expulsion, and in prohibiting their re-entrance. The notion of Eden as a sanctuary was carried on into

[292] Yet what evidence is there that Matthew's readers/hearers associated these angelic figures with the veil of the temple rather than, perhaps, Josephus's description of them, the 'panorama of the universe' (*J. W.* 5.5.4 §214; LCL; ὁ πέπλος ἅπασαν τὴν οὐράνιον, which perhaps better translates 'curtain to all heaven')? The Qumran sectarians, arguably a separatist movement likewise removed from the Jerusalem cult, have very few but telling statements about heaven, comparing it to a temple (see 4Q400–407, 11Q17; cf. *1 En.* 14; cf. 1 Kgs 6:29–32; C. Newsom, 'Heaven', *EDSS* I, pp. 338–40). In the Songs of the Sabbath Sacrifice, we find (from a badly fragmented text) a description in which the reader is led through the heavenly sanctuary. Within the sanctuary the readers are led on their way through the celestial *debir* into the throne room of God (4Q405 f15ii–16:3, 5), yet as they seemingly enter the holy of holies, they bypass the veil of the temple (פרוכת) on which the woven figures of the cherubim found in the Old Testament are singing praises to the Lord. If these accounts are reliable, they may explain how the populace was familiar with the veil and identified it by means of the cherubim on it. Ginzberg's claim (*Legends* III, p. 159, n. 335) that 'during the festivals of the pilgrimage the priests used to raise the curtain from the Holy of Holies to show the pilgrims how much their God loved them as they could see in the embrace of the two Cherubim' finds *no* support from any of the texts he cites (cf. *b. B. Bat.* 99a; *b. Yoma* 54a, b; *Tg. Onk.* Exod. 25:20; *Tg. Jer.* Exod. 25:20; Josephus, *Ant.* 3.6.4 §§124–132; *m. Tamid* 7:1).

[293] Wenham, 'Sanctuary Symbolism', p. 19.

[294] U. Cassuto, *A Commentary on the Book of Genesis* 1 (Jerusalem: Magnes Press, 1961), p. 174.

[295] Wenham, 'Sanctuary Symbolism', p. 21.

[296] Moreover, elsewhere Wenham has argued that the tree in the Garden symbolised the first law that God gave and was subsequently guarded by angelic figures. Similarly, the cherubim on the inner veil and above the atonement slate stood guard over the ark of the covenant, in which were contained the stone tablets of the Law. G. Wenham, *Genesis 1–15* (WBC 1; Nashville, Tonn.: Thomas Nelson, 1987), p. 64.

early Judaism as well; in *Jub.* 8:19, for example, the Garden of Eden is explicitly said to be 'the Holy of Holies' (cf. *Jub.* 3:12–14).[297]

### 3.3 Cessation of Function and Eschatological Restoration

Not only was Eden seen as a temple, but returning to Eden is an important Second Temple and an early Christian eschatological hope (cf. *Jub.* 3:12–14). In Rev. 2:7, for example, 'one who overcomes' will be granted 'to eat of the tree of life, which is in the Paradise of God'. Eden is often depicted as the locus of eschatological blessings for a people restored from exile[298] where God dwelt with humans.[299] It is clear from later texts that Eden was associated with God's heavenly dwelling place, where the righteous and faithful will live.[300] Entering Eden was a recognisable metaphor in Jewish apocalypticism, expressing salvation,[301] and was clearly associated with eschatological blessings.[302] In Rev. 22:14 we see the faithful having the right to the tree of life, with the ban on entering the Garden having been lifted.[303] In *1 En.* 25:4–5 none can partake of the tree until the judgement, after which 'the elect will be presented with its fruit for life'.[304] It was a clear metaphor for heaven and soteriological/eschatological blessings.[305]

Moreover, the Edenic sanctuary was guarded by angels. This tradition is also found in other Christian writings, such as Rev. 21:12b, where Aune draws attention to the correlation between angels guarding the gates of the New Jerusalem and the belief that they guarded the heavenly temple.[306] Indeed, legend has it that it was the angelic figures who drove Adam from Paradise after the fall.[307] They were, in effect, the gatekeepers (cf. *Sib. Or.* 1:60; *2 Bar.* 4:3), the guardians of Eden.[308] Their

[297] Cf. J. Hellerman, 'Purity and Nationalism in Second Temple Literature: 1–2 Maccabees and *Jubilees*', *JETS* 46 (2003), 421–22; Aune, *Revelation* III, p. 1154. Some use caution classifying *Jubilees* as an apocalypse. Cf. Collins, *Apocalyptic Imagination*, p. 5. For an extended discussion of the Garden of Eden and the temple, see P. Lee, *The New Jerusalem in the Book of Revelation*: *A Study of Revelation 21–22 in the Light of its Background in Jewish Tradition* (WUNT II, 129; Tübingen: Mohr Siebeck, 2001).

[298] Ezek. 28:13; 31:9, 16, 18; 36:35. Wallace, 'Eden, Garden of', *ABD* II, pp. 281–83.

[299] Wallace, *ABD* II, p. 282.

[300] *T. Dan* 5.12; cf. *1 En.* 24–25; 28–32; *4 Ezra* 8:52.

[301] *1 En.* 25:5; *3 En.* 23:18; *Apoc. Mos.* 28:4; *Apoc. El. (H)* 5:6.

[302] *Pss. Sol.* 14:2–3, 10; *4 Ezra* 8:52; *2 En.* [A and J] 8:3–7; Ezek. 47:1–12. See Beale, *Revelation*, 235; Aune (*Revelation* I, pp. 152–53) also notes it was a 'metaphor for the elect community' (4 Macc. 18:16; 1QH vi 14–17; viii 5–6; *Odes Sol.* 11:16–21; *Pss. Sol.* 14:3).

[303] Cf. Aune, *Revelation* III, p. 1221.

[304] *OTP* I, p. 26.

[305] *m. 'Abot.* 5:20; *1 En.* 61:12; cf. Brown, *Death* II, p. 1124.

[306] *Exod. Rab.* 18:5 (on Exod. 12:29); *Pesiq. Rab. Kah.* 6:2; cf. *m. Mid.* 1:1.

[307] *L. A. E.* 27:1–28.4; cf. *1 En.* 32:6; *3 En.* 32:1; 35:6; 42:4; *L. A. E.* 1:1.

[308] *L. A. E.* 29:1–2; *Apoc. Mos.* 28:3; *2 En.* 8:8; *T. Levi* 18:10.

presence on the veil, I suggest, may reflect their role as the 'mythical guardians of the Garden of God'.[309] A striking parallel to the notion of removing the angelic guardianship is found in the *Testament of Levi* (18:10–11a), which reports that at the eschaton God 'will open the gates of paradise;/he shall remove the sword that has threatened since Adam,/ and he will grant to the saints to eat of the tree of life'.[310] Here the eschatological entering of Eden is clearly made possible by the removal of its angelic guardians. If Matthew is recognising a similar association, then Matthew's account of the rending of the veil, in part, depicts the removal of angelic protection of Eden (depicted in the rending of the veil), inextricably linked with the death of Jesus.[311] It has disarmed its guardians and, in effect, opened the gates of Paradise 'as a reversal of the events of Eden in Genesis 3'.[312]

309 Aune, *Revelation* III, pp. 1154–55. He has also noted places where such beings were armed and stood guard. Cf. Josh. 5:13; Num. 22:23; 1 Chron. 21:16, 30; *3 En.* 22:6; 4 Macc. 4:10; 3 Macc. 6:18–19; *L. A. E.* 33:1; *Ascen. Isa.* 9:1–4; *Ma'aseh Merkavah* §565 (ed. Swartz, *Prayer*, 237–38); *3 En.* 6:2–3; *Ma'aseh Merkavah* §568; *1 En.* 82:10–20.

310 'The Testaments of the Twelve Patriarchs', translated by H. C. Kee (*OTP* I, p. 795). The association between the temple and creation is, of course, not unique to Matthew. According to *b. Pesaḥ.* 54a, the temple was one of the seven things created before the creation of the world, and according to *2 Bar.* 4:3, it was made when God created Paradise. The heavenly tabernacle, the pattern for the earthly tabernacle described to Moses on Sinai (cf. Exod. 25:9, 40; 26:30; 27:8; *2 Bar.* 4:5–6), is referred to in Wis. 9:8; Heb. 8:1–2; 9:11–12; Aune, *Revelation* II, p. 476. Cf. Brown, *Death* II, p. 1124. Typically only *T. Levi* 2–5 is classified as an 'apocalypse'. Collins, *Apocalyptic Imagination*, p. 5.

311 Jerome likewise associated the death of Christ and the departure of the angelic guardians, though originally doing so in reference to Josephus' account of the destruction of the temple. In *Epistle* 46 (*Paulae et Eustochii ad Marcellam* 4; CSEL 54.333) Jerome associates the rending of the temple veil with Jerusalem's being surrounded by an army and the departure of the angelic guardianship. He cites Josephus in such a way that Josephus seems to say that the voices of the heavenly hosts broke forth 'at that time when the Lord was crucified'. 'We are departing from here' (i.e., the sanctuary) (*J. W.* 6.5.3 §§288–309). Cf. *Commentarium in Isaiam* 3 (CC 73.87); 18 (CC73A.775). Cf. Brown, *Death* II, p. 1117; McNeile, p. 423. Nestle ('Matt. 27,51 und Parallelen', 167; cf. *idem*, 'Sonnenfinsternis bei Jesu Tod', *ZNW* 3 [1902], 246–47) contends that Jerome's *superliminare* = כפתר ('lintel'), which was misunderstood as פרכת ('veil'). This is rightly criticized by Dalman (*Words of Jesus*, p. 56). Cf. Brown, *Death* II, p. 1118, n. 45.

312 Wallace, *ABD* II, pp. 282–83. Finally, although scholars frequently and almost universally associate the rending of the veil with the destruction of the temple in 70 C.E., this discussion seems to suggest precisely the opposite. For while entering Eden, as we have seen, is depicted as salvific, *expulsion* from Eden is explicitly associated with the destruction of the temple, presumably because of the association between fellowship with God and the temple sacrifices (*Gen. Rab.* 16:5 [on Gen. 17:11]; Wenham, 'Sanctuary Symbolism', p. 19. Cf. G. J. Wenham, *Genesis 1–15*, p. 85). Therefore, if Matthew does suggest the removal of angelic guardianship and establishing fellowship with God by his description of the rending of the veil, he cannot also mean that the temple was destroyed, for the temple was seen as the symbol of fellowship with God.

## Analysis of the Matthean *velum scissum* Pericope: Conclusion

That Matthean inclusion of his special material and his depiction of the cessation of the veil's function contributes to Matthean themes recognised by other scholars.[313] This may include the notion of a restoration from exile. Indeed, even prior to Matthew, Jewish texts display a belief that there is a sense that Israel was still in exile and in need of deliverance. Knibb comments,

> Despite many differences in presentation [these] writings all seem to share the view that Israel remained in a state of exile long after the sixth century, and that the exile would only be brought to an end when God intervened in the world order to establish his rule.[314]

Restorational theology in Matthew's gospel has been addressed very recently in the work of P. Yokota,[315] who argues that Jesus' primary messianic role from the beginning of the first gospel is that of Israel's restoration, which is subsequently developed as the narrative progresses.[316] Yokota demonstrates that Jesus' messianic identity from the very beginning of the gospel serves to save his people from their sins and 'to restore the presence of God among them so that all nations may be blessed by him. These are *fundamental expectations* and the reader will read the following narrative in anticipation of their fulfillment'.[317] P. W. L. Walker concurs. Building on a paper by P. Head, Walker rightly indicates that people's being in exile and a cry for restoration resonate throughout

[313] See Bauckham, 'The Restoration of Israel in Luke-Acts', pp. 435–87; S. Talmon, '"Exile" and "Restoration" in the Conceptual World of Ancient Judaism', in *Restoration: Old Testament, Jewish and Christian Perspectives* (ed. J. M. Scott; Leiden: Brill, 2001), pp. 107–46; D. E. Aune with E. Stewart, 'From the Idealized Past to the Imaginary Future: Eschatological Restoration in Jewish Apocalyptic Literature', in *Restoration: Old Testament, Jewish and Christian Perspectives* (ed. J. M. Scott; Leiden: Brill, 2001), pp. 147–78; B. Chilton, 'Temple Restored, Temple in Heaven: Isaiah and the Prophets in the Targumim', in *Restoration: Old Testament, Jewish and Christian Perspectives* (ed. J. M. Scott; Leiden: Brill, 2001), pp. 335–64.

[314] Knibb, 'The Exile in the Literature of the Intertestamental Period', pp. 271–72, cf. Walker, *Jesus and the Holy City*, p. 44; Wright, *The New Testament and the People of God*, p. 386; M. Eloff, 'Restoration from Exile as a Hermeneutical Prism for a Theological Interpretation of Matthew's Gospel' (Th.D. diss.; Stellenbosch University), §4, p. 28; *idem*, 'Exile, Restoration and Matthew's Geneology of Jesus ὁ χριστός', *Neot.* 38 (2004), 82–83.

[315] 'Jesus the Messiah of Israel'. [316] *Ibid.*, p. 318.

[317] *Ibid.*, p. 318. Emphasis his.

Matt. 1–4, with Jesus himself showing the means by which God will bring an end to the exile.[318] That Jesus will 'save his people from their sins' presupposes a previous story[319] already indicated in the opening prologue to Matthew (1:1–17). Wright suggests that

> the geneaology . . . says to Matthew's careful reader that the long story of Abraham's people will come to its fulfillment, its seventh seven, with a new David, who will rescue his people from their exile, that is, 'save his people from their sins'. When Matthew says precisely this in 1:18–21 we should not be surprised.[320]

Through the body of Matthew's gospel, Yokota asserts, the evangelist's notion of restoration gradually escalates while he 'carefully uses the Old Testament throughout the Gospel in order to guide his reader to appreciate the development of the theme of Israel's restoration'.[321] This is especially the case, he argues, with Matthew's strategically located citations of Isa. 40:3 and Isa. 8:23–9:1 which, together, underscore his suggestion that Jesus' 'entire ministry is to be understood as a restorational ministry to Israel'.[322] Indeed, M. Eloff has argued that restoration from exile is a plot in a narrative reading of the first gospel[323] which, using narrative analysis, is 'concerned with the reason for the events and the consequences which they have'.[324]

Though many scholars see restoration depicted in resurrection,[325] Matthew indicates that the restoration is at least inaugurated in *Jesus' death*. It must be said, though, that for Matthew Jesus' resurrection was in Matthew's mind even at the very moment of his death (27:53).[326]

[318] Walker, *Holy City*, p. 44, and P. M. Head, 'Restoration Prophecies and New Testament Fulfillment: A Case Study in Matt. 1–4' (Unpublished paper delivered at Tyndale Fellowship Conference, 1994).

[319] Wright, *The New Testament and the People of God*, p. 385; Eloff, 'Restoration from Exile', §4, pp. 27, 29.

[320] Wright, *New Testament*, p. 386; see Walker, *Holy City*, p. 44; Eloff, 'Restoration from Exile', §4, p. 29. See also J. Willits, 'Reading Matthew's Messianism in the Light of Psalms of Solomon 17? Pursuing the Potential Parallels and Implications' (Paper presented at the British New Testament Conference; Edinburgh, Scotland; September 4, 2004), p. 16.

[321] Yokota, 'Jesus the Messiah of Israel', p. 318. So also Walker, *Holy City*, p. 43; Eloff, 'Restoration from Exile', §4, p. 52.

[322] Yokota, 'Jesus the Messiah of Israel', pp. 318–19.

[323] Eloff, 'Restoration from Exile', §4, p. 2. [324] *Ibid.*, §4, p. 4.

[325] Walker, *Holy City*, p. 45; T. L. Donaldson, *Jesus on the Mount: A Study in Matthean Theology* (JSNTSup 8; Sheffield, JSOT Press, 1985), p. 200; Wright, *Resurrection*, pp. 322, 337.

[326] Indeed, for Wright (*Resurrection*, p. 322, cf. p. 337), Jesus' resurrection indicates the coming of the new age and reverses the effects 'of the present evil age'.

Walker suggests that it is through Jesus' death 'that the restoration of Israel comes into being (26:28; cf. 20:28)' though 'its final completion awaits the *parousia* at 'the end of the age' (28:20)'.[327] In the context of Ezekiel, the deliverance from political captivity is framed in a larger matrix of sin: 'I will save you from all your uncleanness' (Ezek. 36:29); 'They will no longer defile themselves with their idols and vile images or with any of their offenses, for I will save them from all their dwelling places in which they have sinned, and I will cleanse them. They will be my people, and I will be their God' (Ezek. 37:23).[328] This, I have argued, is the purpose of Jesus' death as depicted in Matthew's gospel, and it provides a point of contact: God's deliverance from the captivity of sin is achieved in the death of Jesus. Moreover, Ezekiel's restoration promises include moving his people to follow his decrees and laws (Ezek. 36:27), a unique concern for Matthew (cf. 5:17), and establish an everlasting covenant in which God will dwell among his people forever (Ezek. 37:26, cf. v. 27).

For Matthew, that Jesus was to deliver 'his people' from their sins suggests a collective deliverance from exile and a corporate view of the *participants* in the restoration. Matthew's Jesus is the 'true Israel'[329] and the people of God are defined by their relationship to him, including professing him as 'son of God'. They are the ones who participate in the eschatological restoration in which God's people share fellowship with the God who dwells among them.[330] That Jesus is the true Israel in Matthew has been recognised by many scholars,[331] and is seen, for example, in Matthew's citation of Hosea 11:1. Originally this text referred explicitly to Israel, but it is applied by Matthew to Jesus. This is also seen in the temptation narrative (Matt. 4:1–11), where Jesus re-enacts the Israelite wilderness temptation, though he does so in 'perfect filial obedience'.[332] Indeed, Eloff concludes that Jesus' death has opened the way back to God (citing Matt. 27:51), 'that return from exile is secured

[327] Yokota, 'Jesus the Messiah of Israel', p. 321.

[328] Ezekiel makes no distinction between the physical captivity in which Israel finds herself and the sin that caused it. Greenberg, p. 757. See Deut. 28:36, 64; Ezek. 11:17; 14:3f; 20:39; 36:29.

[329] Eloff, 'Restoration from Exile', §4, p. 18.

[330] Yokota ('Jesus the Messiah of Israel', p. 321) asserts, 'The connexion between the restoration of Israel and the conversion of the nations is hinted at in the beginning of the Gospel (1:1–17; 2:1–11)'.

[331] Walker, *Jesus and the Holy City*, p. 45. See also France, *Matthew: Evangelist and Teacher*, pp. 206–10, for discussion and bibliography.

[332] Walker, *Jesus and the Holy City*, p. 45; France, *Matthew: Evangelist and Teacher*, p. 210. Cf. C. F. D. Moule, 'Fulfilment-Words in the New Testament', *NTS* 14 (1967), 293–320.

for all who will turn to Jesus as saviour (1:21) and submit to him as Lord (28:19–20)'.[333]

Though the people of God who are to participate in the eschatological restoration are defined by their relationship to Jesus,[334] there is an ethical dimension to their participation in restoration as well. For participants must produce fruit worthy of the kingdom (21:43; 22:1–14)[335] regardless of their background. Matthew asserts that the life-giving death of Jesus inaugurates a new age in which the final, eschatological deliverance from bondage to sin is achieved. God's presence now dwells among his people and permits a fellowship between man and God not seen since the Garden of Eden. For Matthew, Jesus is the true Israel and the people of God are defined by their relationship to Jesus. They are the ones who participate in the eschatological restoration with God himself among them forever. Moreover, as Yokota suggests, 'The fact that the nucleus of the renewed Israel is restored through (Jesus') redemptive death enables the disciples to embark on this universal mission' (28:18–20).[336] Yet the final consummation of the eschatological restoration awaits Jesus' return in glory.

[333] Eloff, 'Restoration from Exile', §4, p. 52.

[334] So Davies and Allison, *Matthew* I, p. 210, *pace* Luz, *Matthew* I, p. 105. So also Stanton, *Gospel for a New People*, pp. 378–83; France, *Matthew: Evangelist and Teacher*, pp. 223–31. Some say the 'his people' who will be saved are the nation of Israel (Luz, *Matthew* I, p. 121; Wright, *The New Testament and the People of God*, pp. 385–86). However, Eloff ('Restoration from Exile', §4, p. 35) rightly says that the inclusion of women and others in the geneaology, the faith of the (Gentile) magi, etc., suggests that these boundaries of ethnicity have been removed. So also, Davies and Allison, *Matthew* I, p. 210; Hagner, *Matthew* I, pp. 19–20.

[335] See Yokota, 'Jesus the Messiah of Israel', p. 320.

[336] *Ibid.*, p. 321; see R. J. Bauckham, 'The Restoration of Israel in Luke-Acts', in *Restoration: Old Testament, Jewish and Christian Perspectives* (ed. J. M. Scott; Leiden: Brill, 2001), pp. 480–84.

# 7

# CONCLUSION: MATTHEW'S *VELUM SCISSUM* – RETROSPECT AND PROSPECT

## 1 Retrospect

We have seen that from an early time Christians have variously understood the Matthean *velum scissum* text and looked for solutions to the problems it raises through various avenues and combinations of methods. This has provided an important starting point for the present study, for it allowed us to build upon the helpful work of previous generations of scholars as well as to leave aside those suggestions that now seem less plausible than they may have once seemed. Specifically, I have found the cessation of the veil's function at the *velum scissum* to be a plausible idea, but incomplete. For although scholars relate numerous presumptions about how the veil functioned (after first presuming which veil is in mind), none have given comprehensive attention to the veil in the source widely recognised to be the origin of subsequent discussion of the Jerusalem temple's curtain configuration, the Pentateuchal tabernacle texts – first to identify which curtain was in view, second to examine the implicit and explicit function(s) of each of the curtains translated καταπέτασμα and third to consider the significance of the cessation of those functions depicted in the Matthean *velum scissum* pericope. When we do that, we find that scholars have generally been right to see the inner veil as the one in view and to see that this veil served to separate the holy place from the holy of holies. However, such recognition falls short of accounting for a substantial amount of evidence from the Old Testament that allows us to be a good deal more specific. As I have said in Chapter 3, the inner veil (פרכת) served to separate the holy from the less holy out of cultic necessity. This separation was executed by means of prohibiting physical and visual access to the holy of holies, and therefore to the God enthroned within. Moreover, this prohibition of access was graphically depicted by the presence of cherubim woven into the veil, resonating with imagery of a guardianship role initially played by such figures in Gen. 3:24.

These should not be thought of as separate functions but as one, articulated with specificity and depicted graphically. When we later (Chapter 6) considered the cessation of this function within the particular Matthean context, I found it to be strikingly congruent with recognisable themes both from some aspects of Matthean Christology and from Second Temple soteriological hopes, all immediately related by the evangelist to the death of Jesus and seeming to depict an eschatological turning of the ages. That is, the death of Jesus removed the cultic barriers between the holy (God) and the less holy (humanity). This is quite congruous with later Christian traditions, such as that of Photius, who asserted, 'By means of Christ's crucifixion, the curtain was parted, heralding and announcing to everyone the entrance to heaven'.[1] This meshes nicely with Matthew's unique portrayal of the atoning significance of Jesus' death (26:28; Chapter 5). His death did this by removing the prohibition of physical accessibility to God, as seen especially in Matthew's Emmanuel Christology. It also did this by removing the prohibition of visual accessibility to God, seeming to suggest that those able to see God are now made 'pure in heart', again by means of the death of Jesus. Furthermore, the figures of the cherubim woven into the veil are removed when the veil is torn. They no longer depict the physical and visual inaccessibility of God. They are disarmed, so to speak, and moved out of the way so that descendants of Adam, kept from the immediate presence and view of God by them since Gen. 3:24, are now permitted to re-enter that presence. This resonated with Second Temple 'new creation' motifs and suggested the dawn of the final, eschatological age in which such things were to be made possible.

Yet function was not all that was on the mind of scholars, both ancient and modern, with respect to the *velum scissum*. Some early Christians recognised that the rending was a symbolic image. With no precedent in Judaism or elsewhere for what that symbolism was, scholars frequently conjectured that as discussion of temple destruction is in close proximity to the Matthean *velum scissum* and since, apparently, the *velum scissum* is a negative event, the *velum scissum* must in some respect refer to the destruction of the temple in 70 C.E. However, a different line of reasoning seems more plausible and cognizant of the nature of the imagery employed. For though there is no precedent for what the tearing of the veil symbolises, there *is* evidence for what the veil itself symbolises. Though a few early texts present it as representing the temple itself, we saw that as early as Mark or Josephus, and probably earlier, the veil of the temple was

[1] *Fragmenta in Lucam*. H. L. Kessler, 'Through the Veil: The Holy Image in Judaism and Christianity', *Kairós* 32 (1990), 71–72.

part of a larger Jewish cosmology, dating perhaps to Ezekiel but surely at least to Ben Sira. This cosmology saw the different parts of the temple as representative of different parts of the universe; the veil, in this scheme, represented the heavenly firmament from Gen. 1:6 (Chapter 4). Its rending then connoted the opening of heaven, a well-attested apocalyptic image introducing a revelatory assertion. The veil, as the heavenly firmament, was thought to conceal heavenly secrets, with its removal depicting the revelation of biblical truths. This revelatory assertion designates the following Matthean special material (27:51b–53) as apocalyptic images. These images have been widely seen to reflect the prophecy of Ezek. 37, which shows exiles returning home and God dwelling among his people. It is important that for Matthew these remarkable eschatological events designate the turning of the page in God's soteriological saga; the dawning of the messianic age, which Matthew uniquely and clearly indicates, is inaugurated by the death of Jesus.

This turning of the era inaugurated by the death of Jesus and depicted by the Matthean *velum scissum* text resonates with the language of a restoration of the people of God from the exile of their sins. Indeed, from the beginning of the First Gospel, Jesus' primary messianic role is that of Israel's restoration. This restoration is inaugurated at Jesus' death and awaits his return for final consummation. According to Ezek. 37, such a restoration will involve people defined not by their ethnicity but by their relation to Jesus, the 'true Israel'. Matthew asserts that the life-giving death of Jesus inaugurates a new age in which the final, eschatological deliverance from bondage to sin is achieved, and that God's presence now dwells among his people and permits a fellowship between man and God not seen since the Garden of Eden.

## 2 Prospect

I said at the outset of this project that I expected this not to be the last word on the Matthean *velum scissum* but an early word on a new direction of discussion of the topic, and indeed there is much room for further development on the *velum scissum* itself as well as other issues raised by this study. For example, there is a great deal of room for appropriating our analysis of Matthew's view of the temple into the ongoing discussion of Matthew's relation to Judaism. Furthermore, the role of apocalyptic imagery in Matthew's gospel could be greatly developed not so much with a view to unearthing sociological phenomena pertaining to the 'community' that formed it (Sim), but to its role in the narrative and theology of the gospel's story, particularly as it relates to Matthew's Wisdom Christology.

Furthermore, there is a great deal of room for more thoroughly tracing Matthew's 'special material' in an apocalyptic reading, as I have proposed with the *velum scissum* text. On the Old Testament side there is need for a satisfactory discussion of the role of the פרכת in the 'sin offering' and the meaning of its identity as the 'veil of the testimony'. There is also room for exploration of the intertextual relationship between Ezek. 37. and Zech. 14 and its implications for the Matthean special material.[2] The *velum scissum* itself, in its Matthean context, is in need of further exploration with respect to the relationship between the Passion Narrative and the baptismal account (as well as the transfiguration) with which it is connected. Moreover, a re-examination of Matthew's 'son of God' language is also in order, in light of the correlation our analysis has drawn between its use and allusion in the veil pericope and elsewhere (especially the baptism and transfiguration). There is a great deal of room to appropriate my findings on the *velum scissum* within the contexts of Mark, Luke and the Gospel of Peter, as well as careful analysis of the relation between Matthew's *velum scissum* and veil traditions from Hebrews.[3] Also, I hope to see Eloff's dissertation published and its thesis of return from exile in Matthew taken seriously in the current scholarly discussion. Finally, I hope this book has demonstrated that appropriating familiar methods to an ancient problem in a fresh way can be instructive for furthering our understanding of the richness that can be found in difficult texts.

[2] See especially R. Mason, 'The Use of Biblical Material in Zechariah 9–14: A Study in Inner Biblical Exegesis', in *Bringing out the Treasure: Inner Biblical Allusion in Zechariah 9–14* (ed. M. J. Boda and M. H. Floyd; JSOTSup 370; Sheffield: Academic Press, 2003), pp. 172–200.

[3] See W. R. Telford, *The Theology of the Gospel of Mark* (Cambridge: Cambridge University Press, 1999), pp. 202–3, who suggests that it is tempting 'to see the Epistle's bold theological claim that Christ entered the heavenly sanctuary, opening a "living way . . . through the curtain" (Heb. 10:20), represented in narrative form in the Gospel's statement that at the death of Jesus, "the curtain of the temple was torn in two, from top to bottom" (Mk 15:38)'.

# Diagram

## VEIL LANGUAGE IN THE STRUCTURE OF THE TABERNACLE

**Tabernacle Proper** (Exod. 26:1–37; 36:8–38; 1 Chron. 17:5)
LXX. σκήνη or ἡ σκήνη τοῦ μαρτύριου
MT. ‏מִשְׁכָּן, אֹהֶל מוֹעֵד‎.



**'Veil'** (Exod. 26:31–35)
LXX. καταπέτασμα (94.286%; 31/33x)[1]
MT. ‏פָּרֹכֶת‎ (100.0%; 25/26x)[2]

**'Roof' and 'walls' of the Tabernacle**[3]
**First Layer.** (Exod. 26:1–6)
LXX. αὐλαία (100%; 8/8x)[4]
MT. ‏יְרִיעָה‎ (100%; 21/21x)[5]
**Second Layer.** (Exod. 26:7–13)
LXX. δέρρεις (100%; 13/13x)[6]
MT. ‏יְרִיעָה‎ (83.333%; 10/12x)[7]
**Third Layer.** (Exod. 26:14a; 39:34a)
LXX. κατακάλυμμα (50%; 1/2x)[8]
MT. ‏מִכְסֶה‎ (100%; 2/2x)
**Fourth Layer.** (Exod. 26:14b)
LXX. ἐπικαλύμματα (100%; 1/1x)
MT. ‏מִכְסֶה‎ (100%; 1/1x)

Ark of the Covenant
(Exod. 25:10–22)

Holy of Holies
(‏דְּבִר‎)

Holy Place
(‏הֵיכָל‎)

Altar of Incense
(Exod. 30:1–10)

Framework
(Exod. 26:15–30)

Lampstand
(Exod. 25:31–40)

Table for
Bread of Presence
(Exod. 25:23–30)

**'Screen'** (Exod. 26:36–37)
LXX. καταπέτασμα (40%; 2/5x)[9]
MT. ‏מָסָךְ‎ (100%; 6/6x)[10]

Laver
(Exod. 30:17–21)

Courtyard
(Exod. 27:9–19)

**'Curtain of the courtyard'**
(Exod. 27:9–15)
LXX. ἱστία (100%; 13/13x)[11]
MT. ‏קֶלַע‎ (100%; 16/16x)[12]

Altar of Burnt Offering
(Exod. 27:1–8)

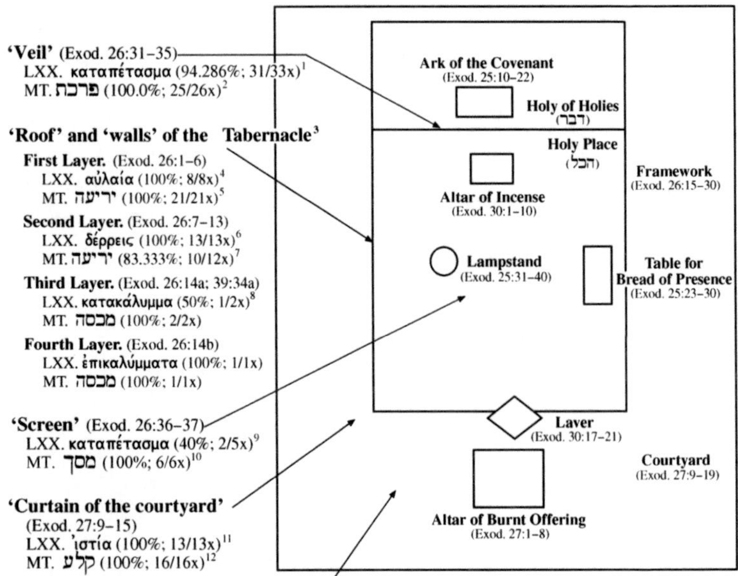

**'Curtain of the entrance of the courtyard'**
(Exod. 27:16)
LXX. καταπέτασμα (62.5%; 5/8x)[13]
MT. ‏מָסָךְ‎ (100%; 8/8x)[14]

[1] LXX Exod. 26:31, 33 (3x), 34, 35; 27:21; 30:6; 35:12; 37:3 (MT 36:35); 38:18 (MT 36:35?); 39:4 (MT 38:27); 40:3, 21, 22, 26; Lev. 4:6, 17; 16:2, 12, 15; 21:23; 24:3; Num. 3:10; 4:5; 18:7; 2 Chron. 3:14. Others: ἐπίκαλυμμα (1x; Exod. 39:20b [34b]); κατακάλυμμα (1x; Num. 3:31).

[2] MT Exod. 26:31,33(3x),35; 27:21; 30:6; 36:35(LXX 37:3); 38:27 (LXX 39:4); 40:3,21,22,26; Lev. 4:6,17; 16:2,12,15; 21:23; 24:3; 18:7; 2 Chron. 3:14. Also ‏מָסָךְ‎ Num. 3:31 (w/‏פָּרֹכֶת‎; Exod. 35:12a; 39:34b; 40:21; Num. 4:5).

[3] Others: καλύμμα/‏מִכְסֶה‎ (Exod. 35:11; Num. 4:25a, b); αὐλαία/‏יְרִיעָה‎(LXX Exod. 37:1[MT 36:8]; 37:2[MT 36:9]); αὐλαία/‏אֹהֶל‎(Exod. 40:19a); κατακάλυμμα/‏מִכְסֶה‎ (Exod. 40:19b); κάλυμμα/‏מִכְסֶה‎ (Num. 3:25a).

[4] LXX Exod. 26:1, 2, 3, 4 (2x), 5 (2x), 6.

[5] MT Exod. 26:1, 2, 3, 4 (2x), 5 (2x), 6; 36:10, 11 (2x), 12 (2x), 13, 14, 15, 16, 12 (2x); 36:8, 9.

[6] LXX Exod. 26:7, 8, 9 (3x), 10 (2x), 11, 12 (3x), 13 (2x).

[7] MT Exod. 26:7, 8, 9 (3x), 10 (2x), 12 (2x), 13. Others: ‏הָאֹהֶל‎ (MT Exod. 26:11); ‏בְּעֵדֶף‎ (MT Exod. 26:13a).

[8] Others: καλύμμα (Exod. 39:20a [MT 34a]; 7.143%; 1/14x).

[9] LXX Exod. 26:37; 37:5 (MT 36:37); Others: ἐπισπάστρον (20%; Exod. 26:36; 1/5x); καλύμμα (Num. 4:25c; 20%; 1/5x); κατακάλυμμα (Num. 3:25b; 20%; 1/5x).

[10] MT Exod. 26:36, 37; 36:37 (LXX 37:5); 40:28; Num. 3:25b; 4:25c.

[11] LXX Exod. 27:9, 11, 12, 13, 14, 15; 35:12b; 37:7 (MT 38:9); 37:12 (MT 38:14); 37:16b (MT 38:18b); 39:19a (MT 40a); Num. 3:26a; 4:26a.

[12] MT Exod. 27:9, 11, 12, 14, 15; 35:17a; 38:9 (LXX 37:7); 38:12 (LXX 37:10); 38:14 (LXX 37:12); 38:15 (LXX 37:13); 38:16; 38:18b (LXX 37:16b); 39:40a (LXX 19a); Num. 3:26a; 4:26a.

[13] LXX Exod. 37:16a (MT 38:18a); 39:19b (MT 40b); Num. 3:26b; 4:32. Others: καλύμμα (Exod. 27:16; 12.5%; 1/8x); αὐλαία (Exod. 3:13 [MT38:15]; Exod. 37:14 [MT38:16]; 25%; 2/8). Exod. 40:5 reference in n. 1.

[14] MT Exod. 27:16; 35:15, 17b; 38:18a (LXX 37:16a); 39:40b (LXX 39:19b); 40:5; Num. 3:26b; 4:26b.

The diagram makes use of the SPIonic and SPTiberian fonts, by kind permission of James R. Adair (http://purl.org/TC/fonts/).

# Appendix 1

## VEIL LANGUAGE IN THE OLD TESTAMENT

| LXX (MT) | Septuagint (LXX) | | | | | | | | | | | Hebrew Bible (MT) | | | | | | | | | | | | | Syriac (Peshitta) | | | | | | | | | | | | | Latin (Vulgate) | | | | | | | | | | | | Description in Context: |
|---|---|---|---|---|---|---|---|---|---|---|---|---|---|---|---|---|---|---|---|---|---|---|---|---|---|---|---|---|---|---|---|---|---|---|---|---|---|---|---|---|---|---|---|---|---|---|---|---|---|---|
| | καταπέτασμα | καλύμμα | καταλύματι | σκηνή | ἐπικάλυμμα | κατακάλυμμα | ἱστία | αὐλαία | δέρρις | ἐπίσπαστρον | παρατάνυσμα | פרכת | מסך | משכן | כפרת | קלע | אהל | יריעה | כסוי | מכסה | נס | רדיד | צמה | מסוה | ܬܪܥܐ | ܦܪܣܐ | ܦܪܣܬܐ | ܚܘܦܝܐ | ܝܪܝܥܬܐ | ܟܣܝܐ | ܚܘܣܝܐ | ܣܪܕܐ | ܓܠܕܐ | ܦܓܠܐ | ܥܛܦܐ | ܟܠܦܐ | ܡܫܟܐ | *velum* | *propitiatorium* | *cortinas* | *cortinari vela* | *sagum* | *tabernaculum* | *tectum* | *velamen* | *pellium* | *signum* | *velamen* | *tentorium* | |
| Gen. 8:13 | O. S | | | | | | | | | | | | | | | | | | |X| | | | | | | |X| | | | | | | | | | | | | | | |X| | | | | | Surface of the ground |
| Exod. 26:1 | | | | | | | |X| | | | | | | | | |X| | | | | | | | | | |X| | | | | | | | | | |X| | | | | | | | | | Sheet of the tabernacle proper |
| Exod. 26:2 | | | | | | | |X| | | | | | | | | |X| | | | | | | | | | |X| | | | | | | | | | |X| | | | | | | | | | Sheet of the tabernacle proper |
| Exod. 26:3 | | | | | | | |X| | | | | | | | | |X| | | | | | | | | | |X| | | | | | | | | | |X| | | | | | | | | | Sheet of the tabernacle proper |
| Exod. 26:4a | | | | | | | |X| | | | | | | | | |X| | | | | | | | | | |X| | | | | | | | | | |X| | | | | | | | | | Sheet of the tabernacle proper |
| Exod. 26:4b | | | | | | | |X| | | | | | | | | |X| | | | | | | | | | |X| | | | | | | | |--|--|--|--|--|--|--|--|--|--|--|--| Sheet of the tabernacle proper |
| Exod. 26:5a | | | | | | | |X| | | | | | | | | |X| | | | | | | | | | |X| | | | | | | | | | |X| | | | | | | | | | Sheet of the tabernacle proper |
| Exod. 26:5b | | | | | | | |X| | | | | | | | | |X| | | | | | | | | | |X| | | | | | | | |--|--|--|--|--|--|--|--|--|--|--|--| Sheet of the tabernacle proper |
| Exod. 26:6 | | | | | | | |X| | | | | | | | | |X| | | | | | | | | | |X| | | | | | | | | | |X| | | | | | | | | | Sheet of the tabernacle proper |
| Exod. 26:7 | | | | | | | | |X| | | | | | | | |X| | | | | | | | | | |X| | | | | | | | | | | | | | |X| | | | | | Goat's hair covering over tent of tabernacle |
| Exod. 26:8 | | | | | | | | |X| | | | | | | | |X| | | | | | | | | | |X| | | | | | | | | | | | |X| | | | | | | | Goat's hair covering over tent of tabernacle |
| Exod. 26:9a | | | | | | | | |X| | | | | | | | |X| | | | | | | | | | |X| | | | | | | | | | | | |X| | | | | | | | Goat's hair covering over tent of tabernacle |
| Exod. 26:9b | | | | | | | | |X| | | | | | | | |X| | | | | | | | | | |X| | | | | | | | | | | | | | |X| | | | | | Goat's hair covering over tent of tabernacle |
| Exod. 26:9c | | | | | | | | |X| | | | | | | | |X| | | | | | | | | | |X| | | | | | | | |--|--|--|--|--|--|--|--|--|--|--|--| Goat's hair covering over tent of tabernacle |
| Exod. 26:10a | | | | | | | | |X| | | | | | | | |X| | | | | | | | | | |X| | | | | | | | | | | | |X| | | | | | | | Goat's hair covering over tent of tabernacle |
| Exod. 26:10b | | | | | | | | |X| | | | | | | | |X| | | | | | | | | | |X| | | | | | | | | | | | |X| | | | | | | | Goat's hair covering over tent of tabernacle |
| Exod. 26:12a | | | | | | | | |X| | | | | | | | |X| | | | | | | | | | |X| | | | | | | | | | | | |X| | | | | | | | Goat's hair covering over tent of tabernacle |
| Exod. 26:12b | | | | | | | | |X| | | | | | | | |X| | | | | | | | | | |X| | | | | | | | | | | | | | |X| | | | | | Goat's hair covering over tent of tabernacle |
| Exod. 26:12c | | | | | | | | |X| | | | | |X| | | | | | | | | | | | | | | | | | | | | | | | | |X| | | | | | | | Goat's hair covering over tent of tabernacle |
| Exod. 26:13a | | | | | | | | |X| | | | | | | | |X| | | | | | | | | | |X| | | | | | | | | | | | |X| | | | | | | | Goat's hair covering over tent of tabernacle |
| Exod. 26:13b | | | | | | | | |X| | | | | |X| | | | | | | | | | | | | | | | | | | | | | | | | | |X| | | | | | | Goat's hair covering over tent of tabernacle |
| Exod. 26:14a | | | | | |X| | | | | | | | | | | | | |X| | | | | | | | | | | | | | | | | |X| | | | | | | | |X| | | | Ram's skin dyed red-covering for tent |
| Exod. 26:14b | | | | |X| | | | | | | | | | | | | | |X| | | | | | | | | | | | | | | | | |X| | | | | | | | |X| | | | Fine leather covering ram's skin (14a) |
| Exod. 26:31 |X| | | | | | | | | | |X| | | | | | | | | | | | | |X| | | | | | | | | | | | |X| | | | | | | | | | | | Veil between the holy place and holy of holies |
| Exod. 26:33a |X| | | | | | | | | | |X| | | | | | | | | | | | | |X| | | | | | | | | | | | |X| | | | | | | | | | | | Veil between the holy place and holy of holies |
| Exod. 26:33b |X| | | | | | | | | | |X| | | | | | | | | | | | | |X| | | | | | | | | | | |--|--|--|--|--|--|--|--|--|--|--|--| Veil between the holy place and holy of holies |
| Exod. 26:33c |X| | | | | | | | | | |X| | | | | | | | | | | | | |X| | | | | | | | | | | |--|--|--|--|--|--|--|--|--|--|--|--| Veil between the holy place and holy of holies |
| Exod. 26:34 |X| | | | | | | | | | |O'| | |X| | | | | | | | | | | | | | | |X| | | | | | | |X| | | | | | | | | | | Textual confusion- veil v. atonement cover |
| Exod. 26:35 |X| | | | | | | | | | |X| | | | | | | | | | | | | |X| | | | | | | | | | | |X| | | | | | | | | | | | Veil between the holy place and holy of holies |
| Exod. 26:36 |U| | | | | | | | |X|Q, S| |X| | | | | | | | | | | | |X| | | | | | | | | | | | | | | | | | | | | | |X| Screen for the entrance to the tent |
| Exod. 26:37 |X| | | | | | | | | | | |X| | | | | | | | | | | | |X| | | | | | | | | | | | | | | | | | | | | | |X| Screen for the entrance to the tent |
| Exod. 27:9 | | | | | | |X| | | | | | | | |X| | | | | | | | | | | | | | | |X| | | | | | | | | | | | | | | | | |X| Curtain of the courtyard (of the tabernacle) |
| Exod. 27:11 | | | | | | |X| | | | | | | | |X| | | | | | | | | | | | | | | |X| | | | | | | | | | | | | | | | | |X| Curtain of the courtyard (of the tabernacle) |
| Exod. 27:12 | | | | | | |X| | | | | | | | |X| | | | | | | | | | | | | | | |X| | | | | | | | | | | | | | | | | |X| Curtain of the courtyard (of the tabernacle) |
| Exod. 27:13 | | | | | | |X| | | | |--|--|--|--|--|--|--|--|--|--|--|--|--|--|--|--|--|--|--|--|--|--|--|--|--|--|--|--|--|--|--|--|--|--|--|--|--|--| Curtain of the courtyard (of the tabernacle) |
| Exod. 27:14 | | | | | | |X| | | | | | | | |X| | | | | | | | | | | | | | | |X| | | | | | | | | | | | | | | | | |X| Curtain of the courtyard (of the tabernacle) |
| Exod. 27:15 | | | | | | |X| | | | | | | | |X| | | | | | | | | | | | | | | |X| | | | | | | | | | | | | | | | | |X| Curtain of the courtyard (of the tabernacle) |
| Exod. 27:16 | |X| | | | | | | | | | |X| | | | | | | | | | | | |X| | | | | | | | | | | | | | | | | | | | | | |X| Curtain at entrance to courtyard |
| Exod. 27:18 |--|--|--|--|--|--|--|--|--|--|--| |X| | | | | | | | | | | | |X| | | | | | | | | | | | | | | | | | | | | | |X| Curtain at entrance to courtyard |
| Exod. 27:21 |X| | | | | | | | | | |X| | | | | | | | | | | | | |X| | | | | | | | | | | |X| | | | | | | | | | | | Veil between the holy place and holy of holies |
| Exod. 30:6 |X| | | | | | | | | | |X| | | | | | | | | | | | | |X| | | | | | | | | | | |X| | | | | | | | | | | | Veil between the holy place and holy of holies |
| Exod. 34:33 | |X| | | | | | | | | | | | | | | | | | | | | |X| | | | | | | | | | |X| | | | | | | | | |X| | | | | Moses' face-veil |
| Exod. 34:34 | |X| | | | | | | | | | | | | | | | | | | | | |X| | | | | | | | | | |X| | |--|--|--|--|--|--|--|--|--|--|--|--| Moses' face-veil |
| Exod. 34:35 | |X| | | | | | | | | | | | | | | | | | | | | |X| | | | | | | | | | |X| | |--|--|--|--|--|--|--|--|--|--|--|--| Moses' face-veil |
| Exod. 35:11 | |X| | | | | | | | | | | | | | | | |X| | | | | | | |X| | | | | | | | | | |--|--|--|--|--|--|--|--|--|--|--|--| General coverings for the tabernacle |

| | | | | | | | | | | | | | | | | | | | | | | | | | | | | | | | | | | | | | | | | | | | | | | | | | | |
|---|---|---|---|---|---|---|---|---|---|---|---|---|---|---|---|---|---|---|---|---|---|---|---|---|---|---|---|---|---|---|---|---|---|---|---|---|---|---|---|---|---|---|---|---|---|---|---|---|---|---|
|Exod. 35:12a|X|||||||||||X|X||||||||||||X|X||||||||||||||||||X||||||Veil between the holy place and holy of holies|
|Exod. 35:12b|||||||X||||||--|--|--|--|--|--|--|--|--|--|--|--|--|--|--|--|--|--|--|--|--|--|--|--|--|--|--|--|--|--|--|--|--|--|--|--|--|--|Curtain of the courtyard (of the tabernacle)|
|Exod. 35:15|--|--|--|--|--|--|--|--|--|--|--||X||||||||||||X||||||||||||||||||||||||X|Curtain of the entrance to the tabernacle|
|Exod. 35:17a|--|--|--|--|--|--|--|--|--|--|--|||||X|||||||||||||||||X||||||||X||||||||||Curtain of the courtyard (of the tabernacle)|
|Exod. 35:17b|--|--|--|--|--|--|--|--|--|--|--||X||||||||||||X|X||||||||||||||||||||||||X|Curtain at entrance to courtyard|
|Exod. 36:10 (MT)|--|--|--|--|--|--|--|--|--|--|--|||||||X||||||||||||X||||||||||||X||||||||||Sheet of the tabernacle proper|
|Exod. 36:11a (MT)|--|--|--|--|--|--|--|--|--|--|--|||||||X||||||||||||X||||||||||||X||||||||||Sheet of the tabernacle proper|
|Exod. 36:11b (MT)|--|--|--|--|--|--|--|--|--|--|--|||||||X||||||||||||X||||||||||||X||||||||||Sheet of the tabernacle proper|
|Exod. 36:12a (MT)|--|--|--|--|--|--|--|--|--|--|--|||||||X||||||||||||X|||||||||--|--|--|--|--|--|--|--|--|--|--|--|Sheet of the tabernacle proper|
|Exod. 36:12b (MT)|--|--|--|--|--|--|--|--|--|--|--|||||||X||||||||||||X|||||||||--|--|--|--|--|--|--|--|--|--|--|--|Sheet of the tabernacle proper|
|Exod. 36:13 (MT)|--|--|--|--|--|--|--|--|--|--|--|||||||X||||||||||||X||||||||||||X||||||||||Sheet of the tabernacle proper|
|Exod. 36:14 (MT)|--|--|--|--|--|--|--|--|--|--|--|||||||X||||||||||||X||||||||||||||X||||||||Goat's hair covering over tent of tabernacle|
|Exod. 36:15 (MT)|--|--|--|--|--|--|--|--|--|--|--|||||||X||||||||||||X||||||||||||||X||||||||Goat's hair covering over tent of tabernacle|
|Exod. 36:16 (MT)|--|--|--|--|--|--|--|--|--|--|--|||||||X||||||||||||X|||||||||--|--|--|--|--|--|--|--|--|--|--|--|Goat's hair covering over tent of tabernacle|
|Exod. 36:17a (MT)|--|--|--|--|--|--|--|--|--|--|--|||||||X||||||||||||X||||||||||||||X||||||||Goat's hair covering over tent of tabernacle|
|Exod. 36:17b (MT)|--|--|--|--|--|--|--|--|--|--|--|||||||X||||||||||||X||||||||||||||X||||||||Goat's hair covering over tent of tabernacle|
|Exod. 36:19a (MT)|--|--|--|--|--|--|--|--|--|--|--|||||||||X||||||X||||||||||||||||||||X||||Ram's skin dyed red-covering for tent|
|Exod. 36:19b (MT)|--|--|--|--|--|--|--|--|--|--|--|||||||||X||||||X|||||||||||||||||||X|||||Fine leather covering ram's skin|
|Exod. 37:1 (MT36:8)||||||||X|||||||||||X||||||||||||X||||||||||||X||||||||||Sheet of the tabernacle proper|
|Exod. 37:2 (MT36:9)||||||||X|||||||||||X|||||||X|||||||||||||--|--|--|--|--|--|--|--|--|--|--|--|Sheet of the tabernacle proper|
|Exod. 37:3 (MT36:35)|X|||||||||||X||||||||||||||X||||||||||||X||||||||||||Veil between the holy place and holy of holies|
|Exod. 37:5 (MT36:37)|X|||||||||A|||X||||||||||||X||||||||||||||||||||||||X|Curtain for the entrance to the tent|
|Exod. 37:7 (MT38:9)|||||||X||||||||||X||||||||||||||||X||||||||||||||||||X|Curtain of the courtyard (of the tabernacle)|
|Exod. 37:10 (MT38:12)|--|--|--|--|--|--|--|--|--|--|--|||||X|||||||||||||||||X||||||||||||||||||X|Curtain of the courtyard (of the tabernacle)|
|Exod. 37:12 (MT38:14)|||||||X||||||||||X||||||||||||||||X||||||||||||||||||X|Curtain of the courtyard (of the tabernacle)|
|Exod. 37:13 (MT38:15)||||||||X||||||||||X||||||||||||||||X||||||||||||||||||X|Curtain of the entrance to the courtyard|
|Exod. 37:14 (MT38:16)||||||||X||||||||||||||||||||||||||||||||||||||||||Curtain of the entrance to the courtyard|
|Exod. 37:16a (MT38:18a)|X|||||A|||||||X||||||||||||X||||||||||||||||||||||||X|Curtain at entrance to courtyard|
|Exod. 37:16b (MT38:18b)|||||||X||||||||||X||||||||||||||||X||||||||||||||||||X|Curtain of the courtyard (of the tabernacle)|
|Exod. 38:16|--|--|--|--|--|--|--|--|--|--|--|||||X|||||||||||||||||X||||||||||||||||||X|Curtain of the courtyard (of the tabernacle)|
|Exod. 38:18 (MT36:35?)|X|||||||||||?||||||||||||||X||||||||||||--|--|--|--|--|--|--|--|--|--|--|--|Veil between the holy place and holy of holies|
|Exod. 39:4 (MT38:27)|X|||||||||||X||||||||||||||X||||||||||||X||||||||||||Veil between the holy place and holy of holies|
|Exod. 39:19a (MT40a)|||||||X||||||||||X|||||||||--|--|--|--|--|--|--|--|--|--|--|--|--||||||||||||X|Curtain of the courtyard (of the tabernacle)|
|Exod. 39:19b (MT40b)|X||||||||||||X||||||||||||||X|||||||||||||||||||X||||||Curtain at entrance to courtyard|
|Exod. 39:20a (MT34a)||X|||||||||||||||||X||||||X||||||||||||||||||||||||X|Curtain of the courtyard (of the tabernacle)|
|Exod. 39:20b (MT34b)|||||X|||||||X|X||||||||||||X|||||||||||||||||||X||||||Veil between the holy place and holy of holies|
|Exod. 40:3|X|||||||||||X||||||||||||||X||||||||||||X||||||||||||Veil between the holy place and holy of holies|
|Exod. 40:5|X|X||||||||TQ, S|||X||||||||||||X||||||||||||||||||||||||X|Curtain at entrance to courtyard|
|Exod. 40:19a||||||||X|||||||||||X||||||||||X||||||||||||X||||||||||||"Tent" covering over the tabernacle|
|Exod. 40:19b||||||X|||||||||||||||X||||||X||||||||||||--|--|--|--|--|--|--|--|--|--|--|--|Covering over the tent (40:19a)|
|Exod. 40:21|X|||||X||||||X|X||||||||||||X|X||||||||||||X||||||||||||Veil between the holy place and holy of holies|
|Exod. 40:22|X|||||||||||X||||||||||||||X||||||||||||X||||||||||||Veil between the holy place and holy of holies|
|Exod. 40:26|X|||||||||||X||||||||||||||X||||||||||||||||||||||||X|Veil between the holy place and holy of holies|
|Exod. 40:28|--|--|--|--|--|--|--|--|--|--|--||X||||||||||||X|X||||||||||||--|--|--|--|--|--|--|--|--|--|--|--|Curtain at the entrance to the tabernacle|
|Lev. 4:6|X|||||||||||X||||||||||||||X||||||||||||X||||||||||||Veil between the holy place and holy of holies|
|Lev. 4:17|X|||||||||||X||||||||||||||X||||||||||||X||||||||||||Veil between the holy place and holy of holies|
|Lev. 16:2|X|||||||||||X|||||||||||||X|||||||||||||X||||||||||||Veil between the holy place and holy of holies|
|Lev. 16:12|X|||||||||||X|||||||||||||X|||||||||||||X||||||||||||Veil between the holy place and holy of holies|
|Lev. 16:15|X|||||||||||X|||||||||||||X|||||||||||||X||||||||||||Veil between the holy place and holy of holies|
|Lev. 21:23|X|||||||||||X|||||||||||||X|||||||||||||X||||||||||||Veil between the holy place and holy of holies|
|Lev. 24:3|X|||||||||||X|||||||||||||X|||||||||||||X||||||||||||Veil between the holy place and holy of holies|

Appendix 1 (*cont.*)

| LXX (MT) | Septuagint (LXX) | | | | | | | | | | | Hebrew Bible (MT) | | | | | | | | | | | | | Syriac (Peshitta) | | | | | | | | | | | | | Latin (Vulgate) | | | | | | | | | | | | Description in Context: |
|---|---|---|---|---|---|---|---|---|---|---|---|---|---|---|---|---|---|---|---|---|---|---|---|---|---|---|---|---|---|---|---|---|---|---|---|---|---|---|---|---|---|---|---|---|---|---|---|---|---|---|
| | καταπέτασμα | κάλυμμα | καταλύματι | σκηνή | ἐπικάλυμμα | κατακάλυμμα | ἱστία | αὐλαία | δέρρις | ἐπίσπαστρον | παρατάνυσμα | פרכת | מסך | משכן | כפרת | קלע | אהל | יריעה | כסוי | מכסה | נס | רדיד | צמה | מסוה | ܦܪܟܬܐ | ܦܪܣܐ | ܦܪܘܣܬܐ | ܟܣܝܐ | ܬܚܝܬ/ | ܡܫܟܢ/ | ܡܫܟܢܐ | ܣܪܕܐ | ܟܠܠܐ | ܦܪܣܬܐ | ܢܝܫܐ | ܦܕܐ | ܟܡܝܐ | *velum* | *propitiatorium* | *cortinas* | *cortinari vela* | *sagum* | *tabernaculum* | *lectum* | *velamen* | *pellium* | *signum* | *velamen* | *tentorium* | |
| Num. 3:10 | X | | | | | | | | | | | -- | -- | -- | -- | -- | -- | -- | -- | -- | -- | -- | -- | -- | -- | -- | -- | -- | -- | -- | -- | -- | -- | -- | -- | -- | -- | -- | -- | -- | -- | -- | -- | -- | -- | -- | -- | -- | -- | Veil between the holy place and holy of holies |
| Num. 3:25a | | X | | | | | | | | | | | | | | | | | | X | | | | | X | | | | | | | | | | | | | | | | | | | | | | | | X | Covering for the tabernacle and tent |
| Num. 3:25b | | | | | | X | | | | | | | X | | | | | | | | | | | | X | X | | | | | | | | | | | | | | | | | | | | | | | X | Curtain at the entrance to the tent of meeting |
| Num. 3:26a | | | | | | | X | | | | | | | | | X | | | | | | | | | | | | | | | | | X | | | | | | | | | | | | | | | | X | Curtain of the courtyard (of the tabernacle) |
| Num. 3:26b | X | | | | | | | | | | | | X | | | | | | | | | | | | X | | | | | | | | | | | | | -- | -- | -- | -- | -- | -- | -- | -- | -- | -- | -- | -- | Curtain at entrance to courtyard |
| Num. 3:31 | | | | | | X | | | | | | | X | | | | | | | | | | | | X | | | | | | | | | | | | | X | | | | | | | | | | | | Veil between the holy place and holy of holies? |
| Num. 4:5 | X | | | | | | | | | | | X | X | | | | | | | | | | | | X | | | | | | | | | | | | | X | | | | | | | | | | | | Veil between the holy place and holy of holies |
| Num. 4:8 | | X | | | | | | | | | | | | | | | | | | X | | | | | | X | | | | | | | | | | | | | | | | | | | | X | | | | Skin cover over table of presence in transport |
| Num. 4:10 | | X | | | | | | | | | | | | | | | | | | X | | | | | | | | | | | | | | | | | X | | | | | | | | | X | | | | Cover for taber. accessories in transport |
| Num. 4:11 | | X | | | | | | | | | | | | | | | | | | X | | | | | | X | | | | | | | | | | | | | | | | | | | | X | | | | Cover for taber. accessories in transport |
| Num. 4:12 | | X | | | | | | | | | | | | | | | | | | X | | | | | | | | | | | | | | | | | X | | | | | | | | | X | | | | Cover for taber. accessories in transport |
| Num. 4:14a | | X | | | | | | | | | | | | | | | | | X | | | | | | | X | | | | | | | | | | | | | | | | | | | | X | | | | Cover for taber. accessories in transport |
| Num. 4:14b | | X | | | | | | | | | | -- | -- | -- | -- | -- | -- | -- | -- | -- | -- | -- | -- | -- | -- | -- | -- | -- | -- | -- | -- | -- | -- | -- | -- | -- | -- | -- | -- | -- | -- | -- | -- | -- | -- | -- | -- | -- | -- | Cover for taber. accessories in transport |
| Num. 4:25a | | X | | | | | | | | | | | | | | | | | | X | | | | | X | | | | | | | | | | | | | | | | | | | | | | | | X | General covering for the tabernacle |
| Num. 4:25b | | X | | | | | | | | | | | | | | | | | | X | | | | | | X | | | | | | | | | | | | | | | | | | | | | | X | | General covering for the tabernacle |
| Num. 4:25c | | X | | | | | | | | | | | X | | | | | | | | | | | | X | | | | | | | | | | | | | X | | | | | | | | | | | | Curtain at the entrance to the tent of meeting |
| Num. 4:26a | | | | | | | X | | | | | | | | | X | | | | | | | | | | | | | | | | | X | | | | | | | | | | | | | | | | X | Curtain of the courtyard (of the tabernacle) |
| Num. 4:26b | -- | -- | -- | -- | -- | -- | -- | -- | -- | -- | -- | | X | | | | | | | | | | | | | X | | | | | | | | | | | | -- | -- | -- | -- | -- | -- | -- | -- | -- | -- | -- | -- | Curtain at entrance to courtyard |
| Num. 4:32 | X | | | | | | | | | | | -- | -- | -- | -- | -- | -- | -- | -- | -- | -- | -- | -- | -- | -- | -- | -- | -- | -- | -- | -- | -- | -- | -- | -- | -- | -- | -- | -- | -- | -- | -- | -- | -- | -- | -- | -- | -- | -- | Curtain at entrance to courtyard |
| Num. 18:7 | X | | | | | | | | | | | X | | | | | | | | | | | | | X | | | | | | | | | | | | | X | | | | | | | | | | | | Veil between the holy place and holy of holies |
| 1 Kings 6:36 | L | | | | | | | | | | | -- | -- | -- | -- | -- | -- | -- | -- | -- | -- | -- | -- | -- | -- | -- | -- | -- | -- | -- | -- | -- | -- | -- | -- | -- | -- | -- | -- | -- | -- | -- | -- | -- | -- | -- | -- | -- | -- | Veil between the holy place and holy of holies |
| 1 Chron. 17:5a | | | | X | | | | | | | | | | | | | X | | | | | | | | | | | | | | | | | | | | | | | | | | | | | | | | | Tabernacle proper |
| 1 Chron. 17:5b | | B | X | | | | | | | | | | | X | | | | | | | | | | | | | | | | | | | | | | | | | | | | | | | | | | | | Tabernacle proper |
| 2 Chron. 3:14 | X | | | | | | | | | | | X | | | | | | | | | | | | | | | X | | | | | | | | | | | X | | | | | | | | | | | | Veil between the holy place and holy of holies |
| Isa 33:23 | | | | | | | X | | | | | | | | | | | | | | X | | | | | | | | | | | | | X | | | | | | | | | | | | | X | | | Sail of a ship or a standard, rallying point |
| Cant. 4:3 | | S | | | | | | | | | | | | | | | | | | | | | X | | | | | | | | | | | | | X | | -- | -- | -- | -- | -- | -- | -- | -- | -- | -- | -- | -- | Woman's face veil |
| Cant. 5:7 | | Q, U | | | | | | | | | | | | | | | | | | | | X | | | | | | | | | | | | | | X | | | | | | | | | | X | | | | City wall |
| Cant. 6:6(7) | | S | | | | | | | | | | | | | | | | | | | | | X | | | | | | | | | | | | | X | | -- | -- | -- | -- | -- | -- | -- | -- | -- | -- | -- | -- | Woman's face veil |

**Key:**

U unknown source(s) T Origen's Theodotion X single occurrence Q Origen's Aquila A LXX Alexandrinus S Origen's Symmachus -- Unrepresented by that version
B LXX Vaticanus L Lucian QmQumran text

# Appendix 2

## VEIL LANGUAGE IN THE TWO TABERNACLE ACCOUNTS

| Referrant | Hebrew | Reference | Translation | Reference | Translation |
|---|---|---|---|---|---|
| Ten curtains of the tabernacle | יריעה | Exod. 26:1 | αὐλαία | Exod. 37:1 (MT36:8) | αὐλαία |
| Ten curtains of the tabernacle | יריעה | Exod. 26:2 | αὐλαία | Exod. 37:2 (MT36:9) | αὐλαία |
| Ten curtains of the tabernacle | יריעה | Exod. 26:3 | αὐλαία | Exod. 36:10 (MT) | -- |
| Ten curtains of the tabernacle | יריעה | Exod. 26:4a | αὐλαία | Exod. 36:11a (MT) | -- |
| Ten curtains of the tabernacle | יריעה | Exod. 26:4b | αὐλαία | Exod. 36:11b (MT) | -- |
| Ten curtains of the tabernacle | יריעה | Exod. 26:5a | αὐλαία | Exod. 36:12a (MT) | -- |
| Ten curtains of the tabernacle | יריעה | Exod. 26:5b | αὐλαία | Exod. 36:12b (MT) | -- |
| Ten curtains of the tabernacle | יריעה | Exod. 26:6 | αὐλαία | Exod. 36:13 (MT) | -- |
| Goat's hair covering over tent of tabernacle | יריעה | Exod. 26:7 | δέρρις | Exod. 36:14 (MT) | -- |
| Goat's hair covering over tent of tabernacle | יריעה | Exod. 26:8 | δέρρις | Exod. 36:15 (MT) | -- |
| Goat's hair covering over tent of tabernacle | יריעה | Exod. 26:9a | δέρρις | Exod. 36:16 (MT) | -- |
| Goat's hair covering over tent of tabernacle | יריעה | Exod. 26:9b | δέρρις | -- | -- |
| Goat's hair covering over tent of tabernacle | יריעה | Exod. 26:9c | δέρρις | -- | -- |
| Goat's hair covering over tent of tabernacle | יריעה | Exod. 26:10a | δέρρις | Exod. 36:17a (MT) | -- |
| Goat's hair covering over tent of tabernacle | יריעה | Exod. 26:10b | δέρρις | Exod. 36:17b (MT) | -- |
| Goat's hair covering over tent of tabernacle | יריעה | Exod. 26:12a | δέρρις | -- | -- |
| Goat's hair covering over tent of tabernacle | יריעה | Exod. 26:12b | δέρρις | -- | -- |
| Goat's hair covering over tent of tabernacle | מִשְׁכָּן | Exod. 26:12c | δέρρις | | |
| Goat's hair covering over tent of tabernacle | יריעה | Exod. 26:13 | δέρρις | -- | -- |
| Ram's skin dyed red-covering for tent | מכסה | Exod. 26:14a | κατακάλυμμα | Exod. 36:19a (MT) | -- |
| Fine leather covering ram's skin | מכסה | Exod. 26:14b | ἐπικάλυμμα | Exod. 36:19b (MT) | -- |
| Veil between the holy place and holy of holies | פרכת | Exod. 26:31 | καταπέτασμα | Exod. 37:3 (MT36:35) | καταπέτασμα |
| Veil between the holy place and holy of holies | פרכת | Exod. 26:33a | καταπέτασμα | -- | -- |
| Veil between the holy place and holy of holies | פרכת | Exod. 26:33b | καταπέτασμα | -- | -- |
| Veil between the holy place and holy of holies | פרכת | Exod. 26:33c | καταπέτασμα | -- | -- |

| Veil between the holy place and holy of holies | כפרת | Exod. 26:34 | καταπέτασμα | -- | -- |
|---|---|---|---|---|---|
| Veil between the holy place and holy of holies | פרכת | Exod. 26:35 | καταπέτασμα | -- | -- |
| Curtain for the entrance to the tent | מסך | Exod. 26:36 | ἐπίσπαστρον | Exod. 37:5 (MT36:37) | καταπέτασμα |
| Curtain for the entrance to the tent | מסך | Exod. 26:37 | καταπέτασμα | -- | -- |
| Curtain of the courtyard (of the tabernacle) | קלע | Exod. 27:9 | ἱστία | Exod. 37:7 (MT38:9) | ἱστία |
| Curtain of the courtyard (of the tabernacle) | קלע | Exod. 27:11 | ἱστία | -- | -- |
| Curtain of the courtyard (of the tabernacle) | קלע | Exod. 27:12 | ἱστία | Exod. 37:10 (MT38:12) | -- |
| Curtain of the courtyard (of the tabernacle) | -- | Exod. 27:13 | ἱστία | -- | -- |
| Curtain of the courtyard (of the tabernacle) | קלע | Exod. 27:14 | ἱστία | Exod. 37:12 (MT38:14) | ἱστία |
| Curtain of the courtyard (of the tabernacle) | קלע | Exod. 27:15 | ἱστία | Exod. 37:13 (MT38:15) | αὐλαία |
| Curtain at entrance to courtyard | מסך | Exod. 27:16 | καλύμμα | Exod. 37:16a (MT38:18a) | καταπέτασμα |
| Veil between the holy place and holy of holies | פרכת | Exod. 27:21 | καταπέτασμα | -- | -- |
| Veil between the holy place and holy of holies | פרכת | Exod. 30:6 | καταπέτασμα | -- | -- |
| Curtain of the courtyard (of the tabernacle) | קלע | -- | -- | Exod. 37:16b (MT38:18b) | ἱστία |
| Veil between the holy place and holy of holies | פרכת | -- | -- | Exod. 39:4 (MT38:27) | καταπέτασμα |
| Curtain of the courtyard (of the tabernacle) | קלע | -- | -- | Exod. 39:19a (MT40a) | ἱστία |
| Curtain at entrance to courtyard | מסך | -- | -- | Exod. 39:19b (MT40b) | καταπέτασμα |
| Curtain of the courtyard (of the tabernacle) | יריעה | -- | -- | Exod. 39:20a (MT34a) | καλύμμα |
| Veil between the holy place and holy of holies | מסך פרכת | -- | -- | Exod. 39:20b (MT34b) | ἐπικαλύμμα |
| Veil between the holy place and holy of holies | פרכת | -- | -- | Exod. 40:3 | καταπέτασμα |
| Curtain at entrance to courtyard | מסך | -- | -- | Exod. 40:5 | κάλυμμα καταπ. |
| "Tent" covering over the tabernacle | אהל | -- | -- | Exod. 40:19a | αὐλαία |
| Covering for the tent | מכסה | -- | -- | Exod. 40:19b | κατακάλυμμα |
| Veil between the holy place and holy of holies | מסך פרכת | -- | -- | Exod. 40:21 | κατακάλυμμα καταπ. |
| Veil between the holy place and holy of holies | פרכת | -- | -- | Exod. 40:22 | καταπέτασμα |
| Veil between the holy place and holy of holies | פרכת | -- | -- | Exod. 40:26 | καταπέτασμα |
| Curtain at the entrance to the tabernacle | מסך | -- | -- | Exod. 40:28 | -- |

# Appendix 3

## AND THE פרכת

| LXX (MT) | Greek | | | | | | Hebrew | | | Greek in Context | Description (from context): |
|---|---|---|---|---|---|---|---|---|---|---|---|
| | καταπέτασμα | ἐπικάλυμμα | καλύμμα | κατακάλυμμα | ἐπίσπαστρον | παρατάνυσμα | פרכת | מסך | כפרת | | |
| Exod. 26:31 | X | | | | | | X | | | ποιήσεις κ. ἐξ ὑακίνθου | Veil between the holy place and holy of holies |
| Exod. 26:33a | X | | | | | | X | | | θήσεις τὸ κ. ἐπὶ τοὺς στύλους | Veil between the holy place and holy of holies |
| Exod. 26:33b | X | | | | | | X | | | ἐσώτερον τοῦ κ. τὴν κιβωτὸν τοῦ μαρτυρίου | Veil between the holy place and holy of holies |
| Exod. 26:33c | X | | | | | | X | | | διοριεῖ τὸ κ. ὑμῖν ἀνὰ μέσον τοῦ ἁγίου | Veil between the holy place and holy of holies |
| Exod. 26:34 | X | | | | | | O' | X | | κατακαλύψεις τῷ κ. τὴν κιβωτὸν τοῦ μαρτυρίου ἐν τῷ ἁγίῳ τῶν ἁγίων | Textual confusion-inner veil/atonement cover |
| Exod. 26:35 | X | | | | | | X | | | τράπεζαν ἔξωθεν τοῦ κ. | Veil between the holy place and holy of holies |
| Exod. 26:36 | U | | | | X | Q, S | | X | | ποιήσεις ἐπίσπαστρον ἐξ ὑακίνθου | Curtain for the entrance to the tent |
| Exod. 26:37 | X | | | | | | | X | | ποιήσεις τῷ κ. πέντε στύλους | Curtain for the entrance to the tent |
| Exod. 27:21 | X | | | | | | X | | | ἔξωθεν τοῦ κ. τοῦ ἐπὶ τῆς διαθήκης | Veil between the holy place and holy of holies |
| Exod. 30:6 | X | | | | | | X | | | ἀπέναντι τοῦ κ. τοῦ ὄντος ἐπί τῆς κιβωτοῦ τῶν μαρτυρίων | Veil between the holy place and holy of holies |
| Exod. 35:12a | X | | | | | | X | X | | τὸ ἱλαστήριον αὐτῆς καὶ τό κ. | Veil between the holy place and holy of holies |
| Exod. 37:3 (MT36:35) | X | | | | | | X | | | ἐποίησαν τὸ κ. ἐξ ὑακίνθου | Veil between the holy place and holy of holies |
| Exod. 37:5 (MT36:37) | X | | | | A | | | X | | ἐποίησαν τὸ κ. τῆς θύρας τῆς σκηνῆς τοῦ μαρτυρίου | Curtain for the entrance to the tent |
| Exod. 37:16a (MT38:18a) | X | | A | | | | | X | | καὶ τὸ κ. τῆς πύλης τῆς αὐλῆς | Curtain at entrance to courtyard |
| Exod. 38:18 (MT36:35?) | X | | | | | | ? | | | κατεχρύσωσεν τοὺς στύλους τοῦ κ. χρυσίῳ | Veil between the holy place and holy of holies |
| Exod. 39:4 (MT38:27) | X | | | | | | X | | | εἰς τάς κεφαλίδας τοῦ κ. ἑκατόν κεφαλίδες | Veil between the holy place and holy of holies |

| | | | | | | | | | | | |
|---|---|---|---|---|---|---|---|---|---|---|---|
| Exod. 39:19b (MT40b) | X | | | | | | | X | | καί τὸ κ. τῆς θύρας τῆς σκηνῆς | Curtain at entrance to courtyard |
| Exod. 40:3 | X | | | | | | X | | | κατεχρύωσεν τοὺς στύλους τοῦ κ. χρυσίῳ | Veil between the holy place and holy of holies |
| Exod. 40:5 | X | | X | | T | Q, S | | X | | ἐπιθήσεις κάλυμμα κ. ἐπὶ τὴν θύραν τῆς σκηνῆς τοῦ μαρτυρίου | Curtain at entrance to courtyard |
| Exod. 40:21 | X | | | X | | | X | X | | ἐπέθηκεν τό κατακάλυμμα τοῦ κ. καὶ ἐσκέπασεν τήν κιβωτόν τοῦ μαρτυρίου | Veil between the holy place and holy of holies |
| Exod. 40:22 | X | | | | | | X | | | ἔξωθεν τοῦ κ. τῆς σκηνῆς | Veil between the holyplace and holy of holies |
| Exod. 40:26 | X | | | | | | X | | | ἐν τῇ σκηνῇ τοῦ μαρτυρίου ἀπέναντι τοῦ κ. | Veil between the holy place and holy of holies |
| Lev. 4:6 | X | | | | | | X | | | ἔναντι κυρίου κατὰ τό κ. τό ἅγιον | Veil between the holy place and holy of holies |
| Lev. 4:17 | X | | | | | | X | | | ἔναντι κυρίου κατενώπιον τοῦ κ. τοῦ ἁγίου | Veil between the holy place and holy of holies |
| Lev. 16:2 | X | | | | | | X | | | εἰς τὸ ἅγιον ἐσώτερον τοῦ κ. εἰς πρόσωπον τοῦ ἱλαστηρίου | Veil between the holy place and holy of holies |
| Lev. 16:12 | X | | | | | | X | | | καὶ εἰσοίσει ἐσώτερον τοῦ κ. | Veil between the holy place and holy of holies |
| Lev. 16:15 | X | | | | | | X | | | ἐσώτερον τοῦ κ. καὶ ποιήσει τὸ αἷμα αὐτοῦ | Veil between the holy place and holy of holies |
| Lev. 21:23 | X | | | | | | X | | | πλὴν πρὸς τὸ κ. οὐ προσελεύσεται | Veil between the holy place and holy of holies |
| Lev. 24:3 | X | | | | | | X | | | ἔξωθεν τοῦ κ. ἐν τῇ σκηνῇ τοῦ μαρτυρίου | Veil between the holy place and holy of holies |
| Num. 3:10 | X | | | | | | -- | -- | -- | ἔσω τοῦ κ. | Veil between the holy place and holy of holies |
| Num. 3:26b | X | | | | | | | X | | τὸ κ. τῆς πύλης τῆς αὐλῆς | Curtain at entrance to courtyard |
| Num. 4:5 | X | | | | | | X | X | | καθελοῦσιν τὸ κ. τὸ συσκιάζον | Veil between the holy place and holy of holies |
| Num. 4:32 | X | | | | | | -- | -- | -- | τοὺς στύλους τοῦ κ. τῆς πύλης τῆς αὐλῆς | Curtain at entrance to courtyard |
| Num. 18:7 | X | | | | | | X | | | τὸ ἔνδοθεν τοῦ κ. | Veil between the holy place and holy of holies |
| 1 Kings 6:36 | L | | | | | | ? | ? | -- | καὶ ᾠκοδόμησε κ. τῆς αὐλῆς τοῦ αιλαμ τοῦ οἴκου τοῦ | Curtain at entrance to courtyard |
| 2 Chron. 3:14 | X | | | | | | X | | | καὶ ἐποίησεν τὸ κ. ἐξ ὑακίνθου | Veil between the holy place and holy of holies |

**Key:**

| | | |
|---|---|---|
| -- = untranslated | U = unknown source(s) | T = Theodotion |
| X = single occurrence | Q = Aquila | A = Alexandrinus |
| | S = Symmachus | L = Lucian |

# BIBLIOGRAPHY


Abbott, Edwin A. *Corrections of Mark: Adopted by Matthew and Luke*. London: Adam and Charles Black, 1901.

*The Fourfold Gospel*. Section 5, *The Founding of the New Kingdom; or, Life Reached through Death*. Cambridge: Cambridge University Press, 1917.

Abbott, Lyman. *Matthew and Mark*. New York, N.Y.: A. S. Barnes, 1875.

Abel, P. F. M. *Les livres des Maccabées*. Paris: J. Gabalda, 1949.

Abrams, Daniel. 'Special Angelic Figures: The Career of the Beasts of the Throne-World in Hekhalot Literature, German Pietism and Early Kabbalistic Literature', *Revue des Études Juives* 155 (1996), 363–86.

Achtemeier, P. J. 'An Apocalyptic Shift in Early Christian Tradition: Reflections on Some Canonical Evidence', *CBQ* 45 (1983), 231–48.

Adams, H. C. *The Greek Text of the Gospels: Part I – St Matthew*. London: David Nutt, 1867.

Ådna, Jostein. *Jesu Stellung zum Tempel: Die Tempelaktion und das Tempelwort als Ausdruck seiner messianischen Sendung*. Wissenschaftliche Untersuchungen zum Neuen Testament 2, 119. Tübingen: Mohr Siebeck, 2000.

Aejmelaeus, Anneli. *Parataxis in the Septuagint: A Study of the Rendering of the Hebrew Coordinate Clauses in the Greek Pentateuch*. Annales Academiae Scientiarum Fennicae: Dissertationes Humanarum Litterarum 31. Helsinki: Suomalainen Tiedeakatemia, 1982.

'What Can We Know about the Hebrew *Vorlage* of the Septuagint', *ZAW* 99 (1987), 58–89.

'Septuagintal Translation Techniques – A Solution to the Problem of the Tabernacle Account', pp. 381–402 in *Septuagint, Scrolls and Cognate Writings*. Septuagint and Cognate Studies 33. Edited by George J. Brooke and Barnabas Lindas. Atlanta, Ga.: Scholars Press, 1992.

Aguirre Monasterio, Rafael. *Exégesis de Mateo, 27, 51b–53: para una teologia de la muerte de Jesus en el Evangelio de Mateo*. Vitoria: Editorial Eset, 1980.

'Cross and Kingdom in Matthew's Theology', *Theology Digest* 29 (1981), 149–53.

Aland, K., ed. *Synopsis Quattuor Evangeliorum*. 9th edn. Stuttgart: Deutsche Bibelstiftung, 1976.

and Barbara Aland. *The Text of the New Testament: An Introduction to the Critical Editions and to the Theory and Practice of Modern Textual Criticism*. 2d edn. Translated by E. F. Rhodes. Grand Rapids, Mich.: Eerdmans, 1989.

Albright, W. F., and C. S. Mann. *Matthew: A New Translation with Introduction and Commentary*. Anchor Bible Commentary 26. New York, N.Y.: Doubleday, 1971.

Alexander, J. A. *The Gospel according to St Matthew*. London: Nisbet, 1761.

Alexander, P. '3 Enoch', *OTP* I, pp. 223–315.

Alexander, T. Desmond, and David W. Baker, eds. *Dictionary of the Old Testament: Pentateuch*. Downers Grove, Ill.: InterVarsity, 2003.

Alexandre, Monique. 'L'épée de flamme (Gen. 3, 24): textes chrétiens et traditions juives', pp. 403–41 in *Hellenica et Judaica: Hommage à Valentin Nikiprovetzky*. Edited by André Caquot, Mireille Hadas-Lebel, and J. Riand. Leuven: Peeters, 1986.

Alford, Henry. *The Greek Testament*. 4 vols. London: Rivingstons, 1871–74.

Allen, Leslie C. *The Greek Chronicles – The Relation of the Septuagint of I and II Chronicles to the Masoretic Text*. 2 vols. Leiden: Brill, 1974.

*Ezekiel*. 2 vols. WBC 28–29. Dallas, Tex.: Word, 1990, 1994.

Allen, Willoughby Charles. *A Critical and Exegetical Commentary on the Gospel according to S. Matthew*. ICC. Edinburgh: T. & T. Clark, 1912.

Allenbach, J., A. Benoît, D. A. Bertrand, A. Hanriot-Coustet, P. Maraval, A. Pautler and P. Prigent, eds. *Biblica Patristica: Index des citations et allusions bibliques dans la literature Patristiqe*. 4 vols. Paris: Editions du Centre national de la recherche scientifique, 1975–87.

Allison, Dale C. 'Matt. 23.39 = Lk 13.35b as a Conditional Prophecy', *JSNT* 18 (1983), 75–84

'Elijah Must Come First', *JBL* 103 (1984), 256–58.

*The End of the Ages Has Come: An Early Interpretation of the Passion and Resurrection of Jesus*. Philadelphia, Pa.: Fortress, 1985.

'The Son of God as Israel: A Note on Matthean Christology', *IBS* 9 (1987), 74–81.

'Matthew: Structure, Biographical Impulse and the *Imatatio Christi*', pp. 1203–21 in *The Four Gospels, 1992*. Edited by Frans van Segbroeck *et al*. Bibliotheca ephemeridum theologicarum lovaniensium 100. Leuven: Leuven University Press, 1992.

*The New Moses: A Matthean Typology*. Edinburgh: T. & T. Clark, 1993.

'Apocalyptic', *DJG*, pp. 17–20.

Anderson, A. A. *2 Samuel*. WBC 11. Dallas, Tex.: Word, 1989.

Anderson, Gary A. 'Worship, Qumran Sect', *EDSS* II, pp. 991–96.

Anderson, Hugh. *The Gospel of Mark*. NCB. London: Oliphants, 1976.

Anderson, Janice Capel. *Matthew's Narrative Web: Over, and Over, and Over Again*. JSNTSup 91. Sheffield: JSOT Press, 1994.

Andreoli, Dante. 'Il velo squarciato nel Vangelo di Matteo', *BSW* 1 (1998), 20–42.

Aquinas, Saint Thomas. *Catena aurea*. Translated by J. H. Newman and A. Nichols. Commentary on the Four Gospels Collected Out of the Works of the Fathers. London: Saint Austin, 1997.

Argyle, A. W. *The Gospel according to Matthew*. Cambridge: Cambridge University Press, 1963.

Arvedson, Tomas. *Das Mysterium Christi: eine Studie zu Mt 11.25–30*. Leipzig: Alfred Lorentz, 1937.

Ascough, R. S. 'Matthew and Community Formation', pp. 96–126 in *The Gospel of Matthew in Current Study: Studies in Memory of William G. Thompson, S. J.* Edited by D. Aune. Grand Rapids, Mich.: Eerdmans, 2001.

Attridge, Harold W. *The Epistle to the Hebrews*. Hermeneia. Philadelphia, Pa.: Fortress, 1989.

Review of Gideon Bohak, *'Joseph and Aseneth' and the Jewish Temple at Heliopolis*, *CBQ* 60 (1998), 555–57.

Aune, David E. *Prophecy in Early Christianity and the Ancient Mediterranean World*. Grand Rapids, Mich.: Eerdmans, 1983.

*The New Testament in Its Literary Environment*. Philadelphia, Pa.: Westminster, 1987.

*Revelation*. 3 vols. WBC 52A–C. Dallas, Tex.: Word, 1997, 1998.

ed. *The Gospel of Matthew in Current Study*. Grand Rapids, Mich.: Eerdmans, 2001.

with Eric Stewart. 'From the Idealized Past to the Imaginary Future: Eschatological Restoration in Jewish Apocalyptic Literature', pp. 147–78 in *Restoration: Old Testament, Jewish and Christian Perspectives*. Edited by James. M. Scott. Leiden: Brill, 2001.

Aus, Roger David. *Samuel, Saul and Jesus: Three Early Palestinian Jewish Christian Gospel Haggadoth*. South Florida Studies in the History of Judaism 105. Atlanta, Ga.: Scholars Press, 1994.

Averbeck, Richard E. 'The Cylinders of Gudea', pp. 417–33 in *The Context of Scripture, Vol. 2, Monumental Inscriptions from the Biblical World*. Edited by W. W. Hallo and K. L. Younger. Leiden: Brill, 2000.

'Sacrifices and Offerings', *DOTP*, pp. 706–33.

'מוֹעֵד', *NIDOTTE* II, p. 873.

'פרכת', *NIDOTTE* III, pp. 687–89.

'Tabernacle', *DOTP*, pp. 807–27.

Avi-Yonah, M. 'The Second Temple', pp. 396–97 in *Sepher Yerushalayim*. Edited by M. Avi-Yonah. Jerusalem: Bialik, 1956 [Hebrew].

Bacon, B. W. 'The "Five Books" of Moses against the Jews', *Expositor* (1918), 56–66.

*Studies in Matthew*. London: Constable, 1930.

Bailey, Kenneth E. 'The Fall of Jerusalem and Mark's Account of the Cross', *Expository Times* 102 (1991), 102–5.

Balentine, Samuel E. *The Hidden God: The Hiding of the Face of God in the Old Testament*. Oxford: Oxford University Press, 1983.

*The Torah's Vision of Worship*. Minneapolis, Minn.: Fortress, 1999.

Balch, David L., ed. *Social History of the Matthean Community: Cross-Disciplinary Approaches*. Minneapolis, Minn.: Fortress, 1991.

Banks, E. J. 'Color', *ISBE* I, p. 743.

Banning, J. van. *Opus Imperfectum in Matthaeum*. Turnholti: Brepols, 1988.

Bar-Efrat, Shimon. 'Some Observations on the Analysis of Structure in Biblical Narrative', *VT* 30 (1980), 154–73.

Bar Hebraeus, Spanuth Johannes. *Gregorii Abulfarag bar Ebhraya in Evangelium Matthaei scholia*. Göttigen: Dieterichaianis, 1879.

Barker, Margaret. *The Gate of Heaven: The History and Symbolism of the Temple in Jerusalem*. London: SPCK, 1991.

'Beyond the Veil of the Temple: The High Priestly Origins of the Apocalypse', *SJT* 51 (1998), 1–21.

*The Revelation of Jesus Christ: Which God Gave to Him to Show to His Servants What Must Soon Take Place*. Edinburgh: T. & T. Clark, 2000.

Barnes, Albert. *The Gospels*. 2 vols. Edinburgh: Blackie & Son, 1841.

Barnett, F. W. 'Characterization and Christology in Matthew: Jesus in the Gospel of Matthew', *SBLSP* 28 (1989), 588–603.

Barr, James. '"Thou art the Cherub": Ezekiel 28.14 and the Post-Ezekiel Understanding of Genesis 2–3', pp. 213–23 in *Priests, Prophets and Scribes: Essays on the Formation and Heritage of Second Temple Judaism in Honour of Joseph Blenkinsopp*. JSOTSup 149. Edited by Eugene Charles Ulrich, Robert P. Carroll and John W. Wright. Sheffield: JSOT Press, 1992.

Barrick, W. Boyd. 'The Straight-Legged Cherubim of Ezekiel's Inaugural Vision (Ezekiel 1:7a)', *CBQ* 44 (1982), 543–50.

Barth, Markus. *Ephesians 1–3*. ABC 34. Garden City, N.Y.: Doubleday, 1974.

Barthélemy, D., and O. Rickenbacher. *Konkordanz zum Hebräischen Sirach mit Syrisch-Hebräischem Index*. Göttingen: Vandenhoeck & Ruprecht, 1973.

Bauckham, Richard J. 'Synoptic Parousia Parables and the Apocalypse', *NTS* 23 (1976), 162–76.

'The Eschatological Earthquake in the Apocalypse of John', *NovT* 19 (1977), 224–33.

'The Delay of the Parousia', *TynB* 31 (1980), 3–36.

'A Note on a Problem in the Greek Version of I Enoch i.9', *JTS* 32 (1981), 136–38.

'Synoptic Parousia Parables Again', *NTS* 29 (1983), 129–134.

'The Apocalypses in the New Pseudepigrapha', *JSNT* 26 (1986), 97–117.

'The Coin in the Fish's Mouth', pp. 219–52 in *The Miracles of Jesus*. Edited by D. Wenham and C. Blomberg. Vol. 6 of *Gospel Perspectives*. Sheffield: JSOT Press, 1986.

'Jesus' Demonstration in the Temple', pp. 72–89 in *Law and Religion: Essays on the Place of the Law in Israel and Early Christianity*. Edited by B. Lindars. Cambridge: James Clarke, 1988.

'Descent to the Underworld', *ABD* II, pp. 145–59.

'The Parting of the Ways: What Happened and Why', *Studia Theologica* 47 (1993), 135–51.

*The Climax of Prophecy: Studies on the Book of Revelation*. Edinburgh: T. & T. Clark, 1993.

*The Theology of the Book of Revelation*. Cambridge: Cambridge University Press, 1993.

'The Relevance of Extra-Canonical Jewish Texts to New Testament Study', pp. 90–108 in *Hearing the New Testament*. Edited by Joel Green. Grand Rapids, Mich.: Eerdmans, 1995.

'The Parable of the Royal Wedding Feast (Matthew 22:1–14) and the Parable of the Lame Man and the Blind Man (*Apocryphon of Ezekiel*)', *JBL* 115 (1996), 447–64.

'Josephus' Account of the Temple in *Contra Apionem* 2.102–109', pp. 327–47 in *Josephus' Contra Apionem: Studies in Its Character and Context with a*

*Latin Concordance to the Portion Missing in Greek*. Edited by L. H. Feldman and J. R. Levison. Arbeiten zur Geschichte des antiken Judentums und des Urchirstentums 34. Leiden: Brill, 1996.

*God Crucified: Monotheism and Christology in the New Testament*. Grand Rapids, Mich.: Eerdmans, 1998.

ed. *The Gospels for All Christians: Rethinking the Gospel Audiences*. Grand Rapids, Mich.: Eerdmans, 1998.

'The Restoration of Israel in Luke-Acts', pp. 435–87 in *Restoration: Old Testament, Jewish and Christian Perspectives*. Edited by J. M. Scott. Leiden: Brill, 2001.

Bauer, David R. *The Structure of Matthew's Gospel: A Study in Literary Design*. JSNTSup 31. Sheffield: Almond Press, 1988.

and Mark Allan Powell, eds. *Treasures New and Old: Recent Contributions to Matthean Studies*. Society of Biblical Literature Symposium Series 1. Atlanta, Ga.: Scholars Press, 1996.

Bauer, Hans, Pontus Leander and Paul Kahle. *Historische Grammatik der hebräischen Sprache des Altes Testaments*. Hildesheim: Olms, 1918–1922.

Bauer, Walter. *Das Leben Jesu im Zeitalter der neutestamentlichen Apokryphen*. Tübingen: Mohr Siebeck, 1909.

*Griechisch-deutsches Wörterbuch zu den Schriften des Neuen Testaments und der frühchristlichen Literatur*. 5th edn. Berlin: De Gruyter, 1963.

Baumgarten, Joseph M. 'The Qumran Shabbath Shirot and Rabbinic Merkabah Traditions', *RevQ* 13 (1988), 199–213.

'Damascus Document', *EDSS* I, pp. 166–170.

'Sacrifice and Worship among the Jewish Sectarians of the Dead Sea', *HTR* 46 (1953), 141–60.

Baumgartner, Walter, and Ludwig Koehler. *Hebräisches und Aramäisches Lexikon zum Alten Testament*. 5 vols. Leiden: Brill, 1967.

Beale, G. K. 'The Use of Daniel in the Synoptic Eschatological Discourse and in the Book of Revelation', pp. 129–53 in *The Jesus Tradition outside the Gospels*. Edited by D. Wenham. Vol. 5 of *Gospel Perspectives*. Sheffield: JSOT Press, 1984.

*The Use of Daniel in Jewish Apocalyptic Literature and in the Revelation of St John*. Lanham, Md.: University Press of America, 1984.

*The Book of Revelation*. NIGTC. Grand Rapids, Mich.: Eerdmans, 1998.

*The Bible and the Church's Mission: A Biblical Theology of the Temple*. NSBT. Downers Grove, Ill.: InterVarsity, 2004.

Beare, Francis Wright. *The Gospel according to Matthew: Translation, Introduction, and Commentary*. Peabody, Mass.: Hendrickson, 1987.

Beasley-Murray, George R. *Jesus and the Future: An Examination of the Criticism of the Eschatological Discourse, Mark 13: With Special Reference to the Little Apocalypse Theory*. London: Macmillan, 1954.

*Commentary on Mark Thirteen*. London: Macmillan, 1957.

*Matthew*. London: Scripture Union, 1984.

*Jesus and the Kingdom of God*. Exeter: Paternoster, 1985.

*John*. WBC 36. Waco, Tex.: Word, 1987.

Beaton, Richard. *Isaiah's Christ in Matthew's Gospel*. SNTSMS 123. Cambridge: Cambridge University Press, 2002.

Beausobre, Isaac de, and Jacques Lenfant. *A New Version of the Gospel according to St Matthew*. London: Whittaker & Co., 1837.

Becker, Hans Jürgen. 'Die Zerstörung Jerusalems bei Matthäus und den Rabbinen', *NTS* 44 (1998), 59–73.

Beckwith, R. *The Old Testament Canon of the New Testament and Its Background in Early Judaism*. London: SPCK, 1985.

Ben-Dov, Meir. *In the Shadow of the Temple: The Discovery of Ancient Judaism*. Translated by I. Friedman. New York, N.Y.: Harper & Row, 1985.

Bendinelli, Guido. *Il commentario a Matteo di Origene: l'ambito della metodologia scolastica dell'antichità*. Roma: Institutum patristicum Augustinianum, 1997.

Bengel, Johann Albrecht. *Gnomon of the New Testament*. Vol. 1. Translated by A. R. Fausset. Edinburgh: T. & T. Clark, 1877.

Ben-Mordecai, C. A. 'The Iniquity of the Sanctuary', *JBL* 60 (1941), 311–14.

Benoit, Pierre. 'La mort de Judas', pp. 341–59 in vol. 4 of *Exégèse et théologie*. 4 vols. Edited by P. Benoit. Paris: Cerf, 1961–82.

*The Passion and Resurrection of Jesus Christ*. Translated by B. Weatherhead. New York, N.Y.: Herder & Herder, 1969.

*L'Évangile selon S. Matthieu*. 4th ed. Paris: Cerf, 1972.

Bentwich, Norman. *Josephus*. Philadelphia, Pa.: Jewish Publication Society, 1914.

Best, Ernest. *A Commentary on the First and Second Epistles to the Thessalonians*. London: A. and C. Black, 1972.

Betz, H. D. 'The Logion of the Easy Yoke and of Rest (Matt 11:28–30)', *JBL* 86 (1967), 10–24.

Bidez, Joseph, *et al.*, eds. *Die Griechischen Christlichen Schriftsteller der Ersten Drei Jahrhunderte*. Berlin: Akademie-Verlag, 1981-continuous

Bieder, W. *Die Vorstelling von der Höllenfahrt Jesu Christi*. Zürich: Zwingli, 1949.

Bietenhard, Hans. *Die himmlische Welt im Urchristentum und Spätjudentum*. WUNT 2. Tübingen: Mohr Siebeck, 1951.

Bilde, P. 'Josephus and Jewish Apocalypticism', pp. 35–61 in *Understanding Josephus: Seven Perspectives*. Edited by S. Mason. JSPSup 32. Sheffield: Academic Press, 1998.

Black, M. 'The Christological Use of the Old Testament in the New Testament', *NTS* 18 (1971), 1–14.

Black, Stephanie L. *Sentence Conjunctions in the Gospel of Matthew: καί, δέ, τότε, γάρ, οὖν and Aysndeton in Narrative Discourse*. JSNTSup 216. SNTG 9. Sheffield: Academic Press, 2002.

Blank, Sheldon H. 'Death of Zechariah in Rabbinic Literature', *HUCA* 13 (1938), 327–46.

Blass, F., A. Debrunner, and Robert W. Funk. *A Greek Grammar of the New Testament and Other Early Christian Literature*. Chicago, Ill.: University of Chicago Press, 1961.

Bleek, Friedrich. *Synoptische Erklärung der drei ersten Evangelien*. Edited by H. Holtzmann. Leipzig: Engelmann, 1862.

Blenkensopp, J. 'The Bible, Archaeology and Politics; or The Empty Land Revisited', *JSOT* 27 (2002), 169–87.

Blinzler, J. 'Zuı Erklärung von Mt 27, 51b–53. Totenauferstehung am Karfrietag?' *T&G* 35 (1943), 91–93.

Block, Daniel I. *The Book of Ezekiel.* 2 vols. NICOT. Grand Rapids, Mich.: Eerdmans, 1997, 1998.

Blomberg, Craig L. *Matthew.* Nashville, Tenn.: Broadman, 1992.

*Jesus and the Gospels: An Introduction and Survey.* Nashville, Tenn.: Broadman & Holman, 1997.

'Interpreting Old Testament Prophetic Literature in Matthew: Double Fulfillment', *TJ* 23 (2002), 17–33.

Bock, Darrell L. *Luke.* 2 vols. BECNT. Grand Rapids, Mich.: Baker, 1994, 1996.

Bockmuehl, Marcus. 'Why Did Jesus Predict the Destruction of the Temple?' *Crux* 25 (1989), 11–18.

*Revelation and Mystery in Ancient Judaism and Pauline Christianity.* Grand Rapids, Mich.: Eerdmans, 1997.

Boda, Mark J. and Michael H. Floyd, eds. *Bringing out the Treasure: Inner Biblical Allusion in Zechariah 9–14.* JSOTSup 370. London: Sheffield Academic Press, 2003.

Bohak, Gideon. *'Joseph and Aseneth' and the Jewish Temple in Heliopolis.* Atlanta, Ga.: Scholars Press, 1996.

Bonnard, Pierre. *L'Évangile selon Saint Matthieu.* Neuchâtel: Delachaux & Niestlé, 1963.

Bonner, C. 'Two Problems in Melito's Homily on the Passion', *HTR* 31 (1938), 175–90.

Borgen, Peder, and Søren Giversen, eds. *The New Testament and Hellenistic Judaism.* Peabody, Mass.: Hendrickson, 1997.

Bornkamm, Günther, Gerhard Barth and Heinz Joachim Held. *Tradition and Interpretation in Matthew.* Philadelphia, Pa.: Westminster, 1963.

'End Expectation and Church in Matthew', pp. 15–51 in *Tradition and Interpretation in Matthew.* Edited by G. Bornkamm, M. Barth, and H. J. Held. Philadelphia, Pa.: Westminster, 1963.

'Μυστήριον', *TDNT* IV, p. 815.

Borowski, Elie. 'Cherubim: God's Throne?' *BAR* 21 (1995), 36–41.

Botha, S. P. ''n Opstanding met verheerlikte liggame in Matteus 27:51b–53? 'Noukeurige lees van die teks', *Hervormde Teologiese Studies* 52 (1996), 270–84.

Bousset, Wilhelm. *Die Religion des Judentums im späthellenistischen Zeitalter.* Tübingen: Mohr Siebeck, 1966.

Box, B. G. H., and W. O. E. Oesterley. 'Sirach', in *Apocrypha,* vol. 1 of *The Apocrypha and Pseudepigrapha of the Old Testament in English.* 2 vols. Edited by R. H. Charles. Oxford: Clarendon, 1913.

Brabar, A. 'Le theme religieux des fresques de la synagogue de Doura (245–56 après J. C.)', *Revue de l'histoire des religions* 123 (1941), 143–92.

Brand, J. 'Concerning an Article on the Second Temple', *Tarbiz* 29 (1960), 210–16 [Hebrew].

Brandon, S. G. F. *The Fall of Jerusalem and the Christian Church: A Study of the Effects of the Jewish Overthrow of A.D. 70 on Christianity.* London: SPCK, 1951.

'The Date of the Markan Gospel', *NTS* 7 (1961), 126–41.

Brenner, A. *Colour Terms in the Old Testament.* JSOTSup 21. Sheffield: JSOT Press, 1982.

Brésard, Luc, Henri Crouzel, and Marcel Borret, eds. *Sources Chrétiennes.* 20 vols. Paris: Cerf, 1991.

Brin, Gershon. 'Issues Concerning Prophets (Studies in 4Q375)', pp. 128–63 in *Studies in Biblical Law: From the Hebrew Bible to the Dead Sea Scrolls.* JSOTSup 176. Sheffield: JSOT Press, 1994.

Broer, Ingo. 'Bemerkungen zur Redaktion der Passiongsgeschichte durch Matthäus', pp. 11–24 in *Studien zum Matthäusevangelium: Festschrift für Wilhelm Pesch.* Edited by Ludger Schenke. Stuttgart: Katholisches Bibelwerk, 1988.

Brooke, Alan England, and Norman McLean, eds. *The Old Testament in Greek: According to the Text of Codex Vaticanus, Supplemented from Other Uncial Manuscripts, with a Critical Apparatus Containing the Varia New Testament Studies of the Chief Ancient Authorities for the Text of the Septuagint.* Cambridge: Cambridge University Press, 1909.

Brooke, George J., ed. *Temple Scroll Studies.* JSPSup 7. Sheffield: JSOT Press, 1989.

'4Q500 1 and the Use of Scripture in the Parable of the Vineyard', *DSD* 2 (1995), 279–85

Brooks, E. W., ed. *Historia Ecclesiastica Zachariae Rhetori Vulgo Adscripta.* 2 vols. Corpus Scriptorum Christianorum Orientalium 83. Leuven: Imprimerie Orientaliste L. Durbecq, 1953, 1965.

Brooks, Stephenson H. *Matthew's Community: The Evidence of His Special Sayings Material.* JSNTSup 16. Sheffield: JSOT Press, 1987.

Bromiley, Geoffrey W., ed. *The International Standard Bible Encyclopedia.* 4 vols. Grand Rapids, Mich.: Eerdmans, 1979–88.

Brotzman, Ellis R. *Old Testament Textual Criticism.* Grand Rapids, Mich.: Baker, 1994.

Brown, Colin, ed. *The New International Dictionary of New Testament Theology.* 4 vols. Exeter: Paternoster, 1975–1986.

Brown, D. 'The Veil of the Temple Rent in Twain from the Top to the Bottom', *Expositor* 5th Series, 2 (1895), 158–60.

Brown, Raymond E. *The Gospel according to John XIII–XXI: A New Translation with Introduction and Commentary.* ABC 29A. New York, N.Y.: Doubleday, 1970.

*The Death of the Messiah: A Commentary on the Passion Narratives in the Four Gospels.* 2 vols. New York, N.Y.: Doubleday, 1994.

'Eschatological Events Accompanying the Death of Jesus, Especially the Raising of the Holy Ones from their Tombs', pp. 43–73 in *Faith and the Future.* Edited by John P. Galvin. New York, N.Y.: Paulist Press, 1994.

Bruce, Alexander Balmain. 'The Synoptic Gospels', pp. 1–651 in vol. 1 of *The Expositor's Greek Testament.* 5 vols. Edited by W. Robertson Nicoll. London: Hodder & Stoughton, 1897.

Bruce, F. F. *Matthew.* London: Scripture Union, 1978.

Bruce, William. *Commentary on the Gospel according to St Matthew.* London: Speirs, 1877.

Brueggemann, Walter. *Isaiah 40–66.* Westminster Bible Companion. Louisville, Ky.: Westminster John Knox, 1998.

Bruyne, Donatien de, and Bonaventure Sodar, eds. *Les Anciennes Traductions Latines des Machabées*. Bruges: Abbaye de Maredsous, 1932.
Bryan, Steven M. *Jesus and Israel's Traditions of Judgment and Restoration*. SNTSMS 117. Cambridge: Cambridge University Press, 2002.
Büchler, Adolf. 'Die Erlösung Eliša b. Abujahs aus dem Höllenfeuer', *Monatschrift für Geschicthe und Wissenschaft des Judentusm* 76 (1932), 412–56.
Budd, Philip J. *Numbers*. WBC 5. Waco, Tex.: Word, 1984.
Bullard, Roger A. Review of O. Hofius, *Der Vorhang vor dem Thron Gottes*, *JBL* 93 (1974), 124–26.
Bultmann, Rudolf. *Die Geschichte der synoptischen Tradition*. Göttingen: Vandenhoeck & Ruprecht, 1921.
Burchard, Christoph. *Untersuchungen zu Joseph und Aseneth: Überlieferung-Ortsbestimmung*. WUNT 8. Tübingen: Mohr Siebeck, 1965.
'Joseph and Aseneth', *OTP* II, pp. 177–248.
Burnett, Fred W. *The Testament of Jesus-Sophia: A Redaction-Critical Study of the Eschatological Discourse in Matthew*. Washington, D.C.: University Press of America, 1981.
Burney, C. F. *Notes on the Hebrew Text of the Books of Kings*. Oxford: Clarendon, 1903.
Burns, Paul C. *The Christology in Hilary of Poitiers' Commentary on Matthew*. Oxford: Oxford University Press, 1977.
Burridge, Richard A. *What are the Gospels? A Comparison with Greco-Roman Biography*. SNTSMS 70. Cambridge: Cambridge University Press, 1992.
Busink, T. A. *Der Tempel von Jerusalem von Salomo bis Herodes*. Studia Francisci Scholten memoriae dicta 3. Leiden: Brill, 1970.
Butler, B. C. *The Originality of St Matthew: A Critique of the Two-Document Hypothesis*. Cambridge: Cambridge University Press, 1951.
Caldecott, W. S. 'Laver', *ISBE* III, p. 76.
Calvin, Jean. *A Harmony of the Gospels, Matthew, Mark, and Luke*. Edited by David W. Torrance and Thomas F. Torrance. Translated by A. W. Morrison and T. H. L. Parker. Grand Rapids, Mich.: Eerdmans, 1972. Translation of *Harmonia ex tribus Euangelistis composite*. Geneva: Vignon, 1555.
Cargal, Timothy B. '"His Blood Be upon Us and upon Our Children": A Matthean Double Entendre?' *NTS* 37 (1991), 101–12.
Carpenter, E. E. 'Sacrifices and Offerings in the OT', *ISBE* IV, pp. 260–73.
Carr, G. L. and Nola J. Opperwall. 'Presence, Bread of the', *ISBE* III, pp. 955–56.
Carr, A. *The Gospel according to St Matthew*. Cambridge: Cambridge University Press, 1887.
Carroll, John T. and Joel B. Green. *The Death of Jesus in Early Christianity*. Peabody, Mass.: Hendrickson, 1995.
Carson, D. A. 'Matthew', pp. 3–599 in vol. 8 of *The Expositor's Bible Commentary*. Edited by Frank Gaebelein. Grand Rapids, Mich.: Zondervan, 1984.
Carter, Warren. *Matthew: Storyteller, Interpreter, Evangelist*. Peabody, Mass.: Hendrickson, 1996.
Review of Ulrich Luz, *The Theology of the Gospel of Matthew*, *RBL* (June26, 2000).
Cassuto, Umberto. 'The Palace of Baal', *JBL* 61 (1942), 51–56.

*A Commentary on the Book of Genesis*. 2 vols. Translated by I. Abrahams. Jerusalem: Magnes Press, 1961, 1964.

*Commentary on the Book of Exodus*. Translated by I. Abrahams. Jerusalem: Magnes Press, 1967.

Celada, B. 'El velo del Templo', *Cultura bíblica* 15 (1958), 109–12.

Charles, R. H., ed. *The Apocrypha and Pseudepigrapha of the Old Testament in English*. 2 vols. Oxford: Oxford University Press, 1913.

*Religious Development between the Old and the New Testaments*. London: Williams and Norgate, 1919.

Charlesworth, James H., ed. *The Messiah: Developments in Earliest Judaism and Christianity*. Minneapolis, Minn.: Fortress, 1982.

ed. *The Old Testament Pseudepigrapha*. 2 vols. New York, N.Y.: Doubleday, 1983, 1985.

*The Old Testament Pseudepigrapha and the New Testament: Prolegomena for the Study of Christian Origins*. SNTSMS 54. Cambridge: Cambridge University Press, 1985.

'The Pseudepigrapha as Biblical Exegesis', pp. 139–52 in *Early Jewish and Christian Exegesis*. Edited by Craig A. Evans and W. F. Stinespring. Atlanta, Ga.: Scholars Press, 1987.

*Graphic Concordance to the Dead Sea Scrolls*. Tübingen: Mohr Siebeck, 1991.

Chevallier, M. A. *L'Esprit et le Messie dans le Bas-Judaïsme et le Nouveau Testament*. Paris: Presses Universitaires de France, 1958.

Childs, Brevard S. *The Book of Exodus: A Critical, Theological Commentary*. Old Testament Library. Philadelphia, Pa.: Westminster, 1974.

*Isaiah*. Old Testament Library. Louisville, Ky.: Westminster John Knox, 2001.

Chilton, Bruce D. 'The Transfiguration: Dominical Assurance and Apocalyptic Vision', *NTS* 27 (1980), 115–24.

*A Galilean Rabbi and His Bible: Jesus' Own Interpretation of Isaiah*. London: SPCK, 1984.

*Targumic Approaches to the Gospels: Essays in the Mutual Definition of Judaism and Early Christianity*. Studies in Judaism. Lanham, Md.: University Press of America, 1986.

'Temple Restored, Temple in Heaven: Isaiah and the Prophets in the Targumim', pp. 335–64 in *Restoration: Old Testament, Jewish and Christian Perspectives*. Edited by James M. Scott. Leiden: Brill, 2001.

Chronis, Harry L. 'The Torn Veil: Cultus and Christology in Mark 15:37–39', *JBL* 101 (1982), 97–114.

Clark, E. G., *et al.*, eds. *Targum Pseudo-Jonathan of the Pentateuch: Text and Concordance*. Hoboken, N.J.: Ktav, 1984.

Clarke, Howard. *The Gospel of Matthew and Its Readers: A Historical Introduction to the First Gospel*. Bloomington, Inn.: Indiana University Press, 2003.

Clemen, Carl Christian. *Religionsgeschtliche Erklärung des Neuen Testaments*. Giessen: A. Töpelmann, 1924.

Clements, Ronald E. *God and Temple*. Philadelphia, Pa.: Fortress, 1965.

*Old Testament Theology: A Fresh Approach*. Marshalls Theological Library. London: Marshall, Morgan & Scott, 1978.

Clermont-Ganneau, Charles. *Le dieu satrape et les Phéniciens dans le Péloponèse*. Paris: Imprimiere nationale, 1878.

Clifford. Richard J. 'The Tent of El and the Israelite Tent of Meeting', *CBQ* 33 (1971), 221–27.

Coghlan, Charles Lambert. *A Scriptural Commentary, on the Book of Genesis and the Gospel according to St Matthew*. London: James Duncan, 1832.

Cohen, Shaye J. D. *Josephus in Galilee and Rome: His Vita and Development as a Historian*. Leiden: Brill, 1979.

*From Maccabees to Mishnah*. Philadelphia, Pa.: Westminster, 1989.

'The Destruction: From Scripture to Midrash', *Prooftexts* 2 (1982), 18–39.

Cole, R. A. *Exodus*. Downers Grove, Ill.: InterVarsity, 1973.

Colemann, Gillis Byrns. 'The Phenomenon of Christian Interpolations into Jewish Apocalyptic Text: A Bibliographical Survey and Methodological Analysis', Ph.D. diss., Vanderbilt University, 1976.

Collins, John J. 'A Throne in the Heavens: Apotheosis in Pre-Christian Judaism', pp. 43–57 in *Death, Ecstasy, and Other Worldly Journeys*. Edited by John J. Collins and Michael Fishbane. New York, N.Y.: State University of New York Press, 1995.

*The Apocalyptic Imagination: An Introduction to Jewish Apocalyptic Literature*. 2d edn. Grand Rapids, Mich.: Eerdmans, 1998.

Colwell, Ernest C. 'A Definite Rule for the Use of the Article in the Greek New Testament', *JBL* 52 (1933), 12–21.

Conder, Colonol. *Tent Work in Palestine: A Record of Discovery and Adventure*. New York, N.Y.: Appleton, 1878.

Conybeare, F. C. and St George Stock. *Grammar of Septuagint Greek*. Peabody, Mass.: Hendrickson, 1995.

Conzelmann, H. 'Historie und Theologie in den synoptischen Passionsberichten', pp. 35–53 in *Zur Bedeutung des Todes Jesu: Exegetische Beiträge*. Edited by H. Conzelmann, *et al.* Gütersloh: Mohn, 1967.

Cook, Stephen L. 'Creation Archetypes and Mythogems in Ezekiel: Significance and Theological Ramifications', *SBLSP* 38 (1999), 123–46.

Cooke, G. A. *The Book of Ezekiel*. ICC. Edinburgh: T. & T. Clark, 1936.

Cope, O. Lamar. *Matthew: A Scribe Trained for the Kingdom of Heaven*. CBQMS 5. Washington, D.C.: Catholic Biblical Association of America, 1976.

'"To the Close of the Age": The Role of Apocalyptic Thought in the Gospel of Matthew', pp. 113–24 in *Apocalyptic and the New Testament: Essays in Honour of J. Louis Martyn* JSNTSup 24. Edited by J. Marcus and M. L. Soards. Sheffield: Aacademic Press, 1989.

Cox, George Ernest Pritchard. *The Gospel according to St Matthew: A Commentary*. London: SCM Press, 1952.

Cranfield, C. E. B. *The Gospel according to Saint Mark*. Cambridge: Cambridge University Press, 1959.

Crosby, Michael H. *House of Disciples: Church, Economics, and Justice in Matthew*. Maryknoll, N.Y.: Orbis Books, 1988.

Cross, Frank Moore. 'The Tabernacle: A Study from an Archaeological and Historical Approach', *Biblical Archaeologist* 10 (1947), 45–68.

'The Priestly Tabernacle', pp. 201–28 in *The Biblical Archaeologist Reader*. Vol. 1. Edited by G. Ernest Wright and David Noel Freedman. Garden City, N.Y.: Doubleday, 1961.

'The Priestly Tabernacle and the Temple of Solomon', pp. 84–95 in *From Epic to Canon: History and Literature in Ancient Israel*. Baltimore, Md.: Johns Hopkins University Press, 1998.

Crossan, John Dominic. *The Cross that Spoke*. San Francisco, Calif.: Harper & Row, 1988.

*The Historical Jesus: The Life of a Mediterranean Jewish Peasant*. San Francisco, Calif.: Harper Collins, 1991.

*The Birth of Christianity: Discovering What Happened in the Years Immediately After the Execution of Jesus*. Edinburgh: T. & T. Clark, 1999.

Curtis, Edward Lewis. *The Books of Chronicles*. ICC. Edinburgh: T. & T. Clark, 1910.

Curtis, John B. 'An Investigation of the Mount of Olives in the Judaeo-Christian Tradition', *HUCA* 28 (1957), 137–80.

Cyril of Alexandria. *A Commentary on the Gospel according to St John*. Translated by Members of the English Church. 2 vols. Oxford: James Parker & Co., 1874.

*Commentary on John*. pp. 639–42 in vol. 2 of *A Library of Fathers of the Holy Catholic Church*. 2 vols. Translator unknown. London: Walter Smith, 1885.

Dahl, N. A. 'The Passion Narrative in Matthew', pp. 53–68 in *The Interpretation of Matthew*. Edited by G. N. Stanton. Edinburgh: T. & T. Clark, 1995. Repr. from *Jesus in the Memory of the Early Church*. Minneapolis, Minn.: Augsburg, 1976.

Dalman, Gustaf. *Orte und Wege Jesu*. 3d edn. Gütersloh: C. Bertelsmann, 1924.

*Jesus-Jeshua: Studies in the Gospels*. Translated by P. P. Levertoff. London: SPCK, 1928.

*Sacred Sites and Ways: Studies in the Topography of the Gospels*. Translated by P. P. Levertoff. London: SPCK, 1935.

*The Words of Jesus: Considered in the Light of Post-Biblical Jewish Writings*. Translated by D. M. Kay. Edinburgh: T. & T. Clark, 1902.

Danby, Herbert. *The Mishnah: Translated from the Hebrew, with Introduction and Brief Explanatory Notes*. Oxford: Oxford University Press, 1933.

Dancy, J. C. *A Commentary on I Maccabees*. Oxford: Basil Blackwell, 1954.

Daniélou, Jean. *Théologie du Judéo-Christianisme*. Paris: Desclée, 1958

Daube, David. *The New Testament and Rabbinic Judaism*. London: Athlone Press, 1956.

Davidson, A. B. *An Introductory Hebrew Grammar*. Revised by John Mauchline. 26th edn. Edinburgh: T. & T. Clark, 1966.

Davies, Graham I. 'The Presence of God in the Second Temple and Rabbinic Doctrine', pp. 32–36 in *Templum Amicitiae. Essays on the Second Temple Presented to Ernst Bammel*. Edited by W. Horbury. JSNTSup 48. Sheffield: JSOT Press, 1991.

Davies, Margaret. *Matthew*. Sheffield: JSOT Press, 1993.

Davies, Philip R. 'The Ideology of the Temple in the Damascus Document', *JJS* 33 (1982), 287–301.

Davies, W. D., and Dale C. Allison. *A Critical and Exegetical Commentary on the Gospel according to Saint Matthew*. 3 vols. ICC. Edinburgh: T.&T. Clark, 1988, 1991, 1997.

Davila, James R. *Liturgical Works*. Eerdmans Commentaries on the Dead Sea Scrolls 6. Grand Rapids, Mich.: Eerdmans, 2000.

D'Costa, Gavin. *Resurrection Reconsidered*. Oxford: Oneworld, 1996.

Deissmann, Adolf. *Light from the Ancient East: The New Testament Illustrated by Recently Discovered Texts of the Graeco-Roman World*. Translated by L. R. M. Strachman. London: Hodder & Stoughton, 1910.

Delamarter, Steve. *A Scripture Index to Charlesworth's 'The Old Testament Pseudepigrapha'*. Sheffield: Academic Press, 2002.

Delcor, Mathias. 'Is the Temple Scroll a Source of the Herodian Temple?' pp. 67–89 in *Temple Scroll Studies*. Edited by G. J. Brooke. JSPSup 7. Sheffield: JSOT Press, 1989.

deSilva, David A. *Introducing the Apocrypha: Message, Context, and Significance*. Grand Rapids, Mich.: Baker, 2002.

Deutsch, Celia M. *Hidden Wisdom and the Easy Yoke; Wisdom, Torah and Discipleship in Mt11, 25–30*. JSNTSup 18. Sheffield: Academic Press, 1987.

'Wisdom in Matthew: Transformation of a Symbol', *NovT* 32 (1990), 13–47.

*Lady Wisdom, Jesus, and the Sages: Metaphor and Social Context in Matthew's Gospel*. Valley Forge, Pa.: Trinity Press International, 1996.

DeVries, Simon J. *1 Kings*. WBC 12. Waco, Tex.: Word, 1985.

De Vaux, Roland, *Ancient Israel: Its Life and Institutions*. Grand Rapids, Mich.: Eerdmans, 1961.

*Studies in Old Testament Sacrifice*. Cardiff: University of Wales Press, 1964.

'Les chérubins et l'achre d'alliance, les sphinx gardiens et les trônes divins dans l'ancien orient', pp. 231–59 in *Bible et Orient*. Edited by R. DeVaux. Paris: Cerf, 1967.

*The Bible and the Ancient Near East*. Translated by D. McHugh. London: Darton, Longman & Todd, 1971.

Dibelius, Martin. *Die Lade Javwes: Eine religionsgeschichtlichte Untersuchung*. Göttingen: Vandenhoeck & Ruprecht, 1906.

*Gospel Criticism and Christology*. London: Ivor Nicholson & Watson, 1935.

*From Tradition to Gospel*. Translated by B. L. Woolf. Philadelphia, Pa.: Westminster, 1971.

Dietrich, Suzanne de. *The Gospel according to Matthew*. Richmond, Va.: John Knox, 1961.

Dietzfeldbinger, C. *Pseudo-Philo, 'Antiquitates Biblicae (Liber Antiquitatum Biblicarum)' in Jüdische Schriften aus hellenistich-römischer Zeit*. Gütersloh: Mohn, 1979.

Di Lella, A. A. *The Hebrew Text of Sirach: A Text-Critical and Historical Study*. The Hague: Mouton, 1966.

Dimant, Devorah. '4QFlorigelium and the Idea of the Community as Temple', pp. 165–89 in *Hellenica et Judaica: Hommage à Valentin Nikiprowetzky*. Edited by Andrew Caquot, Mireille Hadas-Lebel and Jean Riaud. Leuven: Peeters, 1986.

Dirksen, P. B., and A. Van der Kooij, ed. *The Peshitta as a Translation: Papers Read at the II Peshitta Symposium Held at Leiden 19–21 August 1993*. Monographs of the Peshitta Institute, Leiden 8. Leiden: Brill, 1995.

Dodd, C. H. *The Parables of the Kingdom*. London: Nesbet, 1935.

*Apostolic Preaching and Its Developments*. London: Hodder & Stoughton, 1936.

*History and the Gospel*. London: Nesbet, 1938.

Dods, Marcus. 'The Epistle to the Hebrews', pp. 219–381 in vol. 4 of *The Expositor's Greek Testament*. 5 vols. Edited by W. Robertson Nicoll. London: Hodder & Stoughton, 1910.

Donahue, John R. *Are You the Christ? The Trial Narrative in the Gospel of Mark*. SBLDS 10. Missoula, Mont.: University of Montana Press, 1973.

'Temple, Trial, and Royal Christology (Mark 14:53–65)', pp. 61–78 in *Passion in Mark*. Edited by W. H. Kelber. Philadelphia, Pa.: Fortress, 1976.

Donaldson, T. L. *Jesus on the Mount: A Study in Matthean Theology*. JSNTSup 8. Sheffield, JSOT Press, 1985.

Dormeyer, Detlev. 'Die Passion Jesu als Ergebnis seines Konflikts mit führenden Kreisen des Judentums', pp. 211–38 in *Gottesverächter und Menschenfeinde*. Edited by Horst Goldstein. Düsseldorf: Patmost, 1979.

Dowda, R. E. 'The Cleansing of the Temple in the Synoptic Gospels', Ph.D. diss., Duke University, 1972.

Driver, G. R. 'Two Problems in the New Testament', *JTS* 16 (1965), 327–37.

Driver, S. R. *Notes on the Hebrew Text and Topography of the Books of Samuel: With an Introduction on Hebrew Palaeography and the Ancient Versions*. 2d edn. Oxford: Clarendon Press, 1913.

Dulière, W. L. 'Les Chérubins du troisième Temple à Antioche', *Zeitschrift für Religions- und Geistesgeschichte* 13 (1961), 201–19.

Duling, D. 'The Therapeutic Son of David: An Element of Matthew's Christological Apologetic', *NTS* 24 (1978), 392–410.

Dunn, James D. G. *Christology in the Making*. London: SCM Press, 1980.

*Jews and Christians: The Partings of the Ways AD 70 to 135*. Tübingen: Mohr Siebeck, 1992.

'The Significance of Matthew's Eschatology for Biblical Theology', *SBLSP* 35 (1996), 150–62.

Dunwell, Francis. *The Four Gospels, as Interpreted by the Early Church*. London: Clowes, 1878.

Dupont-Sommer, André. *The Essene Writings from Qumran*. Translated by G. Vermes. Gloucester, Mass.: Peter Smith, 1973.

Durham, John I. *Exodus*. WBC 3. Waco, Tex.: Word, 1987.

Ecklebarger, Kermit Allen. 'Authorial Intention as a Guiding Principle in Origen's Matthew Commentary', Ph.D. diss., University of Chicago, 1987.

Edersheim, Alfred. *Theological and Homiletical Commentary on the Gospels of St Matthew and St Mark*. 3 vols. Edinburgh: T.& T. Clark, 1861–62.

*The Life and Times of Jesus the Messiah*. 2 vols. London: Longman, Green & Co., 1883.

*The Temple: Its Ministry and Services*. London: Religious Tract Society, 1874. Repr., Peabody, Mass.: Hendrickson, 1994.

*Sketches of Jewish Social Life*. London: Religious Tract Society, 1976. Repr., Peabody, Mass.: Hendrickson, 1994.

Edwards, James R. 'The use of ΠΡΟΣΕΡΧΕΣΘΑΙ in the Gospel of Matthew', *JBL* 106 (1987), 65–74.

Edwards, Richard Alan. *Matthew's Story of Jesus*. Philadelphia, Pa.: Fortress, 1985.

Ego, Beate. *Im Himmel Wie Auf Erden: Studien Zum Verhältnis Von Himmlischer Und Irdischer Welt in Rabbinischen Judentum*. WUNT II, 34. Tübingen: Mohr Siebeck, 1989.

Eichrodt, Walther. *Theology of the Old Testament*. 2 vols. Translated by J. A. Baker. London: SCM Press, 1961.

*Ezekiel: A Commentary*. Old Testament Library. Translated by C. Quin. London: SCM Press, 1970.

Eliade, Mircea. *Patterns in Comparative Religion*. Translated by R. Sheed. New York, N.Y.: Sheed & Ward, 1963.

Elliger, Karl. 'Zur Analyse des Sündopfergesetzes', pp. 39–50 in *Verbannung und Heimkehr: Beiträge zur Geschichte und Theologie Israels im 6. und 5. Jahrhundert v. Chr.* Edited by A. Kuschke. Tübingen: Mohr Siebeck, 1961.

Ellingworth, Paul. *The Epistle to the Hebrews*. NIGTC. Grand Rapids, Mich.: Eerdmans, 1993.

Ellis, E. Earle, ed. *The Gospel of Luke*. New Century Bible. London: Nelson, 1966.

Ellis, Peter F. *Matthew: His Mind and Message*. Collegeville, Minn.: Liturgical Press, 1974.

Eloff, Mervyn. 'Restoration from Exile as a Hermeneutical Prism for a Theological Interpretation of Matthew's Gospel', Th.D. diss., Stellenbosch University, 2002.

'Exile, Restoration and Matthew's Genology of Jesus ὁ χριστός', *Neotestamentica* 38 (2004), 75–87.

Emmanuel ab Incarnatione. *Matthaeus explanatus, sive Commentarii litterales et morales in sacrosanctum Iesu Christi Euangelium secundùm Matthaeum.* Ulyssipone: Apud Michaelem Deslandes, 1695–1714.

Ernst, Josef. *Matthäus: Ein theologisches Portrait*. Düsseldorf: Patmos, 1989.

Esler, Philip F. 'God's Honour and Rome's Triumph: Responses to the Fall of Jerusalem in Three Jewish Apocalypses', pp. 239–58 in *Modelling Early Christianity*. Edited by P. F. Esler. London: Routledge, 1995.

Essame, William G. 'Matthew xxvii.51–54 and John v.25–29', *Expository Times* 76 (1964), 103.

Evans, C. F. *Resurrection and the New Testament*. Studies in Biblical Theology *Second Series* 12. London: SCM Press, 1970.

Evans, Craig A. 'On the Vineyard Parables of Isaiah 5 and Mark 12', *Biblische Zeitschrift* 28 (1984), 82–86.

'1 Q Isaiah[a] and the Absence of Prophetic Critique at Qumran', *RevQ* 11 (1984), 537–42.

*Noncanonical Writings and New Testament Interpretation*. Peabody, Mass.: Hendrickson, 1992.

'Predictions of the Destruction of the Herodian Temple in the Pseudepigrapha, Qumran Scrolls, and Related Texts', *JSP* 10 (1992), 89–147.

and James H. Charlesworth, eds. *Pseudepigrapha and Early Biblical Interpretation*. Sheffield: JSOT Press, 1993.

'God's Vineyard and Its Caretakers', pp. 381–406 in *Jesus and His Contemporaries*. Arbeiten zur Geschichte des antiken Judentums und des Urchristentums 25. Edited by Craig A. Evans. Leiden: Brill, 1995.

'Jesus' Action in the Temple: Cleansing or Portent of Destruction?' pp. 395–439 in *Jesus in Context: Temple, Purity, and Restoration*. Edited by Craig A. Evans and Bruce Chilton. Leiden: Brill, 1997.

and James A. Sanders, eds. *The Function of Scripture in Early Jewish and Christian Tradition*. Sheffield: Academic Press, 1998.

and Stanley E. Porter, eds. *Dictionary of New Testament Background*. Downers Grove, Ill.: InterVarsity, 2000.

ed. *The Interpretation of Scripture in Early Judaism and Christianity: Studies in Language and Tradition*. Sheffield: Academic Press, 2000.

*Mark 8:27–16:20*. WBC 34B. Nashville, Tenn.: Nelson, 2001.

Review of Darrel L. Bock. *Blasphemy and Exaltation in Judaism: The Charge against Jesus in Mark 14:53–65, RBL* (June 16, 2002).

'Defeating Satan and Liberating Israel: Jesus and Daniel's Visions', *JSHJ* 1 (2003), 161–75.

Eznik of Kolb. *A Treatise on God Written in Armenian by Eznik of Kolb (floruit c. 430–c.450)*. Eastern Christian Texts in Translation. Translated by M. J. Blanchard and R. D. Young. Leuven: Peeters, 1998.

Faber van der Meulen, Harry E. 'One or Two Veils in front of the Holy of Holies', *Theologia Evangelica* 18 (1985), 22–27.

Fabry, Heinz-Joseph, and Helmer Ringgren, ed. *Theologisches Wörterbuch zum Alten Testament*. 8 vols. Stuttgart: W. Kohlhammer, 1987–95.

Faessler, M. 'Marc 15,21–39: La Mort de Jésus', *Bulletin du Centre protestant d'études* 28 (1976), 28–30.

Falk, Daniel K. 'Moses, Texts of', *EDSS* I, pp. 577–81.

Falkenstein, Adam. *Topographie von Uruk*. 3 vols. Leipzig: Harrasowitz, 1941.

Farmer, William R., ed. *Anti-Judaism and the Gospels*. Harrisburg, Pa.: Trinity Press International, 1999.

Fascher, Erich. *Das Weib des Pilatus (Matthäus 27, 19). Die Auferweckung der Heiligen (Matthäus 27, 51–53): Zwei Studien zur Geschichte der Schriftauslegung*. Halle: M. Niemeyer, 1951.

Feldman, L. H., and G. Hata, eds. *Josephus, Judaism and Christianity*. Leiden: Brill, 1987.

Feldmeier, R. 'Der Gekreuzigte im "Gnadenstuhl": Exegetische Überlegungen zu Mk 15,37–39 und deren Bedeutung für die Vorstellung der göttlichen Gegenwart und Herrschaft', pp. 213–32 in *Trône de Dieu*. Edited by Marc Philonenko. Tübingen: Mohr Siebeck, 1993.

Fensham, F. Charles. 'The Curse of the Dry Bones in Ezekiel 37:1–14 Changed to a Blessing of Resurrection', *Journal of Northwest Semitic Languages* 13 (1987), 59–60.

Fenton, John C. *The Gospel of St Matthew*. Harmondsworth: Penguin, 1963.

Fiebig, P. 'Der zerrissene Tempelvorhang', *Neue sächliche Kirchenblatt* 40 (1933), 227–36.

Field, Fridericus. *Origenis Hexaplorum*. 2 vols. London: Macmillan, 1875.

Fillion, Louise Claude and Mark Antoine Bayle. *Évangile selon S. Matthieu*. Paris: P. Lethielleux, 1878.

Filson, Floyd Vivian. *A Commentary on the Gospel according to St Matthew*. London: A. and C. Black, 1971.

Finn, A. H. 'The Tabernacle Chapters', *JTS* 16 (1915), 449–82.

Fishbane, M. 'The Measures of God's Glory in the Ancient Midrash', pp. 53–74 in *Messiah and Christos: Studies in the Jewish Origins of Christianity*. Edited by I. Gruenwald, S. Shaked, and G. Stroumsa. Tübingen: Mohr Siebeck, 1992.

Fitzmyer, Joseph. A. 'Some Observations on the Targum of Job from Qumran Cave 11', *CBQ* 36 (1974), 503–24.

*The Gospel according to Luke*. 2 vols. ABC 28–28A. New York, N.Y.: Doubleday, 1981, 1985.

Fletcher-Louis, Crispin H. T. 'The Destruction of the Temple and the Relativization of the Old Covenant: Mark 13:31 and Matthew 5:18', pp. 145–69 in *Eschatology in Bible & Theology*. Edited by K. E. Brower and M. W. Elliot. Leicester: Appolos, 1997.

'The Cosmology of P and Theological Anthropology in the Wisdom of Jesus ben Sira', Unpublished paper available online at http://www.marquette.edu/maqom.

'Narrative Christologies: The Transfiguration and Post-Resurrection Stories', Third Oxford Lecture on the Development of Christology, undated, unpublished paper.

Forbes, R. J. *Studies in Ancient Technology*. 4 vols. Leiden: Brill, 1964.

Foster, Paul. 'The Use of Zechariah in Matthew's Gospel', pp. 65–86 in *The Book of Zechariah and its Influence: Papers of the Oxford-Leiden Conference*. Edited by Christopher Tuckett. London: Ashgate Press, 2003.

Fox, Douglas J. *The 'Matthew-Luke Commentary' of Philoxenus: Translation and Critical Analysis*. SBLDS 43. Missoula, Mont.: Scholars Press for the Society of Biblical Literature, 1978.

Fox, Michael V. 'The Rhetoric of Ezekiel's Vision of the Valley of the Bones', *HUCA* 51 (1980), 1–15.

*et al.*, eds. *Texts, Temples, and Traditions: A Tribute to Menahem Haran*. Winona Lake, Ind.: Eisenbrauns, 1996.

Fowler, A. *Kinds of Literature: An Introduction to the Theory of Genres and Modes*. Oxford: Clarendon Press, 1982.

Fraenkel, Detlef. 'Die Quellen der asterisierten Zusätze im zweiten Tabernakelbericht Exod 35–40', pp. 140–86 in *Studien zur Septuaginta – Robert Hanhart zu Ehren: Aus Anlass seines 65. Geburtstages*. Edited by Detlef Fraenkel, Udo Quast and John William Wevers. Mitteilungen des Septuaginta-Unternehmens 20. Göttingen: Vandenhoeck & Ruprecht, 1990.

France, R. T. 'Herod and the Children of Bethlehem', *NovT* 21 (1979), 98–120.

'The Formula-Quotations of Matthew 2 and the Problem of Communication', *NTS* 27 (1981), 233–51.

*The Gospel according to Matthew: An Introduction and Commentary*. Grand Rapids, Mich.: Eerdmans, 1985.

'Chronological Aspects of "Gospel Harmony"', *Vox Evangelica* 16 (1986), 33–59.

*Jesus and the Old Testament*. Vancouver, British Columbia: Regent College Publishing, 1988.

*Matthew: Evangelist and Teacher*. Downers Grove, Ill.: InterVarsity, 1989.

*The Gospel of Mark*. NIGTC. Grand Rapids, Mich.: Eerdmans, 2002.

Frankel, Z. *Über den Einfluß der palästinischen Exegese auf die alexandrinische Hermeneutik*. Leipzig: J. A. Barth, 1851.

Frankemölle, Hubert. *Jahwe-Bund und Kirche Christi: Studien zur Form- und Traditionsgeschichte des, Evangeliums' nach Matthäus*. Münster: Aschendorff, 1974.

Fraser, B. 'An Approach to Discourse Markers', *Journal of Pragmatics* 14 (1990), 383–95.

Freedman, D. N. and K. A. Mathews. *The Paleo-Hebrew Leviticus Scroll (11QpaleoLev)*. Winona Lake, Ind.: American Schools of Oriental Research / Eisenbrauns, 1985.

Freyne, Seán and Henry Wansbrough. *Mark and Matthew*. Scripture Discussion Commentaries 7. London: Sheed & Ward, 1971.

Friedlander, G. *Pirke de Rabbi Eleazer*. New York, N.Y.: Sepher-Hermon Press, 1981.

Friedman, Richard Elliot. 'The Tabernacle in the Temple', *Biblical Archaeologist* 43 (1980), 241–48.

'Tabernacle', *ABD* VI, pp. 293–300.

Fritzsche, O. F. *Die Weisheit Jesus-Sirachs*. Leipzig: Wäysenhauses, 1859.

Fuchs, Albert. *Konkordanz zum Protoevangelium des Jakobus*. Druck: Plöchl, Freistadt, 1978.

Gaechter, Paul. *Das Matthäus Evangelium: Ein Kommentar*. Innsbruck: Tyrolia, 1963.

Gall, August Freiherrn von, ed. *Der Hebräische Pentateuch der Samaritaner*. Gießen: Töpelmann, 1914.

Gander, Georges. *Évangile de l'Église. Commentaire de l'Évangile selon Matthieu*. Aix en Provence: Faculté libre de théologie protestante d'Aix-en-Provence, 1969.

Gane, Roy E. 'Re-opening Katapetasma ("Veil") in Hebrews 6:19', *AUSS* 38 (2000), 5–8.

Garland, David E. *Reading Matthew: A Literary and Theological Commentary on the First Gospel*. London: SPCK, 1993.

Gärtner, B. *The Temple and the Community in Qumran and the New Testament: A Comparative Study in the Temple Symbolism of Qumran Texts and the New Testament*. Cambridge: Cambridge University Press, 1965.

Gasque, W. Ward. *New International Biblical Commentary: New Testament Series*. Peabody, Mass.: Hendrickson, 1988.

Gaston, Lloyd. *No Stone on Another: Studies in the Significance of the Fall of Jerusalem in the Synoptic Gospels*. Leiden: Brill, 1972.

Gates, Marie-Henriette. 'Dura-Europas: A Fortress of Syro-Mesopotamian Art', *Biblical Archaeologist* 47 (1984), 166–81.

Geddert, T. J. *Watchwords: Mark 13 in Markan Eschatology*. JSNTSup 26. Sheffield: Academic Press, 1989.

'Apocalyptic Teaching', *DJG* pp. 20–27.

Geist, Heinz. *Menschensohn und Gemeinde: Eine redaktionskritische Untersuchung zur Menschensohnprädikation im Matthäusevangelium*. Würzburg: Echter Verlag, 1986.

Gerhardsson, Birger. 'Sacrificial Service and Atonement in the Gospel of Matthew', pp. 25–35 in *Reconciliation and Hope: New Testament Essays on Atonement and Eschatology Presented to L. L. Morris on His 60th Birthday*. Edited by Robert Banks. Exeter: Paternoster, 1974.

*The Mighty Acts of Jesus according to Matthew*. Lund: Gleerup, 1979.

*The Gospel Tradition*. Coniectanea biblica: New Testament Series 15. Malmö: Gleerup, 1986.

Gibson, John Monro. *The Gospel of St Matthew*. 2d edn. London: Hodder & Stoughton, 1892.

Gibson, Margaret Dunlop., ed. *The Commentaries of Isho'dad of Merv: Bishop of Hadatha (c. 850 A.D.) in Syriac and English*. Horae Semiticae V. 2 vols. Cambridge: Cambridge University Press, 1911.

Gilboa, R. 'Cherubim: An Inquiry Into An Enigma', *Biblische Notizen* 82 (1996), 59–75.

Ginzberg, L. *The Legends of the Jews*. 7 vols. Translated by H. Szold and P. Radin. Philadelphia, Pa.: Jewish Publication Society, 1936–47.

Glanzman, George S. Review of David W. Gooding, *The Account of the Tabernacle: Translation and Textual Problems of the Greek Exodus, Theological Studies* 23 (1962), 106–108.

Gnilka, Joachim. *Das Matthäusevangelium*. 2 vols. Freiburg: Herder, 1986, 1988.

Gnuse, Robert. 'Dream Genre in the Matthean Infancy Narratives', *NovT* 32 (1990), 97–120.

Goldenberg, Robert. 'Early Rabbinic Explanations to the Destruction of Jerusalem', *SBLSP* 21 (1982), 517–25

Goldingay, John E. *Daniel*. WBC 30. Dallas, Tex.: Word, 1989.

Goldstein, Jonathan A. *I Maccabees*. ABC 41. New York, N.Y.: Doubleday, 1976.

Goodenough, Erwin R., ed. *Jewish Symbols in the Greco-Roman Period*. 12 vols. New York, N.Y.: Pantheon, 1953–65.

Gooding, D. W. *The Account of the Tabernacle: Translation and Textual Problems of the Greek Exodus*. Cambridge: Cambridge University Press, 1959.

'Temple Specifications: A Dispute in Logical Arrangement between the MT and the LXX', *VT* 17 (1967), 143–72.

Goodwin, Harvey. *A Commentary on the Gospel of S. Matthew*. Cambridge: Deighton, Bell, & Co., 1857.

Goppelt, L. *Typos: Die typologische Deutung des Alten TestameNew Testament Studies im Neuen: Anhang Apoklyptik und Typologie bei Paulus*. Darmstadt: Wissenschaftliche Buchgesellschaft, 1969.

Görg, Manfred. *Das Zelt der Begegnung: Untersuchung zur Gestalt der Sakralen Zelttraditionen Altisraels*. Bonn: Peter Hanstein, 1967.

'Keruben in Jerusalem', *Biblische Notizen* 4 (1977), 13–24.

Goulder, M. D. *Midrash and Lection in Matthew*. London: SPCK, 1974.

'Fourth Book of the Psalter', *JTS* 26 (1975), 269–89.

Gourgues, Michel. 'Il entendit de son temple ma voix: echos du cantique de David (Ps 18 = 2 S 22) en Mt 27,50–51 et dans le Nouveau Testament', pp. 323–41 in *Ou demeures-tu? La maison depuis le monde Biblique*. Edited by J. Petit. FS G. Couturier. Montréal: Fides, 1994.

Gowan, Donald E. *Theology in Exodus: Biblical Theology in the Form of a Commentary*. Louisville, Ky.: Westminster John Knox, 1994.

Gradwohl, R. *Die Farben im Alten Testament*. Beihefte zur Zeitschrift für die Alttestamentliche Wissenschaft 83. Berlin: Töpelmann, 1963.

'Das 'fremde Feuer' von Nadab und Abihu', *ZAW* 75 (1963), 288–96.

Grässer, E. *Der Glaube im Hebräerbrief*. Marburger Theologische Studien 2. Marburgh: Elwert, 1965.

Grassi, Joseph A. 'Ezekiel XXXVII.1–14 and the New Testament', *NTS* 11 (1965), 162–64.

Gray, George Buchanan. *Sacrifice in the Old Testament: Its Theory and Practice*. Oxford: Clarendon Press, 1925.

Gray, John. 'Canaanite Mythology and Hebrew Tradition', *Transactions of the Glasgow University Oriental Society* 14 (1950), 47–57.

'Cultic Affinities between Israel and Ras Shamra', *ZAW* 62 (1950), 207–20.

Green, F. W. *The Gospel according to St Matthew*. Oxford: Clarendon Press, 1936.

Green, H. Benedict. *The Gospel according to Matthew in the Revised Standard Version: Introduction and Commentary*. Oxford: Oxford University Press, 1975.

Green, Joel B., Scot McKnight and I. Howard Marshall, eds. *Dictionary of Jesus and the Gospels*. Downers Grove, Ill.: InterVarsity, 1992.

Green, Joel B. 'The Death of Jesus and the Rending of the Temple Veil: A Window into Luke's Understanding of Jesus and the Temple', *SBLSP* 30 (1991), 543–57.

'The Demise of the Temple as 'Culture Center' in Luke-Acts: An Exploration of the Rending of the Temple Veil', *RB* 101 (1994), 495–515.

Greenberg, Moshe. 'The Biblical Conception of Asylum', *JBL* 78 (1959), 125–32.

*Ezekiel 21–37*. ABC 22A. New York, N.Y.: Doubleday, 1997.

Grosch, Hermann. *Der Umfang des vom Apostel Matthäus verfassten Evangeliums oder des aramäischen Matthäus*. Leipzig: Werner Scholl, 1914.

Grundmann, Walter. *Das Evangelium nach Matthäus*. Berlin: Evangelische Verlagsanstalt, 1968.

Gundry, Robert H. *The Use of the Old Testament in St Matthew's Gospel: With Special Reference to the Messianic Hope*. NovTSS 18. Leiden: Brill, 1967.

*Matthew: A Commentary on His Handbook for a Mixed Church under Persecution*. Grand Rapids, Mich.: Eerdmans, 1994.

Gurtner, Daniel M. '"Atonement Slate" or the "Veil"? Notes on a Textual Variant in Exodus XXVI 34', *VT* 54 (2004), 396–98.

'Καταπέτασμα: Lexicographical and Etymological Considerations to the Biblical "Veil"', *AUSS* 42 (2004), 105–11.

'The Tearing of the Temple Curtain: A Look Back and a Way Forward', *Them.* 29 (2004), 4–14.

Review of W. G. Olmstead, *Matthew's Trilogy of Parables: The Nation, the Nations and the Reader in Matthew 21.28–22.14, Them.* 30 (2004), 63–64.

'Functionality, Identity, and Interpretation: The Tearing of the Temple Curtain (Matt 27:51a) in Light of Pentateuchal Tabernacle Texts', paper presented at the International Meeting of the Society of Biblical Literature (Groningen, 2004).

'The "House of the Veil" in Sirach 50', *JSP* 14.3 (2005), 187–200.

'LXX Syntax and the Identity of the NT Veil', *NovT* 47.4 (2005), 344–53.

'The Veil of the Temple in History and Legend', *JETS* 49 (2006), 97–114.

'The Biblical Veil in the Dead Sea Scrolls', *Qumran Chronicle* 14 (2006), 57–79.

'The Dividing Wall and the Outer Veil: A Case of Mistaken Identity in the Synoptic Passion Narratives' (in production).

Guthrie, George H. 'Hebrews in Its First-Century Contexts: Recent Research', pp. 414–43 in *The Face of New Testament Studies: A Survey of Recent Research*. Edited by Scot McKnight and Grant R. Osborne. Grand Rapids, Mich.: Baker, 2004.

Habel, Norman. *Literary Criticism of the Old Testament*. Philadelphia, Pa.: Fortress, 1971.

Hadas, Moses. *Aristeas to Philorates (Letter of Aristeas)*. The Dropsie College for Hebrew and Cognate Learning. New York, N.Y.: Harper & Brothers, 1951.

Hagner, D. A. 'Apocalyptic Motifs in the Gospel of Matthew: Continuity and Discontinuity', *HBT* 7 (1985), 53–82.

*Matthew*. 2 vols. WBC 33A–B. Dallas, Tex.: Word, 1993, 1995.

'Matthew's Eschatology', *SBLSP* 35 (1996), 163–81.

Hamerton-Kelly, R. G. 'The Temple and the Origins of Jewish Apocalyptic', *VT* 20 (1970), 1–15.

ed. *Jews, Greeks and Christians: Religious Cultures in Late Antiquity: Essays in Honor of William David Davies*. Leiden: Brill, 1976.

Handmann, Rudolf. *Das Hebräer-Evangelium ein Beitrag zur Geschichte und Kritik des hebräischen Matthäus*. Leipzig: J. C. Hinrichs, 1888. Microform.

Hanson, P. W. *The Dawn of the Apocalyptic*. Philadelphia, Pa.: Fortress, 1975.

Haran, Menahem. 'The Ark and the Cherubim: Their Symbolic Significance in Biblical Ritual', *IEJ* 9 (1959), 30–38, 89–98.

'Shiloh and Jerusalem: The Origin of the Priestly Tradition in the Pentateuch', *JBL* 81 (1962), 14–24.

'The Disappearance of the Ark', *IEJ* 13 (1963), 46–58.

'The Priestly Image of the Tabernacle', *HUCA* 36 (1965), 191–226.

'The Divine Presence in the Israelite Cult and the Cultic Institutions', *Bib.* 50 (1969), 251–67.

*Temples and Temple-Service in Ancient Israel*. Oxford: Clarendon Press, 1978.

'The Shining of Moses' Face: A Case Study in Biblical and Ancient Near Eastern Iconography', pp. 159–73 in *In the Shelter of Elyon: Essays on Ancient Palestinian Life and Literature in Honor of G. W. Ahlstrom*. Edited by W. B. Barrick and J. R. Spencer. Sheffield: JSOT Press, 1984.

'Temple and Community in Ancient Israel', pp. 17–25 in *Temple in Society*. Edited by Michael V. Fox. Winona Lake, Ind.: Eisenbrauns, 1988.

Hare, Douglas R. A. *The Theme of Jewish Persecution of Christians in the Gospel according to St Matthew*. Cambridge: Cambridge University Press, 1967.

*Matthew*. Louisville, Ky.: John Knox, 1993.

'Lives of the Prophets', *DNTB*, pp. 652–54.

'Lives of the Prophets', *OTP* II, pp. 379–99.

Harrington, Daniel J. *The Gospel according to Matthew*. Sacra Pagina 1. Collegeville, Minn.: Liturgical Press, 1983.

'Sirach Research since 1965: Progress and Questions', pp. 164–76 in *Pursuing the Text: Studies in Honour of Ben Zion Wacholder on the Occasion of His Seventieth Birthday*. Edited by J. C. Reeves and J. Kampden. JSOTSup 84. Sheffield: Academic Press, 1994.

'Matthew's Gospel: Pastoral Problems and Possibilities', pp. 62–73 in *The Gospel of Matthew in Current Study: Studies in Memory of William G. Thompson, S. J.* Edited by D. Aune. Grand Rapids, Mich.: Eerdmans, 2001.

Hart, J. H. A. *Ecclesiasticus: The Greek Text of Codex 248*. Cambridge: Cambridge University Press, 1909.

Hartley, John E. *Leviticus*. WBC 4. Dallas, Tex.: Word, 1992.

'Atonement, Day of', *DOTP*, pp. 54–61.

Hartman, Lars. 'Scriptural Exegesis in the Gospel of St Matthew and the Problem of Communication', pp. 131–52 in *L'évangile selon Matthieu: redaction et théologie*. Edited by M. Didier. Bibliotheca ephemeridum theologicarum lovaniensium 29. Gembloux: Duculot, 1972.

Hastings, James, ed. *A Dictionary of Christ and the Gospels*. 2 vols. New York, N.Y.: Charles Scribner's Sons, 1917, 1921.

Hatch, E. and H. A. Redpath, eds. *A Concordance to the Septuagint: And the Other Greek Versions of the Old Testament (Including the Apocryphal Books)*. 2d edn. Grand Rapids, Mich.: Baker, 1998.

Hayward, Robert. 'The Jewish Temple at Leontopolis: A Reconstruction', *JJS* 33 (1982), 429–43.

*The Jewish Temple: A Non-Biblical Sourcebook.* London: Routledge, 1996.

*Hebrew–English Edition of the Babylonian Talmud: Ta'annith.* Translated by J. Rabbinwitz. Edited by I. Epstein; London: Soncino Press, 1984.

Head, P. M. 'Restoration Prophecies and New Testament Fulfillment: A Case Study in Matt. 1–4', unpublished paper delivered at Tyndale Fellowship Conference, 1994.

Hegg, Tim. 'Separating the Most Holy from the Holy: The "Veil" in the Tabernacle and First and Second Temples', paper presented at the Northwest Regional Conference meeting of the Evangelical Theological Society (Portland, Ore., March 4, 2000).

Heil, John Paul. *The Death and Resurrection of Jesus: A Narrative-Critical Reading of Matthew 26–28.* Minneapolis, Mich.: Fortress, 1991.

'The Narrative Strategy and Pragmatics of the Temple Theme in Mark', *CBQ* 59 (1997), 76–100.

Heinrici, Georg. *Des Petrus von Laodicea: Erklärung des Matthäusevangeliums zum ersten Male herausgegeben und untersucht.* Leipzig: Verlag der Dürr'schen Buchhandlung, 1908.

Hellerman, Joseph. 'Purity and Nationalism in Second Temple Literature: 1–2 Maccabees and *Jubilees*', *JETS* 46 (2003), 401–22.

Hellholm, David. 'The Problem of Apocalyptic Genre and the Apocalypse of John', *Semeia* 36 (1986), 13–64.

Hendel, Ronald S. '"The Flame of the Whirling Sword": A Note on Genesis 3:24', *JBL* 104 (1985), 671–74.

Hendrix, Ralph E. 'A Literary Structural Overview of Exod 25–40', *AUSS* 30 (1992), 123–38.

Hengel, Martin. *The Son of God: The Origin of Christology and the History of Jewish-Hellenistic Religion.* Translated by J. Bowden. Philadelphia, Pa.: Fortress, 1976.

*Studies in the Gospel of Mark.* Eugene, Ore.: Wipf and Stock, 1985.

'The Geography of Palestine in Acts', pp. 27–78 in *The Book of Acts in Its Palestinian Setting.* Edited by Richard Bauckham. Vol. 4 of *The Book of Acts in Its First Century Setting.* Edited by Bruce W. Winter. Grand Rapids, Mich.: Eerdmans, 1993.

*The Four Gospels and the One Gospel of Jesus Christ: An Investigation into the Collection and Origin of the Canonical Gospels.* Translated by J. Bowden. London: SCM Press, 2000.

Hertz, J. H. *Leviticus.* The Pentateuch and Haftorahs. London: Oxford University Press, 1932.

Hertzberg, Hans Wilhelm. *I & II Samuel: A Commentary.* Translated by J. S. Bowden. London: SCM Press, 1964.

Hewson, Michael. 'The Commentary on the Gospel of St Matthew by Sedulius Scottus and Its Sources, with a Critical Edition of Chapters 1–2', Ph.D. diss., University College, Dublin, 1955.

Hilary of Poitiers. *Sur Matthieu.* 2 vols. Paris: Cerf, 1978, 1979.

Hill, David. *The Gospel of Matthew.* New Century Bible. London: Oliphants, 1972.

'Son and Servant: An Essay on Matthean Christology', *JSNT* 6 (1980), 2–26.

'The Figure of Jesus in Matthew's Story: A Response to Professor Kingsbury's Literary-Critical Probe', *JSNT* 21 (1984), 37–52.

'Matthew 27:51–53 in the Theology of the Evangelist', *IBS* 7 (1985), 76–87.

Himmelfarb, Martha. 'Apocalyptic Ascent and the Heavenly Temple', *SBLSP* 26 (1987), 210–17.

'Heavenly Ascent and the Relationship of the Apocalypses and the Hekhalot Literature', *HUCA* 59 (1988), 73–100.

*Ascent to Heaven in Jewish and Christian Apoclypses*. Oxford: Oxford University Press, 1993.

Hinnebusch, P. *St Matthew's Earthquake: Judgment and Discipleship in the Gospel of Matthew*. Ann Arbor, Mich.: Servant, 1980.

Hoffmann, Otto. *Die Griechischen Dialekte*. 3 vols. Göttingen: Vandenhoeck & Ruprecht, 1891–98.

Hofius, Otfried. *Der Vorhang vor dem Thron Gottes: Eine exegetisch- religionsgeschichteeliche Untersuchung zu Hebräer 6,19f. und 10,19f.* WUNT 14. Tübingen: Mohr Siebeck, 1972.

Holladay, William L. *A Concise Hebrew and Aramaic Lexicon of the Old Testament: Based upon the Lexical Work of Ludwig Koehler and Walter Baumgartner*. Leiden: Brill, 1988.

Hollander, Harm W., and M. de Jonge. *The Testaments of the Twelve Patriarchs: A Commentary*. Leiden: Brill, 1985.

Holtzmann, Oscar. *The Life of Jesus*. Translated by J. T. Bealby and M. A. Canney. London: Adam and Charles Black, 1904.

*Der Tosephtatraktat Berakot: Text, Übersetzung und Erklärung*. Beihefte zur Zeitschrift für die alttestamentliche Wissenschaft 23. Gieβen: Alfred Töpelmann, 1912.

Horbury, William. 'The Benediction of the *Minim* and Early Jewish-Christian Controversy', *JTS* 33 (1982), 19–61.

Horsnell, M. J. 'Merari, Merarites', *ISBE* III, p. 321.

Houtman, Cornelis. *Exodus*. 3 vols. Historical Commentary on the Old Testament. Leuven: Peeters, 2000.

How, W. Walsham. *The Gospel according to Saint Matthew*. London: SPCK, 1914.

Howald, Johann. *Das Evangelium Matthäus und Markus*. Bärn: Buechhandlung von der Evangelische Gesellschaft, 1944.

Howard, George. *Hebrew Gospel of Matthew*. Macon, Ga.: Mercer University Press, 1995.

Howell, David B. *Matthew's Inclusive Story: A Study in the Narrative Rhetoric of the First Gospel*. JSNTSup 42. Sheffield: JSOT Press, 1990.

Hubbard, B. J. *The Matthean Redaction of a Primitive Apostolic Commissioning: An Exegesis of Matthew 28:16–20*. SBLDS 19. Missoula, Mont.: Scholars Press, 1974.

Hulgard, A. 'The Ideal "Levite", the Davidic Messiah and the Saviour Priest in the Testaments of the Twelve Patriarchs', pp. 93–110 in *Ideal Figures in Ancient Judaism*. Society of Biblical Literature Septuagint and Cognate Studies 12.

Edited by J. J. Collins and G. W. E. Nickelsburg. Chico, Calif.: Society of Biblical Literature, 1980.

Hulteen, Bob. 'The Cherubim Phenomenon', *Sojourners* 23 (1994), 43.

Hummel, Reinhart. *Die Auseinandersetzung zwischen Kirche und Judentum im Matthäusevangelium*. München: Kaiser, 1966.

Humphrey, Edith M. *Joseph and Aseneth*. Guides to Apocrypha and Pseudepigrapha. Sheffield: Academic Press, 2000.

Hurowitz, V. A. 'The Priestly Account of Building the Tabernacle', *JAOS* 105 (1985), 21–30.

'The Form and Fate of the Tabernacle: Reflections on a Recent Proposal', *JQR* 86 (1995), 127–51.

Hurst, Lincoln. *The Epistle to the Hebrews: Its Background of Thought*. SNTSMS 65. Cambridge: Cambridge University Press, 1990.

Hurtado, Larry W. 'First Century Jewish Monotheism', *JSNT* 71 (1998), 3–26.

*Lord Jesus Christ: Devotion to Jesus in Earliest Christianity*. Grand Rapids, Mich.: Eerdmans, 2003.

Hurvitz, A. 'The Usage of שש and בוץ in the Bible and Its Implication for the Date of P', *HTR* 60 (1967), 117–21.

Hutton, D. 'The Resurrection of the Holy Ones (Mt. 27:51b–53): A Study of the Theology of the Matthean Passion Narrative', Th.D. diss., Harvard University, 1970.

Isaacs, E. D. 'Gershon; Gershonites', *ISBE* II, p. 499.

Ishida, Tomoo, ed. *Studies in the period of David and Solomon and Other Essays International Symposium for Biblical Studies: Tokyo, 1979*. Winona Lake, Ind: Eisenbrauns, 1982.

Instone Brewer, David. *Techniques and Assumptions in Jewish Exegesis before 70 CE*. TSAJ 30. Tübingen: Mohr Siebeck, 1992.

Jackson, H. Latimer. *The Eschatology of Jesus*. London: Macmillan, 1913.

Jackson, Howard M. 'The Death of Jesus in Mark and the Miracle from the Cross', *NTS* 33 (1987), 16–37.

Jacob, Benno. *The Second Book of the Bible: Exodus*. Translated by W. Jacob. Hoboken, N.J.: Ktav, 1992.

Jacob, E. *Theology of the Old Testament*. Translated by A. W. Heathcote and P. J. Allcock. New York, N.Y.: Harper & Row, 1958.

Jacobs, Alexander M. 'It's Those Cherubim Again', *Sojourners* 18 (1989), 19.

Jacobus, Melancthon W. *Notes on the Gospels, Critical and Explanatory: Matthew*. Edinburgh: Oliphant, 1862.

Janowski, Bernd. *Sühne als Heilsgeschehen: Studien zur Sühnetheologie der Priesterschaft und zur Wurzel KPR im Alten Orient und im Alten Testament*. Wissenschaftliche Monographien zum Alten und Neuen Testament 55. Neukirchen-Vluyn: Neukirchener, 1982.

Japhet, Sara. *I & II Chronicles*. Old Testament Library. London: SCM Press, 1993.

Jastrow, Marcus. *A Dictionary of the Targumim, the Talmud Babli and Yerushalmi, and the Midrashic Literature*. 2 vols. London: Shapiro, Vallentine & Co., 1926.

Jellicoe, Sidney. *The Septuagint and Modern Study*. Oxford: Clarendon Press, 1968.

ed. *Studies in the Septuagint: Origins, Recensions, and Interpretations*. New York, N.Y.: Ktav, 1974.

Jenner, K. D., and A. Van der Kooij. *The Old Testament in Syriac According to the Peshiṭta Version*. Leiden: Brill, 1998.

Jennings, William. *Lexicon to the Syriac New Testament (Peshiṭta)*. Oxford: Clarendon Press, 1926.

Jensen, Robin M. 'Of Cherubim & Gospel Symbols', *BAR* 21 (1995), 42–65.

Jensen, L. B. 'Royal Purple of Tyre', *JNES* 22 (1963), 104–18.

Jenson, Philip Peter. *Graded Holiness: A Key to the Priestly Conception of the World*. JSOTSup 106. Sheffield: Academic Press, 1992.

Jeremias, Alfred. *The Old Testament in the Light of the Ancient East: Manual of Biblical Archaeology*. 2 vols. Translated by C. L. Beaumont. New York, N.Y.: Putnam's, 1911.

Jeremias, Joachim. *Jerusalem in the Time of Jesus*. Philadelphia, Pa.: Fortress, 1962.

'Hebräer 10:20: tout' estin tēs sarkos autou', *Zeitschrift für die neutestamentliche Wissenschaft und die Kunde der älteren Kirche* 62 (1971), 131.

*New Testament Theology*. 2 vols. Translated by J. Bowden. London: SCM Press, 1974.

Jervell, J. 'Ein Interpolator interpretiert. Zu der christlichen Bearbeitung der Testamente der zwölf Patriarchen', pp. 30–61 in *Studien zu den zwölf Patriarchen*. Edited by W. Eltester. Berlin: Alfred Töpelmann, 1969.

Jobes, Karen H., and Moisés Silva. *Invitation to the Septuagint*. Grand Rapids, Mich.: Baker, 2000.

Johannessohn, M. 'Die Wahrnehmungssatz bei den Verben des Sehens in der hebräischen und griechischen Bibel', *Zeitschrift für vergleichende Sprachforschung auf dem Bebiet der indogermanischen Sprachen* 64 (1937), 141–260.

'Das biblische καὶ ἰδού in der Erzahlung samt seiner hebräischen Vorlage', *Zeitschrift für vergleichende Sprachforschung auf dem Bebiet der indogermanischen Sprachen* 66 (1939), 145–95 and 67 (1940), 30–84.

Johnson, Earl S. 'Mark 15,39 and the So-Called Confession of the Roman Centurion', *Bib.* 81 (2000), 406–13.

Jones, Alexander. *The Gospel according to St Matthew*. New York, N.Y.: Sheed & Ward, 1965.

Jones, Ivor H. *The Gospel of Matthew*. London: Epworth, 1994.

Jonge, Marinas de. *The Testaments of the Twelve Patriarchs: A Study of their Text, Composition and Origin*. Van Gorcum's Theologische Bibliotheek XXV. Assen: van Gorcum, 1953.

'Christian Influence on the Testaments of the Twelve Patriarchs', *NovT* 4 (1960), 99–117.

'Once More: Christian Influence in the Testaments of the Twelve Patriarchs', *NovT* 5 (1962), 311–19.

'Christelijke elementen in de Vitae Prophetarum', *Nederlands Theologisch Tijdschrift* 16 (1962), 161–78.

*Testamenta XII Patriarchum. Edited according to Cambridge University Library Ms Ff I.24 fol. 203a–262b*. Pseudepigrapha Veteris Testamenti Graece 1. Leiden: Brill, 1964.

'De berichten over het scheuren van het voorhangsel bij Jesus' dood in de synoptische evangelien', *Nederlands Theologisch Tijdschrift* 21 (1966), 90–114.

'Het motief van het gescheurde voorhangsel van de temple in een aantal vroegchristelijke geschriften', *Nederlands Theologisch Tijdschrift* 21 (1967), 257–76.

ed. *Studies on the Testaments of the Twelve Patriarchs*. Leiden: Brill, 1975.

'Two Interesting Interpretations of the Rending of the Temple-Veil in the Testaments of the Twelve Patriarchs', *Bijdragen* 46 (1985), 350–362.

'Matthew 27:51 in Early Christian Exegesis', *HTR* 79 (1986), 67–79.

*Jewish Eschatology, Early Christian Christology and the Testaments of the Twelve Patriarchs*. Leiden: Brill, 1991.

'The Main Issues in the Study of the Testaments of the Twelve Patriarchs', *NTS* 26 (1980), 508–24.

Juel, Donald. *Messiah and Temple: The Trial of Jesus in the Gospel of Mark*. SBLDS 31. Missoula, Mont.: Scholars Press, 1977.

*Messianic Exegesis: Christological Interpretation of the Old Testament in Early Christianity*. Philadelphia, Pa.: Fortress, 1988.

Kähler, M. *The So-Called Historical Jesus and the Historic Biblical Christ*. Philadelphia, Pa.: Fortress, 1964.

Kappler, Werner, ed. *Maccabaeorum libri I–IV*. Göttingen: Vandenhoeck & Ruprecht, 1936.

Käsemann, Ernst. *Das wandernde Gottesvolk: Eine Untersuchung zum Hebräerbrief*. Göttingen: Vandenhoeck & Ruprecht, 1957.

*The Wandering People of God: An Investigation of the Letter to the Hebrews*. Translated by R. A. Harrisville. Minneapolis, Minn.: Augsburg, 1984.

Kautzsch, E. ed. *Die Apokryphen und Pseudepigraphen des Alten Testaments*. Tübingen: Mohr Siebeck, 1900.

Kee, Howard Clark. *Community of the New Age: Studies in Mark's Gospel*. London: SCM Press, 1977.

*Jesus in History: An Approach to the Study of the Gospels*. New York, N.Y.: Harcourt Brace Jovanovich, 1977.

*The Gospels: A Commentary on Matthew, Mark, Luke, John*. Nashville, Tenn.: Abingdon, 1983.

'Testaments of the Twelve Patriarchs', *OTP* I, pp. 775–828.

Keel, O. *The Symbolism of the Biblical World*. New York, N.Y.: Seabury Press, 1978.

Keener, Craig S. *A Commentary on the Gospel of Matthew*. Grand Rapids, Mich.: Eerdmans, 1999.

Keil, Carl Friedrich. *Commentar über das Evangelium des Matthäus*. Leipzig: Döfferling und Franke, 1877.

Kelber, Werner H., ed. *The Passion in Mark: Studies on Mark 14–16*. Philadelphia, Pa.: Fortress, 1976.

Kelly, William. *Lectures on the Gospel of Matthew*. London: G. Morrisch, 1868.

Kennedy, H. A. A. *Sources of New Testament Greek: The Influence of the Septuagint on the Vocabulary of the New Testament*. Edinburgh: T. & T. Clark, 1895.

Kerr, A. R. *The Temple of Jesus' Body: The Temple Theme in the Gospel of John.* JSNTSup 220. Sheffield: Academic Press, 2002.
Kessler, Herbert L. 'Through the Veil: The Holy Image in Judaism and Christianity', *Kairós* 32 (1990), 53–77.
Kilpatrick, G. D. *The Origins of the Gospel according to St Matthew.* Oxford: Clarendon Press, 1946.
Kim, Kwang Won. 'The Matthean Text of Origen in his Commentary on Matthew', Ph.D. diss., University of Chicago, 1946.
Kingsbury, Jack Dean. *Matthew: Structure, Christology, Kingdom.* Minneapolis, Minn.: Fortress, 1975.
'The Figure of Jesus in Matthew's Story: A Literary-Critical Probe', *JSNT* 21 (1984), 3–36.
'The Figure of Jesus in Matthew's Story: A Rejoinder to David Hill', *JSNT* 25 (1985), 61–81.
*Matthew.* Proclamation Commentaries. Philadelphia, Pa.: Fortress, 1986.
*Matthew as Story.* 2d edn. Philadelphia, Pa.: Fortress, 1988.
'Reflections on 'The Reader' of Matthew's Gospel', *NTS* 34 (1988), 442–60.
Kinzer, Mark. 'Temple Christology in the Gospel of John', *SBLSP* 37 (1998), 447–64.
Kiraz, George Anton. *Comparative Edition of the Syriac Gospels: Aligning the Sinaiticus, Curetonianus, Peshîṭtâ and Ḥarklean Versions. Vol. 1, Matthew.* Leiden: Brill, 1996.
Kirk, Albert. *A Commentary on the Gospel of Matthew.* New York, N.Y.: Paulist Press, 1978.
Kittel, G., and G. Friedrich, eds. *Theological Dictionary of the New Testament.* Translated by G. W. Bromiley. 10 vols. Grand Rapids, Mich.: Eerdmans, 1964–76.
Kiuchi, N. *The Purification Offering in the Priestly Literature: Its Meaning and Function.* JSOTSup 56. Sheffield: Academic Press, 1987.
Klauser, Theodor. 'Der Vorhang vor dem Thron Gottes', *Jahrbuch für Antike und Christentum* 3 (1960), 141–42.
Klein, Ralph W. 'Back to the Future: The Tabernacle in the Book of Exodus', *Interpretation* 50 (1996), 264–76.
Klijn, Albertus Frederik Johannes. *Jewish-Christian Gospel Tradition.* Supplements to Vigiliae Christianae 17. Leiden: Brill, 1992.
Klostermann, Erich. *Das Markusevangelium.* Handbuch zum Neuen Testament. Tübingen: Mohr Siebeck, 1926.
*Das Matthäusevangelium.* Handbuch zum Neuen Testament. Tübingen: Mohr Siebeck, 1927.
Knabenbauer, Joseph. *Commentarius in quatuor S. Evangelia Domini N. Jesu Christi. I, Evangelium secundum S. Matthaeum.* Parisiis: P. Lethielleux, 1892. Microform.
Knibb, Michael A. 'The Exile in the Literature of the Intertestamental Period', *HeyJ* 17 (1976), 253–72.
Knipe, David M. 'The Temple in Image and Reality', pp. 105–38 in *Temple in Society.* Edited by Michael V. Fox. Winona Lake, Ind.: Eisenbrauns, 1988.
Knowles, Michael. *Jeremiah in Matthew's Gospel: The Rejected-Prophet Motif in Matthean Redaction.* JSNTSup 68. Sheffield: JSOT Press, 1993.

Koch, K. *Die Priesterschrift von Exodus 25 bix Leviticus 16*. FRLANT 53. Göttingen: Vandenhoeck & Ruprecht, 1959.

*Spuren des hebräischen Denkens: Beiträge zur alttestamentlichen Theologie*. Gesammelte Aufsätze Band 1. Edited by Bernd Janowski und Martin Krause. Neukirchen-Vluyn: Neukirchen Verlag, 1991.

Koch, O. 'Kenntnis und Verwendung des Matthäus-Evangeliums bei den apostlischen Vätern', pp. 157–78 in *Studien zum Matthäusevangelium: Festschrift Für Wilhelm Pesch*. Edited by Ludger Schenke. Stuttgart: Katholisches Bibelwerk, 1988.

Koester, Craig R. *The Dwelling of God: The Tabernacle in the Old Testament, Intertestamental Jewish Literature and the New Testament*. CBQMS 22. Washington, D.C.: Catholic Biblical Association of America, 1989.

'The Epistle to the Hebrews in Recent Study', *CBS* 2 (1994), 123–145.

*Hebrews: A New Translation with Introduction and Commentary*. ABC 36. New York, N.Y.: Doubleday, 2001.

Koester, Helmut, ed. *Ancient Christian Gospels: Their History and Development*. London: SCM Press / Philadelphia, Pa.: Trinity Press International, 1990.

Kohler, K. 'Asenath, Life and Confession or Prayer of', pp. 172–76 in vol. 2 of *The Jewish Encyclopedia*. 12 vols. Edited by I. Singer *et al.*. New York, N.Y.: Funk & Wagnalls, 1901–6.

Kohler L., and W. Baumgartner. *Lexicon in Veteris Testamenti Libros*. 2 vols. Leiden: Brill, 1958.

Köhler, Wolf-Dietrich. *Die Rezeption des Matthäusevangeliums in der Zeit vor Irenäus*. Tübingen: Mohr Siebeck, 1987.

Konkel, M. *Architektonik des Heiligen: Studien zur zweiten Tempelvision Ezechiels (Ez 40–48)*. Bonner Biblische Beiträge 129. Berlin: Philo, 2001.

Korner, Ralph J. '"And I Saw . . .": An Apocalyptic Literary Convention for Structural Identification in the Apocalypse', *NovT* 42 (2000), 160–83.

Kozar, Joseph Vlcek. 'The Tragedy of Israel's Religious History as Portrayed in the Story of Matthew's Gospel', *Proceedings of the Eastern Great Lakes and Midwest Biblical Societies* 13 (1993), 47–54.

Kraeling, C. H. 'The Meaning of the Ezekiel Panel in the Synagogue at Dura', *BASOR* 78 (1940), 12–18.

*The Synagogue, The excavations at Dura-Europas: Final Report*, VIII/1. New Haven, Conn.: Yale University Press, 1956.

Kraemer, Ross Shepard. *When Aseneth Met Joseph: A Late Antique Tale of the Biblical Patriarch and His Egyptian Wife, Reconstructed*. Oxford: Oxford University Press, 1998.

Kraft, Robert A. 'The Pseudepigrapha in Christianity', pp. 55–86 in *Tracing the Threads: Studies in the Vitality of Jewish Pseudepigrapha*. Edited by John C. Reeves. Society of Biblical Literature Early Judaism and Its Literature 6. Atlanta, Ga.: Scholars Press, 1994.

Kratz, Reinhard. *Auferweckung als Befreiung: Eine Studie zur Passions- und Auferstehungstheologie des Matthäus (besonders Mt 27,62–28,15)*. Stuttgart: Katholisches Bibelwerk, 1973.

Kraus, Hans-Joachim. *Worship in Israel: A Cultic History of the Old Testament*. Translated by G. Buswell. Oxford: Basil Blackwell, 1966.

Kugler, Robert A. *The Testaments of the Twelve Patriarchs*. Guides to Apocrypha and Pseudepigrapha. Sheffield: Academic Press, 2001.

Kuhn, K. G. *Sifre zu Numeri*. Stuttgart: Kohlhammer, 1959.

Künzel, Georg. *Studien zum Gemeindeverständnis des Matthäus-Evangeliums*. Stuttgart: Calwer Varlag, 1978.

Kupp, David D. *Matthew's Emmanuel: Divine Presence and God's People in the First Gospel*. SNTSMS 90. Cambridge: Cambridge University Press, 1996.

Kurtz, J. H. *Sacrificial Worship in the Old Testament*. Edinburgh: T. & T. Clark, 1863.

Lachs, Samuel Tobias. *A Rabbinic Commentary on the New Testament: The Gospels of Matthew, Mark, and Luke*. Hoboken, N.J.: Ktav, 1987.

Ladd, George Eldon. 'Apocalyptic and New Testament Theology', pp. 285–96 in *Reconciliation and Hope: New Testament Essays on Atonement and Eschatology Presented to L. L. Morris on His 60th Birthday*. Edited by Robert Banks. Exeter: Paternoster, 1974.

Lagrange, Marie-Joseph. 'L'Évangile selon les Hébreux', *RevB* 31 (1922), 321–49.

*Évangile selon saint Matthieu*. Paris: J. Gabalda, 1948.

Laible, Heinrich. 'Der zerrissene Tempelvorhang und die eingestürzte Obenschwelle des Tempeleingangs vom Talmud bezeugt', *Neue kirchliche Zeitschrift* 35 (1924), 287–317.

Lamarche, Paul. 'La mort du Christ et le voile du temple selon Marc', *La nouvelle revue théologique* 106 (1974), 583–99.

Lambdin, Thomas O. *Introduction to Biblical Hebrew*. New York, N.Y.: Charles Scribner's Sons, 1971.

Lampe, G. W., ed. *A Patristic Greek Lexicon*. Oxford: Clarendon, 1961–68.

Lane, David J. '"The Curtains of Solomon": Some Notes on the "Syriacizing" of *ŠÎR-HAŠŠÎRÎM*', pp. 73–84 in *The Peshitta as a Translation: Papers Read at the II Peshitta Symposium Held at Leiden 19–21 August 1993*. Monographs of the Peshitta Institute Leiden. Edited by P. B. Dirksen and A. Van der Kooij. Leiden: Brill, 1995.

Lane, William L. *The Gospel of Mark*. NICNT. Grand Rapids, Mich.: Eerdmans, 1974.

*Hebrews*. WBC 47A–B. Dallas, Tex.: Word, 1991.

Lange, Joachim. *Das Erscheinen des Auferstandenen im Evangelium nach Mattäus: Eine traditions- und redaktionsgeschichtliche Unterzuchung zu Mt 28, 16–20*. Würzburg: Echter Verlag, 1973.

Lange, Johann Peter. *The Gospels of St Matthew and St Mark*. 3 vols. Edinburgh: T. & T. Clark, 1862.

and Philip Schaff. *The Gospel according to Matthew*. New York, N.Y.: Charles Scribner's Sons, 1915.

Lapham, Fred. *An Introduction to the New Testament Apocrypha*. London: T. & T. Clark International, 2003.

LaRondelle, Hans K. *The Israel of God in Prophecy: Principles of Prophetic Interpretation*. Berrien Springs, Mich.: Andrews University Press, 1983.

Latourette, Kenneth Scott. *A History of Christianity*. London: Eyre and Spottiswoode, 1954.

Laughlin, John C. H. '"The Strange Fire" of Nadab and Abihu', *JBL* 95 (1976), 559–65.

Lee, Pilchan. *The New Jerusalem in the Book of Revelation: A Study of Revelation 21–22 in the Light of its Background in Jewish Tradition.* WUNT II, 129. Tübingen: Mohr Siebeck, 2001.

Lefort, L. T. *Les Manuscrits Coptes de l'Université de Louvain.* Leuven: Bibliothèque de l'Université, 1940.

Légasse, Simon. 'Jésus et l'impôt du Temple', *Science et Esprit* 24 (1972), 361–77.

'Les voiles du temple de Jérusalem: Essai de parcours historique', *RevB* 87 (1980), 560–89.

*Les récits de la Passion.* Cahiers Évangile 112. Paris: Cerf, 2000.

Legg, S. C. E. *Novum Testamentum Graece: Evangelium Secundum Matthaeum.* Oxonii: E. Typographeo Clarendoniano, 1940.

Lehmann, Manfred R. '"Yom Kippur" in Qumran', *RevQ* 3 (1961), 117–24.

Leitier, Nechama. 'Assimilation and Dissimilation Techniques in the LXX of the Book of Balaam', *Textus* 12 (1985), 79–95.

Le Maistre de Sacy, Isaac-Louis. *Le Saint evangile de Jesus-Christ selon Saint Matthieu.* Paris: Guillaume Desprez et Guillaume Cavelier, 1746.

Lentzen-Deis, Fritzleo. 'Das Motiv der "Himmelsöffnung" in verschiedenen Gattungen der Umweltliteratur des Neuen Testaments', *Bib.* 50 (1969), 301–27.

*Die Taufe Jesu nach den Synoptikern: Literarkritische und gattungsgeschhichteliche Untersuchungen.* Frankfurt: Josef Knecht, 1970.

Lenski, R. C. H. *Interpretation of St Matthew's Gospel.* Peabody, Mass.: Hendrickson, 1998.

Levenson, J. D. *Sinai and Zion: An Entry into the Jewish Bible.* Minneapolis, Minn.: Winston Press, 1985.

*Creation and the Persistence of Evil: The Jewish Drama of Divine Omnipresence.* 2d edn. Princeton, N.J.: Princeton University Press, 1994.

Levey, Samson H. *The Targum of Ezekiel.* Aramaic Bible 13. Edinburgh: T. & T. Clark, 1987.

Levine, Amy-Jill. *The Social and Ethical Dimensions of Matthean Salvation History.* Studies in Bible and Early Christianity 14. Lewiston, N.Y.: Edwin Mellen Press, 1988.

Levine, Baruch A. 'The Descriptive Tabernacle Texts of the Pentateuch', *JAOS* 85 (1965), 309–18.

*In the Presence of the Lord.* Studies in Judaism in Late Antiquity 5. Leiden: Brill, 1974.

*The JPS Torah Commentary: Leviticus.* Philadelphia, Pa.: Jewish Publication Society, 1989.

*Numbers.* 2 vols. ABC 4A–B. New York, N.Y.: Doubleday, 1993, 2000.

Levine, Lee I. 'Josephus' Description of the Jerusalem Temple: *War, Antiquities,* and Other Sources', pp. 233–46 in *Josephus and the History of the Greco-Roman Period: Essays in Memory of Morton Smith.* Edited by Fausto Parente and Joseph Sievers. Studia Post-Biblica 41. Leiden: Brill, 1994.

Lewis, Agnes Smith. *The Old Syriac Gospels.* London: Williams & Norgate, 1910.

Liddell, Henry George, Robert Scott, *et al.*. *A Greek–English Lexicon.* 9th edn. Oxford: Oxford University Press, 1996.

Liebaert, Jacques. *Deux Homélies Anoméenes pour l'Octave de Paques.* Paris: Cerf, 1969.

Lightfoot, John. *A Commentary on the New Testament from the Talmud and Hebraica, Matthew – 1 Corinthians*. Peabody, Mass.: Hendrickson, 1989. Translator unknown. Translation of *Horae Hebraicae et Talmudicae*. Oxford: Oxford University Press, 1859. Repr. of *Horae Hebraicae et Talmudicae*. Cantabrigiae: Johan, 1674.

Lightfoot, John, and John Rogers Pitman. *The Temple-Service: And the Prospect of the Temple*. London: J. F. Dove, 1823.

Lightfoot, R. H. *History and Interpretation in the Gospels*. London: Hodder & Stoughton, 1935.

*The Gospel Message of St Mark*. Oxford: Clarendon Press, 1950.

Lindeskog, Gösta. 'The Veil of the Temple', pp. 132–37 in *In honorem A. Fridrichsen sexagenarii*. Edenda curavit Seminarium Neotestamenticum Upsaliense. Coniectanea neotestamentica: New Testament Series 11. Lund: Gleerup, 1947.

'Vorhang', p. 2119 in vol. 3 of *Biblisch-historisches Handwörterbuch: Landeskunde, Geschicth, Religion, Kultur, Literatur*. 4 vols. Edited by B. Reicke and L. Rost. Göttingen: Vandenhoeck & Ruprecht, 1979.

Linnemann, Eta. *Studien zur Passionsgeschichte*. FRLANT 102. Göttingen: Vandenhoeck & Ruprecht, 1970.

Livermore, Abiel Abbot. *The Four Gospels: With a Commentary*. Boston, Mass.: Lockwood, Brooks, & Co., 1881.

Lohmeyer, Ernst. 'Das Gleichnis von de bösen Weingärtnern', *Zeitschrift für systematische Theologie* 18 (1941), 242–59.

*Das Evangelium des Markus*. 12th edn. Göttingen: Vandenhoeck & Ruprecht, 1953.

*Das Evangelium des Matthäus*. 4th edn. Göttingen: Vandenhoeck & Ruprecht, 1967.

Lohse, E. *History of the Suffering and Death of Jesus Christ*. Translated by M. O. Dietrich. Philadelphia, Pa.: Fortress, 1967.

'Πρόσωπον', *TDNT* III, pp. 768–80.

Loisy, Alfred. *Les Évangiles Synoptiques*. Vol 1. Paris: Ceffonds, 1907.

Longenecker, B. W. 'Rome's Victory and God's Honour: The Jerusalem Temple and the Spirit of God in Lukan Theodicy', pp. 90–102 in *The Spirit and Christian Origins*. Edited by G. N. Stanton, B. W. Longenecker and S. C. Barton. Grand Rapids, Mich.: Eerdmans, 2004.

Lotz, W., M. G. Kyle and C. E. Armerding, 'Ark of the Covenant', *ISBE* I, pp. 291–94.

Luomanen, Petri. *Entering the Kingdom of Heaven*. WUNT II, 101; Tübingen: Mohr Siebeck, 1998.

Luria, B. Z. 'The Temple Mount Precincts', *Beth Mikra* 13 (1968), 3–15 [Hebrew].

Lust, J, E. Eynikel, and K. Hauspie. *A Greek–English Lexicon of the Septuagint*. 2 vols. Stuttgart: Deutsche Bibelgesellschaft, 1996.

Luther, Martin. *Lectures on Titus, Philemon, and Hebrews*. Luther's Works 29. Edited by Jaroslav Pelikan. St Louis, Mo.: Concordia, 1968.

Lutteroth, Henri. *De L'Evangeline selon Saint Matthieu*. Paris: Librairie Sandoz et Fischbacher, 1876.

Luz, Ulrich. *Das Evangelium nach Matthäus*. EKKNT. 4 vols. Zürich: Benziger Verlag, 1985–2002.

*Matthew 1–7: A Commentary*. Minneapolis, Minn.: Augsburg, 1989.

'Eine thetische Skizze der matthäischen Christologie', pp. 221–35 in *Anfänge der Christologie*. Edited by C. Breytenbach and H. Paulsen. Göttingen: Vandenhoeck & Ruprecht, 1991.

*Matthew in History: Interpretation, Influence, and Effects*. Minneapolis, Minn.: Fortress, 1994.

*The Theology of the Gospel of Matthew*. Translated by J. B. Robinson. Cambridge: Cambridge University Press, 1995.

*Matthew 8–20*. Hermeneia: Minneapolis, Minn.: Fortress, 2001.

'Intertexts in the Gospel of Matthew', *HTR* 97 (2004), 119–37.

Maahs, K. H. 'Curtain', *ISBE* I, p. 838.

Maas, A. J. *The Gospel according to Saint Matthew with an Explanatory and Critical Commentary*. St Louis, Mo.: Herder, 1898.

MacAskill, Grant. 'Restored-Creation Eschatology in Matthew's Gospel and Early Judaism', paper presented at the Annual Postgraduate Research Conference, University of Glasgow, June 2, 2004.

Macdonald, J. 'An Assembly at Ugarit?' *Ugarit-Forschungen* 11(1979), 515–26.

Mach, Michael. 'Angels', *EDSS* I, pp. 24–27.

Madvig, D. H. 'τὸ καταπετάσμα', *NIDNTT* III, p. 794.

MacRae, G. W. 'Some Elements of Jewish Apocalyptic and Mystical Tradition and their Relation to Gnostic Literature', Ph.D. diss., 2 vols., Cambridge University, 1966.

Magen, Y. 'The Gates of the Temple Mount according to Josephus and the Mishnah', *Cathedra* (1980), 47–53 [Hebrew].

Maier, Gerhard. *Matthäus-Evangelium*. 2 vols. Neuhausen-Stuttgart: Hänssler, 1979–80.

Maier, Johann. *The Temple Scroll: An Introduction, Translation and Commentary*. Translated by R. T. White. JSOTSup 34. Sheffield: JSOT Press, 1985.

'The Architectural History of the Temple in Jerusalem in the Light of the Temple Scroll', pp. 23–62 in *Temple Scroll Studies*. Edited by George J. Brooke. JSPSup 7. Sheffield: JSOT Press, 1989.

'Temple', *EDSS* II, pp. 921–27.

'Zu Kult und Liturgie der Qumrangemeinde', *RevQ* 14 (1990), 543–86.

*Die Tempelrolle vom Toten Meer und das 'Neue Jerusalem'*, Munich: Reinhardt, 1997.

Maisch, Ingrid. 'Die Österliche Dimension des Todes Jesu: Zur Osterverkündigung in Mt 27, 51–54', pp. 96–123 in *Auferstehung Jesus – Auferstehung der Christen: Deutungen des Österglaubes*. Edited by FS A. Vögtle and I. Broer. Freiburg: Herder, 1986.

Maldonado, Juan de, and George J. Davie. *S. Matthew's Gospel*. London: John Hodges, 1888. Microform.

Mangan, Céline. 'Some Observations on the Dating of Targum Job', pp. 67–78 in *Back to the Sources: Biblical and Near Eastern Studies in Honour of Dermot Ryan*. Edited by K. J. Cathcart and J. F. Healey. Dublin: Glendale, 1980.

*The Targum of Job*. Aramaic Bible 15. Edinburgh: T. & T. Clark, 1991.

Manicardi, Ermenegildo. 'Gesu e la sua morte secondo Marco 15:33–37', pp. 9–28 in *Gesu e la sua morte*. Edited by G. Boggio, A. Bonora, S. Cipriani *et al*. Brescia, Italy: Paideia Editrice, 1984.

Mann, C. S. *Mark*. ABC 27. New York, N.Y.: Doubleday, 1986.
Manson, T. W. *The Sayings of Jesus: As Recorded in the Gospels according to St Matthew and St Luke Arranged with Introduction and Commentary*. London: SCM Press, 1949.
Mara, M. G. *Évangile de Pierre*. Paris: Cerf, 1973.
Marcus, Joel, and Marion L. Soards, eds. *Apocalyptic and the New Testament: Essays in Honor of J. Louis Martyn*. JSNTSup 24. Sheffield: Academic Press, 1989.
Marcus, Joel. *The Way of the Lord: Christological Exegesis of the Old Testament in the Gospel of Mark*. Louisville, Ky.: Westminster John Knox, 1992.
Martling, C. H., and S. E. Staxäng, eds., *Kommentar till evangelieboken, Högmässotexterna*. Stockholm: Uppsala, 1964.
Mare, Harold. *The Archaeology of the Jerusalem Area*. Grand Rapids, Mich.: Baker, 1987.
Marguerat, Daniel. *Le Judgment das l'Evangile de Matthieu*. Genève: Labor et Fides, 1981.
Marmorstein, Emile. 'The Veil in Judaism and Islam', *JJS* 5 (1954), 1–11.
Marshall, I. Howard. *The Gospel of Luke*. NIGTC. Exeter: Paternoster, 1978.
Martin, Ralph P., and Peter H. Davids, eds. *Dictionary of the Later New Testament and Its Development*. Downers Grove, Ill.: InterVarsity, 1997.
Martinez, Florentino Garcia, and Eibert J. C. Tigchelaar, eds. *The Dead Sea Scrolls: Study Edition*. 2 vols. Grand Rapids, Mich.: Eerdmans, 1997, 1998.
Martinez, E. 'The Gospel Accounts of the Death of Jesus: A Study of the Death Accounts Made in the Light of New Testament Traditions, the Redaction and the Theology of the Four Evangelists', Ph.D. diss., Rome, 1969.
Martínez, G. 'Temple Scroll', *EDSS* II, pp. 927–29.
Mason, Rex. 'The Use of Biblical Material in Zechariah 9–14: A Study in Inner Biblical Exegesis', pp. 1–208 in *Bringing out the Treasure: Inner Biblical Allusion in Zechariah 9–14*. Edited by Mark J. Boda and Michael. H. Floyd. JSOTSup 370. Sheffield: Academic Press, 2003.
Mason, Steve, ed. *Understanding Josephus: Seven Perspectives*. JSPSup 32. Sheffield: Academic Press, 1998.
*Flavius Josephus: Translation and Commentary*. Leiden: Brill, 2001.
*Josephus and the New Testament*. 2d edn. Peabody, Mass.: Hendrickson, 2003.
Massaux, Édouard. *The Influence of the Gospel of Saint Matthew on Christian Literature before Saint Irenaeus*. 3 vols. Edited by Arthur J. Bellinzoni. Translated by N. J. Belval and S. Hecht. Macon, Ga.: Mercer University Press, 1993.
Matera, Frank J. *The Kingship of Jesus: Composition and Theology in Mark 15*. Chico, Calif.: Scholars Press, 1982.
*Passion Narratives and Gospel Theologies: Interpreting the Synoptics through Their Passion Stories*. New York, N.Y.: Paulist Press, 1986.
May, Herbert G. 'The Departure of the Glory of Yahweh', *JBL* 56 (1937), 309–21.
McCarter, P. Kyle. *2 Samuel*. ABC 9. Garden City, N.Y.: Doubleday, 1984.
McCasland, S. Vernon. 'Portents in Josephus and the Gospels', *JBL* 51 (1932), 323–35.
McConnell, R. A. 'Law and Prophecy in Matthew's Gospel', Ph.D. diss., University of Basel, 1964.

McDonald, J. I. H. *The Resurrection: Narrative and Belief*. London: SPCK, 1989.

McKay, John W. 'When the Veil Is Taken Away: The Impact of Prophetic Experience on Biblical Interpretation', *Journal of Pentecostal Theology* 5 (1994), 17–40.

McKeating, Henry. *Ezekiel*. Old Testament Guides. Sheffield: Academic Press, 1993.

McKelvey, R. J. *The New Temple: The Church in the New Testament*. London: Oxford University Press, 1969.

McKnight, Scot. 'Jesus and His Death: Some Recent Scholarship', *CR: BS* 9 (2001), 185–228.

McNamara, Martin. *Targum Neofiti 1: Genesis*. Aramaic Bible 1a. Edinburgh: T. & T. Clark, 1992.

McNeile, A. H. *The Book of Exodus*. 3d edn. London: Methuen & Co., 1931.

*The Gospel according to St Matthew*. London: Macmillan, 1915.

Meier, John P. *The Vision of Matthew: Christ, Church and Morality in the First Gospel*. New York, N.Y.: Paulist Press, 1979.

*Matthew*. New Testament Message 3. Wilmington, Del.: Michael Glazier, 1981.

'Salvation History in Matthew: In Search of a Starting Point', *CBQ* 37 (1975), 203–15.

Meisner, Norbert. 'Aristeasbrief', pp. 35–87 in *Jüdische Schriften aus hellenistisch-römischer Zeit*. Edited by Werner Georg Kümmel. Gütersloher: Verlag Gerd Mohn, 1977.

Mettinger, Tryggve N. D. 'Yhwh Sabaoth: The Heavenly King on the Cherubim Throne', pp. 109–38 in *Studies in the Period of David and Solomon, and Other Essays – International Symposium for Biblical Studies, Tokyo, 1979*. Edited by Tomoo Ishida. Winona Lake, Ind: Eisenbrauns, 1982.

'Cherubim', *DDD*, pp. 362–67.

Metzger, Bruce M. *The Text of the New Testament: Its Transmission, Corruption, and Restoration*. 3d edn. Oxford: Oxford University Press, 1992.

Meyer, Ben F. *The Aims of Jesus*. London: SCM Press, 1979.

Meyer, Heinrich August Wilhelm. *Critical and Exegetical Commentary on the New Testament: Matthew*. 2 vols. Edinburgh: T. & T. Clark, 1879.

Meyers, Carol. 'Screen', *ABD* V, p. 1011.

'Temple, Jerusalem', *ABD* VI, pp. 350–69.

'Veil of the Temple', *ABD* VI, pp. 785–86.

Michaelis, Wilhelm. *Das Evangelium nach Matthäus*. 2 vols. Zürich: Zwingli, 1948–49.

'ὁράω', *TDNT* V, pp. 315–67.

Michaels, J. R. 'The Centurion's Confession and the Spear Thrust', *CBQ* 29 (1967), 102–9.

Michel, Otto. 'The Conclusion of Matthew's Gospel: A Contribution to the History of the Easter Message', pp. 39–52 in *The Interpretation of Matthew*. Translated by R. Morgan. Edited by G. N. Stanton. Edinburgh: T. & T. Clark, 1995. Repr. from *Evangelische Theologie* 10 (1950), 16–26.

'Ναός', *TDNT* IV, pp. 880–90.

and Otto Bauernfeind. *Flavius Josephus, De Bello Judaico – Der Jüdische Krieg*. Darmstadt: Wissenschaftliche Buchgesellschaft, 1969.

Micklem, Philip A. *St Matthew*. London: Methuen, 1917.

Milgrom, Jacob. *Studies in Levitical Terminology, 1: The Encroacher and the Levite; The Term 'Aboda*. Near East Studies 14. London: University of California Publications, 1970.

'Sin-Offering or Purification-Offering?' *VT* 21 (1971), 237–39.

*Cult and Conscience: The* ASHAM *and the Priestly Doctrine of Repentance*. Leiden: Brill, 1976.

'Israel's Sanctuary: The Priestly "Picture of Dorian Gray"', *RB* 83 (1976), 390–99.

*Studies in Cultic Theology and Terminology*. Leiden: Brill, 1983.

*The JPS Torah Commentary: Numbers*. Philadelphia, Pa.: The Jewish Publication Society, 1990.

*Leviticus 1–16*. ABC 3. New York, N.Y.: Doubleday, 1991.

'Ethics and Ritual: The Foundations of the Biblical Dietary Laws', pp. 159–91 in *Religion and Law: Biblical–Judaic and Islamic Perspectives*. Edited by E. Firmage, B. Weiss and J. Welch. Winona Lake, Ind.: Eisenbrauns, 1990.

Review of Bernd Janowski, *Sühne als Heilsgeschehen. Studien zur Sühnetheologie der Priesterschrift und zur Wurzel KPR im Alten Orient und im Alten Testament, JBL*104 (1985), 302–4.

'Sacrifice', *EDSS* II, pp. 807–12.

'The Two Pericopes on the Purification Offering', pp. 211–15 in *The Word of the Lord Shall Go Forth.*Edited by C. Meyers and M. O'Connor. Winona Lake, Ind.: Eisenbrauns, 1983.

'Two Kinds of *ḤAṬṬĀ'T*', pp. 70–74 in *Studies in Cultic Theology and Terminology*. Studies in Judaism in Late Antiquity 36. Leiden: Brill, 1983.

R. E. Gane. 'פרכת', *TWAT* VI, pp. 755–56.

Miller, James E. 'The Mælæk of Tyre (Ezekiel 28,11–19)', *ZAW* 105 (1994), 497–501.

Miller, R. J. 'The Rejection of the Prophets in Q', *JBL* 107 (1988), 225–40.

Mitchell, H. G., J. M. P. Smith and J. A. Bewer, *Haggai, Zechariah, Malachi and Jonah.*International Critical Commentary. Edinburgh: T. & T. Clark, 1912.

Moeller, Edmond, ed. *Corpus Christianum*. Turnholti: Brepols, 1992–continuous.

Moffitt, David M. 'Righteous Bloodshed, Matthew's Passion Narrative and the Temple's Destruction: Lamentations as a Matthean Intertext', *JBL* 125 (2006). 299–320.

Montefiore, Claude G. *The Synoptic Gospels*. 3 vols. London: Macmillan, 1909.

*Rabbinic Literature and Gospel Teachings*. London: Macmillan, 1930.

*Josephus and the New Testament*. London: Mowbray, 1962.

Montefiore, H. W. 'Josephus and the New Testament', *NovT* 4 (1960), 139–60.

Montgomery, James A. *Arabia and the Bible*. Philadelphia, Pa.: University of Philadelphia Press, 1934.

*The Books of Kings*. ICC. Edinburgh: T. & T. Clark, 1951.

Moo, Douglas J. *The Old Testament in the Gospel Passion Narratives*. Sheffield: Almond, 1983.

'Jesus and the Authority of the Mosaic Law', *JSNT* 20 (1984), 3–49.

Moore, George Foote. *Judaism*. 3 vols. Peabody, Mass.: Hendrickson, 1997.

Morböck, Johannes. 'Die "Geschichte Israels' als 'Bungesgeschichte" nach dem Sirachbuch', pp. 177–97 in *Neue Bund im Alten*. Edited by Erich Zenger. Freiburg: Harder, 1993.

'Der Hohepriester Simon in Sir 50: Ein Beitung zur Bedeutung von Priester Turm und Kult im Sirachbuch', pp. 215–29 in *Treasures of Wisdom*. Edited by Nuria Calduch-Begades. Leuven: Peeters, 1999.

Morgenstern, J. 'Moses with the Shining Face', *HUCA* 2 (1925), 1–27

Morgentstern, J. 'The Ark, the Ephod and the Tent of Meeting', *HUCA* 17 (1942), 153–57.

Moses, A. D. A. *Matthew's Transfiguration Story and Jewish–Christian Controversy*. JSNTSup 122. Sheffield: Academic Press, 1996.

Moulton, J. H., and G. Milligan. *Vocabulary of the Greek Testament*. Peabody, Mass.: Hendrickson, 1997. Repr. of *Vocabulary of the Greek Testament*. London: Hodder & Stoughton, 1930.

Morison, James. *Commentary on the Gospel according to Matthew*. London: Hamilton & Adams, 1870.

Morris, Leon. *The Gospel according to Matthew*. Grand Rapids, Mich.: Eerdmans, 1992.

Mossman, Thomas W., ed. *The Great Commentary of Cornelius a Lapide: St Matthew's Gospel*. London: John Hodges, 1876.

Motyer, Stephen. 'The Rending of the Veil: A Markan Pentecost?' *NTS* 33 (1987), 155–57.

Moule, C. F. D. *The Gospel according to Mark*. Cambridge: Cambridge University Press, 1965.

'Fulfilment-Words in the New Testament', *NTS* 14 (1967), 293–320.

*The Phenomenon of the New Testament: An Inquiry into the Implications of Certain Features of the New Testament*. London: SCM Press, 1967.

Moulton, Mark. 'Jesus' Goal for Temple and Tree: A Thematic Revisit of Matt 21:12–22', *JETS* 41 (1998), 561–72.

Mowery, Robert L. 'God, Lord and Father: The Theology of the Gospel of Matthew', *Biblical Research* 33 (1988), 24–36.

'The Activity of God in the Gospel of Matthew', *SBLSP* 28 (1989), 400–411.

'The Matthean References to the Kingdom: Different Terms for Different Audiences', *ETL* 70 (1994), 398–405.

'From Lord to Father in Matthew 1–7', *CBQ* 59 (1997), 642–56.

'Son of God in Roman Imperial Titles and Matthew', *Bib.* 83 (2002), 100–110.

Muirhead, Lewis A. *The Eschatology of Jesus*. London: Andrew Melrose, 1904.

Mulder, Otto. *Simon the High Priest in Sirach 50: An Exegetical Study of the Significance of Simon the High Priest as Climax to the Praise of the Fathers in Ben Sira's Concept of the History of Israel*. JSJSup 78. Leiden: Brill, 2003.

Mullen, E. T. *The Assembly of the Gods*. Harvard Semitic Monographs 24. Camridge, Mass.: Harvard University Press, 1980.

Müller, Morgens. 'Salvation-History in the Gospel of Matthew: An Example of Biblical Theology', pp. 58–76 in *New Directions in Biblical Theology: Papers of the Aarhus Conference, 16–19 September 1992*. Edited by Sigfred Pedersen. Leiden: Brill, 1994.

Münster, Sebastian. *Evangelium secundum Matthæum in lingua hebraica, cum versione latina, atque annotationibus Seb. Munsteri. Una cum epistola D. Pauli ad Hebræos hebraice & latine*. Basileœ: Henricum Petri, 1557.

Muraoka, Takamitsu. *Classical Syriac for Hebraists*. Wiesbaden: Harrassowitz, 1987.

Myers, Jacob M. *I Chronicles*. ABC 12. Garden City, N.Y.: Doubleday, 1965.
*II Chronicles*. ABC 13. Garden City, N.Y.: Doubleday, 1965.
Neander, Johann A. W. *The Life of Jesus Christ*. Translated by J. M'Clintock and C. E. Blumentahl. London: H. G. Bohn, 1851.
Neirynck, F., J. Verheyden and R. Corstjens, eds. *The Gospel of Matthew and the Sayings Source Q: A Cumulative Bibliography 1950–1995*. Leuven: Peeters, 1998.
Nelson, Milward Douglas. *The Syriac Version of the Wisdom of Ben Sira Compared to the Greek and Hebrew Materials*. SBLDS 107. Atlanta, Ga.: Scholars Press, 1988.
Nelson, Russell David. 'Studies in the Development of the Text of the Tabernacle Account', Ph.D. diss., Harvard University, 1986.
Nepper-Christensen, Poul. *Das Matthäusevangelium: Ein judenchristliches Evangelium?* Aarhus: Universitetsforlaget, 1958.
Nestle, Eberhard. 'Matt 27,51 und Parallelen', *Zeitschrift für die neutestamentliche Wissenschaft und die Kunde der älteren Kirche* 3 (1902), 167–69.
'Sonnenfinsternis bei Jesu Tod', *Zeitschrift für die neutestamentliche Wissenschaft und die Kunde der älteren Kirche* 3 (1902), 246–47.
Neusner, Jacob. 'Judaism in a Time of Crisis: Four Responses to the Destruction of the Second Temple', *Judaism* 21 (1972), 313–27.
*The Idea of Purity in Ancient Judaism*. Studies in Judaism in Late Antiquity 1. Leiden: Brill, 1973.
ed. *The Tosefta: Translated from the Hebrew*. 6 vols; Hoboken, N.J.: KTAV, 1979–86.
*Rabbinic Judaism: Structure and System*. Minneapolis, Minn.: Fortress, 1995.
Neuss, W. *Das Buch Ezechiel in Theologie und Kunst bis zum Ende des XII. Jahrhunderts*. Münster: Aschendorff, 1912.
New, David S. *Old Testament Quotations in the Synoptic Gospels and the Two-Document Hypothesis*. SBLSCS 37. Atlanta, Ga.: Scholars Press, 1993.
Newsom, Carol. *Song of the Sabbath Sacrifice: A Critical Edition*. Harvard Semitic Studies 27. Atlanta, Ga.: Scholars Press, 1985.
'Heaven', *EDSS* I, pp. 338–40.
'Songs of the Sabbath Sacrifice', *EDSS* II, p. 889.
Nicholson, Edward W. B. *A New Commentary on the Gospel according to Matthew*. London: C. Kegan Paul, 1881.
Nickels, Peter. *Targum and Testament: A Bibliography Together with a New Testament Index*. Rome: Pontifical Biblical Institute, 1967.
Nickelsburg, G. W. E. *Jewish Literature between the Bible and the Mishnah: A Historical and Literary Introduction*. London: SCM, 1981.
'Apocalyptic Texts', *EDSS* I, pp. 29–35.
Nicklas, Tobias. 'Die altsyrische Sinaiticus-Handschrift ($Sy^s$) als Zeuge antijüdischer Tendenzen', *AS* 1 (2003), 29–54.
Nolland, John. *Luke*. 3 vols. WBC 35A–C. Dallas, Tex.: Word, 1989, 1993.
Review of David D. Kupp, *Matthew's Emmanuel. Divine Presence and God's People in the First Gospel*, *JTS* 49 (1998), 741–43.
Review of David C. Sim, *Apocalyptic Eschatology in the Gospel of Matthew*, *JTS* 49 (1998), 225–29.
Noth, Martin. *Leviticus: A Commentary*. Translated by J. E. Anderson. London: SCM Press, 1977.

O'Connell, Kevin G. *The Theodotionic Revision of the Book of Exodus: A Contribution to the Study of the Early History of the Transmission of the Old Testament in Greek*. Cambridge: Cambridge University Press, 1972.

Odeberg, Hugo. *3 Enoch or The Hebrew Book of Enoch*. Cambridge: Cambridge University Press, 1928.

Oden, T. C., and C. A. Hall, eds. *Mark*. Ancient Christian Commentary Series: New Testament 2. London: Fitzroy Dearborn, 1998.

Oerke, Albrecht. 'Κάλυμμα', *TDNT* III, pp. 558–60.

Oesterley, W. O. E. *The Wisdom of Jesus the Son of Sirach or Ecclesiasticus*. London: SPCK, 1916.

*Sacrifices in Ancient Israel: Their Origin, Purposes and Development*. London: Hodder & Stoughton, 1937.

Ó Fearghail, Fearghas. 'Sir 50,5–21: Yom Kippur or the Daily Whole-Offering?' *Bib*. 59 (1978), 301–13.

Ohly, Dieter. 'Die Göttin und Ihre Basis', *Mitteilungen des deutschen Archäologischen Instituts, Athenische Abteilung* 68 (1953), 25–50.

Olmstead, Wesley G. *Matthew's Trilogy of Parables: The Nation, the Nations and the Reader in Matthew 21.28–22.14*. SNTSMS 127. Cambridge: Cambridge University Press, 2003.

Olyan, S. M. *A Thousand Thousands Served Him: Exegesis and the Naming of Angels in Ancient Judaism*. TSAJ 36. Tübingen: Mohr Siebeck, 1993.

Orchard, Bernard. *Matthew, Luke & Mark*. Manchester: Koinonia, 1977.

Origen. *Contra Celsum*. Translated with an introduction and notes by H. Chadwick. Cambridge: Cambridge University Press, 1965.

Ornan, Tallay. 'Symbols of Royalty and Divinity', *BAR* 21 (1995), 38–39.

Orton, D. E. *The Understanding Scribe: Matthew and the Apocalyptic Ideal*. JSNTSup 25. Sheffield: JSOT Press, 1989.

Otzen, B. 'בדל', *TWOT* II, p. 3

Overman, J. Andrew. *Matthew's Gospel and Formative Judaism: The Social World of the Matthean Community*. Minneapolis, Minn.: Fortress, 1990.

Ouellette, J. 'The Basic Structure of the Solomonic Temple and Archaeological Research', pp. 1–20 in *The Temple of Solomon: Archaeological Fact and Medieval Tradition in Christian, Islamic and Jewish Art*. Religion and the Arts 3. Missoula, Mont.: Scholars Press, 1976.

Paige, Lucius R. *A Commentary on the New Testament*. Boston, Mass.: A. Tompkins, 1855.

Pallis, Marco. 'The Veil of the Temple: A Study of Christian Invitation', *Studies in Comparative Religion* 15 (1983), 81–88.

Patte, Daniel. *Early Jewish Hermeneutic*. Missoula, Mont.: Society of Biblical Literature, 1975.

*The Gospel according to Matthew: A Structural Commentary on Matthew's Faith*. Philadelphia, Pa.: Fortress, 1987.

Patrich, J. 'Reconstructing Herod's Temple Mount in Jerusalem', *BAR* 15 (1989), 23–43.

Payne Smith, J. *A Compendious Syriac Dictionary*. Oxford: Clarendon Press, 1903.

Pearlman, Moshe. *The Maccabees*. Jerusalem: Weidfeld and Nicolson, 1973.

Pelletier, André. 'Le "Voile" du Temple de Jérusalem est-il devenu la "Portière" du Temple d'Olympie', *Syria* 32 (1955), 289–307.

'Le grand rideau du vestibule du Temple de Jérusalem', *Syria* 35 (1958), 218–26.

'La tradition synoptique du "Voile déchiré" à la lumière des réalités archéologiques', *Recherches de science religieuse* 46 (1958), 161–80.

*Lettre d'Aristée a Philocrate: Introduction, Texte Critique, Traduction et Notes, Index Complet des Mots Grecs*. Sources Chrétiennes 89. Paris: Cerf, 1962.

'Le "voile du temple" de Jérusalem en termes de métier', *Revue des etudes grecques* 77 (1964), 70–75.

Penar, Tadeusz. *Northwest Semitic Philology and the Hebrew Fragments of Ben Sira*. Rome: Biblical Institute Press, 1975.

Penney, D. L. 'Finding the Devil in the Details: Onomastic Exegesis and the Naming of Evil in the World of the New Testament', pp. 37–52 in *New Testament Greek and Exegesis: Essays in Honor of Gerald F. Hawthorne*. Edited by A. M. Donaldson and T. B. Sailors. Grand Rapids, Mich.: Eerdmans, 2003.

Pennington, Jonathan T. 'Heaven and Earth in the Gospel of Matthew', Ph.D. diss., University of St Andrews 2005.

Perrot, Charles. *Jésus et l'histoire*. Paris: Desclée, 1979.

Pesch, Wilhelm. *Matthäus der Seelsorger*. Stuttgart: Katholisches Bibelwerk, 1966.

Peters, Norbert. *Hebräische Text des Buches Ecclesiasticus*. Freiburg: Herdersche Verlagshandlung, 1902.

Petersen, William L. *Tatian's Diatessaron: Its Creation, Dissemination, Significance, and History in Scholarship*. Supplements to Vigiliae Christianae XXV. Leiden: Brill, 1994.

Review of Robert F. Shedinger, *Tatian and the Jewish Scriptures: A Textual and Philological Analysis of the Old Testament Citations in Tatian's Diatessaron*, *JBL* 122 (2003), 391–95.

Pinches, T. G. *The Old Testament in the Light of the Historical Records of Assyria and Babylonia*. 2d edn. London: SPCK, 1903.

Plastaras, James. *The God of Exodus: The Theology of the Exodus Narratives*. Milwaukee, Wis.: Bruce Publishing Co., 1966.

Plummer, Alfred D. *An Exegetical Commentary on the Gospel according to S. Matthew*. London: Paternoster Row, 1909.

Plumptre, E. H., and C. J. Ellicott, C. J. *The Gospel according to St Matthew*. London: Cassell and Co., 1900.

Popper, Julius. *Der biblische Bericht über die Stiftshütte: Ein Beitrag zur Geschichte der Composition und Diaskeue des Pentateuch*. Leipzig: Heinrich Hunger, 1862.

Porten, Bezalel. 'The Structure and Orientation of the Jewish Temple at Elephantine: A Revised Plan of the Jewish District', *JAOS* 81 (1961), 38–42.

Powell, J. Enoch. *The Evolution of the Gospel: A New Translation of the First Gospel with Commentary and Introductory Essay*. New Haven, Conn.: Yale University Press, 1994.

Powell, Mark Allen. *What Is Narrative Criticism?* Minneapolis, Minn.: Fortress, 1990.

'Direct and Indirect Phraseology in the Gospel of Matthew', *SBLSP* 30 (1991), 405–17.

Review of D. C. Sim, *Apocalyptic Eschatology in the Gospel of Matthew*, *JBL* 117 (1998), 534–36 and *RBL* (Jan. 15, 1998).

Preuss, H. D. 'בּוֹא', *TDOT* II, pp. 22–23.

Pritchard, James B., ed. *Ancient Near East in Pictures Relating to the Old Testament.* 2d edn. Princeton, N.J.: Princeton University Press, 1969.

ed. *Ancient Near Eastern Texts Relating to the Old Testament.* 3d edn. Princeton, N.J.: Princeton University Press, 1969.

Propp, William H. 'Gershon', *ABD* II, pp. 994–95.

Provence, Thomas E. 'Who Is Sufficient for These Things: An Exegesis of 2 Corinthians 2:15–3:18', *NovT* 24 (1982), 54–81.

Przybylski, Benno. *Righteousness in Matthew and His World of Thought.* SNTSMS 41. Cambridge: Cambridge University Press, 1980.

Purvis, James D. *The Samaritan Pentateuch and the Origin of the Samaritan Sect.* Harvard Semitic Monographs 2. Cambridge, Mass.: Harvard University Press, 1968.

Qimron, Elisha. 'New Readings in the Temple Scroll', *IEJ* 28 (1978), 161–72.

*The Hebrew of the Dead Sea Scrolls.* Harvard Semitic Studies 29. Atlanta, Ga.: Scholars Press, 1986.

'Further New Readings in the Temple Scroll', *IEJ* 37 (1987), 31–35.

*The Temple Scroll: A Critical Edition with Extensive Reconstructions.* Jerusalem: Israel Exploration Society, 1996.

Rabe, Virgil W. 'The Identity of the Priestly Tabernacle', *JNES* 25 (1966), 132–34.

Radermakers, J. *Au fil de l'Évangile selon Saint Matthieu.* 2 vols. Heverlee-Louvain: Institut d'études théologiques, 1972.

Rattey, Beatrice Katherine. *The Gospel according to Saint Matthew in the Revised Version, with Introduction and Commentary.* Oxford: Clarendon Press, 1938.

Reed, Stephen A. 'Merarites', *ABD* IV, pp. 698–99.

Reicke, Bo. 'Synoptic Prophecies on the Destruction of the Temple', pp. 121–34 in *Studies in New Testament and Early Christian Literature.* Novum Testamentum Supplement Series 33. Edited by D. Aune. Leiden: Brill, 1972.

Reuss, J. *Matthäus-Kommentare aus der griechischen Kirche.* Berlin: Akademie-Verlag, 1957.

Reventlow. H. G. '"Sein Blut komme über sein Haupt"', *VT* 10 (1960), 311–27.

Rice, George. 'Heb 6:19: An Analysis of Some Assumptions Concerning Katapetasma', *AUSS* 25 (1987), 65–71.

Riches, John. *Matthew.* New Testament Guides. Sheffield: Academic Press, 1997.

Ridderbos, Herman N. *Matthew's Witness to Jesus Christ: The King and the Kingdom.* New York, N.Y.: Association Press, 1958.

*The Coming of the Kingdom.* Translated by H. de Jongste. Phillipsburg, N.J.: P&R, 1962.

Riebl, M. *Auferstehung Jesu in der Stunde seines Todes? Zur Botschaft von Mt 27, 51b–53.* Stuttgart: Katholisches Bibelwerk, 1978.

Riesenfeld, Harald. *The Resurrection in Ezekiel xxxvii and in the Dura-Europos Paintings.* Uppsala: Uninversitets Årsskrift, 1948.

Riesner, Rainer. 'Back to the Historical Jesus through Paul and His School (The Ransom Logion – Mark 10.45; Matthew 20.28)', *JSHJ* 1 (2003), 171–99.

Robertson, A. T. *Commentary on the Gospel according to Matthew.* New York, N.Y.: Macmillan, 1911.

Robinson, James M., Paul Hoffmann and John S. Kloppenborg. *The Critical Edition of Q.* Hermeneia. Minneapolis, Minn.: Fortress, 2000.

*Documenta Q: Reconstructions of Q Through Two Centuries of Gospel Research Excerpted, Sorted, and Evaluated.* Leuven: Peeters, 1996.

Robinson, Theodore Henry. *The Gospel of Matthew*. Moffatt New Testament Commentary. London: Hodder & Stoughton, 1928.
Rogerson, John W., R. W. L. Moberly and William Johnstone. *Genesis and Exodus*. Sheffield: Academic Press, 2001.
Roloff, Jürgen. 'Anfänge der soteriologischen Deutung des Todes Jesu (Mk. X. 45 und Lk. XXII. 27)', *NTS* 19 (1972), 38–64.
Rosenthal, Franz. *A Grammar of Biblical Aramaic*. 6th edn. Wiesbaden: Harrasowitz Verlag, 1995.
Roth, Cecil. 'Ecclesiasticus in the Synagogue Service', *JBL* 71 (1952), 171–78.
Roth, Wolfgang M. W. 'The Secret of the Kingdom', *Christian Century* 100 (1983), 179–82.
Rowland, Christopher. *The Open Heaven: A Study of Apocalyptic in Judaism and Early Christianity*. Eugene, Ore.: Wipf & Stock, 1982.
'Apocalyptic, the Poor, and the Gospel of Matthew', *JTS* 45 (1994), 504–18.
Rowley, H. H. *Worship in Ancient Israel: Its Form and Meaning*. London: SPCK, 1967.
Rudman, Dominic. 'The Crucifixion as *Chaoskampf*: A New Reading of the Passion Narrative in the Synoptic Gospels', *Bib.* 84 (2003), 102–7.
Rudolph, Wilhelm. 'Problems of the Books of Chronicles', *VT* 4 (1954), 401–9.
*Chronikbücher*. Handbuch zum Alten Testament. Tübingen: Mohr, 1955.
Ryou, Philip Ho-Young. 'Apocalyptic Opening, Eschatological Inclusio: A Study of the Rending of the Heaven and Temple Curtain in Mark's Gospel with a Special Reference to the Motif of Seeing', Ph.D. diss., University of Glasgow, 2004.
Ryssel, V. 'Die Sprüche Jesus' des Sohnes Sirachs', pp. 230–475 in vol. 1 of *Apokryphen, Die Apokryphen und Pseudepigraphen des Alten Testaments*. Edited by E. Kautzsch. Tübingen: Mohr Siebeck, 1900.
Runia, David T. *The Studia Philonica Annual: Studies in Hellenistic Judaism*. Vol. 8. Atlanta, Ga.: Scholars Press, 1996.
Rutgers, L. V., *et al..*, eds. *The Use of Sacred Books in the Ancient World*. Leuven: Peeters, 1998.
Sabbe, Maurits. 'The Johannine Account of the Death of Jesus and its Synoptic Parallels', *ETL* 70 (1994), 34–64.
Sabourin, Leopold. *The Gospel according to St Matthew*. Bandra, Bombay: St Paul Publications, 1982.
'Apocalyptic Traits in Matthew's Gospel', *Religious Studies Bulletin* 3 (1983), 19–36.
Sacchi, Paolo. *Jewish Apocalyptic and Its History*. Translated by W. J. Short. JSPSup 20. Sheffield: JSOT, 1990.
Sadler, M. F. *The Gospel according to St Matthew*. London: Bell, 1906.
Sahlin, Harald. 'Zum Verständnis der christologischen Anschauung des Markusevangeliums', *Studia Theologica* 31 (1977), 1–19.
Saldarini, Anthony J. 'Varieties of Rabbinic Response to the Destruction of the Temple', *SBLSP* 21 (1982), 437–58.
*Matthew's Christian–Jewish Community*. Chicago, Ill.: University of Chicago Press, 1994.
Sand, Alexander. *Das Gesetz und die Propheten: Untersuchungen zur Theologie des Evangeliums nach Matthäus*. Regensburgh: Friedrich Pustet, 1974.
*Das Evangelium nach Matthäus*. Regensburg: Friedrich Pustet, 1986.

Šanda, A. *Die Bücher der Könige. Übersetzt und Erklärt.* 2 vols. Münster: Aschendorffsche Verlagsbuchhandlung, 1911.
Sanders, E. P. *Jesus and Judaism.* London: S.C.M. Press, 1985.
*Judaism: Practice and Belief, 63 BCE–66 CE.* London: S.C.M. Press, 1992.
Sanderson, J. E. *An Exodus Scroll from Qumran.* Harvard Semitic Studies 30. Atlanta, Ga.: Scholars Press, 1986.
Sandmel, Samuel. 'Parallelomania', *JBL* 81 (1962), 1–13.
Sarna, Nahum M. *The JPS Torah Commentary: Exodus.* New York, N.Y.: Jewish Publication Society, 1991.
Satran, David. *Biblical Prophets in Byzantine Palestine: Reassessing the 'Lives of the Prophets'.* Leiden: Brill, 1995.
Schaeffer, Charles Frederick. *Annotations on the Gospel according to St Matthew.* Philadelphia, Pa.: United Lutheran Publication House, 1895.
Schäfer, Peter, *et al.*. *Synopse zur Hekhalot-Literatur.* TSAJ 2. Tübingen: Mohr Siebeck, 1981.
Schaff, Philip. *The Gospel according to Matthew.* New York, N.Y.: Charles Scribner's Sons, 1882.
Schenk, G. 'τὸ ἱερόν', *TDNT* III, pp. 230–41.
Schenk, Wolfgang. *Der Passionsbericht nach Markus.* Gütersloh: Mohn, 1974.
Schenke, Hans-Martin. 'Erwägung zum Rätsel der Hebräerbriefes', pp. 421–37 in *Neues Testament und christliche Existenz.* Edited by H. D. Betz and L. Schottroff. Tübingen: Mohr Siebeck, 1973.
Schenker, Adrian. 'Das Zeichen des Blutes und die Gewissheit der Vergebung im Alten Testament', *München theologische Zeitschrift* 34 (1983), 195–213.
'Once Again, the Expiatory Sacrifices', *JBL* 116 (1997), 697–99.
Schiffman, Lawrence H. 'The Sacrificial System of the *Temple Scroll* and the Book of Jubilees', *SBLSP* 24 (1985), 217–33.
'The Dead Sea Scrolls and the Early History of the Jewish Liturgy', pp. 33–48 in *The Synagogue in Late Antiquity.* Edited by L. I. Levine. Philadelphia, Pa.: American School of Oriental Research, 1987.
and James C. VanderKam, eds. *Encyclopedia of the Dead Sea Scrolls.* 2 vols. Oxford: Oxford University Press, 2000.
Schlatter, Adolf. *Zur Topographie und Geschichte Palästinas.* Suttgart: Calwer Verlag, 1893.
*Das Evangelium nach Matthäus.* Stuttgart: Calwer Verlag, 1947.
*Der Evangelist Matthäus: Seine Sprache, sein Ziel, seine Selbständigkeit.* Stuttgart: Calwer Verlag, 1957.
Schleiermacher, Friedrich. *The Life of Jesus.* Translated by S. M. Gilmour. Philadelphia, Pa.: Fortress, 1975. Translation of *Das Leben Jesu. Vorlesungen an der Universität zu Berline im Jahr 1832.* Edited by K. A. Rütenik. Berlin: Georg Reimer, 1864.
Schmid, Josef. *Das Evangelium nach Matthäus.* Regensburg: Friedrich Pustet, 1965.
Schmidt, Thomas E. 'The Penetration of Barriers and the Revelation of Christ in the Gospels', *NovT* 34 (1992), 229–46.
Schnackenburg, Rudolf. *Matthäusevangelium.* 2 vols. Würzburg: Echter Verlag, 1987.
Schneemelcher, Wilhelm, ed. *New Testament Apocrypha.* 2 vols. English translation edited by R. McL. Wilson. Louisville, Ky.: Westminster John Knox, 1991.

Schniewind, Julius. *Das Evangelium nach Matthäus*. Göttingen: Vandenhoeck & Ruprecht, 1954.

Schneider, C. 'Der Hauptmann am Kreuz. Zur Nationalisierung neutestamentlicher Nebenfiguren', *Zeitschrift für die neutestamentliche Wissenschaft und die Kunde der älteren Kirche* 33 (1934), 1–17.

'Καταπέτασμα', *TDNT* III, pp. 628–30.

Schneider, Gerhard. '"Im Himmel – Auf Erden", Eine Perspektive Matthäischer Theologie', pp. 285–97 in *Studien Zum Matthäusevangelium: Festschrift Für Wilhelm Pesch*. Edited by Ludger Schenke. Stuttgart: Katholisches Bibelwerk, 1988.

Schonfield, Hugh J. *An Old Hebrew Text of St Matthew's Gospel*. Edinburgh: T. & T. Clark, 1927.

Schuon, Frithjof. 'The Mystery of the Veil', *Parabola* 19 (1994), 49–50.

Schürer, Emil. *History of the Jewish People in the Age of Jesus Christ*. 4 vols. Edinburgh: T. & T. Clark, 1984.

Schüssler Fiorenza, Elisabeth. 'Cultic Language in Qumran and in the NT', *CBQ* 38 (1976), 159–77.

and Shelly Matthews. *Searching the Scriptures*. New York, N.Y.: Crossroad, 1994.

Schwartz, Baruch J. 'The Bearing of Sin in the Priestly Literature', pp. 3–21 in *Pomegranates and Golden Bells: Studies in Biblical, Jewish, and Near Eastern Ritual, Law, and Literature in Honor of Jacob Milgrom*. Edited by D. P. Wright, D. N. Freedman and A. Hurvitz. Winona Lake, Ind.: Eisenbrauns, 1995.

Schwartz, Daniel R. 'The Three Temples of 4 Q Florilegium', *RevQ* 10 (1979), 83–91.

'Viewing the Holy Utensils (P Ox V,840)', *NTS* 32 (1986), 153–59.

Schweitzer, Albert. *The Mystery of the Kingdom of God: The Secret of Jesus' Messiahship and Passion*. Translated by W. Lowrie. London: Adam and Charles Black, 1914.

*The Mysticism of Paul the Apostle*. Translated by W. Montgomery. London: A. & C. Black, 1931.

Schweizer, Eduard. *Matthäus und seine Gemeinde*. Stuttgart: K. B. W. Verlag, 1974.

*The Good News according to Matthew*. Translated by D. E. Green. London: SPCK, 1976.

Schwemer, Anna Maria. 'Gott als König und seine Königsherrschaft in den Sabbatliedern aus Qumran', pp. 45–1118 in *Königsherrschaft Gottes und himmlischer Kult im Judentum, Urchristentum und in der hellenistichen Welt*. Edited by Martin Hengel and Anna Maria Schwemer. Tübingen: Mohr Siebeck, 1991.

*Studien zu den frühjüdischen Prophetenlegenden* Vitae Prophetarum. 2 vols. TSAJ 49. Tübingen: Mohr Siebeck, 1995, 1996.

Schwier, Helmut. *Tempel und Tempelzerstörung: Untersuchungen zu den theologischen und ideologischen Faktoren im ersten jüdisch-römischen Krieg (66–74 n. Chr.)*. Göttingen: Vandenhoeck & Ruprecht, 1989.

Segal, Peretz. 'The Divine Verdict of Leviticus x 3', *VT* 39 (1989), 91–95.

Senior, Donald P. *The Passion Narrative according to Matthew: A Redactional Study*. Leuven: Leuven University Press, 1975.

'Escatologia e soteriologia nella passione secondo Matteo', pp. 95–105 in *La sapienza della croce oggi*. Vol. 1. Edited by C. Duquoc, M. Adinolfi *et al.*. Turin: Elle Di Ci, 1976.

'The Death of Jesus and the Resurrection of the Holy Ones (Matthew 27:51–53)', *CBQ* 38 (1976), 312–29.

*Invitation to Matthew: A Commentary on the Gospel of Matthew*. Garden City, N.Y.: Image Books, 1977.

'The Death of God's Son and the Beginning of the New Age', pp. 31–59 in *The Language of the Cross*. Edited by A. Lacomara. Chicago, Ill.: Franciscan Herald Press, 1977.

*The Passion of Jesus in the Gospel of Matthew*. Wilmington, Del.: Glazier, 1985.

'Matthew's Special Material in the Passion Story: Implications for the Evangelist's Redactional Technique and Theological Perspective', *ETL* 63 (1987), 272–94.

'The Death of Jesus and the Birth of the New World: Matthew's Theology of History in the Passion Narrative', *CTM* 19 (1992), 416–23.

'Revisiting Matthew's Special Material in the Passion Narrative: A Dialogue with Raymond Brown [The Death of the Messiah, 1994]', *ETL* 70 (1994), 417–24.

*The Gospel of Matthew*. Interpreting Biblical Texts. Nashville, Tenn.: Abington, 1997.

'Between Two Worlds: Gentiles and Jewish Christians in Matthew's Gospel', *CBQ* 61 (1999), 1–23.

Seow, C. L. 'Ark of the Covenant', *ABD* I, pp. 386–93.

Shea, William H. 'A Further Reading for the Hobab Inscription from Sinai', *AUSS* 27 (1989), 193–200.

Sherlock, Charles. 'Ezekiel 10: A Prophet Surprised', *Reformed Theological Review* 42 (1983), 42–44.

Shiner, W. T. 'The Ambiguous Pronouncement of the Centurion and the Shrouding of Meaning in Mark', *JSNT* 79 (2000), 3–22.

Shuler, P. L. *A Genre for the Gospels. The Biographical Character of Matthew*. Philadelphia, Pa.: Fortress, 1982.

Shutt, R. J. H. 'Letter of Aristeas: A New Translation and Introduction', *OTP* II, pp. 8–18.

Sim, David C. 'The "Confession" of the Soldiers in Matthew 27:54', *HeyJ* 34 (1993), 401–24.

'The Gospel of Matthew and the Gentiles', *JSNT* 57 (1995), 19–48.

*Apocalyptic Eschatology in the Gospel of Matthew*. SNTSMS 88. Cambridge: Cambridge University Press, 1996.

*The Gospel of Matthew and Christian Judaism: The History and Social Setting of the Matthean Community*. Edinburgh: T. & T. Clark, 1998.

'Matthew's Anti-Paulism: A Neglected Feature of Matthean Studies', *Hervormde Teologiese Studies* 58 (2002), 767–83.

Simian-Yofre, H. 'פָּנִים', *TWOT* XI, pp. 595–96.

Simon, Marcel. *Verus Israel: A Study of the Relations between Christians and Jews in the Roman Empire (135–425)*. Translated by H. McKeating. Oxford: Oxford University Press, 1986.

Simonetti, Manlio. *Biblical Interpretation in the Early Church: An Historical Introduction to Patristic Exegesis*. Edinburgh: T. & T. Clark, 1994.

*Matthew. Ancient Christian Commentary on Scripture*. 2 vols. Downers Grove, Ill.: InterVarsity Press, 2001, 2002.

Singer, I., *et al.*, eds. *The Jewish Encyclopedia*. 12 vols. New York, N.Y.: Funk & Wagnalls, 1901–6.

Skehan, Patrick W., and Alexander A. Di Lelli. *The Wisdom of Ben Sira*. ABC 39. New York, N.Y.: Doubleday, 1987.

Slomovic, E. 'Toward an Understanding of the Exegesis in the Dead Sea Scrolls', *RevQ* 7 (1969), 3–15.

Smend, Rudolf. *Die Weisheit des Jesus Sirach: Erklärt*. Berlin: Georg Reimer, 1906.

*Griechisch-Syrisch-Hebräischer Index zur Weisheit des Jesus Sirach*. Berlin: Verlag von Georg Reimer, 1907.

Smid, Harm Reinder. *Protevangelium Jacobi: A Commentary*. Assen: VanGorcum, 1965.

Smith, Harold, ed. *Ante-Nicene Exegesis of the Gospels*. 6 vols. London: SPCK, 1925–29.

Smith, J. Z. 'The Temple and the Magician', pp. 233–47 in *God's Christ and His People: Studies in Honour of Nils Alstrup Dahl*. Edited by J. Jervell and W. A. Meeks. Oslo: Universitetsforleget, 1977.

Smith, Ralph P. *Micah-Malachi*. WBC 32. Waco, Tex.: Word, 1984.

Smith, Robert H. *Matthew*. Minneapolis, Minn.: Augsburg, 1989.

'Lampstand', *ISBE* III, pp. 69–71.

Smyth, H. W. *Greek Grammar*. Cambridge, Mass.: Harvard University Press, 1956.

Snaith, John G. *Ecclesiasticus or The Wisdom of Jesus Son of Sirach*. Cambridge: Cambridge University Press, 1974.

Snodgrass, K. *The Parable of the Wicked Tenants: An Inquiry into Parable Interpretation*. Tübingen: Mohr Siebeck, 1983.

Soden, Wolfram von, ed. *Akkadisches Handwörterbuch*. 3 vols. Wiesbaden: Harrassowitz, 1972.

Soisalon-Soininen, I., Anneli Aejmelaeus and Raija Sollamo. *Studien zur Septuaginta-Syntax*. Helsinki: Suomalainen tiedeakatemia, 1987.

Sokoloff, M. *The Targum of Job from Qumran Cave XI*. Ramat-Gan: Bar-Ilan University, 1974.

Soloweyczyk, Elias, and Moritz Grunwald. *Die Bibel, der Talmud, und das Evangelium*. Leipzig: F. A. Brockhaus, 1877.

Stanton, Graham N. *The Gospels and Jesus*. Oxford: Oxford University Press, 1989.

*A Gospel for a New People: Studies in Matthew*. Louisville, Ky.: Westminster John Knox, 1992.

ed. *The Interpretation of Matthew*. Edinburgh: T. & T. Clark, 1995.

'The Fourfold Gospel', *NTS* 43 (1997), 317–46.

Stecchini, Livio C., and Jan Sammer 'The Gospel according to Seneca', http://www.metrum.org/gosen/portenjesus.htm.

Steck, O. H. *Israel und das gewaltsame Geschick der Propheten: Untersuchungen zur Überlieferung des deuteronomistischen Geschichtsbildes im Alten Testa-*

*ment, Spätjudentum, und Urchristentum*. WMANT 23. Neukirchen-Vluyn: Neukirchener Verlag, 1967.

Steinmann, A. E. 'Cherubim', *DOTP* pp. 112–13.

Stemberger, Günter. Review of O. Hofius, *Der Vorhang vor dem Thron Gottes*, *Kairos* 17 (1975), 303–6.

Stendahl, Krister. *The School of St Matthew and Its Use of the Old Testament*. Uppsala: Almqvist & Wiksell, 1954.

'Matthew', pp. 769–98 in *Peake's Commentary on the Bible*. Edited by M. Black and H. H. Rowley. London: Nelson, 1962.

Stern, E. 'The Babylonian Gap', *BAR* 26.6 (2000), 45–51.

*Archaeoology of the Land of the Bible*. 4 vols. New York, N.Y.: Doubleday, 2001.

Stern, Menahem. 'Josephus and the Roman Empire as Reflected in the Jewish War', pp. 71–80 in *Josephus, Judaism and Christianity*. Edited by L. H. Feldman and G. Hata. Leiden: Brill, 1987.

Steudel, Annette. *Der Midrasch zur Eschatologie aus der Qumrangemeinde (1QMidrEschat$^{a-b}$)*. Studies on the Texts of the Desert of Judah 13. Leiden: Brill, 1994.

Stock, Augustine. *Saint Matthew*. Conception, Mo.: Conception Abbey Press, 1960.

Stone, M. E. 'List of Revealed Things in the Apocalyptic Literature', pp. 414–52 in *Magnalia Dei: The Mighty Acts of God: In memory of G. E Wright*. Edited by Frank M. Cross, Werner E. Lemke and Patrick D. Miller. New York, N.Y.: Doubleday, 1976.

Strack, Hermann L., and Paul Billerbeck. *Kommentar zum Neuen Testament aus Talmud und Midrasch*. 6 vols. Munich: C. H. Beck, 1922–61.

Strack, Hermann L., and Günter Stemberger. *Introduction to the Talmud and Midrash*. Translated and edited by M. Bockmuehl. Minneapolis, Minn.: Fortress, 1992.

Strange, John. 'The Idea of Afterlife in Ancient Israel: Some Remarks on the Iconography in Solomon's Temple', *PEQ* 117 (1985), 35–40.

Strauss, David Friedrich. *The Life of Jesus Critically Examined*. Translated by G. Eliot. London: SCM Press, 1973.

Strecker, Georg. *Der Weg der Gerechtigkeit: Untersuchung zur Theologie des Matthäus*. Göttingen: Vandenhoeck & Ruprecht, 1962.

Streeter, B. H. *The Four Gospels: A Study of Origins*. London: Macmillan, 1924.

Strickert, Fred. 'Philo on the Cherubim', pp. 40–57 in *Studia Philonica Annual*. Atlanta, Ga.: Scholars Press, 1996.

Stroumsa, Gedaliahu G. 'Le couple de l'Ange et de l'Esprit: traditions juives et chrétiennes', *RB* 88 (1981), 42–61.

Strugnell, John. 'The Angelic Liturgy at Qumran – 4QSerek Šîrôt 'Olat Haššabbāt', pp. 318–45 in *Congress Volume: Oxford, 1959*. Supplements to Vetus Testamentum 7. Leiden: Brill, 1960.

'Moses-Pseudepigrapha at Qumran: 4Q375, 4Q376, and Similar Works', pp. 221–56 in *Archaeology and History in the Dead Sea Scrolls: The New York University Conference in Memory of Yigael Yadin*. Edited by Lawrence J. Shiffman. JSOTSup 8. Sheffield: JSOT Press, 1990.

Strycker, Émile de. *La Forme la Plus Ancienne du Protévangile de Jacques*. Bruxelles: Société des Bollandistes, 1961.

Suggs, M. Jack. *Wisdom, Christology, and Law in Matthew's Gospel*. Cambridge, Mass.: Harvard University Press, 1970.

Swanson, Dwight D. *The Temple Scroll and the Bible: The Methodology of 11QT*. Leiden: Brill, 1995.

Swart, G. J. 'Twee aardbewings of een? Die assosiasie van liter ^re motiewe in die eksegese van Matteus 27:51–54 & 28:2–4', *Hervormde Teologiese Studies* 49 (1993), 255–265.

Swedenborg, Emanuel, Robert S. Fischer and Louis G. Hoeck. *Commentary on the Gospel according to Matthew: Compiled from the Theological Works of Emanuel Swedenborg*. Boston, Mass.: Massachusetts New-Church Union, 1906.

Swete, Henry Barclay. *An Introduction to the Old Testament in Greek: With an Appendix Containing the Letter of Aristeas*. Edited by H. St J. Thackeray. Cambridge: Cambridge University Press, 1900.

*The Gospel according to St Mark: The Greek Text with Introduction Notes and Indices*. London: Macmillan, 1909.

Syreeni, Kari. 'Between Heaven and Earth: On the Structure of Matthew's Symbolic Universe', *JSNT* 40 (1990), 3–13.

Sylva, Dennis D. 'The Temple Curtain and Jesus' Death in the Gospel of Luke', *JBL* 105 (1986), 239–50.

Talbert, C. H. *What Is a Gospel? The Genre of the Canonical Gospels*. Philadelphia, Pa.: Fortress, 1977.

Talmon, Shemaryahu. '"Exile" and "Restoration" in the Conceptual World of Ancient Judaism', pp. 107–46 in *Restoration: Old Testament, Jewish and Christian Perspectives*. Edited by James M. Scott. Leiden: Brill, 2001.

Tarragon, Jean M de. 'La kapporet est-elle une fiction ou un élément du culte tardif', *RB* 88 (1981), 5–12.

Tasker, R. V. G. *The Gospel according to St Matthew, an Introduction and Commentary*. Grand Rapids, Mich.: Eerdmans 1961.

Taylor, C., and S. Schechter. *The Wisdom of Ben Sira*. Cambridge: Cambridge University Press, 1899.

Taylor, Vincent. *Jesus and His Sacrifice: A Study of the Passion-Sayings in the Gospels*. London: Macmillan, 1937.

*The Gospel according to St Mark*. London: Macmillan, 1952.

'Narrative of the Crucifixion', *NTS* 8 (1961), 333–34.

*The Passion Narrative of St Luke: A Critical and Historical Investigation*. London: Cambridge University Press, 1972.

Tedesche, Sidney, and Solomon Zeitlin. *The First Book of Maccabees*. New York, N.Y.: Harper & Brothers, 1950.

Telford, W. R. *The Barren Temple and the Withered Tree: A Redaction-Critical Analysis of the Cursing of the Fig-Tree Pericope in Mark's Gospel and Its Relation to the Cleansing of the Temple Tradition*. JSNTSup 1. Sheffield: JSOT Press, 1980.

*Mark*. T. & T. Clark Study Guides. Sheffield: Academic Press, 1997.

*The Theology of the Gospel of Mark*. Cambridge: Cambridge University Press, 1999.

Thackeray, H. St J. 'The Letter of Aristeas', pp. 501–18 in *An Introduction to the Old Testament in Greek*. Edited by H. B. Swete. Cambridge: Cambridge University Press, 1900.

*A Grammar of the Old Testament in Greek according to the Septuagint.* Hildeschein: Georg Olms Verlag, 1978.

Thackston, Wheeler M. *Introduction to Syriac: An Elementary Grammar with Readings from Syriac Literature*. Bethesda, Md.: Ibex, 1999.

Thayer, Joseph Henry. *A Greek–English Lexicon of the New Testament.* 4th edn. Edinburgh: T. & T. Clark, 1896.

*The Ante-Nicene Fathers*. Edited by Alexander Roberts and James Donaldson. 1885–87. 10 vols. Repr., Peabody, Mass.: Hendrickson, 1994.

Theissen, Gerd. *Untersuchungen zum Hebräerbrief.* Studien zum Neuen Testament 2. Gütersloh: Mohn, 1969.

Review of O. Hofius, *Der Vorhang vor dem Thron Gottes. Theologische Literaturzeitung* 99 (1974), 426–28.

*The Nicene and Post-Nicene Fathers*, Series 1. Edited by Philip Schaff. 1886–89. 14 vols. Repr., Peabody, Mass.: Hendrickson, 1994.

*The Nicene and Post-Nicene Fathers*, Series 2. Edited by Philip Schaff. 1886–89. 14 vols. Repr., Peabody, Mass.: Hendrickson, 1997.

Thureau-Dangin, F. *Rituels accadiens*. Paris: E. Leroux, 1921.

Thompson, A. L. *Responsibility for Evil in the Theodicy of IV Ezra: A Study Illustrating the Significance of Form and Structure for the Meaning of the Book*. SBLDS 29. Missoula, Mont.: Scholars Press, 1977.

Thomson, J. E. H. *The Samaritans: Their Testimony to the Religion of Israel.* Edinburgh: Oliver and Boyd, 1919.

Thornhill, Raymond. Review of David W. Gooding, *The Account of the Tabernacle: Translation and Textual Problems of the Greek Exodus*, *JTS* n.s. 11 (1960), 124–27.

Thysman, Raymond. *Communauté et directives éthiques: La catéchèse de Matthieu*. Gemblous: J. Duculot, 1974.

Tolbert, Mary Ann. *Sowing the Gospel: Mark's World in Literary-Historical Perspective*. Minneapolis, Minn.: Fortress, 1989.

Tomasino, A. 'יְרִיעָה', *NIDOTTE* II, p. 542.

Toorn, K. van der. *Sin and Sanction in Israel and Mesopotamia: A Comparative Study*. Assen: Van Gorcum, 1985.

Bob Becking and Pieter W. van der Horst, eds. *Dictionary of Deities and Demons in the Bible*. Leiden: Brill, 1995.

'The Significance of the Veil in the Ancient Near East', pp. 327–39 in *Pomegranates and Golden Bells: Studies in Biblical, Jewish, and Near Eastern Ritual, Law, and Literature in Honor of Jacob Milgrom*. Edited by David P. Wright *et al.*. Winona Lake, Ind.: Eisenbrauns, 1995.

Torrey, C. C. 'The Foundry of the Second Temple at Jerusalem', *JBL* 55 (1936), 247–60.

*The Lives of the Prophets: Greek Text and Translation*. JBL Monograph Series 1. Philadelphia, Pa.: Society of Biblical Literature and Exegesis, 1946.

Tov, Emmanuel. *Textual Criticism of the Hebrew Bible*. 2d rev. edn. Minneapolis, Minn.: Fortress, 1992.

*The Text-Critical Use of the Septuagint in Biblical Research*. 2d edn. Jerusalem: Simor, 1997.

Trafton, Joseph L. *The Syriac Version of the Psalms of Solomon: A Critical Evaluation*. SBLSCS 11. Atlanta, Ga.: Scholars Press, 1985.

Tramontano, Raffaele. *La Lettera di Aristea a Folicrate*. Naples: Ufficio succursale della civiltà cattolica in Napoli, 1931.

Trilling, Wolfgang. *Das Wahre Israel: Studien zur Theologie des Matthäus-Evangeliums*. Müngen: Kösen, 1964.

*The Gospel according to Matthew*. Translated by K. Smyth. London: Burns & Oates, 1969.

*Christusverkündigung in den synoptischen Evangelien*. Biblische Handbibliothek 4. München: Kösel, 1969.

Troxel, R. L. 'Matt 27.51–54 Reconsidered: Its Role in the Passion Narrative, Meaning and Origin', *NTS* 48 (2002), 30–47.

Tucker, Gene M. *Form Criticism of the Old Testament*. Philadelphia, Pa.: Fortress, 1971.

Tuell, Steven Shawn. *The Law of the Temple in Ezekiel 40–48*. Harvard Semitic Monographs 49. Atlanta, Ga.: Scholars Press, 1992.

Ulansey, David. 'The Heavenly Veil Torn: Mark's Cosmic Inclusio', *JBL* 110 (1991), 123–25.

'Heaven Torn Open: Mark's Powerful Metaphor Explained', *Bible Review* 7 (1991), 32–37.

'The Transfiguration, Cosmic Symbolism, and the Transformation of Consciousness in the Gospel of Mark', paper presented at the annual meeting of the Society of Biblical Literature, New Orleans, La., Nov. 1996.

Um, Stephen T. 'The Theme of Temple Christology in the Fourth Chapter of John's Gospel in Light of Early Jewish Understanding of Water and the Spirit', Ph.D. diss., University of St Andrews, 2001.

Upton, J. A. 'The Potter's Field and the Death of Judas', *Concordia Journal* 8 (1982), 214–16

Valdés, Juan de. *Commentary upon the Gospel of St Matthew*. Translated by J. T. Betts and Eduard Boehmer. London: Trübner, 1882.

Van Aarde, Andries G. 'Matthew 27:45–53 and the Turning of the Tide in Israel's History', *BTB* 28 (1998), 16–26.

Van Dam, C. 'בדל', *NIDOTTE* I, pp. 604–605.

VanderKam, James C. *The Dead Sea Scrolls Today*. Grand Rapids, Mich.: Eerdmans, 1994.

*An Introduction to Early Judaism*. Grand Rapids, Mich.: Eerdmans, 2001.

VanGemeren, Willem A. *Interpreting the Prophetic Word: An Introduction to the Prophetic Literature of the Old Testament*. Grand Rapids, Mich.: Zondervan, 1990.

ed. *The New International Dictionary of Old Testament Theology and Exegesis*. 6 vols. Carlisle: Paternoster, 1997.

van Unnik, W. C. 'Die 'geöffneten Himmel' in der Offenbarungsvision des Apokryphons Johannes', pp. 269–80 in *Apophoreta*. Edited by W. Eltester. Berlin: Töpelmann, 1964.

Vargas-Machuca, Antonio. '(Καὶ) ἰδού en el estilo narrative de Mateo', *Bib.* 50 (1969), 233–44.

Vattioni, Francesco. *Ecclesiastico: Testo ebraico con apparato critico e versioni greci, latina e siriaca.* Napoli: Istituto Orientale di Napoli, 1968.

Verheyden, J. 'L'Ascension d'Isaïe et l'Évangile de Matthieu: Examen de AI 3,13–18', pp. 247–74 in *The New Testament in Early Christianity: La reception des écrits néotestamentaires dans le christianisme primitif.* Edited by Jean-Marie Sevrin. Leuven: Leuven University Press, 1989.

Vermes, Geza. *The Complete Dead Sea Scrolls in English*. London: Penguin, 1997.

Verseput, Donald J. 'The Role and Meaning of the "Son of God" Title in Matthew's Gospel', *NTS* 33 (1987), 532–56.

'Jesus' Pilgrimage to Jerusalem and Encounter in the Temple: A Geographical Motif in Matthew's Gospel', *NovT* 36 (1994), 105–21.

Via, D. *Ethics of Mark's Gospel in the Middle of Time*. Philadelphia, Pa.: Fortress, 1985.

Vielhauer P., and G. Strecker. 'The Gospel of the Nazareans', pp. 154–65 in vol. 2 of *New Testament Apocrypha*. 2 vols. Edited by W. Schneemelcher. Translated by R. M. Wilson. Louisville, Ky.: Westminster John Knox, 1991.

Vincent, H. 'La description du Temple de Salomon. Notes exégétiques sur I Rois VI', *RB* 16 (1907), 515–42.

'Jérusalem d'après la Lettre d'Aristée', *RB* 5 (1908), 520–32.

'Jérusalem d'après la Lettre d'Aristée (*Suite*)', *RB* 6 (1909), 555–75.

Vincent, L. H. 'Le temple hérodien de'après la Mišnah', *RB* 61 (1954), 5–35, 398–418.

Voigt, Gottfried. *Der zerrissene Vorhang, 2 v: Homiletische Auslegung der Predigttexte der Reihe 4*. Berlin: Evangelische Verlagsanstalt, 1969.

Volz, P. *Jüdische Eschatologie von Daniel bis Akiba*. Tübingen: Mohr Siebeck, 1903.

Von Rad, G. *Old Testament Theology*. 2 vols. Translated by D. M. G. Stalker. Edinburgh: Oliver & Boyd, 1962.

Vriezen, T. C. 'The Term *HIZZA*: Lustration and Consecration', *Oudtestamentlisch Studiën* 7 (1950), 201–35.

Wade, Martha Lynn. 'Translation as Interpretation in the Old Greek Exodus', paper delivered at the Fellowship of Professors, Johnson Bible College, Knoxville, Tenn., 1999.

'Evaluating Lexical Consistency in the Old Greek Bible', *BIOSCS* 33 (2000), 53–75.

*Consistency of Translation Techniques in the Tabernacle Accounts of Exodus in the Old Greek*. SBLSCS 49. Leiden: Brill, 2003.

Wagner, Guy. 'Alliance de la lettre, alliance de l'esprit: essai d'analyse de 2 Corinthiens 2:14 a 3:18', *Etudes Théologiques et Religieuses* 60 (1985), 55–65.

Walker, P. W. L. *Jesus and the Holy City: New Testament Perspectives on Jerusalem*. Grand Rapids, Mich.: Eerdmans, 1996.

Walker, Rolf. *Die Heilsgeschichte im ersten Evangelium*. Göttingen: Vandenhoeck & Ruprecht, 1967.

Wallace, Daniel B. *Greek Grammar beyond the Basics: An Exegetical Syntax of the New Testament*. Grand Rapids, Mich.: Zondervan, 1996.

Wallace, Howard N. 'Eden, Garden of', *ABD* II, pp. 281–83.

Waltke, Bruce K., and M. O'Connor. *An Introduction to Biblical Hebrew Syntax*. Winona Lake, Ind.: Eisenbrauns, 1990.

Warner, A. R. 'Fulfilling All Righteousness: The Death of Jesus in Matthew', *CTM* 29 (2002), 12–19.

Waters, K. L. 'Matthew 27:52–53 as Apocalyptic Apostrophe: Temporal-Spatial Collapse in the Gospel of Matthew', *JBL* 122 (2003), 489–515.

Watt, J. W. *Philoxenus of Marbug: Fragments of the Commentary on Matthew and Luke*. Leuven: Corpusco, 1978.
Watts, Rikki. *Isaiah's New Exodus in Mark*. Tübingen: Mohr Siebeck, 1997.
Weaver, Dorothy Jean. *Matthew's Missionary Discourse*. Sheffield: JSOT Press, 1990.
Weinrich, O. 'Türöffnung im Wunder- Prodogien- und Zauberglauben der Antike, des Judentums, und Christentums', *Tübinger Beiträge zur Altertumswissenschaft* 5 (1929), 200–464.
Weir, T. H. 'Veil', pp. 790–91 in vol. 2 of *Dictionary of Christ and the Gospels*. 2 vols. Edited by J. Hastings. Edinburgh: T. & T. Clark, 1917.
Weiss, Bernhard. *Das Matthäus-Evangelium*. Göttingen: Vandehoeck & Ruprecht, 1890.
Wellhausen, J. *Das Evangelium Matthaei*. Berlin: Georg Reimer, 1904.
*Prolegomena zur Geschichte Israels*. 6th edn. Berlin: Gruyter, 1927.
Wenham, D. 'The Resurrection Narratives in Matthew's Gospel', *TynB* 24 (1973), 21–54.
Wenham, Gordon J. *The Book of Leviticus*. NICOT. Grand Rapids, Mich.: Eerdmans, 1979.
'The Theology of Unclean Foods', *Evangelical Quarterly* 53 (1981), 6–15.
'Sanctuary Symbolism in the Garden of Eden Story', pp. 19–24 in *Proceedings of the Ninth World Congress of Jewish Studies. Division A, The Period of the Bible*. Jerusalem: World Union of Jewish Studies, 1986.
*Genesis 1–15*. WBC 1. Nashville, Tenn.: Thomas Nelson, 1987.
Wenschkewitz, Hans. *Die Spiritualisierung der Kultusbegriffe: Tempel, Priester und Opfer im Neuen Testament*. Leipzig: E. Pfeiffer, 1932.
Wentling, Judith L. 'Unraveling the Relationship between 11QT, the Eschatological Temple, and the Qumran Community', *RevQ* 14 (1989), 61–73.
Weren, W. J. C. 'The Use of Isaiah 5, 1–7 in the Parable of the Tenants (Mark 12, 1–12; Matthew 21, 33–46)', *Bib.* 79 (1998), 1–26.
Werner, Martin. *Die Enstehung des christliche Dogmas problemgeschichtlich darstellt*. Bern/Leipzig: Haupt, 1941.
Westcott, B. F. *The Gospel according to St Matthew*. London: Macmillan, 1890.
*The Epistle to the Hebrews*. London: Macmillan, 1903.
Westerholm, S. 'Tabernacle', *ISBE* IV, pp. 698–99.
Westermann, Claus. *Isaiah 40–66*. Philadelphia, Pa.: Westminster, 1969.
Wevers, John William, ed. *Numeri. Septuaginta: Vetus Testamentum Graecum Auctoritate Academiae Scientiarum Gottingensis editum* III, 1. Göttingen: Vandenhoeck & Ruprecht, 1982.
ed. *Leviticus*. Septuaginta: Vetus Testamentum Graecum Auctoritate Academiae Scientiarum Gottingensis editum II, 2. Göttingen: Vandenhoeck & Ruprecht, 1986.
*Notes on the Greek Text of Exodus*. Septuagint and Cognate Studies 30. Atlanta, Ga.: Scholars Press, 1990.
'PreOrigen Recensional Activity in the Greek Exodus', pp. 121–39 in *Studien zur Septuaginta – Robert Hanhart zu Ehren: Aus Anlass seines 65. Geburtstages*. Edited by Detlef Fraenkel, Udo Quast and John William Wevers. Mitteilungen des Septuaginta-Unternehmens 20. Göttingen: Vandenhoeck & Ruprecht, 1990.

ed. *Exodus*. Septuaginta: Vetus Testamentum Graecum Auctoritate Academiae Scientiarum Gottingensis editum II, 1. Göttingen: Vandenhoeck & Ruprecht, 1991.

*Notes on the Greek Text of Leviticus*. Septuagint and Cognate Studies 44. Atlanta, Ga.: Scholars Press, 1997.

Wheeler, Frank. 'Textual Criticism and the Synoptic Problem: A Textual Commentary on the Minor Agreements of Matthew and Luke against Mark', Ph.D. diss., Baylor University, 1985. Microform.

Wiefel, Wolfgang. *Das Evangelium nach Matthäus*. Leipzig: Evangelische Verlagsanstalt, 1998.

Wilckens, Ulrich. *Weisheit und Torheit: eine exegetisch-religions-geschichtliche Untersuchung zu 1. Kor. 1 und 2*. Tübingen: Mohr Siebeck, 1959.

Williams. Ronald J. *Hebrew Syntax: An Outline*. 2d edn. Toronto: University of Toronto Press, 1976.

Williams, Rowan. 'Between the Cherubim: The Empty Tomb and the Empty Throne', pp. 87–101 in *Resurrection Reconsidered*. Edited by Gavin D'Costa. Oxford: Oneworld, 1996.

Williamson, R. 'The Background of the Epistle to the Hebrews', *Expository Times* 87 (1975), 232–37.

Willits, Joel. 'Reading Matthew's Messianism in the Light of Psalms of Solomon 17? Pursuing the Potential Parallels and Implications', paper presented at the British New Testament Conference, Edinburgh, Scotland, September 4, 2004.

Winden, J. C. M. Van. 'Quotations from Philo in Clement of Alexandria's Protrepticus', *Vigiliae Christianae* 32 (1978), 208–13.

Winkle, Ross E. 'The Jeremiah Model for Jesus in the Temple', *AUSS* 24 (1986), 155–72.

Wintzer, Friedrich. Review of G. Voigt, *Der zerrissene Vorhang, 2 v: Homiletische Auslegung der Predigttexte deer Reihe 4*, *Theologische Literaturzeitung* 97 (1972), 227–29.

Winter, Michael M. *A Concordance to the Peshịtta Version of Ben Sira*. Leiden: Brill, 1976.

Wischnitzel-Bernstein, R. 'The Conception of the Resurrection in the Ezekiel Panel of the Dura Synagogue', *JBL* 60 (1941), 43–55.

Wise, M. O. 'Temple', *DJG* pp. 811–817.

'Temple Scroll (11QTemple)', *DNTB*, p. 1185.

Witherup, Ronald D. 'The Cross of Jesus: A Literary-Critical Study of Matthew 27', Ph.D. diss., Union Theological Seminary in Virginia, 1985.

'The Death of Jesus and the Raising of the Saints: Matthew 27:51–54 in Context', *SBLSP* 26 (1987), 574–85.

Wright, Benjamin G. *No Small Difference: Sirach's Relationship to its Parent Text*. Septaugint and Cognate Studies 26. Atlanta, Ga.: Scholars Press, 1989.

Wright, D. P. 'The Gesture of Hand Placement in the Hebrew Bible and in Hittite Literature', *JAOS* 106 (1986), 433–46.

Wright, G. Ernest, ed. *The Bible and the Ancient Near East: Essays in Honor of William Foxwell Albright*. London: Routledge & Kegan Paul, 1961.

'The Significance of the Temple in the Ancient Near East: Part III. The Temple in Palestine Syria', pp. 169–84 in *The Biblical Archaeologist Reader*.

Vol. 1. Edited by G. Ernest Wright and David Noel Freedman. Garden City, N.Y.: Doubleday, 1961.

Wright, J. Edward. *The Early History of Heaven*. Oxford: Oxford University Press, 2000.

Wright, N. T. *The New Testament and the People of God*. London: SPCK, 1992.

*The Resurrection of the Son of God*. Minneapolis, Minn.: Fortress, 2003.

Würthwein, Ernst. *Text of the Old Testament*. Translated by E. F. Rhodes. 2d edn. Grand Rapids, Mich.: Eerdmans, 1994.

Yadin, Y. 'Excavations of Hazor, 1958: Preliminary Communiqué', *IEJ* 9 (1959), 74–88.

ed. *The Temple Scroll*. 3 vols. Jerusalem: Israel Exploration Society, 1983.

Yamauchi, E. M. *Pre-Christian Gnosticism*. Grand Rapids, Mich.: Eerdmans, 1973.

'Gnosticism and Early Christianity', pp. 29–61 in *Hellenization Revisited: Shaping a Christian Response within the Greco-Roman World*. Edited by Wendy Helleman. Lanham, Md.: University Press of America, 1994.

Yates, J. E. *The Spirit and the Kingdom*. London: SPCK, 1963.

Yerkes, R. K. 'The Unclean Animals of Leviticus 11 and Deuteronomy', *JQR* n.s. 14 (1923), 1–29.

Young, Richard. *Intermediate New Testament Greek*. Nashville, Tenn.: Broadman & Holman, 1994.

Yokota, Paul. 'Jesus the Messiah of Israel: A Study of Matthew's Messianic Interpretation of Scripture as a Contribution to Narrative Study of his Christology', Ph.D. diss., University of St Andrews, 2004.

Zahn, Theodor. 'Der zerrissene Tempelvorhang', *Neue kirchliche Zeitschrift* 13 (1902), 729–56.

*Das Evangelium des Matthäus*. Leipzig: Deichert, 1922. Repr., Wuppertal: R. Brockhaus, 1984.

Zeller, D. *Die weisheitlichen Mahnsprüche bei den Synoptikern*. Würzburg: Echter, 1977.

Zerwick, M. *Biblical Greek, Illustrated by Examples*. Rome: Scripta Pontificii Instituti Biblici, 1963.

Zimmerli, Walther. *A Commentary on the Book of the Prophet Ezekiel, Chapters 1–24*. Translated by R. E. Clements. Philadelphia, Pa.: Fortress, 1979.

*A Commentary on the Book of the Prophet Ezekiel, Chapters 25–48*. Translated by J. D. Martin. Philadelphia, Pa.: Fortress, 1983.

Zohar, N. 'Repentance and Purification: The Significance and Semantics of חטאת in the Pentateuch', *JBL* 107 (1988), 609–18.

Zuurmond, R. 'Der Tod von Nadab und Abihu', *Texte und Kontexte* 24 (1984), 23–27.

# INDEX OF TEXTS

## 1. Old Testament

**2. New Testament**

## 4. Philo



## 5. Flavius Josephus

## 6. Dead Sea Scrolls



## 7. Rabbinic Writings

## 8. Christian Writings

## 9. Greco-Roman Literature



## 10. Papyri

# INDEX OF SELECT SUBJECTS

# INDEX OF MODERN AUTHORS

# INDEX OF SELECT TERMS